The Micmac Indians of Eastern Canada

WILSON D. WALLIS AND
RUTH SAWTELL WALLIS

University of Minnesota Press, Minneapolis

Copyright 1955 by the
UNIVERSITY OF MINNESOTA

All rights reserved. No part of this book may be reproduced in any form without the written permission of the publisher. Permission is hereby granted to reviewers to quote brief passages in a review to be printed in a magazine or newspaper.

PRINTED AT THE NORTH CENTRAL PUBLISHING COMPANY, ST. PAUL

Library of Congress Catalog Card Number: 54-10292

PUBLISHED IN GREAT BRITAIN, INDIA, AND PAKISTAN BY
GEOFFREY CUMBERLEGE: OXFORD UNIVERSITY PRESS, LONDON, BOMBAY, AND KARACHI

Acknowledgments

OUR first words in this book should express gratitude and most heartily they do so. Immediate thanks go to Canadian officials and friends across the border which their cordiality has made almost invisible: to the Department of Citizenship and Immigration, Indian Affairs Branch, for permission to work among the Micmac in 1950 and 1953; in particular to the Honorable Laval Fortier, deputy minister, for an understanding interest and encouragement; to the following cooperative superintendents of Indian agencies, E. J. Blakey, Miramichi, N.B., C. R. Nadeau, Restigouche, Que., H. C. Rice, Shubenacadie; to the chiefs and councilors of Restigouche, Big Cove, Burnt Church, Eel Ground, Indian Island, and Micmac, with whom rested the consent to our presence and the success of our visits to their reserves.

The basic information for this study was secured in 1911 and 1912 through the financial support of the University Museum, University of Pennsylvania. We are indebted to the director for permission to publish the results and for supplying the drawings and photographs of ethnologic materials made by the late William C. Orchard. The specimens here illustrated were secured by WDW for the collection of George G. Heye; most of them are now in the Museum of the American Indian, New York City.

Our field work in 1950 and 1953 was financed by the Department of Anthropology and the Graduate School of the University of Minnesota, and encouraged by Vice President Malcolm M. Willey and Dean Theodore C. Blegen. In 1953 additional funds were supplied by the American Philosophical Society.

Borrowings from minds of the past have been greatly facilitated by J. Russell Harper, archivist-librarian, New Brunswick Museum, St. John, and by Blanche Moen, chief reference librarian, University of

The Micmac Indians of Eastern Canada

Minnesota. For the opportunity to consult and use field data collected among the Micmac in 1950, we are indebted to three young anthropologists, William C. Martin, William C. Sayres, and Sheila Craig Steen; and also to Mrs. Mary M. Macy, mother of the late Mr. Martin, to Professor Clyde Kluckhohn of Harvard, and Professor A. Irving Hallowell of the University of Pennsylvania, who put these notes in our hands.

Even with these various aids, considerable as they have been, our efforts would not have reached present fruition without the aid of the Staff members of the University of Minnesota Press. To them we render sincere thanks.

W. D. W.
R. S. W.

South Woodstock, Connecticut
September 1954

Table of Contents

PART ONE *Tribal Life*

I   STUDIES OF THE MICMAC 3

II *ELNU*, THE PEOPLE 14
The Name, 14. Population and Distribution, 16. Geographic Environment, 18. Physical Traits, 20. Language, 21.

III ECONOMIC LIFE 25
Fishing, 27: capture of sea mammals, 29. Hunting, 31: bow and arrow, 31, hunting dogs, 33, game, 34, skinning animals and tanning hides, 40. Means of Transport, 42: *muskweakwitan*, the birch-bark canoe, 42, other types of canoe, 50, toboggans and sleds, 51, snowshoes, 52. Travel, Maps, and Messages, 53: travel, 53, maps, 54, messages, 55.

IV SHELTER, FOOD, CLOTHING, CRAFTS 57
The Wigwam, 57. The Smokehouse and the Preservation of Foods, 61. Food and Its Preparation, 63: meat and fish, 63, eggs, 65, salt, 65, vegetable foods, 66, beverages, 66, bread, 67, maple sugar, 67. Tobacco and Pipes, 68. Utensils and Tools, 68: birch-bark vessels, 70, basketry, 73, knives, 75, tools, 76, household utensils, 76, thongs, 77. Clothing, 78: foot covering, 79, caps, 80, pins, 81, raincoat, 81, cleaning, 81, traditional dress, 83. Hairdo, 83. Adornment, 85. Arts and Crafts, 87: weaving, 87, dyes, 87, moose-hair and quill work, 89, carving and modeling, 92, ornamental designs, 95.

V CONCEPTS OF THE NATURAL WORLD 97
Celestial Phenomena, 97: the heavens, 97, the sun, 97, the moon, 98, the stars, 98, rainbow, 98, thunder and lightning, 99. Cold, 100. Fog and Dew, 100. Springs and Streams, 100. Weather Signs, 101. Local Geography, 102. Time Divisions, 103. Numerals, 105.

The Micmac Indians of Eastern Canada

VI ZOOLOGY AND BOTANY 106

Transformation of Species, 106. Respect for Animals, 107. Tabooed Animal Foods, 109. Beliefs about Animals, 109: bear, 109, beaver, 110, moose, 111, caribou and deer, 111, skunk, 111, other land animals, 112, sea mammals and fish, 113, snakes and serpents, 113, domestic animals, 114, rats, 116, birds, 117. Learning Songs from Birds, 118. Botany, 119.

VII THE BODY IN SICKNESS AND IN HEALTH 120

Physiology, 121: sense organs, 121, alimentary system, 121, blood, 122. Disease and Its Treatment, 123: sweat lodge, 123, seventeenth-century treatments, 125, medicines, 127, the seventeenth-century medicineman, 134.

VIII MENTAL PROCESSES 137

Dreams, 138: dream experiences of John Newell, 138, dreams of other Pictou men, 140.

IX RELIGION 142

Sun Worship, 142. The Medicineman as Diviner, 146. The Land of the Dead, 149.

X THE SUPERNATURAL 151

Supernatural Beings, 151: *skadegamutc*, 151, Gluskap, 153. Supernatural Races, 154. Supernatural Power, 156: *ginap*, 156, *buoin*, 156, *keskamzit*, 162, *keskamzit* objects, 163. Everyday Magic, 166. Signs and Omens, 167. Everything Is a Sign of Something, 169.

XI SOCIAL AND POLITICAL ORGANIZATION 171

The Chief, 171. Assistant Chief, 174. Settlements, 175. Bonds of Unity, 176. Feasts, 178: in the seventeenth and eighteenth centuries, 179, St. Anne's Day, 183.

XII DANCE, SONG, AND GAMES 191

Dances, 191. Songs, 192. Games, 195: *waltes*, 195, other games, 200.

XIII INTERTRIBAL ORIENTATION AND RELATIONS 202

Attitudes toward Other Tribes, 202: Maliseet and Penobscot, 202, northern Indian tribes, 205, Eskimo, 206, Mohawk, 208. Warfare, 211: causes, 211, preparations, 212, methods, 217, return of the warriors, 218, captives and slaves, 219. Peace, 221. Alliance and Confederacy, 222.

Table of Contents

XIV FAMILY, KIN, AND MARRIAGE 226

Wigwam Life, 226. Relationship and Social Status, 230: terms of relationship, 230, joking relationships, 233, age status, 233. Marriage, 234: John Newell's marriage, 235, how Peter Ginnish got his wife, 235, love story, 235, choice, 236, age at marriage, 237, tribal marriage, 237, the wedding, 239, polygyny, 239, early marriage customs, 240. The Status of Women, 243.

XV FROM BIRTH TO DEATH 248

Pregnancy and Childbirth, 248. Childbirth and Infant Care in the Seventeenth and Eighteenth Centuries, 251. Childhood, 253. Orphans and Adopted Children, 256. The Aged, 256. Death and Burial Rites, 258. Death and Burial in the Seventeenth Century, 261: the dying, 262, the soul, 262, messengers, 263, preparation of the body, 263, funeral rites, 264, cemeteries, 266, mourning, 267.

XVI THE MODERN MICMAC 270

Material Culture, 274. Recreation and Holidays, 283. Weddings and Funerals, 293. Medicine and Disease, 294. Beliefs about the Supernatural, 296. Micmac Attitudes, 306.

GENERAL BIBLIOGRAPHY 309

PART TWO *Folktales and Traditions*

INTRODUCTION by Wilson D. Wallis 317

I TALES ABOUT GLUSKAP 321

1. Gluskap's Early Adventures, 322. 2. Gluskap and the Animals, 323. 3. Gluskap Turns People into Frogs, 325. 4. Gluskap Wins a Contest with Pesadasixunji [scalped], 327. 5. Animals and People Get Muscles, 327. 6. Gluskap Has Power to Grant Wishes, 328. 7. Gluskap Leaves Instructions with the Dogs, 328. 8. How the Beaver Got his Tail, 329. 9. Gluskap Gives the Frogs Their Voices, 329. 10. The Origin of the Cedar's Twist, 329. 11. The Origin of the Canoe, 330. 12. Gluskap as Transformer, 330. 13. Gluskap and the Two Kings, 332. 14. Gluskap Visits the King, 335. 15. Gluskap Supplies a French Warship, 335. 16. Gluskap Assists the Indians in a Fight, 336. 17. Gluskap's Prophecy Fulfilled, 337.

II SUPERNATURAL BEINGS 338

Kitpusiagana, 338: 18. Kitpusiagana's Beginnings, 338, 19. Kitpusiagana Gets Summer, 341, 20. Djenu and Kitpusiagana, 343. Djenu, 343: 21. A

The Micmac Indians of Eastern Canada

Djenu Tamed by Kindness, 343, 22. The Djenu Are Cannibals, 344, 23. A Newfoundland Djenu, 344, 24. A Man and a Woman Become Djenu, 344. Tcipitckaam, 345: 25. A Man Became a Tcipitckaam, 345, 26. A Man Is Chased by a Tcipitckaam, 346. 27. An Encounter with a Tcipitckaam, 347.

III MYTHIC PEOPLES 348

28. The Very Large and Very Strong People, 348. 29. The Halfway People, 349. 30. The Appearance of the Halfway People Is Ominous, 349. 31. The Halfway People Must Be Respected, 350. 32. The Girl Who Visited Aadaiik [Halfway], 351. 33. The Salstog, 354. 34. The Puktesadulkwultidjik [the People Who Smoke], 356. 35. The Migamawesu, 356. 36. Migamawesu Cure Disease, 357. 37. The Migamawesu Facilitate Travel, 357. 38. An Encounter with a Migamawesu, 358. 39. Two Migamawesu at Burnt Church, 358. 40. Migamawesu at a Lumber Camp, 361. 41. The Pugulatamutc [Stone Indians], 362. 42. Appearance and Habits of the Pugulatamutc, 363. 43. At Cape Breton, 365. 44. At Mount Katahdin, 366. 45. The Pugalatamutc Help the Indians, 367.

IV GHOST, WILL-O'-THE-WISP 368

Skadegamutc, 368: 46. Personal Adventures with *Skadegamutc*, 368, 47. One Who Was Not Afraid of *Skadegamutc*, 370, 48. An Encounter with *Skadegamutc*, 370, 49. The Behavior of *Skadegamutc*, 370, 50. *Skadegamutc* Is a Fearless Fighter, 371, 51. Fear of *Skadegamutc*, 371, 52. *Skadegamutc* Clothed as a Woman, 372, 53. *Skadegamutc*, 373, 54. *Skadegamutc* Causes the Echo, 373, 55. A Ghost Story, 374, 56. *Skadegamutc* Can Bring Help, 374, 57. *Skadegamutc* of a Drowned Man, 374, 58. *Skadegamutc* in the House, 375.

V SUPERNATURAL POWERS 376

Ginap, 376: 59. A Young *Ginap* at Richibucto, 376, 60. A *Ginap* in Cape Breton, 377, 61. A *Ginap* at Campbellton, 377, 62. A *Ginap* in Disguise, 377. People Who Live under Water, 384: 63. The Man Who Lived under Water, 384, 64. Atweumisel, the Man Who Said He Had Lived under Water, 385. *Buoin*, 385: 65. Atuen, 385, 66. A *Buoin* Saves Her Son, 386, 67. Tcedjaginwit, 387, 68. A *Buoin* in Red Bank Kills a Woman in Cape Breton, 387, 69. A *Buoin* Caught at Her Own Game, 388, 70. Old Sallie and the Conductor, 389, 71. The Result of a Wish, 389, 72. Walking under Water, 390, 73. A *Buoin* Travels Fast, 390.

VI KESKAMZIT [MAGICAL GOOD LUCK] 392

74. For Finding Money, 392. 75. For Violin Playing, 392. 76. For Making Tubs, 393. 77. For Cutting Wood, 393. 78. *Keskamzit* Indicated by Hearing a Bell, 394.

Table of Contents

VII SUPERNATURAL PLACES 395
79. Halfway River, 395. 80. The Lake with the Water Lily, 395.

VIII ORIGINS OF MATERIAL CULTURE 396
81. Fire-Maker, 396. 82. Bow and Arrow, 396. 83. Origin of the Eel Spear, 397. 84. Origin of the Snowshoe, 397. 85. Origin of Weaving, 399. 86. Origin of Dyes, 399. 87. Origin of Corn, 399.

IX HUMAN ADVENTURES 401
Deserted Women, 401: 88. Orphan girl, 401, 89. A Wife Escapes Murder, 401. Marriages, 402: 90. A Marriage That Reconciled Two Communities, 402, 91. Transaction in Eels That Resulted in Marriage, 403, 92. Married at a Crane-Picking, 404, 93. A Girl Who Was Married While Catching Trout, 404, 94. How a Certain Snowshoe Traveler Was Married, 405, 95. A Widow Must Not Cherish the Dead Husband, 407. Hunting Stories, 408: 96. A Man Who Killed Many Bears, 408, 97. Djako: A Story of Acculturation, 409.

X ANIMAL STORIES 413
98. Rabbit the Gentleman, 413. 99. Rabbit and His Grandmother, 414. 100. Rabbit and Wolverine Visit Kitpusiagana, 417. 101. Wolverine's Behavior, 430. 102. Gugwes and the Origin of Mosquitoes, 430. 103. A Boy Who Lived with the Bears, 431. 104. The Man Who Was Transformed into a Snake, 431. 105. The Crow Which Found a Whale, 432. 106. The Service Rendered by Pigeon and by Crow, 433. 107. The Dog and the Otter, 433. 108. Eagle and Fishhawk, 433. 109. Whale [*pudap*], 434. 110. Why the Whale Chews His Food, 435. 111. How the Beaver Obtained His Broad Tail, 435. 112. Adventures with Geese and Spider, 435. 113. Moose and Caribou, 437. 114. Partridge and his Family, 441. 115. The Kalu, 445.

XI HISTORY AND TRADITION 447
Other Tribes, 447: 116. Maliseet, 447, 117. Montagnais, 448, 118. Western Indians, 448, 119. Mohawk, 448, 120. Gainskugwak, 449, 121. Mohawk Magic and Micmac Magic, 450, 122. Mohawk Fights at Barney River, 451, 123. A Micmac *Buoin* and His Wife Fight Mohawk, 452, 124. Fights with Mohawk and English, 453, 125. Wedjibokwedjik [the Little Boy Who Has Fits]: A Micmac Ginap Who Slew Mohawk, 456, 126. Duneil's Adventures with the Mohawk, 459, 127. Duneil's Encounter with the French and English, 461, 128. Sabiesagamac and His Sons, 463. Micmac and Europeans, 469: 129. Columbus' Visit, 469, 130. The First French Visitors, 469. Why Micmac Have a Treaty with the King, 470: 131. Father Maillard, 470, 132. A Woman *Buoin*, 471, 133. Bill Dumfy's Story, 471. Miramichi Traditions, 472: 134. The History of Burnt Church and Its Church, 472, 135. Scots Civilize the Micmac, 476, 136. The Miramichi Fire, 476, 137. The Campbellton Fire, 479.

The Micmac Indians of Eastern Canada

TALES TOLD IN 1950 AND 1953 481

138. Gluskap's Uncle, 481. 139. Gluskap and Turtle, 482: 140. The Creation of Mankind, 482. 141. The End of the World, 484. 142. Mount Katahdin, 484. 143. Old Margaret, the *Buoin*, 488. 144. Micmac and Caughnawags, 490.

BIBLIOGRAPHY ON MICMAC FOLKLORE 493

APPENDIX A ZOOLOGICAL TERMS 497

APPENDIX B BOTANICAL TERMS 502

APPENDIX C ANATOMICAL TERMS 505

KEY TO ABBREVIATIONS 507

INDEX 508

List of Illustrations

1. The Micmac Country 4
2. Peter Ginnish of Burnt Church, N.B. 8
3. John Newell of Pictou Landing, N.S. 8
4. Micmac Script 24
5. Wooden Fish Spears 27
6. Hunter's Light Snowshoes and Bow and Arrow Shafts 32
7. Section of an Arrow Shaft 33
8. Birch-Bark Moose-Caller 37
9. Typical Micmac Canoes 43
10. Detail of Snowshoe Construction 52
11. Micmac Notice 55
12. Wigwam at Dartmouth, N.S., 1912 58
13. Bark Boxes 71
14. Section of a Birch-Bark Roll 71
15. Birch-Bark Tray and Attachment of Bottom and Cover of a Circular Box 72
16. Circular Bark Box 73
17. Birch-Bark Bucket 74

18. Birch-Bark Dipper 75
19. Method of Making a Splint Basket 76
20. Implements and Tools 77
21. Chief's Coat 82
22. Articles of Traditional Dress 82
23. Micmac Woman Wearing a Squaw Cap 83
24. Types of Quahaug Beads 84
25. Mrs. Peter Ginnish, of Burnt Church, N.B. 84
26. The Process of Quillwork on Birch-Bark Boxes 90
27. Quillwork on Birch-Bark Boxes 91
28. Quillwork Designs on Birch-Bark Boxes Resembling Those of Ursuline Nuns in the Eighteenth Century 91
29. Varieties of Ribbon Appliqué 92
30. Designs Incised on Circular Birch-Bark Box 93
31. Designs on the Sides of Circular Birch-Bark Boxes 93
32. Designs on Bone Dice 94
33. John Sark of Prince Edward Island 95
34. Bead Design on Moccasin 96
35. Sash Pattern 96
36. *Keskamzit* Objects 164
37. *Keskamzit* for Maternity 165
38. Sainte Anne des Micmac 182
39. St. Anne's Day Shrine at Burnt Church 189
40. Beads, Medals, and Equipment for Playing *Waltes* 196
41. Men Playing *Waltes* 197
42. Types of Counters Used in *Waltes* 198

List of Illustrations

43. Social Arrangement of Micmac Life 226

44. Micmac Family Group in Nova Scotia 227

45. An Old Woman of 1912 257

46. Ste Anne de Restigouche, Quebec 272

47. Maria, Quebec 273

48. Drawing of a Man Dragging a Wood-Sled 280

49. Drawing of a Village Scene 280

PART ONE *Tribal Life*

CHAPTER I

Studies of the Micmac

THE Micmac as a subject for ethnographic study was suggested to me in 1911 by the late Frank G. Speck. His interest in the eastern Algonkin peoples was then centered on Penobscot and Passamaquoddy. East and northeast of these tribes lived the Micmac, scattered along the eastern and southern shores of the Gaspé Peninsula and, except for the St. John River region, throughout the three Maritime Provinces. Each settlement was a culture island in an encroaching sea of foreign concepts and social structure. If a knowledge of their tribal life was to be obtained, the attempt could not be long delayed.

The field study of the Micmac on which the following account is mainly based was begun in the summer of 1911 at Restigouche, Que., Red Bank, Eel Ground, and Burnt Church, N.B., Pictou Landing and Tuft's Cove (near Dartmouth), N.S.; and continued in 1912 at Burnt Church, Tuft's Cove, and Pictou Landing, at Lennox Island, P.E.I., and at Truro, Shubenacadie, Elmsdale, Enfield, New Germany, and Bear River reserves and the sites of three former settlements, Musquodoboit Harbor, Merigomish, and Grand Lake, all in Nova Scotia. Almost four decades later I returned to the Micmac country in 1950 with Ruth Sawtell Wallis for a preliminary study at Burnt Church, N.B., and Shubenacadie, N.S. In 1953 we spent eight weeks at Restigouche and Maria on the Gaspé, and at Eel River, Burnt Church, Eel Ground, and Big Cove, N.B. We have not visited settlements in Cape Breton or in Newfoundland. (See illustration 1.)

The purpose of the original study was to obtain as complete an ethnographic account as possible. The aim of the later trips was threefold: to discover how extensive had been the loss of Micmac culture in the

NOTE: Throughout this volume, *I* refers to Wilson D. Wallis; *we* to both authors.

3

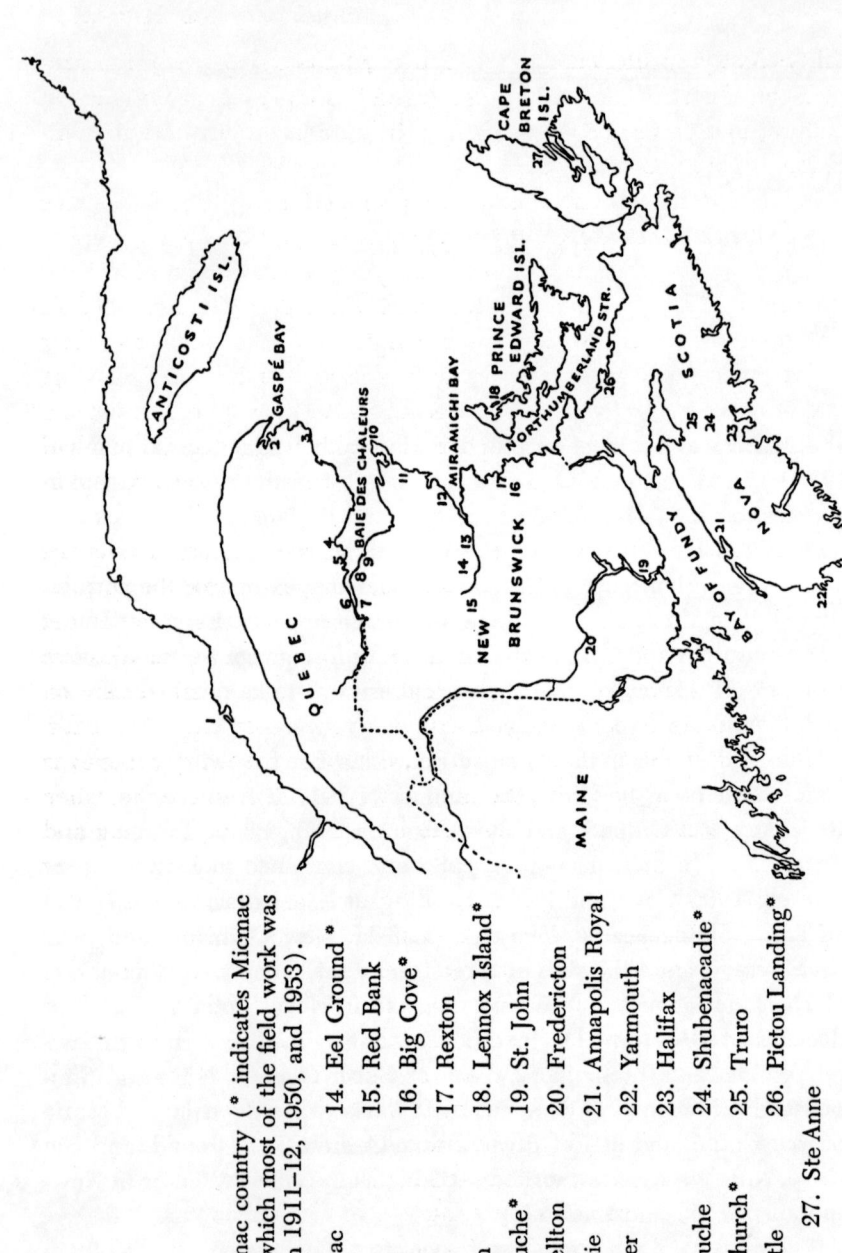

1. The Micmac country (* indicates Micmac reserves at which most of the field work was conducted in 1911–12, 1950, and 1953).

1. Tadoussac
2. Gaspé
3. Percé
4. Maria*
5. Carleton
6. Restigouche*
7. Campbellton
8. Dalhousie
9. Eel River
10. Miscou
11. Pokemouche
12. Burnt Church*
13. Newcastle
14. Eel Ground*
15. Red Bank
16. Big Cove*
17. Rexton
18. Lennox Island*
19. St. John
20. Fredericton
21. Annapolis Royal
22. Yarmouth
23. Halifax
24. Shubenacadie*
25. Truro
26. Pictou Landing*
27. Ste Anne

thirty-eight-year interval, and which hardy traits had persisted; to supplement, if possible, information gathered in 1911–12 regarding the old culture; to observe and assess changes in material culture and in orientation, drives, and motivations.

At the present day one could ask for no more friendly and talkative people than the Micmac. Questioned about old times by a white stranger who shows a little sympathetic knowledge, men and women of all ages answer promptly and as fully as they can. But in 1911 the old men, with whom rested the final sanction, were suspicious of the whites and their ways. During their youth and until late middle age, habits of cooking, eating, and posture had departed little from aboriginal type. The son of a white man who had been adopted in infancy by a Micmac couple, had later married a French girl, and had left the reserve, gave an account of these Indians:

"When my father's adoptive parents were very old and feeble, he brought them to our house to live; but they could not accept our ways. They would not sit at a table to eat, but squatted cross-legged on the ground, a piece of skin spread out in front of them as a table. We gave them a bed, but they removed the mattress and the covers and slept on the floor. Such things as pies, custards, and sweets they did not care for, and they did not like bread unless it was cooked in the coals, without the use of a vessel. They craved the flesh of wild animals. In the fall, when this craving was strongest, they were in such a state of dejection and drooping spirits that, if you did not know them, you would think they were sick. Whenever I killed a rabbit, squirrel, or porcupine for them, they were delighted, and the meat lasted them three or four days. They insisted, however, on having the meat put on spits and cooked on a grate or roasted over a fire. This was about 1890."

Men and women of seventy in 1911 who had been brought up in this fashion, though they might now sleep on a board bed with a straw-stuffed tick, lived in a world psychologically far removed from the Canadian life that encompassed all sides of their small reserves, and felt the impossibility of explaining their beliefs and fears to intruding whites. Within the constricted boundaries they wanted to be let alone to pursue the old culture to the limit of that narrow scope.

Fortunately, among the suspicious old men on each reserve there was at least one good storyteller who, although he would answer few questions put by a young white man, could not resist an invitation to enter-

PART ONE *Tribal Life*

tain with his specialty. Myths, folktales, and accounts of personal adventure were the high road and sometimes the only discoverable road to many phases of ethnographic information. With them and from them I embarked upon practically all topics. The following story about a Micmac hero, Sako, illustrates the detailed value of some of the tales:

"Each Micmac always kept four or five arrows in his wigwam. An old man saw an animal swimming across a stream. He went to his wigwam to get his bow and arrows. When the animal came to the bank, he shot an arrow into its forehead. He went to the animal and removed the arrow. His wife brought a dish and kept the blood for him and the children; they would drink it. His wife said, 'Here is your portion.' He would not drink it.

"That morning he had shot a moose. He dragged the moose away and cut it up. After removing the hide and cutting the meat into pieces, each person in the settlement was given a share. This moose provided a breakfast for everybody. The man who had killed it received no more than the others.

"The people were getting berries of all kinds for winter — blueberries, rockberries, cranberries, huckleberries, and others — intending to save as many as possible. They made of these a kind of soup by mixing them with fish cut up into small pieces and cooking all of this in one vessel. After they had gathered all they wanted, they looked about in the woods for a place in which to store them — they never stored them along the water for use in winter.

"No one knows what kind of animal that was. They think it was sent by Providence. The chief said so, and when the chief says a thing, the others must accept his word. The chief was Sako; he it was who killed the animal."

No direct inquiry would elicit the details of social life that form the background of a story and, because they are unstressed and are almost unconscious elements, they are, by so much the more, important and convincing. These unconscious elements often contradicted the narrator's expressed statements and alleged convictions. An example is the case of the young man who insisted that he was not afraid of a *skadegamutc*, will-o'-the-wisp, although one chased him about five miles one night; and who then, in proof, related the incident — a story which shows that his flight of five miles was one of terror, terminating in complete physical and mental exhaustion.

Studies of the Micmac

The results of this method of working from folktale to straightforward questioning of an informant with whom I had now established rapport gave me most of the material for Part One of this book; about two thirds of the stories which I collected in 1911–12 are published in Part Two.

During the field trips of 1950 and 1953 the changed attitude of Micmac toward whites, and in a considerable degree toward their own culture, was hospitable to the interview, free or directed; which was well, for, unlike certain beliefs which maintain a vigorous though half-hidden life, myths and tales are today feeble fragments.

Informants spoke English and no interpreter was employed. Although they had had little or no schooling and were firmly oriented in reserve life, most Micmac men in 1911–12 had been thrown among whites by economic necessity and thus forced to learn English; some could also speak French. As basket sellers, makers and venders of woodenware, loggers, and guides for sportsmen they had had from boyhood periodic contacts with French and British Canadians, whose European folk beliefs they had unconsciously taken over in part along with the two languages.

Foremost among the informants of 1911–12 was Peter Ginnish, of Burnt Church, N.B., a blind man, a canoe maker with a fund of detailed information about material culture and an almost endless flow of narratives well told. (See illustration 2.) Among whites and the younger Indians he had the reputation of being a colossal liar, a reputation no doubt in part deserved, in part attributable to his narration of tales that represented beliefs foreign to whites and shared by only a few Micmac, in part earned by his boasts of the days when he guided the Prince of Wales, who always addressed him as "Mr. Ginnish Esquire." However, all his information was in accord with Micmac culture, which is fundamentally the same throughout Quebec and the Maritimes, and several of his statements which sounded bizarre were confirmed by seventeenth-century accounts of the Micmac. Another important informant was John Newell, an old man at Pictou Landing, N.S., born in Cape Breton, where he lived until about the age of twenty. (See illustration 3.) He spoke French and English well, could read, and prided himself on his knowledge of people and affairs. A third, Thomas Meuse, originally from Truro, N.S., was not more than thirty years of age. A wanderer, he was very intelligent, and had learned a great deal from French and British Canadians in numerous contacts. Confirmatory in-

PART ONE *Tribal Life*

2. Peter Ginnish, of Burnt Church, N.B., shows the method of measuring the dimensions of a canoe. 3. John Newell, of Pictou Landing, N.S.

formation was gathered from other men, mainly elderly, on the reserves at which the principal informants resided, and at other reserves.

Micmac women in 1911–12 were extremely shy. I seldom saw one at the house of an informant. With the exception of a tale or two told by a few of the quite old, the only material gathered from a woman was about medicines and their use — from Mrs. Peter Ginnish, then about fifty years of age. In 1950 and 1953 this situation was quite different. While it is not without significance that we were working as a husband-and-wife team, and that in forty years I had moved from age twenty-five to the "old man" group — a Micmac term of respect — there had been a basic change in Micmac culture and in the woman's role. In all houses where I worked with a man informant the woman of the family came and went as naturally as in a white household. Frequently I talked with husband and wife, and some of our most fruitful sessions were held by us jointly with one of several Micmac couples ranging in age from thirty to eighty.

In 1953, when our objective was to concentrate on certain phases of the culture and check the data at each reserve, we interviewed twenty-five women from twenty-four to eighty-one years of age and about the

Studies of the Micmac

same number of men within a comparable age range. The topics stressed were knowledge of natural phenomena, persistence and modification of belief in witchcraft and magic, concepts of disease and methods of treatment, first menstruation, pregnancy, childbirth, infant feeding and training, adoption, teen-age problems, and current ways of making a living. A portion of the data from our recent field work is presented in Chapter XVI.

The core of our book is the ethnographic study made in 1911–12, compared with accounts of Micmac culture recorded earlier, in some instances three hundred years earlier, by shrewd, if not unprejudiced, observers. One of the satisfactions in studying Micmac culture, and also a source of major exasperation, stems from the long period of European contacts. Four hundred years is time enough for an intricate interweaving and snarling of cultural threads into a fabric which the Micmac consider wholly aboriginal. Much of it is native, for the Micmac have been strong resisters as well as comfortable adopters and adapters of foreign traits.[1] To a greater extent than in most Indian cultures there are, in some phases of Micmac belief — for example, witchcraft, ghosts, and dreams — unsolved problems of the amount of French or British acculturation.

Records of Micmac life begin in 1606, with Lescarbot, and practically end in 1739, with Maillard; within that period of 133 years detailed descriptions of highly selected activities in one place may be followed after an interval of thirty or forty years by an account written at a different locality whose subject matter has little in common with any preceding one. A fairly wide dissemination of generalized knowledge about the existence of this early history and about even earlier contacts with Europeans has given rise to two clichés which the student of Indians in eastern Canada hears repeatedly: "What aboriginal culture can you expect to find when whites have been there for all that time?" And, "All the ethnographic accounts we will ever have are in the *Jesuit Relations.*" As a matter of fact, Micmac culture, although in many respects differing greatly from its pre-European character, was in 1911–12 an integrated and closely woven culture, not a tangle of loose and ill-assorted traits; and in 1953 tribal concepts still influenced the aim and frequently hampered the accomplishment of a life-way which in material aspects is Canadian. The Jesuit chronicles are invaluable; so also are

[1] Bailey, 1937. Wallis and Wallis, 1953, 100–2.

PART ONE *Tribal Life*

many contemporary descriptions, and some that were written nearly seventy years after the last of the Jesuit accounts.

The first European to encounter the Micmac was Jacques Cartier. In 1534 he entered the Miramichi Bay, or Bay of Boats, as he christened it in reference to the many canoes that surrounded his ship.[2] The discoverers of the country, the first settlers, and the first missionaries were French. During the seventy years that intervened between Cartier's visit and the founding of Port Royal, now Annapolis Royal, the Micmac could have had many contacts with fishermen and traders. In 1578, 150 French vessels participated in the Newfoundland trade, and Basque, Dutch, and other peoples were vigorously engaged in the fisheries. French boats put into the bays on the coast of New Brunswick to dry their catch; in 1605 they were in the habit of landing in the Miramichi region. Throughout this period the small resident French colony in Newfoundland carried on trade with mainland Indians as far south as the Potomac.[3]

The founding, in 1605, of the short-lived agricultural colony of Port Royal was significant for the Micmac and also for us, mainly because of three men: Marc Lescarbot, Father Pierre Biard, and Membertou. The most important Indian in the Acadian region, Membertou was a medicineman as well as chief, a combination which, in conjunction with a personality impressive to French and Indians, gave him more power than was common in a loosely organized tribe. In 1610 Jessé Fleché, a secular priest, baptized Membertou and twenty members of his family. The French knew no Micmac, the Micmac knew no French. Membertou, by acts of grace, or of graciousness to the strangers, became and has remained a symbol: the first Christian Micmac. On June 24, 1910, at Ste Anne de Restigouche in Quebec, French, English, and Micmac from Cape Breton to the Gaspé gathered for the tercentenary celebration of his baptism.

Father Biard, a Jesuit missionary who arrived in New France in 1611, and Marc Lescarbot, a Parisian lawyer who preceded him by five years, were observant, recorded what they saw, and became the first ethnographers of the Micmac. With the advent of Biard, directed acculturation began. He, like other missionaries who followed him, in part in-

[2] Wright states that Cartier did not enter this bay. We have accepted the identification given by Biggar, 45.
[3] JR, I, 177. Lescarbot, *History*, II, 284. References to the *Jesuit Relations* are to the Thwaites edition. References to Lescarbot, Denys, LeClercq, Dièreville, and Maillard are to the English translations. See Bibliography.

Studies of the Micmac

spired by the belief that civilization and Christianity must advance together, in part because with nomadic bands it was impossible to maintain the steady contact necessary to a lasting conversion, instituted a policy of introducing French traits. "If they are savage," he wrote, "it is to domesticate and civilize them that people came here." [4]

The first missionaries had spent only two years at Port Royal and on the St. John River (1611-13) when the first Acadian colony was attacked by the British. In 1616 four Recollect Fathers met with Champlain in Quebec to report on a survey of the mission field: those natives down the river and to the north (Montagnais, Etchemins [Maliseet], Eskimo) lived in too wild a country and were too superstitious to be good preliminary subjects, but missionaries "who have even penetrated by land to Cadie, Cape Breton, and Chaleurs Bay, Isle Percé and Gaspé" reported the country as more temperate and susceptible of civilization. "There would be found dispositions less estranged from Christianity as the people had more shame, docility and humility than the others." [5]

The choice was good; for the Micmac relations with the French were to be mutually pleasant and helpful. "The Souriquois [Micmac] were so jovial and so confiding that they easily attached themselves to the French and became their faithful friends; also, for their part, the French were attracted to these people. Therefore, later on, when Acadia fell under the power of the English, the Acadians [Indians] stubbornly refused to make war on their former allies. 'We have lived together,' they said, 'we have prayed together, we have shared the same dangers, these are our brothers; we will never attack them.' " [6]

Because of territory shifts from French to British and back again, the missions were not firmly established, nor were French settlements, until the treaty of Breda (1667) returned the country to France, which had developed the fisheries of the Grand Banks most fully in the century following their discovery. The French had to maintain colonies at the places visited for catching or for drying fish — Newfoundland, Cape Breton, Percé, and the coasts of Acadia — in order to hold these free of dispute. Basque as well as French ships went there to obtain oil from whales, seals, or porpoises. To serve these French colonists and to convert the savages, "the ardent charity of the Jesuits" spread among the

[4] JR, I, 141.
[5] LeClercq, *First Establishment*, I, 109–10.
[6] Ferland, I, 72.

PART ONE *Tribal Life*

nations up and down the river St. Lawrence, the coast of Acadia, and the islands of Cape Breton and Miscou. Missions among the Micmac or serving them were Holy Cross, at Tadoussac; St. Anne at Cape Breton; St. Charles at Miscou; Our Lady of Consolation at Nipisiguit, "whence they spread to Cadie and Chaleurs bay." Other missions included Restigouche, Rivière-du-Loup, and Port Royal.[7]

After 1671, when the Recollet order of Franciscans took over the work abandoned by the Jesuits, there were missions among the Micmac at Beaubassin (Chignecto), Miramichi, Nipisiguit (Bathurst), Restigouche, and Percé. To this last-named place, on the Gaspé, came Father Chrétien LeClercq. At Isle Percé, in 1675, a busy spot in summer, were gathered four to five hundred French fishermen. Besides serving them LeClercq, before his departure in 1683, visited the Micmac at Restigouche, Nepisiguit, Miramichi, and on the Gaspé; invented and taught his ideographic system; and compiled the notes for his valuable book about the Indians.[8] Fifty years after his departure there arrived among the Micmac the last missionary priest and historian to come to them from France, Father Maillard, hero of several folktales told in 1911.[9]

The following chapters of our book reveal the debt which the ethnographer owes to these men and to a few others who from 1606 to 1755 observed the Micmac and wrote about them. Without their work, some phases of the culture would have been forever lost; other aspects remembered today would be difficult to assess without confirmation from a source close to aboriginal life; also, clues from these seventeenth- and eighteenth-century accounts help to uncover otherwise unsuspected present-day concepts and practices. These accounts are not perfect; the writers were hurried, their purpose and interest were not ours; descriptions break off at the most exciting point with "but the rest is too long," or "too dull," or "too superstitious" — or words to that effect. We must, however, be grateful to the missionaries who describe with fair detail the funeral rites or the curing ceremonies they were bent on destroying. I did not read Maillard or LeClercq until after my return from field work in 1911; it was very satisfying to discover then that my informants' insistence that the aboriginal religion had been sun worship was not so unlikely as I had supposed. I could learn nothing from informants about

[7] LeClercq, *First Establishment*, I, 313–14, 383, 384, 404.
[8] *Ibid.*, II, 80.
[9] See Part Two, Tale 131.

Studies of the Micmac

a hierarchy among tribal chiefs, except a sentence in a story about the hero-transformer Gluskap: When he left the Micmac, he decreed that all chiefs should be equal. In the *Jesuit Relations* Father Biard said they were equal, and added that therefore they seldom reached a decision.

The *Jesuit Relations* are an important source of information about Micmac customs. From 1632 to 1674 the Jesuit Superior at Quebec sent an annual *Relation* to his Superior, the Provincial at Paris. Sometimes he wrote an original narrative based on notes and interviews. More often, the *Relation* incorporated reports from missionaries throughout New France, either edited or sent on without change. The Provincial caused them to be published, in order to disseminate this information among the French public. They contain, in addition to Father Biard's *Relations*, a contribution by the layman Lescarbot and shorter accounts written at missions from Cape Breton to Miscou.

Other sources include books by Lescarbot, who spent the year 1606–7 at Port Royal in Acadia; Nicolas Denys, merchant and provincial official, who from 1622 to 1672 knew many Micmac from Cape Breton to Baie des Chaleurs; Father LeClercq, 1675–83; the traveler Dièreville (1710); and Abbé Maillard, 1735–62. When citing or quoting these writers we shall identify the source by the years which the writer spent in New France, rather than by the time of publication, which, as in our own case, was sometimes much later.

CHAPTER II

Elnu, the People

THE Micmac are an Algonkin-speaking people of Eastern Woodland culture, one of the six Wabanaki tribes which include Passamaquoddy, Maliseet, Penobscot, Wowenock, Abenaki. Most of them live on reserves where they retain a semblance of their old life and a strong sense of group identity — maintained by the constant use of their own language, by loyalty to the chief and council elected under the Canadian governmental system, in accord with the old Micmac way, and by homogeneity of religion. All profess the Roman Catholic faith. The Protestant missionary Silas Rand labored among them many years, mastered the language, and familiarized himself with their customs and with many of their beliefs; yet today there is not one professing Micmac Protestant.

THE NAME

The Micmac are the Souriquois of the *Jesuit Relations*, and the Gaspesians of LeClercq. The old name for the tribe, used now by the Micmac, is *El'nu*, "People," although they commonly refer to themselves as *Mikmok*. Rand in his *Dictionary* gave *ulnoo* as the term for *Indian*, but said its original meaning signified *man* as distinguished from all other animals or objects; he stated that *Megumawaach* was the Micmac designation for themselves. This was recorded before 1888. Rand seldom gave regional or dialectic differences.

The people themselves offer no derivation for the name *Micmac*. Peter Ginnish of Burnt Church did, however, give the following explanation of outside recognition of them as Micmac. (*Kwe* means "Greetings.")

"One day, after the Indians had settled here, a strange Indian came. He entered a wigwam and said, '*Kwe!*' To this '*Kwe!*' was responded.

"The stranger remarked, 'I must *kwe* when I find a Micmac.' No one

Elnu, the People

knows where he went; he was never heard of after that. That is how other people came to call us Micmac. This was before the coming of the whites. The name which we gave ourselves is *Elnu*, 'People.'

"After we were given the name 'Micmac,' we began to observe the Sabbath. Six days are ours; on the seventh day there is no work, and no travel. A great many say that the man who said to us '*Kwe!* I must *kwe* when I find a Micmac' came from the sky."

Micmac, by a process we cannot fully trace, is derived from *Miscou*. Early in the seventeenth century, Miscou, an island at the southern end of the Baie des Chaleurs where it opens into the Gulf of St. Lawrence, was a central point for fish and trade. Here in 1634 at the Denys trading post the Jesuits established the mission of St. Charles, primarily for the French settlement, but with the added purpose of converting the savages. By 1659 the Indians there were said to be "the most populous and best disposed to Christianity" in Acadia. In the *Jesuit Relations* of 1651–52 the writer said that at Port Tadoussac (at the mouth of the Saguenay) "every day, for a while, God's praises were sung in French, in Huron, in Algonquin, in Montagnais, and in the Canadian [or] Miscouien language." [1] This is the first known reference to the tribe as Miscouien. The editor added: "The term 'Canadian' was applied by early explorers and settlers, to all the Indians whom they encountered on the coasts of the gulf and lower river of St. Lawrence. Most of these were Micmacs on the south side of that stream, and, as Miscou was a central point of trade with these tribes, the name of that part was naturally applied to their language." [2]

We have not been able to ascertain when the word *Miscouien* (*Miscouienne*) became *Micmac*. It was once spelled *Mic Macs*. The first designation of the people as *Micmac* appears to be in a memoir by M. de la Chesnaye, in 1676, where this spelling was used. This may be an editorial alteration. In a Cadillac memoir, 1692, the spelling was *Mikemakes*; and *Micmaks* appeared in a 1693 French list of tribes which were to receive presents. Dièreville, 1710, used the spelling *Miquemaques*. It first appeared on a map, in 1703, as *Micmaques*, to designate natives in the eastern part of the peninsula of Nova Scotia, those occupying the western part being called *Souriquois*. The word *Micmaks* occurred in the 1744 edition of Charlevoix' *Histoire et description générale de la Nou-*

[1] XXXVII, 191.
[2] II, 205. See also JR, III, 41; VII, note 19; XXXVII.

PART ONE *Tribal Life*

velle France.³ He referred to the Gaspesians as members of the same tribe as the Acadians.

Today the name is known to and used by neighboring tribes, who have evolved their own unflattering derivations. "The Micmac, *Mi'k'makik* (singular *Mi'k'moi*), are well known to the Penobscot, who regard them as large strong people, but poor and inclined to be mean. The name *Mi'k'moi* is evidently, though obscurely, related to the term *Mi'koimwe's* referring to a class of dwarf-like supernaturally gifted human creatures who inhabit the dense woods. The connection between these names is brought out more clearly through the Malecite *Mi k'am*, 'Micmac' or 'Wood Spirit'." ⁴

POPULATION AND DISTRIBUTION

The reserves, homes of most present-day Micmac, are in Quebec at Restigouche and Maria on the south shore of the Gaspé Peninsula; in New Brunswick at Eel River on Baie des Chaleurs, on the Miramichi Bay and River at Burnt Church, Eel Ground, and Red Bank, and on the Richibucto River at Big Cove and Indian Island; at Lennox Island off the north coast of Prince Edward Island. All these are old Micmac sites. In Nova Scotia a centralization program, begun in 1944, resettled about half of the Indians on two reserves: Micmac, near Shubenacadie (Hants County) and Eskasoni in the Bras d'Or Lake region of Cape Breton; the remainder stayed on twenty old reserves, including Truro and Pictou Landing, and others have drifted back to their old homes.

In the early days of European contact Micmac lived at the present Percé and Barachois at the tip of the Gaspé Peninsula, in Newfoundland, and throughout the Maritimes, in much the same places where they are now settled. Hunting, fishing, trade, and war took them to the shores of the St. Lawrence at Rivière-du-Loup and Tadoussac, into the gulf to Anticosti Island, and along the north shore to Labrador.

Whether any Micmac group was permanently settled on the St. John River at the western border of New Brunswick is not certain. They are said to have frequented the river's mouth after the arrival of Europeans. The Jesuit missionary Enemond Massé passed the winter of 1611–12 on the St. John with the family of Louis Membertou, son of the chief at Port Royal, in order to continue his study of the Micmac language. Cadillac

³ I, 124, 279, 658.
⁴ Speck, *Penobscot Man*, 17–18.

Elnu, the People

stated that thirty miles up the St. John was a Micmac fort. However, Raymond identified this as Villebon's fort at Nashwak, where Micmac from eastern New Brunswick and Nova Scotia often gathered for raids on New England.[5] Dièreville said there were some on the lower St. John River; but they later withdrew from that region and went to Nova Scotia. Webster believed "they . . . occupied the lower portion of the Saint John river (to above the site of Fredericton), for all the place names on this area are of Micmac origin. . . . Undoubtedly, they had extended as far as the Passamaquoddy, judging by the place names, but they gradually withdrew eastward."[6]

Before the days of the census, the population of the Micmac was variously estimated at 2000 (by Biard in 1612[7]), 3000, and 3500 (by the same writer a few years later[8]). In 1760 a colonel stationed at the isthmus of Chignecto gave the number of Micmac as "near 3000 souls."[9]

As early as 1610 the malign influences of civilization were getting in their deadly work. Chief Membertou of Port Royal assured Biard that in his youth he had seen *chimonitz*, that is to say, Savages, as thickly planted there as the hairs upon his head. It is maintained that they have thus diminished since the French have begun to frequent their country; for, since then they do nothing all summer but eat; and the result is that, adopting an entirely different custom and thus breeding new diseases, they pay for their indulgence during the autumn and winter by pleurisy, quinsy and dysentery, which kill them off. During this year alone sixty have died at Cape de la Heve, which is the greater part of those who lived there; yet not one of all M. de Pountrincourt's little colony have even been sick, notwithstanding all the privations they have suffered.[10]

According to Canadian government reports the Micmac population in 1910 was stationary at 4000 on sixty reserves in the Maritimes and Quebec, with populations from 6 to 506. The 1949 Census of Indians in Canada gives a total of 5083 Micmac. Thus the people who were barely holding their own at the time this study was begun, thirty-eight years later when the check was made had achieved a gain of 27 per cent. In New Brunswick and Quebec, where the organization of reserves was the same in the two periods, the increase was 32 per cent.

[5] Pp. 7, 10.
[6] In Dièreville, 216.
[7] JR, II, 73.
[8] In 1616. JR, III, 111.
[9] MHSC, X, 116.
[10] JR, I, 177.

PART ONE *Tribal Life*

GEOGRAPHIC ENVIRONMENT

The physical environment which permitted aboriginal Micmac culture to exist and to develop was predominantly a region of forests, rivers, lakes, and coasts.

In the seventeenth century

as for the trees of the forests, the most common in Port Royal be oaks, elms, ashes, birch, (very good for joiner's work), maples, sycamores, pine-trees, fir-trees, whitethorns, hazeltrees, willows, bay-trees, and some others . . . There is in certain places store of strawberries. Item, in the woods small fruit, blue and red. I have seen there small pears very delicate; and in the meadow all the winter long there be certain small fruits like to small apples coloured with red, whereof we made marmalade.

There be store of gooseberries like unto ours, but they grow red. Item, those other small round gooseberries which we do call *guedres*. And peas in great quantity along the seashores.[11]

Before the coming of white men and guns the waters were plentifully supplied with fish, the forests abounded with game. The most common and important game were deer, moose, bear, porcupine, squirrel, rabbit, wolverine, hedgehog, weasel, fox, beaver, otter, hair seal, walrus, muskrat, and fowl, including several species of wild duck, wild goose, loon, and crane.

Rivers and lakes were highways for travel for the light and convenient bark canoes, which draw little water and are easy to carry over the short portages. Thus the Micmac could travel to any region of the tribe, and at several points, through the eastern affluents of the St. John River, could enter the Maliseet country.

They took long voyages in their sea-going canoes, as witness the expeditions against the Iroquois and the Montagnais. A Jesuit Father wrote in 1610–13:

The Savages of Port Royal can go to Kebec [Quebec] in ten or twelve days by means of the rivers, which they navigate almost up to their sources; and thence, carrying their little bark canoes for some distance through the woods, they reach another stream which flows into the river of Canada [the St. Lawrence], and thus greatly expedite their long voyages, which we ourselves could not do in the present state of the country.[12]

The inland water routes that connected all parts of interior New Bruns-

[11] Lescarbot, *History*, III, 1606, 256–57.
[12] JR, I, 101.

Elnu, the People

wick long remained important to Micmac and also to whites. In 1832 Cooney wrote:

All the principal rivers of New Brunswick are intimately connected with each other either by small streams or short portages. Thus, the Restigouche approximates to the Saint John, by an eight mile portage leading to the Grand River. The Miramichi is connected with the Nipisiguit by a still shorter route; and the latter approaches the Restigouche by an Indian road leading to the Upsalquitch. The Saint John is also linked with the Miramichi and the Nipisiguit, by the Lakes that supply the main and little Tobique, and the Miramichi mingles with the Richibucto by two or three of its tributaries, while the latter approaches the Saint John by Salmon River, along the Grand Lake, and thence down the Jemseg. The same route inverted leads from the Saint John to the Miramichi, by a portage connecting Salmon River with the Etinne. There is also a route from the Madawaska to the Bay des Chaleurs; and the Chicktocook falls into the Saint John near the Presque Isle, and runs by a short vista upon the branch of the Miramichi, while the Buctouch rises near the New Cannaan, a River discharging with the Washademoak Lake which empties itself about thirty miles above the city.[13]

Intratribal travel to and from Nova Scotia was along a highway, formed of a series of lakes extending north of Halifax toward the Minas Basin and the Bay of Fundy, and thence to the St. John River. Within Nova Scotia small streams and lakes gave an almost continuous waterway north through the west-central part of the province to the northern shore. That these routes were often followed the homogeneity of Micmac culture seems to attest.

So far as is known, the pre-European Micmac never grew corn. Living north of the commercial corn belt and within the short-summer climatic zone, they would have been threatened by killing frosts and no crop for their labor.[14] They must have been aware of the possibility of agriculture, for in 1500 corn grew on the present site of Montreal and, at least by the seventeenth century, Maliseet were raising crops on the St. John River. Lescarbot reported that "Our Souriquois formerly . . . tilled the ground; but since the French bring them kettles, beans, peas, biscuits, and other food, they are become slothful, and make no more account of those exercises";[15] and LeClercq repeated a tale in which corn was brought back from the land of the dead by members of the tribe who

[13] Pp. 23–24.
[14] Byers, 1946, 11. Tale 87 suggests that corn growing was not native to the Micmac.
[15] *History*, III, 195, 250.

PART ONE *Tribal Life*

had won it in gambling with Papkootparout, the master of souls. The plants were set out and cultivated according to instructions, and for a time they flourished, but through negligence, the art was soon lost.[16] LeClercq made no comment on this item embedded in a long story, and nowhere else was early agriculture mentioned. French writers from first to last berated the Micmac because they did not till the soil. This early apparent self-accusation of Micmac sloth and negligence is so heartily in accord with French sentiment that one wonders how the motive got into the tales.

PHYSICAL TRAITS

Only the early visitors could describe the racially pure Micmac. Lescarbot wrote:

All they which I have seen have black hairs, some excepted which have auburn colour hairs; but of flaxen colour I have seen none, and of red still less . . . The beard of the chin (which our savages call *migidoni*) is with them as black as their hairs. They all take away the producing cause thereof [pull the hairs out by the roots], except the Sagamos, who for the most part have but a little. Membertou hath more than all the others, and notwithstanding, it is not thick as it is commonly with Frenchmen . . . As for the inferior parts, our savages do not hinder the growing or increasing of the hairs there . . . [Women, but not men, plucked the pubic hair.]

These people have generally less hairs than we; for along the body they have none at all . . . Concerning their eyes, they have then neither blue or green, but black for the most part, like to a decent greatness. And I may say assuredly and truly that I have seen there as fair boys and girls as any can be in France . . . As for the mouth, they have no big moorish lips, as in Africa and also in Spain; they are well-limbed, well-boned, and well-bodied, competently strong; and nevertheless we had many in our company who might have wrestled well enough with the strongest of them; but, being hardened, there would be made of them very good men for the war, which is that wherein they most delight . . . If there be any blind with one eye, or lame (as it happeneth sometimes), it is a casual thing, and cometh of the hunting. Being well composed, they cannot choose but be nimble and swift in running . . . I will affirm nothing . . . of our savages, because I took no heed to it; but it is very certain that all can swim very cunningly. For the other parts of their bodies they have them very perfect, as likewise the natural sense. For Membertou (who is above an hundred years old) did see sooner a shallop or canoe of the savages, to come afar off unto Port Royal than any of us.[17]

[16] *Gaspesia*, 213.
[17] *History*, III, 140–41.

They have no beards, the men no more than the women, except some of the more robust and virile. They have often told me that at first we seemed to them very ugly with hair both upon our mouths and heads; but gradually they have become accustomed to it, and now we are beginning to look less deformed. Generally speaking, they are of lighter build than we are; but handsome and well-shaped, just as we would be if we continued in the same condition in which we were at the age of twenty-five. You do not encounter a big-bellied, hunchbacked, or deformed person among them: those who are leprous, gouty, affected with gravel, or insane are unknown to them.[18]

In 1635 Father Le Jeune described the Cape Breton natives as having

nothing anomalous in their physical appearance; you see well-formed men, good-looking, of fine figures, strong and powerful. Their skin is naturally white, for the little children show it thus; but the heat of the Sun, and the rubbing with seal oil and moose fat, make them very swarthy, the more so as they grow older . . . One sees here old men, of eighty and a hundred years, who have hardly a gray hair.[19]

At present Micmac are so intermixed with whites, especially French, that it is doubtful whether there is a pure-blooded individual among them. In northern New Brunswick intermarriage with the French was so considerable that a century ago Cooney ascribed to the French settlers at Caraquette

more of the color and features of the Micmac Indians than is generally discernible in Acadians. This personal distinction, however, is also observable at *Petit Roche,* another French settlement farther up the Bay; and there is little doubt that the peculiarity in both cases, is the result of early settlers having intermarried with the Savages.[20]

The policy of adopting white children has added a degree of mixture which it is equally difficult to assess. Only in the last few years, because of the expense involved in an increasing Indian population, has the Canadian government forbidden this. At each reserve visited in 1953, at least two adults, Micmac in speech and culture, were whites adopted in infancy.

LANGUAGE

Micmac is a dialect of eastern Algonkin. There are local differences in pronunciation and vocabulary which distinguish Gaspé speech from that common to the Miramichi region, and both from that of Nova Scotia,

[18] JR, III, 73, 75.
[19] JR, VIII, 159.
[20] P. 184.

PART ONE *Tribal Life*

particularly Cape Breton; but a Micmac from any settlement is readily understood by any other Micmac.

In 1950 and 1953 Micmac at Burnt Church, in the Miramichi region, said that the most old-fashioned language is spoken in Newfoundland; and that their own and its close counterpart, the speech at Restigouche and elsewhere on the Gaspé, are next in conservatism. Nova Scotia speech they consider easy to understand.

In addition to the dictionaries compiled more than sixty years ago by Silas Rand, studies of the language have been made by Michelson,[21] Mechling,[22] Father Pacifique,[23] and Voegelin and Voegelin.[24] Mechling, in 1911, recorded and translated several texts.

With the exception of a few songs, none of our information was recorded in text. In 1911–12 native words were recorded according to the system employed in the *Handbook of American Indian Languages*; the difficulty of printing this phonetic alphabet prohibits its use here.

Vowels have Continental values (as in German); there is an obscure *u*, as in *but*, originally indicated by *A*, now represented by *a*. The consonants *d* and *t*, and frequently *g* and *k*, are heard interchangeably in many words and are probably intermediate, as are *p* and *b*; *r* does not occur except in a few borrowed words, and is not trilled. Some speakers substitute *l* for *r* in the pronunciation of English or French words which contain this consonant, as *Lestigouche* for *Restigouche*. Final *k* approximates German posterior *ch*; initial or medial *k* is a palatal medial. A glottal stop at the end of a word ending in *k*, *g*, or *tc* is common; *c* has the sound of *sh*.

The attitude of the Micmac toward their language is highly personal and conservative. In the present times of rapid social change it is the trait that identifies, symbolizes, and unites the entire group. All adults speak or at least understand English, but very few children understand more than a few words when, at the age of seven, they enter school. The delight expressed in 1911 when a white person used the Micmac language, if only a word correctly pronounced, may be less today, but has by no means disappeared; the utterance of *buoin* will almost invariably bring the response that inasmuch as the speaker already knows about Micmac witchcraft it will do no harm to tell him more. However, this

[21] "Preliminary Report," 1912.
[22] Manuscript in the Canadian National Museum, 1911–12.
[23] *Leçon grammaticales et théoretiques pratiques*, 1939.
[24] In *Man in Northeastern North America*, 1946, 188–92.

Elnu, the People

feeling expressed by an informant in 1911 is now probably rare: "If you pronounce a word correctly, an Indian will listen and will answer you; but if you do not pronounce it correctly, he will think you are making fun of him, and you will receive no reply. Some persons cannot say Indian words, because they cannot twist the tongue enough; there is too much English in them."

On each reserve some persons can still read and write Micmac. The teaching of reading and writing in the native language was greatly retarded because of an unfortunate inspiration of the otherwise admirable Father LeClercq. After observing that Micmac children while repeating prayers made mnemonic strokes on birch bark, he invented an elaborate and laborious method to facilitate learning by using arbitrary characters, each of which stood for a word — in Chinese fashion. The characters themselves soon assumed spiritual powers in Micmac eyes, but as a visual aid to education their value might be questioned by all except their inventor.[25]

Father LeClercq's little folly made strong secret appeal to Father Maillard, who, without due acknowledgment, took over the ideographs and turned out documents in the name of the Micmac, in their "native" symbols; the earliest known is a declaration made by "les Sauvages Micmaks" to British officials in 1740. (See illustration 4.) A hundred years later the missionary Father Charles Kauder, impressed by Maillard's "invention," persuaded the Austrian government to print, for distribution among the Indians, an edition of the prayer book and catechism in Micmac ideographs. An edition was printed at Restigouche in 1866, and later the famous Father Pacifique, Capuchin missionary at Restigouche from 1894 until 1943, turned out a *Manuel hiéroglyphique de religion*, which brought him the congratulations of the Congregation of Propaganda. On the reserves there are today a few copies of the old prayer book, and a few old women can read them — more or less as a stunt; but the Micmac do not now know the history of the characters. The only explanation of their origin offered in 1911 was that they came from Providence, and probably were made before the world was made.

During the vogue of these tortuous devices the missionaries did not concentrate on teaching the reading and writing of Micmac. When such teaching was introduced, it was almost too late; for the need of English to obtain employment, and the Canadian policy of compulsory educa-

[25] *Gaspesia*, 126, 131, 133–35.

PART ONE *Tribal Life*

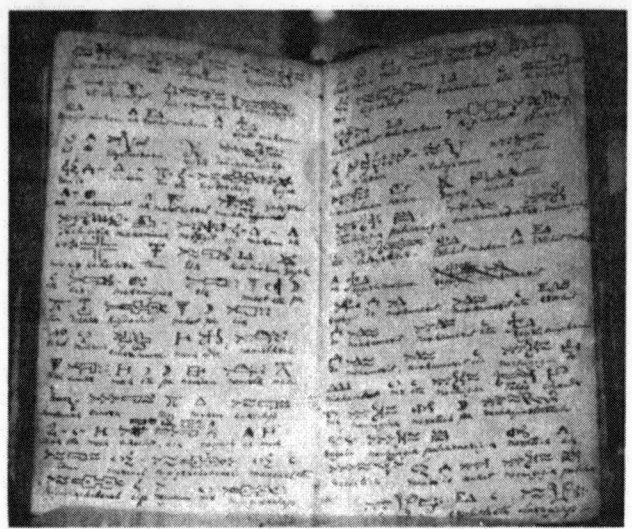

4. Micmac script. Below the ideograph is an interlinear translation into Micmac written in Roman script. The manuscript, by the Abbé Maillard, was photographed in the library of the Archbishop of Quebec, with the permission of the librarian, Father Lidsay.

tion, ended the desirability of formal knowledge of Micmac. Old persons remember attending "Indian school" held in someone's house at Restigouche, about 1885. Knowledge of the printed Micmac language was spread through a column instigated by Father Pacifique, which appeared in the weekly St. John *New Freeman* from May 31, 1903, until April 25, 1908, and through his *Micmac Messenger*, issued monthly at Restigouche from 1906 until 1936 and distributed throughout the Maritimes.

In 1911–12 a Micmac expressed the need for English in dealing with practical problems: "We found this out in an instance in which we had difficulty with our bank account. Consider, too, all the bracing and rigging on a vessel. We cannot pronounce these words in Micmac. The English language has more words than that of any other people. On the other hand, there are no words in Micmac that one cannot say in English." Even so, the more conservative believed that if an Indian had too much education he was no good at all. "The natural way is his way." An Indian who could read and write was more likely to be distrusted than to be respected by his fellows.

CHAPTER III

Economic Life

LONG before 1911 the exclusively hunting-fishing economy and its inevitable seasonal migrations had vanished, but many old men knew the basic pattern, could recount the details of activities long obsolete, and respected the ancestral wisdom of their forebears. The old-time Micmac, they felt, knew, with an instinct like that of the beasts, what was good to eat and what was harmful, what was medicine and what was poison. To get enough food they had to move around during the year. Spring, summer, and early autumn were spent by a river; in late autumn they moved into the woods, and camped near a spring or a brook where water could be obtained, and in a spot which promised plentiful game. Even so, now and then times were very hard.

The autumn removal to a hunting camp, a feature of many folktales,[1] impressed seventeenth-century priests and travelers from France, who described its occurrence at Miscou, Percé, and Port Royal.[2]

In 1616 Father Biard, at Port Royal, recorded the month-by-month hunting calendar of the Micmac:

In January they have the seal-hunting: for this animal, although it is aquatic, nevertheless spawns upon certain Islands about this time. Its flesh is as good as veal. In the month of February and until the middle of March, is the great hunt for beavers, otters, moose, bears (which are very good), and for the caribou, an animal half ass and half deer. If the weather then is favorable, they live in great abundance, and are as haughty as Princes and Kings, but if it is against them, they are greatly to be pitied and often die of starvation. The weather is against them if it rains a great deal, and does not freeze; for then they can hunt neither deer nor beavers. Also, when it snows a great deal, and does not freeze over, for then they cannot put their dogs upon the chase, because they

[1] See Part Two, Tales 97 and 125.
[2] JR, I, 83–87, XXXII; LeClercq, *Gaspesia*, 80.

25

PART ONE *Tribal Life*

sink down; the savages themselves do not do this; for they wear snowshoes on their feet which help them to stay on top; yet they cannot run as fast as would be necessary, the snow being too soft. They have other misfortunes of this kind which it would be tedious to relate.

In the middle of March, fish begin to spawn, and to come up from the sea with certain streams, often so abundantly that everything swarms with them. Any one who has not seen it could scarcely believe it. You cannot put your hand into the water, without encountering them. Among these fish the smelt is the first; this smelt is two or three times as large as that in our rivers; after the smelt comes the herring at the end of April; at the same time bustards, which are large ducks, double the size of ours, come from the south and eagerly make their nests upon the Islands. Two bustard eggs are fully equal to five hens eggs. At the same time come the sturgeon, and salmon, and the great search through the Islet for eggs, as the water-fowl, which are there in great numbers, lay their eggs then, and often cover the Islets with their nests. From the month of May up to the middle of September, they are free from all anxiety about their food; for the cod are upon the coast, and all kinds of fish and shellfish; and the French ship with which they traffic; and you may be sure they understand how to make themselves courted.

Water game abounds there, but not forest game, except at certain times birds of passage, like bustards and gray and white geese. There are to be found there gray partridges which have beautiful long tails and are twice as large as ours; there are a great many wild pigeons, which come to eat raspberries in the month of July, also several birds of prey and some rabbits and hares. Our savages in the middle of September withdraw from the sea, beyond the reach of the tide, to the little rivers, where the eels spawn, of which they lay in a supply. In October and November comes the second hunt for elks [moose] and beavers; and then in December comes a fish called by them ponamo, (translated as "dog-fish" or "tom cod") which spawns under the ice. Also then the turtles bear little ones, etc. . . . In order to thoroughly enjoy this, their lot, our foresters start off to their different places with as much pleasure as if they were going on a stroll or an excursion; they do this easily through the skillful use and great convenience of canoes.[3]

The preceding picture, abnormally bright from absence of dark and frequent famine, continued for at least two centuries to represent the ideal Micmac economic life, gradually fading as game diminished and hunting grounds shrank. In the accounts of economic life and material culture which follow, in this and in the succeeding chapter, informants spoke for the most part of materials and methods before their time. All such descriptions have been placed in the past tense; the present tense

[3] JR, III, 77, 83.

Economic Life

is used for activities current in 1911–12, and such terms as "now," "still," and "at present" refer to these years.

FISHING

At low tide, lobsters were dug out of the flats with a stick, caught by the tail, and put into a bark vessel. Shellfish were dug out at low tide and were roasted on coals. Mussels and clams were located by their breathing holes and by their "spitting."

A bone gorge served as a fishhook. This was an oblong piece of bone, sharp at both ends, one end slightly larger than the other. At the larger end a hole was made through which a line composed of twisted yellow-birch twigs passed. Sometimes people fished without hooks, using bait attached to the line. The teeth of the fish caught in the bait, or the fish swallowed it and was pulled out before it could disgorge. Trout, salmon, and smelt were procured in this way.

Fish are still taken with a wooden spear, the sharp point being flanked by two flanges lashed to the shaft on either side, extending beyond the middle point, and so shaped as to hold the speared fish on the barbs. (See illustration 5.) The spear was most effectively used at night, when

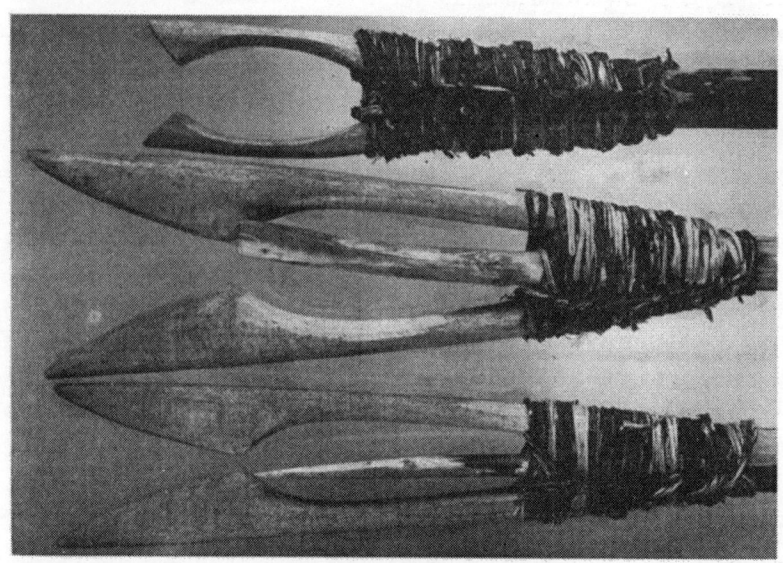

5. Wooden fish spears.

PART ONE *Tribal Life*

a torch of cedar bark was held in the split end of a stick in front of the canoe. The fisherman's wife, or a man, paddled and steered the canoe. In this manner, especially in autumn, large quantities of salmon were taken.

A net, *a'bi*, sometimes fifty yards in length, is made of intertwined branches of birch, elder, or other tree or bush. It is put into the water near the shore and extends into deep water. While some tend the net, others in canoes splash water to drive the fish into the apex of the triangle formed by shore, net, and canoes. The deep-water end of the net is then drawn toward the shore and gradually pulled into shallow water, where the fish can be taken.

A semicircular weir, *a'bilokteg'an* (net-trap), is employed to catch fish close to shore. A swinging door in the center opens sufficiently with the incoming tide to allow the fish to enter, and is closed by the receding water, thus imprisoning the fish.

A weir made of brush, *lokaskadeg'an*, of similar construction, was used in the Richibuctou River and at Eel Ground, N.B., about the middle of the last century. Horizontal sticks were put up, crossed alternately in and out with smaller ones. A door at the middle and one at the end, each about three feet wide, extended the depth of the weir. The doors were left open until high tide, and then were closed. Each door, four vertical sticks intertwined with brush, was held in place by a horizontal stick, *tci'bila'an*, the ends of which were inserted into the weir on the side of the door. At low tide, fish were speared from canoes. To attract the fish into the weir, a bait of meat was put on a stake, and the stake was driven into the mud to keep it in place. The bait was called *wa'adegan*; the stake holding it, *kulnade'gandjitc*; the doors of the weir, *ka'agan*.

In constructing this weir, which was from fifty to a hundred feet in length, the first step was to drive vertical sticks, about three feet apart, into the mud. They were then interwoven by a man who stood in the water. The intertwining was done at the surface, and the branches were pushed down, layer by layer, until the work was completed. Usually two or three men, working together, built a weir. It belonged to those who had cooperated in its construction, and they shared equally in the catch, irrespective of who attended it. The ice destroyed it in the winter, and it was rebuilt every spring, before the big run of fish. A great many fish, especially trout, bass, and salmon, were taken in these weirs.

Essentially the same type of construction was described by Marc Les-

Economic Life

carbot in 1606, when dolphin, sturgeon, and salmon were taken in that manner.[4]

Ice fishing is still practiced in an old-time way. In winter the fisher cuts a hole in the ice and lies by it when the tide is running, watching for fish. The first day, he watches all day, to ascertain when the fish are running — whether at high tide, low tide, or when the tide is strong. The time of his return trip is governed accordingly. He sits on a piece of hide and under a shelter of hides supported by seven *pasi'dal*. A small hole for each pole is dug in the ice, and the poles are bound together at the top with a spruce root. The structure, called *mtu'ma'anewi'gwamtcitc*, is used only during the day. The shanties which are now used during winter nights, when men spear smelt by the aid of a torch, are called *wendji'gwamtci'dal*.

Capture of Sea Mammals

Seal, walrus, and porpoise are no longer caught off the Maritimes, but Micmac of New Brunswick and Nova Scotia know that this great game was once most common at Point Miscou and near the Magdalen Islands and can give full accounts of the native method of seal hunting. Seals drifted into Miramichi Bay and other northern waters on ice floes, and the hunter approached them over the floe. In securing the hair seal the hunter imitated a playing seal, until he was close enough to shoot. In Nova Scotia decoy seal was used. The hunter remained in hiding near the decoy, which was usually put on the beach close to the water's edge. The decoy, made of a piece of dead wood about the color of a seal, resembled a seal in shape and size. A mouth was cut in it, and charred depressions represented the eyes. If the wood was too light in color, it was charred slightly here and there and was rubbed until the appropriate shade was obtained. Hard, smooth wood was too glossy. When placed on a rock, beach, or sand bar frequented by seals, the decoy often lured them out of the water. A sealskin stuffed with moss might also be used.

Occasionally a man covered himself with sealskin and lay on the beach, or moved about in imitation of a seal, and sometimes succeeded in his deception. This method, of course, could be used only when the wind was from the proper quarter. Seals, if they could be reached on ice, were sometimes killed with a club. A man who hunted the animal in this way had to keep directly in front of it and deliver his blow from that

[4] *History*, III, 236.

PART ONE *Tribal Life*

quarter. If he approached it from behind, or from the side, he would almost certainly be killed, for a seal can turn and strike with deadly rapidity a foe that approaches from the rear or from the side. It can, however, jump straight ahead only a few inches, and a man can easily keep out of danger if its head is toward him. A seal that has been shot sinks. To raise it to the surface, a long pole with a barbed stone head lashed to it on one side was employed. The barb was made by breaking away some of the flint at a right angle to the longitudinal axis of the stone implement, and near the point.

Harpoons (*ap'skantcitc*) were most frequently used to take seals. The point was made of bone of moose or caribou, split with a large stone, and sharpened on a stone.[5] Near the larger end a hole was cut or bored with a piece of sharp flint. Barbs were made near the head. The head was fastened to the shaft by means of a long moose-hide thong. When the harpoon was thrown, the thong, which was held in the hand, was dropped. The seal was allowed to run until it drowned, and was then hauled in by means of the thong, which was passed through a slit cut in the lower jaw of the captive. The harpoon was used at least as far south as Pictou, N.S.[6]

From the literature, items reinforce the accounts of hunting sea mammals given by my informants. Walrus in 1764 entered Shediac Bay, N.B. As late as 1866 Micmac from Prince Edward Island roved as far as the Magdalen Islands, Anticosti, Labrador, and Newfoundland in search of seal.[7]

Porpoise in 1836 were so common in the Bay of Fundy that Micmac engaged commercially in their capture; when Levinge's ship entered the strait (Digby Gut) between the bay and Annapolis Basin "the canoes of the Micmac hunting the porpoise . . . covered the water."[8] A hundred years later, Indians in the region described in detail, and fully reconstructed, the porpoise hunt for Dr. Alexander Leighton:

The method . . . was simple and direct. Two men put out, each in a twenty-foot birch-bark canoe. The canoes were the usual Micmac shape, no up-curl to the bow and stern, and therefore fine for open and windy water. There were no seats. The bow man knelt and leaned back against

[5] Before 1672, iron points manufactured especially for sale to the Indians had replaced bone in arrows, spears, and harpoons. Denys, II, 442–44.
[6] George Patterson ("The Stone Age in Nova Scotia," TNSINS, 7:235–36) described, among the local archeological specimens in Dalhousie Museum, an artifact which appears to be a bone harpoon-head.
[7] Smethurst, 377, 385; Vetromile, 123.
[8] Levinge, 210.

Economic Life

a thwart, and while the stern man sometimes sat at the back where the gunwales came together, he usually slipped down on his knees when any exertion or skillful work was required. The bow man was equipped with a ten-bore, long-barreled muzzle-loader called a "porpoise gun," and a twelve-foot spear. The gun was an instrument with a terrible kick, and the shot used was very coarse, larger than buckshot. Powder horn and shot bag were kept close by. The spear was fixed with the butt caught under one of the middle thwarts and the point projecting beyond the bow. Thus it could be quickly seized. It was really a gaff, the sharp part made of iron, about a foot long and barbed at one end, and at the other fitted into a light spruce shaft of eleven feet or more.

Out on the sea the canoes went their way fairly individually. To keep together increased the danger of shooting each other. They set forth on the rising tide and met the porpoises coming in toward the rivers and estuaries in pursuit of herring and mackerel. As soon as a porpoise rose close enough, he was shot and then transfixed with the spear before he could escape or sink. The spear was never thrown, but held by the bow man, who rode his canoe like a horse and used the spear like a boar hunter. In a rough sea with a wild porpoise, both bow and stern man had to fight hard to keep the canoe right side up. To capsize miles from land, in water chilled by the Labrador current, would have been fatal. When the porpoise was dead he was pulled in over the side by the Indian at the stern — another difficult job, even in calm weather. The usual day's catch was about six porpoises per canoe, but some men could get as many as twelve and come home with their gunwales almost awash.[9]

HUNTING

Bow and Arrow

Bows were made of fir, spruce, or rock maple. Some of the old-time Micmac preferred fir, because it was considered the most elastic wood. White maple, if used for a bow, was cut when green. Informants now say it is more efficient when green than when dry. To increase the pliability, the ends were sometimes dampened. The simple bow was used. A notch was cut in each end to hold the bowstring. The string was made of deer or caribou thong, preferably from the large flank muscle or tendon, which was rubbed to and fro between the hands to make it pliable and elastic. An extra bowstring was always carried. One informant said yellow birch was used as a bow and was reinforced with a backing of moose-hide thong. Later cord was substituted for the thong. (See illustration 6, center.)

The bow was grasped between the middle of the first finger and the

[9] P. 411.

PART ONE *Tribal Life*

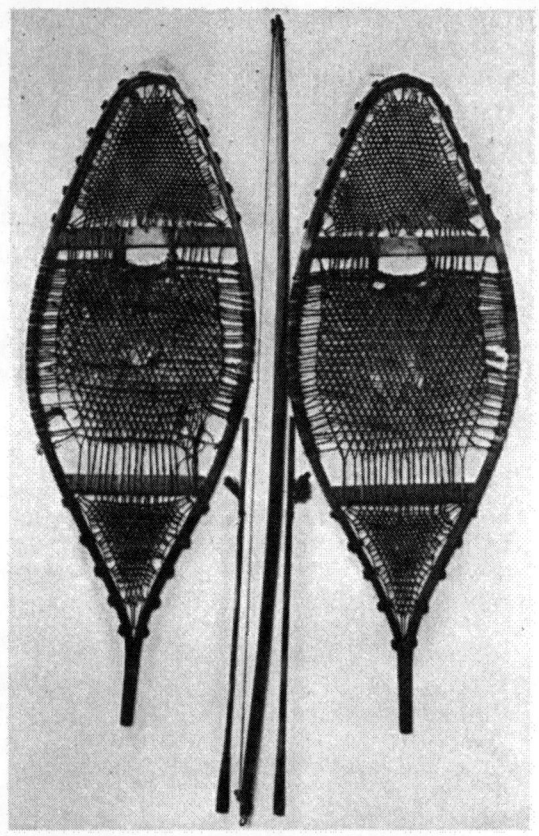

6. A hunter's light snowshoes from Pictou Landing, N.S., and bow and arrow shafts with blunt ends.

thumb of the left hand — the primary release. The wrist guard, *mato'ktaligan*, consisted of a small root wrapped around the wrist.

Arrow shafts were about two and one-half feet long. Neither arrow straighteners nor arrow-shaft rubbers were used. Shafts, before they were straightened, were scraped with a sharp flint and were heated over a fire. About six inches from the head of the arrow, three feathers were attached. The tail feathers of the woodpecker, because they are stiff and straight, were preferred.[10] The quills were trimmed down, fitted into

[10] In 1607 eagles' tail feathers, because of their firmness, were attached to the arrows to make them carry well through the air, and were so prized that as much as one or even two beaver skins would be traded for one such feather. Lescarbot, *History*, III, 191, 192.

Economic Life

very small grooves cut at equal intervals on the shaft, and bound with thong. (See illustration 7.)

An otter-skin quiver, *wiskwo'kuksummug'agane*, was used. This was carried over the back, the arrow shafts projecting above the right shoulder, low enough to avoid contact with limbs and bushes while the hunter or warrior walked through the woods. The quiver was kept in position by a strap or thong which passed over the left shoulder and under the right arm. This larger thong, *pi'daladil*, was fastened to the

7. Section of an arrow shaft, showing insertion and fastening of the feathers.

coat by means of a smaller string, the *tcibila'an*, which held the quiver in position.

In warfare, the arrows were aimed considerably above the target. They were "poisoned" with a preparation made from bark, root, and a bush, the identity of which is not known (or was not revealed in 1911). "Poisoned" arrows were used only in fighting, never in hunting.[11]

The Micmac shield was oblong, of platted basswood bark, backed with the short ribs of moose-hide thong, and was provided with a loop of thong to serve as a grasp. An oblong piece of hard wood was hung under the skin jacket as a breastplate, and was kept in position by a thong which rested on the back of the neck. It afforded some protection, but would split after being struck two or three times.

Hunting Dogs

The earliest description of Micmac dogs was given by Lescarbot:

They have dogs, or hounds, almost like to foxes in form and bigness, and of hairs of all colours, which follow them, and, although they do not

[11] For the origin myth of the bow and arrow, see Tale 82.

PART ONE *Tribal Life*

spend nor call, nevertheless, they can very well find the haunt of the beast which they seek for, which being found they pursue her courageously, and they never give her over until they have her down.[12]

Game

Beaver. To capture beaver, one side of a beaver dam is cut through. The hunter stands above the opening through which the water flows out. After it is out, the beavers leave. The old one leads the way. Watchers stand with raised clubs and bring them down over the middle of the beaver's back, breaking it if a well-directed blow is given. A beaver is a fierce animal and, at close quarters, dangerous.

Beaver traps are built in a lake or river on two split logs placed on the bottom. If the beavers have a path to the water, a deadfall — a log of fir about a foot in diameter and two strides in length — is put over this. The log must be carried some distance from the spot where it is cut, for a beaver readily detects human odor. The deadfall is visited only when the wind is favorable, and after a rain, when one's tracks leave no odor.

A detailed account of winter methods for hunting beaver was given by Nicolas Denys, who for fifty years observed the Micmac from Cape Breton to the Baie des Chaleurs:

In winter . . . Dogs . . . were only used to find the houses in which they smelled the Beavers through the ice. Having found them, the Indians cut through the ice and made a hole large enough to let through a Beaver. Then they made another hole twenty-five or thirty paces away, on the open surface of the lake. In this place an Indian or two took their stand with a bow and an arrow which has a harpoon of bone at the end, made like a barbed rod, like that which was used in fishing the Sturgeon, but smaller. It has also a cord to which it is attached at one end, and the Indian took hold of the other. Everything being ready, another Indian went to the other hole near the house of the Beavers. Lying down on his belly upon the ice, he placed his arm through the hole to find the Beavers' opening, that by which they place their tail in the water. There they are all arranged one against the other, that is to say, all those of one Beaver family. Having found them, the Indian passed his hand very gently along the back of one several times, and, approaching little by little to the tail, tried to seize it.

I have heard it said by the Indians that they have kept the arm so long in the water that the ice froze all around the arm. When they once seized the tail they drew the Beaver all at one swoop out from the water upon the ice, and at the same time gave it the axe upon the head. They

[12] *History*, III, 221.

Economic Life

killed it for fear lest the Beaver bite them, for wherever these set their teeth they take out the piece. Having thus drawn one out they tried to obtain another, which they did in the same way, rubbing them gently. That does not put them to flight, for they imagine they are touching one another. But nevertheless three or four of them having been removed, the remainder take to flight and throw themselves into the water. Not being able to remain long without breathing, the daylight which shows over the hole out on the surface leads them to go there to get the air. The other Indians who are there in ambush, so soon as they appear, give them an arrow shot; the harpoon, which has teeth, holds in some part of the Beaver from which it cannot be drawn out. The cord is then pulled and the Beaver is drawn out through the hole; then comes another which is taken in the same way. Few in a house are saved; they would take all. The disposition of the Indians is not to spare the little ones any more than the big ones. They killed all of each kind of animal that there was when they could capture it.[13]

The winter beaver hunt was earlier related by Lescarbot, and a little later in more general terms by LeClercq, who made it sound more difficult by giving credit to the beaver. "These animals," he said, "make sport of the hunter, scorn him, and very often escape his pursuit by slipping from their pond through a secret outlet, which they have the instinct to leave in their dam in communication with another neighboring pond."

Bear. In New Brunswick, bears were caught in a baited snare of a strong bough or young bush. The tension of the snare string was so great that in one instance a man was killed by a thong which slipped loose while he was setting the snare. In Nova Scotia, where bear is still hunted, a snare is made by boring a hole horizontally in a tree, close to the ground. Into this hole a stick is inserted. Two heavy bushes or young trees are bent and fastened to the first stick, the trigger on which the bait is placed. Interference with the bait loosens the trigger and springs the snare; the thongs draw the animal to the tree and choke it. This device, informants say, was borrowed from the whites.

For the seventeenth-century bear hunt, Nicolas Denys is again the authority:

As to the Bears, if they killed them in winter, it was necessary that they should happen upon them when hunting. Coming upon some large trees they looked to see whether there came out any breath in the form of vapour from within. If they saw any it was a sign that the Bear was there. They mounted upon the tree and killed the Bear with their spears; then they drew it out. In the spring they met them in the woods, when they

[13] II, 429, 431–32.

PART ONE *Tribal Life*

followed their track. Or they killed them sometimes upon an Oak where they were eating acorns. Then a shot of an arrow straightway brought it to the ground, and so soon at it was down they gave it another arrow, and then they killed it with blows from axes. If they meet it upon the ground, and they draw upon it, according to whether the Bear is hurt [or not] it [either] flees or comes to the man, who has immediately another arrow ready. If he does not bring it down, the Bear embraces him, and will very soon have torn him to pieces with its claws. But the Indian to escape this throws himself face down upon the ground. The Bear smells him, and if the man does not stir, the Bear turns him over and places its nose upon his mouth to find if he is breathing. If it does not smell the breath, it places its bottom on the [man's] belly, crushes him as much as it can, and at the same time replaces its nose upon the mouth. If it does not then smell the breath, and the man does not move, it leaves him there and goes fifteen or twenty paces away. Then it sits down on its haunches and watches [to see] if the man does not move. If the man remains some time immovable, it goes away. But if it sees him move, it returns to the man, presses him once more upon the belly for a long time, then returns to smell at his mouth. If it perceives that the man breathes it will press him like that until it believes it has suffocated him, if in the meantime its wounds do not bring it down. To guard against this, it is necessary to take good care neither to breathe nor to move until it is far off. They do not do any other harm. When one has Dogs one is guaranteed against all this.[14]

Moose and Deer. Moose and deer were taken in overhead snares made of twisted white-birch branches. Two strong young trees, one on each side of the path used by these animals, were bent down to make the spring. When released, they caught the animal around the neck, and sometimes strangled it. A deer walks with head down, and a snare set for it had to be low; a moose carries its head high, and for it, a high snare was set.

The following device, Micmac say, is native: Two parallel rows or large stakes were driven into the ground a short distance apart, and the stakes in each separate row were tied together by yellow-birch twigs. Over this rested a deadfall. The bait, rolled up in bark, was placed below the deadfall, and was fastened to it with birch twigs or thongs. When the animal pulled the bait, the deadfall dropped.

Moose were sometimes stalked by hunters in disguise. In the evening two men would approach a grazing moose, each concealed in the hide of a moose or that of a cow. The men, when close enough, threw the

[14] II, 433–34.

Economic Life

disguise aside and shot their arrows. Probably imitation moose's antlers were sometimes used.[15]

Frequently in the deep snow of winter, the hunter, who wore snowshoes, and could sometimes outrun and easily capture a moose, drove these animals close to camp.

The hunter's best aid in taking moose in early days and now is the "moose call." The call is made with hands to mouth, or with a rolled conical piece of birch bark, in the shape of a trumpet. (See illustration 8.) The bark is held in position by a thread of spruce root. If the bull answers, the call of the cow moose is repeated. Sometimes the bull is lured to within a few feet of the hunter. If the call of the cow moose elicits no answer, the call of the bull is given, and sometimes this attracts the female. The moose call is most successful during the mating season,

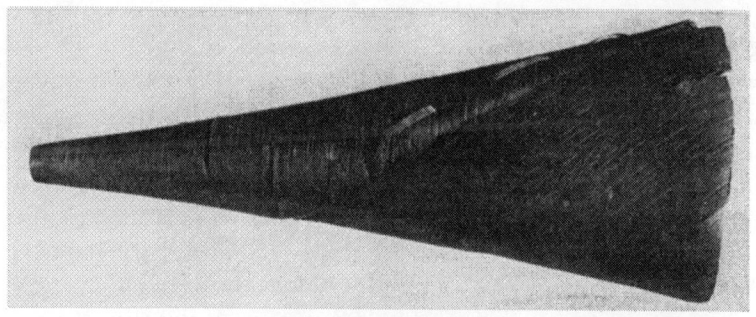

8. Birch-bark moose-caller.

in the autumn, when the bulls are in fighting mood as well as in mating temper. At this season a bull moose is dangerous. At other times he will run away, unless wounded or held at bay, when he is likely to charge.

A similar procedure, followed in the late seventeenth century, was set down by LeClercq, and by Denys:

At rutting time the moose were hunted at night upon the rivers in a canoe. Counterfeiting the cry of the female, the Indians with a dish of bark would take up some water, and let it fall into the water from a height. The noise brought the male, who thought it was a female making water. For this object they let themselves go softly along the stream; if they were ascending, they paddled very softly, and from time to time

---

[15] Manslaughter charges sometimes rose from fatal accidents due to this type of hunting. See below, pp. 172–73.

PART ONE *Tribal Life*

they made water fall, counterfeiting always the female. They went all along the border of the river, and if there was any male in the woods who heard the sound of this water, he came there. Those who were in the canoe would hear him coming, because of the noise the beast made in the woods, and they kept on constantly imitating the cry of the female, which made him come close up to them. They were all ready to draw upon him and never missed him. The darkest night was best for this hunting, and also the most calm, since the wind prevented the noise made by the fall of the water from being heard.[16]

Micmac, like other hunters, make considerable claims to a high development of the senses. The following "true" story illustrates the alleged keenness of the ancient hunters. The narrator cited it in proof of his assertion that at sundown, when all is quiet, a man can, by putting his ear to the earth or to a rock, hear a moose walking, even though the animal is a mile away.

"Two men had been calling moose. They heard one coming. It went directly to the men, but did not answer their call. It was close to them. One tried to fire his flintlock musket, but the powder did not explode. The moose saw the spark, and charged. The man fired, struck the animal on the flank, but did not kill it. They listened, with ear to the ground, until they heard an end of the moose's running. 'In half an hour we will learn whether we killed it,' said one of the men. With loaded muskets, the men went in pursuit. It became cloudy, and they were forced to halt and camp for the night. The hunter knew where the moose had stopped, although this was two or three miles from the place where they had shot it. Next morning, to avoid the telltale scent on the wind, they made a big detour, and found the moose, dead, at the very spot where the man had predicted they would find it."

A remarkable sense of taste as well as hearing is an aid to moose hunting. According to LeClercq, hunters knew the places where the moose had their retreat from certain gnawed or broken tips of branches which they called *pactagnae*, that is to say, the depredations of the moose. The hunters chewed this wood and could tell from the taste of the branches how long a time had elapsed since these animals had passed the place.

Birds. Informants agreed on the method of hunting partridge and small owls. A man who sees a spruce partridge sitting on a low limb stretches out his arm toward the bird, points a finger at it, and gradually moves closer. When he has almost touched it, he grasps it quickly with

[16] II, 427–28.

Economic Life

the other hand. If the bird is beyond reach, he fastens spruce root to the end of a stick, makes a slip-noose in the root, and puts this over the bird's head. The man must keep his eye steadily on the bird, and push the pole gradually through the extended left hand, with a steady right hand. The ordinary partridge can sometimes, but not often, be taken in this way. The *kup'ketc* (saw-whet, small owl) can be taken in the same way. It will open its eyes and look at you. You must remain still until it closes them, then go closer, very slowly; soon you will be able to grasp the bird.

I did not see an exhibition of these methods; but the straightforward and matter-of-fact way in which these accounts were corroborated by all who were questioned about them convinced me that they are, or were, employed as described.

A similar capture of the partridge, and the pursuit of the hummingbird was recorded by LeClercq:

The Partridges of Canada perch and roost in trees; and they eat the birch or the fir, which imparts to them a little of its bitter taste. Their stomachs are white and delicate like that of a capon, and those which eat only birch are excellent, in whatsoever manner one prepares them. The hunting of them is easy, especially in Spring, when they seek to lay their eggs; because then they make a noise by beating with their wings, and this reveals them to the hunter. And they are so little wild that one can drive them like chickens before him; and they even allow themselves to be approached near enough to permit one to extend a noose attached to the end of a pole, through which they pass the head, and thus render easy this method of capture.

The Humming-bird, which some call the Bird of Heaven, is of the size of a nut. Our Gaspesians call it Nirvido, and it is hunted solely as a curiosity. The guns are loaded with sand, because even the smallest shot would be too large for killing this tiny bird, which is dried in the oven and in the sun, for fear lest decay come in a body which seems wholly plumage.[17]

Denys described the capture of ducks and geese by night:

They had still another kind of hunting by night, and one rather interesting. In certain closed coves which are under cover from the wind, the Wild Geese, the Brant, and the Ducks go to sleep out upon the surface, for on land they would not be safe because of the Foxes. To those places the Indians went, two or three in a canoe, with torches which they made of Birch bark; these burn more brightly than torches of wax. Reaching the place where all these birds are, they laid down in the canoe, which they allowed to drift without their being seen. The current carried

[17] *Gaspesia*, 279–81.

them right into the midst of all these birds, which had no fear of them, supposing them to be logs of wood which the sea was carrying from one place to another, something that often happens, which makes them accustomed to it. When the Indians were in their midst they lighted their torches all at once. This surprised the birds and obliged them all at the same moment to rise into the air. The darkness of the night makes this light very conspicuous, so that they suppose it is the sun or other [such] thing. They all proceeded to wheel in confusion around the torches which an Indian held, always approaching the fire, and so close that the Indians, with sticks they held, knocked them down as they passed. Besides, by virtue of much wheeling about, these birds became dizzy, so that they fell as if dead; then the Indians took them and wrung their necks. As a result in a single night they filled their canoe.[18]

Skinning Animals and Tanning Hides

In skinning deer or moose, the hide was first cut lengthwise along the middle of the belly. If it was to be used in making moccasins, it was cut around the middle of the upper leg and was pulled down. Some began at the hind legs, then at the front legs, and then along the belly.

One old informant said that deerskin was removed by inserting a tube through the hide of a lower hind leg and blowing air into this until the skin up to the flanks was inflated; and similarly with the other hind leg. Two men, one at each leg, then pulled off the hide. The tube was made of three telescoped quills of the wild goose. A Maliseet who was then at Burnt Church said this method was not possible — the skins of deer were too tough; it could be employed only on rabbits, whose skin was easily sloughed off. Later, at Magnolia, Massachusetts, I mentioned the matter to another Maliseet and to a Penobscot. The Penobscot laughed and said my Micmac informant had given me ridiculous accounts. The Maliseet, however, remarked that in his youth he had received many a whipping for skinning rabbits in this way, for it was an insult to the animal. This taboo suggested that the custom was recent among the Maliseet. The Micmac informant declared this was an old Micmac method; and said that he had seen it used on sheep, on a French war vessel, and that the French said they had learned it from the Indians.[19]

[18] II, 435–36.
[19] An account published in 1863 in *Harpers' New Monthly Magazine* (27:291) describes this method of skinning sheep in Italy and quotes the following from W. J. C. Moens' *English Travelers and Italian Brigands: A Narrative of Capture and Captivity* (Harper). The locality, it seems, is the neighborhood of Naples. "The sheep was taken in hand by two men. One doubled the fore legs of the sheep across

Economic Life

After the hide was removed, the flesh side was washed with water, dried in the sun, and scraped with a *ka'e guk'*, a stone knife furnished with a wooden handle. It was then stretched over a framework of poles, to which it was fastened by means of thongs penetrating it at intervals; this was put outside, flesh side up, and exposed there for a night or longer, but not sufficiently long for it to become stiff.

In tanning, a hide is rubbed with pine or oak punk, or with the fat of an animal, usually deer, bear, beaver, skunk, or raccoon; or with fat and oil from bass or trout. It is salted, and rolled up with the hair inside. The operator stands on this roll and kneads it by placing his weight first on one foot and then on the other. He continues the kneading, usually for about an hour, until all parts have been worked and the entire hide is pliable. He then unrolls it, spreads it out on the ground, and with the hands man and wife knead every portion of it. This last-mentioned task occupies from three to four hours. The hide, hairy side down, is left over a slow fire throughout the night. It is not allowed to become very hot. The slow steaming loosens the hair, so that it can be pulled out in large bunches. The hide is scraped to remove hair that remains, fat is applied, and the kneading is continued.

Tanning in the seventeenth century was performed as follows:

To dress their skins, these are soaked and stretched in the sun, and are well-heated on the skin side for pulling out the hair. Then they stretch them and pull out the hair with bone instruments made on purpose, somewhat as do those who prepare a skin for conversion into parchment. Then they rub it with bird's liver and a little oil. Next, having rubbed it well between the hands, they dress it over a piece of polished wood made shelving on both sides just as is done to dress the skins for

the head; the other held the head back, inserting a knife into the throat, and cutting the windpipe and jugular vein. It was then thrown down and left to expire. When dead, a slit was made in one of the hind legs near the feet and an iron ramrod taken and passed down the leg to the body of the animal; it was then withdrawn and the mouth of one of the men placed to the slit in the leg, and the animal was inflated as much as possible, and then skinned." I am indebted to the late Dr. Frank G. Speck for this reference.

In the summer of 1913, Dr. Benjamin F. Schappelle, at my request, made inquiry in Barcelona about this custom. He found it used there among the peasants and in the large *abbattoirs* of Barcelona, where machinery is employed to inflate the hides. He photographed the process and supplied me with copies of the photographs.

Dr. C. Marius Barbeau reported a record of its use in France in the seventeenth century. For a further account of the use of this process in Spanish America and among Indians and others who have had contacts with Spanish or with French, see my note, "Removing the Skins of Animals by Inflation," AA, 18:587–601 (1916). Inflation is no longer practiced by the Micmac.

PART ONE *Tribal Life*

making gloves upon an iron. They rub it until it becomes supple and manageable. Then they wash it and twist it with sticks many times, until it leaves the water clean. Then they spread it to dry. For the skins dressed with the hair, these are only treated with the livers, with which they are well rubbed by hand; they are passed repeatedly over the sticks to dress them well. If they are not then soft enough, more of the livers is added and they are once more rubbed until they are pliable; then they are dried. All of those robes, whether for men or for women, are made like a blanket.[20]

MEANS OF TRANSPORT

To facilitate pursuit of game and the seasonal migrations involved in a hunting culture, Micmac make toboggans, sleds, the snowshoe indispensable in winter hunting, and canoes.

Muskweakwitan, the Birch-Bark Canoe

The making of the first canoe required supernatural assistance which is ascribed to Gluskap, the culture hero,[21] or to the special gifts of the human creator, Mateo, who, when asked how he learned to do it, replied, *"Kes'kamzit."*[22] No one had taught him; it came out of his head or his heart.

From early times to the last days of canoe construction, there were recognized canoe builders to whom others came to obtain their crafts. In 1911 few Micmac canoe makers remained. Most of the following information was obtained from Peter Ginnish of Burnt Church. The wife of this old canoe builder, following precedent, was a valued assistant and seemed to understand the construction as well as did her husband and to have been almost as competent a canoe builder. The pronounced curve amidships is typical of Micmac canoes. (See illustration 9.)

Construction, New Brunswick. Large sheets of birch bark are removed whole and brought to camp. Sometimes a canoe, it is said, is made of a single piece of bark. If more than one strip is used, a strip forms the bottom of the canoe, deepest in the middle and sloping gradually at the sides, to conform with the shape of the bottom of the canoe. Bark is laid along the gunnels, the upper edge higher than the levels to which the ends of the ribs will come.

[20] Denys, II, 412.
[21] See Tale 11.
[22] For an explanation of this concept, see below, Chapter X and Tales 74–78.

Economic Life

9. Typical Micmac canoes on the shore at Burnt Church, N.B.

The maker places one end of an upright stick on the ground by his elbow, arm parallel to it, fingers outstretched or bent in the manner indicated in illustration 2; then he measures the heights for the respective segments of the canoe, and at these points makes notches on the stick. The tip of the outstretched forefinger of the left hand, with the arm in this position, is the height at the middle of the gunnel; the nearest knuckle of the finger, below the tip, is the height of the gunnel midway between the ends and the middle; and the additional width of the three horizontal fingers of the right hand indicates the height of the gunnel at the ends. These fixed points determine the degrees of dip in the curvature of the gunnel. The gunnel, viewed horizontally, with the eye on a level with the middle, presents an undulating surface. To ascertain the proper height of the middle of the ground where the canoe is to be placed while being built, the maker lies at full length on the ground, rests the outer side of his hand on the ground, forefinger up and pointing straight ahead, and places his chin on this extended forefinger. His eye is then on a level with this middle portion. A stick is placed upright at each end of the area on which the canoe will be built, to aid in "getting the level."

The bark is laid in the channel prepared for it, and sticks are driven into the ground, vertically, around the bark, to hold it in place. A cedar plank is placed inside along the bottom, and the ribs are inserted. The forward rib is inserted first. It is shoved into position by the foot, which

PART ONE *Tribal Life*

is placed on the middle of it and is pressed on it until the rib fits the bark evenly along its entire length. Each of two or three workers simultaneously inserts a rib. When the ribs are in position, the bark along the gunnel is turned down, inside, to cover the ends of the ribs, and is then sewed in place. The ends of the canoe are packed with shavings to prevent the sides there from bending inward. The builder sights along the bottom of the overturned canoe to ascertain whether it has the proper curvature and proportions.

To determine the length of the canoe the measure is taken from end of thumb to end of second (middle) finger, the two placed as far apart as possible, the extended hand pointed down. This measure is called *moptibiltc'acik*. The span of the middle of the canoe is measured by the compass of the arms extended horizontally, the chest representing the bottom of the canoe, and the arms the transverse median curve of the sides.

At the ends, where the strain is greatest, spruce pins about an inch in length are inserted. The sewing is done with bark from spruce root. Spruce root grows, tendril-like, near the surface. Sometimes a piece three fathoms in length can be obtained; if it is found along the beach, or near water, in damp ground, it may be four or five fathoms long. It is of almost uniform thickness throughout its entire length. The root is cut off at the larger end, and from that end is split lengthwise; one part is held in the teeth, and the other by the hand. In this way, it is easily split down to the smaller end of the root. This method of separating the root into fibers is called *elikpe'tk*.[23] If more than one strip of bark has been used, several people assist in sewing the strips together.

To prevent leakage at the stitching, spruce gum is smeared over the stitches. It is obtained by boiling spruce sap in the fat of codfish, bear, beaver, moose, or other animal, to make it adhesive. Before the prepared threads of the roots are used, they are soaked in warm water. This prevents brittleness. May or June is the best month to gather it, as is true also of the birch bark for the canoe; but the root can be pulled whenever the ground is soft. The root or bark of birch, maple, or hazel is twisted before it is used; spruce root or bark is not twisted.

For sewing the bark, an awl made from a leg bone of caribou or of moose is used. It is heated in a fire until it splits lengthwise. The heat

[23] *Elikpe'tkal* means "splitting," as when strips of ash are cut for basket weaving. It refers to anything in which the teeth are used in splitting or indenting. Thus indenting birch bark into designs by the teeth is *elikpetk*.

Economic Life

hardens it. A piece of suitable size is selected, is split again to secure a good point, and is sharpened by rubbing it on a stone. Sometimes the sharp solid antlers of young deer are used as awls.

The cedar ribs are two and one-half to three inches wide, about one-fourth inch thick at the ends, and one-half inch thick in the middle. They are slightly wider in the middle than at the ends. The maker, when shaping them, holds each at arm's length, in front of him, and with his eye measures the proportions. If it is properly shaped, he gives it the desired curvature by holding each end in one hand and pressing out the middle with his knee. To make the ribs pliable, and also to speed the drying, they have previously been soaked in hot water. They are then placed in the sun to dry and to ensure retention of the proper shape.

Between the ribs and the bark cover, thin pieces of split cedar run lengthwise in the canoe. They are wider in the middle than at the ends, and lie close to one another. When the craft has been constructed, two long narrow sticks are laid along the outside of the canoe, a few inches below the gunnel. They extend the entire length of the canoe, are sewed together at the ends, and strengthen it.

Micmac claim that a good builder, without assistance, could with "hurry-work" and fine weather build a canoe in about eight days. Dry weather is the best; it is almost impossible to do the work in wet weather. An ordinary man not especially versed in the art requires about twelve days to construct a canoe.

A good canoe, well cared for, will last about twenty years. Several canoes at Burnt Church have been in commission for twelve to fifteen years and are still serviceable, though most of them are patched and evidently the worse for wear.

Construction, Nova Scotia. The account of canoe building in Nova Scotia is practically identical with that given above. A canoe can be built only in dry weather; and the warmer the day, the better. If the weather is cool, hot water is poured over the bark to keep it from breaking and to render it pliable.

The bark is ordinarily hard, but becomes soft in the heat of the sun or of fire. To secure the bark, a birch tree of proper size is cut down with a stone axe. A log is placed nearby for the tree to fall on, so that the bark will not be injured. A fire is built on each side of the log; the heat loosens the bark and makes it pliable. The bark is then pulled off. The bark is measured off in units of the full span of the outstretched

45

PART ONE *Tribal Life*

arms; four of these for a large canoe, and an extra half-span — from the middle of the chest to the tip of the middle finger — for a very large canoe. For an even larger one, the length is extended by the length of the middle finger.

Sometimes the bark, after being wrapped with thong to prevent its breaking, is cut from a standing tree. If the bark is not first heated, it will peel off, when it is cut, with a rapidity that is likely to cause it to crack in some places. It is put in the hot sun until it becomes pliable.

In some settlements ribs of spruce or of juniper are preferred to cedar, because cedar, when wet, becomes soft.

The heights of the gunnel of the birch-bark canoe are determined by the distances from the elbow to the ends of the fingers of the outstretched hand, in the following manner: to the end of the little finger for the height at the ends; to the end of the third finger for the height at the middle; to the end of the thumb for the height midway between the ends and the middle. The longitudinal strips between the bark and the ribs are of fir.

Stones are put on the bottom of the canoe to hold the bark firmly in place; and from time to time the canoe is floated to ascertain whether it has the proper balance and proportions. Sometimes all the work is done by men; frequently, however, women assist with the sewing and sometimes do all the sewing.

Paddles and Anchor. The typical shape of the Micmac paddle is shown in illustration 42g. In shallow water, especially rapids, a pole is used for punting.

The canoe usually carried an anchor stone, sometimes spherical, sometimes flat, one and one-half to two feet in length and about eight to twelve inches in circumference. A groove was cut around the middle, to accommodate the attached thong. In shallow water, spruce root was frequently employed as an anchor rope. For deep-water anchorage, rawhide thong was preferred, because it was thought to be safer.

Sails. Almost every canoe at Burnt Church is equipped with a canvas sail. Formerly, two kinds of sail were used. A young spruce tree — spruce because of its dense foliage, was especially suitable — was cut, the end shaved down so that it would fit into the hole prepared for it, and the tree, with its limbs and needles, used as a sail. At the present day the board in which the mast is set is placed under the ribs. Formerly a flat plank about two feet long and seven inches wide was placed over the

Economic Life

ribs. It was held in place by means of four sticks, each about two feet long, two at each end of this board, driven between the ribs and the bottom of the boat at an angle which brought them against the board and thus pinned the board down.

Another type of sail consisted of a small pole four or five feet high and three or four pieces of concave cedar bark. The pole pierced the bark in two places. By means of strings attached to either side of the bark, and held by the steersman, the bark could be turned to catch the breeze. If the wind was stiff, one or two of the top pieces of bark were removed. Peter Ginnish had seen these used, and believed they antedated the white man. The Pugula'tamutc, or "Stone Indians," are said to have used them.[24]

At Pictou, N.S., a birch-bark sail was employed in the canoe. This was extended by two small strips of wood, near either edge, running vertically and piercing the bark here and there. It was fastened to a mast. Strings of spruce root tied to one side of the canoe held one side of the bark sail in position; the other side was kept in position by similar strings held in the hand and made taut or loose, to catch the breeze to advantage. The use of a tree or bush for a sail was not known.

Size. Formerly, canoes were about twelve feet in length. This information is corroborated by Rand.[25] The canoes are now much larger. One at Burnt Church has the following dimensions: length, 23 feet, 9 inches; greatest width at middle, 3 feet, 11 inches; inner width of thwarts at middle, 3 feet, 3 inches; vertical height in middle from the cedar strips on which the ribs rested to level of gunnel, 1 foot, 9½ inches; inside height of prow, 1 foot, 11 inches; vertical height of prow above ground, 2 feet, 4½ inches. This canoe carries seventeen yards of sail, and the owner said it can carry fifteen people in quiet water and twelve people in rough water. Another man made the more conservative statement that a canoe of this size might carry twelve people in quiet water, and that its load capacity is about eighteen hundred pounds. Very heavy loads are sometimes transported in the canoes, which seem able to carry almost as much as can be gotten into them.

Navigability. Micmac canoes sail well with the wind; but owing to

[24] See Tale 42.
In a Timagami Ojibwa story there is reference to the use, by an animal, of "a big bark sail." Frank G. Speck, *Mythology and Folk-Lore of the Timiskaming Algonquin and Timagami Ojibwa*, CDM, GS, AS, 1915, No. 9, p. 47.
[25] *History, Manners, Customs . . . of the Micmac Indians*, 1850.

PART ONE Tribal Life

their flat bottom and lack of keel, the steering being done with a paddle, they do not sail well in a breeze from any other quarter. One man claimed that he had sailed from the lighthouse on Portage Island to the point at Burnt Church in fifteen minutes — a distance estimated at about five miles; and the same exaggerator claimed to have made the trip from Newcastle to Burnt Church, a distance of thirty-two miles, in fifty-three minutes, having on board a passenger and a barrel of flour.

The canoes are light and graceful sailing craft. They respond readily to a breeze and skim the water with seemingly little resistance. The upward curve in the middle of the gunnel is said to be so placed because the wave is highest at the middle of the canoe. The canoeman, when taking breakers, attempts to enter the wave when it breaks and follow on it to shore. If overtaken by a storm, the occupants of the canoe go to shore, pull up the canoe, turn it bottom up, and lie or sit under it for shelter. By elevating one side of it, room is obtained for a fire in front, and the craft furnishes shelter overhead and to windward.

Terms. Rand in his *Dictionary* states that there are "about 70 terms connected with making and operating a birch bark canoe." They include the Micmac terms for the following: to bend the ribs; to get the upper "timbers"; thwarts; gunwale; ribs; the timber; midships, in the middle of the canoe; the sitting place, i.e., the crosspiece on which the paddler sits; the ribs of the sitting place; ribs for the end next to the sitting place; small (ribs); ribs next to the end.

In 1911, the following designations were given the parts of the canoe:

akwit'an, canoe. Generally called *mu'skweakwi'tan,* birch-bark canoe (*mus'kwe,* birch bark).

samwatcit'c, "frog," the upright stick at the end of the canoe between the bark and the shavings.

uk'tcidabig'awan, the upright stick placed on the other side of the shavings, toward the middle of the canoe, to hold them in place. It was kept in position by means of wedges driven tightly between it and the bottom and the sides.

tca'awele'wagan, the spruce-tree sail. The canvas sail is called *se'gigan.* (Mast is *u'togan;* sprits are *me'ndjinaskobi la'an.*)

u'kwat, the flat board of the old-type canoe in which the mast was set.

kade'kan'abi, the ropes by which the sail was held in place by the steersman (*kade',* eel, *ababi,* rope). As the name implies, they were made of eelskin.

kundo'wie kul'bisan, the stone anchor. *kul'bisan,* anchor.

kul'bisan tu'a kwa'bi, anchor rope.

Economic Life

prilao'k, horizontal sticks laid on the outside of the canoe to strengthen it.

mindjitca'mantci'tc, the thwart nearest the stern.

olipul'iemund'jiteaman, the thwart between the middle and the end. (There are five thwarts. The fore and aft halves of the canoe are identical, and either end can be used as bow or stern.)

ka'dalukwemun'djitca'man, the middle thwart. The paddler usually sits on the thwart nearest the stern.

priga'nk, the ribs.

maunk, the horizontal strips of cedar laid between the ribs and the bark.

pukta'an, paddle.

ki'gamkon, pole used for punting. The height of the canoe at any place is called *ta'makkwi'tanek*.

In 1611, and in 1616, Father Biard, at Port Royal, described the Micmac canoes as "little skiffs made of birch bark, narrow and closed at both ends, like the crest of a morion; the body is like a large hollow cradle; they are eight or ten feet long; moreover so capacious that a single one of them will hold an entire household of five or six persons, with all their dogs, sacks, skins, kettles, and other heavy baggage." A heavily loaded canoe drew only half a foot of water; unloaded it was light enough to be picked up and carried away with one hand. Paddles were made from a single piece of beechwood; the blade was an arm's length by about a half foot-breadth, the handle somewhat longer than the blade. Three, four, or five persons, both men and women, paddled together. In good weather they could make thirty or forty leagues a day.[26]

At this early period, according to Lescarbot, Father Biard's contemporary, a sail was not used. Some fifty years later Denys wrote: "They also went with a sail, which was formerly of bark but oftener of a well-dressed skin of a young Moose. Had they a favourable wind they went as swiftly as the throw of a stone. One canoe carried as many as eight or ten persons."[27]

The craft is used (1911) only in the Miramichi region of New Brunswick, the probable spot where, four hundred years earlier, Cartier had to frighten the crowding canoes away from his ship. Even there they are few; at Burnt Church fifteen are in use; two at Eel Ground; two unsea-

[26] JR, III, 83–85; I, 160–61.
[27] Denys gives a full account of canoe building, pp. 420–22. For Lescarbot's account, see *History*, III, 192.

PART ONE *Tribal Life*

worthy ones linger at Red Bank. At Restigouche, two or three still do service.

Micmac attribute the disappearance of the canoe to the fact that the modern flat-board boats are not so quickly worn out by the grinding pebbles and sand, and suitable birch bark and spruce-root thread are very difficult to procure and can be obtained only after a two or three days' tramp into the woods. The large birch trees have been cut for timber, and the tramplings of cattle have broken the spruce roots, so that now only short and unserviceable pieces can be obtained.[28]

Other Types of Canoe

Formerly a great many *ta'a ulk* were in use; but now none exist. They are believed to have been obtained from the Maliseet and to have derived their name from the Ta'a (Ottawa) tribe. Some informants say they were procured from the English. They consisted of a ribless sheet of spruce bark, the sides kept apart by sticks inserted near the top. It was essential to have a piece of bark not penetrated by limbs. In some instances a few ribs were inserted. The ends of the bark were sewed together with cedar root. A Micmac is said to have traveled in one of these from Tobique to Chatham, and thence to Burnt Church, a distance of about two hundred miles.

The *mkisaneg'it* were made of the hide of a horse, cow, ox, deer, or moose. Before the coming of the whites, moose, deer, and caribou skins were used. The skin of the moose was most frequently used; a canoe made of moose hide was called *mu'su u'lk*. The hair was first scraped off with a stick. Skins which have been thus used are soft and pliable. The hides of two moose, or a hide and a half, were used in making the *musu ulk*, which usually was about two and one-half to three feet wide and about ten inches deep. This and the ribless spruce-bark canoe were most frequently made in the spring, when hunters who had been in the woods throughout the winter wished to transport their catch and their possessions to the shore and were loath to take the time and trouble involved in making the more serviceable birch-bark canoe.

Sometimes in summer a hunter who had killed a moose far from camp

---

[28] As early as 1661 Indians on the Gaspé bought small boats from French fishermen, handled them with great skill, and were fast rowers. Crude wooden gangplanks allowed them to embark dry-shod. In these shallops they set forth on war parties into the Gulf of St. Lawrence. JR, XLVII, 225.

Economic Life

and canoe removed the skin, used it as a canoe, and carried most of the meat downstream in it. Or he improvised a canoe, in a few minutes, out of a piece of spruce bark. The *musu ulk* is said to have been the only canoe in use until Gluskap gave the Micmac the birch-bark canoe. At Pictou informants said this was the only type of canoe which was made there. The *taa ulk* was known, and was said to have come from a tribe to the west. Nothing was known of the Taa tribe.

The *kumu'dju'lk* is a dugout canoe, made from a poplar log, used on the Restigouche River, but not found south of there. Other types of dugout used in this region are the *wasakta* and the *biaro'*. Before the arrival of the whites, dugouts were not used. Micmac now use in the shallower waters of the Restigouche a canoe or boat called *esk a'djidjitc* (probably a combination of "scow" and *djitc*, diminutive), locally known as a "go-devil."

Toboggans and Sleds

The toboggan, *taba'gan*, was employed by the Micmac, and from them, probably, the English name is derived. Its width varied from a foot and a half to two feet; it was from six to eight feet in length and about one-half inch in thickness. It consisted of a single slab turned up in front. The front portion was held up by two thongs attached to the body of the *tabagan*.

There was also a sled, *wa'aski'bidek* (a word which refers to the noise made by the abrasion of one limb on another in the woods). Two runners, about four inches in width, were made of hard wood. In each runner were cut three holes, over which as many cross-sticks were bound loosely with twine, so that one runner could be brought in advance of the other, thus lessening the width between them. If, for example, the sled was to be drawn through a narrow place, one runner could be pulled ahead of the other, the loose cross-sticks allowing it to move a certain distance forward while the other runner remained stationary; the width of the sled was thus diminished, and the passage accomplished.

Rand (before 1894) described the *ootabakunaskook* as

a kind of sledge, made flat and wide, of several pieces bent over, like the iron of a pair of skates, at the forward end. The several pieces of which it is composed are about three or four inches wide and half an inch thick, and sometimes ten feet long. No nails are used in its construction, but it is fastened together with green hide strings.

PART ONE *Tribal Life*

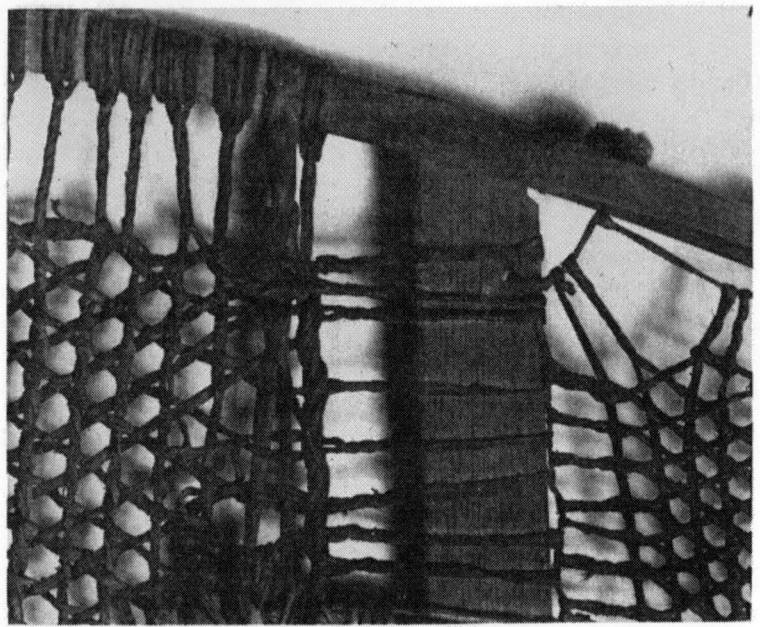

10. Detail of snowshoe construction.

Several pieces of wood are laid across, and holes are pierced through the slats; these cross bars are tied down firmly, the string on the outside being sunk into a groove to keep it from catching and wearing off. Rock-maple or beech is preferred as the material for construction. A small round stick runs along on the top lengthwise, on each side, to which the load is bound. The whole forms a light, convenient, yielding, yet strong sledge for conveyance through the woods. Such sledges are especially adapted for hunting on snowshoes, as they readily yield to the uneven surfaces, slipping over the snow and windfalls; and even if they capsize, they sustain no injury, — the load, being bound on, can be readily righted. This was the *tobakun* of olden times.[29]

Snowshoes

The Micmac snowshoe is said to have a "square toe," that is, the front border is almost straight. To determine from the track the tribe of the wearer, the front portion of the track is carefully examined. Maliseet and Montagnais snowshoes have come into vogue in some places, by trade or by copying, but are not confused with the square-toed type. The snow-

[29] *Legends*, 451.

Economic Life

shoes shown in illustration 6 are long and light, made for travel and hunting rather than for use while carrying burdens.

Thongs of moose or of caribou form the network of the snowshoe. A heavy thong is used in the middle of the shoe, and a lighter thong is used at toe and heel. (See illustration 10.) Women and boys use snowshoes of light frame. The method employed in weaving the net for the snowshoe is described in Tale 84.

Rand gives sixteen designations for parts of the snowshoe. These include the bow or hoop, the two wooden crosspieces, and the fine filling at the toe and heel. The toe is called "his head." Snowshoes were made in several sizes, a large size for use on light snow, and the smallest and lightest type for use on the crust formed by freezing after rain.[30]

To the French, the first Europeans who saw them, these "rackets, thrice as great as ours" which the Indians tied under their feet and thus used to run over the snow, were a marvel to relate to their fellow-countrymen in France whose own rackets were used in the game of court tennis (*jeu de paume*).[31]

TRAVEL, MAPS, AND MESSAGES

Travel

In pre-European days Micmac were frequent travelers, with well-defined canoe routes and portages throughout New Brunswick and Nova Scotia. In the annual search for food they wandered as far as Rivière-du-Loup on the south shore of the St. Lawrence, and Tadoussac on the north shore at the mouth of the Saguenay. West of the present Rimouski was Maliseet territory; a missionary stationed at Rivière-du-Loup in 1677 wrote that Micmac who appeared there seemed "as if in a foreign country." [32]

Micmac families from Gaspé and the Baie des Chaleurs made annual hunting trips to Anticosti Island in April and May, where they met Montagnais from Mingan and Sept-Isles. In the last year in which they visited the island (1893) the Indians killed 150 martins, 25 silver foxes, 12 otters, and 17 bears.[33]

Warfare, trade, tribal and intertribal gatherings, and frequent visiting

[30] *Dictionary*, 193.
[31] JR, 247; Lescarbot, *History*, III, 221.
[32] Pacifique, *Etudes Historiques et Géographiques*, 316.
[33] Schmitt, 1906.

PART ONE *Tribal Life*

among relatives also necessitated knowledge of directions and means of communication. Some of this lore still remains in Micmac memory and practice. When two or more go through the woods together, they move in single file, and liken themselves to moose or cattle. Old-time ways of finding directions, still followed, are thus explained: In the forest, on a cloudy day, one is likely to lose one's way, and will then go in a circle to the right; when, however, one walks through the woods at night, one will go straight. The direction of the sun can be ascertained, even on a cloudy day, by holding up a stick and noting the shadow. Directions can be told, also, by the thickness of the bark on the trees, for the bark is thickest on the north side. "If you were there, you would put thicker clothes on the north side, for from that direction comes the wind. This is the way the old-time Indians reasoned." They also observe the inclination of the tops of the pine trees, for these hang toward the south. One infers directions in the woods from the fact that windfalls are to the east and southeast; and limbs of trees are more numerous on the south side.

In a fog on water one orients oneself by the direction of the waves, after having observed, on shore, the direction of the wind. Cracks in the ice run in one general direction; in winter they are guides to direction while one is traveling over the ice.

Similar signs were noted in the seventeenth century. LeClercq wrote of the exact knowledge of all rivers and landmarks which enabled the Micmac, given only slight indication of a wigwam's location, to find it successfully at a distance of a hundred leagues and through dense forests. (The present-day survival of detailed local geography for some six hundred miles is described in Chapter V.) Distances were reckoned by naming the points or capes along river or coast and by the length of time required for the journey in terms of the number of nights which they were obliged to sleep en route. In this enumeration, neither the day of departure nor that of arrival was included.[34]

Maps

That maps were regularly made or kept seems improbable; however, they were made for temporary needs. If, for example, a man had left a moose up the river and wished to send someone for it, he scratched on a piece of birch bark a representation of the stream, and indicated the tributary streams, points, and other landmarks, seriatim, as they would

[34] *Gaspesia*, 136.

Economic Life

be seen by the canoer. He thus indicated clearly the exact location of the moose. The canoer would probably carry the map, after it had been explained to him.

Such maps of native origin were described in the seventeenth century: "They have much ingenuity in drawing upon bark a kind of map which marks exactly all the rivers and streams of a country of which they wish to make a representation. They mark all the places thereon exactly and so well that they make use of them successfully, and an Indian who possesses one makes long voyages without going astray." [35]

Messages

A man who intends to leave camp, and wishes to inform people who may come that day or the following day how long he will be away, leaves a bough of spruce or fir for each day that he expects to be gone. Or he may put up a piece of bark with notches in the upper part to indicate the number of days. If he does not expect to return to camp, and wishes to inform others of that fact, and also to indicate how long he has been there, he cuts notches in the lower surface of the bark. If he desires to leave information about a canoe party, he makes incisions in the bark of a tree near the stream through which the canoe travels. The direction

11. Micmac notice. "A notice by Micmac scouts, which tribe was then at war with the Passamaquoddy, erected on a tree, to warn the rest of the tribe that ten Passamaquoddy Indians have been observed in canoes on the lake going toward the outlet of the lake and probably down the river." After Mallery, ARBAE, 10:341 (1888–89).

in which the arrow points indicates whether the party has gone upstream or downstream. Close to this are made vertical marks, one for each person in the canoe. Sometimes a piece of bark is placed over this, to protect it from the weather. (See illustration 11.)

If a man wishes to indicate a path through the woods, or a place where a path branches, he throws down a twig of evergreen, the broken stem

[35] *Ibid.* For reference to such a map, see Tale 124.

PART ONE *Tribal Life*

pointing in the direction he has taken. These guides enable him easily to retrace his steps through a maze of paths or to find an article hidden to one side. Or, the path is indicated by breaking twigs, here and there, and leaving them hanging on trees.[36]

The twigs are broken by bending them downward, so that the cleavage of the bark is from above; bears break twigs in the opposite direction, by bending them upward and cleaving the bark from beneath. Hence, there is no difficulty in distinguishing the work of man from that of a bear.

Hagar said in 1895: "Sticks are placed in the ground; a cut on one of them indicates that a message in picture-writing on a piece of birch bark is hidden nearby under a stone. The direction in which the stick leans from its base upward indicates that in which the party moved, and thus serves as a convenient hint to those who follow to keep off their hunting grounds."[37]

Informants alleged that long ago it was a custom of chiefs to send letters on birch bark (*ju'duskwa'du*) from one settlement to another by means of a messenger, *ladiu*, assigned this particular function; special persons served as writers, *muduwigiget*, i.e., one who can read and write. The message was enclosed in a birch-bark envelope, *mundetc*, sealed with spruce gum. A sharp stick was used to scratch the message; later juice from a plant or from berries was used as ink.

Kaluswa'anabil' was a beaded string used as a message from a chief of one settlement to another. The wampum belts of the Wabanaki Confederacy are discussed in Chapter XIII.

Signaling by fire and smoke is referred to in the *Jesuit Relations*.[38]

---

[36] This is not very different from a custom in vogue in fourteenth- and fifteenth-century England, when "strange men ofte erre and go out of the waye: and take uncerten waye, and the waye that is unknowe, tofore the waye that is knowen. . . Therefore ben ofte knottes made on trees and in bushes, in bowes and in braunches of trees: in token and marke of the highe way, to showe the certen and sure waye to wayfaring men." J. Trevisa (trans.), *Bartholomew, de Proprietatibus Rerum*, lib. VII.C.20 (London, 1535; translated 1398); quoted in H. S. Bennett, *The Pastons and Their England: Studies in an Age of Transition* (Cambridge: Cambridge University Press, 1922), 129.

[37] "Micmac Customs and Traditions," AA, 8:31.

[38] II, 1612, 171.

CHAPTER IV

Shelter, Food, Clothing, Crafts

THE WIGWAM

ON EACH reserve visited in 1911 and 1912, two or three birch-bark wigwams were set up for the summer season. The following account of their construction was obtained at Burnt Church. (See illustration 12.)

The conical wigwam (*wi'gwam*) varies in height, and varies considerably in ground circumference. The first task before erecting one is to level the ground with an adze of stone or of bone, or with a wooden hoe. Four poles, each about fourteen feet in length, are cut to serve as the *pasi'dal*, inwardly slanting poles, the framework over which the bark will be placed. They are from three to four inches in diameter, and usually are of spruce or of fir; however, any straight wood will suffice. The bark is not removed from the poles. The four poles are laid together, parallel, on the ground, and spruce root, or fiber from the inner bark of cedar, is bound loosely around them at a point about three feet below the smaller ends. The binding is so arranged that it will retain its position while the four poles are raised and the larger ends are placed in the four holes that have been dug to receive them. The binding holds the tops of the poles in place while the poles are being arranged, one on another, at the apex. Between these four main *pasidal* are placed as many smaller poles as seem necessary. The smaller *pasidal* are tied to the larger ones with spruce root or cedar bark, to make the structure stable. Sometimes a crotched stick is driven into the ground about midway between the center and the circumference of the wigwam. On it one end of a stick lies, the other end resting on the ground at the circumference of the wigwam. This helps to hold out the lower bark and keeps it from crowding the apex of the wigwam.

Strips of birch bark are put horizontally over the outside, beginning

57

PART ONE *Tribal Life*

12. Wigwam at Dartmouth, N.S., 1912.

at the bottom. They are sewed together with spruce root. Each layer slightly overlaps the one below it, as shingles are laid. When the family wishes to move, the wife builds a small fire under the bark, to make it pliable, rolls it into bundles, and carries it with her, to use again.

Immediately below the apex of the *pasidal* a band of yellow-birch twigs, *awis'tiada'an*, is put around the poles and is fastened to them with spruce root. This holds them tightly together and provides a place from which the cooking vessel can be hung. Small sticks, *koa'di*, are put on top of this band, the ends placed between opposite *pasidal*. To them are attached the thongs to which the vessel is fastened.

Usually the bark is put directly on the *pasidal*, but sometimes they are first covered with flag or swamp grass, *se'suusk*, woven into a mat, *e'laama'sit*. It forms an inside lining which helps to keep out the rain and the wind. These mats are three to four feet in length, and about two and a half feet in width — practically the same width as the bark placed over them.

Along the edge of the roll of birch bark (to keep it from tearing) is put a stick, *bala'an*, sewed to the edge with spruce root. It has a little flap, *anagwe'djk*, to which the adjoining piece of bark can be fastened

Shelter, Food, Clothing, Crafts

without piercing the cover. The width of the roll should not be greater than a *na'nobiltca'sik*, that is to say, five *biltca'sik*. A *biltcasik* is the distance from the end of the thumb to the end of the middle finger when thumb and middle finger are held as far apart as possible. If it is wider than this, it will be difficult to sew.

After the bark has been put on, several sticks, *malkwi'gan*, are placed against it from the outside, between the *pasidal* and parallel to them. They hold the cover in position, despite the wind. In addition to hanging the pot in the manner described, a long V-shaped yellow-birch stick is put in the ground at a slant, one arm of the stick extending over the fire; the other arm is bent upward and is tied with spruce root to a strong stake that gives stability to the fixture.

The entrance, *ka'gamuk* (*pan'tadukag'am*, open the flap, or door; *il'tadu*, close the flap of the entrance) faces the midday sun. It is supported by two vertical sticks which join the *pasidal* about five feet from the ground and are tied to the *pasidal* with spruce root. From top to top of these two sticks, the *kulmadeg'andjitc*, extends the *ci'bila'an*, a cross-stick from which hangs the *suskwadeg'an*, the skin flap that covers the entrance. The hair side is turned out.

To the lower part of this skin flap is sewed, with spruce root, another stick similar to the horizontal hinge from which it hangs. This keeps the flap spread out at the bottom and holds it down. This lower stick falls a short distance below a horizontal one against which the flap is held in position. A piece of bark, *la'kai igam*, is placed over the upper hinge of the flap to keep out the rain.

The earth floor is covered with small fir branches, gathered by the women. They begin a short distance from the middle, where the fire will be, and lay the branches one over another, butt ends on the ground. The result is a soft carpet of fir twigs and needles; and there are no sharp projections. The ground between the fire and the entrance is bare. The exposed ends of the twigs toward the fire are held in position by means of *an'iökteg'an*, forked sticks driven down tightly over them into the ground. Over the branches are placed moose hides, or hides of other animals, and over these are put beaver skins, on which the occupants lie. Over this is placed a bearskin, to cover the person.[1] Deerskin stuffed with moose hair constitutes a bed. A roll of hide serves as a pillow. Sometimes a long swamp-grass mat under a bark cover is placed over the

[1] See Parsons, in JAFL, 39: 462–63 (1926).

PART ONE *Tribal Life*

ground, or over the fir branches, between the fire and the door. The portion of the wigwam used as one's sitting or resting place is called *ki'sanaksit*. Formerly an oblong structure, *susadi*, in which wood was kept and meat was hung, was occasionally built adjoining the wigwam at the entrance.

During the first two hundred years of white contact, several observers recorded their impressions of the Micmac wigwam. All described it as circular, although the Jesuit Biard (1616) stated that this was the form erected in winter; the summer habitation was broad and long "that they may have more air." [2] On the Gaspé and in the Miramichi region, a half-century later, Father LeClercq described circular bark wigwams, decorated by the women with bright painted designs. Some, constructed from the bark of seven or eight trees, contained four fires and lodged fifteen to twenty persons. "They are so light, and portable," he wrote, "that our Indians roll them up like a paper, and carry them thus upon their backs very much like the tortoises which carry their own houses.[3] Other priests and travelers plied less idyllic pens: they pictured smoke and suffering eyes; stench from filth and refuse; the constant danger of burning alive from too large a fire on a winter night, or a worse death from burns and slow gangrene.

Dièreville (1710) gave the following description of the method of erecting the wigwam:

Fifteen or sixteen Poles, more or less according to its size, are set up in a circle, two feet apart; they are a fathom or a fathom and a half in height, and their upper extremities are joined in a point, and fastened together; the Poles are covered with branches of Fir, and large pieces of

---

[2] JR, III, 77. Biard described a Micmac band setting up camp: "Arrived at a certain place, the first thing they do is to build a fire and arrange their camp, which they have finished in an hour or two, often in half an hour. The women go to the woods and bring back some poles which are stuck into the ground in a circle around the fire and at the top are interlaced in the form of a pyramid, so that they come together directly over the fire, for there is the chimney. Upon the poles they throw some skins, matting, or bark. At the foot of the poles, under the skins, they put their baggage. All the space around the fire is strewn with leaves of the fir tree, so that they will not feel the dampness of the ground; over these leaves are often thrown some mats or sealskins as soft as velvet; upon this they stretch themselves around the fire with their heads resting upon their baggage; and, what no one would believe, they are very warm in there around that little fire, even in the greatest rigors of the winter. They do not camp except near some good water, and in an attractive location. In summer the shape of their houses is changed; for then they nearly always cover them with bark, or mats of tender reeds, finer and more delicate than ours made of straw, and so skillfully woven, that when they are hung up the water runs along their surface without penetrating them."

[3] *Gaspesia*, 100.

Shelter, Food, Clothing, Crafts

bark from the same tree, or from Birch, and sometimes with skins; a hole is left at the bottom that is only large enough to go in and out of, on all fours. Inside, a Pole traverses it at a height of four or five feet, and on it the Kettle is hung over a fire, which is kept low, and built in the center of the rear part of Wigwam.[4]

Well into the nineteenth century the wigwam continued to be the standard Micmac dwelling. In 1831 all Nova Scotia Indians were said to be living "in neat birch bark wigwams — a house was a rare exception";[5] and Duncan Campbell, in 1873, declared that

they adhere pertinaciously in the construction of their peculiar habitations to the form which obtained in the days of their fathers. In the wigwam there is a place for everything and everything in its place. Every post, every bar, every fastening, every tier of bark, and every appendage, whether for ornament or use, in this curious structure, has a name, and every section of the limited space has its appropriate designation and use. Perhaps it would be impossible to plan a hut of equal dimensions in which the comfort and convenience of inmates could be so effectively secured.[6]

THE SMOKEHOUSE AND THE PRESERVATION OF FOODS

A Burnt Church informant described a smokehouse, *bo'ksano'gwum* (*bo'ksa*, smoke), which was used to smoke fish for preservation. Often a smokehouse was erected and owned by three or four men jointly.

This one was about twenty-four feet long — that is to say, two men with outstretched arms could reach from the middle to the end — about four feet wide, and eight to twelve feet high. Four posts were erected, with crotched top, on which were laid pieces to form the support for the roof. Against these were placed several slanting poles, fastened in place with spruce root. They were about a foot apart, and extended along both sides. Both ends of the structure were open. Over the poles was put birch bark, for it allowed the heat to enter and also kept the smoke in. The top was open, if the weather permitted. In time of rain it could be closed by means of two long strips of bark, one on each side, fastened with spruce root to the outer longitudinal pole. Such a flap was known as *i'kjaswi'gan*. The spruce-root hinge was *iktci'bila'an*; this word now means also the hinge of an ordinary door.

[4] P. 177.
[5] Gilpin, in *Canada, An Encyclopedia*, I, 244.
[6] Pp. 17–18.

PART ONE *Tribal Life*

The split fish were placed on spruce-covered racks. Wood and bark of white birch were used as fuel; the smoke of this wood was believed to impart the best flavor. The fish were smoked for a day or two, and usually were tended by two men, who turned them frequently. They were then packed in boxes of birch bark, covered with sticks, and over these sticks stones were placed as weights to force the contents into a compact mass. Or a piece of *tci'bila'endjidal*, a strand of spruce root, was tied around the tail of each fish, and this strand encircled a stick, the ends of which were tied to an overhead rafter. From six to nine fish were suspended from a stick. One end of the stick could be taken out of the supporting loop, a fish, or several, slipped off, and the stick put back into the loop.

Storehouses near Port Royal, in 1616, were made of interlacing tree branches; from these hung sacks of smoked meat, roots, shelled acorns, and the peas, beans, and prunes bought from the French, who were astonished to see them left unguarded when the owners set out on the winter hunt.[7]

A hundred and fifty years later, a white man took refuge with an Indian band near Pokemouche, Miramichi Bay, who were living in a fashion not strikingly different from that described in this chapter. In a wigwam large enough to hold twenty people, ten or a dozen men, women, and children slept on spruce boughs, rolled in blankets around the central fire. Above them hung shredded fish, dried without salt, and geese and game, boned, cut in thin strips, and dried in smoke.[8]

The flesh of deer, moose, and other large animals is cut into slabs about the thickness of one's hand and from one to two feet in length, and smoked for four or five days until they become hard (1911). Pieces are sometimes left in the sun in order to ascertain whether the smoking process has continued long enough.

Eels are smoked on rock-maple sticks; only this treatment gives them the proper flavor. If soaked before being skinned, the flesh would be flabby. Eels which are to be kept for winter use are hung on sticks in the wigwam. The sticks are passed through the lower jaw. The eels are smoked until the following day, and the entrails are then removed. Inner bark of yellow birch twisted into fibers is threaded through the gills by means of a sharp stick. On hot summer days the eels are split and are

[7] JR, III, 107-9.
[8] Smethurst, 1764.

Shelter, Food, Clothing, Crafts

dried in the sun; a fire is built near them, and the smoke keeps the flies away. This is done also when drying fish.

FOOD AND ITS PREPARATION

Meat and Fish

By far the most desirable food has always been meat.

Fish are sometimes fastened in a split stick, which is wrapped to hold the fish in place, and are then roasted. Shellfish are freely used as food. The flesh of the muskrat is considered to be very sweet because it lives solely on marsh grass.

The flesh of any edible animal is highly prized. Formerly, dog meat was much valued, especially at feasts. In the old days meat was seldom if ever eaten raw, but the preparation of it was hasty and, by our standards, not thorough. The feathers, dry, were pulled off birds preparatory to roasting them on spits before the fire. One informant said the intestines of all animals were cut up and roasted, or were boiled with the other meat, and all the internal organs were eaten except the gall bladder, the contents of which were kept as an ointment. The intestines of most birds were not eaten; but those of the goose and the brant, which live on seaweed, and are "not as fishy and dirty as are other fowl," were eaten.

The porcupine was roasted on spits, without removing the quills. The quills, when well roasted, were scraped off. If the skin is removed before the animal is roasted, the flesh has a distinctive flavor; if roasted over the smoke, it has a different flavor.

Fresh moose meat was boiled to obtain soup. It was considered salty enough without seasoning. Or it was roasted on long sticks, stuck into the ground and slanted toward the fire, and turned from time to time; or it was placed directly on the coals. Cooking was never done by dropping heated stones in water.[9] The meat was dipped into a vessel of sea water to season it, and often into a vessel of blood which was used as gravy.

Supplementing these descriptions of cooking meat is the following account from a tale:

"After cooking their meal they burned the table — a piece of bark — and carefully extinguished the fire. The smaller intestines of moose, caribou, and deer were turned inside out and dried as sausage. These

[9] This is contrary to early accounts, beginning with Lescarbot who said, "A thing which I have admired . . . is to put stones made red hot in the fire in the . . . trough and to renew them until the meat is sodden."

PART ONE *Tribal Life*

and the meat of the bear were hung on sticks which rested on parallel bars that were supported by crotched sticks, about the height of one's head, and were smoked there. The meat was washed in a running stream. The tripe was dried and smoked, but the contents of the stomach were not eaten."

Methods of meat cookery in the seventeenth century were explained by Denys:

To roast the meat they cut it into fillets, split a stick, placed it therein, then stuck up the stick in front of the fire, each person having his own. When it was cooked on one side, and in proportion as it cooked, they ate it. Biting into it, they cut off the piece with a bone, which they sharpened on rocks to make it cut. This served them in place of knives of iron and steel, the use of which we have since introduced among them.

Having eaten all of it that was cooked, they replaced the meat in front of the fire, took another stick and went through the same process. When they had eaten all the meat from a stick, they always replaced it with more, keeping this up all the day.

They had another method of roasting, with a cord of bark from trees, attached to a pole which extended across the top of their wigwam, or from one tree to another, or upon two forked sticks stuck in the earth. The meat was attached to the lower end of the cord, through which was thrust a stick with which it was twisted several turns. After it was let go, by this means the meat turned a long time first one side then the other to the fire. When it turned no longer, the cord was again twisted by means of the stick through its middle, and again allowed to go. The surface of the meat being cooked, they would bite the outside, and cut off the piece close to the mouth, continuing thus until the whole was eaten. They also roasted it upon coals.

As for fish, they roasted it on split sticks which served as a grill, or frequently upon coals, but it had to be wholly cooked before it was eaten. All the children do their cooking like the others, with split sticks and upon the coals.[10]

The preparation of fat, which was an essential item to early Micmac living on an almost entirely meat diet, is known to their present-day descendants, who thus describe the process: Fat was melted on a grooved stone and run into a birch-bark vessel. This, when full, was emptied into a *putckadju* (birch-bark box), or into a seal bladder or a seal stomach. The fat from the back of the bear — in the autumn the bear is very fat — was packed in boxes.

According to LeClercq, Micmac made

[10] II, 400–1.

Shelter, Food, Clothing, Crafts

a loaf of cacamos of nine to ten pounds . . . a kind of grease which is taken from the bones of the legs and thighs of the moose. After they have eaten all the marrow, they pound and crush these bones until they have reduced them almost to powder; then the fragments are placed in a huge kettle of boiling water, so that every remaining trace of marrow or grease in these broken bones floats upon the water because drawn out by the heat of the fire. They then collect this grease, and preserve it carefully, as something very choice and delicate. As to the soup, it becomes as white as milk, and according to their idea, they believe it as good for the chest as a large glass of brandy, or as the best of our meat broths.[11]

Other Micmac table delicacies of LeClercq's day were moose intestines. Washed, boiled, and made into rolls "much like puddings," they "made the most delicious desserts." Most delicate in the opinion of French as well as Indians were moose nose and tongue.

Sometimes as a diversion, the entire head of a young elk, called *nigaiou*, was roasted. "They do not remove therefrom either the nose or the tongue; but simply, without other arrangement, they attach to some pole a cord by which this head is hung directly in front of the fire, so that by giving it from time to time a twist with a stick, it turns and returns to the right and the left without burning until it is cooked." A smoked dog's head, "the teeths and tongue still standing," found hanging in an empty Indian camp near Restigouche, was a welcome morsel to the starving Smethurst in 1764.[12] Another treat for Micmac gourmets was to "hunt after the lice in their heads and regard them as a dainty."[13]

Eggs

At nesting time eggs of geese and bustard in all degrees of freshness were gathered along shore and packed into the canoe.[14]

Salt

Salt, it is claimed, was formerly procured in the following way: A large thick stone was placed, slanting, close to a hot fire, and a bark vessel was placed under a portion of the stone. Salt water was brought from the shore and poured slowly over this heated stone, which evaporated the water. This was continued until a thick layer of salt was de-

[11] *Gaspesia*, 118.
[12] Ganong (ed.), 1905.
[13] JR, II, 79.
[14] Lescarbot, *History*, III, 172.

PART ONE *Tribal Life*

posited on the stone. The salt was then removed, and the process resumed. (The informant alleged that the Eskimo use the same method.) Informants insist that prior to the coming of the whites salt was obtained by boiling sea water and pouring it on heated stones. With regard to *salawa*, the word for salt, Rand said: "There is evidence that the Indians used no salt before they obtained it from the Whites, since they had no name for the article." [15] Lescarbot stated that the Micmac had no salt.[16]

Vegetable Foods

The *sage'ban*, the so-called "wild potato," more properly, "wild carrot," which has the shape and flavor of the carrot and grows in marshes and on the edges of the woodland, was boiled and eaten as a vegetable, as were also the roots of *wiskabodama'djkal*, *mas'kusidal*, and *a'djuk*, all of which grow in the woods.

Beechnuts were much enjoyed. The Indians frequently procured these by robbing the stores of ground squirrels (chipmunks?).

Huckleberries, blueberries, and the Indian pear or service berry were and are eaten. Cranberries, huckleberries, and blueberries are gathered, boiled three or four hours, compressed into disc-shaped cakes, and dried in the sun on pieces of birch bark. They are turned every two or three hours. The drying requires three or four days. They are put into a large birch-bark box, which contains meats and other provisions. When dry, they do not freeze. The Micmac soak them, then boil them. *Gol'kimawe*, the designation of these cakes of dried blueberries, now means also the hard commercial biscuit.

Beverages

The twigs of yellow birch, winterberries, and the roots of labrador and of sassafras are boiled to make tea. Tea is also made from waxberries and from spruce leaves, the latter boiled about five minutes; tips of young maple trees, boiled about ten minutes; leaves or bark of hemlock, boiled about ten minutes; and chips of rock maple. These beverages, like the commercial tea, are sweetened with molasses. All are believed to be medicinal and stimulating.

Spruce tea, or spruce beer, is the only native drink now commonly used as a beverage. There may have been a nonalcoholic spruce drink native

[15] *Dictionary*, 224.
[16] *History*, III, 172.

Shelter, Food, Clothing, Crafts

to the Micmac. Spruce beer was brewed by the Acadian French, "a strong decoction . . . put into a cask with yeast and molasses,"[17] a formula still followed by the Micmac.

Bread

Nothing about the Micmac astonished the French more than their lack of bread, the more extraordinary, it seemed, because corn was grown and ground to meal by other Wabanaki tribes. The main explanation which occurred to the Europeans was Indian laziness. At Port Royal, in 1606, Micmac employed around the fort "never wanted bread," and steadily refused to undertake for the French the tough job of grinding grain in hand mills even when offered half the grinding for their own use.[18]

Lescarbot was certain that "the chief defect in their lives is that they have no bread. Indeed bread is a food very natural to man, but it is easier to live on flesh or fish than on bread alone. They are slothful at . . . exercise such as tilling the ground, and at our mechanical trades; even at grinding corn for their own use. For sometimes they will boil it whole rather than grind it by hand labour."[19] However, articles the Micmac desired in trade included hard biscuits.[20]

According to my informants, bread, when finally accepted, was cooked in the sand. Live coals were scraped away, the dough was put into the subjacent hot sand, covered with it, and left there for about an hour. As late as 1890 some old people refused to eat bread unless it had been baked in this fashion.[21]

Maple Sugar

In the early seventeenth century, maple sap was drunk from the tapped tree to quench thirst.[22] In the region now New Brunswick the ten or a dozen gallons of sap obtained from each tree was boiled and reduced to one third its original volume and hardened into small loaves, a delicacy which gave equal pleasure to Micmac and French.[23]

[17] Dièreville, 9.
[18] JR, I, 141.
[19] *History*, III, 171, 217.
[20] *Ibid.*, 128.
[21] See Tale 97 and Chapter I.
[22] Lescarbot, *History*, III, 194.
[23] LeClercq, *Gaspesia*, 122–23.

PART ONE *Tribal Life*

TOBACCO AND PIPES

Tobacco was the one plant cultivated by Micmac at the time of the first white settlement. Lescarbot stated: "Our savages plant great store of tobacco. When they have gathered this herb, they dry it in the shade, and have certain little leather bags, hanging about their necks, or at their girdles, wherein they always have some, with calumet or tobacco pipe."[24] Ganong identified the plant as *Nicotiana rustica*, said to be grown occasionally by Nova Scotia French as late as 1914.

This is the sole evidence of pre-European cultivation, but tradition maintained that the art had formerly flourished after tobacco had been bestowed by Papkootparout, master of souls; through negligence the art had soon been lost.[25]

Men, women, girls, and boys smoked tobacco in pipes. The Micmac pipe in Lescarbot's day was "a little horn with a hole at one side." A long quill or pipe was fitted into the hole "out of which they suck the smoke of the tobacco which is inside the said horn, after lighting with a coal which they lay upon it."[26] Pipes observed by Denys (1622–72) were made of wood or of stone. The wooden pipe bowl was fitted with a lobster claw. Also a single piece of red or of green stone was used for pipe and stem. Stem and bowl were hollowed out by a bone somewhat flattened and sharpened, which was turned back and forth on the stone. "By virtue of time," said Denys, "they came to the end of it. None of their work was very pressing, and all that they did of this sort was only for amusement."[27] Maillard described (1755) "a sort of spungeous reed, which may furnish, according to its length, a number of calumets, each of which is about a foot long, to be lighted at one end, the other serving to suck in the smoak at the mouth, and is suffered to burn within an inch of the lips."[28] The simplest kind of pipe was made by rolling a narrow strip of birch bark and fastening the tube in place with a spruce root. (See illustration 20.) An informant fashioned one of these for me in 1911, but this type was then not used.

UTENSILS AND TOOLS

The simplest aboriginal cooking vessels were rough wooden kettles or tubs made from a tree trunk, cut down at the spot where a moose was

[24] *History*, III, 252.
[25] LeClercq, *Gaspesia*, 213. Corn had also been bestowed. See Chapter II.
[26] *History*, III, 252. [27] II, 422. [28] *Customs and Manners*, 53.

Shelter, Food, Clothing, Crafts

killed.[29] Sometimes a tree stump two or three feet high was hollowed out by hot coals and by stone tools, and the pot was ready for water, heated stones, and meat.[30]

Such pots were also carefully made for permanent use:

The kettle was of wood, made like a huge feeding-trough or stone watering-trough. To make it they took the butt of a huge tree which had fallen; they did not cut it down, not having tools fitted for that, nor had they the means to transport it; they had them ready-made in nearly all the places to which they went. For making them, they employed stone axes, well-sharpened, and set into the end of a forked stick [where they were] well tied. With these axes they cut a little into the top of the wood at the length they wished the kettle. This done they placed fire on top and made the tree burn. When burnt about four inches in depth they removed the fire, and then with stones and huge pointed bones, as large as the thumb, they hollowed it out the best they could, removing all the burnt part. Then they replaced the fire, and when it was again burnt they removed it all from the interior and commenced again to separate the burnt part, continuing this until their kettle was big enough for their fancy, and that was oftener too big than too little.[31]

Lescarbot said that the Micmac formerly made earthen cooking pots "in the shape of a nightcap, like those made by the Armouchiquois," but ceased to do so when they could get French kettles.[32]

European copper kettles were an early trade article in great demand; their use and care in Micmac hands was described to repletion by LeClercq:

Our Gaspesians never clean their kettles except the first time they use them, because, they say, they are afraid of the verdigris, which is in no danger of attaching itself to them, when they are well greased and burnt. Nor do they ever skim it off, because it seems to them that this is removing grease from the pot, and just so much good material is lost. This causes the meat to be all stuffed with a black and thick scum, like little meat balls which have nearly the appearance of curdled milk. They content themselves with removing simply the largest moose hairs, although the meat may have been dragged around the wigwam for five or six days, and the dogs also may have tasted it beforehand.[33]

[29] Lescarbot, *History*, 194.
[30] Ferland, I, 73.
[31] Denys, II, 401–2.
[32] *History*, III, 194. According to Ganong, archeological research in Maliseet territory has turned up pottery. See *Bulletin of the Natural History Society of New Brunswick*, No. III, 1884, p. 6; and later articles in the same publication.
[33] *Gaspesia*, 121.

PART ONE *Tribal Life*

Birch-Bark Vessels

The characteristic Micmac container and cup was made of birch bark, cut, folded, and sewed. Needles of sharpened bone pierced the bark and through these holes passed cedar roots split in thirds, some of it very fine.[34] Their current manufacture was described by my informants in 1911. (See illustrations 13–17.)

Boxes are made by folding birch bark and sewing the upper corners with spruce root. A large square one, known as *wiskwe'djala'an*, is employed to catch the sap of the maple when it is gathered to be used for maple sugar. *Muska'nadi* is a large storage birch-bark box used in the dwelling; usually the baby's clothes are kept in it. *Mintedju* is a small birch-bark box, square at the bottom and round at the top. The top is kept in position by a hoop sewed within it. A cover is fitted over the *mintedju*.

Wisko'madi is a square box; *ula'an*, a conical bark vessel, larger at the top than at the bottom, is used for carrying water. Birch-bark vessels were formerly hung over the fire for cooking meat, or, as a rule, were placed directly on coals of hemlock. Although green birch bark burns easily and rapidly, cooking vessels when in use do not burn below the water line.

A piece of birch bark folded at one end forms a drinking cup, *intce'dju*. With thumb and finger the user holds the bark in position. Sometimes one end of a stick of hard wood is split and the folded bark is inserted into the split. Sometimes a long handle is attached, a small groove being cut in it and in the bark to permit lashing, and the cup is used as a ladle. (See illustration 18.) The handle can be easily removed, the cup put in the pocket, and used subsequently as a cup or as a ladle. If birch bark is not obtainable, a large leaf, preferably of hazel, is substituted. It is bent lengthwise along the middle, and each end is turned up, by thumb and finger, to hold the folds in position during use. To make the drinking vessel known as *wiskwe'djala'an*, the term applied to the unsewed birch-bark vessel used for gathering maple sap, a piece of birch bark is folded at both ends. It is actually a box or a trough, rather than a cup. In some districts, a short-handled drinking cup is called *mkwantcitc*, a long-handled one (used as a ladle rather than as a drinking cup), *la'ama'g-ancitc*, and one without a handle, *li'ntcetcutc*.

[34] Denys, II, 406.

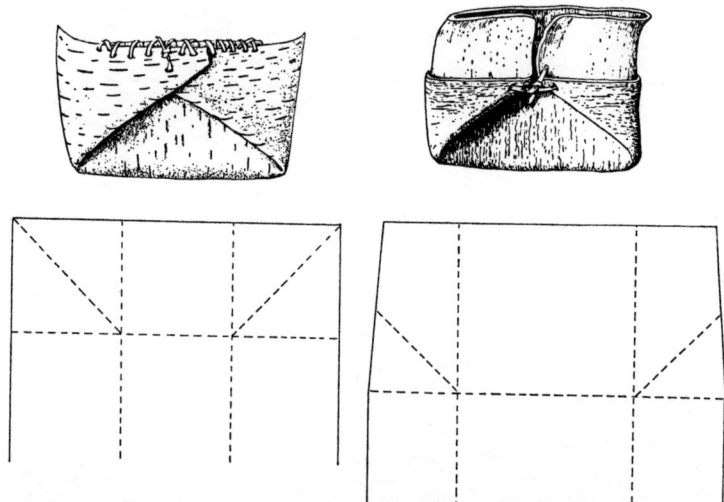

13. *Top.* Bark boxes. Left, the upper flap is represented as turned up, to show the manner of folding and sewing the bark. Right, the box is folded and tied. *Bottom.* Methods of sewing and folding bark to make a box, without cutting and without reinforced rim or bottom, are shown. The dotted lines indicate creases along which the bark is folded.

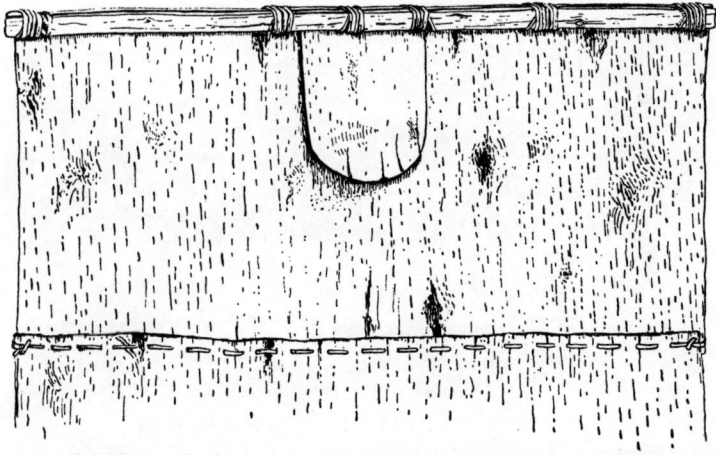

14. Section of a birch-bark roll showing the little flap, *anagwedjk*, used to keep the pieces together. The stitch as seen at the overlap has the same appearance when seen from the inner or the under side of the bark.

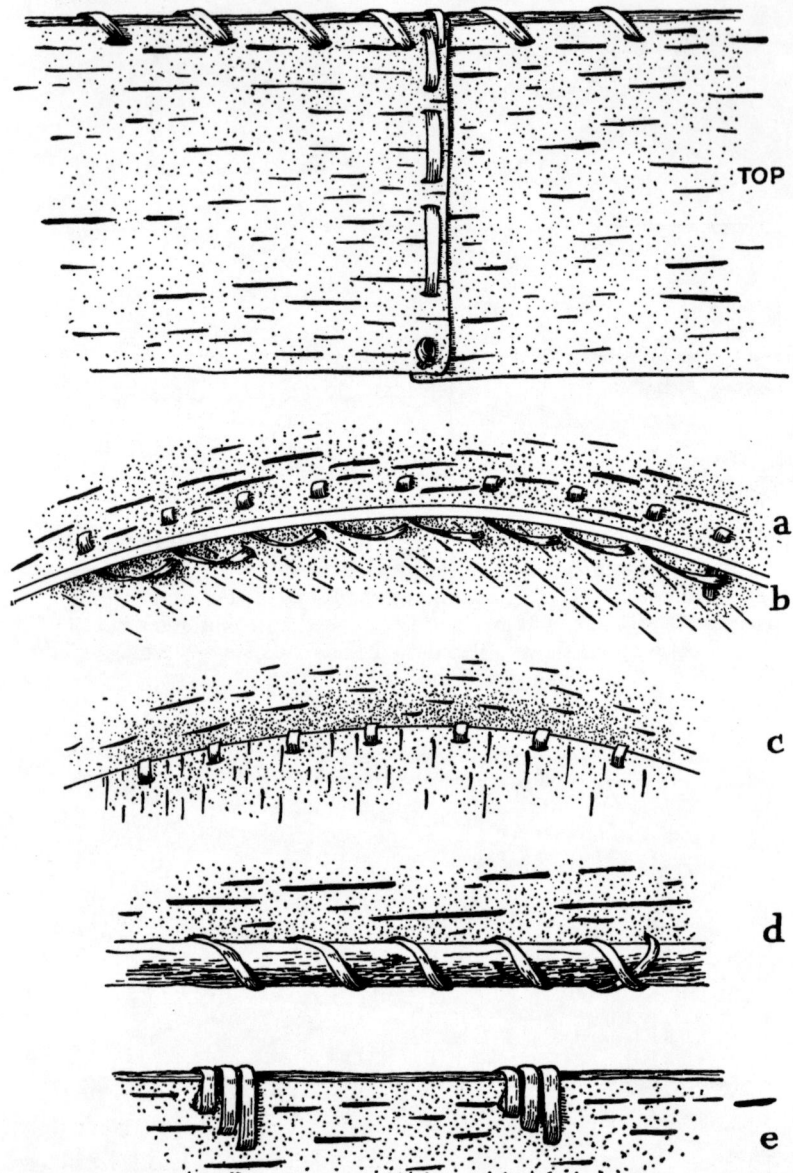

15. *Top.* Birch-bark tray, showing the manner of attaching the rim and the vertical stitch used at the overlap. *Bottom.* Attachment of the bottom and the cover of a circular box: *a* is the outside, *b* the bottom, *c* the inside view of the stitch, *d* the attachment of a splint reinforcement on the outer side of the lower rim to the cover, and *e* the attachment of a splint to the outside of the rim of the cover.

Shelter, Food, Clothing, Crafts

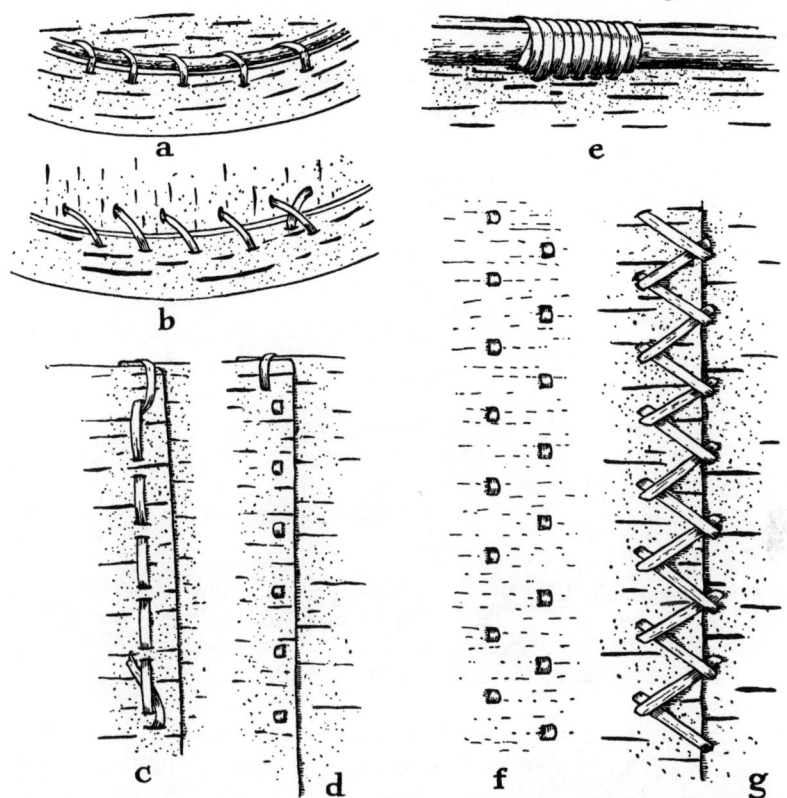

16. Circular bark box. Figures *a* to *d* show a different stitch from that used in illustration 15: *a* is the outside of the top edge of the cover, *b* shows the stitches as they appear on the inside, *c* represents the outside vertical attachment where the bark overlaps, and *d* shows the inside view. The rim attachment on the box is shown in *e*. Horizontal stitching on a circular box where the bark overlaps is shown in *f* as it appears on the inside and in *g* as it appears on the outside of the box.

Basketry

Splints of cedar, spruce, juniper, and other woods are used in making baskets; formerly only roots were employed. Hazel roots are sometimes placed around the outside horizontally to fortify the ribs. (See illustration 19.)

The following story told by Peter Ginnish explains the origin of basket making and the method of procedure:

"A lazy woman was lying down. She rose, scratched the ground, and

PART ONE *Tribal Life*

17. A small birch-bark bucket with square bottom and rim. The sketch shows the manner in which the rim is let into the handle and the way in which the rim is fastened to the bark and the handle kept in place by the spruce root thread.

found a long root. She split it at one end with her teeth; then, holding one end in her teeth, and grasping the other end with her hand, split it lengthwise, into two long fibers. She removed the bark. She did the same with another root. She wrapped the root around her finger several times, leaving eight strands sticking out. The eight pieces served as eight ribs, the warp around which she wove another root, running it alternately in and out of the ribs until the basket was finished. This she showed to the people. No one could name it. It was the first time one had been made, and no one knew what to call it. Next day, people came to see the thing which she had made. They noticed that the bottom of the basket was round, and that the ribs had been filled in to the top. They thought it queer; for they had never seen anything like it. Thereafter, the people made baskets. Green cedar is very easy to split, and it splits into pieces as small as one desires. The woman made a little handle, and the basket was finished. From that time to the present, baskets have been made; and no one knows how long they will continue to be made. Ai'ip is the name of the woman who first made baskets by twisting roots around her finger."

Shelter, Food, Clothing, Crafts

Splint basketry, now commonly of cedar or spruce, it is said, replaced birch bark among the Micmac more slowly than it did in other Wabanaki tribes. My best informant on material culture declared that no baskets were made before the coming of the whites. However, Lescarbot as early as 1607 saw provision baskets made by the Indian women from rushes and roots.[35]

Knives

Informants knew that sharp pieces of flint for cutting were once obtained by putting a piece

18. Birch-bark dipper.

of thin stone in the fire. When heated, it split, and very sharp pieces were thus procured. If a scratch was made where the splitting was desired, the stone would break apart along this line. Such a knife used for cutting up animals or for removing the hide was called *pe'soasik*; *ta'lawo* was another old stone knife; and *wis'wesk* was another, an exact description of which I could not obtain. In the seventeenth century a knife was commonly carried at the chest, not for ornament, but for necessity.[36]

The tomahawk, a stone knife used for cutting wood, or for fighting, was called *tami'gan*. *A'lnaanak* was a grooved stone adze hafted to a bent sapling of hard wood. The ends were brought together. Lashings around the haft and the axe held the axe in position in the curved end of the bent sapling. It was used also as an adze, to level the floor of the wigwam.

Soft stone was bored with a piece of flint, later replaced by the white man's triangular file. The bow drill, informants say, was adopted from the whites and was not used in pre-European days. Knives, when carried, were usually wrapped in a piece of hide.

[35] *History*, III, 201.
[36] *Ibid.*, III, 158.

PART ONE *Tribal Life*

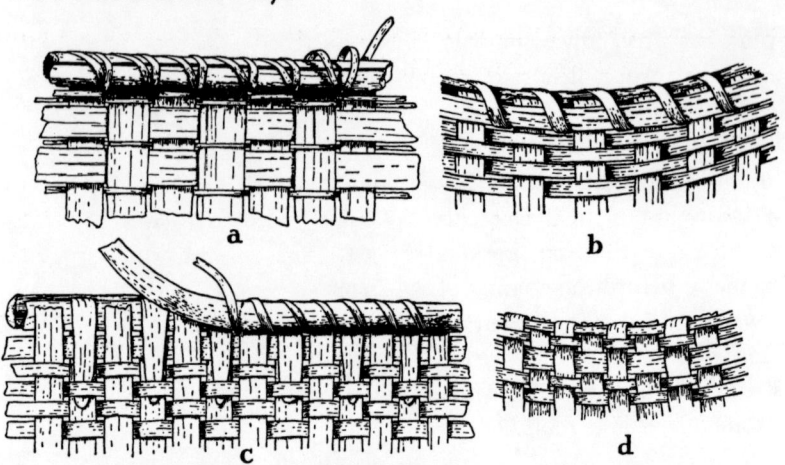

19. Method of making a splint basket: *a* and *b* show types of weave and ways of attaching the upper rim; *c* illustrates the manner in which the ends are tucked under one of the horizontal splints; in *d* the upper rim framework is without reinforcement.

Tools

A wooden hoe, *elge'gankamud'je*, of one piece of wood, also was used for leveling the ground when making a wigwam floor. It was of poplar or cedar, with a blunt edge. A bone adze, *wa'ando*, hafted like the stone adze described above, was used for similar purposes. The ulna of the sable was used as an awl. It was small, sharp at one end, and nearly flat at the other. (See illustration 20, left.)

Household Utensils

Brooms were made from the branches of fir or of spruce, broken off and utilized without further preparation. Later, possibly in imitation of the brooms of the whites, small pieces of the branches of yellow birch were bound into a bundle, wrapped with twisted yellow-birch branches, and used as a broom. A broom procured at Pictou, N.S., was made by shaving down a stick of yellow spruce and bending these shaved pieces down toward the end of the stick so as to give a bunch of attached shavings that would serve as a broom. It is the only specimen of the kind that I saw.

The shell of the quahaug served as a spoon. Spoons were also made of bark or of hard wood, particularly maple. They were said to be better

Shelter, Food, Clothing, Crafts

than iron ones. Those which were cut out of wood were boiled until soft, and the handle was then bent into the desired shape.

Thongs

The inner bark of cedar was split into convenient sizes and used for packstraps and similar purposes. Peter Ginnish related this anecdote: "One time an Indian [at Burnt Church] was given an old horse. He

20. Implements and tools: mallets, awls, chine knives, splint knives, a crooked knife, a wooden spoon, and a pipe made of birch bark. The mallet from Pictou, N.S. (lower left) bears nineteen incised designs which include a barrel, a bucket, a pipe or mallet, two stave drivers, a crooked knife, a chine knife, a compass, a shovel(?), the figure 2, and a portion of a design used on bone dice.

PART ONE Tribal Life

went to a house and procured an old horse-collar and harness. In the spring he went in the woods and peeled off cedar bark, saving only the inner layers of the bark. Out of this he made a complete set of harness for his horse. In the winter he used it for his sleigh and drove with it from Burnt Church to Chatham. Everyone came out to see it. They told him his grandmother must have given him that set of harness." Cooney mentioned the use of the sinews of the moose as thong.[37]

Branches of yellow birch were cut in the spring and gently beaten with a stone hammer to loosen the fibers and make them pliable. They were boiled, with a small amount of fat, in water. The fibers could then be easily separated and remained pliable for a long time. Ordinarily a yellow-birch branch is twisted with the hands and used, without further preparation, as a thong.

Other tools used by the Micmac are pictured in illustration 20; these include fleshers for hides (chine knives), a wooden mallet for softening birch bark, and so-called splint knives of wood fitted with metal blades for cutting strips of cedar to be used in making baskets.

CLOTHING

The aboriginal Micmac dress was fully described by informants in 1911–12, although no specimens had been preserved. In summer, men and women wore merely a waist girdle. On very hot days a light jacket of deer hide was worn over the back as protection against the sun.

Usually the clothing was cut from the belly of the moose. The skin of the fore part of the belly and that around the shoulders, in one piece, served as a coat, and the legs as sleeves. A slit was cut, through which the head was thrust when one put the jacket on.[38] It was fastened around the waist by a thong which penetrated it and the trousers here and there, and held the trousers in place.

The trousers were made of moose skin or, for lighter wear, of deer or caribou. They reached only to the knee. Sometimes a skirt, laced tight in front, was worn. In addition to the trousers, or sometimes replacing them, a robe (*pitkasan*) was used. The woman's was called *mad'alet*.

Sex differences in these robes were thus described by Denys:

The men wear them upon their shoulders, tying the two ends with

[37] P. 231.
[38] Denys, II, 413.

Shelter, Food, Clothing, Crafts

strings of leather under the chin, while all the remainder is not closed up. They show the whole body with the exception of their privy parts, which are hidden by means of a very supple and very thin skin. This passes between their legs and is attached at the two ends to a girdle of leather which they have around them; and it is called a truss [brayer]. The women wear this robe in Bohemian fashion. The opening is on one side. They attach it with cords in two places, some distance apart, in such a way that the head can pass through the middle and the arms on the two sides. Then they double the two ends one above the other, and over it they place a girdle which they tie very tightly, in such manner that it cannot fall off. In this way they are entirely covered. They have sleeves of skin which are attached together behind.[39]

In winter a skin cloak or mantle with separate sleeves was worn, together with leather leggings and moccasins. The head was usually bare.

Lescarbot (1607) described the Micmac as "well clothed with a cloak furred with beavers and sleeves on the arms tied together with a latch."[40] Ten years later, Biard, also at Port Royal, wrote that the skin clothing was fringed and ornamented with painted designs in a lace-like pattern. Men rejected trousers as a hindrance which "placed them, as it were in chains." Women's clothing was like the men's except for two girdles, one above, the other below, the stomach, and they were "less nude" than the men.[41]

At Cape Breton in 1634, these traits of similar clothing for men and women and greater female modesty were again set down; the almost total absence of beards, and hair worn long by each sex, made it difficult for the French priests to distinguish between male and female.[42]

The European bed blanket, worn double from shoulder to mid-leg, girdled with beadwork and wampum, was an early adaptation. Furs were traded eagerly for hats, caps, shoes, woolens, shirts, and linen for cleaning babies.[43]

Foot Covering

The skin of muskrat, rabbit, or woodchuck was used for socks.

Leggings for adults were made from shanks of moose, and children's from those of deer, because the latter were small and light. The leggings

[39] II, 413.
[40] *History*, III, 132.
[41] JR, III, 73, 75–77.
[42] JR, VIII, 159.
[43] JR, III, 75–77; LeClercq, *Gaspesia*, 94.

PART ONE *Tribal Life*

were warm and watertight. They were split down the front, almost to the instep, and through holes along the split part a thong was inserted to hold the uppers together. The ends of this thong were wrapped around the top and were tied there.

The moccasin (*mka'san*) was made from a folded piece of deer or of moose skin, sewed at both ends. Through holes along each side, near the top, ran a drawstring of moose sinew or moose thong. This held the moccasin snugly to the foot. Inasmuch as it had the same shape at heel and toe, the tracks did not reveal the direction in which a man had gone.

Old moose-skin robes were made into moccasins and, being more greasy, were considered better than new skins. Denys, who recorded this, said the sewing of the moccasin was redoubled at the front and very finely gathered.[44] Young girls trimmed the seams of their moccasins with quills dyed red and violet.

"The great and high stockings" of leather which seventeenth-century Micmac wore on hunting and fishing expeditions were tied to their girdles. Micmac of the Gaspé and the Miramichi wore these stirrup-like, footless hose in summer and winter. Moccasins were lined with moose skin to keep the feet warm.[45]

The immediate ancestors of modern Micmac used the skin of the young seal for moccasins; it was "as durable as ox hide." A northern New Brunswick informant believed the Micmac had learned the use of sealskin from the Eskimo. He said, however, that the Micmac did not hunt the fur seal, and had had the fur of the seal only after the coming of the whites; later they ate the flesh of the seal.

Caps

Caps and hats made currently or until a short time prior to 1912 were fully described by the Micmac. They were usually made from the *sawade'k* of the moose, that is, the skin under its neck. The skin of deer or the fur of the mink was also employed.

The skin caps of the men were pointed in front. A flap at the back could be tied down on a cold day, or for protection against the sun, or could be tied up by means of strings pendant from the sides. Women's hats were much higher than those of the men; they came to a sharp ridge

[44] II, 413.
[45] Lescarbot, *History*, III, 132; LeClercq, *Gaspesia*, 93.

Shelter, Food, Clothing, Crafts

or crest, as did the hat worn by a chief. Men's hats had the fur outside; women's had the fur inside. The conical cap, *a'gwesan*, was worn only by a chief or a councilor.

A few years before this study Micmac wore hats and caps made of birch bark. The sharp-pointed bark cap is called *ka'niskwed'jkawe*, that is, woman's hat. The bunch of feathers worn on the front is *tcigo'antcitc*, the crest is *tcigoa'n* (the same term is applied to the comb of a rooster or that of a bird). The hat worn by a chief is *o'kta'gwisan*. The strand of sweet grass worn around the cylindrical bark hat is *e'ltagade ge'nipke we*; the piece of bark worn on the front of the birch-bark hat is *uksiskuwe*, "face."

At the time of this study they made hats of ash or of sweet grass in good imitation of those worn by the whites.

Pins

Pins (*kamiskwig'an*) were made of maple or other hard wood. They were large at one end and tapered to a sharp point at the other. Sometimes they were made of moose or caribou bone, or of antlers; the last mentioned, however, were difficult to sharpen. Three or four of these pins were inserted in the front of the jacket to hold it together.

Raincoat

A man when out in a rain procured a large sheet of birch bark, square or round, cut in the middle an opening large enough for the insertion of his head, and used this as a cape over his shoulders. It could not be worn while one was walking through the woods or through bushes, but was useful in a canoe or in a clearing.

Cleaning

Clothes were cleaned with a brush (*jwig'aan*) made from a piece of moose hide removed from the neck of the animal. Ashes were added to assist in the cleaning. Soap, believed by the Micmac to be aboriginal, was made in the following way: Ashes were boiled in water and strained out. The strained water was poured back into the vessel, and animal fat was added. This was boiled, removed from the fire, stirred until cool, and then was ready for use.

21. Chief's coat.

22. Articles of traditional dress. *Top row.* Beaded tabs for jackets, trousers, moccasin tops, epaulets, tabs, and bag.
Bottom row. Women's caps.

Shelter, Food, Clothing, Crafts

Traditional Dress

Throughout the nineteenth century the Micmac wore on ceremonial and festive occasions the costumes described below and represented in illustrations 21–23, 33, 41, and 44.

23. Micmac woman wearing a squaw cap.

Women and men were clothed in coarse blue cloth. The men wore blue frocks with scarlet edges on the shoulders and the arms. A scarlet or gay-colored sash bound this to the waist, at the back of which hung a tobacco pouch of moose skin. They wore, also, knee breeches and long gaiters of the same blue, with the selvage edge left long and ornamented with scarlet. The stocking was a long roller of blanket, wound from the toe to the knee. A silver brooch, the size of a large watch, usually held the frock at the neck, and the foot was covered by an untanned moccasin. . . .

The women [in 1831] wore a high-pointed cap of blue cloth, often ornamented with scarlet cloth and white beads; a short gown and petticoat reaching to the knee, with a gaiter trouser, and the selvage left loose to the ankles. In cold weather a blanket was worn over the head, and always brought square across the back. This pleasing dress . . . we infer, was their habit from the time they ceased to wear skins.[46]

In 1911 men donned on special tribal occasions, such as St. Anne's Day, knee-length coats of blue wool heavily beaded at shoulders, wrist, and hemline, and on bands down the front; or the more elaborate "chief's" coat. (See illustrations 21, 33, 41, 44.) The more conservative women covered their heads with tight scarves and with a shawl fastened and draped from the crown of the head. (See illustrations 44 and 45.) On festive days they wore the traditional beaded cloth "squaw" cap which came down to the lower angle of the jaw, full dark skirt with embroidered and beaded bands, bodice with beaded tabs, and ropelike bead necklaces. (See illustrations 22, 23, 24, 40, and 45.)

HAIRDO

The old Micmac hair styles are still well known. Men and women wore the hair long, parted in the middle. It was made up in two strands,

[46] Gilpin, in *Canada: An Encyclopedia*, I, 244.

PART ONE *Tribal Life*

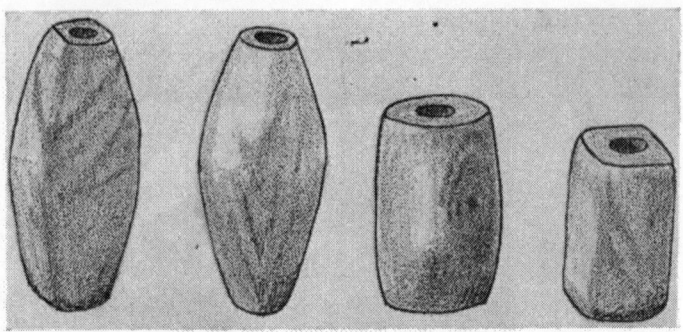

24. Types of quahaug beads (actual size).

which were doubled and sometimes redoubled, then tied close to the head with a piece of eelskin or deer-hide thong. (See illustration 25.) One informant said the hair was taken down every night and put up every morning; but this is doubtful. A strand (*e'lumvelat*) was allowed

25. Mrs. Peter Ginnish, of Burnt Church, N.B., with her hair arranged in old Micmac style.

to hang down in front of each shoulder, as is done by many of the old women today. According to informants, there was no difference in the hairdress of men and that of women. The men had by 1911 discarded the old hairdress.

In 1606 Lescarbot saw men and women always with their hair loose over their shoulders. Men, however, tied the hair at the crown of the head with a piece of leather, letting it hang down behind. On holidays

Shelter, Food, Clothing, Crafts

and festivals, and when they went to war, men wore about their heads a sort of crown made of long moose hairs painted red and glued or otherwise fastened to a filet of leather three fingers broad.[47]

The everyday hairdo was the same in LeClercq's day (1675), but sometimes hair was arranged in braids ornamented with small strings of beadwork or wampum. Men often wore a kind of crown made from two wings of a bird killed in hunting.[48]

A later style, predating 1845, was said to be fashionable among the women: The long hair was doubled up at the back, with artificial addition if the roll was not large enough to please, and all was tied together with a hair string. These strings, *sakulo bee*, were often made of eelskin, an effective stimulant to growth, and are said to have possessed supernatural power.[49]

Great pride was taken in the hair, which was rubbed with a special oil to darken it. There was also frequent anointment less special; for, lacking napkins, after eating they "sedulously rubbed their hands" on moccasins and hair.

ADORNMENT

Aboriginal adornments, described by informants and by early French writers, were simple and few. A piece of spruce root was used to attach an ornamental strip of skin to the outside of the trouser leg. *Oktcigwod'en* were the feathers used as headdress by the chief; the *akusitc* (assistant to the chief) wore around his head a band of skin about two inches wide, called *aptu'gabila'an*. At dances, the chief wore eagle feathers on his cap and on the right and left sides of his coat. One informant said that the chief wore a flower, known as *wa'suwek*, tied with a string to the inside of his cap, which flower he himself gathered in the woods. Until about 1900, on festive occasions, the chief wore on the anterior part of each sleeve, below and near the shoulder, a bunch of feathers from the black duck, and pendant from his cap, a little wooden tomahawk, bow, and arrow.

In the early period, Biard said, women more frequently than men were ornamented with "chains, gewgaws and such finery after their fashion."[50] Gewgaws mentioned by LeClercq included bits of bead-

[47] *History*, III, 160.
[48] *Ibid.*, 133, 160; *Gaspesia*, 99.
[49] Rand, *Legends*, 24, 163.
[50] JR, III, 73.

PART ONE *Tribal Life*

work, shells, and small bells dangling from pierced ears, and on ceremonial occasions collars, belts, and bracelets decorated in a very simple manner with beadwork and porcupine quills dyed red or yellow.[51]

Porcupine quills, dyed black, white, and red, were the main local material for ornaments throughout the aboriginal Micmac area. Beads shaped like quills and made of glass combined with lead and tin were brought from France and traded in large quantities. The preferred bead was shell, which the Micmac got from Algonkin peoples in Maine.[52] Small squares of various colored beads sewed together were tied to the hair of little children.

When dressed in festive garb, the Micmac decorated their faces with vertical stripes of red ocher. All informants agreed that neither tattooing nor scarification was practiced. However, they said, in former days men put burning coals on their arms and other parts of the body as tests of courage. The resulting scars were proudly worn.[53]

The first report of tattooing came from Dièreville (1710) who referred to Micmac at Port Royal. In 1758 Maillard described it as a betrothal custom.[54] Dièreville stated: "The colors are differentiated under the skin, and all kinds of Devices are reproduced, Crosses, Names of Jesus, Flowers; anything in fact that may be desired, and these marks never come off."[55]

Face painting for feasting or for mourning as practiced in 1675 was described by LeClercq:

When, now, we say that the Indians paint themselves, that is equivalent to saying that they daub their faces, which is done sometimes with black and sometimes with red, just as it pleases them. The most capricious make a mixture of these two colours. Some paint themselves with a single colour, or with several; others daub all the forehead with red, and the remainder of the face with black. Others again, still more fanciful than the first, draw a line wholly of black from the middle of the forehead clear to the end of the nose, while the two cheeks will be all mottled and streaked with white, yellow, black and red. This painting is precisely that of which they make use on the days of their feasts, and of their leading diversions. They use it also even in mourning, for, in order to mark their sorrow and affliction when they hear of the death of some one of their kinsmen, they paint the whole face in black.

[51] *Gaspesia*, 94–95, 98–99.
[52] Lescarbot, *History*, III, 158.
[53] *Ibid.*, 188.
[54] *Customs and Manners*, 55.
[55] 1710, 170.

Shelter, Food, Clothing, Crafts

But when they go to war, then they make use of red, in order, say they, that neither their enemies nor yet their own companions may be able to detect different expressions of countenance which fear very often causes to appear in even the most intrepid and bravest persons.[56]

Grease as a cosmetic from the earliest times was applied to the face by women and girls before attending a public gathering.

ARTS AND CRAFTS

Weaving

Socks and mitts are made from moose hair. It is combed out with the fingers, until fine, then twirled between flat open palms into a strand. It is wrapped on the *makwe'gan*, a stick with three or four branches growing from the main stock in approximately the same plane. The thread is then wound around a rock-maple spindle, *elta'ani'gane*, the lower end of which rests on a board, the upper end being grasped and turned by hand. A wooden or a stone disc near the bottom gives momentum to the spindle. As the yarn is formed, it is wound into skeins around the upper left arm as one terminus, and the extended thumb of the left hand (the arm is flexed at the elbow) as the second terminus. These threads are then washed out and hung up to dry. The knitting is done with two small smooth sticks. A stick of uniform size throughout is said to be commonly employed for knitting socks. "Commonly" is not quite the word; for I saw only one piece of moose-hair knitting and found comparatively few women who understood the technic. Some declared it was aboriginal. An old informant at Burnt Church said it was taught to the Micmac by an old Indian woman by the name of St. Anne, whose husband was Swa'san. She came with the French, upon their first arrival, and taught the Indians how to do this work. In corroboration, he pointed to a picture of St. Anne in which the spindle, represented in the group of which she was one, was identical with that which had been described to me.[57]

Dyes

All early observers of the Micmac remarked on the fine bright colors with which they dyed porcupine quills for decoration. Particularly strik-

[56] *Gaspesia*, 96–97, 99.
[57] See Tale 85.

PART ONE *Tribal Life*

ing was the red obtained from a small plant identified as *Galium tinctorum*, a bedstraw.[58]

Before contact with whites, and long afterward, the Micmac had only four colors: red, white, black, and yellow, and no words for expressing colors other than these.[59] The list of dyes known in 1911 shows how greatly the Micmac have added to their aboriginal color assortment. For these, new names had to be invented or old names adapted. Women, the craft workers, seem to have made these names more fully a part of their speech; men as late as 1950 named fewer colors.

The dyes known and prepared in 1911–12 at Pictou Landing, N.S., were the following:

Black. (1) Boil the dark blue wood found under decayed portions of an old log, and add a little salt water. (2) Boil white maple and elm together. (3) Boil fir bark.

Red. (1) Scrape off elder bark, *tapi*; chew; put on a plate; put a little of this in water and keep the water almost at the boiling point for nine or ten hours. (2) Boil the bark of *maldewia'djkal* (*ma'ldo*, blood), a bush about three feet high, which grows in the swamps. It yields a very dark red.

Brown. Boil the moss found growing between the wrinkles in the bark of maple trees.

Yellow. (1) Boil "gold root" (*wisankwe'skal*), which is obtained from the woods. (2) Boil the leaves and the tip of *mkasil'*, a swamp plant (not identified), until the water is yellow.

Green. Boil moosewood a little longer than the time required in cooking potatoes (the latter requires about half an hour). When soft, take out and crush; then boil again for about half an hour.

The following list of dyes was obtained at Burnt Church, N.B.:

Yellow. The top of the hazel, a bush that grows in the marshes, is cut into small pieces, about the size of grains of wheat; these are crushed, rubbed together, and boiled until the water is yellow.

Purple. The bark of white maple is boiled from one-half hour to one hour. Alum is added to enrich the color.

Green. The bark is removed from a princess-pine bush, the root is pulled up and wrapped around the bark, and these are boiled.

Red. Hemlock root near the surface of the ground is procured, the outside bark is scraped off, and the remainder is boiled.

Black. To purple, made by boiling white maple bark about an hour, ashes from a hard wood are added. The result is a pure black.

Blue. The bark of beech is boiled about an hour; a tablespoonful of

[58] For the supernatural origin of dyes, see Tale 86.
[59] LeClercq, *Gaspesia*, 95.

Shelter, Food, Clothing, Crafts

hard wood ashes which have been put into a half-gallon of boiled water are added.

Brown. Add white ashes, or soda, to yellow, prepared as described above. If a small amount is used, blue results. According to the amount added, green, pink, and purple, in various shades, can be obtained.

The *wi'gigan*, a small stick about six inches long and one-half inch in circumference at the larger end, was used to hold the pigment when porcupine quills were being dyed. At the larger end a notch was cut to hold the dye. The tapered smaller end was used as a handle. This stick, it seems, was not in use in 1911–12.

Moose-Hair and Quill Work

Moose-hair thread and porcupine quills were undoubtedly used in pre-white Micmac culture. All early travelers speak of the brilliantly dyed quills employed for bracelets, necklaces, and belts, sewed on moccasins, robes, purses, and tobacco bags. Quills are said to have outlined the designs of insignia on a chief's robe at least as early as the sixteenth century,[60] and quills adorned the canoes, snowshoes, and other articles shipped as curiosities to France by 1670.[61]

There is no seventeenth-century mention, however, of anything suggesting the mosaic of quills covering the small birch boxes which became the characteristic souvenir article made during the nineteenth century. A Micmac informant in 1912 said that before the whites came, no quillwork was made, for there was no one to buy it. The source of these precisely made and decorated boxes was, probably, the Ursuline nuns of Quebec. Supplying the growing number of mission churches with vestments and articles for the altars was an important purpose of the nunnery. Poverty forced the Ursulines to use materials indigenous to Canada, and today at that monastery are preserved little packets of moose-hair thread and porcupine quills.[62] More important, there also exist dated objects of the nuns' handiwork, including boxes (1795) of birch bark covered with quillwork which, in form and designs, nearly duplicate certain examples in the collection made in 1912 for the Heye Museum. (See illustrations 26–28.[63])

A second duty of the Ursulines, to which they were avowed from

---

[60] Ganong, footnote to LeClercq, *Gaspesia*, 191.
[61] *Ibid.*, 95.
[62] Barbeau, *Québec*, 56–57.
[63] Compare 28, left, with Barbeau, 55.

PART ONE *Tribal Life*

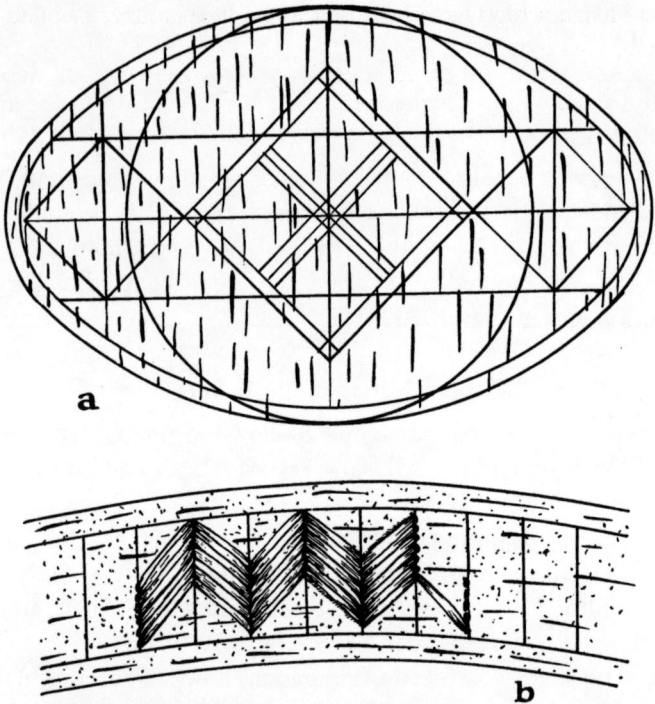

26. The process of quillwork on birch-bark boxes. *a.* Lines incised on the lid before the insertion of the quills. The design will follow these lines. The symmetry of this figure does not exaggerate the accuracy and balance of the lines on the actual box. *b.* The side of a circular box partly worked, showing marking off of equal horizontal areas within which the quills will be put when applying the design. Quills of another color will be used above those already inserted, and quills of a third color will be used below the central band.

1639 to 1729, was the education of *les petites sauvagesses*. A few years after the school opened, the Indian pupils numbered forty-five Huron, Algonkin, Iroquois, and Eskimo whom the nuns found particularly apt at embroidering the needed vestments.[64] Indirectly over the years technics and designs reached the most eastern of the Canadian Indians. Huron at Lorette in the nineteenth century are credited with great export of such arts and crafts to Penobscot and Maliseet, and an early and direct contact with Micmac was also possible. For by 1683 two

[64] Barbeau, 48.

Shelter, Food, Clothing, Crafts

Micmac girls from the Gaspé or the Miramichi had attended the Ursuline school. The young ladies, as Father LeClercq tells us, could read and write. It seems not unlikely that they had also acquired the accomplishment, more congenial to Micmac culture, of elegant embroidery.

Such diffusion from French sources is particularly evident in certain of the designs on clothing. The actual making of the mosaic quillwork covering the birch-bark box came late to the Micmac and seems to have had a restricted adoption. E. S. Dodge, director of the Peabody Museum,

27. Quillwork on birch-bark boxes, Nova Scotia.

28. These quillwork designs on birch-bark boxes from Nova Scotia are remarkably close to those of the Ursuline nuns in the eighteenth century.

PART ONE *Tribal Life*

Salem, Massachusetts, has stated that they were made almost exclusively in Nova Scotia (where in 1912 were collected all the examples shown in illustrations 26–28), and that the earliest in the Museum collection dates from about the second quarter of the nineteenth century. The craft was supposed to have died out some years ago, but in 1950 at least two women on the Micmac reserve at Shubenacadie, N.S., were carrying it on at a high level; one of these was sixty-five years of age, the other under fifty. Lack of interest and a birch blight will probably inhibit any considerable revival of this application of quillwork.

29. Varieties of ribbon appliqué on women's bonnets.

No moose-hair embroidery was seen in 1911–12. However, the craft was formerly carried on by a Micmac group who for some years after 1850 had a sales booth near the steamboat landing at Rivière-du-Loup on the St. Lawrence. In contrast to the pine and star designs in moose hair appliquéd on skin, which spread from Huron Lorette, the Micmac examples in the Peabody Museum at Salem are of birch bark decorated with miniature human and animal figures.[65]

Carving and Modeling

Small figurines were made in aboriginal days. According to Lescarbot, birds, beasts, and men were carved in stone and wood in the form of pipes or simply to please the eye.[66] Little figures molded from pigment, and quills, beadwork, or wampum, according to LeClercq, adorned cradles.[67]

[65] Speck, "Huron Moose Hair Embroidery," AA, n.s., 13:1–14 (1911). I am indebted to E. S. Dodge for the opportunity to see this moose-hair work and for the description given above.
[66] *History*, III, 99.
[67] *Gaspesia*, 89.

30. Designs incised on a circular birch-bark box. *a.* Design on the rim of the cover. *b.* Design on half of the cover; the other half is a duplicate.

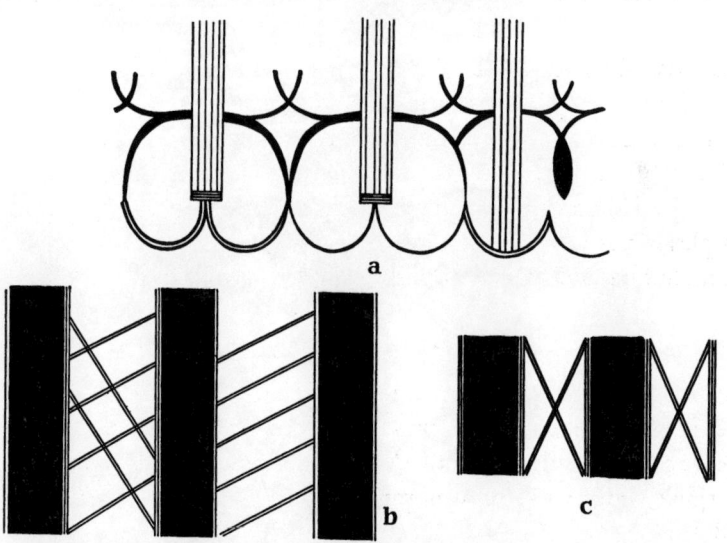

31. Designs on the sides of circular birch-bark boxes. *a.* The variation at the right does not occur elsewhere on this box or on any other specimen in the Heye Micmac collection. *b.* The variation at the left occurs only once on this box. *c.* The design is repeated.

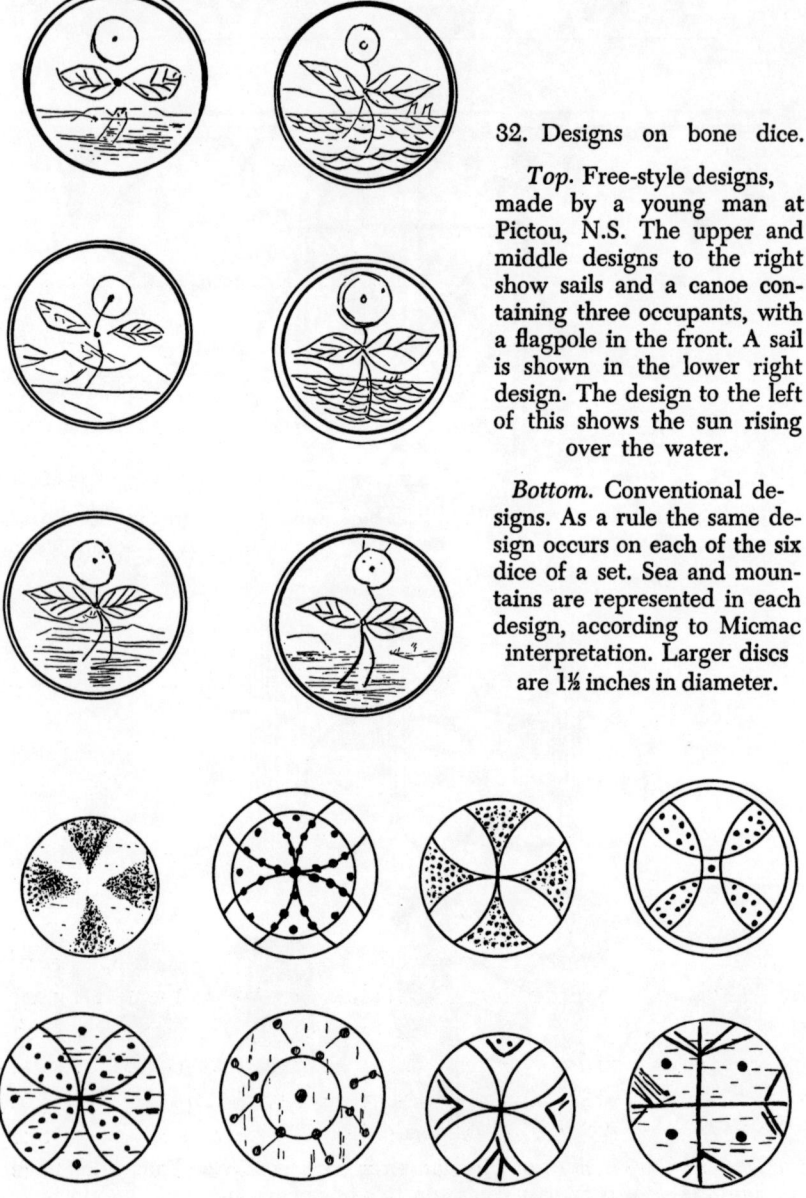

32. Designs on bone dice.

Top. Free-style designs, made by a young man at Pictou, N.S. The upper and middle designs to the right show sails and a canoe containing three occupants, with a flagpole in the front. A sail is shown in the lower right design. The design to the left of this shows the sun rising over the water.

Bottom. Conventional designs. As a rule the same design occurs on each of the six dice of a set. Sea and mountains are represented in each design, according to Micmac interpretation. Larger discs are 1½ inches in diameter.

Shelter, Food, Clothing, Crafts

Ornamental Designs

Micmac seem always to have enjoyed painting gay figures on wigwams and robes. Beasts and birds "adorned their skin garments, and on the birch bark of the wigwams women sketched moose, otter, beaver," a thousand different pictures.[68] Colors applied with specially prepared and heated bone were waterproof. Embroidery on summer robes of white mooseskin was in the form of broken chevrons or of animals "according to the fancy of the workman."[69]

Designs in the present century occur most frequently in the porcupine-quill work and bead work. Ribbon appliqué appears on women's bonnets and skirts. (See illustration 29.) Ornamental scratches on birch bark are also found (see

33. John Sark, of Prince Edward Island, in his chief's coat.

illustrations 30 and 31), and occasionally indentations with the teeth on a thin sheet of bark. All bone dice of the game *waltes* (see illustration 32) bear designs, incised and filled with color.[70]

Except on a few sets of these dice, the aboriginal free style has been replaced by formal arrangements of patterns. In these the double curvilinear motive characteristic of Eastern Woodland culture predominates,[71] mingled with floral designs of Iroquois, and ultimately of French, origin. A personal touch is the heart design on the chief's coat from Prince Edward Island (see illustration 33); the hearts on each breast were put on by a Maliseet while the owner of the coat, Chief John Sark, was visiting a Maliseet reserve; they signify that he had a good heart toward the Maliseet. A double-V in the center of the yoke was applied by Micmac whom he was visiting at Cape Breton, and are

[68] *Ibid.*, 95, 100–2.
[69] Denys, II, 411.
[70] See below, Chapter XII, and illustration 40.
[71] Speck, *The Double-Curve Motive*, 7.

PART ONE *Tribal Life*

34. Bead design on the instep piece of a moccasin. Heavy lines indicate beads, the fine line a border of braid.

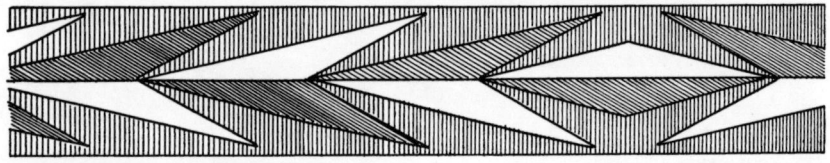

35. Sash pattern. At the right is the middle of the sash where the pattern reverses. Vertical lines are red, slanting lines are blue, and blank spaces are white.

said to be the special symbol of that group. Bands around the cuffs were of European manufacture.

The older Micmac beadwork had a fineness and delicacy not approximated in the introduced Iroquois style; the specimens reveal this difference more clearly than do photographs or drawings of them. Moccasin-top design, such as that shown in illustration 34, is probably Mohawk.

Sashes (see illustration 35), into which beads are woven to outline the dominating designs possibly are, as alleged, of native workmanship. I could not secure information regarding the method of weaving these sashes.

CHAPTER V

Concepts of the Natural World

THE orientation of the Micmac in his aboriginal world cannot be ascertained. Early seventeenth-century French observers were seldom interested in the philosophic or speculative attitudes of *les sauvages*; what little they noted comes to us dimly in the light of prejudices concerning noble innocence or devil-inspired jugglery.

From these fragments one might be tempted to infer that so far as natural phenomena are concerned, the Micmac stood rather comfortably in their midst, regarding the features close at hand with perceptive eyes which seldom turned to the heavens above or the earth beneath.

In 1911–12, informants, although they were aware that worship of the rising sun had been the principal feature of the native religion, showed little knowledge of celestial phenomena, and little interest in them; and they had not annexed much lore from the whites, although they had adopted many beliefs regarding supernatural beings.[1] Their explanations of the natural world follow, much as they expressed them.

CELESTIAL PHENOMENA

The Heavens

The earth is round and is completely enveloped by the heavens. Hence the heavens are curvilinear, like the surface of the earth. The sun shines through the intervening space.

The Sun

Naguset is the sun. *Naguset aniolusink*, a halo around the sun, indicates rain, and an opening in it will show the direction from which a

[1] The best account of sun-and-moon worship is by Maillard, *Customs and Manners*, pp. 22–27 and 47–48. See Chapter IX below.

97

wind will blow. A red sun means that a big fire is raging somewhere. When the sun is angry, he hides himself and there is an eclipse. In the old days people said to one another, "Perhaps Se'sas is angry with us." They would go to each wigwam, asking, "Have you done anything amiss? Sesas is angry with us." If a misdeed was discovered, the wrongdoer was killed. At an eclipse of either sun or moon, women went out of the wigwam, nursed their infants, and prayed to the celestial body.

The Moon

Tepkanuset is the moon. A halo around it is called *ac a lu'sink* or *el'tepkanuset*; the second is more complex.

The man in the moon holds a basket. He once picked chips on Sunday. Providence saw him doing this. He was not far from Providence, who said: "Leave the chips alone; today is Sunday." "It is not very wrong to pick a few chips?" "It is wrong. You should have done it yesterday." The Lord sent him to the moon. You can see him and the basket today. The priests and the bishops say this; perhaps it is true, perhaps not. When the moon is full, the man tries to hide his face.

The Stars

The stars are called *aklo we'djiwi*. Many of them have names, for example, *ohtadab'an*, morning star seen in the east. The North Star, called *go'gwadane glo'go wetc*, meaning "north," was a guide to travelers. The constellation of the Great Dipper is called *mu'in* (bear), or *adjalkatc*. In the seventeenth century it was called *mouhinne*, and *mouhinchiche* was the Little Bear or Little Dipper.[2] The three guards of the North Star are three Indians in a canoe who embarked to catch the bear but have not done so yet.

Rainbow

A rainbow is called *welkwun*. Formerly, when a rainbow was seen, people placed the two forefingers together, held the arms outstretched, then separated them, and swung them horizontally, through a semicircle, to the side. They then gestured as though they were pulling strands from the rainbow and placing them over the shoulder to serve as thongs to support a carrying bag. They did this in the belief that the rainbow was

[2] LeClercq, *Gaspesia*, 135–36.

Concepts of the Natural World

made of fine strands.³ When the sun penetrates the clouds, we see a rainbow, though the sun must be beyond the rainbow before we can see that too.

Thunder and Lightning

Thunder stays under a cliff, in a fog or thick mist. The following account is by Peter Ginnish:

"When the world was made, thunder, too, was made. It is like the wind, sometimes here, sometimes there. Occasionally it brings a very heavy storm. You should cease walking until the thunder has passed over, though a great many do not observe this precaution. Thunder is not always at the same altitude; some of it is high, some is low. When it is close to the ground, the lightning strikes. The noise of the thunder is made by the heat going up and coming into contact with the frost. But the old-time story says that there are people up there talking, just like ourselves. The sharp, loud, quick thunder is the voice of the young men talking about the hunt. The low, rumbling, rolling thunder is the voice of the old people telling the young ones to be careful in the hunt, not to hurt anyone, and so on, as is the case among ourselves when a party of young men are preparing to go into the woods to hunt."

Another informant said:

"One time three little boys came running into the house, their clothes wet, trying to get out of the rain. They looked out, saw a man come to the edge of the cloud, and then go back quickly, when it thundered. They called to their mother: 'Oh mother! Did you see that man?' She could not see him. I would rather take the word of three little boys than that of an old man of forty or fifty — they are too young to lie. I myself saw part of a cloud go round and round and then disappear."

If lightning strikes a man, he must not be touched until the next thunderstorm comes. He will then revive and get up. Some, however, say that a man killed by lightning must be left for twenty-four hours where he fell; during that time no one may touch him. When the thunder arrives home, he will tell the other thunders about the man. They will say, "Go back and bring him to life." The thunder will do so.

Lightning originated at the crucifixion of the Saviour, when the people saw a black cloud.

---

³ The magic or other significance of the act is not clear. Like the sun, the rainbow seems to have figured in old religious beliefs.

PART ONE *Tribal Life*

COLD

Cold is caused by the wind's striking the North Pole; a north wind, therefore, is a cold wind. The stories about the North Pole cannot be true, said one sage, because people cannot go where it is so cold that fire will not burn. The Eskimo can endure it, because it is their country; but other people cannot live in it, for they are not used to such low temperatures.[4]

FOG AND DEW

Fog (*un*) comes from the water. If the sun draws water, there will be rain the next day. The sun draws only fresh water; hence rain is never salty. There is fresh water below the surface of the sea, and this the sun draws up through the surface of salt water.

Dew falls only in the morning.

SPRINGS AND STREAMS

A spring in Prince Edward Island spouts up from three openings to the height of five or six feet and makes a great noise. About two or three hundred cartloads of stones have been put into it, but these have never had the slightest perceptible effect on the flow of the water. John Newell, the old man who described this phenomenon, frequently expressed the native philosophy which implies that whatever is natural is good. The following words illustrate this point of view:

"I was one day walking along the road to New Glasgow. I met a man who was going there on foot. I was very thirsty. We came to a spring, and he said, 'You can get some water there, John.' 'I won't drink that,' says I. Farther on we came to another puddle. 'You can get a drink here,' says he. 'I'll eat snow first,' says I. The water was muddy, running from the road. 'It's too muddy for me,' says I. 'You're making a mistake, John,' says he. 'How so?' says I. Says he, 'When the soldier ran his spear into the Almighty, blood flowed over the whole earth, because He is the owner of the whole earth. Wherever you find water on the ground, and no animal was there to make it bad, it is all right.' That man was correct and I was a fool. When he said that, I couldn't answer him. I drank the water. No water anywhere will hurt you, unless it is in a spring or some other place where an animal has spoiled it."

[4] For attitudes toward Eskimo, see Chapter XIII.

Concepts of the Natural World

If you go into the woods at twilight, when all is quiet, you will hear words from the brook. It sounds as if someone is laughing, then speaking, though with such indistinctness that you can scarcely understand what is said. When, however, you pass by in the daytime, you do not hear anything. Sometimes the voice seems so close to you that you can almost distinguish what it says. The old-time Indians obtained in that way a great deal of information and many words. There is something inside a spring that keeps the water flowing. If this something leaves, the flow will stop.

WEATHER SIGNS

A rain that starts Friday morning "hangs well." One that begins Friday afternoon will not stay long. An echo, "the sun drawing water," a mackerel sky, a cool morning breeze, or small dark patches of clouds, all are signs of rain. If the early morning breeze is warm, there will be no rain that day. Light, fleecy clouds over the water are a sign that wind is coming.

The very bright red clouds often seen in the autumn toward the west, about twilight, contain fire. From such clouds came the fire which started the great Miramichi fire.[5]

If "waves" from the sun (i.e., a succession of light shadows caused by fleeting clouds, but not thus interpreted by the Micmac) pass over a stone axe turned edge up, there will be rain or snow in a day or two. (The Micmac now use a steel axe when making this observation.)

Moose-tree berries do not grow every year. Their appearance foretells deep snow during the coming winter. An abundance of beechnuts or of mooseberries foretells a severe winter.

If moose rest under big trees, there will be good weather; if they feed on bushes, away from the big trees, one must expect bad weather. If they are very fat, there will be a hard winter; if only moderately fat, a mild winter will follow. If cattle are fat in the autumn, there will be a severe winter.

If partridges huddle together in the woods or under bushes, expect a storm or a cold night. If they wear feathers over the entire leg, or if the spruce partridge feeds all the time, and is fat, or the porcupine does not go far from its den, but constantly gnaws on nearby trees, the winter will be severe.

[5] See Tale 136.

PART ONE *Tribal Life*

LOCAL GEOGRAPHY

In contrast to the meager evidence of concern with the remote features of nature, informants showed in 1911 a continuation of the interest in their surroundings that had made possible the extended journeys of aboriginal days. Individual differences in degree of interest were marked. John Newell, a good informant for many topics, produced two dozen Micmac names of places between Caribou and Abercrombie, N.S., the neighborhood of his reserve, Pictou Landing; many of these had the air of *ad hoc* inspiration; whereas the blind Peter Ginnish, when asked if he knew any Indian names for places, took an orderly journey of some 600 miles.[6]

The route Ginnish described was from the tip of the Gaspé Peninsula to the end of its south shore at Restigouche; along the opposite shore of the Baie des Chaleurs to Point Miscou, and southward along the Gulf of St. Lawrence to Miramichi Bay; up the Miramichi River to Red Bank, and back along the opposite bank to the Gulf; down the coast to the Richibucto River, and then up and down that stream; finally from the mouth of the Richibucto along the coast to Shediac Bay at the Isthmus of Chignecto, which joins New Brunswick to Nova Scotia. In relating the features of this land, Ginnish started from Red Bank on the north bank of the Miramichi, and proceeded toward the bay on which he lived and from there north to Point Miscou; this is 60 per cent of the entire account. He then began inland on the other bank of the Miramichi and moved down the coast. Finally he returned north to Point Miscou and went around the Baie des Chaleurs, and then to Gaspé; the two hundred miles from Restigouche to Gaspé, the point farthest from Burnt Church, had the briefest treatment.

It is of some interest to compare Ginnish's 305 place names with those gathered by Father Pacifique for the same area. The method of collection is not stated by Father Pacifique. Before publication he checked and compared his lists with those of Anderson and Ganong.[7] The tabulation shows for certain regions the number of place names covered by Peter Ginnish from memory compared with Father Pacifique's research study. Those regions in which Ginnish's list is the longer are nearest to the Burnt Church reserve. The Gaspé region, nearest to Father Pacifique's

[6] The complete list of place names in Micmac, with Ginnish's derivations in English, omitted here because of limitations of space, we expect to publish elsewhere.
[7] "Le Pays des Micmac," in *Etudes Historiques et Geógraphiques*, 175–321; Anderson, 1919; Ganong, 1896.

Concepts of the Natural World

station at Restigouche, gave him far fewer names than did relatively remote Kent County.

	Pacifique	Ginnish
Gaspé Point to Restigouche	39	9
Tidehead to Caraquet	68	47
Caraquet to Tracadie	41	44
Tracadie to Red Bank	123	133
Kent County, N.B.	120	59

TIME DIVISIONS

Given their general lack of contemplation and of scientific curiosity, the primitive calendar of the Micmac, similar to that of neighboring Algonkin tribes, is to be expected. Seasons and lunar months were recognized and were expressed mainly in terms of the food cycle. Only LeClercq described the seventeenth-century concepts and gave the four names: spring (*paniah*), the time when leaves sprout, wild geese appear, moose fawns attain a certain size in the mother's belly, and seals bear the young; summer (*nib*), the time when salmon run up the rivers, and wild geese shed their feathers; autumn (*taouak*), marked by the southward migration of waterfowl; winter (*kesik*), which brings cold, snow, and the bears' retirement to hollow trees. Three of these four ancient names for the seasons were given at Burnt Church in 1953: spring, *tsuk*; summer, *nip*; fall, *tokwa*; winter, *kesik*.

The year was divided into twelve lunar months; a thirteenth was added if plants and animals arrived at the wrongly named moon. Biard says that thirteen moons made a year; LeClercq, who, it seems, was present at a moment of miscalculation, stated that the Micmac at Gaspé and on the Miramichi "confounded one moon of the Spring with those of the Summer and one of the Autumn with those of the Winter." Both men suggested that each moon bore the name expressive of seasonal occupation, but neither of them named the twelve. Biard, at Port Royal, suggested that the moons were called after the hunting for seal, beaver, moose, and the fishing for herring, eel, and tomcod. According to LeClercq, the calendrical year began with November, *tkours* (Rand: *skools*), a word indicating that the rivers are about to freeze.[8] December, the only other moon which LeClercq named, is *bonodemeguiche*, "when tomcods ascend the river" (Rand: *poonamoo*, tomcod).

[8] JR, III, 79; LeClercq, Gaspesia, 137–39. Abenaki designate the October moon "there is ice on the banks." Vetromile, 1866.

PART ONE *Tribal Life*

In 1890, Micmac translated the names of the twelve moons for Roth,[9] but no one who was asked about them in 1911–12 could do better than the man who said each was named after a flower! However, forty-one years later we did better. These late-garnered names are compared here with Roth's list.

1890 (Roth)	1953 (Wallis)
January ......Frost-fish	Spawn of tomcod
February .....Snow-blinding	Strong, cold weather; *or* sore eyes
March ....Spring	Springtime beginning
April ....Egg-laying	Hens start laying; *or* bird-hatching; *or* we make [maple] sugar
May ....Young seals	Frogs croaking; *or* everything growing; *or* we get herring
June ....Summer; or leaf-opening	Planting time; *or* growing up
July ....Sea-fowl shed feathers	St. Anne's moon; *or* we make hay
August ....Young birds are full-fledged	Harvest time
September ....Moose-calling	Cranberry-picking
October.......Fat, tame animals	Potato-picking
November ....*skools-goos* [tomcod moon]	All Saints' Day moon
December ....The chief moon [Christmas]	Christmas moon

Subdivisions of the thirty days may not have been formerly made but they could have been specified when need be; for words exist for many phases of the moon. *Tep'kanuset* (Rand: *depkunoosat*) indicated moon used as month. The following phases with their names were obtained in 1911–12. By 1950 only five were remembered: new moon; first quarter; half moon; last quarter; full moon.

New moon ....*tepkanusetdjitc*
First quarter ....*pegat tepkanuset*
Half-moon
   Waxing ....*aga dada cink tepkanuset*
   Waning ....*tepkanuset pemga'ayet*
Third quarter
   Waxing ....*gaayet tepkanuset*
   Waning ....*tepkanuset pemga'ayet*
Full moon ....*tepkanuset wadjuwet (wasjuwet)*
Last quarter ....*ote'tc ka we a'adat*

Days as time intervals were counted by nights, for example, a three-night journey. There is a Micmac word for yesterday, yesternight, the day before yesterday. The words for divisions of the day are given below.

Darkness before dawn ....*akadabani'ek* (1950)
Daybreak ....*wedjkwabania'k* (1950)
Sunrise to midday ....*kis'kadjibagabo'oiek* (1911)
About 9 o'clock ....*kiskiga'djikukwik na'guset* (1950)
Noon ....*meia'lagwe'dak* (*meliugwek*, 1950)

[9] P. 39.

Concepts of the Natural World

Noon to sunset .... *kip'kwadek* (1911)
Sundown .... *kalkwaisiek* (1950)
Dark after sundown .... *kakibiluomukwi'ak* (1911)
Midnight .... *ak'takba* (1911)

The direction of the shadows cast by the vertical sticks which supported the crane over the fire, one to the east, one to the west, and a third one to the south, midway between the others, gave the time of day. On a cloudy day one end of a stick was placed on the ground and the other end was held in the hand; this gave a perceptible shadow. In the woods, the huntsman had merely to place one end of his bow on the ground. Also, the hand could be held out at arm's length between the face and the sun, the open palm toward oneself, and one, two, three, or four fingers extended until they hide the intervening space between the sun and the horizon. The number of fingers thus required indicated the time of day.

A clock is *nagusadewe* (*nagu'set*, sun); a watch, *la mudala we*. A minute or a second is *ne a a task* ("one moved").

NUMERALS

The Micmac have native words for the numerals one to ten: *neo'xctc, ta'bo, sist, ne'o, nan, as'agum, e'luwig'anax, i'xmultcin, pes'xunadex*, and *amtelan*.

CHAPTER VI

Zoology and Botany

THE Micmac attitude toward animals, a mixture of kinship, awe, and the pragmatic is most clearly conveyed in their manner of expression, if not in their exact words.

Animal species are like tribes. Each species has a speech of its own which no other animal understands. There is no "headman" of all the animals, according to John Newell; each species has a headman, which is larger than the others. Some Micmac, however, say the moose is chief of all animals, and the whale is king of all life in the sea. Each beast, bird, or fish has a mate; and to designate each of these females there is a separate word.

TRANSFORMATION OF SPECIES

No hunter in the world can say, "I saw a moose, bear, or caribou so old that it could not get up." If you find a carcass, this signifies that some one has killed the animal (John Newell).

Aged animals transform themselves into a different species. Bear, caribou, and especially moose become whales; whales turn into moose.

Old moose go to the shore, enter the water, and become whales. Close similarities in the flesh of the two animals demonstrate this. Whale meat is salty like that of moose, and they have the same color and almost the same texture, both the fat and the lean. If you have the two meats together, you cannot tell them apart. The disappearance of the moose from the Maritime Provinces is explained by this transformation.

The following story is one of several based on allegedly actual observation:

"One time the Indians in Cape Breton could procure no moose, and could find no beaver. They were compelled to boil their moccasins in

Zoology and Botany

the spring of the year and to drink the broth along with salt water. They also had to kill and eat their dogs. They saw moose tracks leading away from the shore. They followed the tracks, and soon found and killed the moose. They discovered seaweeds in its stomach and in its intestines, and few traces of bushes.

"Beavers, which used to be very plentiful in Nova Scotia, turned into black ducks. This explains also why the black ducks frequent the lakes and inland waters and will not go out to sea. Like a beaver, a black duck will smell you, and if the wind is from your direction, will fly away.

"Squirrels turn into snakes. When squirrels are scarce, snakes are plentiful; when snakes are scarce, squirrels appear in abundance. The hiding place of the ground squirrel [chipmunk] is in an old log, and contains many stored beechnuts. They are splendid to eat.

"My brother saw a squirrel go into the hole of a tree, in Cape Breton. He was with another Indian. They dug there to hunt for beechnuts. At the very end of the hollow they saw the ground squirrel. It was not a ground squirrel at all; it was the ugliest snake they had ever seen. 'From this time on I will never dig out a squirrel,' said my brother. The squirrel had not gone out past him. I have noticed that when there are few snakes in the woods, the ground squirrels are plentiful."

RESPECT FOR ANIMALS

You should not bother animals that you cannot use. Leave them alone. It is wrong to kill them unless you have need of them. Let them go where they wish to go. You should not strike an animal with a stick or a stone that has blood on it.[1] You should not throw away a bone that has flesh on it, but should leave it there on the ground. It will bring starvation to you even if you pitch the bone to a dog. A stick on which fish or meat has been roasted should be treated in the same way. If you do not observe this, you will not be able to kill animals of that species.

This concern with the disposal of animal remains, current in 1911, is a weak survival of early Micmac practice. In 1675:

The bones of the beaver are not given to the dogs, since these would lose, according to the opinion of the Indians, the senses needed for the hunting of the beaver. No more are they thrown into the rivers, because the Indians fear lest the spirit of the bones of this animal would promptly

[1] A pregnant woman was warned particularly to show respect to animals. See Chapter XV.

PART ONE *Tribal Life*

carry the news to the other beavers, which would desert the country in order to escape the same misfortune.

They never burned, further, the bones of the fawn of the moose, nor the carcass of martens; and they also take much precaution against giving the same to the dogs; for they would not be able any longer to capture any of these animals in hunting if the spirits of the martens and of the fawns of the moose were to inform their own kind of the bad treatment they had received among the Indians.[2]

In 1710:

What remains of their superstition is the practice of tearing out the eyes of Fish, Birds and Beasts, and throwing them away, saying that otherwise they would be observed by their kind and would no longer be able to approach them; and they never burn the bones of Animals or Fish. Because of a similar delusion, they never singe the feet of Ducks, Geese, Swans, or any other web-footed Waterfowl, believing those that survived would no longer be able to alight on the sand, and for that reason few would be caught.[3]

Above all, the early Micmac believed the spirit of an important food animal must be protected from the contamination resulting from contact of its flesh with women. Menstruation, parturition, and death carried contagion and insult, particularly to moose and beaver. Only a bad girl or woman would eat beaver while menstruating; for the smart beaver, discovering this, would not allow itself to be captured by a man who had permitted it to be eaten by his unclean daughter or wife. For two months following childbirth women might not eat moose or beaver. Neither they nor menstruants might eat meat or drink soup from a bark kettle or a container in which beaver or moose had been cooked. Only if this taboo was observed could good hunting continue.

A widow might not eat meat killed by a young man. "So scrupulously do they observe this superstitious custom that they still at this day relate with admiration how a Gaspesian widow allowed herself to die of hunger rather than eat moose or beaver which was left in her wigwam even in abundance, because it was killed by young men, and widows were not permitted to eat it."[4]

Greatest respect was given to a slain bear. A new entrance was made in the wigwam, because women and girls did not deserve to pass through the same opening as the bear. Girls and women who had not yet

[2] LeClercq, *Gaspesia*, 225–29.
[3] Dièreville, 161.
[4] LeClercq, *Gaspesia*, 228. See 225–29.

108

Zoology and Botany

borne children left the wigwam as soon as the dead bear approached, and did not return until it was wholly eaten.

TABOOED ANIMAL FOODS

Micmac now and in the past seem fairly free of food taboos. Unlike many Indians, they have no fear that any kind of food eaten by a pregnant woman will mark the child. Certain animals are not eaten because, Micmac say, they do not like them. Their 1911 list — snake, frog, toad, lizard, skunk, insects are not universal favorites. In 1607 Lescarbot named wolf, otter, conies, and mussels.[5]

Certain meats were forbidden to young hunters because of associated traits that would impair their skill: porcupine, because it travels so slowly, and bear, which would bring shortness of breath or loss of courage. The finest morsels — bear entrails, and marrow and fetuses of bear, beaver, moose, otter, and porcupine — were reserved for the old men; young men were told that eating them would give them pains in their feet while they were hunting.[6]

BELIEFS ABOUT ANIMALS
Bear

Bear (*mu'in*) is very much afraid of fire, and goes away as soon as he sees it. During the winter he hides under the snow and lives on blueberries which he gathers and stores for winter. He sucks his paws by way of getting nourishment. He goes into the brooks and, with one or both paws, throws out smelts.

If you so much as look into a bear's den, the bear will not enter it again. It goes into a den, pulls bushes and leaves in behind it, and thus closes the opening. Before it moves from there, it cleans out the den as thoroughly as though it had been swept.

"A certain black bear has two cubs. In the middle of the spring the cubs become hungry and begin to cry. After a while the bear goes to the shore, and in a little brook sees smelts. She sits in the brook, so that the water comes up over her back. The young ones go up the stream and drive the smelts down to her. (Bears can talk in a language of their own.) The smelts come into her extended paws, and she throws them out upon

[5] *History*, III, 172.
[6] LeClercq, *Gaspesia*, 225–29.

PART ONE *Tribal Life*

the bank. The bear has not seen the Indian, for the wind is from another quarter. When the cubs have eaten enough, the old one again goes into the brook and pitches out smelts. She does this until there is a large pile of them. She shakes the water from her body, and lies down.[7]

"The cubs come to her and nurse. She says, 'Nurse away! Nurse away!' The Indian aims his gun, to shoot them. He is not more than three to four hundred yards away. He thinks better of it, and decides not to kill them. He watches them, to see how they will act. After a while, the bear begins to growl, walks to the smelts, gathers them into a pile, covers them with brush, and on top of this puts leaves, and earth over the leaves, until she completely conceals the fish. She behaves precisely as an Indian would do. 'If she comes toward me,' says the Indian, 'I will shoot her; but if she goes the other way, I will do her no harm. I do not wish to kill her, for her young ones would then have no one to take care of them.' The man goes about a hundred yards up the brook. He sees the bear removing the bark from a long stick. She then licks the sap from it, and the young ones come up and lick it, to get the sap.

"Often, when we walk through the woods, we see places where a bear has peeled off bark in order to obtain the sap. I have often seen such places. The bear comes out [of hibernation] about March. When he travels, he must have a bed. Accordingly, he pulls off cedar bark, and with it makes a bed for himself. One April we were in the woods peeling bark for a canoe. Two men were walking on one side of a brook, and I was on the other side. I heard a crackling. I walked in that direction, saw a piece of bark that had been peeled off, and found it warm. I heard sticks crackling. I went toward the sound and saw two bears pulling off bark. The bear must have a bed to sleep on — he will not sleep on the ground." (Thomas Meuse.)

Beaver

Beaver (*ko'bit*) lives on maple bark. He has a plan by which he gets a livelihood, just as do people. Nova Scotia Micmac believe he lives solely on poplar bark. Beavers turn into black ducks. There are two kinds of beavers: one you can shoot in the evening; the other you cannot catch in a trap, because he seizes the trigger in his mouth and trips the trap. Sometimes you can catch one in a deadfall, but the deadfall must be so far away that the beaver will not know what it is. Beavers know as much

[7] See Tale 103.

Zoology and Botany

as a person, and possibly more. The old Indians could tell the age of any killed beaver, and knew how many beavers remained in the den. A beaver from birth to about three months is known as *ki'djibantci'tc*; during the next age period, *ki'djibaumi'djit*; then *ki'djibantcidjmi'djit*; the next to oldest, *webahumskumi'djitc*; the oldest, *webahumsk*.[8]

Micmac admiration for these beasts amused Father LeClercq. The Indians told him that beavers have sense and form a separate nation, and that

they would cease to make war upon these animals if these would speak, howsoever little, in order that they might learn whether the Beavers are among their friends or their enemies. . . . "In truth, my brother, the Beaver does everything to perfection. He makes for us kettles, axes, swords, knives, and gives us drink and food without the trouble of cultivating the ground."[9]

Moose

Moose (*di'am*), chief of all the animals, lives on the leaves and branches of moosewood, roundtree, hazel, and princess pine. He eats moss in winter. Feeding moose walk with the wind, so that they can detect the odor of anyone following their tracks. Moose cure themselves of epilepsy by scratching the head behind the ear with the left hind foot. This belief was also reported by Dièreville (1710).[10]

Caribou and Deer

Caribou (*kalibu*) eats the moss pendant from trees. In Newfoundland there is a large black caribou; wherever it goes, all the others follow.

Deer (*le'ntuk*) lives on the leaves of yellow birch. A deer hears through eight (six?) parts of its body: through its two ears and its four hooves.

Skunk

Skunk (*abi'kstciluk*) is a dirty brute. No moose, caribou, or deer will go near him. He is alone all the time. No other animal will keep him

---

[8] Rand: a young beaver of the first year, *kujebancheech*; second year, *peewech*; third year, *pulumskw*.

[9] *Gaspesia*.

[10] In 1954 the mad moose of Nova Scotia was still news. The *New York Times* of February 19 reported that "about half of the moose in the province are believed to be out of their minds . . . they lope around the countryside, their sensory and motor nerves out of order." Reporters — non-Micmac — are biologists of the Nova Scotia Lands and Forestry Department.

PART ONE *Tribal Life*

company, for he stinks horribly. The odor from the skunk is emitted in the form of air from the rectum. If you catch him in a burrow, grasp his tail and two hind legs, and hold his tail down; he cannot then emit the disagreeable odor. Formerly his smell was stronger than it is now — so strong that it would kill people. The Almighty [doubtless, formerly, Gluskap in his role of Transformer] altered him so that he would not smell so strongly.

Sometimes a skunk goes into a wigwam when people are within, walks about, and looks for something to eat. His tail is always ready, and one must not make the slightest movement. If people do not move, he will not "open fire," but if a person moves, he will turn his artillery on that person.

Other Land Animals

Weasel (*eskcus'*) is a queer animal, which barks like a dog. He is a rascal; we do not like him at all. If he follows in the tracks of a man, the man will have bad luck. If the man kills it immediately, the bad luck will be averted.

Wolverine (*gigwa'dju*, "Indian devil") is a very queer animal. If he finds a lumber camp, he walks all about it. Wherever he makes water, there is a fearful odor. He looks for powder, and if he finds any, puts it in the fire. Sometimes he burns himself in this way. He is always full of mischief.[11]

Porcupine (*ma'dawes*) eats the bark from the trunk and limbs of trees. If you wash a porcupine after singeing off its hair, there will be a heavy shower. If it is not clean, you must wipe it with a rag or something else.

A raccoon will "play possum" if you come on it suddenly and surprise it.

A mole will die if it goes across the road. "I have seen them run across the road and drop as soon as they reach the other side."

The belief was current at Pictou Landing in 1911–12 that a vessel which has on board the skin of a black fox can enter any port duty-free and wharfage-free. The Micmac were puzzled as to the reason for this alleged fact, and supposed it was associated with the great value and the rarity of that article. The skin of a black fox was believed to be a shipowner's talisman.

[11] Gigwadju figures prominently in folktales. See Tales 99–101.

Zoology and Botany

Sea Mammals and Fish

The whale (*pu'dup*) is known to be a mammal. *Pu'dupes* is the calf. The whale is the largest creature in the ocean and the king of them all. Shad (*sadadimak*) is messenger for the whale and chief of all the fishes.

The island seal (*wa'spuk*) goes to a small island to bear its young. The rock seal (*kunda'mwee'tc*) leaves its young on the rocks. The sand seal (*si'galadi'*), said to have a skin as rough and hard as sandpaper, leaves its young in the sand along the beach. (The same name was assigned the shag fish.)

A sea otter can prevent your firing a gun. If it pursues you, you cannot escape it.

Brush fish (*sa'dasu*) is "quick as lightning," has long whiskers around its mouth, which is curved like the claw of a young owl. It will spit on you. If it spits into your eyes, you will lose your sight. *Pi'ter* (a species of cod) has a mark on the back of its neck where St. Joseph caught hold of it in a pond; it is so called because it is St. Peter's fish. The name is believed to be the old Micmac name (sometimes called *pier*, from Pierre).

When the swallows come, the salmon have arrived. When yellow (pollen?) floats to the shore, the bass have come.

The shag fish (also called sand seal) bears a great many young at one time. It does not spawn slowly like other fish, but emits all its eggs simultaneously. It lives principally on smelts. Hence, when seals come, this is a sign that the smelts will soon appear.[12]

Snakes and Serpents

Snakes are disliked because they give one a "creepy" feeling. About the middle of September, large numbers of snakes climb into trees and entangle themselves. This is their breeding season. They then sing in quiet, sweet voices, somewhat like the chirping of a bird. Lizards behave in the same way. At the end of the month the snakes and lizards fall to the ground, burrow into it, and remain underground until spring.

In a lake near Pictou, a Micmac saw creatures half-frog with a tail like a trout. "After seeing them," he declared, "I never ate trout." (Eating frog legs is abhorrent to Micmac.)

Near Pictou one can sometimes see a sea serpent not less than fifty

---

[12] For further lists of animals, see Appendix A.

PART ONE *Tribal Life*

yards long. It is hard to tell how big he is because he wriggles so rapidly through the water, half-submerged. A sea serpent whose body is as large as a barrel enters bays or rivers on August 15, when all the animals forgather. Only since the coming of the whites have the Indians known that date; the white people read it out of books. (Probably the concept of an animal assembly on a given date is borrowed from the whites.)

Tcipi'tcka'am is an alligator-like creature that lives in lakes and woods. He eats toads, frogs, geese, and ducks. He catches waterfowl in his mouth as they fly over. His head is as big as that of a horse. The eyes, two crystal-like substances, one of each side of the head, are potent "medicine." He is chief of the reptiles. Snake is his fast messenger. The old-time Indians killed Tcipitckaam by putting "medicine" on his head.

Belief in a giant serpent is spread so widely throughout the world that it is impossible to say that Micmac knew no Tcipitckaam before the coming of the whites with their dragon tales. Like various other mythic beings in the Micmac world, this monster is both an individual and a species or race. At Lake Ainslie, Cape Breton, John Newell once encountered two Tcipitckaam.

"They stood up in the water about an hour. I saw half of their bodies. They came up there every year. The male was black, and probably was the larger; the other, brown, was the female. The head is shaped somewhat like that of a horse, but is larger. Sometimes you see, at the bottom of a spring, a small worm about six inches long. If you tie a hair from your head around the middle of this, you will see a Tcipitckaam.[13] If you untie it, it will not hurt you. But if you do not do so, it will certainly find you and injure you.

Domestic Animals

Micmac declare that before the coming of the whites they used dogs to assist them in hunting. Father Biard, writing in 1612 from Port Royal, said that the only animal which was not wild was the dog. He referred to the slaughter of dogs on the eve of the death of a man, that he might have their assistance in the next world.[14]

According to one informant, who on the whole was very unreliable, the old Indians tamed the fox and fed it regularly, principally on the flesh of the partridge. The fox was caught while young and was kept at

[13] Tales 25–27, and Rand, *Legends*, II, IV, VII, XIII.
[14] JR, II, 11, 17.

Zoology and Botany

the camp. Each morning and each evening the trainer took the young fox to the water's edge, fed it a piece of partridge flesh, and threw the remainder of the meat into the water. The fox secured this and brought it back. This was done to attract the birds; when birds see a fox run to the edge of the water, they fly there in search of food; and the waiting hunter shoots one or two of them. The same method was used to decoy ducks. None of his statement was corroborated by any other informant.

At the present time dogs are used in northern New Brunswick to pull sleds, but it is not alleged that they aided in transportation in the old days.

Dogs. Every dog understands his master's language. The following designations are used: *e'lmutc,* "dog"; *e'lmutcitc,* "pup." "*Kus!*" is said to a dog in our sense of "Be gone!" or "Go away!"

To make a dog a good hunter, take boiled meat, sulfur, the ashes of birch bark, and pieces scraped from beech bark, mix with beef tea and a little raw meat, and have the dog drink the broth from this mixture. This will make the animal a good hunter, able to track game. To make it an especially good porcupine hunter, mix the ashes of porcupine quills with the mess. The mixture will make the dog fat and well. It should be given only to a young dog, and at the age when dogs will eat anything. (The informant had given his dog sulfur.) The dog is man's best friend. Even if you beat him, he remains attached to you. If he has a lump on his head you can teach him anything.

"A certain man was always kind to his dog, and another was never kind to his dog. The former man heard the following conversation between these two dogs: 'Why don't you go hunting for your master?' 'He is never kind to me; he gives me only hard bones and no meat. You are treated well, and you hunt for your master. When it is cold, he drives me out of the wigwam and I almost freeze. That is why I do not hunt for my master.'"

"The man told this to his friend. 'I don't know whether you have had bad luck,' he said, and related the dogs' conversation. The friend took the dog into his wigwam and treated him well. Soon it captured moose, and later much other game. The man, because he had shown no kindness to his dog, had nearly starved."

In the seventeenth century dogs were eaten as ordinary food only when people were starving. Even then a certain respect was due. Jesuits at Miscou in 1645 described such an incident:

One day, when a dog had been killed to save the lives of numerous persons who were starving, this boy [a Frenchman] who was not satisfied with the little that they had given to him as to the others, seized the liver of the animal that had been thrown away, and cooked and ate it. He was warned to leave that meat, that it would do him harm, and make his skin fall off. He would not believe it, and continued his repast, but to his regret, for it cost him his skin, which fell off in great flakes without any pain, so that in a short time his skin was entirely changed. The Savages know by experience this result on those who have eaten that meat.[15]

European Domestic Animals. The cat is *mia'ktc, mia',* or *miatcitc* (the last usually applied to a kitten). Cats are kept as pets, but are regarded as uncanny. Few Micmac will allow a cat to remain in the house at night. They associate cats with witchcraft. They tell stories about a beast, in the shape of a cat, called Winchester, of frightful appearance. It is so called, they say, because nine bullets fired at it from a Winchester rifle failed to kill it. In Restigouche the name for cat is identical with that for wildcat — *utokwetc.* A man at Pictou stated that he would never allow a cat to remain in the house at night, although it might be there during the day. He had been told that a cat was no good after it was a year old, and he thought they should be killed then. He also told of a place near St. John, N.B. — though whether the story was true he was not sure — where cats became so plentiful that they attacked people and horses which passed through the place, and at night swarmed over the roofs of the houses. They were finally gotten rid of by burning the place.

The cow has been called "French moose," *wendju'diam,* since its first appearance in New France. Another term, *elagoduk,* is also used.

Animals under the Sea. On the bottom of the sea are animals like those found on land; for example, cows, pigs, and little pigs which suckle the mother.[16]

Rats

Rat is *me'skil* (large), *abiktci'tc* (mouse). According to an informant, before a fire breaks out in the city, all the rats will leave, even though this involves swimming a river. They will leave a vessel if it is destined to sink. It is the same way with the Indians when something is about to

[15] JR, XXVIII, 27.
[16] This is a belief held in European countries, especially Sweden. Paul Sébilot, *Légendes, Croyances, et Superstitions de la Mer* (Paris, 1886), 196.

Zoology and Botany

befall them—they have a presentiment of it. Some people once said they intended to sit up all night to kill the rats which were rampant in the house. The rats heard the conspiracy, left, and not one of them was killed. Another time the rats heard people saying they intended to set traps for them; that night the rats turned the traps upside down. They heard people say they would poison the potatoes which the rats were carrying away; the rats continued to carry away the potatoes, but after this, did not eat them.

Birds

Micmac information about birds includes the natural and certain additional elements of the marvelous.[17] Information in the main came from three informants, none of whom claimed complete knowledge. To quote one of them: "There are a great many things in the woods. We do not know them all." In the three accounts contradictions occur. For example: *gu'gwetc* to Peter Ginnish is a small owl, frightening but not otherwise harmful. To John Newell, *kupketc* (*gugwetc*) is the saw-whet owl which, if mocked, burns one's possessions with secret fire. These are the actions ascribed by Tom Meuse to the *glo'edjidjit*, a name given by Ginnish to a puffin.

According to Ginnish: Gugwetc is invisible, but will frighten you in the daytime or at night. He may call to you, or make a noise to frighten you. You may go where you hear him singing, yet you cannot see him. So it is. If you become frightened and run, he will follow and frighten you. He will not, however, do you any other injury. A mother will quiet her child by telling it to stop crying or Gugwetc will get it—"Gugu! gugu!" goes the mother, in imitation of Gugwetc. If you hear something queer in the woods while you are walking there, it is Gugwetc that frightens you. It makes a noise like a person. It is sometimes male, sometimes female. It goes about in the woods, living there just like the Mi'gamawe'su.[18]

Meuse's Glo'edjidjit, St. James bird, is so called because its song is *glo'e* and *djidjit*, that is, "doing tricks with gloe [fire]." Gloedjidjit does not like people to imitate his singing. If you do so, he will come back and punish you, and whatever you have that you prize highly, that he will get and burn. No one knows how he procures the fire with which

---

[17] For lists of birds, see Appendix A.
[18] Compare Tales 35–40. The cry of a larger owl, the "whooper," is interpreted as the harbinger of a *skadeg'amutc* (ghost).

PART ONE *Tribal Life*

to burn it, but the treasured object will surely be burned into holes. He does this while you are sleeping, never while you are awake. For this reason, people very seldom tease it by imitating its cry. If you imitate its cry, in a dream, the bird will come to you and say: "My work and your work are different. I must look after my work, and you must look after yours." You will then awake and find a treasured object burned full of holes. This owl is a *buoin* (witch). You will not see the bird, for it is a tiny one. Even though you lock your property in an iron chest, it will, nevertheless, be burned.[19]

Wa'lawedj, the nighthawk, is a queer bird and a *buoin*. He can twirl a burning stick in one "hand" and catch it with the other. Pigeon, a very fast traveler, is his messenger. Eagle can catch any bird except the pigeon. A large eagle, hawk, or crow circling about is a spy looking over the country, maybe a Mohawk in disguise.

To disturb a bird's nest brings bad luck. "A bird may say to you, 'For God's sake, go away and don't disturb my little ones!' You don't understand what it says, but it will be bad for you."

"Pigeons," said Newell, "will not stay at a house in which husband and wife quarrel. "My wife heard [contentious] words between a man and his first wife. They had two pigeons. The pigeons left, and stayed away four days. About a week later she heard them quarreling again; they did not fight, but there were loud words. The pigeons left again, and did not return." Newell did not know why this had happened, but seemed to consider that the pigeons' aversion to domestic incidents of this nature was in keeping with their gentle dovelike nature.

LEARNING SONGS FROM BIRDS

John Newell gave the following account of songs: The Micmac learned songs from birds. (See, for example, the Loon Song, Chapter XII, p. 195.) The Indians did not understand what the birds were saying, and hence the words in these Micmac songs have no meaning. They learned them especially from the wild turkey and the sea gull. "Ka ka ka kwi't," sings the wild turkey to herald a storm. Gulls which fly around together and herald a storm or a high wind for the following day furnished inspiration

[19] John Newell identified this bird as the saw-whet. The note of the saw-whet is described by Chapman and Reed as "a frequently repeated whistle; sometimes high, sometimes low; generally begins slow and ends rapidly; resembles noise of a saw-filing." The ornithological name, *Nyctala acadica*, suggests its presence in the Maritime Provinces.

to the Micmac composer. The gull sings "ka'ni! ka'ni! ka'niak! ka'niak! ka'niak!" three times, then flies away. One old Indian listened to the gull until it had finished its song. Thus he learned its song, and said to the others: "If you people care to dance to it, dance. If not, then merely listen to me." He then took a stick and beat time. But as he sang he wanted to put some words into the tune. He was thinking about a woman who was hunting for something, and accordingly he sang about this.

Many songs were learned from owls. One can almost understand their language. They speak words distinctly, "wi ya'," (long drawn out) is said by the owl, plainly, when he has finished his song. This is what the Micmac sings at the end of his song. After this the owl leaves and another takes his place, and sings "wuk'wa ha, wuk'wa ha." After he has finished, he goes off to one side, sits by himself, and gives a "hu'a" (rising inflection on first syllable, falling inflection on second), then a "wa'hi! wa'hi!" and at each syllable nods his head.

A Micmac learned a song from the owl. He was camping in the woods. The owl smelled the fire and came close to it. After a while he heard someone singing "ru! ru! ru! ru! ru! ru! ru! hua'wa! hua'wa!" finishing with "hi'a! hi'a! hi'a!" Soon another owl sang; and then another. The owl commenced with high notes, in a very sweet voice, and ended with "hu'a," a deep guttural. It sounded as though he was choking. After this, three or four sang in chorus, the refrain of one answering the syllables of the other. The man said, "I have his song now, and will sing it hereafter as a *ne'skawe't* (greeting song)."

BOTANY

Micmac men and women have an intimate knowledge of the trees, plants, and herbs of the locality, and know their names, uses, and seasons. They know the names and virtues of almost every flower, weed, bush, tree, or vine that grows in the Maritime Provinces. Chapter VII contains a discussion of plants used in the treatment of disease. A list of botanical names in Micmac will be found in Appendix B.

CHAPTER VII

The Body in Sickness and in Health

To OLD men in 1911–12, the Micmac of their day were degenerated organisms, small and feeble in comparison with their tall, long-lived ancestors. Formerly people attained great age. A man at Red Bank lived to be one hundred and fourteen years old; and many passed the century mark.¹ They were also of great stature. Stories about skeletons that have been found usually attribute to the deceased an enormous stature. John Newell's grandfather told him the following story:

"My brother had a wigwam at Mabou, in Cape Breton. While he was digging holes in which to put the poles of his wigwam, he found some human bones. They were bones of the old-time Indians. The bone of the upper leg was about four fingers longer than those of the Indians of my day."

The Micmac language, as Silas Rand has shown, is rich in evidence that the speakers are interested observers of human form and features. Such distinctions as a large-nosed person, a large crown-of-the-head person, a long-tongued person abound. *Kokwodumae* means walking with the toes straight in front as an Indian does; white people turn their toes out when they walk. Talk of that sort in 1616 evidently went around Port Royal in a most informal way, for Biard wrote to Paris:

Any of our people who have some defect, such as the one-eyed, squint-eyed, and flat-nosed, are immediately noticed by them and greatly derided, especially behind our backs and when they are by themselves. For they are droll fellows, and have a word and a nickname very readily

---

¹ The belief that the old-time people were wont to reach a ripe old age, frequently going beyond the century mark, seems to have been shared by many of the early Fathers. Membertou, the first Micmac baptized (1610), was declared by a pious Jesuit to be "at least a hundred years old, and may in the course of nature live more than fifty years longer." JR, I, 75, 109.

Body in Sickness and in Health

at command, if they think they have any occasion to look down upon us.[2]

PHYSIOLOGY

In 1911 close observation and detailed "knowledge" of anatomy was shown only by Thomas Meuse. His long list of anatomical parts is given in Appendix C. The following descriptions of physiological processes also are his. Other informants tested on these topics had almost nothing to say. Nothing could be learned about reproduction or other vital processes.

Sense Organs

The aperture of the ears extends the entire distance through the head and forms a continuous canal from one ear to the other. The nasal apertures open into the middle portion of this canal, the name of which is *widina'biusidiwa'an nidotcal'kok*. At the juncture of the nasal apertures and the ear canal are two small valves, *edalauki kepsaktes'kal*, which move up and down, like bellows, with each inhalation. When they close, deafness results. *Mus'kwuisei'k* is the mucous membrane in the posterior portion of the nose by means of which smell is possible. *U'kwuda'an* is the mucous membrane in the back portion of the mouth where taste has its origin. *Wi'lnu* is the tongue.

The interior of the eyeball is hollow. The pupil of the eye reaches from the surface of the eyeball to this hollow portion. If an object gets between the surface of the eye and this hollow, the *ne'midegump*, the "inner" sight, is lost. *Utuga'bie'lankuk* is a tough but soft membrane at the back of the eye which holds the eye in position and also allows it to move. This membrane is fastened to a bone. *Kli'gan* is a small muscle fiber at the back of the eye which grows into the *utugabielankuk* and holds the eye attached to it.

Alimentary System

Uto'ala wa'anabil is the esophagus. A little below the esophagus is the beginning of the trachea, *tcu'asanabi*, a much smaller tube. When one drinks or swallows, it closes; this is shown by the fact that one cannot breathe while drinking. It is a very small tube. Choking of the esophagus is caused by food getting on the *utugabielankuk* at the back

[2] JR, II, 3.

PART ONE *Tribal Life*

of the eye. The cause of tracheal strangling is not known. *Wendjusum* is the Adam's apple. (Literally, "apple," from *wenwutc*, "Frenchman," and *sun*, "cranberries.") The *wendjusun* must move before one swallows. It enables one to swallow, and is working steadily while one swallows. If it fails to work, food goes into the trachea.

Utkla'mihi is the stomach. No information could be given about this organ. Pains in the stomach are caused by foul air moving to and fro, trying to escape. If there were no air in the stomach, food would never move through the bowels. Air forces out the contents of the intestines. Food in the body remains fresh for one day; thereafter it is putrid.

Blood

Blood vessels are called *midja'witc*. They penetrate the entire body. No explanation was given of the circulation of the blood, beyond the assertion that the body makes it go. A man should cut himself now and then, to permit the old blood to go out and fresh blood to come in; otherwise, he will retain the blood which he had when a child. When blood is old, it becomes sluggish; hence, formerly, old men bled themselves occasionally, in order to have a supply of fresh young blood. The instrument used for this purpose is known as *e'tkcac'digan*. It is composed of three strips of wood, one of which has a sharp flint in the end. The fingers of one hand are placed between these, and the flint is given, with the free hand, a sharp blow that drives it a half-inch to an inch into the flesh. At each operation one to two quarts of blood are extracted.

The seventeenth-century practice was described by LeClercq:

They are great lovers of blood-letting; they even open their veins themselves with flint stones or the points of their knives. If any swelling makes its appearance, either on arm or leg, they lance the places where the evil is, and they make several incisions with the same instruments, in order more readily to suck out the foul blood, and to remove all its corruption.[3]

Thomas Meuse's information about blood ends his descriptions of Micmac physiology. Beliefs expressed by the old men were limited to these few: Continued heat, such as that of the tropics, softens the bones and a person is nearly cooked. Diet affects body and mind. If one constantly feeds a dog meat, the dog becomes very savage. The constant meat diet made the old-time Indians wild. Because of the great quantities

[3] *Gaspesia*, 297–98.

Body in Sickness and in Health

of dark moose meat which they ate, they were darker in complexion than are present-day Micmac. The fact that eating moose meat makes one dark can be learned by observing the black excrement which results from eating this meat.

DISEASE AND ITS TREATMENT

Attitudes toward health and disease in 1911 were expressed thus:

There was no sickness among the old-time Micmac. A white man came to North America and brought smallpox in his small ship and left some of his sick crew here. There was then no cure.

Houses are not as healthy as wigwams. There is a great deal of poison in the woods, and there is also a great deal of medicine. In the spruce boughs and limbs which were put under the wigwams there was always good medicine. One could not smell it, and no one could say precisely what it was, but the occupants breathed the air from it and were benefited. From the floors of the houses one does not get this.

In the wigwam there was a draught up through the top, at the middle, and the dust went out there. In the houses there is no such draft, and the dust and dried spittle of people, well and sick alike, float about and go into one's lungs. Now the women die at an earlier age than formerly. They get heated while working in the houses, and when they go out in the wind, catch cold and have rheumatism.

According to the old precepts, bathing when the tide is coming in brings sickness and ills into one. One should bathe when the tide is going out, for then the ills will be carried away.

The cause of unexplained disease, the kind no doctor can cure, was as widely attributed to witchcraft in the twentieth century as it was in the seventeenth century; in the earlier days it was described as the presence in the afflicted part of the body of a worm introduced by the witch and removable only by a medicine man.

Preventive treatments were formerly emetics and the sweat bath. LeClercq described an emetic made from a root resembling chicory, or from certain seeds gathered from the trees, which were steeped for ten or twelve hours in a bark dish filled with water or broth.

Sweat Lodge

The sweat lodge, formerly used throughout the Maritimes, is no longer employed; only the older men in 1911 knew about it. It was the

PART ONE Tribal Life

custom, after returning to the coast from a winter spent in the woods, to dig a shallow hole, put bent sticks over this, each end thrust into the ground, and make a dome-shaped structure. This was covered with leaves and earth to make it airtight.

The structure was called *na'ganame wog'wum*, i.e., "sweat wigwam." No further details of the structural characteristics could be obtained.

A fire was made in it, and stones were heated in the fire. Everything was then removed except the heated stones. Over them were placed hemlock boughs, whereupon three or four men entered, made the entrance airtight, and remained to have a good sweat. No water was employed. This treatment was taken by men of all ages upon the return from winter quarters in the forest, to remove from the system the cold of autumn and winter. One informant stated that boys used the sweat lodge and, rarely, the women also used it; the bodies of the latter were "too soft."

A somewhat different version of the lodge and associated practices is as follows: When the grass begins to sprout and the trees begin to bud, the bark of seven different trees, viz., black cherry, choke cherry, juniper, white maple, fir, pine, and a second growth of ash, are boiled together until the mixture has the consistency of syrup or molasses.

Poles about five feet in length are driven into the ground to a depth of about a foot, and are set firmly. Spruce bark is put alternately in and out along these stakes, so that it is strongly braced and held in position. It is then covered with a blanket and made as nearly airtight as possible. A large stone is placed in the center, and three stones are placed around it. Over these a fire is built. The medicine made from seven kinds of bark, and the poles and the spruce, are now ready. The stones are heated to a white heat. Three or four men go in naked, and sit on the fir boughs placed there for this purpose. A man pours medicine on the stones, and vapor fills the lodge. It goes to lungs and bones.

Each man has a towel of moose or caribou skin with which he rubs the back of one of his fellows, and is the recipient of similar treatment. The sweat is like slime — so full is it of impurities from one's entire system. Before he leaves the lodge, each wraps himself in a blanket. They then go to bed and cool off gradually. Cooling suddenly would bring sickness.

The sweat bath of the seventeenth century was a more strenuous affair, at least in the Miramichi region, involving the use of water and a subsequent plunge into the river.

Body in Sickness and in Health

The sweat-house is a kind of a hot room, built in the form of a little wigwam covered with bark, or with skins of beaver and moose, and so arranged that it has no opening whatever. In the middle thereof the Indians place some hot stones, which heat those inside so much that the water soon starts from all parts of their bodies. They throw water upon those hot stones, whence the steam rises to the top of the wigwam, then it falls upon their backs, much like a hot and burning rain. This continues until some of them, unable to endure this heat, are obliged to rush out as quickly as they can.

This proceeding, which serves to torment some of them, is never-theless a matter of amusement to others, who take a particular pleasure in throwing water from time to time upon the stones, in order to see who will have most endurance. They even sing and joke among themselves, giving vent to their usual whoops. Then, rushing quickly from this wigwam, they throw themselves into the river in order to cool themselves. This would, without doubt, cause serious illness, and even death itself, to people less robust than our Gaspesians, who set to eating with unequalled avidity immediately after they have issued from the sweat-house and the river.[4]

The final plunge from "these sudorific Ovens" was also part of a sweat bath that Dièreville saw in Nova Scotia.[5]

Seventeenth-Century Treatments

Aboriginal methods for treating the frequent wounds and fractures were greatly admired by the Micmac's French neighbors. Dièreville's account, while not the earliest, is the most complete:

They injure themselves very frequently, but Nature has placed under the bark of the Balsam-fir, trees which are very common in all parts of Acadia, a marvelous remedy for all their wounds; it is a Turpentine, finer in quality, and more balsamic than that obtained from Venice, and it is found wherever it might be needed for a dressing. If the Indians break their Arms or Legs, the bones are reset evenly, and large pads of soft fine moss are made, which are saturated with their Turpentine, and wrapped around the broken limb; outside of that is placed a piece of Birch-bark,

---

[4] LeClercq, *Gaspesia*, 296–97.
The Beothuck had a similar sweat lodge. "The remains of a vapour bath were found, the construction was ingenious; large stones were heated in the open air by burning [sic] stones around them, the ashes were then removed, a hemispherical frame work, closely covered with skins to exclude the external air was fixed over the stones. The patient crept in under the skins, taking with him a birch rind bucket of water and a small dish to dip it out; on pouring water on the hot stones he could raise the steam at pleasure." A. Macdougall, "The Beothuck Indians," TCI, 2:100 (1891).
[5] Pp. 175–76.

PART ONE *Tribal Life*

which readily conforms to the shape of the part; splints are not forgotten, and, to hold all secure, they use long strips of thinner bark which make suitable bandages. The Patient is then laid in position on a bed of moss, and this method always succeeds very well. If such an accident were to overtake an Indian when he was alone, he would fire his Musket to summon help; or, if he had no arms, he would make smoke, the usual signal between them, one that never fails in time of need. A Wigwam is made at the place where the accident has occurred.[6]

Primitive preparation and application of turpentine was described by LeClercq:

Since this balsam is a little too irritating to the patients, they have the ingenuity to temper its activity by masticating the pellicle which is found attached to the fir after they have removed the outer bark. They spit the water which comes from it upon the affected part, and make of the remainder a kind of poultice, which alleviates the evil and cures the wounded man in a very short time.[7]

The medicineman in Lescarbot's day (1606–7) licked and sucked a wound and then put a slice of beaver's kidney on it.[8]

A few years later Father Biard, at Port Royal, noticed the good effect the Micmac attained by massage, followed up by rubbing the whole body with eel oil. This noisome oiling not only protected the skin against heat, cold, and mosquitoes; it also kept their loose-hanging hair from catching in branches, and from blowing and drenching in storms.[9]

To Dièreville we are again indebted for knowledge of treatment in such diverse crises as epilepsy and drowning:

To resuscitate a drowned person they fill with Tobacco smoke the bladder of some animal, or a long section of large bowel, commonly used as receptacles for the preservation of their Fish and Seal oil, and having tied one end securely, they fasten a piece of Pipe or Calumet into the other, to serve as an injection Tube; this is introduced into the backside of the Men who have been drowned, and, by compressing it with their hands, they force into them the smoke contained in the bowel; they are afterwards tied by the feet to the nearest tree which can be found and kept under observation; almost always follows the satisfaction of seeing that the smoke Douche forces them to disgorge all the water they had swallowed. Life is restored to their bodies, and before long this astonishing and beneficent result is made manifest by the twitching movements of the suspended Men. Don't forget this blessed

[6] Pp. 176–77.
[7] *Gaspesia*, 296.
[8] *History*, III, 186.
[9] JR, III, 115, 117.

Body in Sickness and in Health

restorative, attested by a thousand experiences; its virtue, in time of need, would be no less effective among your friends, than among the Indians.[10]

The treatment for epilepsy, witnessed by Dièreville, was as follows:

An Indian squaw . . . went into the neighboring forest [and] brought back two doses the size of two broad Beans, scrapings of a plant root; she made him take one when his attack had passed off, and had him well covered, making him understand that he would sweat profusely and that he would void a great amount, both above and below . . . She allowed him to rest on the next day, and, as she was leaving on that day, she said that he was to be given the remaining dose on the day following, and that he would then be completely cured; he did as she told him, and the remedy produced the same results as before, and, since that time, the Patient has never had an attack of his malady. I saw him a long time afterward in perfect health. When seven or eight days had gone by, and it was seen that his trouble no longer recurred as usual, the Commandant was very sorry that he had not inquired into the composition of a remedy so rare and so beneficial.[11]

LeClercq stated that epilepsy was cured by using the left hind hoof of a moose which had been seen to cure its epilepsy by scratching behind the ear with the same hoof.[12]

Moose also contributed a remedy for easing the spasms of childbirth. A small bone, called *oagando hi guidanne*, "found in its heart," was ground to powder, cooked in a broth, and administered to the patient.[13]

Medicines

Informants in 1911 believed much of the old lore concerning the good and evil inherent in nature, particularly in plant life.

"Go out into the woods in the spring when the leaves are putting forth, and you will be invigorated." The informant had spent about a week in the woods, and consequently felt splendid. "The opposite is true if you go into the woods while the leaves are falling."

If people get dew on themselves from along the edge of a certain large lake in Shelburne County, N.S., or go too close to the edge of it, they will have the palsy. A great many people in this county are affected with this shaking. Some say it is caused by snow.

[10] P. 180.
[11] Pp. 181–82.
[12] *Gaspesia*, 275. See above, 111.
[13] *Gaspesia*, 275.

PART ONE *Tribal Life*

At *Sugulagadis* (literally, "Rotten"), a large burying ground about thirty miles from Pictou, are two large rocks, *kukamadjino*, "grandmother of all of us," and *miskunidjino*, "grandfather of all of us." They have moved from the bank toward the water's edge and are now near the shore. They are man and wife, and are moving slowly, all the while endeavoring to get closer to each other. If you are sick, you will obtain a certain cure from the roots of medicinal plants which grow back of these rocks in places where they (supposedly) were before they moved to their present positions. You should put a penny, pin, or something else on one of them whenever you pass them. Perhaps you put a penny on one of them and cover the coin with a stone; when you come there later, the coin is not there. No one knows what becomes of these things. They are offered, it is alleged, as a "sort of charity."

In March of each year a certain man turns over in his grave and says: "Help me! All my strength is gone. In the place where I have been lying there will be for you people potent medicines." This is the strongest medicine for smallpox.

Some of the most valuable medicines are the most difficult to find. There is a medicine that goes "tick! tick! tick!" like a clock, but you cannot locate it. You hear it at one place, and when you go to that spot, you hear it at another place; it persistently eludes you. An old man told me that when he was with other men he heard the "tick! tick! tick!" and hunted for the plant a long time, but with no success. Another said: When, in the evening, you are near a swamp or a marsh, you will hear "ticks" from a plant. This sound can be heard in the marsh at Amherst, N.S. Though you search for the plant a hundred times, you cannot find it. You hear the ticks in one place, and when you go there, you hear them in another place. To find the plant, procure a spider and a black lizard — these are the worst poisons in the world — put them alive into water, and you will hear this *me'didesxe'we* (the plant), ticking. Go at midnight, strip off all clothing, and take a step at each tick, which comes every second or two. You will find the plant. Finally, you will hear it at your feet. Do not look down or stoop, but squat, dig in the ground there, and you will find the sought-for root. Carefully replace all the removed soil. If you do not put it back, you will not be able to find the plant again. A very small piece of root will suffice for a very long time. Boil the root, together with a spider and a lizard. It is fine medicine, but dangerous. A very small amount, if it gets into the blood, will kill. Formerly this

Body in Sickness and in Health

"poison" was used on arrows. The informant said he had heard this "ticking" in the marsh near Charlestown, Massachusetts.

Another good medicine, equally elusive, is a tall plant which has six leaves, in pairs, one pair directly over the other. Some men who found it blazed a tree alongside it, so that they could find it later. When they returned to get it, they searched for it diligently, for three hours, but could not find it. "I myself, in company with some others, found one. We left our axes by it, and went to dinner. When we returned after dinner, it was gone. An old woman once told me, 'You must put a penny on the ground, over the roots; the plant will then not go away.'" In the old days people placed the kneecap of an animal over its roots, and the plant would then not go away.

If you drink tea made from it and rub some of the plant on your hands and face, you can sleep next to a person with the smallpox or anything else, and you will not contract the disease.

Sweet grass, if put in a room, will keep sickness away. Probably every Micmac house contains some of it. Steeped calamus root, *kiw'eswa'skul*, makes a good drink, and is good medicine for any sickness. At Burnt Church last winter (1910), it cured a case of smallpox. The woods contain medicines capable of curing every ill — if only one knows the proper things to use; unfortunately, our knowledge is only partial. (A precaution that should be observed in procuring medicine was one day brought to my attention when my informant attributed his indisposition to his pulling up on the previous day medicinal roots. "You should not get medicine before you are sick," he said; "if you do so, you are likely to become sick." I noticed, however, that most medicinal plants, when found, were usually pulled up and taken home.)

Micmac say that Indian medicine will not act as quickly as that of a white physician, though it will cure a white man more speedily than it will cure a Micmac; and a white physician's medicine is more effective when taken by a Micmac than when taken by a white man.

Sometimes the observer finds it difficult to distinguish between Micmac medicines and mere beverages. Thus, the bark of hemlock, tips of juniper, bark of white, yellow, or black spruce, white pine, sassafras, labrador (*Ledum latefolium Groenlandicium*), dogwood, and moosewood are boiled and used as teas or "drinks," and also are taken as medicines. Black spruce, juniper, sassafras, and labrador are not specifics but are "good for anything," stress being placed on their value as tonics.

PART ONE *Tribal Life*

The leaves, berries, and bark of the waxberry (*kwa'saniman*) are boiled as tea, and are considered exhilarating.

The following list of diseases and their treatment was obtained at Pictou Landing, N.S.[14] This information I submitted to Dr. Wilson Wood, then of the Medical School of the University of Pennsylvania, who furnished observations, here appended, regarding the value of the treatments. Dr. Wood's observations are bracketed. Many of the remedies, like many of the diseases, are of European origin.

Diarrhea. "Wild chocolate," *egwitkewe*, will stop it gradually, though not suddenly.

Purgatives. Bark of hazel tea is a purgative if, after taking it, the abdomen is rubbed from above downward; if rubbed from below upward, it causes vomiting. Pipe-stem wood (*nickanamusi*; alder?) is a good physic. When boiled and mixed with fat of porcupine it is as effective as castor oil. [The good effect of this combination is presumably due to the fat, which is laxative. Alder bark, which contains tannic acid, would tend to have the opposite effect.] Molasses [molasses alone is also laxative] and lard combined is a good physic much used by adults; a newborn child is given as a physic the fatty oil of raccoon or porcupine. Root and bark of gooseberry vine, scraped and mixed with grease and a little sugar, "will go right through you." One who takes this physic will suffer no ill effects from getting wet or from working. *Sagebanigewe* (a species of wild carrot?), a red-blossom plant with three leaves clustered around the stalk, which grows along brooks, is steeped, and is a mild purgative. The roots of *ukskusaligan*, a plant which grows in low swampy places, is beaten until soft, then applied around the waist, as a poultice. It is as effective as salts.

Whooping Cough. Mix skunk grease with grease from the red squirrel and, if desired, a little fat of the latter. It induces vomiting, and ensures recovery. A dose should be given three or four times a day. [It is possible that this nauseous dose causes vomiting and, by effecting a general relaxation, relieves the spasm of coughing, but it can have no effect on the course of the malady.]

Colds, Coughs, and Influenza. A tea made of hemlock bark and of the bark, needles, and twigs of the white pine is used. [The volatile oils contained in these evergreens have long been credited with a good effect in bronchitis. This is probably due to the fact that in their passage through the lungs they stimulate the bronchial secretions.] A tea is made from wild turnip and the bark of moose-wood, pounded together and sweetened. Ground- or spruce-hemlock is boiled and whiskey is added. This is good for the bowels also; and for any internal trouble. The bark of black spruce [see statement in the last brackets] and of

[14] Wilson D. Wallis, AA, 24:24–30 (1922).

Body in Sickness and in Health

white maple of second growth, i.e., the shoots from the stump of an old tree, are scraped and steeped. A physic should be taken prior to a dose of this. The tops and leaves of *masusidjal*, "sweet palm," are boiled. This will also ward off tuberculosis, and will gradually cure diarrhea.

The *kaad jumanaktsi* (literally, "crow's nest plant" — the mistletoe?) is good medicine for any ailment, especially for colds, particularly in the case of infants. The staghorn sumach (*Rhus typhira* or *hirta*) is good for sore throat. [The astringent properties of its tannic acid accounts for the good result.] The *madaweswalu* (yarrow, *Achillea millefolium*), by inducing a sweat, cures a cold. [Yarrow and juniper contain volatile oils which act as a counterirritant, relieve pain, and possibly account for their reputation as beneficial agents for sprains or bruises.] It should be boiled about an hour, and taken in warm milk. In about a half-hour it causes the patient to sweat, and drives out the cold. Lay it on coals for about half an hour, leave it there until thoroughly dried, then remove, and mash with a stone into a fine powder. Rub this dry powder, using for this purpose bark or green leaves, over a swelling, bruise, or sprain. On the following day, a cure will be effected. *Tcigawabi*, "bass root," spikenard, is good for a cold or for sore eyes.

Cuts and Wounds. Tea from bark of white spruce is a good salve; muskrat roots (*kiweswusk*), for open wounds. Resin and mutton tallow are used. [The mutton tallow acts merely as a protectant. The resin is slightly antiseptic. Juniper is used for this purpose by the Hudson Bay Indians.[15]]

Tcigawabi, spikenard, is boiled until it becomes soft, and is then applied to the wound. To treat a severe cut, wash the wound with castile soap and apply beeswax; remove this, and apply mutton tallow. The wound will soon heal. Juniper gum will make it heal too rapidly. If you put juniper gum [see statement in last brackets] on a wound, it will heal so quickly that you will think you have never been cut. The informant added: "I knew an Englishman who cut his knee badly into the bone, put excrement on it, then covered this with balsam, to keep the odor in. In two or three weeks the flesh and bone were entirely healed. Another man broke his collarbone. An old Micmac woman from Restigouche put excrement and balsam gum over the fracture and cured it."

Red willow chewed fine and placed on a fresh cut will stop the bleeding. Bark of white pine scraped and boiled until soft, mixed with grease, will cure a wound. To stop bleeding, chew the leaves of the pigeonberry plant until they are soft and pliable, and apply to the wound. Boil alder bush until the bark is soft, then remove it. The bark will be soft almost immediately after the boiling point is reached. If it boils long, it will be too strong. For bleeding or for hemorrhage of the lungs, chew and swallow the boiled bark. [All these contain tannic acid, which, when locally applied, tends to stop bleeding by constricting the blood vessels.

[15] Cree?

PART ONE *Tribal Life*

The natural inference among the ignorant that they are beneficial also in hemorrhage from the lungs is without foundation.]
For hemorrhage, drink the sap and the water found in the little bark (cones?) on pine trees, mixed in a little warm water. Relief will be almost instantaneous.

Tuberculosis of the Lungs. A person who has tuberculosis should move about, outside, and should not spit on the floor. Peel the bark from a juniper tree, as far up as possible, then cut the tree down. In the exposed wood are little lumps. Cut into these, collect the sap which exudes from them, mix this with brandy, and allow the decoction to stand overnight. Scrape off a small amount of skunk cabbage and add the scraped portions to this. When the patient is better, he should take a physic to purify the blood. A walk in the morning and one in the evening will further aid recovery.

Defective Hearing. The urine from a porcupine's bladder dropped into the ear and kept there by wads of cotton will improve defective hearing.

Earache. Pour into the ear either tea made from boiled sumach or warm skunk grease. [The oil retains heat, which relieves the pain.]

Sore or Weak Eyes. Pour vinegar on a porous pebble, allow the pebble to dry, then tie it over the eye. The vinegar will go into the eyeball and cure sore eyes or defective sight. The sore eyes of a man are cured by the urine of a little girl about four or five years old; those of a woman, by the urine of a boy of about that age. "When I injured my eyes last year, I treated them with the urine of a little girl about a year and a half old. But for that I should have been entirely blind. Now my eyes are as well as ever they were. Do not tell anyone what you are doing, but if your eyes become sore and you have the opportunity, try the urine of a little girl."

Toothache. Scrape the bark of *kaldjimanaksil* (wax root) and steep it. Place this on cotton and put in the affected tooth. Wash the face in cold water, throw the water away, and forget about the tooth and the water.

Headache. Tie skunk cabbage in a bundle and smell it. [Nervous or hysterical headache may be relieved by this ill-smelling plant. Bad odors seem to have a beneficial psychic effect in such conditions.] Do the same with the roots of the waxberry plant. The shed skin of a snake worn in the hatband or tied around the head will cure headache. (One old man, because of his aversion to snakes, disapproved of this treatment.) Grate waxberry root fine and snuff it.

Rheumatism. Rub with raccoon grease, or, preferably, skunk grease. Porcupine grease is equally good. [These oils merely facilitate massage.] The grease is procured by skimming the broth. The fat of turtle and the contents of the gall bladder of any animal are good lubricants.

Sprains. Wrap juniper gum around the affected part, with eel skin; or merely apply the eel skin as a tight bandage. "My wife had sprained her

Body in Sickness and in Health

back and could walk only by putting each hand on a knee; juniper gum cured her." A plaster of juniper gum removes the soreness and pain. The plaster will move around, of itself, and will not stay in one place long, no matter on what part of the body it has been put. "A man was badly injured by a fall and could not sit or walk. My grandmother's mother told the people to put juniper gum on the helpless portions of his body. Soon he was sitting up straight, and was as well as any one."

Childbirth. Fresh milk and boiled ground hemlock (not too strong) are given to the mother. [Ground hemlock yew is used by ignorant Negroes in the southern states to produce abortion, but has caused many fatalities.] A tea made from the black haw or stag-bush sloe (*Viburnum pomifolium*) is given to women both before and during parturition. A tradition is current to the effect that the Virgin Mary carried this latter plant about with her when she was with child. [Many physicians credit *Viburnum* with distinct virtues, but there is a grave doubt of its value.]

Colic. Tea made from the tips or combs of balsam trees cures colic. [The volatile oil in balsam gives a sense of warmth and comfort in the stomach, grateful in cases of mild colic.] To alleviate pain in the stomach, the bark of the round tree (*epsimusi*, mountain ash) is chewed raw.

Diphtheria. Drink alder-bark tea.

Convulsions. To cure a person of fits, cut the feet from a mole or from a moleskin and place these on any part of his body. If possible, open the patient's mouth and put one of them down his throat. If you cannot split the feet of the mole, open the skin and scrape the inside of it. This will cure for the time being, but not permanently. A final cure is effected by the use of the codfish louse, a parasite found on the gills or other part of the cod. A woman was cured in a few hours by hanging a piece of this, sewed in canvas, pendant from her neck, and resting over her chest. She had suffered during an entire summer. It is essential that the patient should not know what is effecting the cure.

Worms. Eat raw dulse (a seaweed).

Saltrheum. Apply axle grease.

Ringworm. Spit on ink powder and rub this on the afflicted part.

Corns. Rub with sulphur from matches.

Measles. Drink the fresh dung of sheep dissolved in water. Previously the dung of deer was used. This will drive the measles out and ensure speedy recovery.

Kidneys. For trouble with the urine, use white pine tea. [Tea made from white pine causes an increase in the action of the kidneys, chiefly because of the large amount of water, but also to a slight extent from the stimulating effect of the volatile oil of pine.]

Festers. For festers or fever cover the entire body with alder leaves, after removing the stems. Allow them to remain on until they wither. A cure is then effected. If it is winter and the leaves cannot be had, cover the body with alder bark.

PART ONE *Tribal Life*

Smallpox. Drink a strong potion of princess pine, black cherry bark, wild turnip, beavers' castors, and honey. Take a teaspoonful in the morning and at evening. Smallpox is hard on Indians because of the texture of their skin. The skins of white people break easily, whereas the skin of the Indian is very tough.

Miscellaneous. If a dog gets porcupine quills in it, feed it fat pork; the quills will then pass out of the animal's body.

The buttercup is good for cancer. When laid over the diseased part, it draws out the sickness.

Gold-root (*wisakiwes*) chewed raw cures chapped or cut lips.

Lambkill (*kagipul*, or, more commonly, *nebitck*) draws out the pain. For this purpose it should be pounded into a powder, mixed with oatmeal porridge, and applied as a poultice.

Roots of *koldjimanaksil* (*Myraca cirifera*), wax myrtle, will cure inflammation. They should be pounded, soaked in water, and applied at a temperature just below the boiling point.

Wabegpagosi, the rough cow parsnip (*Heracleum sphondylium*), when green and light in color, is good medicine for women; when dark and riper, it is good for men.

The buttercup, the virtues of which have already been recorded, is effective medicine if picked after one returns from church service on St. Anne's day (July 26), but not if gathered on other days.

In concluding his observations regarding these remedies of the Micmac, Dr. Wood said: "Many of the statements made by the author's informant are obviously too indefinite to understand or criticize. Most of the practices recommended are unquestionably based on superstition, and some, if followed, must be absolutely harmful. A few seem to be the result of favorable experience and have their analogues in methods employed by more civilized peoples. Nearly all of these, however, are, as might be expected, extremely crude."

The Seventeenth-Century Medicineman

The simple skills necessary for the preparation and administration of aboriginal medicines were universal among the Micmac. But if the illness was serious, if the patient refused to eat and lay silent by the fire, the medicineman was summoned. This practitioner, called *Autmoins* by Lescarbot and Biard, and *Bohinne* by LeClercq, was a religious leader as well as doctor.[16] For treating the sick he received payment in meat or

[16] *Buoin* is the modern Micmac word for a person possessing magic power, a wizard or witch. Rand: *Boooin*, wizard, juggler. See Chapter X and Tales 65–73.

Body in Sickness and in Health

skins. He was said to be the one member of the group to whom all was given and no return required.

Initial treatment was described by Lescarbot, Biard, and LeClercq. Subsequent stages, sometimes necessitated by persisting disease, are summarized below from Biard's vigorous but highly prejudiced account.[17]

On arrival the medicineman looked over the patient to judge where the germ, evil spirit, or whatever was causing the illness was centered. He then blew all over the body, particularly on the affected part. Sometimes the spot was sucked or incised. Blowing was accompanied by invocations, contortions, and cries.

If no improvement occurred after several days, the medicineman announced that the evil must be driven out by force. Everyone then set about preparing for a three-hour ceremony that would be filled with danger. The angered spirit might attack and strangle anyone in the crowd. Each person was assigned a role in the proceeding. (But, says Biard, this would be too tedious to describe!)

The medicineman dug a deep hole and within it buried a stick tied to a protruding cord. He chanted, danced, and howled over the hole and, alternately, over the sick man who lay nearby. He then entered into active combat with the evil, slashing about so furiously or (said Lescarbot) pulling so hard at the rope that he broke out in sweat. Suddenly he roared out that the moment of peril was at hand. All grew pale and trembled. Then: "We have him. He is exterminated at last." Now the crowd pulled at the rope; but in vain. More howls and slashes from the medicineman, more tugs at the rope. Little by little the stick was uncovered and torn out. On the end were some decayed bones or a piece of skin covered with dung. This was the evil.

The medicineman then stated that whether the spirit was dead, damaged, or merely gone a short distance away, he could not tell until he had slept and dreamed. The next day he again viewed the patient and decided whether or not he would recover. If the man would die, the medicineman announced the duration of life — a matter of days.

The patient was then given up by his family who no longer fed him. If at the end of the stated time he still lived, it was believed that the evil spirit in him would not let him die easily, and to hasten relief from suffering, cold water was poured on the naked abdomen.

[17] JR, III, 117–25.

PART ONE *Tribal Life*

This hastening of death in hopeless cases was also described by a more sympathetic observer, LeClercq, who stated that sometimes, at the time of migration, the family of a patient who could no longer eat, drink, or smoke, broke the sick man's head.

CHAPTER VIII

Mental Processes

THE way in which sensory stimuli are believed to reach the Micmac brain has been recorded in the preceding chapter. The brain is called *tabal;* there is no name for nerves, but *ne'sawet* or *ne'sai* means "nervous."

The mind of a living person is called *klidaswa'anum*; the mind or soul of the dead is *skadegamutc*. As an informant phrased it, when the mind is in your head, it is *klidasawaanum*. *Skadegamutc* leaves the face at death. A watcher who fell asleep beside a dying man whose face was covered with a cloth woke to find the face bare. The departing mind had removed the covering. This dead soul or ghost is identified with phosphorescence, but is not confined to old stumps outdoors at night; *skadegamutc* is everywhere. A resolve made by the living mind, *klidaswaanum* (for example, to fight someone), may be carried out by *skadegamutc*.[1]

The Micmac seem to have few ideas about thought processes or consciousness, and questions regarding these matters elicited almost nothing. A rare exception follows: "The memory of a person is like the tide — it comes in slowly and rises gradually. What the Micmac learn they carry along with them. In the old days therefore, young people had much respect for their elders. Suppose an old man should say, 'This is good for that,' and 'That is good for the other.' Then later that young fellow can tell someone else. It was like the tide coming up, gradually; just carrying along in the memory what was learned from other people." This is practically the only abstract native account of psychic processes that I obtained.

In other contexts a few concepts were spontaneously offered. From

[1] For further concepts see Chapter X.

PART ONE *Tribal Life*

these scattered items one can tentatively conclude that outstanding mental ability is unnatural, unsafe, and un-Micmac.

Precocity is undesirable. If a boy is too clever when he is young, he will have no sense when he grows up. The unusual, particularly the mentally precocious, leads to trouble.

DREAMS

Micmac dreams frequently contain much culture reference. A recurrent theme is the necessity to master an attacking person or animal; actually the dreamer believes he must conquer the witch, *buoin*, who has sent the dream; otherwise he will be defeated in a daytime encounter.[2]

Impressed by the strength of the Micmac belief in dreams, the early French missionaries led planned attacks on "the bonds that held [them] down in [their] wretchedness." But all they attempted to destroy was not misery; according to a 1607 report, those who had auspicious dreams rose in the middle of the night to hail the omen with song and dance.[3]

Some of the success and failure of the good fathers is reflected in the dreams related by John Newell, of Pictou Landing, N.S.

Dream Experiences of John Newell

1. In a dream, Joe Martin's wife's mother and I started from home. We traveled until we saw a large church. We said our prayers on the steps.

A man came out and invited us to go in. We went in. All the people there wore white clothes. The man took me to the pulpit. "Do you know this man?" "No." "That is God." "What am I to do?" "Kneel down and ask pardon."

I did as I was told. The Saviour waved his hand, indicating that I was to get up, made the sign of the cross, and told me to sit in the chair. The Saviour said, "You are not ready to come yet." He told the woman, "You go with this man and come back soon." Three days later she died.

2. The only good dream I had was this one: I dreamed twice that I killed the devil. A big bull was chasing two of us. "That's the devil," I

[2] See Chapter X and Chapter XVI.
[3] JR, II, 75; XLV, 63–65, 227.

Mental Processes

said. "How can we escape?" "I'm not going to run away, I'm going to kill him." Big steel horns protruded from the bull's forehead. He jumped into the doorway of an old house nearby. When he came out, I struck him with a stick, and beat him until I broke a horn. He cried, and said he would not do anything to me. I pounded him until I killed him.

3. I dreamed that I saw, in a rock, along a bank, a door which opened and admitted five schooners. A woman came, but was too late — the door had closed. A short time after this dream experience five people of my acquaintance died. I had seen the road to Heaven.

4. Another time I dreamed that I saw a big mountain. There was a severe storm and a heavy sea. A large tall man came out on it, bowed, and cried. I did the same. He turned back and climbed the mountain. The sun rose, and went back. It happened a second time. I thought, "I had better say my prayers; it is the Saviour." Again the sun rose and went back. The Bible hung from my neck, and I was reading it. I told the others to kneel: "Maybe it is the last day. If he goes back, we shall be here yet a while." Finally, he stopped, moved twice in a straight line, and then at right angles to this [made the sign of the cross] and went back. "We are safe," I said, "the world is saved" — for he had gone back.

5. I was hunting with another man. I had a dream. I dreamed I was in a big dance in which the women wore fine white dresses. I was having a splendid time. (As a matter of fact, I never dance or attend these functions.)

I was sure then to get a big fat moose the next day. Next morning there was a noise in my ears. [Possibly suggestive of the roar from a gunshot.] I am then sure that I shall have success while hunting. That is dreaming. I do not believe that, but still it's so.

6. I had come in from a long hunting trip and was tired. It was late afternoon. I lay down, and soon went to sleep. I dreamed that I saw a bull with long horns, running at my father to kill him. (My father was planning to butcher a bull.) I picked up an axe and ran toward it, to strike it on the head. I gave it a blow. When I looked again, it was not a bull, but a man, and I had taken off the top of his head. He held his head down, and said nothing. I said, "I have committed a crime, and

PART ONE *Tribal Life*

they will hang me for it. I may as well finish the job and kill him." I raised the axe and gave him a heavy blow on the head. I then awoke, in a cold sweat. My wife said, "What is the matter?" "Nothing," I told her. "You were throwing your arm around this way and that," she said, "but I did not touch you." "It is a good thing you did not touch me," I said.

Before I married, I used to go with a girl. I left her, and married another. She was jealous of me and had tried to hurt me this way. Next time I saw her, her head was bandaged, there was a long bruise on one cheek, and another on her forehead.

7. In Bathurst, I had a dream which indicated that someone wished me ill. I was sleeping with another man. I dreamed that I was a carpenter and had been making a coffin for a little girl, because another girl had told me to do so. While I was fastening down the screws in the lid, she pushed the lid off and came to me. She clung to my legs, her head very close to my knees, and insisted that I go to a certain place. I would not do it. I had a hard time, but finally I brought my knees up with a quick jerk and struck her, with one knee, in the face, and with the other, below the neck.

She then left. Next day I passed the house of the girl who had sent this other girl to me in the dream and the former was standing in the doorway. On her face, at a spot corresponding with the one on which I had kicked the girl who visited me in my dream, was a big bruise. If I had not done that, something bad would have happened to me. I do not know precisely what would have happened — it is not possible to say. I expect that when I was working with lumber my legs would have been cut off or crushed. If I had not kicked her as I did, I would have been in a bad way.

It was about three o'clock when I had the dream. When I awoke, I was trembling and overcome with fear — a terrible feeling of something awful that I cannot explain.

Dreams of Other Pictou Men (John Newell, Narrator)

1. The chief at Pictou dreamed that he would see a row. We were in Restigouche. "How do you know?" "I dreamed of a fine time — people happy, running about, and everyone glad." That afternoon the people chose a new policeman. He and the former one had had a fight. Such was the fulfillment of the dream. [Dreams go by contraries?]

Mental Processes

2. A father said to his two sons, "You can't get any game," and laughed at them. They went into the woods and, a long way from their father's house, set one hundred and seventy traps. That night, in a dream, the older son saw his father go with upraised hands to every trap and cry, "Shu! Shu! Shu!" and frighten away the animals. Next morning their traps contained only two squirrels and a hare. The next night, the older boy, in a dream, saw his father do the same thing. The following morning they caught nothing. Five nights in succession this happened, and on each succeeding morning the traps were empty. The older son said to his brother: "Our father has been frightening away the animals. I have seen him on five [successive] nights. That is why we get nothing. I shall go home and kill him." The younger one told him not to kill their father. They returned; they had been seventy-five or eighty miles away in the woods. The older son told his father about these events, and threatened to kill him if he should frighten away the game again. They returned to the place where they had been trapping, for they had left their blankets and other things there. They could not find any of these. To this day no one has seen their possessions or knows what became of them. [The informant thought it probable that their father had secretly murdered them.]

3. A man who was in the woods, trapping, saw in a dream a man going about, frightening the animals away from his traps. The next night he saw him doing the same; he threw his arms about, and said, "Shu! Shu! Shu!" and frightened the game away. He then went to the wigwam, raised the flap, and started to walk in. The man was there, waiting for him. He struck the intruder several times, as hard as he could, on the right arm. The dreamer awoke, and found that he had torn away the flap of the wigwam. A few days later he returned to the settlement and went to the house of the man who had frightened away these animals. The man was nursing a sore arm. A few days later he died from it. And it served him just right — the old rascal!

CHAPTER IX

Religion

SUN WORSHIP

MICMAC can recall only one thing about their native religion. The rising sun was greeted each morning by a short prayer, which asked for blessing. No one could repeat the prayer formula, but knowledge of the act of worship was general. The sun was addressed as *Sa'gama*, an honorary title applied to a chief or to a white man.

To reinforce this meager evidence of sun worship, the early accounts afford frequent though brief evidence. "They believe in a God, so they say," remarked the always scornful Biard, "but they cannot call him by any name except that of the Sun." "Their God was formerly the Sun," Dièreville stated a century later. "*Nichekaminou*, which means . . . the Very-Great; they gave thanks to him for his kindness to them."

To LeClercq we owe more. The sun is the Micmac creator, he said, to whom they owe — and have always shown — devotion, homage, and adoration. Because it is the sun's command that they live content, the Micmac quietly endure the misfortunes of nature. The only religious ceremony was the morning and evening greeting and invocation. At the first ray of sunrise they came out of their wigwams, and turning their faces to the sun, addressed it with the ordinary Micmac greeting repeated three times (*Ho, ho, ho*), bowing low and gesturing with arms above the head. They then asked for protection for family, power over enemies, good hunting, a great catch of fish, a long life, and a long line of posterity. At sunset the ceremony was always repeated; this was considered the more propitious time for presenting requests. Possibly only the head of the family performed the rite.[1]

A young medicineman told Father Biard that when the people were

[1] *Gaspesia*, 143–44.

Religion

in great need "he put on his sacred robe and turning toward the East said, *Niscaminon hignemouy minem narcodam*:[2] 'Our Sun, or our God, give us something to eat,' that after that they went hunting cheerfully and with good luck."

LeClercq thought that the end of "false worship" had come; he had seen the sun ceremony performed by only one person, an aged man. Some fifty years later the Abbé Maillard saw or heard about a great deal more. Micmac religion observed in the mid-eighteenth century was in general as vague as had been noted earlier: Manitoo was an indeterminate being or source of power, which sent the spirits of the dead to tell the living of distant happenings, to forewarn them, and to give advice. Instigation to revenge also came from Manitoo. There were no accounts of the origin of the world or of mankind: Micmac cosmology consisted of the assertion that all their ancestors were good at everything.[3]

Sun worship continued, and aid in war was sought by sacrifice and by invocation. More rarely, hunters and night travelers besought help from the moon. In 1755 we find set down the words and concepts of these petitions. Micmac metaphor and allegory, "in which even their conversation abounds," appealed to the Abbé Maillard. To him, learning the Micmac language included adopting the "measured cadence in delivery" and an elegance of expression which, he boasted, equaled that of the best of the women "who most excel in this point." Maillard's version of an invocation to the sun preceding a sacrifice on the eve of war (given in full in Chapter XIII), refers to the "beauteous luminary" as Father of the Day. He is eternal, regular in appearance, all-seeing and all-penetrating, the source of growth and vigor. His rays, impregnating the womb of earth, produced human beings, who then grew up like the herbs and trees, whose father is also the sun, essential to the development and functioning of mind and body.[4]

Second in importance to the sun is the moon, who protects life from the malignant night air, a substitute for the Father of the Day. Micmac consider regularity of appearance among the orb's high qualities. Wife of the sun and always a mother to mankind, the moon protects women in childbirth, and bestows children and the milk to feed them. Maillard gave this hunter's prayer:

[2] This name and the preceding Nichekaminou suggest the Kitchimanitu of Central Woodland Algonkin.
[3] *Customs and Manners*, 44.
[4] *Ibid.*, 22-27.

143

PART ONE *Tribal Life*

How great, O moon! is thy goodness, in actually, for our benefit, supplying the place of the father of the day, as, next to him, thou hast conceived to make us spring out of that earth we have inhabited in the first stages of the world, and takest particular care of us, that the malignant air of the night should not kill the principle and bud of life within us. Thou regardest us, in truth, as thy children. Thou hast not from the first time, discontinued to treat us like a true mother. Thou guidest us over nocturnal journies. By the favour of thy light it is, that we have often struck great strokes in war; and more than once have our enemies had cause to repent their being off guard in thy clear winter-nights. Thy pale rays have often sufficiently lighted us, for our marching in a body, without mistaking our way; and have enabled us not only to discover the ambushes of the enemy, but often to surprise him asleep. However we might be wanting in ourselves, thy regular course was not wanting to us. Beautiful spouse of the sun! give us to discover the tracks of the elks, moose-deer, martins, lynxes, and bears, when urged by our wants, we pursue by night the hunt after these beasts. Give to our women the strength to support child-births, render their wombs prolific, and their breasts inexhaustible fountains.[5]

The concept that man came from the ground, expressed in the invocation to both sun and moon, is recorded in almost identical words by Roth:

The Micmacs believed themselves to have sprung from the ground, in which the Great Spirit planted them as he did the flowers and trees. Lossing says, "A Micmac chief in Nova Scotia said to Colonel Cornwallis of the British army, a century and a quarter ago [1765]: 'The land you sleep on is ours. We sprung out of the earth like the trees, the grass and the flowers.'"[6]

Long before this date, however, the sun had become thoroughly entangled in Christianity. Here is a Micmac version of Genesis, or as much of it as LeClercq thought worthy of preservation:

When the sun, which [the Micmac] have always recognised and worshipped as their God, created all this great universe, he divided the earth immediately into several parts, wholly separated one from the other by great lakes: that in each part he caused to be born one man and one woman, and they multiplied and lived a very long time: but that having

---

[5] *Ibid.*, 47–48.
In a Cape Breton story collected by Frederick Johnson in the 1930s, a hungry old man addresses the moon: "Bright, you know I have never asked you for anything yet, but now I am going to ask you to get me a moose. I am an old man and can't get one." Next morning a moose appeared so near his door that he could easily shoot it with his bow and arrow. P. 75.
[6] Pp. 43–44.

Religion

become wicked along with their children, who killed one another, the sun wept with grief thereat, and the rain fell from the heaven in such great abundance that the waters mounted even to the summit of the rocks, and of the highest and most lofty mountains. This flood, which, say they, was general over all the earth, compelled them to set sail in their bark canoes, in order to save themselves from the raging depths of this general deluge. But it was in vain, for they all perished miserably through a violent wind which overturned them, and overwhelmed them in this horrible abyss, with the exception, however, of certain old men and of certain women, who had been the most virtuous and the best of all the Indians. God came then to console them for the death of their relatives and their friends, after which he let them live upon the earth in a great and happy tranquillity, granting them therewith all the skill and ingenuity necessary for capturing beavers and moose in as great number as were needed for their subsistence. They add also certain other wholly ridiculous circumstances, which I purposely omit, because they do not bear at all upon a secret which is unknown to men, and reserved to God Alone.[7]

With the rising prestige of the French priests, certain Micmac who began aping ceremonies and hearing confession were revered as persons who held converse, spoke familiarly to, and had direct communication with, the sun. An old woman particularly successful in this role, who owned an unthreaded rosary, gave a bead now and then to a follower, saying that they came from the sky whenever she went out of her wigwam and rendered homage to the sun. "I have only to hold up my hand and open it in order to bring down from heaven these mysterious beads which have the power and property not only of succouring the Indians in their sicknesses and all their most pressing necessities, but also of preserving them from surprise, from persecution, and from the fury of their enemies."[8]

Such raw religious mixtures have long since passed away, but an element of the native sun worship may still be present in Micmac Catholicism. In accepting the Church, the sun symbolism of the monstrance may have increased group receptivity. In the seventeenth century this was often designated by the word *soleil* rather than *ostensior*. As late as the tercentenary of the first Micmac baptism Father Pacifique feared that his Restigouche flock did not have quite the orthodox concept of the sun's role in Christian religion.[9]

[7] *Gaspesia*, 84–85.
[8] *Ibid.*, 229–30.
[9] "Le Pays des Micmac" in *Etudes Historiques*, 108, footnote.

PART ONE *Tribal Life*

Micmac reverence for the sun provided the early French writers with half of the necessary appeal for contributions to missions: the heathen had a god. But to name the Indian devil was not so simple and clear. The word *devil* they used repeatedly (Dièreville [10] calls the demon *Mendou*; so does Rand's *Dictionary*), but inasmuch as there seems to have been no personified evil in Micmac concept, a variety of spirits good or bad filled the role to the satisfaction of the good Fathers and the confusion of their present-day readers.

THE MEDICINEMAN AS DIVINER

The Micmac medicineman, known to us only through the early writers, was an important personage, honored and well paid. In addition to the ceremonial robe already mentioned, his official equipment consisted of a medicine bag. Membertou, headman in the vicinity of Port Royal, who was also a famous shaman (*Aoutmoin*), wore around his neck a triangular bag covered with wampum beads. In it he carried, said Lescarbot, "I know not what as big as a small nut. This was his devil, *Aouten*." [11]

In almost identical words LeClercq described the *oüahich* of a Gaspesian medicineman as "the size of a nut." But LeClercq knew what this devil was; it was a stone.[12] This suggests the *keskamzit* stones in 1911 still current among Micmac.[13] The bags used in the Miramichi region and northeastward in 1675–87 had for decoration the owner's *oüahich* in the form of a wolverine, a monster, or a headless man.

Here is the inventory of that which I found in this little bag of the Devil. It was made of the skin of an entire head of a moose, with the exception of the ears, which were removed.

There was, first of all, this juggler's Oüahich, which was a stone of the size of a nut wrapped in a box which he called the house of his Devil. Then there was a bit of bark on which was a figure, hideous enough, made from black and white wampum, and representing some monster which could not be well distinguished, for it was neither the representation of a man nor of any animal, but rather in the shape of a little wolverene, which was adorned with black and white beadwork. That one, say the jugglers, is the master Devil, or Oüahich. There was, in addition, a little bow a foot in length, together with a cord, two

[10] P. 160.
[11] *History*, III, 110.
[12] *Gaspesia*, 220–25.
[13] See Chapter X and Tales 74–78. In Tale 65, *Atuen* is the designation of a wizard.

146

Religion

fathoms long, interlaced with porcupine quills. It is this fatal bow which they use to cause the death of little children in the wombs of their mothers.

In addition to these things, this bag contained also a fragment of bark, wrapped in a delicate and very thin skin, on which were represented some little children, birds, bears, beavers, and moose. Against these the juggler, using his little bow, shot his arrow at pleasure, in order to cause the death of the children or of some other thing of which the figure is represented upon this bit of bark. Finally, I found there a stick, a good foot in length, adorned with white and red porcupine quills; at its end were attached several straps of a half-foot in length, and two dozen dew-claws of moose. It is with this stick that he makes a devilish noise, using these dew-claws as sounders — an arrangement which seems more suitable for amusing little children than for juggling. Finally, the last article in the bag was a wooden bird, which they carry with them when they go hunting, with the idea that it will enable them to kill waterfowl in abundance.[14]

In addition to treating the sick, as already described, the medicineman was called upon to predict the future, to answer whether a missing person was alive or dead, to name the place to hunt for game, and to approve or disapprove of war plans. If his answer proved later to be wrong, the practitioner explained that his spirit, when angry with him, had led him astray — "an impertinent excuse," said LeClercq.[15] Medicinemen seem to have been adept illusionists, raising up visions of spirits and "snakes and other beasts that go in and out of the mouth while they are talking."[16]

Two descriptions of the *modus operandi* of medicinemen follow; the first written in 1607 at Port Royal; the second in 1710, probably in Nova Scotia.

When that these *Aoutmoins* make their mows and mops, they fix a staff into a pit, to which they tie a cord, and, putting their head into this pit, they make invocations and conjurations in a language unknown to the others that are about, and this with beatings and howlings, until they sweat with very pain. . . . When this devil is come, this master *Aoutmoin* makes them believe that he holdeth him tied by his cord, and holdeth fast against him, forcing him to give him an answer before he let him go. By this is known the subtlety of this enemy of nature, who beguileth thus these miserable creatures. . . . That done, he beginneth to sing some thing (as I think) to the praise of the devil, who hath

[14] *Gaspesia*, 220–25.
[15] *Ibid.*, 296.
[16] Biard, JR, III, 121.

PART ONE *Tribal Life*

discovered some game unto them; and the other savages that are there do answer, making some concordance of music among them.[17]

Dièreville said he had seen medicinemen perform the following trick:

They chew a piece of flintstone in their mouths, and grind it up like Gravel; they spit it out into their hands, to show it to you, and afterwards they swallow it to the last grain. . . . When the flintstone, ground to gravel, is in their stomachs, they take a little stick about a foot long and very smooth; they smoke, and offer it the fumes of the Tobacco, mumbling some words from the Black Book; then they thrust it down their throats, their faces become completely livid and it seems as though they were about to choke; they rummage, so to speak, with the stick, and, after a few grimaces, they draw it out with the flintstone whole at the end of it. . . . The skin of an Otter which had been flayed, perhaps six months before, is made to walk, and this is how they go about it. After spreading it on its belly, they bring the head toward the hinder part by means of folds, made in such a way that it appears to be all in one piece.

A little tin mirror is placed on the right of the head, at a distance of four or five feet; they like to look at their own reflections so much, that they doubtless believe it is the same with animals; but whether that be so or not, there is the skin of the Otter, ready to walk on its own four feet, for these are always left in the skinning when they wish to keep the pelt whole, without slitting it along the belly, *Chipotis*, as it is termed. . . .

Then the Indian, who by craft or by magic . . . is trying to make the skin move, performs grotesque manoeuvres around it.

> He dances and capers, and then he leaps over it,
> Throws himself on the ground, rolls and wallows,
> Beats together his hands and his feet, then he rises
> And makes the air ring with a thousand shrill cries.
> Like a Demon, he tortures himself, and he sweats,
> He's covered with water, his eyes flash with fire,
> There's foam at his lips; so much does he do,
> That one does see the skin walk in the end.

It is only with great difficulty that it moves at first, but, little by little, it stretches out and drags itself as far as the Mirror where it stops. When the skin is slow in starting to walk, the Indian says to Onlookers from other Countries, before whom he is doing this trick, that their Spirit is stronger than his . . . by his own, he means only the Demon. This malign Spirit beats them occasionally with a strange violence, bruising and marking every part of their body with contusions.[18]

[17] Lescarbot, *History*, III, 185–86.
[18] Pp. 183–84.

Religion

Such beatings by the devil were once rife in the Gaspé, said Father LeClercq, and hideous specters appeared to terrify the Micmac. Sometimes "frightful carcasses" fell in the midst of a wigwam and the inhabitants dropped dead of fright. In such circumstances there was always one man brave enough to go forth to kill the tormenting devil, who could guess his path to the camp and lie in wait, armed with a gun.[19]

The diviner of Maillard's day (1755), was a milder but somewhat devious operator. The "juggler," he said, fills a bowl with water from a river known to have beaver houses. He walks in a certain number of circles around the bowl, muttering. He bends low over the bowl, lies over it, looks at himself. If the water is the least muddy or unsettled, he stands and circles again, until it is clear. He then pronounces magic words two or three times. If he then does not find the answer in the water, he says in a loud voice that the Manitoo or Miewudoo would not declare himself until all present whispered their greatest secrets to the juggler. He rises, laments, accuses the spectators. Then going around the company he makes them whisper whatever is in their minds.

By these means it is that these artful Jugglers render themselves formidable to the common people, and by prying into the secrets of most families acquire a hank over them. . . . When the juggler has collected all they will tell him he again bends over the bowl two or three times with face close to the water, makes evocation, and then says to the audience that he can get only a half-answer. Manitoo says there is one obstructionist present. The Juggler will not name him — he will light a signal fire at an unnamed place at night and he is to meet the Juggler there.[20]

THE LAND OF THE DEAD

In contrast to these grim encounters and connivings with the supernatural (not understated, one surmises, by priestly pens) is an account of a journey to the land of the dead from which one returned to tell the tale, a phase of Micmac religious belief recorded only by Father LeClercq:

From these false premises, based upon a tradition so fabulous, they have drawn these extravagant conclusions, — that everything is animated and that souls are nothing other than the ghost of that which had been animated: that the rational soul is a sombre and black image of the man himself: that it had feet, hands, a mouth, a head, and all other parts of

[19] *Gaspesia*, 220–25.
[20] *Customs and Manners*, 37–39.

PART ONE *Tribal Life*

the human body: that it had still the same needs for drinking, for eating, for clothing, for hunting and fishing, as when it was in the body, whence it comes that in their revels and feasts they always serve a portion to these souls which are walking, say they, in the vicinity of the wigwams of their relatives and of their friends: that they went hunting the souls of beavers and of moose with the souls of their snowshoes, bows, and arrows: that the wicked, on their arrival at the Land of Souls, danced and leaped with great violence, eating only the bark of rotten trees, in punishment for their crimes, for a certain number of years indicated by Papkootparou: that the good, on the contrary, lived in great repose at a place removed from the noise of the wicked, eating when it pleased and amusing themselves with the hunting of beavers and of moose, whose spirits allowed themselves to be taken with ease. Such is the reason why our Gaspesians have always observed inviolably the custom of burying with the deceased everything which was in their use during life.[21]

No knowledge of this spirit land with its rewards and punishments exists today, nor do the Micmac retain even a fragmentary memory of the medicinemen and their arts. Except for the general statement about respect for the sun, we are almost wholly dependent on early French accounts. One feels considerable sympathy for Charlevoix, who remarked: "You will perhaps ask me . . . if they have a religion. To this I answer, that it cannot be said they have not one, though it is difficult to give a definition of what it is."

[21] *Gaspesia*, 213–14.

CHAPTER X

The Supernatural

SUPERNATURAL BEINGS

THE Sun God long ago left the Micmac sky but the earth is still inhabited by beings which the seventeenth-century missionaries would certainly have classified as devils: some, aboriginal, which the Fathers probably missed; others, introduced by their fellow countrymen.

Skadegamutc

The most prevalent and most feared spirit is *skade'gamutc*, primarily the ghost of a dead person, but often the apparition of a living person. It is everywhere; it is not confined to the woods or the swamps, or to the hours of the night. Micmac have words to express the apprehension of a hovering spirit: at Burnt Church, N.B., *nesit*; at Pictou, N.S., *giwakit*, "frightened, nervous, afraid to go outside." [1]

When death draws near, the *skadegamutc* of the dying may leave the body and show itself in various ways. "When you are sick, you think about a great many things; whatever you think of will rattle, or a person will see your *skadegamutc* hovering about that thing. If you say that you will fight a certain person before you die, then, when you are sick, your *skadegamutc* will appear to that person and will fight him. Two women were once seen fighting in a wigwam and pulling each other's hair in the usual way, while nearby in another wigwam a woman lay dying. That night she was found dead with one hand full of hair. Her *skadegamutc* had been called to help in the fight."

A lonely night walk in the woods is the most frequent setting for the appearance of *skadegamutc*, made manifest by his voice (the whooper

[1] See Tale 46, third adventure. These words and their meaning were given by Thomas Meuse.

151

PART ONE *Tribal Life*

owl), by pursuing footsteps, white light or flames (phosphorescence in decaying wood), or as a human figure vaguely seen. He is a fearless fighter; men have fought him all night, and when daylight came, found themselves holding the dead tree stump into which he had changed himself. He is a great runner; the more his victim runs, the better he likes it. One who answers his call will die.

The appearance of a ghost usually signifies an approaching death, but there are other beliefs, such as the following:

"At night you see *skadegamutc* coming. Sometimes he brings news to you. Sometimes he speaks to you. He may call you by your name. If you answer and ask what he wants, he will answer. But few men can ask him. If you answer him, he will tell you what he wishes to say — for example, to get your hay in, or to attend Mass. He does not call you without some purpose. Sometimes he comes into a house; you can hear him rattling dishes or rustling paper. People see a house lighted and hear noises; when they go in, all is quiet; they see nothing unusual. That is *skadegamutc*.

"If you see *skadegamutc* standing, dressed in white, and go after him, he becomes constantly smaller while you approach him, and finally vanishes. Perhaps you will see a stump or a little stick where it has been, but nothing more. If you run from him, he will chase you, and remain the same size. Not every one is able to chase a *skadegamutc*. [In over twenty accounts of personal adventures with the ghost, in only one was he pursued and caught.] Every will-o'-the-wisp (jack o'lantern) is *skadegamutc*."

Norman and Breton methods of dealing with ghosts migrated with the French to Canada and are current on Micmac reserves in New Brunswick and Nova Scotia; for example, carrying a pin, because the ghost will not pass its point; or setting up a needle, through whose eye the spirit must crawl slowly, thus allowing the pursued a chance to escape. French belief that ghosts will not cross a stream which bears a saint's name is seen in the Micmac statement that they will not cross a bridge unless you call "Come over."[2] Other elements, such as women in white shrouds and an unseen emanation which it is impossible to pass, are common in French folk belief.

There is a suggestion from Cape Breton that there the present *skade-*

[2] See Tales 46–58. Farrer, "Miracles in French Canada," *Popular Science Monthly*, 48:238 (1896).

The Supernatural

gamutc was preceded in pre-European times by a different concept of the will-o'-the-wisp. A text recorded in 1900 explained that formerly he was seen primarily as a hunter seeking food for his children and should not be whooped at. For many years no Micmac ever whooped at a will-o'-the-wisp, but now people do not care about the old-time stories. Nowadays when they see the jack o'lantern, they say, "This means news. Perhaps someone is dead."

Song of the Jack O'Lantern
For the little animal which they seek I will sing.
For the little animal which they seek I will sing.
The beasts they hung for them I will sing.
The beasts they hung for them I will sing.
After all had flown aloft, then those ones danced.
Then the old man sang thus:
"*eiiko ellilo kuko aio ellilo*"
Were they beasts, those I sang for?
No, no beasts are they; only
Hunters of wild beasts.[3]

Gluskap

Unquestionably aboriginal is Gluskap, the Wabanaki culture hero, apparently not known to early French writers. To him are attributed certain basic inventions, such as the canoe which he fashioned from the breastbone of a bird.[4] His transformations of the landscape from the Gaspé to Cape Breton and along the St. John River are preserved today in rock (his grandmother, his footprints, his dogs). Micmac sometimes pick up stones which they identify as bones or eggs left over from his contests with beaver and partridge. To the finder, such stones are powerful sources of *keskamzit*. (See illustration 36.)

Certain places, associated with Gluskap's exploits, have magic potentialities. John Newell said:

"There is a place in the lake at Baddek, Cape Breton, where some strange things happen. It is fine, clear, calm water. One day when I was there I said to a man: 'If I take a paddleful of water and throw it on the other side of that rock, you will see what a rain we'll have.' 'Nonsense!' I threw two paddlefuls on it. Before we arrived at the bridge, it was raining so hard that we could scarcely draw our breath. This can be

[3] Prince, "A Micmac Manuscript," ICA, 15:119 (1906).
[4] See Tale 11.

PART ONE *Tribal Life*

done today. The rock is at Middle River, near Nianza. It must be there that Gluskap ate the young beaver which he had killed."

A large rock near Upper Musquodoboit, N.S., is said to bear a striking likeness to the recumbent figure of a sleeping man covered by a blanket. Micmac called it "grandfather," and say it is an old Indian who went there to hunt. After he lay down to sleep, he was transformed into the stone, as he is seen today. In 1912 the older Indians laid a penny or some small offering by it and "made their wishes on it," in the expectation of fulfillment. At this spot, my Micmac guide did not specifically name Gluskap.

Culture hero and transformer, Gluskap was also a protector. He performed such deeds as removing the whale from a small lake to the ocean where he cannot harm people, cutting malicious dwarfs down to scale, and in later days helped fight white invaders, and stood up to the kings of England and France.[5]

Gluskap went away long ago. He lives just beyond the clouds, and to Micmac who have visited him there he has granted every request except eternal life. In time of danger he will return. During a moment of tension in 1911, I was reminded often that if there should be any trouble, the people of Burnt Church had Gluskap on their side.[6]

SUPERNATURAL RACES

Micmac shared their woods and shores with a half-dozen supernatural races whose native and European antecedents are not clear. Least frequently encountered were the giants, who harmed no one, although a giant girl might disconcertingly scoop up a Micmac, canoe and all, to use as a doll.[7] Mermen had been seen by several old informants in 1911; one insisted he had found a mer-child on the beach. These halfway people sometimes stuck up their heads and asked fishermen for tobacco or a knife. Within memory they had taken two Micmac as marriage partners. If they were angry at a man, they might raise a storm.[8]

Closer to the Micmac were several tiny races, to them natural, Indians miniature but "real." Although an informant might occasionally use the word "fairies" when telling a tale about such beings, he would make it clear that this was what whites would say, and that he knew no word in

[5] See Tales 12–17.
[6] See below, p. 209.
[7] See Tale 28; Michelson, 1925.
[8] See Tales 29–32.

The Supernatural

English that exactly expressed the Micmac idea. In the following paragraphs, Micmac describe mythic peoples in their own way.

Two groups of tiny people live underground. The Salstog are a tribe of Indians who speak Micmac but never wanted to be civilized; they kill only small animals. Puktesadulkwultidjik, the People Who Smoke, are red, and though very small, kill only big animals; and like to learn civilized ways.[9]

The Migamawesu live in the woods. You can hear them at almost any time, and see them if they wish it so. They are people of splendid appearance, well dressed and good-looking, especially the women. [The informant, obviously, is a man.] Women encounter only male Migamawesu; men see only females.

You talk with Migamawesu and then suddenly they disappear like a snap of the fingers. They utilize everything that is in the woods. When they are alone there, the fine clothes like ours are gone, and they are covered with hair just like the beasts.[10] They watch the Indians day and night. Sometimes they help with the gift of a magic herb to cure illness, or transport someone long distances through the air. To refuse the request of a Migamawesu is asking for trouble. Suppose they tell you to kill wife, father, or mother. That is very hard. But if they tell you to do it, you must do it. If you do not do what they tell you, you will surely suffer for it; but if you do it, everything will be all right. At the present time there is too much religion. The priests teach that it is a sin like murder to call on these people for help. And there is too much confession.[11]

Best known are the Stone Indians, Pugulatamutc, a race who live in mountain caves.[12] They are small people, but they do a big work. They live and dress like the old-time Indians, and eat only wild meat. They live on Tracadegash Mountain on the Gaspé, and in Cape Breton where Gluskap told them to stay, not meddle with the Micmac, and await his return.[13] They have small legs and arms and big bodies like bullfrogs.

[9] See Tales 33–34.
[10] See Tales 35–40.
[11] *Mi'gwida'sawa'an* is used with respect to a thought or hidden word that suddenly comes into one's mind. Possibly the suddenness of its appearance indicates that the Migamawesu have placed it there.
[12] I could find no confirmation of S. Hagar's observation that "According to the Micmacs, there are now several such hermits [the comparison is to the *kavigtok* of the Eskimo] of their tribe dwelling on the mountains in the almost unexplored wilderness around Cape North, Cape Breton Island." HERE, Vol. 1, p. 433. Possibly this refers to the Pugulatamutc.
[13] See Tale 12.

PART ONE *Tribal Life*

Like other supernatural beings they can help and they can harm. They can give a man furs, or warn of coming evil, and they can perform bad tricks around the house and barn.[14]

SUPERNATURAL POWER

Great supernatural power, known as *ginap* and *buoin*, may reside in human beings, otherwise normal and ordinary.

Ginap

A *ginap* is a very strong person who does not necessarily possess any other extraordinary power. There are male and female *ginap*; they can pick up tremendous loads, drink a bucket of boiling grease, and bend guns like butter. The quality appears in childhood; some great victories over Mohawk raiding parties have been won by a single *ginap* Micmac child.[15] A *ginap* is sometimes also a *buoin*, but his power is never evil.

Buoin

The *buoin* — wizard, witch — is the last descendant of the Micmac medicineman, the *Bohinne* of LeClercq. Micmac know that *buoin* formerly meant medicineman, but say that it also means strength and power of a particular kind. It does not connote the strange and mysterious as does *wigwasik* or *biltuasik*. The hardwood maple, *unkwoktc*, out of which game bowls are made, possesses *buoin*; so does the punk (*mespibaan*), which is dug up in low places and is used as tobacco or as tinder.

Examples of *buoin* behavior were given by several informants:

A *buoin* smokes his stone pipe, shuts his eyes, and sees everything. Sometimes he smokes and sings throughout the night, concocting his bad wish. A man struck by this bad wish (*teladasit*) feels a twitching at his heart, or a quivering of the flesh in some part of his body. The *buoin*, after giving the wish, turns into a fly, then into a little bird, and flies away to observe the effect of his magic.[16]

Buoin sometimes go into turtles; if you cut off a turtle's head, the feet move for a long time.

[14] See Tales 41–45.
[15] See Tales 59–62, 125–28; for a 1953 concept of *ginap*, see Chapter XVI.
[16] An account of divination by Cape Breton *buoin* is given by Johnson, 68–79.

The Supernatural

"My uncle was a *buoin* and could do wonderful things. His collarbone was as large as the lower arm of an ordinary man. His chest was always exposed, so that people could see the large collarbone."

The institutional role of the medicineman in the seventeenth century is remembered only in part. The wrestling with spirits to cure sickness, prediction of game, and other services performed for the good of the group and reinforced by group participation are gone. However, a *buoin* seems to have served until recent times as an assistant to the chief of each settlement, functioning mainly in a crisis. He would then smoke his pipe, hand it to the chief, who smoked it and saw all that the *buoin* wished to convey to him. Sometimes the *buoin* acted as a dispenser of justice. If two jealous chiefs were fighting, a third chief might call on the *buoin* to part them. If he could not himself do it, his *skadegamutc* would arrive instead with the speed of lightning, and settle the fight. It is felt (1911) that, although no such assistant now exists, in time of great danger one would come forward.[17]

The *buoin* is believed to possess some of the powers of the early medicineman. He can predict the future; and he can walk under water. People have walked on the bottom of the Miramichi River from Eel Ground, and some from Red Bank to Burnt Church. Formerly many people did it, and some still do it. A man walked from Burnt Church to Cape Breton, and back, on the bottom of the ocean — "a fish could not do that."

A Micmac in Cape Breton said French war vessels go a thousand miles under the water. People laughed at him; but in a few years the submarine came. He said that an insect would destroy their crops, and butterflies would eat their cattle. In a few years the potatobugs came, and the hornflies troubled the cattle. One day he put on a vest which he wore only at uncommon times. His children, when they saw him wearing this, did not know what to expect. He came into a room in which there were some people. "I put on this vest," said he, "only when something bad is about to happen. Some strange Indians will come and attack us." The people only laughed. He went to one end of the settlement, played *waltes'*, and won seven games. In the afternoon, he went to the other end of the settlement, played *waltes*, and won more games. "Now," said he, "I have beaten them. They will not hurt us." The people only laughed at him. But two days later two strange Canadian (i.e., northern or

[17] In 1953 such potential helpers were called *ginap*.

157

PART ONE *Tribal Life*

eastern) Indians were there, walking around, and not knowing just what their business was.

Although nowadays the influence and performance of the *buoin* are almost always evil, he may wet his finger, put earth on it, rub this on the chest of a sick person, and cure him.

Formerly one *buoin* could protect against the power of another, and sometimes did so. When a man had made, or acquired, a pair of new snowshoes, before he wore them he would, to secure good luck, go to an old woman *buoin* and tell her he had a pair of new snowshoes. She would come to see them, and say, "Will you give them to me?" He handed them to her, whereupon she wrapped her socks around his feet. "Leave these snowshoes with me until morning," she would say. "It is the same as big medicine to you, and no witchcraft can prevail against you when you use them." She would walk about on them, return them, and say, "Nothing will disturb you." If this was not done, perhaps while the man was hunting moose, he would entangle his snowshoes in bushes, and would be killed, or other misfortune would befall him. A long time ago, when twelve-and-a-half-cent pieces (sixpence?) were current, an Indian who wished to become a good runner would put one of these in his sock, so that it lay against the skin, in the middle of his instep. Thus equipped, he could run so fast that no witchcraft could outdo him for speed.

However, most of the accounts and all of the attitudes toward the Micmac witch paint him in black. A *buoin* is easily recognized by the instinctive fear aroused in the normal person and by his behavior; the only peculiarity specified was the bent head and averted gaze particularly characteristic of the seated witch. The basic concept of witchcraft and the means of combating it are much the same throughout the Micmac world, with individual or local differences. The following accounts were given by an informant in each of the three Maritime Provinces.

John Sark, chief at Lennox Island reserve, Prince Edward Island (see illustration 33) began with a description of magic which suggests the medicine bag and associated practices described by LeClercq:

"Witches drew on a board the picture of a certain man and shot at it twice with a gun. They struck one side of the head. In two days the man who was represented by this was nearly crazed. If they had shot his heart, he would have been killed.

The Supernatural

"If you are in the woods, perhaps two hundred yards from a person whom you wish to kill, you can effect that person's death in this way: Put a certain medicine [of the exact nature of it, the Chief declared ignorance, but I am convinced that he knew] on an arrow and shoot it into the air. It will fall on the head of the intended victim and kill him. The Micmac, when they were fighting the Mohawk, successfully used a magic of this kind.

"A *buoin* can make you sick by merely looking at you and saying: 'What is the matter with you? Are you sick?' If you see him in a dream that night, all is well; otherwise, you will be sick, and perhaps will die.

"If one wishes you ill, an animal — for example, a bear — will come to you while you are asleep [that is to say, in a dream], and will fight you. You must fight it and not allow it to injure you. If you kill or injure it [in your dream], the bad wish will return to the source and be visited upon the head of the ill-wisher."

"There ought to be a law against witches. Suppose a person goes along this road here, while we are sitting by it, and I wish that he will fall over the bridge; then another comes along, and I wish that he shall fall over; and a third, and I wish the same.

"It is not right that I should make all of those people fall over the bridge. Such doings are a dirty trick, and there should be a law to punish people who make wishes like that. *Buoin* can kill people by means of wishes which send an animal or a person to them in a dream. *Buoin* did not exist in the old days. I know that an old *buoin* in Burnt Church has been trying to do me harm. [Others, too, believed this old woman, referred to by the informant, was a *buoin*, and feared her.]"

John Newell, my old Nova Scotia informant, gave this account of his struggle with a *buoin*:

"Witchcraft can be worked this way: Take a spruce bough on which someone has been lying, get a hair of his head, use the bough as a bow, and the strand of hair as the bowstring. Draw a picture of the person, make an arrow out of a twig, and shoot it at that part of the person which you wish to injure. Burn all of these things. In three days, the person will suffer injury in that part of the body. If, for example, the knees have been shot at, he will not be able to walk.

"I injured a woman [a *buoin*] that way. She asked me to take her in my canoe, and I refused to do so. Three days later my knees became sore. I consulted a doctor, but nothing helped me.

PART ONE *Tribal Life*

"An Indian from Restigouche came. We had more provisions than we needed, and I gave some of them to children who did my errands. I could not move. I told him, 'I can't move, but get yourself something to eat.' One day he looked at my knee. It was not better. 'Help yourself,' said he. 'If you don't help yourself, you'll lose your leg. Look me in the eyes,' he said. 'What is the matter with my leg?' 'What did you do to that old woman at Pictou?' I told him about the incident. 'That's her,' he said. 'What shall I do?' 'When your wife has gone to bed, take an arrow and a bow, and a little hair for a string, make a drawing of the woman, and shoot once at her head.' (If I should shoot three times, I would kill her.) I told my wife to bring in a piece of bark, for I might want to smoke, and would use it to light my pipe. I did as I had been told. Three days later this woman was very sick and nearly died. My leg then began to get better. She continually grew worse, while I constantly improved.

"One day this [Restigouche] man came in. 'Well, John, how are you getting on?' 'I'm getting better.' He laughed. 'She will know now what kind of trouble she gave you! Never mind, she will not die,' said he. When we went to the Island to attend a communion service, we saw the old woman there, smoking.

"When my wife heard the cause of my trouble, she wanted to kill that woman. That night the woman's daughter came in and gave me some medicine. It was flagroot. She told me to boil it and rub it on my head. I did so, and soon was well.[18] How did she know I was sick? If that man had not helped me, I would have been in a bad fix. I had seen the old woman in a dream. She said, 'You will have this [affliction] because you refused to take me in your canoe.'"

The only personal experience told me by an actual or potential wizard was, again, John Newell's:

"I believe that I could have become a *buoin*, and that if trouble had come to my people, I would have had the power. Sometimes, when I was smoking, with my eyes closed, I would feel myself rising, rising to about the height of the house. When I dream, things are as real and as clear as when I am awake. I have thrown out my hand in my dream, fighting, and bruised it and made it bleed, because I struck the side of the house so hard. I am afraid of striking my little girl some night, when I am asleep. One time I dreamed I was walking over the water, as *buoin*

[18] Informants in 1953 stated that only the witch can cure the effects of his or her "bad wish."

The Supernatural

often do, and I saw a wigwam on the bottom, way out there. This does not happen to me as often as it formerly did—it is going from me. If, however, the need came, and any harm befell my people, I think I would have the power to help them."

Peter Ginnish related:

"In the case of some men, whatever they say will come true. I have known some cases in which a man would say to another, 'You are going to die tomorrow'; and the next day that man was dead.

"At one time most of the *buoin* were women. They could do anything. They talked like any ordinary person, but they had a power somewhere. There was one here a long while ago. I did not know her, but I married her daughter. She hated all of her children and her sons-in-law. But she did not disturb me. People said she was afraid of me. At the present time, when you ask *buoin* what they want, they turn and reply. Formerly, they would not reply; and they were afraid of nothing.

"One time a young man was making bread for dinner. When he uncovered the bed of hot coals, he had no stick with which to stir the hot sand. He put his hand into the red-hot sand, stirred it, put in the dough, and covered the dough with the hot sand. His hand was not burned in the least. I myself saw that. He is still alive, near here, but he would not hurt anyone. Twice he was beaten in a fight. He did not wish to hurt anyone. If he had wished to do so, he could easily have killed the man with whom he was fighting. The following day I asked him, 'Why did you not play a trick on that man?' He replied, 'I did not want to. If I had slapped him hard, I would have killed him.'

"There were a great many *buoin* in the old days. In North Sydney [C.B.] there are two *buoin*. No one knows how much strength they have; they themselves do not know. However, they are very quiet now. Indians are something besides Indians—they are not merely Indians. Where does that power come from? They have no learning, though they are being tamed now."

Although witchcraft was a serious concern to old people in 1911, it was felt to be on the wane. One opinion: Some Indians say little when you talk to them, but their eyes work. That is the way with these people — they say little but you do not know what power they have. If a *buoin* does not like you, she will give you sickness at once; or, the next day you will cut your foot or your hand. But they are very quiet now; they would not injure anyone unless forced to do so.

PART ONE *Tribal Life*

"We must not tell the young people these things," another old informant said, after a confidential talk about them, in the recesses of the woods, "till they are old enough to have sense. Sometimes they come to me with a penny and say, 'Now, old man, tell us a tale of the old times.' I say, 'My children, I do not know any.' But if I am spared ten years, I shall tell them."

The reason given for withholding such knowledge was that if people understood magic they would use it to injure others.

Keskamzit

Magic good luck which comes suddenly to an individual in the form of unusual ability, capacity, or power is called *kes'kamzit*. It is acquired as the result of a wish, but no one fully understands how it originates. *Keskamzit* is personal and specific. It must be kept secret; to mention it is to lose it forever.

Informants gave numerous accounts of the acquisition of this luck:

Keskamzit may come in this way. Perhaps you are passing through the woods at night and hear a fiddle being played. When that is finished, another tune is played. You move in the direction of the sound, and soon find the fiddle. If you take it home, that night or the next morning you will be able to play the tune which you heard. But you must not tell anyone. If someone asks you about the fiddle, say, "I bought it." If you tell anyone how you acquired it, the *keskamzit* leaves.

Or, suppose you wish to learn to play the violin. Go to a crossroads late some dark night and play a violin there. People will come from hell and dance. They will teach you tunes; on the following day and ever after, you will be able to play these tunes. A young man at Pictou thus learned a tune, but was so frightened that he ran home and lost his senses. He has been crazy since the night during which he acquired *keskamzit* for violin playing.

A young man at Burnt Church acquired great *keskamzit* for reading. He was chopping wood, and in one chip that came off he could read letters of the alphabet. He had never gone to school, but after that, he could read any Micmac or English words. The chip was of no value, but he retained the *keskamzit* which it gave him.

A man acquired *keskamzit* for running. While he was walking, he found tracks, and followed in them. As he went farther, the distance between them gradually increased, until they were very far apart, and

The Supernatural

he was taking them in immense strides. Thereafter he had *keskamzit* for fast running.

Sometimes something runs after you. However far or fast you run, you continually hear it running behind you. It will not hurt you. It is your *keskamzit*. If you tell no one about the adventure, you will be a fast runner.

Everyone at Burnt Church knows about the prowess of John Francis, a renowned woodcutter. He could cut down, in a day, two hundred to three hundred trees. He never chopped at this rate if someone was watching him. If he left his axe for a while, when he returned he would look at it to see whether someone had used it. As soon as he saw it, he knew whether a person had touched it. If he found that someone had used it — and no one knew how he could tell this — he would not use it. Any man who chopped near him did an extraordinary day's work. John Francis' *keskamzit* was contagious.

Almost anything strange can bring this magic power. Frank Cope would have had *keskamzit* for hunting, if he had not told of the incident which indicated it. He had caught a rabbit and a squirrel together in the same snare. He said: "A squirrel's head is much lower than a rabbit's; I do not see how a squirrel could have gotten into a rabbit's snare, and the rabbit, too, in there." When he went home, he told what he had seen, and so no *keskamzit* came to him. If you catch a fish with two heads, or one with three heads, throw it back into the water and say nothing about it to anyone. After that you will have *keskamzit* for fishing.

Keskamzit Objects

Finding stone, wood, or fungus of a peculiar shape, suggesting a specific object, is a certain means of acquiring an appropriate *keskamzit*. A man who was in the woods hunting found a piece of wood resembling a beaver, with eyes, nose, mouth, feet, and tail indicated. After that he had big *keskamzit* for beaver. If you find a stone that resembles a fish, you will have *keskamzit* for fishing. Always secrecy is essential.

Almost anything is taken home that is of unusual shape or found under unusual circumstances. A stone resembling a toad had been found on a Cape Breton mountainside in the following way: While an old man was descending, suddenly the stones rolled out from under him and he had a bad fall. He examined the stones and finally found a "toad" which he knew at once had caused his fall. He sold it to me but with great re-

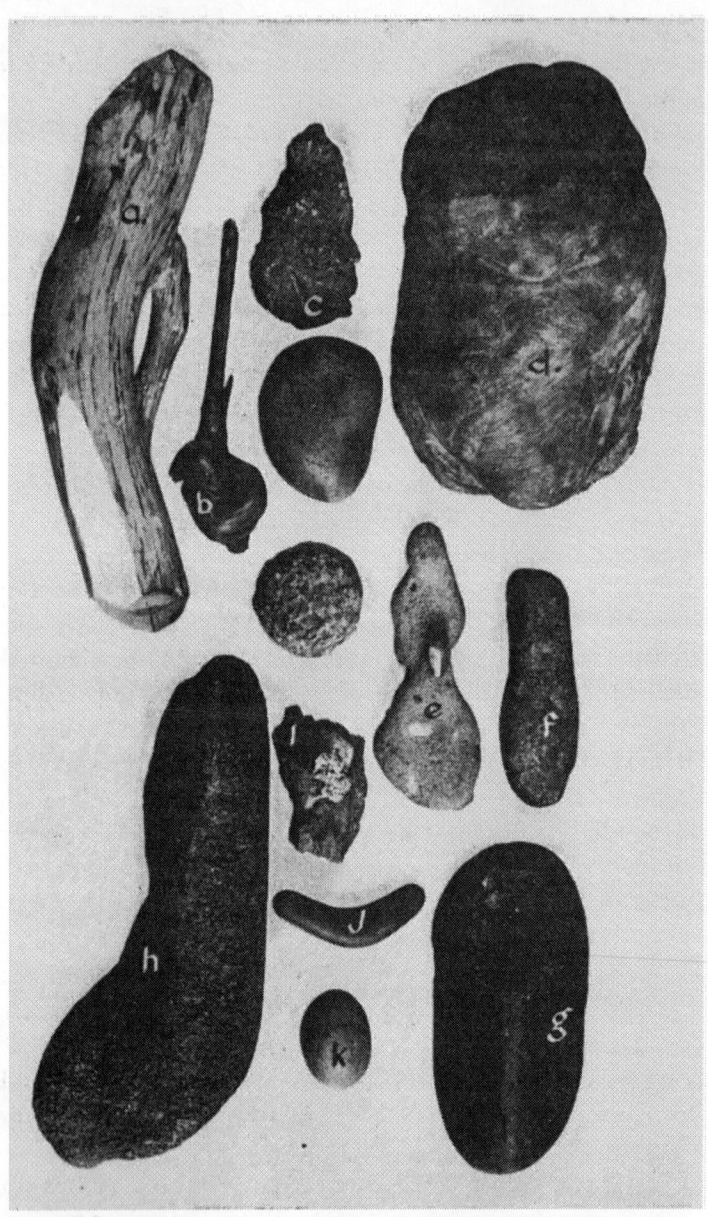

36. *Keskamzit* objects. *a* and *b*. Odd natural growths of wood.
c. Stone toad. *d*. Wood resembling a woolly sheep. *e*. Soaring
pigeon of stone. *f*, *g*, and *h*. Feet of stone. *i*. A lamb on a rock.
j and *k*. Stone collarbone and partridge egg
associated with Gluskap.

The Supernatural

luctance; for, he said, in doing so he would lose part of his "strength," his "witchcraft," his *keskamzit*. (See illustration 36c)

A curious fungus growth I purchased at Pictou Landing had been kept for three years by the finder, a woman, without anyone else knowing of its existence. Its appearance suggests an old woman with a large nose, and a protuberant abdomen, which latter probably suggested *keskamzit* for maternity. The finder had treated it with great care; she had made for it a bonnet and shawl and a chair to sit upon, but in spite of this attention and of the secrecy maintained, she had borne no living children,

37. *Keskamzit* for maternity. A fungus growth resembling a woman with protuberant abdomen, clothed and throned by a Micmac who wanted children.

and therefore parted with this object of false hope. (See illustration 37.)

At Lennox Island, P.E.I., a wooden object which brought *keskamzit* was a growth, resembling an animal, which had been cut from a tree. Nostrils, mouth, and eyes had been added by the owner. The finder said it resembled a seal, or, especially if one observed the grain of the wood, a sheep, for the whorls suggested matted wool. (See illustration 36d.)

Some Micmac told me that the thing which confers *keskamzit* is of no value at all; one throws it away or leaves it where it was found. Others, however, parted with the objects only after persuasion, or not at all. Two such objects are associated with mythic beings which appear in the folktales. The first of these is a stone foot broken at the ankle, the work of *Tcedjaginwit* (Clean Life), a medicineman whose magic was stronger

PART ONE *Tribal Life*

than a priest's.[19] (See illustration 36g.) The second is the egg of a spruce partridge left by Gluskap in the sand along the shore of Merigomish Island,[20] where John Newell found it. (See illustration 36k.) In the same illustration is another souvenir of Gluskap, a man's collarbone, now stone, which Gluskap had placed in a tree. (See illustration 36j.) Money and assurance that the objects would be properly respected and cared for induced the owners to part with these; but in almost every instance it was only with the greatest reluctance that an owner did so. In some instances, neither money nor persuasion, nor both, availed. Several of the objects here illustrated came from a man at Pictou Landing who did not tell me of their existence until the second summer in which I visited him, and only after our acquaintance had ripened.

Keskamzit is believed to have functioned since the beginning of Micmac life. Through its power the invention of each basic tool, such as eel-spear and canoe, was made. Such a gift is not without an ethical aspect. *Keskamzit* improves the life of the individual in its particular way, but it leads to general deterioration of character. Ease in earning money or in acquiring skill results in laziness and indolence. If abused, it may disappear; a successful hunter who forgets the fundamental virtue of sharing his game liberally with others will lose his *keskamzit*.

EVERYDAY MAGIC

Some magic requires no special power inherent in the practitioner.

A medicinal plant which grows in the woods is potent enough to take a man from his wife, or a wife from her husband. Chew it and spit some of it on a woman's clothes; she will leave her home and go to you. Even if you go outside and hide, she will find you, no matter where you are. It has the same effect if you put some of the spittle in an apple or an orange and give the fruit to her; or if you spit it onto your handkerchief, rub this on something, and give that thing to her. This is said to be Maliseet medicine, but is employed by the Micmac.

Suppose I lose my dog in the winter. He was a good dog, and I am very sorry not to have him. I set up my bow and arrow, pointing toward the place where I lost the dog. On these I put tobacco, flint, and a pouch. The dog, if alive, will return that night. This will work at any time of the year, but only in the case of a dog.

[19] See Tale 67.
[20] See Tale 3.

The Supernatural

The twelve-and-a-half-cent piece possessed a magic that would prevent a dog from barking, if the user was committing a crime in the vicinity of the animal. (How this power was made to prevail, and what medicine possessed this potency, was not known to my informant, he assured me.) If, however, you comb the dog from nose to tail, and from back to belly, with a fine-toothed comb, and hang round his neck a twelve-and-a-half-cent piece in which a hole has been bored for suspension, he will bark all night, if there be any cause, and no magic will avail against him.[21]

The following method was used to find one who had lost his way in the woods — apparently not a rare occurrence in the old days: Get spruce boughs from the place in the wigwam where he was accustomed to lie, crush them into a powder, carry them on a piece of bark, and sprinkle them on the path he was wont to take while moose hunting. When you come to forked roads, sprinkle this on each of the roads that you think he may have taken. At night, when all is quiet, close the lost one's wigwam, put a blanket over your head, and with birch bark or punk start a fire along the line of this powdered spruce. It will run to the forks of the road, and on one of these branch roads the smoke will have an odor resembling that of singed hair. On that road you will find him dead. This was the old way of finding the dead, and can be employed with equal success today. If the man is not dead, but has only lost his way, the fire will return. Even in the water, if you know the track, you can find the exact place where a boat has sunk. The fire will run to the spot at which the ship has gone down, and will then go out. "When young people hear this, they say, 'Ach! Not true.' They do not believe, because they do not know."

SIGNS AND OMENS

Signs and omens, like dreams, are not the same for each person. Some have signs peculiar to, and perhaps known only by, themselves. For one old woman, for example, a quivering above the eyebrow is a sure sign that she will see a drunken man. The common interpretation is that if an eyebrow or an eyelid twitches, the person will soon cry, or will soon see someone crying. Some say it signifies news of a death.

If the lip twitches, one will soon quarrel with someone, or will see two persons having a lively quarrel. If the palm of the left hand twitches,

---

[21] Presumably this is the European belief that a silver piece will keep away spirits.

PART ONE *Tribal Life*

one will soon receive money. If the palm of the right hand twitches, one will shake hands with one's best friend. If the right thigh or the right foot twitches, a friend is coming to see that person or is going somewhere else.[22]

Belching is a sign that one will obtain food. An old man who belches usually says, "Thank you, God." If one is going hunting, a belch indicates good luck; if one is going fishing, one will have a good catch. An ear-bell or ear-drum signifies that one will hear something bad — "perhaps a row or a fight." (One old man stated that he had never heard that any significance attaches to this phenomenon. He said it was due to the presence of hard wax in the ear, and was relieved by removing the wax.)

To lose one's way signifies that a friend will soon die. "I have lost my way in the bushes and woods very close home, and each time thereafter within two weeks someone died. I never knew this sign to fail."

To have good luck for money, carry a small red lizard in the pocket. A moleskin is equally effective and has the additional virtue of being efficacious even when kept elsewhere, in a box or in a chest.

The following is possibly only an individual sign: "I was a maker of coffins, here, almost all my life. If I was in the woods and smelled pine, as I did when I was working with pine boards — and in the woods I smelled it plainly on two or three occasions — I would surely hear of a death in a few days. Also, if I made a coffin too short or too long, and not according to the measure I had taken — sometimes the cover would touch the deceased's chest, or his head would have to be turned to one side — there would be another death soon."

Finding a roll of birch bark in the woods means that the finder, if unmarried, will soon be married. (This omen was not generally known among the young people at Burnt Church, where the belief was recorded.) In the wigwam is a crosspiece from which the pot hangs. To find out whether you will marry, try to make a skin sock or a moccasin hang on this by pitching it up on it. If, after three attempts, you do not succeed in getting it to hang there, you will not be married for a long time — perhaps not for thirty or forty years. If you succeed in one of these three attempts, you will soon be married.

It is useless to make traps on a rainy day. Make them on a clear day, and set them on a rainy day. Friday is lucky for any undertaking; Monday, Tuesday, and Wednesday are unlucky. People who work on

[22] See Tale 128.

The Supernatural

Sunday never have any luck. A man who does not observe the Sabbath will never get along well. If a man works on Sunday, he will not prosper. "Some people were working on the log drive on Sunday, last spring, and now see where the logs are! If they had worked only on week days, perhaps the logs would now be down all right." (In 1911-12, "several million" logs were held up in the log drives of New Brunswick, because of lack of spring rains.) If you work on Sunday, you will not feel right.[23]

EVERYTHING IS A SIGN OF SOMETHING

Some wrongdoing is behind the selective course of every disaster in the world.

Micmac say there is something strange about the way in which the Indians' Catholic churches are burned or are blown down. (Two or three have successively burned at Burnt Church, N.B.; the mission at Restigouche, Que., burned; and a large church on Merogomish Island, N.S., was blown from its foundation.) This misfortune seldom happens to Protestant churches. There is something very queer about that.

The fire which burned the church and the Capuchin Monastery at Restigouche, in 1912, is uniformly considered "something strange." It is said that the fire first appeared above the floor, along the altar, as shooting flames. Some attributed it to "too much Catholicism"—the priests had worked too vigorously in inculcating Christianity, and this was a punishment.

The sinking of the Titanic off Newfoundland in 1912 was the result of wrongdoing upon the part of someone.

Certain fires seem to make the opposite type of selection. According to the Micmac, the Miramichi fire of 1825 was sent to punish the whites for their treatment of the Indians. Nearly all the English and their property were destroyed; not one Indian wigwam burned. When fire came to a wigwam, it went around it. It came on a night when whites had been planning to kill all of the Indians. One white man had refused to join the murder plan, and only his house was saved. All Protestant churches were burned; all Catholic churches were spared.[24]

[23] These superstitions are European. They are now general among northeastern Algonkin and northern Iroquois, and many of them are found in numerous other tribes which have had contacts with whites.
[24] See Tales 134, 136-37.

PART ONE *Tribal Life*

A similar cause lit the Campbellton fire in 1910. A mistreated Indian wished the town misfortune.[25]

There exists a French-Canadian precedent for a part of these beliefs. When Wolfe was harrying the St. Lawrence River parishes during the siege of Quebec (1759), St. Anne saved Beaupré and those farmhouses in which she was especially venerated.

[25] After the Rimouski fire (1950) Micmac said the poor of that town had been badly treated.

CHAPTER XI

Social and Political Organization

THE structure of Micmac society was simple and not sharply defined. Small settlements (*udan*) consisted of a family or group of related families, each with a chief of limited power.

THE CHIEF

The old method of selecting a chief could not be definitely ascertained. Chieftainship, said some informants, was hereditary and went to the oldest son. If the oldest son was dead, the dying chief chose his successor. At a meeting held after the chief's death, the assembled men simultaneously pointed a finger at the designated one, thus signifying approval of his appointment. Other informants said that the oldest son succeeded to office only if fitted for the position; all informants said that a chief, when he believed he was about to die, designated his successor.

In this matter of choice, early French observers were not much more helpful than were the Micmac of 1911. Lescarbot, who was at Port Royal in 1607–8, said that the office went from father to son if the son had the proper qualifications; Biard, his closest contemporary observer, remarked only that the chief was the oldest son in a powerful family. A century later, Dièreville was certain that the office was never hereditary either in direct or in collateral line, and that it was conferred on an outstanding and ambitious hunter who thereafter could not be deposed except for commission of a crime.[1]

The chief who headed a small band, composed of several families, was addressed as *sa'gama* (in 1911 spoken of as *mui sagama* in distinction

[1] P. 149.

PART ONE *Tribal Life*

from a white gentleman, who is addressed as *sagama*). Authority of the chief, which was not absolute, was symbolized by a baton, *a'ptuan*, which only he might carry. Lashed on it with spruce roots were choice feathers from the wingtips of the duck and brightly colored feathers of other birds. The handle was covered with weasel fur, which is soft and silky.

One role of the chief was to question strangers who appeared in his settlement and to exclude those of whom he was suspicious.[2] The most important function named by 1911 informants was the allotment of land to the families under him, which numbered from two to fifteen. Each family was assigned territory on which only its members might hunt. The boundaries were indicated by blazings on trees; no particular sign or emblem was used for this purpose. According to one informant, the hunting grounds were designated by the chief annually; according to another, every seven years. I could not learn of any clan or totemic organization; or ascertain the method of determining what families would be associated in a common hunting territory.

In LeClercq's day the chief assigned territory to individuals at spring and autumn assemblies held especially for this purpose. Hunting limits were strictly enforced.[3]

If a serious crime was committed, group opinion, according to informants, rather than chiefly power decided upon and carried out the punishment. In the old days the group were of one mind. One man said something and all gave their assent. (Now, as a result of education, each has a different opinion and there is no harmony.) A murderer's hands and feet were tied with several thongs. A score of people grasped these and pulled on them until death relieved the sufferer. This might continue until the body was badly mangled. Or, the offender was tied to a tree and was shot with bow and arrows.

A distinction was made between murder and manslaughter. One night a man went to hunt moose, gave the moose call, and heard an answer. He was wearing, as a disguise, antlers of bark, in imitation of a moose. He called again, and this time was sure that the answer came from a moose. The other, who was in fact a man, saw the antlers in the bushes and shot at it. He heard a fall, and went over to look at his kill. He peeled off a piece of bark, lighted it, held it up as a torch, and saw a fallen man,

[2] See Tale 39.
[3] *Gaspesia*, 237. See Speck, AA, n.s., 17, 302–3 (1915).

Social and Political Organization

shot through the heart. He carried the body home, and explained how the misadventure had happened. He was not punished. If the hunter had known that he was shooting a Micmac, the people would have torn the offender to pieces.

In the seventeenth century, in settling disputes and ending hair-pullings between members of a band, and in punishing serious crime, the chief seems to have been only one of the possible arbiters. Biard said local quarrels were settled by either Sagamores or common friends, and LeClercq agreed. The "great offenses" of murder and wife stealing, according to Biard, were left for individual vengeance or, if the victim was dead, vengeance by his relatives. "When this happens, no one shows any excitement over it, but all dwell contentedly upon this word habenquendonic. 'He did not begin it, he has paid him back; quits and good friends!' But if the guilty one, repenting of his fault, wishes to make peace, he is usually received with satisfaction, offering presents and other suitable atonement."[4]

In the Gaspé and Miramichi districts, however, group opinion condemned a deliberate murderer to death. "'Take care, my friend,' say they, 'If thou killest, thou shalt be killed.' This is often carried out by command of the elders, who assemble in council upon the subject, and often by the private authority of individuals, without any trial of the case being made, provided that it is evident the criminal has deserved death."[5]

According to those who saw the institution functioning in the seventeenth century, the duties of a chief were advisory in time of peace and active leadership in warfare. Young unmarried men and others without family were a part of his household. How human nature worked under these conditions in Acadia was described by Father Biard:

All the young people of the family are at his table and in his retinue; it is also his duty to provide dogs for the chase, canoes for transportation, provisions and reserves for bad weather and expeditions. The young people flatter him, hunt, and serve their apprenticeship under him, not being allowed to have anything before they are married, for then only can they have a dog and a bag, that is, have something of their own, and for themselves. Nevertheless they continue to live under the authority of the Sagamore, and very often in his company; as also do several others who have no relations, or those who of their own free will place them-

[4] JR, III, 87–97.
[5] LeClercq, *Gaspesia*, 236–37.

PART ONE *Tribal Life*

selves under his protection and guidance, being themselves weak and without a following. Now all that the young men capture belongs to the Sagamore; but the married ones give him only a part, and if these leave him, as they often do for the sake of the chase and supplies, returning afterwards, they pay their dues and homage in skins and like gifts. From this cause there are some quarrels and jealousies among them as among us, but not so serious. When, for example, some one begins to assert himself and to act the Sagamore, when he does not render the tribute, when his people leave him or when others get them away from him; then as among us, also among them, there are reproaches and accusations, as that such a one is only a half Sagamore, is newly hatched like a three days' chicken, that his crest is only beginning to appear; that he is only a Sagamochin, that is a Baby Sagamore, a little dwarf [*sagamotcitc*]. And thus you may know that ambition reigns beneath the thatched roofs, as well as under the gilded, and our ears need not be pulled much to learn these lessons.[6]

And these were Father LeClercq's observations from the Gaspé:

The most prominent chief is followed by several young warriors and by several hunters, who act always as his escort, and who fall in under arms when this ruler wishes particular distinction upon some special occasion. But, in fact, all his power and authority are based only upon the good will of those of his nation, who execute his orders just in so far as it pleases them.[7]

ASSISTANT CHIEF

According to 1911 informants the chief's assistant, *mudjekdidegwinu*, foresaw everything. "If he should say, 'That schooner must go into the field at once,' it must go at once; if he said 'It must go back into the water,' it must go back. He had power to do anything, but seldom, except in time of trouble, did anything superhuman. If trouble should now come to the Indians at Burnt Church, one would assert himself, although no one now knows who he would be. One is certainly here. If we need news from Cape Breton in half an hour, he will get the news to us in that length of time."

This assistant to the chief, or "captain," as he is now called, is represented in the present (1911) political organization of the Micmac. Probably he was formerly a medicineman and adviser. Some declare that in times of difficulty he had sole charge of affairs and the chief was then subordinate to him. In the seventeenth century, the *autmoin* was the

[6] JR, III.
[7] *Gaspesia*, 234.

Social and Political Organization

only person other than sagamores who made a speech at tribal gatherings. If the chief was also a medicineman, he was "greatly dreaded." Membertou was such a medicineman, famous war leader, and chief.[8]

A Nova Scotia informant (1911) asserted that in each settlement there were two assistant chiefs or, literally, a second watcher, *ud'jenkap'toget ta'boac't*, and a third watcher, *sisto wadj ud'jenkap'taget*. In northern New Brunswick the *ä'kusitc* was said to be the leader in time of war, and in peace was second in authority. Every fortnight, or at least once a month, a messenger (*aganudamaanetc*) went from each reserve to one or more neighboring ones to learn the news and ascertain whether help was needed. The chief dispatched the messenger, and might choose any available man. Sometimes two or more men (*eskemadjik*), "watchers," were detailed for this purpose. Small stone beads, *elnu'pskul*, were mnemonic devices for conveying messages: Each bead suggested a story or a bit of information. Only one specimen was in existence (near Sydney, C.B.); I did not see it.

The use of the *elnupskul* was explained as follows: "Suppose a Micmac is out in the woods and hears a crackling or something there. He knows the Mohawk are coming. He runs to the chief as fast as he can. He does not say a word, but takes these beads and arranges them thus [indicating the arrangement]. The chief watches, and as soon as the man has arranged them, he orders the men to get ready for a fight."

SETTLEMENTS

The local chiefs were of equal power; no settlement was superior to another.

From the most distant times, each settlement seems to have had a distinguishing symbol done in quillwork on the clothing and marked on the canoes. At Restigouche the symbol was a salmon; at the present Red Bank, Little Southwest Miramichi, a beaver; on the Northwest Miramichi (Eel Ground), a man with drawn bow and arrow; on the Main Southwest Miramichi, the sturgeon.[9] Each canoe on a ceremonial visit carried a banner, *kwitantawegan*. Canoes visiting a reserve on St. Anne's Day in the nineteenth century are described by John Newell as carrying each a distinctive color.[10]

[8] JR, I, 75–77; III, 87–97.
[9] Ganong, footnote to LeClercq, *Gaspesia*, 39–40. See also 192–93.
[10] See Chapter XIV.

PART ONE *Tribal Life*

More importance attached to the chief of a group of settlements. At the beginning of white contact the country was divided into districts bounded by geographic features, usually bays and rivers. Along the Pentegoet, St. Croix, and St. John rivers, in New Brunswick, there was one sagamore for each.[11]

Similarly, the Burnt Church settlement, according to a local resident, was the *ju'ktâ*, "fire," or meeting place for the chiefs of reserves as far north as Baie des Chaleurs and as far south as Point du Chêne. He designated as belonging to this, about 120 years ago, Eel Ground, Red Bank, Restigouche, Bathurst, Pokemouche, Tracadie, Shippegan, Richibucto, Shediac, and Southwest (near Red Bank). The chief at Burnt Church was recognized as head chief of these eleven settlements.

The chief over a district of settlements was known as *bun*. The local chiefs met at Burnt Church every summer and every winter, to discuss tribal affairs. Another district included settlements in western Nova Scotia and about a third of the settlements in Cape Breton and eastern Nova Scotia. A district chief was also the chief of his own settlement.

It was also stated that there was a chief of the entire tribe. This office may be no older than the Wabanaki Confederacy (mid-eighteenth century); in the early days there was no tribal hierarchy, and the presence at a council of several chiefs of equal power frequently resulted in adjournment without reaching a decision.[12]

BONDS OF UNITY

Without firm and elaborate social structure, the Micmac tribe was held together by the recognition of common need, reinforced by formal courtesy and by frequent meetings for fellowship as well as for tribal business. The hungry were always fed. If a hunter had been successful and others were short of supplies, he shared his bag equally with the group. Communism seems to have been practiced only in times of scarcity. In January or February, when many were near starvation, the man who killed the first moose would carry meat even to distant wigwams and urge the dwellers to move nearer him so that he could supply them with food more often. Highly skilled hunters sometimes gave furs and meat to a friend who needed help to pay off a debt, or made a present to widows and orphans.[13] In time of hunger, a man who shot no

[11] JR, III, 87–97.
[12] JR, III, 97. See Chapter XIII.

Social and Political Organization

more than a single teal, barely sufficient to restore his own strength, would take it to a wigwam and share it with others.[14] However, by subterfuge, too painful hospitality might be averted. Biard related such an instance:

Once when we had gone a long way off to a fishing place, there passed by five or six women or girls, heavily burdened and weary; our people through courtesy gave them some of our fish, which they immediately put to cook in a kettle, that we loaned them. Scarcely had the kettle begun to boil when a noise was heard, and other Savages could be seen coming; then our poor women fled quickly into the woods, with their kettle only half boiled, for they were very hungry. The reason of their flight was that, if they had been seen, they would have been obliged by a rule of politeness to share with the newcomers their food, which was not too abundant. We had a good laugh then; and were still more amused when they, after having eaten, seeing the said Savages around our fire, acted as if they had never been near there and were about to pass us all by as if they had not seen us before, telling our people in a whisper where they had left the kettle; and they, like good fellows, comprehending the situation, knew enough to look unconscious, and to better carry out the joke, urged them to stop and taste a little fish; but they did not wish to do anything of the kind, they were in such a hurry, saying *Coupouba, Coupouba*, "Many thanks, many thanks." Our people answered: "Now may God be with you since you are in such a hurry."[15]

Traveling Micmac who had shot no game were accustomed to help themselves to provisions of dried fish and meat found hanging in any wigwam they reached during the owner's absence, a custom still followed in 1764.[16]

In 1911 the old hospitality to any member of their tribe was fully practiced. A visitor might stop at any house and remain a welcome guest for weeks. According to Rand, it was the custom to stop at the first wigwam in the settlement; but my informants said that a man entered whatever wigwam or house he felt prompted to go to.

To a visitor whom one has invited into the house the greeting is *up'chila'si*, "come in and sit down." The visitor, before entering a dwelling, must knock. If welcome, he is greeted with *up'chila'si tcim'ana*, "come up and be seated" (that is, take the seat back of the fire, the freest from draughts and the most comfortable in the wigwam).[17]

[13] LeClercq, *Gaspesia*, 117.
[14] Dièreville, 163.
[15] JR, III, 87–97.
[16] Smethurst, 375.
[17] Tale 128 describes the ceremonial greeting of a Micmac stranger.

177

PART ONE *Tribal Life*

To strangers who are not of their tribe Micmac are hospitable, provided the stranger frees himself from suspicion — not an easy thing to do. They then treat him as though he were a tribesman.

In the old days the first sign of hospitality and friendship was the proffered pipe. Frenchmen in 1607 watched with amusement the reception of guests by the chief, Membertou:

We have many times seen savage strangers to arrive in Port Royal, who, being landed, without any discourse went straight to Membertou's cabin, where they sat down taking tobacco, and, having well drunken of it, did give the tobacco-pipe to him that seemed the worthiest person, and after consequently to the others.

Then some half an hour after they did begin to speak. When they arrived at our lodgings, their salutation was: 'Ho, ho, ho!' and so they do ordinarily; but making courtesies and kissing of hands they have no skill, except some particulars which endeavoured themselves to be conformable unto us, and seldom came they to see us without a hat, to the end they might salute us with a more solemn action . . . But our savages have not any salutation at the departure, but only the '*A Dieu*' which they have learned of us.[18]

FEASTS

Binding the members of the tribe together in the days before government interference were the feasts of meat, accompanied by song, speeches, and dance, held on any possible occasion — one might say excuse — if the host had sufficient food. "There were feasts of health, of farewell, of hunting, of peace, of war, of thanks," said LeClercq; and Denys added to the list marriages and funerals. Food was especially abundant at spring feasts to rejoice over a successful winter of hunting, but as at all feasts, the meat was limited to the flesh of a single species of animal: beaver, bear, and moose were never mixed at the same meal. At special feasts grease and oil were drunk straight. To procure success in future hunting, an "eat-all" feast was held; everything had to be consumed before anyone might leave the wigwam; and even the smallest scrap might not be fed to a dog. One who could not finish his portion might present it to a more expandable neighbor. Remainders were thrown on the fire, but these were kept to a minimum, because of the glory attached to him who could eat more than the others.

[18] Lescarbot, *History*, III, 176.

Social and Political Organization
Feasts in the Seventeenth and Eighteenth Centuries

The host, as a rule, did not eat with his guests; he should not diminish their portions. Only men "in condition to go to war against the enemy responded to his cry of *Chigoudah ouikbarino*, 'Come here to my wigwam for I wish to entertain you'." It is not clear whether this means the exclusion of the aged as well as the sick and the ritually unclean. Crying "Ho, ho, ho!" three or four times, the men, carrying their dishes, entered the festive wigwam, sat down in the first vacant place, smoked some of the chief's tobacco, and were tossed some meat or offered it on a pointed stick. When all had eaten, two or three distinctive cries summoned the women, children, and the young boys who had not yet killed a moose, and any disqualified men, to receive the remains of the meat outside the wigwam.[19]

All feasts began with speeches, including one from the host explaining the reason for the invitation. Nicolas Denys, who considered the Micmac good orators and good laughers, mentioned the customary recital of genealogies at marriages and funerals:

in order to keep alive the memory, and preserve by tradition from father to son, the history of their ancestors, and the example of their fine actions and of their greatest qualities, something which would otherwise be lost to them, and would deprive them of a knowledge of their relationships, which they preserve by this means; and it serves to transmit their [family] alliances to posterity. On these matters they are very inquisitive, especially those descended from the ancient chiefs. This they sometimes claim for more than twenty generations, something which makes them more honoured by all the others.[20]

All seventeenth-century feasts closed with dances and songs in tribute to the host.

A century and a half later, the Abbé Maillard, writing from "Micmaki Country," March 27, 1755, viewed these still popular feasts with ambivalence. That part of him which considered it his priestly duty to spur the savages on to "make copious chase," so that furs would pay the Micmac debts to French traders, deplored the waste of time, meat, and peltry. But his weakness for Indian oratory has given us a detailed account of the speeches following a friendly feast of undercooked dog (de-fleaed) and hot seal grease. After dinner, when pipes were half-smoked, the most noted man present gave a speech in praise of the

[19] LeClercq, *Gaspesia*, 290–92.
[20] II, 410.

feast and of the giver. He compared the host to a tree, "whose large and strong roots afford nourishment to a number of small shrubs; or to a medicinal herb, found accidentally by such as frequent the lakes in their canoes." At winter feasts, the host was compared to a "turpentine tree" that never fails to supply sap and gum, or to the mild days that occur in the midst of even the worst winters. Next, the lineage of the host was mentioned:

"Your great-great-great-grandfather was a great-great-great-hunter. His skill was no better than others, but he had some miraculous secret way of seizing creatures by springing upon them. Your great-great-grandfather was wonderful with beavers, those animals who are almost men. Your great-grandfather was an expert trapper of moose-deer, martins, and elks. Your grandfather has a thousand and a thousand times regaled the youth with seals. How often in our young days have we greased our hair in his cabin. Your father never missed his aim at game flying or sitting. He was particularly admirable in decoying bustards by his imitations. He had better inflections in his voice than most of us; he moved his body to sound like the clapping of their wings; he even deceived us. As for you — I am too full of good things to say more but thanks."

A younger and less important man then rose and summarized the first speaker and praised his manner. He did the thanking, shook the host's hand, and said: "All the steps I am going to take as I dance lengthwise and breadthwise in thy cabin are to prove to thee the gaiety of my heart and my gratitude." He now does his *Netchkawet*,

advancing with his body erect, in measured steps, with his arms a-kimbo. Then he delivers his words, singing and trembling with his whole body, looking before and on each side of him with steady countenance, sometimes moving with a slow grave pace, then again with quick and brisk ones. When he makes a pause, he looks full at the company, as much as to demand their chorus and the word *Heh!* which he pronounces with great emphasis. Then they often repeat *Heh!* fetched up out of the depths of their throats — when he pauses, they cry aloud in chorus, *Hoh!*

The dancer got his breath and then praised the host and asked the company to agree with him. He shook everyone's hand, danced again, "sometimes to a pitch of madness." He kissed his hand as a final salute to all and resumed his place. All the other men did the same thing.

Then girls and women entered, the eldest at their head, carrying a great piece of heavy birch bark which she struck as a drum. All the

Social and Political Organization

women danced, "springing round on their heels, quivering with one hand lifted, and the other down; other notes they have none but a gutteral loud aspiration, of the word *Heh! Heh! Heh!* as often as the old female savage strikes her bark drum. As soon as she ceases striking, they set up a general cry, expressed by *Yah!*" If approved, they repeated the dance.

When they withdrew, an old woman gave thanks in the name of all the women,

the introduction of which is too curious to omit as it so strongly characterizes the sentiments of the savages of that sex, and confirms the general observation that where their bosom once harbours cruelty, they carry it to greater lengths than even the men whom frequently they instigate to it.

"You men! who look on me as of an infirm and weak sex and consequently of all necessity subordinate to you, know that in what I am, the Creator has given to my share, talents and properties at least of as much worth as yours. I have had the faculty of bringing into the world warriors, great hunters, and admirable managers of canoes. This hand, withered as you see it now, whose veins represent the roots of a tree, has more than once struck a knife into the hearts of prisoners, who were given up to me for my sport. Let the river-sides, I say, for I call them to witness me, as well as the woods of such a country, attest their having seen me more than once tear out the heart, entrails, and tongue of those delivered up to me, without changing color, roast pieces of their flesh, yet palpitating and warm with life, and cram them down the throats of others whom a like fate awaited. With how many scalps have not I seen my head adorned, as well as those of my daughters! With what pathetic exhortations have not I, upon occasion, roused up the spirit of our young men to go in quest of the like trophies that they might achieve the reward, honor, and renown annexed to the acquisition of them: but it is not in these points alone that I have signalized myself. I have often brought about alliances which there was no room to think would ever be made, and I have been so fortunate that all couples whose marriages I have procured have been prolific and furnished our nation with supports, defenders, and subjects to eternalize our race, and to protect us from the insults of our enemies. These old firs, these ancient spruce-trees, full of knots from the top to the roots, whose bark is falling off with age, and who yet preserve their gum and powers of life, do not amiss resemble me. I am no longer what I was; all my skin is wrinkled and furrowed, my bones are almost everywhere starting through it. As to my outward form, I may well be reckoned amongst the things fit for nothing but to be totally neglected and thrown aside; but I have still within me wherewithall to attract the attention of those who know me."[21]

[21] Maillard, *Customs and Manners*, 2–18.

PART ONE *Tribal Life*

38. Sainte Anne des Micmac. The statue was erected for the tercentenary (1910) of the baptism of the Micmac chief Membertou and his family. Behind the fence is the *Marquis de Malauze*, French ship sunk in 1760 off Restigouche and raised in 1936.

More praises followed. This pleased the hunters and spurred them on in that essential occupation.

A twentieth-century survival enacted at the mission of Ste Anne de Restigouche at the tercentenary celebration of Membertou's baptism was described by an attending priest (see illustration 38):

An unscheduled and unrehearsed part of the three-day celebration was the performance by the Micmac of a mixture of songs, speeches and dances, which it is Micmac custom to hold in honor of an individual in the great moments of family or group life, such as mourning, marriage or the departure of an important member of the tribe. They gather together to give each in turn a eulogy of the dead, the fiancé, or the one about to depart. Exaggeration is permitted and is even *de rigueur*. From time to time the orator raises his voice and chants in rhythm, "*Iouana, oouana, Haiouana, yo, ha, yo, aahe, aahe, aahe*"; then suddenly he stops and throws towards the audience a searching and pleading look to get their approbation of the praises of the hero. . . . In one voice they respond, "*ha! ha! ha!*"

Women and young girls are commonly allowed to take part in the celebration; they may even address the gathering — and do so — but only after the men have spoken, and not until they have presented their

Social and Political Organization

apologies to the gathering. This office is generally entrusted to the oldest Micmac woman present. On this occasion, in respect to the presence of many priests, the Indian women had the delicacy to limit their participation to applause of their chiefs.[22]

Great ceremony and prolonged feasting attended the summer meetings of the tribal chiefs which, Father Biard said (1616), were held to consult about peace and war and to make "treaties of friendship and treaties for the common good." The host chief feasted his guests for as many days as he could. The guests made him some presents, but expected that each visiting chief would receive a parting gift; the host was not required to present anything to men of lesser rank.[23] Of particular importance in tribal ritual was the ceremonial arrival of the visiting chief and his followers, a feature complied with by French traders eager for Micmac furs. This account dates from 1675–87:

They are fond of ceremony, and are anxious to be accorded some when they come to trade at the French establishments; and it is, consequently, in order to satisfy them that sometimes the guns, and even the cannon, are fired on their arrival. The leader himself assembles all the canoes near his own and ranges them in good order before landing, in order to await the salute which is given him, and which all the Indians return to the French by the discharge of their guns. Sometimes the leader and chiefs are invited for a meal in order to show to all the Indians of the nation that they are esteemed and honoured. Rather frequently they are even given something like a fine coat, in order to distinguish them from the commonalty. For such things as this they have a particular esteem, especially if the article has been in use by the commander of the French.[24]

St. Anne's Day

Long after the political purpose of the summer councils had died, tribal gatherings flourished in cultural syncretism as the proper way to celebrate St. Anne's Day.

The future patron saint of the Micmac was first established in New France in 1628 when, at the Cape Breton mission, the priests Vimont and Vieuxpoint kept the promise made to their patroness, Anne of Austria, Queen Mother of France, by dedicating the first chapel they built in the New World to Sainte Anne d'Apt. Ste-Anne au Cap-Breton antedated by twenty-nine years the establishment of Ste Anne de Beaupré.[25]

[22] *Souvenir of the Micmac Tercentenary Celebration*, 1910, 11. Translated.
[23] JR, III, 87–97.
[24] LeClercq, *Gaspesia*, 247.
[25] Pacifique, "Sainte-Anne au Cap-Breton," in *Etudes Historiques*, 52.

PART ONE *Tribal Life*

Here in eastern Canada, as in many other times and places, the Roman Catholic Fathers found an aboriginal institution—the summer tribal gathering—and a saint whose festal day would fuse pleasantly with it. St. Anne's Day, July 26, is the most important date in the Micmac calendar. She is their own saint; a great helper of the Micmac, a sort of culture hero who taught them moose-hair weaving, a trait of relatively recent introduction.[26] St. Anne is described as the wife of an Indian named Swasan (a common family name on New Brunswick reserves). She is of very good family and is the mother of the Virgin Mary. At her first meeting with Micmac she told them that she wanted to show them how to do things, and said she would like to meet them again on July 26. They remembered the day and have observed it ever since.

Two accounts of early St. Anne's Day celebrations were obtained in 1911; one at Burnt Church, N.B., the other at Pictou, N.S. The Pictou version, John Newell's, though told as a St. Anne's celebration, is entirely lacking in religious reference and in political significance; the people gathered for a good time. The following description, given in an approximation to Newell's words, contains many aboriginal traits: the ceremonial arrival by canoe, the role of chief and assistant chief, *waltes* games, and a *ginap* drinking a pint of grease. Social solidarity is evidenced in the blood-brotherhood rite. In a sequel to the gathering, one of the chief's assistants, called *nudjlulkuldegat u'kit mal'tcewedjc*, the Watcher of the Young People, arranges for the intersettlement marriages which are one objective of the celebration. (See Chapter XIV.) Although, probably for clarity, Newell speaks as if a single visiting band arrived, he mentions at one point that several chiefs and their followers were present.

Old-Time St. Anne's Day in Nova Scotia. This is a description of the ceremony of putting the gun or arrow on the shoulder of the visiting chief, or as we call it, *gu'daluktadimpk sa'awegik hicigugiga*. In the old days the Indians went in canoes to some place for a good time, and took their families with them. When the canoes arrive at the shore of the visited settlement, all the people in the settlement go to the shore to welcome the visitors. The visiting men get out into the water, to the depth of their chests. Before the party lands, the two chiefs greet each other. The visiting chief then sings the *neskawe't* song. When he begins to sing, the home chief lays an old flintlock [formerly an arrow and a bow

[26] See Tale 85.

Social and Political Organization

were used] on the shoulder of the visiting chief, and discharges it. The home people carry the canoes of the visitors and their crews onto the beach and far beyond. Two shots are fired for the chief, and one for each other man (known as the *ä'sadamket wedulitcinam*) in charge of a canoe while they are each carried ashore. The people at the settlement erect wigwams to accommodate the visitors.

Three to six men go into the woods with bows and arrows to hunt moose, and three men go fishing. The moose is taken to the wigwam of the visitors, cooked whole, and is not cut up before being eaten. Two poles are set up with crotched tops, and from them the moose is hung. After roasting the moose, they fry the flesh in bear's grease. A visitor steps forward to test his capacity for the boiling bear's grease. (A *ginap* could drink about a pint of it. Such a man could do anything; he could change stone into wood and make it float on water.) The *ginap* must make the test before the visitors eat. If he can drink the proffered amount, the chief says, "We will try the rest; give the women and children their food." Meanwhile the women on the reserve have been cooking food.

The dry meat and the fresh meat are cooked rare; some boil bear's grease, some make fish chowder, and some cook *säge'bin* [so-called wild potato]. The men have a canoe race with the visitors — the *bi'luwedj* [the word means also "stranger" or "enemy"]. If the home people win, they must again go hunting and procure game. They now hold a foot-race. The feast, *tiwig'oba'ktim*, then starts. The old men of each party arrange themselves in two rows, facing each other, the food between them. The women and children are a short distance away. All are now out in the open air. They shout "e! Ahi, i!" after which the visiting chief stands by the food and gives the war whoop, to which everyone responds with "A hi, i!" The visiting chief makes a short address in which he says that he is glad to be once more with these people and his friends; that the contests pleased him, and he would not be averse to seeing them renewed; concluding with, "I can look after my *udan* [settlement]; you do the same with yours and with the visitors who come to you from the other *udan*." At the conclusion of this speech from the visiting chief, the home chief shouts "e! hi, i!" stands, acknowledges the good words of the visiting chief, and declares himself grateful for all that has been said. After this interchange of pleasant words, the two chiefs shake hands. One of the chiefs now sings a war song, and each of them dances between the row of men and the food. The visiting chief is next to the row

PART ONE *Tribal Life*

of home people, the home chief is next to the row of visitors. When they arrive at the end of the row, at the place where the respective assistants to the chiefs are sitting — the chief had been seated at one end of the row, and his assistant at the other end — they shake hands again, and continue to sing.

The home chief goes to the visiting assistant to the chief, shakes hands with him, and then with his own assistant. They remain on the side of their own people, dance between them and the food, and resume their places. They are no sooner seated than they rise again, shake hands as before, and repeat the whole procedure. The assistant to the visiting chief goes to the assistant to the chief, who is the host, and they shake hands. The chief who is host says to his assistant, "Stand and do your part." The visiting chief says the same to his assistant. The assistants dance, and wave a tomahawk in the right hand, as though in the act of scalping. They address each other pleasantly, and each declares he is glad to see the other. The visiting assistant goes to the people who are hosts, places his tomahawk in his moose-hide belt, and distributes among them the food which is on a birch-bark plate provided for the purpose. The men eat. Two men share from one plate. They eat a second plateful. Large plates, *e'ptân*, at each of which four men sit, are now provided.

After the meal has been eaten, the visiting assistant and the home assistant stand, give the war whoop, and, singing, dance toward the end of the table. At the end of the table or place where food is spread they whoop and shout, *"el'bikut ki'luwälol,"* "women's meal." This elicits a whoop from the women. After the women have eaten, the men dance. Everybody is in high spirits.

The women dance apart from the men. Time is kept for both the men and the women by a man who sings, and beats on a roll of birch bark.

Each man who dances carries a *jitkasog'andjitc*, a hollow moose antler in which are small pieces of the antler of the moose. These they rattle while they dance. After two circuitings they shout *"dalio!"* Each woman who dances carries an *o'pkuma'an*, a club about two and a half feet long.

The women, after they have danced, choose partners, and play *waltes*. Two visiting women play against two of the women hostesses. The men take their bows and arrows and go off to shoot squirrels.

One of the home people, or one of the visitors, brings in the arrows, the clothes, or the moccasins of a person whose identity and place of

Social and Political Organization

residence are not known. All the men prepare for the hunt. The property of the unknown person is sold. One pays for an article the foreleg of a moose; one, the thigh; one, a partridge; one, half a partridge; and so on, until all the possessions have been disposed of. After they return from the hunt, the various articles agreed to be paid for these things are taken to the auctioneer, the *mid'jentie'skwet*, who, after dark, takes these things to the man whose possessions he has sold. (He alone knows the identity of that person.) The recipient is a man who has no provisions and whose family is in need, or perhaps three or four needy persons who took some of their possessions to the *mid'jentie'skwet* during the night.[27]

The women, the men, the young children, and the girls, respectively, sleep in separate groups, on the skins of animals. When the visitors are ready to leave, they sit in their canoes and the home people carry the laden canoes into the water. At the shore good-byes are said. The home women give the first whoop, *"hup! hup! hup! ha! wi'a!"* The women guests answer with the same whoop. The women then talk about the games of *waltes* which they played and the great fun they were. The anchors are up, and the women await the men. The men are busily exchanging blood. They use for this purpose a small flint knife, a *taktamut*, that is employed only for this purpose. When two men decide to mingle their blood, each mixes the blood from his hand with blood from the hand of the other, and blood from his foot with blood from the foot of the other. No one knows how many do this; the women are apart from the men, and no one is present at this interchange except the two men. [The informant believed that about a quart of blood was taken from each man; he said he did not know the meaning of the custom.]

While the men go to their canoes, they dance the war dance. They first perform it in the circle in which they danced after landing. They dance and sing the *lugwa'oda*, during which they go once around in a circle, then dance toward the canoes. All the men participate in this dance. A man keeps time on a birch-bark drum until all have arrived at the shore.

A *ginap* says he will show them something that will make them open their eyes with astonishment. While he dances, he brings each foot down about a foot and a half into the ground, at every step, no matter what the nature of the soil is.

The visiting chief says, "We will meet again. Take care of yourselves

[27] Something of this custom survives today in the sale of possessions following a death. See Chapter XVI.

PART ONE *Tribal Life*

and send us word if anything goes amiss." The hosts reply to this in unison with a long drawn out "Ah!" [28]

John Newell's account of St. Anne's Day must greatly antedate his own life. Peter Ginnish, of Burnt Church, however, tells what he remembers from his youth, after the religious element in the holiday had long ago become strong.[29]

St. Anne's Day at Burnt Church. Perhaps fifteen or sixteen canoes come from Richibucto [Big Cove Reserve] bringing the chief and the priest, for St. Anne's. Everyone knows that people come here to celebrate St. Anne's. They are met on the shore at the cove below the church. They have spent the previous night on Portage Island, where they made a big fire, the length of a house, in order to show the people here that they were on the way, and would soon arrive at Burnt Church. During that night no one sleeps.

About eight o'clock in the morning they arrive. A pennant flies from the place where the chief stays, and one from the house of the priest. The canoes approach the shore, some ahead of others. When they are about twelve feet from land, they form abreast, and stop. The visiting chief stands, addresses a greeting to everyone on shore, and says that he is coming for St. Anne's; that he has his own priest with him; and that he will not bother the chief at Burnt Church. The Burnt Church priest is at the shore with the others who have gathered to welcome the visitors. The visiting chief speaks few words; he merely announces to the people under what circumstances and with what motives he has come, and then sits down. The chief's assistant goes into the water, which comes nearly to his knees, and walks to the shore. He sings a song. All then place their guns over the left shoulder and shoot.[30] After the song of the visiting chief's assistant has been sung, the Burnt Church chief and his assistant reply with a song of welcome.

The visitors then go to shore, get out of their canoes, and march, in

[28] The departure of the canoes and the backward glances of those in love are described in Chapter XIV.
[29] In 1835, Levinge remarked: "The Micmac Indians meet annually [at Burnt Church] on the feast of St. Anne, (26th July) to arrange all the business of the year. They remain together about a fortnight, when chiefs are elected or deposed, marriages contracted, children baptized, and the priests who attend instruct the young in the articles of the Catholic faith, to which all the Indians of New Brunswick belong."
[30] A man was killed by the explosion of a large wooden cannon used at the celebration about 1886; and since that time guns have not been employed.

188

Social and Political Organization

procession, to the church. [See illustration 39.] After a service at the church, the visitors build a wigwam for themselves. On the day after the procession, the 27th, the fun commences. There is no sleep at night. The visitors, while preparing to leave, roll up the bark with which they have covered their wigwam, and store it away, to be kept for use on the next St. Anne's.

39. St. Anne's Day shrine at Burnt Church. This is used once a year for the procession bearing St. Anne's image from the church. The cross, erected in 1952, replaces one raised in 1858.

The celebrations proper are initiated by the visiting assistant to the chief, who sings, goes about, and shakes hands with the Burnt Church people. There is a big dinner. The Burnt Church people kill a large ox, provide a barrel of flour, and all have abundance to eat. Throughout the night there is dancing. The departure of the guests is quiet and without formality.

Previously marriages were celebrated only at St. Anne's; and this is still the chosen time. During the St. Anne's celebration, Indians who

PART ONE *Tribal Life*

were not Micmacs would hide, and would not show themselves until it was over. If a stranger openly declared who he was, and why he was there, he would not be molested, and might participate as freely as any other.[31]

Fear of the presence of a stranger at these celebrations seems to be an inheritance from the period when these assemblies, or their antecedents, were important intersettlement meetings. Although intersettlement visiting by groups has shrunk to this one much-acculturated holiday, individual trips are frequent from reserve to reserve throughout the Maritimes; and without the chief's magically propelled messengers, news travels from Cape Breton to the Baie des Chaleurs with fair speed.

[31] Rand, about 1869, was told by a Micmac that "a few years ago, the Indians were assembled in Potlodek, Cape Breton, on Saint Ann's Day; and by what they heard and saw they were led to conclude that there were *owwiscooks* (spies) from Canada on the island. It was proposed by the young men to use their guns upon them; but the old chief, Tooma, would not allow it. One night, however, one of the boys fired upon them. The next day they traced the blood to where he had been carried and buried; a *luscun* (signboard) was set up, informing them that there were twelve of the strangers, who had no evil intentions, and need not have been fired upon. The Indians have the impression, however, that spies deserve to be killed even in times of peace." *Legends*, 244.

CHAPTER XII

Dance, Song, and Games

THE importance of song and dance in tribal gatherings has appeared on nearly every page of the preceding chapter. Many of the tales, particularly war stories, stress the magic power of song. Birds are said to be the inspiration or direct teachers of Micmac composers.

DANCES

In early days dances were held to entertain visitors; to express thanks as guests; at feasts of any sort; to honor "the devil who guides to the deer"; in preparation for war and in celebration of victory.

Musical instruments, known in 1911 but in 1953 no longer used, were drum, rattle, and trumpet. The drum, a birch-bark box, was struck with the knuckles of the fist. A rattle of birch bark, which contained pebbles, and a horn with shot were used. The conch was blown. When thus used as a trumpet it was called *pugua'mawes*. Birch bark rolled into the shape of a speaking trumpet is said to have been used for that purpose. The *bi'bigwa'an*, a thin piece of bark fastened like the lip of a flute, was blown by children.

Two highly unsympathetic accounts of Micmac dancing follow, the first from 1607–8.

The dances of our savages are made without removing from one place, and, notwithstanding, they are all in a round (or very near) and do dance with vehemency, striking with their feet upon the ground, and lifting themselves up as in half a leap. And as for their hands they hold them close, and their arms in the air, in form of a man that threateneth with a motion of them. As for the voice, there is but one that singeth, be it man or woman: all the rest do and say *Het, het!* as some that breatheth out with vehemency.

And at the end of every song they all make a loud and long exclama-

PART ONE *Tribal Life*

tion, saying *Heeee*. For to be more nimble they commonly put themselves stark naked, because that their gowns made of skins do hinder them. And, if they have any of their enemies' heads or arms, they will carry them about their neckes, dancing with this fair jewel, which they will sometimes bite, so great is their hatred even against the dead.[1]

The second came from observations in 1675–87.

They dance as a rule in a ring, in time to the noise which they make by striking with a stick upon a bark plate or upon a kettle. They do not hold one another by the hands, but all keep their fists closed. The girls cross theirs over one another, a little out from the stomach. The men raise theirs in the air, and make sundry movements with different postures as if they were at war, representing fighting, winning victory, and removing the scalps from their enemies. They do not jump, but in lieu thereof, they strike the ground, sometimes with one foot, sometimes with both together.

The special dances of the women and the girls are very different from those of the men, for they make some horrible contortions in dancing. They draw back and push out the arms, the hands, and the whole body, in a manner altogether hideous, looking intently on the earth as if they would draw out something therefrom by the very strength and force of their contortions. This they continue until they are all of a perspiration. They do not force from the bottoms of their stomachs, as do the men, those hues and cries of ho, ho, of ha, ha, of he, he; but their only sound is made with their lips, and is a certain hissing like a serpent. This is the usual tune of their dance, which can properly be designated an innocent Indian racket.[2]

SONGS

The Micmac in 1911 recognized three classes of songs: *neska wet*, a song not accompanied with dance and sung at a big festival; *tcigamaan*, a song sung at a festive occasion and danced to; *neska winto*, a song sung when a lone singer is present, who sometimes but not invariably accompanies it by a dance.

The following are some of the songs which were recorded in New Brunswick and Nova Scotia in 1911. Any one of them is repeated ad lib. The records of a few of the songs have not been transcribed, and for some of those that have been transcribed the text was not obtained. The transcriptions were made by Jacob D. Sapir, father of the well-known linguist and anthropologist Edward Sapir.

[1] Lescarbot, *History*, III, 181–84.
[2] LeClercq, *Gaspesia*, 292–94.

Dance, Song and Games

Gu'gwetc (Game Song)

kampate'la bali tcika'nwe twe'labala twen'kam asetlabodji ke'mpato debala da bo'.
(At each word a mark is rubbed out.[3])

Tes'kamwe Tabe'giana (Snake Song)
Sung by Peter Swason

e'du gwe dug' edu'gwa. (Repeated ad lib.)
(No meaning.)

Ucatolte Tabe'giana (Toad Song)
Sung by Peter Swason

e'du egwe edug' gwa. (Repeated ad lib.)
(No meaning.)

Neskâwe'tan
Sung by Simon Basque

Ulä nige	no'ga madut	neskâwa' audjit	Akta'mkia
This little song	my dear friends	little neskâ waan	beginning
ma'ktuadan	su iltudanu, täu	kaugigi na'ik	idalin tu didis.
not to forget	the way	our forefathers	their songs.

Words spoken at the end of the song:

na'tali Sa'gala ma luk no'gamaduk dante'siuk na'ni ge uba nes'kâ wâ audijitc ta'ntaleginasik mo'k wanda'salti nenu kiuiskamidjin a kwetc telibnadu'dis.
(Free translation: Now thus I initiate you into the memory of the songs our forefathers used to sing in the days when they ruled our country.)

Ad'iu an'ietcitc' (Goodbye, Little Annie)
Sung by Thomas Meuse

A boy from another reserve had come to visit a girl, and they had become engaged. The girl was very proud of the engagement, and talked about it too much. The boy was angered by her free talking. While he walks along a path about two miles away from the reserve, but where, as he knows, all can hear him, he sings:

She wants to see me only in the dark, but I don't want it so. I can't show my face on the reserve — I'm ashamed of her much-talking. Now I'm going to leave. I shall carry no birch-bark writing paper, but I'll take the news myself. I'll be back next summer, and then I can tell you a little more plainly than I can tell you now. I'll meet you anywhere when I come back in the summer. Ad'iu an'ietcitc'.

Comment by Thomas Meuse at the end of the recording:

[3] For another Gugwetc song, see p. 201 below.

PART ONE *Tribal Life*

I told him myself that I could not sing very well. Probably on St. Anne's Day I'll be a little better. That boy went home and was ashamed; I'm ashamed, too, because I'm a stranger, and I've been painting that old flagpole. If I can't sing this on St. Anne's Day this year, perhaps I can sing it on St. Anne's Day next year.

War dance (Sung before Going to War)

Song:

Ma'liauswa' un: Walneg' dik dja'diek
Ma'liauswa' un okum'la mum ed hi äs ho' dä sitk be' dan tcitc
Mo' gwcä ge' dji duk du dju lma' la diu kew dedj
ke dan' dji wa' git du'pop kun de'a si äk hau' e ya da ho!

Speech:

Neduptcitctut utsi dun mok kwäe ge lu'lt nuk ga' duk gelu'l ta do se da'u' e wimpick mu gehi'lk nuk ab bau'i a muk tci'poduk gehil' ta do.

Song:

e' go kwa'n u da i' gan e a'dj i ga ai'na tcu'gat luk
tcu ga' du in na ni'gamaauit ges' u se gel wu'dj i noeu.

Translation: Ma'liauswa'un [the name of a girl], I have been to the cove. Her heart is beating up the river [near me]. She does not know what time the Mohawk will take her home [with them]. There are as many Indians here in Munagit [i.e., Cape Breton] as there is dirt. Hâ e ya da ho. [At this all yell da ho, greatly prolonging the last syllable.]

Comment at the end:

When the Mohawk took her home, it made me lonely. (He then gives the war dance.) You dance right and get her back. (This song makes some of the Indians cry, and angers others.)

Kiste' djuwe tabe'giau (Captive Song)
Sung by John Newell

| *ke'si* | *babe'labewit* | *we'tckwi* | *ne' abiet* |
| You are | with your thin face | showing yourself | looking at me |

| *ka'du* | *jadeladi'ktukc* | *e'dala dalupc.* | (Repeated ad lib.) |
| and then | at the table | you have been eating. | |

(This was sung around the captives brought by returning warriors. The women sang it while they danced around the captives, who were tied to a stake, and from whom they cut off pieces of flesh, until death relieved the sufferers.)

Amkawamk tabe'gian (Treaty Song)
Sung by John Newell

| *Nige'itc* | *amalka'ldiek* | *kelu'lk.* | *Wes'awaduk* | *no'ktabu'ntuk.* |
| Now | we are dancing | well. | We are taking | one year. |

Dance, Song and Games

A'mkatamu'k   tan   kla'idu   na   a'mk wa'mka.
We shall go to see   then   how it will do   now   the treaty.
(Repeated ad lib.)
(Meaning, that the treaty is to be tried for one year. Said to have been sung at the last treaty between the Mohawk and the Micmac, which is still in force.)

Ama'lka'mkewe tabe'giana (Dancing Song)
Sung by John Newell

We'sawa'duk   kelu'lk   nige'itc   wela'gwa.
We are having   (a) good   (time) now   this evening.
(These words are used in two other songs sung by John Newell.)

Ne'dabahinkewe tabe'giana
(Going to Hunt Song; A Welcoming Song to Returning Warriors)
Sung by John Newell

A'bintebali   ku'laman.'   We'ligalo'lk   tau.
I am returning from the hunt   now.   We did well   then.
(i.e., from the fight)

Te'lado'adiek   nige'itc?   Aba'sidâek   amsit
What are we doing   now?   We are all returning   all   (as)
poktamkida'iek.   Nige'itc amsit   abadjida'iek.   Mokwe'dj
when we started.   Now   all   are coming back.   Nobody,
nokte'djit   tale'idjik.   (Repeated ad lib.)
not one,   was killed.

Nidietcweik tabe'gian (Loon Song)
Sung by Peter Swason

Telidalsu'ltciok   mo'kwa   he i mo'k   uteimog   uksitra'muk
You thing   not   here   world.
mo'kweimu' tcinama miamutc
neia'cidu amudju nemiado'lksut neiasi'tca akmiamu'tc ka'midu tâdet etane'iacitca mia'mutc kisigala'digadu u'ktu lugawa'ana ka'du mapu' umugwi tan is'tilada'addja istigene'gam kadu e'ik tanu'an kisuli'gede to is'tigene'gam.

GAMES

Waltes

Like all their neighbors, Micmac are great gamblers. Games and contests are a favorite diversion at all social gatherings. Most popular from

PART ONE *Tribal Life*

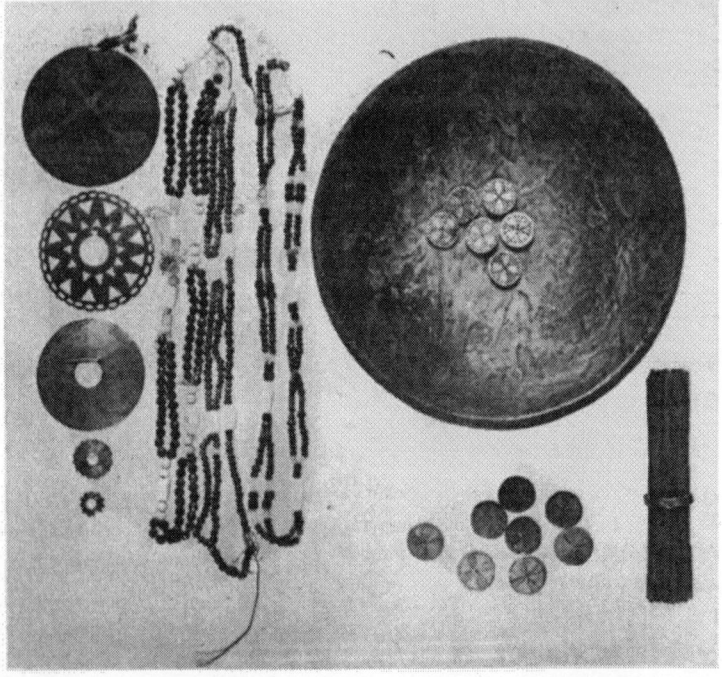

40. Beads, medals, and equipment for playing *waltes*. Beads are of glass and shell. The stone medal at the upper left bears crossed hockey sticks, insignia of the owner's trade. The four silver medals below are used as ornaments. The game bowl contains a set of dice. Beside a second set of dice is a bundle of tally sticks.

pre-white days and still played often in 1911 was *waltes'*, the dice game. The equipment consists of a bowl of hard wood made from a burl, six bone dice, and a bundle of thirty-eight sticks used in keeping score. *Waltes*, "plates," can be played by an even number of people, each for himself, or with partners. The usual number of players is perhaps two or four. Formerly it was never played without stakes, and it is still a gambling game. Anything may be put up as the stake.[4] (See illustration 40.)

The players squat in a circle. The *waltes*, "plate," is in the middle, usually on a cushion or other yielding substance. It is essential that when

[4] A description of the game of *waltes* is given by Hagar, AA, 8:31, and Gatschet, "Micmac Fans and Games," BFMUP, 2:190–94. For Lescarbot's account, see *History*, III, 197–98.

Dance, Song and Games

pitching the dice the plate be brought down with a thud, for this makes a good throw. There seems to be no rule as to who shall begin the game. The play goes from left to right, that is to say, counterclockwise. (See illustration 41.)

The dice are placed on the bowl haphazardly, are pitched, and are caught on it. If a score is made, the player is entitled to another throw, and another, until no score is made by him.

If only one marked side or only one unmarked side of the dice turns up, a score of one is made, and three ordinary sticks are put aside. (There are thirty-four ordinary sticks, three intermediate ones, called *tra'moi*, and a notched one, called *ki'cigu*, "old man." See illustration 42.)

If a play of only one marked or only one unmarked side is repeated, each play scores two; that is to say, the player has scored a total of four points.

If this is thrown three successive times, each play scores three sticks; and the total score for the three consecutive plays is nine sticks. If this is done four times, it is a *tramoi* — four times four sticks. If all marked, or all unmarked, sides turn up, the score is one *tramoi*; if this is repeated, the total score is two plus two *tramoi*; if thrown a third time, a *kicigu*

41. Men playing *waltes*. The player at the left donned the ceremonial coat before he would consent to the photograph.

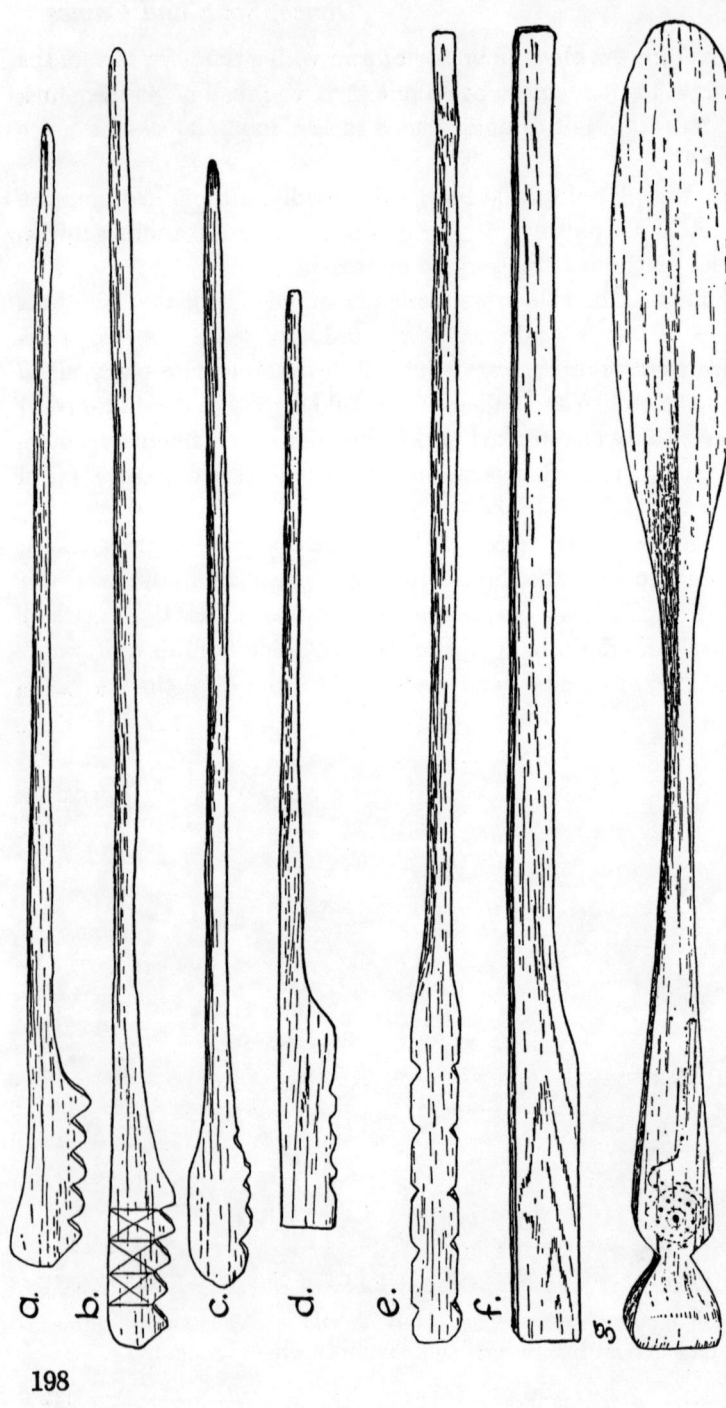

42. Types of counters used in the game of *waltes*. *a–e.* "Old man." *f.* A *tramoi*. *g.* A counter which accurately represents a Micmac canoe paddle. The actual length is fourteen inches.

is taken. A *tramoi* is the equivalent of four ordinary sticks. When the same score is made four times running, the player is entitled to a *tramoi* stick. *Kicigu* is the equivalent of five sticks.

Eventually all the sticks, save one ordinary one, are taken, there being always an ordinary stick left over.[5] Sometimes the sticks are counted out when won and are laid by the side of the respective players; frequently, however, they remain in the main pile, and a tally is kept by taking one stick for each three (four?) sticks to which the player is entitled. In the latter case, when all the sticks have been won, some one says *"na'skwieskit"* (*naskwadu*, "divide," or "apportion"), that is, "apportion the sticks," and each takes his share of them. The game continues in the same way, except that the sticks must be won from opponents; for there are now no sticks in the common pile. The object of the game is to win all the sticks. A tally for each player is kept, and when all the sticks have been won, they are counted and laid aside. Each opponent then has an opportunity to make five scores in succession. One who succeeds in doing this wins the game. This is called "drifting" (*ela'lagwet*).

(One old man asked me whether I understood the game; and when I said that I did, responded that he could not say as much, for there were plays whose score he could not count.)

It is the custom when playing, especially if the player is very anxious to make a good score, to wave the right hand rapidly over the plate and say *"tramoi!"* the idea being that the hand will cause the dice to give a *tramoi* score. Some players constantly throw the hand across the plate. If a die rolls about, the hand is waved over it violently. Some plates have a small hole in the center — it was only in Nova Scotia that I saw such plates — said to be put there because the air coming up through it causes the dice to turn well. The dice are called *walteestaank*, the sticks, *kitimaank*, of which the ordinary ones are called *wesaadam*, the larger ones *tramoi*, and the five-score piece, *kicigu*. When all of a kind are up, *"tramoi"* is said; when only one of a kind is up, *"wesaadam."* The latter means "good shot," and is said if one hits the mark when shooting.

The old word for *walteestaank* is said to be *waltesigaan buoinwe*, the *buoinwe* referring to its use in magic. A man would play *waltes*

[5] According to the informant's statement. The above description of the method of scoring does not ensure this remainder.

PART ONE *Tribal Life*

with another to find out whether he would win in an approaching fight; and the game was played by the women in camp while the men were away on a war expedition. The idea seemed to be that as the women were happy, so would the men be in good spirits and therefore be able to overcome the enemy. It is said also that the large burl from which the waltes is made is *buoin* (magical).

Although both men and women play *waltes*, it is more particularly a woman's game, and the bowl and dice invariably belong to the wife. I purchased several sets and attempted to buy others; in no instance were they sold by the husband; invariably the husband referred me to the wife, and she received the money. However, in the seventeenth century, *waltes* was a game on which men sometimes staked all their property, including their wives.[6]

Other Games

Wabanaank, "white" dice game, an old game, was in 1911 so seldom played that I was nowhere able to obtain a complete description of it, although in almost every reserve at which I made inquiry it was known that such a game was once in vogue. A set of these dice is in the Halifax Museum. I procured a set at Pictou Landing, and only one other was known to be in existence. One old man attempted to give me a description of how the game was played; but evidently he did not understand it in detail. It was played with eight dice, larger than those used in *waltes*, but of the same shape, marked similarly, and made of walrus tusk. They were thrown, all together, from the hand, upon a piece of moose hide or a piece of birch bark spread out on the ground. If all fell the same side up, the score was *wabitramoi*. If all except one was of the same side, it was *we'saatck*.

Another informant gave the following account: *Wa'bana'ank* are made of tusks of walrus. Pick them up so that all decorated sides are turned up in the hand. Throw onto a moose hide laid, to give the hide firmness, over a piece of birch bark. The hand is sometimes placed fingers down on the moose hide, then given a sudden twist, and the dice are pitched out when the hand turns and opens. The player has three throws. The object is to have all the dice fall marked side up. One who accomplishes this at the first throw wins. If this does not happen, those that fall smooth side (bottom side) up are thrown again. This is re-

[6] Lescarbot, *History*, III, 197.

Dance, Song and Games

peated for a third throw. The dice which fall face up remain on the board.

The *wabanaank* which I procured were made of walrus tusk. Only one old man at Pictou reserve knew how to play and score this game, although all of the older people knew something about it. It was the men's gambling game par excellence. Coats, caps, canoes, game — anything was wagered. It is said that a stake was always played for. Speck refers to the Micmac game of *wabana'yan*, played with eight ivory discs, or dice, an inch in diameter. The players, who may be of any number, take turns throwing the discs upon a blanket. There are only three throws that give a score. A throw which results in two discs with the same side up counts one (*ma'xtewi 'txamo'wi*); one only facing up, and seven facing down, scores five (*wa'bite witxamo'wi*). If the player throws all flat side down, the throw is called *mi'ktcik tciwa'wa'*, "turtle eggs," and he wins the game. This is said to be "the manner in which it is played in Cape Breton."[7]

The Halifax Museum contains the materials of a game called *comugesjokontc*, which, the label says, was played like jackstraws. I was not able to obtain a specimen or a description of this game.

The game of *gugwetc* (ghost, literally owl) is played by boys. They sit in a small circle in the sand, each with three lines in the sand in front of him. The lines represent, respectively, *tcabudjidjain*, brook, *iktakti*, path, and *iksidaamitc*, soul. One of them, the *gugwetc*, sings a song, in monotone, consisting of the three words in the order given, and the song is repeated until the game is finished. While the singer drones this song, he scratches out a line in front of each player as his hand goes around the circle; the one whose line is last to be rubbed out jumps up and runs away, the *gugwetc* attempting to hit him with a pebble, a club, a stick, or whatever is at hand. If the *gugwetc* strikes him, the latter becomes the *gugwetc* for the next game. The game is seldom played, and is little known south of Miramichi Bay.

[7] Speck, *Beothuk and Micmac*, 80.

CHAPTER XIII

Intertribal Orientation and Relations

FOLLOWING an old tribal pattern of speech, or overcompensating for the wretched reserve existence, Micmac in 1911 invariably represented themselves as the most powerful of peoples — all other Indians, from Maliseet of New Brunswick to strange tribes encountered in the western harvest fields, fear the very mention of the word Micmac. Micmac have never lost a war, and have never fought except to avenge a wrong. Today, quiet as they are, the old power lies below the surface and danger would bring it forth in the person of an unknown "captain" who would protect and save.

According to most informants, the Micmac have always dwelt in their present territory, but some said that they came long ago from the west, and moved into Nova Scotia from the direction of the present St. John, N.B., a territory then in the hands of the Mohawk.[1]

ATTITUDES TOWARD OTHER TRIBES

Maliseet and Penobscot

The best known neighbors, the Maliseet of the St. John River region, their Maine branch, the Passamaquoddy, and the Penobscot, received short treatment by Micmac informants and raconteurs. When the whites first came to what is now New Brunswick, Micmac were in the habit of traveling from the Miramichi to the St. John, making use of five or six portages. Maliseet journeyed into Micmac territory; at Richibuctou Bay in 1625 the two tribes met for trade with the French.[2] To the Abbé Maillard, missionary to Micmac and Maliseet, the two differed in lan-

[1] Rand (*Legends*, 110) stated that Micmac tradition placed their ancestral home to the southwest.
[2] Esther Clark Wright, *The Miramichi* (Sackville, N.B., 1945); JR, XLV, 59.

guage but had the same customs and the same way of thinking and acting. It is this difference in language that Micmac stress in their name for their neighbors, which whites have adopted, and which is explained in the following tale:

Before the whites came, the Micmac held a pow-wow and a feast at Prince Edward Island. Two dogs fought over some bones. The master of one dog struck the other dog. The second dog's owner said, "You and your dog are one," and hit the first man. The followers of the two men now joined the two fighting men. The vanquished party were pushed off the island. From that time onward they were so afraid of the other Micmac that they changed their speech so that they could not be understood. *Maliseet* means "corrupted speech."[3]

In 1911 no information could be obtained regarding a league or alliance with Maliseet, and only one tale (Tale 124) refers to a joint war expedition. In this story three Maliseet join two Micmac against innumerable Mohawk, and as usual, win because of their powerful magic; the event, which is said to have occurred over 400 years ago, before the French came to America, concludes with a fight against a British man-of-war. This is as close a reference as I could obtain to the joint participation of Micmac and Maliseet under French leadership against the British in Nova Scotia and in New England; in raids on Maine forts Penobscot Indians also participated. During King William's War (1689–97) Micmac from the Miramichi, Chignecto, and Cape Breton, and their allies, destroyed Dover, Pemaquid, and other frontier towns, and during the winters helped build forts for the French. In Lovewell's War (1722–25) and later, when the Maritimes became a battleground, Maliseet came to fight at Chignecto and Port Royal. The following account is typical:

In June 1724 thirty Maliseet came by canoe to "the mysterious and lonely island at the headwaters of the Bay of Fundy, 'Isle Haut.' There they met with fifty Micmac arrayed in war paint. A feast of dog flesh was eaten to give them courage to battle and the war dance was held." They then set out on one of the many attacks on the Port Royal fort. Maliseet from Aucpaque Island in the St. John, stirred up by Father Germain, their warrior priest, fought the British often between 1740 and 1763, aided by Micmac and their fiery leader, the Abbé Le Loutre. During the American Revolution, however, Micmac were cool to over-

[3] L. W. Watson, "The Origin of the Malicites," JAFL, 20:160–62 (1907).

PART ONE *Tribal Life*

tures from Boston and Machias, and did not join Maliseet and Penobscot against the British.[4]

Micmac in 1911 said Maliseet never fought Micmac because their tribe was never large enough, and Micmac are much bigger men. Neither statement is true.[5] A few tales were told of the wary way members of the two groups behave at a chance meeting.

The talk about Penobscot was similar. Micmac never fought them, for they were too inferior. Penobscot similarly regarded Micmac as large strong people, but poor and inclined to be mean. The name *Mikma* is evidently, though obscurely, related to the term *Mikamwes* referring to a class of dwarflike supernaturally gifted human creatures who inhabit the dense woods. . . . The Micmac know the Penobscot as Ganibax. . . . They in turn consider the Penobscot very much their inferiors. The feeling is manifested in a statement which I heard a Micmac woman make to the effect that the Penobscot used to eat people. Persons from Prince Edward Island, both Micmac Indian and White, are collectively called Enigwi'tak, 'Blue Noses,' by the Penobscot. In early times a war between the Penobscot and Micmac is said to have taken place, in which the Micmac claim the Penobscot were defeated.[6]

The following account of Penobscot-Micmac relations was obtained at Pictou, N.S.

"Dja'djaginwi't, a Micmac chief, fought the Penobscot. Later they made peace, and as a record painted with alder (red or brown) an eel and a turtle on one side of a bearskin. They crossed a tomahawk, spear, bow, and arrows and buried them thus. Over this spot they erected a small birch-bark wigwam; and at the top of it put bearskin. This was at Peter Denys Point [Princeton], Maine. After this, Micmac and Penobscot intermarried. The Micmac told the Penobscot: 'If you break this treaty, there is the Sun above you to see you. If you break it, you will be like salt on the ground when water is poured on it.'

"Those who intermarried lived at that place and soon had a language of their own," explained the informant. "This is proved by the numerals from one to ten, which are very similar in Micmac and Penobscot, whereas Maliseet is very different."

The early French records told of anything but peace. Parkman asserted that Algonkin tribes in New England were "in a chronic state

[4] Raymond, 38, 41–42, 262–63. Bird, 36.
[5] Maillard, *Customs and Manners*, 18–33, summarized below in section on warfare.
[6] Speck, *Penobscot Man*, 17–18.

Intertribal Orientation and Relations

of war with the tribes of New Brunswick and Nova Scotia," and Lescarbot noted (1607) that there had always been war between the Souriquois and the Armochiquois, the latter probably Penobscot. Trade between these two groups was so frequently interrupted that the Micmac, deprived of the shell beads they highly prized, were more willing to trade for French-made glass beads. Still, trade went on in peaceful intervals, and at that period and later Penobscot probably obtained "white bone" (ivory) from Micmac walrus hunters.[7]

Northern Indian Tribes

Accounts of other neighboring tribes given in 1911 were brief.

Montagnais-Naskapi. Montagnais, John Newell boasted, were just as afraid of the Micmac as the Maliseet were. He met some in Labrador and although he was alone, the whole bunch went off when he walked toward them.

The Montagnais-Naskapi were known to old-time Micmac of New Brunswick, who, before the whites came, used to travel far north up the coast, but disliked the intense cold. Montagnais were said never to have entered Micmac territory and had not been seen by present-day Micmac. The tribe was better known as the Osegamah (the people living along the Saguenay River).

Raids on two Montagnais bands, the Bersiamites (1648) and the Papinachioneski (1661), cited in the *Jesuit Relations*, will be described below.

Ottawa. Some Micmac remembered fighting with Taa from whom they obtained the *taaulk*, a type of canoe known throughout the Micmac area. The dried head and face of a captured Ottawa, I was told, was preserved in Cape Breton.

Ojibwa. The Tcibwe (Ojibway), the Micmac said, still wore skin clothes, and some had two or three wives.

Beothuck. The Makwe'djit ("Red Indians," the extinct Beothuck) were once very dangerous and used to fight the Micmac. In New Brunswick they were little more than a name and were sometimes located north of the St. Lawrence. In Nova Scotia, they were known to have lived in Newfoundland and said to have used a great deal of red paint, fought the Micmac, and also to have been greatly afraid of their enemies from

[7] Parkman, *Jesuits in North America*, xxi; Lescarbot, JR, I, 105. Speck, *Penobscot Man*, 109–10.

PART ONE *Tribal Life*

the mainland. Some said they once occupied a portion of Nova Scotia. Their dwellings were correctly described as being partly subterranean, with a tunnel exit, and having around the sides a bench of earth on which to sit. An old woman at Pictou Landing had heard an aged aunt of hers, long since dead, relate many stories about the Makwedjit. She said they were once in Nova Scotia and in Cape Breton. They spoke a language totally different from Micmac, as different from it as is Mohawk, and not bearing any similarity to it such as is found in Maliseet, Penobscot, or Montagnais. They were a wild people, and were very much afraid that the Micmac would do them harm. They lived in dwellings dug down into the ground two or three feet, circular in form, and covered like the Micmac birch-bark wigwams. A bench was around the interior, sunk in the earth, and in it a separate seat was cut for each occupant, and so if you found a dwelling you would know how many occupants it had. People of all ages and of both sexes painted the entire face with red ocher. A Micmac man married a Makwedjit woman. After she washed her face, it was the same color as that of the Micmac.[8]

Eskimo

To 1911 informants as far south as southern Nova Scotia the Eskimo were well known and were described as follows:

"Eskimo have been visited by many Micmac. They are always clothed in skins, and except in the summer live exclusively on raw meat. In the summer they kill a small seal, put it on the rocks, and allow it to rot until the flesh runs. When they are hungry, they cut off its forepaws and suck the oil from them. Codfish and other meat they treat similarly. [No information about their winter food was known.]

"They have a habitation in the ground, like that of a muskrat, and cover it with earth. They have been visited by whites, and are not as wild as they used to be. If they are treated well, they behave properly; if they are frightened, they immediately run away.

"Two Eskimo once drifted away on a large iceberg and were carried to

[8] The Beothucks' "winter *mamateeks*, or wigwams, were conical. Their frames were of poles covered with skins or birch bark, stoutly constructed, though they looked very light. Several had withstood the storms of over thirty winters. They were made to accommodate from six to eighteen persons. The fire was in the centre; round it were a number of holes, one for each person, in which the occupant sat, and, it is supposed, slept. For increased comfort the holes were lined with moss." A. Macdougall, "The Boeothic Indians," TCI, 2:100 (1891).

Intertribal Orientation and Relations

Prince Edward Island. Later the iceberg drifted to Margaree Harbor, Cape Breton. A short time before the French came, some Eskimo visited the Micmac at Pictou. They gave their name as *Eskimo*, 'Eaters of Raw' flesh."[9]

The duration of Micmac-Eskimo contacts can be in part ascertained from Leland:

"Even at the present day [1884] there are men among Micmac and Passamaquoddies who have gone on their hunting excursions even to the Eskimo. I myself know one of the latter who has done so, and the Rev. S. T. Rand, in answer to a question on the subject, writes to me as follows:

"Nancy Jeddore, a Micmac woman, assures me that her father, now dead, used to go as far as the wild (heathen) Eskimo, and remained once for three years among the more civilized. She has so correctly described their habits that I am satisfied that her statement is correct."[10]

In the seventeenth century Eskimo were living on the Gulf of St. Lawrence at two points along the North Shore of the present Quebec: at Mingan, the mouth of the Romaine River, opposite Anticosti Island, known today as Eskimaux Point; and also at Bradore Bay, at the beginning of the strait of Belle Isle. The river which here forms the boundary between Quebec and Labrador is named the Eskimo. At Bradore Bay Basques had extensive cod fisheries and here, following the murder and mutilation of an Eskimo girl by a Basque sailor, her fellow tribesmen killed and ate Basque fishermen. Their arrows, said to have a barb which remained in the wound when the shaft was pulled out, were particularly deadly.[11] In 1660 the Jesuits sent to Paris this description: "It is wonderful how these Savage mariners navigate so far in little shallops, crossing vast seas without compass, and often without sight of the Sun, trusting to instinct for their guidance."[12] The missionary's account of kyaks and houses leaves no doubt that the people referred to were Eskimo.

To the priests at Miscou, and at Percé on the Gaspé, they were best known as the goal of Micmac war parties which stopped off at the missions on the way to combat, or on their return laden with captives and scalps. In the early period of white contact, when Micmac were

[9] *Nutcit*, eat, *eskadalk*, raw. The Cree have a similar etymology and nomenclature.
[10] *Algonquin Legends*, 10–11.
[11] LeClercq, *Gaspesia*, 268.
[12] JR, XLV, 65–69.

PART ONE *Tribal Life*

described as warlike in general and given to fighting their southern neighbors, and in the late seventeenth century when LeClercq says they were generally peaceful, all accounts agree that their main enemies were the Eskimo. Micmac invaded Eskimo territory; such raids are mentioned as occurring from 1620 to 1675. There are no accounts of Micmac country invaded by Eskimo. According to LeClercq they were hereditary enemies who thoroughly feared the Micmac.[13] No evidence of this long hostility appeared in accounts by 1911 informants, nor is there any reference in folktales.

Mohawk

To Micmac in 1911 and for at least three hundred preceding years the foes most feared were the Iroquois, generally referred to as Mohawk, and occasionally as Caughnawags. A hundred years after the end of hostilities Mohawk were still a living threat in the minds of each Micmac community.

"The Mohawk send spies every year to find out the strength of the Micmac. These spies transform themselves into squirrels, and throw stones at our houses." This statement made repeatedly in 1911 represented a sort of fantastic reality, as I soon learned. Before going to Burnt Church, I had taken head and body measurements of some Maliseet, near Frederickton. Soon after my arrival at the reserve, a Maliseet from the St. John River settlement, accompanied by a friend of mine, came to Burnt Church. The Maliseet, to assist me – so he later said! – went from house to house and told the Indians how necessary it was that they should be measured; that from these measurements I could make statues which would look so much like the person measured that no one would be able to distinguish between statue and man; that by this means anyone could tell the difference between a Micmac, a Maliseet, or any other Indian. His efforts bore fruit in an increasing suspicion, by the Micmac, of my motives. A meeting of the men on the reserve was held, and it was decided that I might not take any measurements on people there. I had connived with the Maliseet to send these measurements to the Mohawk, who could then distinguish between Micmac and Maliseet and would sweep down and exterminate the Micmac. The Burnt Church chief wrote to reserves at Pictou, N.S., Lennox Island,

[13] *Gaspesia*, 266; Ferland, I, 73; JR, XXX, 133; XXVIII, 34, 105; XLV, 65; XLVII, 221.

Intertribal Orientation and Relations

P.E.I., and Big Cove, N.B. to forewarn the Micmac of my sinister intentions. The incident placed me under a suspicion that remained in the minds of several influential men and undoubtedly was a considerable handicap in winning their confidence. The younger men merely laughed at the idea; but often one of the older men would recount to me the fighting abilities of the Micmac, the aid they would get from Gluskap in time of trouble, and so on, in a strain that suggested they knew the danger and meant to show themselves capable of countering it.

This is not an isolated remnant of belief held by the old men on a single reserve. In 1910 representatives of the entire tribe met at Ste Anne de Restigouche to celebrate the tercentenary of the baptism of Membertou. At the end of the mass the Grand Chief of the Micmac, Jean Baptiste Denis, of Cape Breton, found it necessary to begin his speech with soothing words to his people; for a bad joker, himself a Micmac, had spread around reports designed to arouse fear in certain groups of the Indians present.

Said the Chief, "the Iroquois, our cruel enemies of the old days should have been sent a letter telling them to come to Restigouche for this occasion and they should have been given an order to make the most of this celebration to descend upon the Micmac and wipe them out! Who else but the devil, the Big Liar, *Gjimento*, could have invented such a lie! He and he alone, jealous of the announcement of this celebration, the preparations made and the happy circumstances that resulted from these rites, could find such a means of compromising success by attempting to disturb our minds. Let our hearts from this moment be given over completely to happiness and gratitude." [14]

According to accounts current in 1911 the Mohawk came in large war parties. If the Micmac discovered them in time, they surrounded them and killed a great many. The French paid the Mohawk to kill the Micmac, and gave them two shillings and sixpence for each Micmac head. The man who fought the Mohawk at Truro and was compelled

---

[14] Fr. Casimir de Cieutat, in *Souvenir of the Micmac Tercentenary Celebration*, 1910, 8. Translated and adapted.

An earlier episode at Restigouche is recorded by the Reverend J. C. Herdman. About 1863 there was a report that Mohawk were about to descend upon the Micmac. When a few friendly canoes appeared, "not a canoe in Restigouche would venture from shore. It was said that two gigantic forms clothed in unwonted garb had appeared in the neighborhood upon a mountain height, as if to spy out the best chances of attack." SJDS, January 10, 1883.

In 1804 Nova Scotia had a Mohawk scare that led to canoe building and other preparations for war, which the whites misinterpreted as a sign of hostility toward themselves. Murdoch, III, 233.

PART ONE *Tribal Life*

to lift up his shirt in order to let fall the bullets which had flattened against his body and collected there is typical of the exaggeration in these stories. Although the Micmac declare that in every fight with an enemy they were victors, their great fear of the Mohawk suggest that they fared badly at Mohawk hands. All our recorded stories of fighting with Indians refer to the Mohawk.[15]

Actually the Micmac suffered frequently from Iroquois conquest, intensified and continued because of the French alliance with the Algonkin-speaking peoples, which placed the Iroquois usually on the British side. At least one spot on the south shore of the St. Lawrence is haunted by an Iroquois-borne disaster of pre-white days. Off shore from Bic, east of Rimouski, lies L'Islet au Massacre, where the dreaded *bil'wedji* from Caughnawaga found two or three hundred (which tradition do you choose?) Micmac — men, women, and children — hiding in a cave. All but five were slain. "The quaint villagers of Bic tell, with striking emphasis, the story of L'Islet au Massacre, the departure of the lonely Micmac survivors, the weird cries heard, and the strange specters seen by their forefathers, as they gazed upon the Islet on stormy nights.[16]

Mohawk stories are told also by Maliseet and Penobscot. The latter have created a spirit, Awusjhowa, "spy," who goes from tribe to tribe gathering information about men and resources which he carries back to Caughnawaga.[17] Joint raids into Iroquois territory were sometimes carried out by warriors of the several tribes. Father Richard wrote (1642–43) about Micmac who went to Tadoussac that "some particularly of the youth may proceed as far as Kebec [Quebec] or beyond in order to go to war against the Hiroquois."[18] In 1652 "ten or eleven shallops arrived at Quebec, Savages from Gaspé, and some Etechemins [Maliseet] and Montagnais, going to war against the Iroquois."[19]

During the early eighteenth century when Micmac and Maliseet aided the French in assaults on Annapolis, the harried British built a fort nearby for their imported Mohawk allies whose power to terrify the Micmac they well knew. From this period, probably, date many of the tales of roasted babies, and spies transformed into clams and perched on the rim of the wigwam's smoke hole. Today at Annapolis Royal there

[15] See Tales 119–28.
[16] MacLean, 127. See also JR, XXX, 305, editor's note.
[17] Speck, JAFL, 48:17.
[18] JR, XXIV, 147.
[19] JR, XXXVIII, 179; II, 207.

Intertribal Orientation and Relations

is a tablet on an iron standard erected in 1938 and inscribed: "Site of fort built in 1712 by Mohawk Indians under Major Livingston, employed as allies of the British to intimidate the Micmacs."

WARFARE

Causes

My Micmac informants had comparatively little information about methods of warfare and gave none about the cause or declaration of intertribal conflicts. The accounts of Marc Lescarbot and of Fathers Biard and LeClercq are colored by their own culture, but on most points they agree. Wars were generally waged between groups of different language and in different territories, but trouble sometimes arose within a language group.[20]

No wish for land or property motivated war; the urge to show superior strength over another group or the desire to avenge an injury were the instigating forces. This is Lescarbot's opinion: "Our savages . . . make war . . . that they may say I have beaten you, or else for revenge in remembrance of some injury received, which is the greatest vice that I find in them, because they never forget injuries." And this is LeClercq's: "If we investigate the motives and the particular causes which have inspired these people in going to war, we find nothing other than a desire to avenge an injury they have received, or, more often, the ambition to make themselves feared and dreaded by foreign nations."[21]

War was sometimes waged by a tribe to avenge the wrong of a single member (Lescarbot), but on occasions when the tribe refused to go to war, the injured man, or a small group, might travel a great distance through the snow with only a little corn for food, and in the enemy country lie in ambush for ten to fifteen days to fall upon a victim or two, and return with the scalps that would prove to their tribe that they had the courage and ability to avenge insults (LeClercq).

Sometimes a deceased ancestor appeared in a dream to say that his spirit could not rest until the descendant had avenged a wrong done him in life. Father André Richard interpreted this (1661) as a demand for any human life and said that a group of warriors who had resolved

[20] JR, III, 87–97; II, 73.
[21] *History*, III, 263–64. *Gaspesia*, 265.

PART ONE *Tribal Life*

to carry out such a plan would brood on it all winter and set forth as soon as spring came.[22]

The decision for or against war was made in a tribal or an intertribal gathering. Three observers described these occasions. Lescarbot, at Port Royal in 1606–7, commented:

When they will make wars, the sagamos who hath most credit among them maketh them to know the cause why, the rendezvous, and time of assembly. Being arrived, he maketh long orations unto them upon the occasion which is offered and for to encourage them. At every proposition he demandeth their advice, and if they give consent they all make an exclamation, saying "Hau!" — if not, some Sagamos will begin to speak and say what he thinketh good of it: being both the one and the other well heard.

Father André Richard, at Gaspé in 1661 wrote:

When, therefore, some proposed in their Councils and feasts a hostile expedition, they were listened to by one party and opposed by another. But when the braves and Ruffians ridiculed those peacefully inclined, about thirty young men raised their hatchets in sign of the advocacy of war.

And Father LeClercq, at Gaspé in 1675–87, said:

War is never declared except by advice of the old men, who alone decide, in the last resort, the affairs of the country. They prescribe the order which must be followed in the execution of their military undertakings; they fix the day of departure; and they assemble the young warriors to the war feast. These come there with their usual arms, firmly resolved to fight valiantly for the good of the nation.

All early writers stressed the Micmac ideal of courage. "To have the name of Great Heart, *Meskir Kameramon*, among them is the crowning virtue," said Biard. Men told LeClercq that before starting on a raid they painted their faces red to conceal any changes of natural color that might reveal fear. To the French and British, however, Micmac and in fact all other Indians, because of their manner of fighting, seemed to be cowards and traitors. The use of darkness, surprise, and ambush were deceit and trickery: "they never place themselves in a line of battle."

Preparations

When war had been decreed, the preparations began: the war dance, the feast of dog meat, and various magic practices to ensure or to pre-

[22] JR, XLVII, 221.

Intertribal Orientation and Relations

dict success. According to 1911 informants, the warriors rubbed themselves with a medicine which protected them against injury. The old people would not tell what kind of medicine they employed; for if they had done so, everyone would know how to protect himself. The men, before going to battle, in order to get magic power, played *waltes* for two or three days. While the men were away the women who remained in camp spent their time playing *waltes*. If they did not keep active and bestir themselves, misfortune would befall the absent warriors. Accordingly, they played, continually moved about, and were lively and cheerful, as though there was nothing to worry about. If they should sit and be quiet and inactive, as though under a gloom, misfortune would befall the warriors.

At earlier periods in Micmac history women were more actively engaged in magical prediction. In the Port Royal region (1607) the warriors, before setting out, built and entered a stockade, and this was besieged by the women. The men tried to make sallies; the women endeavored to keep them inside. Men who were caught were beaten and stripped. The women's victory was a good sign for the war expedition; if the men escaped, evil would result (Lescarbot). On the Gaspé, the affair was even livelier but there it was the women who were stripped by members of their own sex:

While the warriors were plying their oars on the River Bacadensis, behold, two canoes issued as if from an ambuscade and started directly toward them to attack them, plunder them, and prevent their expedition. They were filled with young women, very active and well dressed, who came to convey an idea and present a picture of the battle these warriors were to fight with their enemies. They passed and repassed, turning and executing a thousand caracoles around these Shallops, trying to board them for the purpose of pillaging them, or, at least, of carrying off some little plunder. Bravely attacked, bravely defended. The men repulsed them, discharging their muskets frequently, rather to make a noise than to harm them. At length the young women withdrew, thoroughly tired, and without succeeding in plundering a single article. They returned to the bank where the other women, who were waiting for them, received them with shouting and hooting as if they had been vanquished enemies, pouncing upon them, stripping them of their new robes and of their ornaments, and giving them some old rags instead. One of these Amazons was ridiculed and mocked because she had not on her handsome robe and fine attire, having strongly suspected that she would be robbed of them. These women are very willing to be thus

213

PART ONE *Tribal Life*

despoiled for the sake of furnishing a happy omen of the victory which they desire for their relatives and friends.[23]

Informants in 1911–12 stated that frequently war canoe-parties tested one another's magic power by song. While one side danced and sang their magic song, the other responded with ha! ha! ha! and they, in turn, danced and sang while the others made response. They might be of equal power; if one was mightier than the other, the weaker side would be prevented from continuing the response of ha! ha! ha! Tales contain various instances of the magic power of song.

Omens at the start of a war expedition were matters of great concern. Gaspé warriors who, by 1661, were in the habit of embarking in the wooden boats purchased from French fishermen, by way of a small gangplank, would abandon their raid if in this process a man fell into the water or "wetted himself." Similarly if a boat ran aground or was unduly delayed, the war party turned back. A remembered promise to a deceased relative, even if recalled when the boats were well out in the Gulf of St. Lawrence, might cause a man to turn back; in this event all other relatives of the dead man in the party would also return to the settlement.

In an attempt to obtain, perhaps, all possible kinds of supernatural aid, a war party from Acadia passing Miscou in 1644 stopped at the mission of St. Charles and attended mass. (They stopped on the way back and held a scalp dance.)[24]

Solemn preparation for a war against the Maliseet in 1755 received detailed treatment by the Abbé Maillard. The Micmac were the aggressors. They had suffered insult, but the first move was made by them. A summary of Maillard's account follows.

First. They select a raiding party to ravage enemy country to destroy game and ruin beaver huts. They come home laden with game and furs. A meat feast is then held "for the whole nation"; while gorging meat, they all swear by sun, moon, and the name of their ancestors to do likewise to their enemies. If they have brought back a live beast from the enemy country, they cut its throat, drink the blood, and "even the boys with their teeth, tear the heart and entrails to pieces," and devour them, as symbolic of what will happen to the enemy at their hands.

[23] JR, XLVII, 223–35.
[24] JR, XXVIII, 37.

Intertribal Orientation and Relations

Second. The painting begins. Blood from the animal is added to a bark bowl full of the coarse vermillion found on the coast of Chibucto and on the west side of Acadia (N.S.). Old and young smear face, belly, and back. They trim their hair shorter, some on one side of the head, some on the other; some leave only a small tuft at the crown; others cut it entirely off on the right side; some leave on top of the forehead only one lock, and this falls back to the nape of the neck. Some bore their ears and insert the fine fir roots (*toobec*) commonly used as thread, and string shells on it.

Third. All the skins of animals from the enemy country are put in a pile. The oldest sagamo rises and asks, "What weather is it? Is the sky clear? Does it shine?" If so, he orders the young men to carry the heap to an eminence near the camp. He follows them and thus addresses the sun:

Be witness, thou great and beauteous luminary, of what we are this day going to do in the face of thy orb. If thou didst disapprove, thou wouldst this moment, hide thyself, to avoid affording the light of thy rays to all the action of this assembly. Thou didst exist of old and still existeth. Thou remainest forever as beauteous, as radiant, and as beneficent as when our forefathers first beheld thee. Thou wilt always be the same. The father of the day can never fail us, he who makes everything vegetate and without whom, cold, darkness, and horror would everywhere prevail. Thou knowest all the iniquitous procedure of our enemies toward us. What perfidy have they not used, what deceit have they not employed, whilst we had no room to distrust them? There are not more than five, six, seven, eight moons revolved since we left the principal amongst our daughters with them, in order thereby to form the most durable alliance with them (for, in short, we and they are the same thing as to our being constituted, and blood), and yet we have seen them look on these girls of the most distinguished rank *kayhecpidetchque*, as mere playthings of them, an amusement, a pastime put by us into their hands to afford them quick and easy consolation for the fatal blow we had given them in the preceding war. . . . Beautiful, all seeing, all penetrating luminary, without whose whole influence the mind of man has neither efficacy nor vigor, thou has seen in what a pitch . . . that nation has carried its insolence towards our principal maidens. Our resentment would not have been so extreme in respect of the girls of common birth. But here we are wounded in a point there is no passing over. Beauteous luminary! Who are thyself so regular in thy course and in the wise distribution thou makes in thy light and in the morning and in the evening, wouldst thou not have us imitate thee? . . . There are certain places where thy influence does not suffer itself to be felt . . .

PART ONE *Tribal Life*

But as for us, we are thy children; for we can know no origin but that thy rays have given us, when first marrying efficaciously, and the earth we inhabit, they impregnated its womb, and caused us to grow out of it like herbs in the field, and the trees in the forest, of which thou art equally the common father. To imitate these, then, we cannot do better than no longer to countenance and cherish those, who have proved themselves unworthy. . . . They shall dearly pay for the wrong they have done us. They have not, it is true, deprived us of the means of hunting . . . they have not cut off the free passage of our canoes . . . but they have done worse; they have supposed in us a tameness of sentiments which does not, nor cannot, exist in us. They have defloured [*sic*] our maidens in wantonness and lightly sent them back to us. This is just motive which cries out for vengeance. Sun, be thou favorable to us in this point, as thou art in that of our hunting. . . . Be propitious to us, that we may not fail to discover the ambushes that may be laid for us; that we may not be surprised unawares in our cabins, or elsewhere and, finally, that we may not fall into the hands of our enemies. Grant them no chance against us, for they deserve none. Behold our skins and their beasts now a burnt-offering to thee. Accept it, as if the firebrand I hold in my hands, and now set on the pile, was lighted immediately by thy rays, instead of our domestic fire.

He sets fire to the pile of skins. All listen to the invocation "with a kind of religious terror, and in profound silence."

Fourth. As soon as the pile blazes, all shout and give war cries and curses. Some vow so and so many skins to be burned here to the sun if they should kill a specified enemy. They throw stones into the fire and take out the best pieces to fasten on sticks, slit at one end, and they tie the stone in the cleft with fir thread; these are to split the enemies' skulls. Long poles are made, fitted with pointed elk-bone, edged on both sides. Arrows are made at the same time, and are pointed with bone. The wood for the arrow shafts and also the gut for the bow, must be dried in the "mysterious" fire. (Maillard adds that he is describing what happened earlier than 1755, "before European goods were common.")

Fifth. Now enter the women, who "come like so many furies," to howl and dance around the fire. Their rage turns against the men. They utter threats that for those who bring back no scalps there will be no "lawful pleasures," and their daughters will be given only to good fighters. The men consult together and order the women to withdraw, promising them plenty of prisoners to torture.

Sixth. Messengers are sent to declare war on the enemy. They go to

Intertribal Orientation and Relations

the largest village. They speak to no one on the way. Arrived at the village, they strike the earth with their hatchets, as a signal of hostility, shoot two arrows into the village, and leave hastily. They carry home some indubitable proof that they actually reached the enemy country.

Seventh. Each side now holds its councils about fortifications, plans of attack, and so forth. There is great display of eloquence. A favorite strategem is to hide on the outskirts of the enemy territory and give animal cries that might draw the young men into an ambush. An ambush in a narrow defile where the enemy must pass to hunt is sought; sometimes in such spot the two parties almost completely destroy each other.

Eighth. In the course of the torture that follows, if prisoners were taken, there is usually cannibalism; at least some limbs of prisoners are eaten and their blood is drunk.

It is now some time since our Micmakis especially are no longer in the taste of exercising such acts of barbarity. I have yet lately seen amongst them some remains of that spirit. I am now only speaking, upon my knowledge, of the Micmakis and the Mariquects, who, though different in language, have the same customs and manners, and are of the same way of thinking and acting.[25]

Methods

Micmac informants in 1911–12 knew that shields were carried in war. John Tenass, at Red Bank on the Miramichi, explained a series of pits on the south bank as holes where men and women of the settlement formerly hid and watched their enemies on the north side of the river. They had to be watched night and day; the enemy crossed in canoes or swam, and there was always fighting.

Vetromile asserted that the Micmac tracked enemies by using their powerful sense of smell. His example, of a Micmac smelling out a bottle of brandy in the house of a Nova Scotia Frenchman who had told him the cupboard was bare, is not the best evidence. The only possible reference in my notes is the somewhat scatalogical account of discovering the first French spoor.[26]

A more formal type of battle than the customary sneak raid was described by a 1911 informant: Fighting would, at a given signal, stop; or before beginning the fight both sides would agree to stop when the

[25] *Customs and Manners*, 18–33.
[26] Vetromile, 76. See Tale 130.

PART ONE *Tribal Life*

sun reached a certain place in the heavens. Hands were clapped loudly for the beginning and for the end of the fight. This signal was given by the *ä'kusitc*, the chief's assistant. "If you see a wild Indian in the woods today and clap your hands," said an informant, "he will suddenly disappear into the ground." None of the recorded stories refers to this custom.

Return of the Warriors

After the fight had ended, the 1911 account continues, the victors set out for home bearing "the glorious mementoes of their valour and spirit." Each man wore hanging from his neck a knife ready to make incisions in the head of an enemy and remove the scalp. As mentioned above, an informant said he had seen in Cape Breton the dried head and face of an Ottawa man who had been captured by a Micmac in a war between the two tribes. He said it was kept for the young men to see, as a model of the scalping of an enemy. A man would take it, sing about how he had fought, captured, and overcome his enemy, and so on, after which he would hand it to another, who would do the same.

In the early seventeenth century, Lescarbot said that captives' heads were carried as trophies, and that on any occasion dancers who had heads or arms of their enemies wore them around their necks and sometimes bit them.[27]

When the canoes of returning heroes came in sight, the women rushed to the shore to seize the scalps. LeClercq wrote of the Gaspé women:

They even throw themselves in blind haste into the water in order to receive them, and plunge into the river or the sea every time the warriors make their hues and cries of joy. These cries indicate the number of the enemies they have killed outright, and of the prisoners whom they are bringing to make suffer the usual torments and tortures.[28]

A party of Acadian Micmac returning from a fight with Montagnais stopped to show their prowess to a Micmac band at Nipisiguit.

They threw on the shore at landing, the scalps of the poor massacred people, and at the same time spread joy throughout the cabins. The women vied with one another who should first seize these Trophies, and who should sing and dance the best. Neither rain nor wind could stop them, from morning to night. It is strange that this constant and

[27] *History*, III, 181–84.
[28] *Gaspesia*, 265–66.

Intertribal Orientation and Relations

continued dancing and singing for several days did not tire and weary them. But a false alarm, and the rumor that the enemy had appeared, interrupted their rejoicing, threw them into fear and apprehension of falling into the hands of the Hiroquois, and made them think of flight. They all withdrew to Miskou, where for a long time they continued their baleful songs to the cadence of the waving scalps.[29]

The special treatment of a man who had gone on a solitary raid and returned with an enemy's head was described by Lescarbot:

They make great feasts, dances, and songs for many days; and, whilst these things be in doing, they strip the conqueror and give him but some bad rag to cover himself withal. But at the end of eight days or there about, after the feast every one doth present himself with some thing, to honour him for his valour.[30]

Captives and Slaves

There are many accounts of return with war captives: Eskimo, Montagnais, Penobscot, and — in folktales — English. In the raid on the Montagnais, mentioned above, thirteen or fourteen prisoners were taken, most of whom were children. Although some have said that Micmac never tortured prisoners, there is abundant evidence to the contrary, including statements made in 1911–12 and in 1950 by my informants. Burning at the stake, they said, was not practiced. Instead, the captives brought back to the home settlement were tied to trees; the women danced around them, singing, and slashed them with knives until death put an end to their misery.[31]

A Micmac family in 1689 traveled from Nova Scotia to Meductic, on the St. John River, to get a chance to torture an English captive because, some time before, a son had been killed in a fight with the British.[32] Even Lescarbot, who stated that captive warriors were put to death without torture, recorded that prisoners who attempted to escape or who aided others to do so were executed. In the instance he described, a Penobscot woman who, after stealing a tinderbox and hatchet from the headman's wigwam, had helped a fellow tribesman to escape, was ordered to be put to death by members of her own sex. A young maid of eighteen years of age, plump and fair, gave her the first knife stroke

[29] JR, XXXII, 33–37.
[30] History, III, 162.
[31] For the Captive Song, see Chapter XII.
[32] Giles, 84.

PART ONE *Tribal Life*

in the throat. Two other young girls followed; the last of these, daughter of the chief, gave the death blow.³³

In 1661 Jesuit fathers at the Gaspé mission witnessed an inglorious return from Montagnais territory with a single little captive:

When they were yet at a considerable distance from their proposed landing-place, they indulged in a bit of cruel barbarism toward their poor little prisoner, throwing him into the water, wounded as he was in various places. At the same time they threw in the scalps they had taken, surrendering to plunder all the spoils they had captured from their pretended foes. Forthwith most of the Savages, both men and women, plunged in and swam, the women straight toward the floating scalps, and the men toward the little boy, who was drowning. The women, after seizing the scalps, wished to snatch the little prisoner from the men, and the poor child found himself pulled and torn about like a victim fallen into the clutches of wolves or lions; but finally, after much altercation, he was adjudged and given to the Captain's wife. She, wishing to show that she had courage as well as her husband, and that she could witness human bloodshed without shrinking and without weakness, drew a large knife from her bosom and plunged it with inhuman cruelty into the arm of that child, — half-dead as he already was, both from the wounds received in the encounter, and from the cruelty with which he had been treated in the water. Yet he was forced to sing as he beheld his own blood, which drew from him neither tear nor cry. The training which parents give their children to display courage in such circumstances and the noise and din made by those Barbarians, cause such a stupefaction of their prisoners' senses that even the youngest are not wanting in the manifestation of fortitude.³⁴

Micmac now deny that any of their captives were used as slaves or were absorbed into the tribe. The evidence, however, is otherwise. Lescarbot wrote that captive women and children of Algonkin tribes from New England were "kept as prisoners to serve them." Eskimo in 1657 were taken as slaves to Cape Breton, where one was ransomed by the French.³⁵

Moreover, in Tale 124, an Englishman was kept as a slave in the chief's house, "where he worked all the time." This story was said to be approximately four hundred years old; and the incident was dated as pre-French.

The *Jesuit Relations* of 1645 described the treatment of "an Esqui-

³³ *History*, III, 216.
³⁴ JR, XLVII, 235–41.
³⁵ *History*, II, 215. JR, XLV, 65–69.

Intertribal Orientation and Relations

mau by nation, taken in war," who "served as a menial to a family of Savages."

This poor captive falls sick in his master's cabin, near our new settlement, and is reduced to such extremity that he resembled a skeleton rather than a living man; the bones had already pierced the skin, in some parts of his body. And, for climax of his misfortune, some one of those whom he had fed, for the space of several years, by his toils in the chase, had, with a cruel compassion, prepared a rope to take from him what remained of his life.[36]

PEACE

Tale 127 describes the symbolic close of hostilities between Micmac and European settlers with the burial of weapons in a hole four feet deep. Similarly, the traveler Dièreville in 1710 said it was the custom at the conclusion of a war to bury the hatchet in the deepest hole that could be dug.[37]

The following account, written at Miscou in 1646, describes a peace concluded there between "the Betsiamites, who inhabit the lands of the North side, 60 leagues below Tadoussac, and the Savages of our coasts and those of Acadia, who bore each other a mortal hatred."

This peace was concluded at the beginning of the month of July, at Isle Persée [Percé] where by good fortune I chanced to be . . . After these good Christians had satisfied their devotion, they prepared themselves to treat of peace more by action than by words. The Captain of the Savages of our coasts, together with Ignace Onandagareau, loads a young man with a bag of porcelain [wampum]; two others carry on their shoulders two dozen new blankets; others, thirteen fine arquebuses, powder, lead, and some javelins longer and broader than usual. Then they had everything carried into a great cabin, where many Savages — Montagnais, Algonquins, three of the nation of Sorcerers [Nipissings] and two Betsiamites were assembled. The Captain of our coasts takes the floor in the name of the captains of Acadia, and of him of the Bay of Rigibouctou [Richibuctou] his kinsman, from whom he says he has his commission to treat for peace; they assert that they all have banished from their hearts the former enmity, in confirmation whereof they offered all these presents to testify their kind affection. Simeon Boyer, who served as interpreter to the Betsiamites, answered that they accepted the presents, that they would be for the future only one heart; then he caused to be brought a goodly number of bundles of

[36] JR, XXX, 133, 135.
[37] Dièreville, 172.

PART ONE *Tribal Life*

beaver skins, of which he made a gift. The rest of the day, and several others following, were spent in dances and feasts.[38]

ALLIANCE AND CONFEDERACY

Not all Micmac warfare was carried on by them alone, nor was peace maintained without formal, although generally unstable, alliances. For the most part this side of tribal life has dropped out of memory; informants added little or nothing to the subject.

Father Biard, in 1616, spoke of assemblies of local groups called together in crises, and of occasional alliances extending outside the tribe:

Now in these assemblies, if there is some news of importance, as that their neighbors wish to make war upon them, or that they have killed some one, or that they must renew the alliance, etc., then messengers fly from all parts to make up the more general assembly, that they may avail themselves of all the confederates, which they call *Ricmanen*, who are generally those of the same language. Nevertheless the confederation often extends farther than the language does, and war sometimes arises against those who have the same language. In these assemblies so general, they resolve upon peace, truce, war, or nothing at all, as often happens in the councils where there are several chiefs without order and subordination, whence they frequently depart more confused and disunited than when they came.[39]

Relying proudly on their own courage whenever possible, the Micmac summoned their allies only in dire need. "Nevertheless," said LeClercq, "they ask for auxiliary troops from their allies if they cannot themselves settle their quarrels; and they send ambassadors with collars of wampum, to invite them to take up the hatchet against another nation." [40]

The past existence and function of wampum was well known in 1911, but I saw none. It is called *ankuwamk*, "meeting," as contrasted with the separation involved in fighting. The word also indicates splicing, for example, splicing wood. Dièreville was probably referring to wampum when he wrote: "They make themselves understood by means of little pieces of wood arranged in different ways. They make Necklaces of these little sticks, which serve to declare war or to sue for peace, and they are sent to the tribes with which they are at variance." [41]

Perhaps in Biard's day the messengers bearing the wampum actually

[38] JR, XXX, 139-41.
[39] JR, III, 87-97.
[40] *Gaspesia*, 269.
[41] P. 171.

Intertribal Orientation and Relations

"flew" from one group to another, but speed was not the Indian custom where ceremony must smooth a path always potentially hostile. The procedure described in a Passamaquoddy text, which accords with the accounts of other ceremonial visits (see Chapter XI) was probably followed whenever time allowed. The visit of Passamaquoddy messengers to the Micmac on the occasion of the death of a Passamaquoddy chief evidently dated from the days of the Wabanaki Confederacy when a tribe must consult with others about the choice of a new headman.[42]

Alliances between these Algonkin-speaking neighbors in historic times antedated the Wabanaki Confederacy. As early as the end of the seventeenth century "the Souriquois, the Abenoquis, and the Malecites" were joined to furnish mutual aid in war against the English colonists.[43] In 1847 Gesner stated: "the Chiefs and Delegates of the Penobscots, Micmacs, and Melicetes hold a council annually at Point Pleasant, on the St. Croix, where they renew their friendship and establish regulations for the public weal. Each tribe has laws peculiar to itself, and the measures adopted by the Grand Council prevent collision in hunting and fishing."

This period was toward the end of the Wabanaki Confederacy which was created a century earlier as an outgrowth, Speck said, of the organizing tendency of the Iroquois. Oldtown, on the Penobscot, was the capital of the eastern branch. In historic times the Confederacy included only Penobscot, Passamaquoddy, Maliseet, and Micmac. All these tribes had suffered at the hands of the Mohawks, who seemed to be trying to force them to join the Iroquois League.[44] To these eastern Algonkins, however, the only motive for confederation was protection against Mohawk cruelty. The Ottawa acted as arbiters between the two warring groups, and an alliance was formed between the Wabanaki, headed by Penobscot, and the Mohawk at Caughnawaga and Oka. Regular meetings were held at Caughnawaga.

Delegates were sent, and symbolic ceremonies were held. These meetings led to wide diffusion of Iroquois culture, including the mnemonic use of wampum, and the election of chiefs. It was perhaps then

[42] John Dyneley Prince, "Passamaquoddy Texts," *Publications of the American Ethnological Society*, 10:11–15 (1921).
[43] Ferland, I, 66. Quoted in JR, XII, 274.
[44] "The Eastern Algonkian Wabanaki Confederacy," AA, 17:492–508 (1915). Rand (Legends, xxxi) wrote in 1850 that a council of ten tribes "extending from Cape Breton to Western Canada" held periodic meetings which the Micmac seemed to consider as important as they had ever been.

PART ONE *Tribal Life*

that they developed the means of communication with fellow tribesmen as well as with Europeans which Gamaliel Smethurst noted among Miramichi Micmac in 1761:

A look or a gesture is often sufficient intimation of their thoughts. They were very shrewd in their remarks, and significant in their signs. When they wanted to inform me that the French and them were in one interest, they said they were *so*, (pointing the same way with the forefingers of their right and left hands, and holding them parallel); and when, that the English and Indians were in opposite interests, this they described by crossing their forefingers. Their chief made almost a circle with his forefinger and thumb, and pointing at the end of his forefinger, said there was Quebec, the middle joint of his finger was Montreal, the joint next the hand was Boston, the middle joint of the thumb was Halifax, the interval betwixt his finger and thumb was Pookmoosh [Pokemouche], so that the Indians would soon be surrounded, which he signified by closing his finger and thumb.[45]

According to tradition, the Ottawa presided at Confederacy meetings. If a tribe failed to send a delegate to the triennial gathering at Caughnawaga, at the next session at which one appeared his head would be cut off and set up on a pole in front of the council house — not a very strong inducement to be a delinquent's successor. Mohawk guarded the central council fire.

All transactions were recorded by means of wampum belts and strings in conventional designs, to be held in the delegate's hand while he reported from the Confederacy to his home council. Hanging up these wampum belts at each grand council meeting was called "adding brands to the fire."

The Wabanaki Confederacy died long ago. Speck found no remembrance of it at Caughnawaga. In 1915 the Penobscot still remembered it, and a few Micmac still played a part without function. Even this Micmac survival was slight and isolated. Within the Confederacy the tribe had been the weakest and the newest member, called "the younger brothers," a position symbolized in the Caughnawaga meetings by putting the oldest Micmac present on a cradleboard and keeping him there, undressed, tied, and fed like a baby, for an entire day.[46] Speck said the strength of the Confederacy among Micmac lessened from west to east, but in 1915 he found it alive, seventy-five years after active functioning had ceased elsewhere, only in Nova Scotia and Cape Breton,

[45] P. 372.
[46] Nicolar, 139.

Intertribal Orientation and Relations

where the office of Grand Chief still existed. Grand Chief John Denys explained to Speck: "From the earliest times Mohawk warred against Micmac . . . At the close of the first overtures for peace a belt of wampum was sent by the Mohawk to the Micmac chief, symbolizing their new relationship. Regularly till 1872 delegates went from Eskasoni to Caughnawaga. A new belt was always brought back. At the Micmac national reunion on St. Anne's Day the chief now calls the council together, wampum belts are shown, and there are accompanying speeches. This ceremony takes an entire day."

Speck said the office of Grand Chief was hereditary in the Denys family; but Parsons' informants in 1923 denied this. In that year John Denys, of Eskasoni, was succeeded by Gabriel Sylliboy of Whycocomagh, also in Cape Breton. The Grand Chief was chosen by the chiefs in annual meeting at Chapel Island. The priest installed the chief and presented him with the insignia of office, saying, "Use your people like children."[47] A few Micmac from Nova Scotia, and the chief and his wife from Prince Edward Island, came to this "national reunion"; all others were from Cape Breton. Attendance was said to be decreasing year by year.

[47] Parsons, JAFL, 39:472-73 (1926).

CHAPTER XIV

Family, Kin, and Marriage

THE basic social group was the band made up of a few related families who wandered through the woods in winter in search of game, often in single family units, and returned each spring to the same neighborhood on the shore of river or bay.

WIGWAM LIFE

Within the wigwam each person was assigned his place according to age, sex, and family role. The wigwam of a young couple had a single entrance until the birth of a child. The wigwam of a single family is

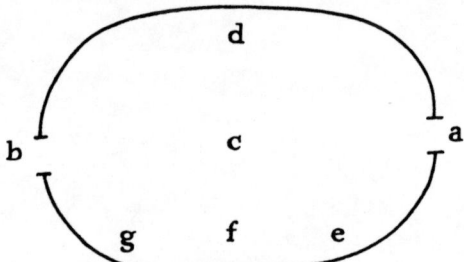

43. The social arrangement of wigwam life. *a.* Hunters' entrance. *b.* Girls' entrance. *c.* Fire. *d.* Boys' place. *e.* Girls' place. *f.* Parents' place. *g.* Grandparents' place.

represented in illustration 43. Some wigwams were circular, others eliptical, with the entrance at either end, *a* or *b*. The entrance at *b*, the girls' entrance, is called *ebidesawe*; that at *a*, the hunters' entrance, *aktategiwimwe*. Grandparents were assigned a place between the girls' entrance and the place occupied by the father and the mother. Only males

226

Family, Kin, and Marriage

44. A Micmac family group in Nova Scotia.

used the hunters' entrance. Father and grandfather might enter or leave by the girls' entrance. A widow might use either entrance. A girl who left or entered by the wrong opening would at once be given in marriage; she was "spoiled," no longer a girl, and her parents must find a husband for her.[1]

Often there were two, and sometimes three, families in a large wigwam, which might be ten or twelve feet in diameter. The same rules in regard to the use of entrances applied as when a single family occupied the wigwam. At such times, however, the children frequently slept with their parents, each family thus having a place to itself. (Illustration 44 shows a Nova Scotia family in 1912.)

The wife assigned each person to his proper place. It was the husband's duty to keep up the fire during the night. Man and wife slept back to back.[2] They ate from one plate, the children from another. (In the tales, however, girls eat from one plate, boys from another; this was probably the old custom.)

Within the crowded space etiquette was taught to children and main-

[1] There were further taboos on use of entrance at the holding of a bear ceremony or on the occasion of a death. See pp. 108 and 263.

[2] Rand (*Legends*, 24) says they slept *witkusoodijik* – "heads and points, i.e., the woman's head is at her husband's feet."

PART ONE *Tribal Life*

tained by adults. The father kept a long stick beside him with which to stir the fire or strike his son's foot if a boy stretched his leg out. Boys who slept with legs outstretched would not become swift runners. Under no circumstances would a woman step over the legs or the feet of a male. This restriction is observed today. No reason for it could be obtained except "it is not nice for a woman to step over a man." Informants said that nothing would befall a violator of the rule or the man so treated, but they insisted it never happened, except that a woman within her own wigwam might step over her son.

Sister and brother kept apart from one another and one did not converse with the other.

Custom decreed that a man might not enter the wigwam of another if the husband was away; and a woman might not enter another wigwam if the mistress was not in.

The above information given in 1911 is confirmed at a few points by earlier observers. In Father LeClercq's day, the seating arrangement within a wigwam was as follows:

The place of the head of the family is on the right. He yields it sometimes, as an honour and courtesy to strangers, whom he even invites to stop with him, and to repose upon certain skins of bears, of moose, of seal, or upon some fine robes of beaver, which these Indians use as if they were Turkey carpets. The women occupy always the first places near the door, in order to be all ready to obey, and to serve promptly when they are ordered.[3]

Two hundred years later, a Nova Scotian, Duncan Campbell, wrote:

In the centre is the fire. On each side is what is called the *kamigwom*, where sit, on the one [side] the master and mistress, and on the other the old or young people. The wife has her place next the door, and by her side sits her lord. In no case does the wife sit above the husband. Towards the back part of the wigwam is the place of honor. They say to a stranger that is made welcome — "*Kutakumagual upchalase*," "Come up to the back part of the wigwam." The men sit crosslegged, in Oriental fashion, the women with their feet twisted round to one side, and the young men of the family, with their feet extended, in front. The etiquette observed in this limited domicile is as exact and rigid as in more polished society. When a neighbour comes to the wigwam at night he never presumes to enter without ceremony.[4]

The strict etiquette compulsory between brother and sister greatly

[3] *Gaspesia*, 102.
[4] Pp. 18–19.

Family, Kin, and Marriage

interested Dièreville. A brother, he said, never spoke an immodest word in his sister's hearing or contradicted anything she said. Rather than break wind in her presence he would have burst. Dièreville then repeated what he called a "characteristic incident" which moved him to poetry. A girl saw on the forehead of her brother as he entered the wigwam a smear of his excrement:

> She saw the stain, with horror shuddering,
> Nor could she overcome her quick despair,
> And, that excessive modesty from shame
> Might suffer less, she ran to hang herself.[5]

One suspects that this "characteristic incident" is a modification of the brother-sister incest folktale motive, in which the sister, by putting soot on her nocturnal lover, later discovers that he is her brother. This is a prominent motive in Eskimo folklore; and Chippewa have a variant of it.

The role of husband and wife in making a winter camp was described by LeClercq:

It is the business of the head of the family, exclusively over all others, to give orders that camp be made where he pleases, and that it be broken when he wishes. That is why, on the eve of departure, he goes in person to trace the road which is to be taken, and to choose a place suitable and ample for the encampment. From this place he removes all the useless wood, and cuts off the branches which could be in the way. He smoothes and opens out a road to make it easy for the women to drag over the snow on their toboggans, the trifle of furniture and of luggage which comprises their housekeeping outfit. He marks out, also all by himself, the plan of the wigwam, and throws out the snow with his snowshoes until he has reached the ground, which he flattens and chops out in pieces until he has removed all the frozen part, so that all of the people who compose his family may lodge in the greatest possible comfort. This done, he then cuts as many poles as he considers suitable,[6] and plants them in a circle around the border of the hollow which he has made in the earth and the snow — always in such a manner, however, that the upper ends come together in a point, as with tents or belfrys. When this is finished, he makes preparations for hunting, from which he does not return until the wigwam has been completely put in order by the women, to whom he commits the care thereof during his absence, after assigning to each one her particular duty. Thus some of the women go to collect branches of fir, and then they

[5] P. 164.
[6] Biard, at Port Royal, said women always cut the poles. JR, III, 77.

place the barks upon the poles: others fetch dry wood to make the fire: others carry water for boiling in the kettle, in order to have the supper ready when the men return from the hunt. The wife of the head of the family, in the capacity of mistress, selects the most tender and most slender of the branches of fir for the purpose of covering all the margin inside the wigwam, leaving the middle free to serve as a common meeting-place. She then fits and adjusts the larger and rougher of the branches to the height of the snow, and these form a kind of little wall. The effect is such that this little building seems much more like a camp made in the spring than one made in winter, because of the pleasing greenness which the fir keeps for a long time without withering.[7]

A hundred and fifty pages later LeClercq drew a less fragrant picture:

They are filthy and vile in their wigwams, of which the approaches are filled with excrements, feathers, chips, shreds of skins, and very often with entrails of the animals or the fishes which they take in hunting or fishing. In their eating they wash their meat only very superficially before putting it upon the fire, and they never clean the kettle except the first time that they use it. Their clothes are all filthy, both outside and inside, and soaked with oil and grease, of which the stink often produces sickness of the stomach. They hunt for vermin before everybody, without turning aside even a little. They make it walk for fun upon their hands, and they eat it as if it were something good. They find the use of our handkerchiefs ridiculous; they mock at us and say that it is placing excrements in our pockets. Finally, however calm it may be outside of the wigwam, there always prevails inside a very inconvenient wind, since these Indians let it go very freely, especially when they have eaten much moose, of which one can say *Corruptio optimi pessima*.[8]

RELATIONSHIP AND SOCIAL STATUS

Terms of Relationship

So far as could be ascertained in 1911, the Micmac have a fairly simple system of kinship terms, differing little from our own system. The terms do not distinguish between maternal and paternal kin. On the other hand, they carry certain age distinctions which our terms lack, connotations of married or of unmarried, and a term connoting all married siblings. Direct descendants and ancestors are designated for four generations — to the great-great-grandparent and the great-great-grandchild.

[7] *Gaspesia*, 100–2.
[8] *Ibid.*, 253.

Family, Kin, and Marriage

Some single terms connote persons for which we have separate designations. Thus, in each of the following pairs, one term, not two, is employed: grandfather and stepfather; grandmother and stepmother; grandchild and stepchild. There is a separate designation for an adopted child — used, probably, only in reference and not in address. In 1953 the distinctions made in speech were, in Quebec and New Brunswick, identical with those in English, though spoken in Micmac.[9]

The terms are as follows:

Father, *nutc*. (*My* is implied for each recorded term.)
Mother, *nkitc*.
Mother's father, father's father, *niskomitc*. (Also stepfather, according to Parsons.)
Great-grandfather (paternal or maternal), *pidawiniskamitc*.
Great-grandmother (paternal or maternal), *pidawinugamitc* (*pi'dawi*, going through).
Great-great-grandfather, *uksimikskamitc*.
Great-great-grandmother, *uksigunamitc* (*uksi*, large, big, great).
Mother's mother, father's mother, stepmother, *migamitc*.
Daughter, *untus*.
Son, *unkwis*.
Granddaughter, stepdaughter, stepson, grandson, *midjitc*.
Great-grandaughter, great-grandson, *pidawinudjitc*.
Great-great-granddaughter, great-great-grandson, *sistuwepidawinudjitc* (*sistuwe*, third).
Siblings, married, *wedjigimkudjiek*.
Sisters, *amsitnanabemk*.
Sister, married, *widjigudiek*, or *ebit*.
Older sister, unmarried, *namisk*.
Older sister, married, *namisktepkatka*.
Younger sister, married, *unkwedjitcebides*.
Younger sister, unmarried, *unkwedjitc*.
Brother, *widjigudiek*. (No distinction is made between married and unmarried brothers.)
Older brother, *nsisk*.
Younger brother, *untciganumk*.
Father's or mother's older or younger sister, *msowis*.
Cousin (maternal or paternal), *nogama*.
Father-in-law, *ntciltc*.
Mother-in-law, *ntagwidjitc*.
Brother-in-law, *namaktum*.
Sister-in-law, *nilumus*.

[9] For kinship terms used in Cape Breton, see Parsons in JAFL, 39:475–77 (1926).

PART ONE *Tribal Life*

Adopted child, "raising-up child," *nigwena delnutcuwatcl.*
Husband, *tcinamum.* (Rand gives *wetabiteme,* "one who has a wife.")
Wife, *ntebidem.*
Two men whose wives are sisters, *wechoosteek* (Rand).

The following are used in a descriptive sense (as, for example, when we say father's brother's son, instead of nephew):

Father's sister, *nutcwidjigadedidal.*
Father's older sister, *nutcumisal.*
Father's younger sister, *nutckwedjidjal.*
Uncle, *nkelomoksis* (1950).
Father's brother, *nutcwidjigadedidal.*
Father's older brother, *nutcuksisal.*
Father's younger brother, *nutcuktciganamal.*
Mother's older brother, *unkitcuksisal.*
Older brother, *unsiswidjigadididal.*
Younger brother, *unkitcuktciganamal.*
Brothers and sisters, *amsitwidjigadoltidjik.*
Older sister, *amkitcumisal.*
Younger sister, *amkitcukwedjidal.*

Rand gives mother's sister, *mulis;* father's sister, *nsoogwis;* mother, *nkech;* mother-in-law, *nchugweejich;* father, *nooch;* father-in-law, *nchilch;* uncle, *nkulamooksis.*

No distinction, Rand says in his *Dictionary,* is made between paternal and maternal uncle. For nephew he gives *nulooks;* for niece, *nsum,* which is applicable to the "daughter of my brother or sister, or my first cousin, or second cousin, or third cousin, etc. etc., as far as the line can be traced." Grandmother is *noogumich;* grandfather, *nikskamich;* grandchild, *moojeech;* brother, *wijegideek cheemum;* a brother older than the speaker, *nsees.* A woman calls her brother-in-law *melumoos;* a man calls his brother-in-law *mumaktem;* a man calls his wife's brother-in-law *mechoos.* Sister is either *mumees* [male speaking?] or *mkwajeech* [female speaking?]; sister-in-law (male speaking) is *melumoos,* or (female speaking) *memaktem.* Son is *mkwis;* son-in-law, *mtloosook;* daughter, *mtoos;* daughter-in-law, *looswaaskw.*

In Lewis H. Morgan's *Systems of Consanguinity and Affinity of the Human Family* (1870), the following information is given on the authority of Rand:

My brother's son and daughter [and] . . . my sister's son and daugh-

Family, Kin, and Marriage

ter, Ego a male, are my nephew and niece. With Ego a female, they are my son and daughter. My father's brother is my little father. My father's brother's son and daughter are my brother and sister, elder or younger. My father's sister is my aunt. My mother's brother is my uncle. My mother's sister is my little mother. My mother's sister's son and daughter are my brother and sister, elder and younger. My grandfather's brother is my grandfather. The grandchildren of my brothers and sisters, and of my collateral brothers and sisters, are my grandchildren.

Morgan's account is not altogether consistent with that contained in Rand's *Dictionary*; it seems to be his own interpretation of data supplied by Rand.

Joking Relationships

In 1911, when ethnographers were just discovering the existence of the joking relationship as an institution, I did not inquire about it. At Burnt Church in 1950 informants said that a mild, informal relationship existed between two men. This applies only to a few men, and is not based on any specific relationship, such as in-law. In the instances cited reference to illicit sexual relations always occurred.

For example, a man will say to the one with whom he has this reciprocal relationship: "You were drunk last night and talked foolishly." Or, "I saw you last night walking with a woman not your wife." At the beginning of the interchange both probably laugh. Other examples are "You are an awful man. I was at your house and saw you going away with that widow." "You did see me?" "Yes, I did. I saw you going into the bushes with her." "Well, maybe; but if so, it was another woman." "Yes, I know it was another woman as well as that one." Both then laugh heartily. Joking friends like one another.

Age Status

Micmac have clearly defined terms for age levels. Many of these also connote sex. Young people at age seventeen are considered adults and make their own decisions. The earlier maturity of the girl, both physical and social, is recognized in defining the terms and in further explanation: "A girl of sixteen is a woman; lots of girls get married at sixteen. A boy of sixteen is just a child."

The following terms were used in 1950:

Newborn, *weskadjiniwit*.
Infant, to one year, *nudjiwadjitc*.

PART ONE *Tribal Life*

Child, under 9 years, *bidjawadjitc*.
Male child, *elbadutc*.
Female child, *ebidedjitc*.
Girl, about 10 to 16, *ebides*.
Boy, about 17 or 18, *elbadus*.
Young adult, female, *ebit*; male, *tcinum*.
A person 40–59, *akadibunad* ("middle" or "half").
Old man, about 60 or over, *kisigudjitc*.
Old woman, *kisiguwisku*.[10]

MARRIAGE

Micmac uniformly asserted that in the old days relations between the sexes were ideal: a boy and a girl never even spoke to one another; stable marriages were the rule; adultery was unknown. None of this applied in 1911.

To enforce the concept of a virginity so extreme that a word or even a glance could violate it was the threat of immediate marriage. If a boy spoke to a girl, and she responded, his parents would say, "That is your wife." If she responded to a boy's greeting, by saying, even "Good morning," or, "It's a nice day (*weligiskuk*)," her response signified acceptance of his implied offer of marriage. If the incident was reported to the girl's father, and he did not thereafter greet the boy as "son-in-law," the failure to do so signified his disapproval, and the contemplated marriage did not take place. Some informants said that after an expression of agreement between a boy and a girl refusal was never given.

Folktales of marriage (90–93) describe in oversimplified terms this type of meeting and subsequent—indeed, consequent—marriage; in one story, however (94), a young man is attracted by the adventurous spirit shown by a girl who had made a daring trip on snowshoes to his settlement, and persuades his chief to marry them, before consulting her father. When the father learns of the *fait accompli*, he remarks: "That was her time. It was right for her to get a husband then." The same tone of inevitable fate is expressed by father to son in another story: "When the time comes to find a wife, you cannot stop"; to which the narrator adds, "It is like death, you must obey."

The approximation of fact to fiction is clear in the stories of the marriages of two principal informants of 1911–12, both then over seventy years of age.

[10] Compare Parsons, JAFL, 39:479.

Family, Kin, and Marriage

John Newell's Marriage

"My home is in Cape Breton; that is, I was born there. When I was a young man I came here [Pictou Landing], intending to go to the States. Some old people here told me, 'You better not go! Perhaps you will be murdered, or something [bad] will happen to you. There is a young girl here without father or mother. You should marry her and stay here. She is a good girl and a good housekeeper.'

"When they said this, I told them, 'If that girl will agree, I will marry her.' Next day I met her. I said, 'Good morning.'

"'Good morning,' said she. 'Will you marry me?' I asked. 'I am a poor girl and have no home.' She went her way, and I went mine.

"Next day I saw her going to get water. I went to the well while she was filling her bucket. I had been watching her. 'It is a nice day,' I said. 'Yes,' she said. 'Did that old woman say anything to you?' I asked. 'Yes.' 'What did you tell her?' 'I told her I would marry you if you wished me to do so. But I have no home.' 'Neither have I,' said I, 'but we will have a home after we marry, and I will have some place to go to get my meals.' 'When will you be ready?' she asked. 'I shall not keep you waiting two or three years,' said I, 'I'll be ready tomorrow morning.' 'All right, I'll be ready for you and will wait for you at the house at seven o'clock.'

"That woman and I lived together for fifty years."

How Peter Ginnish Got His Wife

"My woman's man [wife's former husband] died in the winter. About a month later, my wife died. My present wife and I lived close to each other. We did not speak one word [about marriage] to one another until the next spring. One Sunday that spring I was alone and wishing I had a drink of fresh water. While I was at the gate, this woman came by. I said, 'I wish I had someone to bring me a drink of fresh water.' 'I will bring you some water,' she said. She brought the water and gave it to me. 'That is the finest water I have ever drunk,' I said, 'I wish I had someone to bring me water all the time.' 'I will bring water for you — all you want,' she said. 'Do not say anything about this to anyone,' I told her. Neither one of us told anyone about this until the following autumn, when we were married."

Love Story

This is the true story, told in 1953, of a marriage that began in 1903 and is still in force. When Mrs. Philip Muskrat was seventeen, her best

PART ONE *Tribal Life*

friend up river wrote to invite her to her wedding. Mrs. Muskrat had always promised she would come whenever her friend should marry. At a big dance the night before the wedding, she met Philip Muskrat, the prospective bridegroom. A man came up to her and said, "Mr. Muskrat wants to talk to you outside. The wedding is off."

She wouldn't go out and talk to him. He came to the house where she was staying and asked her to marry him. She said, "My father isn't here. He has to decide. I am too young."

She returned to her home reserve. Philip Muskrat, aged nineteen, followed her there and asked her father's permission. Her aunt (her father's sister) said, "You had better marry while you have the chance." Two weeks later they married.

Her girl friend never spoke to her again.

Choice

In a dozen autobiographical accounts of marriages which took place between 1890 and 1912, only one other woman named or implied mutual choice as a factor. Father, mother, or grandmother chose the husband or accepted the suitor for the girl, usually very young, who scarcely knew the man until the wedding day.[11]

In selecting these husbands the parent seemed to follow the old Micmac way as described by men in 1911–12. Wealth and social status were of little importance. Sometimes but not always in aboriginal times the son of a chief married the daughter of a chief. The very poorest man might marry a chief's daughter. LeClercq found this lack of self-interest in marriage true of his day also, and said that no dowry was asked or given.[12]

Only members of the biological family were forbidden intermarriage. A man might marry the sister of his mother, the sister of his father, or a sister-in-law. After a spouse died, no one was by custom or regulation his or her successor.

According to LeClercq it was permissible to marry the wife of one's deceased brother in order to produce children "of the same blood," if she had had no child by her former husband.

---

[11] The accounts given by women informants in this and the next chapter were recorded in 1950 and 1953 by RSW.

[12] *Gaspesia*, 237.

Family, Kin, and Marriage

Age at Marriage

Micmac informants in 1911–12 believed that in the old days a man at marriage was from thirty to forty years of age, and a woman about thirty. This late age was insisted on, they claimed, to keep down the population. No evidence seems to support this statement, which is made rather frequently by North American Indians.

In the eighteenth century, Maillard said, Micmac men of twenty to thirty years of age married girls just past puberty. Betrothal and matrilocal residence began about two years before the girl was mature. Because early marriage was discouraged, something had to be arranged for young men returning from war or hunting. Without the relaxation of sexual intercourse, it was believed that they would suffer severe pains in the loins. A woman divorced because of sterility might without scandal practice sexual promiscuity; if she rejected this way of life, she might even be forced to serve the young hunters and warriors.[13] Troubled by this situation, the Abbé wondered what could be done to get the boys married as soon as their voices changed. His distant successors, the French missionary priests, at least during the period 1890–1912, seem to have worked with parents on the converse of the problem: marrying off the girls while still virgins. Many girls between the ages of 12 and 15 married men from 45 to 59. In the same decades Maliseet girls were forced into similar marriages; this suggests other than tribal influence. One Micmac woman stated that her father talked over such a proposed marriage for her with the priest, who then came to her and said, "You are a good little girl, teaching catechism. The man is serving mass. You can make me a little acolyte." She was not quite 14; the man was 45, and she became his third wife. The child-wife custom, apparently a fusion of the aims of two cultures, Micmac and priestly, each seeking to keep a girl "unspoiled," died about the time of World War I. No old man's darling of the period helped to perpetuate it in her children's generation.

Tribal Marriage

In former days the tribe or a local division took an interest in marriages of the young people whom they wished to keep within their boundaries. The annual tribal meeting in the summer, precursor of St. Anne's Day, provided an opportunity for young people to see one another and, within

[13] *Customs and Manners*, 51–52.

PART ONE *Tribal Life*

the narrow limits of modesty, express a preference for one another under the eye of the host chief's special assistant, the *nudjialkatdegat ukcit maltewdj*, "Watcher of the Young People." John Newell, a native of Cape Breton, presumably the most conservative of Micmac culture areas, gave the following account as part of his description of the old celebration of St. Anne's Day.[14]

During the several days of feasting and games the boys and girls do not speak to one another. A local girl may long for one of the visiting boys. She has been seen turning her head toward him and laughing, and he has responded in the same manner. There are perhaps four or five such couples. When all of the visitors have embarked, the "Watcher of the Young People" goes to the home chief and tells him the names of the canoes (which is the same as the names of their "captains," the men in charge) in which are the boys or girls who have been looking in this manner at a local young person of the other sex.

Later, the "Watcher of the Young People" and the assistant chief go to the settlement of the returned guests to tell the chief of that place the names of these young people. Before they land, however, the same ceremonies of greeting must be performed that are customary when visitors arrive at a settlement. Canoes had already been sent from the settlement of the visitors, however, and these meet the canoes from the visited settlement about halfway between the two places. When they meet, the occupants give a whoop. The *muudumpkit*, the canoe captain, raises his paddle and gives a whoop, the signal for the others to join in.

When the canoes of the Watcher of the Young People and the assistant chief arrive, and people hear from them the news, the chief of the settlement puts aside a short stick for each girl named, and a long one for each boy. Sometimes the stick of a boy is colored as is the canoe in which he traveled, and that of a girl as are the beads which she wore. The chief then lays down as many short sticks as there are days intervening between that day and the day on which the people of the two settlements will again meet. (On the seventh day after this the engaged couple eat no breakfast; and thereafter, until the wedding, every seventh day is for them a fast day.) When the chief has finished laying down the sticks, the canoe starts back home with the news. Three or four days later the crew returns again with further news to the settlement.

[14] At Burnt Church, N.B., marriages were arranged on St. Anne's Day at least as late as 1835. Levinge, 39.

Family, Kin, and Marriage

Soon the people of the two settlements meet again. The one with the lesser number of girls to be married visits the one with the greater number. The marriages take place in the wigwam of the chief, which is always a large one. The chief marries the couples the day after they arrive. The home chief always presides at the wedding of a girl who comes from another settlement.[15] He delivers to the visitors an address of welcome, and gives to the couple he marries advice about living together peacefully and without quarreling. After the wedding, there is a marriage dance and song. Each boy takes his wife to his wigwam. He must live in his own settlement; the chief would not consent to his quitting it permanently.

Some informants, however, asserted that at marriage the boy went to live in the *udan*, or settlement, of the girl. At Lennox Island, P.E.I., it was said that formerly after marriage the boy went to the *udan* of his wife and lived with her parents until the birth of the first child; they then went to his village and lived with his father. Man and wife usually went to a wigwam of their own after the birth of the first child, although this custom was not invariably observed.

In the rare cases of extratribal marriage the man joined his wife's tribe.

The Wedding

The wedding celebration, as described in 1911–12, was mainly a feast held soon after the acceptance, given usually by the bride's parents. From time to time someone would rise, entertain with song and dance, and shout, "Matamaliahe!" Those who are about to start the dance shout "ha! ha! ha!" as a signal to begin it. Dancers respond to the song with "Ahe! Ahe!" and vary this with such pleasantries as *iksamamiek*! ("move ahead"); *wetskiulag*! ("night is coming"); or *atiginag*! ("keep busy"). Marriages often were held at St. Anne's Day; partly because it was the traditional gathering time, and partly because a priest was certain then to be on each reserve.

Polygyny

Informants in 1911 alleged that among co-wives, in the old days, there was little dissension, "because the husband was boss." The first wife was accorded better treatment than the others, who had to do most of the

[15] See Tales 94 and 128.

239

work, under the supervision of the first wife. In a dispute among co-wives, the husband would probably champion the first wife.

Polygyny was practiced by most chiefs; and others who could afford the luxury had two or three wives. A man might give a wife to a friend to relieve himself of the burden of support.

Micmac told early French visitors that extra women were needed in a chief's household to do the work involved in caring for the numerous retainers and guests, and to provide children who would strengthen the group through alliances.[16]

Quarrels among wives and among children of different mothers enlivened the scene. The Jesuit Fathers extolled the virtues of Membertou, the great chief who "even before his conversion never cared to have more than one living wife." Elsewhere they record his age at conversion as one hundred years.

Early Marriage Customs

No 1911 informant mentioned the marriage custom uniformly recorded in the seventeenth century: the year of residence between acceptance and marriage during which the young man had to work for the girl's father.[17]

A boy wishing to marry a girl approached her father and asked if he might enter his wigwam for the probationary year of work. If both the father and the girl disliked the suitor, refusal ended the affair. A girl was never forced to take a man she did not care for, and often a father would accept as son-in-law a man who pleased his daughter far more than he satisfied her parents.

Hence it is that the fathers and mothers of our Gaspesians leave to their children the entire liberty of choosing the person whom they think most adaptable to their dispositions, and most conformable to their affections, although the parents, nevertheless, always keep the right to indicate to them the one whom they think most likely to be most suitable for them. But in the end this matter turns out only as those wish who are to be married; and they can very well say that they do not marry for the sake of others, but for themselves alone.[18]

The next step was the offering of presents ("dogs, beavers, kettles,

[16] JR, II, 23, 79, 228–29; III, 101, 103.
[17] Lescarbot, *History*, III, 162–63; Biard, JR, III, 99; LeClercq, *Gaspesia*, 237, 259–62; Denys, II, 407–9; Maillard, *Customs and Manners*, 53–60.
[18] *Gaspesia*, 259–60.

Family, Kin, and Marriage

axes," etc.) and their acceptance by the future father-in-law, after which the young man returned home to say farewell to his parents for a year. During that year, he had to hunt and turn over all game and furs to the girl's father, thus showing that he was capable of supporting a family and also, by his behavior, that he was a pleasant person to live with.

The girl, for her part, also does her best with that which concerns the housekeeping, and devotes herself wholly, during this year, if the suit of the boy be pleasing to her, to making snowshoes, sewing canoes, preparing barks, dressing skins of moose or of beaver, drawing the sled — in a word, to doing everything which can give her the reputation of being a good housewife.[19]

Sex relations were strictly prohibited during the betrothal year and the prohibition, it seems, was generally observed. This period over, if the couple were congenial and the boy had been a good worker, the marriage feast took place. Lescarbot wrote of one young man whose choice of occupation did not please the girl's father. Bituani, a young Micmac, "finding good relish" in the kitchen of Monsieur de Monts, at Port Royal (1607), took service there, a job that did not impress the father of the girl whom he wished to marry. Consent was withheld on the grounds that loitering around a kitchen was not proof that he could support a family: Bituani should exercise himself a-hunting. Bituani obtained the girl; but her father took her away and kept her in custody until, after "a great quarrel" involving Monsieur de Monts and many of her father's friends, Bituani "goeth a-fishing, taketh great store of salmons, and the next day following, he came clothed with a fair new gown of beavers . . . bringing his wife with him as a triumph for the victory, having gotten her, as it were by dint of sword." [20]

The accepted husband must go hunting and provide meat for the marriage feast. Speeches, song, and dance accompanied the consumption of a meal "more or less magnificent according as he makes a hunt or fishery more or less successful." In the presence of the guests the girl was handed over to the boy as his wife. Even then, however, she could refuse; and "everybody is as content and satisfied as if the marriage had been accomplished, because, say they, one ought not to marry only to be unhappy the remainder of one's days" (LeClercq; Denys).

A more detailed account of the marriage probation at a later period

[19] *Ibid.*, 261.
[20] Lescarbot, *History*, II, 247.

PART ONE *Tribal Life*

(1751) was given by Maillard. When a young man wants to marry, his father or near relative selects a girl: "he rarely consults his fancy." After negotiations between both sets of parents; and a formal exhortation to the young man, the latter lights a calumet and enters the girl's wigwam. If she has no particular aversion to him, she asks for the calumet. In some regions, but not at the locality in which Maillard was writing, the girl signifies her acceptance by blowing out the fire in the calumet; in Maillard's region, she sucks it, blows smoke towards his nostrils, sometimes so hard that she makes him "qualm-sick," to her great delight. Thereafter, their behavior to one another is modest, but she performs certain services for him. She will braid his hair, paint his face, and will tattoo his body in various places with "curious devices and flourishes, all relating to their love," pricked in, and rubbed over with a composition that makes it indelible.

If her parents are pleased, at the end of two years they inform the young man that the period of probation is ended. At once he leaves the wigwam, with bow and arrow, hurries home, and announces that he will go into the woods and will not return until the girl sends for him. He hunts for two or three days. All the young men of his village then fetch him and carry back his game. Many seal and sea cows are also provided for the wedding feast.

The medicineman meets the bridegroom, who heads the procession, takes him by the hand, and leads him to the bride. He lies down by her side, and they are motionless and silent, while the medicineman, the parents, and the oldest relatives make "long tedious harrangues." The couple then rise and are led, he by the young men, she by the girls, to the place of entertainment, while all sing, shoot, and dance.

The bridegroom sits among the young men at one side; the bride, among the girls on the other side. One of his friends heaps an *oorakin*, a birch-bark dish, with meat, and sets it beside him. An identical dish and serving is set beside the girl. The medicineman then utters some magic words; he foretells, especially for the bride, that the meat will bring her dreadful consequences if she should ever be unfaithful to her husband in word or deed or act as a spy against her tribe; but if she remains true-hearted and loyal, the *oorakin* will bring her happiness.

While the medicineman talks, the girl's best friend and the man's best friend keep their eyes on the *oorakins*; as soon as he finishes, these two young people, apparently spontaneously, but actually rehearsed, pick up

Family, Kin, and Marriage

an *oorakin*; the man takes the bride's and gives it to the groom; the girl hands the groom's dish to the bride. The guests are then served.

The two young friends then confer, pretending that the dishes had been mixed up, and each accuses the other of having done so. The medicineman announces: "The manitoo has had his design in this mistake." It is a sign of his approval of the marriage. "What is the one's is the same as the other's. May they multiply without end!"

The guests rise and shout, and embrace bride and groom. All then "sit very gravely down again" and finish the food in silence. The day ends with dancing.

Fairly free choice of partners did not ensure stable unions. From Cape Breton to the Gaspé, missionary priests wrote despairing reports of a people who would not acknowledge the indissolubility of marriage. A couple who after a few years had had no children generally parted. LeClercq was probably not the only missionary to be shocked by Micmac reasoning: "'Dost thou not see,' they will say to you, 'that thou hast no sense? My wife does not get on with me, and I do not get on with her. She will agree well with such a one, who does not agree with his own wife. Why does thou wish that we four be unhappy for the rest of our days?'"

THE STATUS OF WOMEN

In aboriginal Micmac society women suffered from the many disadvantages and the few benefits customary to a primitive food-gathering culture. Overburdened and overworked, periodically unclean and dangerous to the men, bearing and losing many children, they nevertheless were essential to the life of the group and sometimes were so recognized.

The woman had specific duties and skills. She made all bark vessels and ornamented them with quills, plaited rushes for bags, brought in the game, skinned and cut it up, heated rocks to cook it, dressed and tanned the skins, made robes, sleeves, stockings, and moccasins, and corded the snowshoes. She put up and took down the wigwam, and when the band changed location, carried everything and the baby. Her daughters big and little carried goods, water, or firewood according to their strength, and early learned all kinds of work, including the chewing of resin for caulking canoes, a service which gave them teeth much whiter than those of the men — or those of the ladies of France. Men made all the wooden articles: bows, arrows, handles for spears and knives, snowshoe frames, baby-boards, and their tobacco pipes.[21]

Within their sphere, the men trusted the women to carry on:

> The men leave the arrangements of the housekeeping to the women, and do not interfere with them. The women cut up, slice off, and give away the meat as they please, but the husband does not get angry; and I can say that I have never seen the head of the wigwam where I was living ask of his wife what had become of the meat of moose and of beaver, although all that he had laid in had diminished very quickly.[22]

For causes that to the missionaries seemed slight, husbands frequently beat their wives, and gave the not inappropriate answer to snooping Frenchmen, "How now, have you nothing to do but to see into my house every time I beat my dog?"[23] Recalling certain characteristics displayed by these tender wives on the eve of, or on the night after, a battle, it may be surmised that those who could dish it out could probably also take it.

Certainly women did not lack spirit. A desperate gambler might stake a wife, like other property, in a game of *waltes*, but she was no great profit to the victor, because a woman lost at play was not easy to get hold of and was likely to greet the winner with jeers and mocking gestures.[24] As for the girls, Lescarbot warned his compatriots that "touching maidens that be loose, if any man hath abused of them, they will tell it at the first occasion, and therefore it is bad jesting with them."[25]

However, because of her periodic physical strangeness, the Micmac woman remained a frequently feared inferior. Menstruation required seclusion in a separate wigwam for four days. A menstruant might not eat with others, and cooked her food in a separate vessel. Contact with a man or with any of his possessions would bring disability to him and his weapons. Even a beaver would be insulted if it knew that a man had allowed its flesh to be eaten by "unclean daughters." Infection was inherent in menstrual blood.[26]

A hundred years later, a man still feared contact with a menstruant, for, he believed, this would deprive him of the use of his legs. Should

[21] Denys, II, 422–25.
[22] LeClercq, *Gaspesia*, 263.
[23] JR, III, 103–5.
[24] Lescarbot, *History*, III, 197.
[25] *Ibid.*
[26] JR, III, 105.

Family, Kin, and Marriage

this happen, he would not attempt to take a step, convinced that he was helpless, and would remain in bed "until the imaginary cause of his malady, no less imaginary, had passed away." If the woman touched a musket, it would not fire. Married women, to prevent sexual contact, at once told their husbands of their condition.[27]

As late as 1755, the Abbé Maillard stated that menstruants never had sexual relations or attended ceremonies. The old ideas prevailed in 1873, when Duncan Campbell wrote: "In passing from one part of a wigwam to another a woman must not, however crowded it may be, step across a man's feet or his fish spear if it happen to be in the way. To do so would be regarded as a gross insult."

No reference to menstruants was made by male informants in 1911-12, unless we so interpret their refusal to explain why a woman should not step over a man. All women questioned in 1950 and 1953 who were young wives in 1912 agreed that the menstrual wigwam was news to them and sounded "like Eskimo" — their idea of the primitive. However, most of them had experienced at first menstruation a survival of a form of aboriginal seclusion. The girl is instructed (1912, and in many instances, 1953) by her mother or grandmother to sit quietly in her own room — if she has one — and to do nothing, or to knit. She must not touch her hair, lest it fall out, or her face, to avoid pimples. An older woman washes the girl's face, combs her hair, and does her laundry for three days, admonishing her against stepping over men or women and to follow all instructions so that later she will be strong in childbirth.

Micmac women, as presented through the words of my male informants appear to have shared most of the economic pursuits of the men. Frequently a man and his wife fished from the same canoe. In war, women carried arrows on their back with which to supply the male fighters, and themselves used the bow and arrow against the enemy. Their essential role in war magic we have described.

They knew how to make canoes, and assisted their husbands in this occupation. The wife of the old canoe maker at Burnt Church, Peter Ginnish, seemed to know as much about its construction as did her husband, whom she had frequently assisted in his specialty.

Husbands professed no control over the possessions of a wife, and usually a man would not sell any of his own property until he had consulted his wife about it.

[27] Dièreville, 161–62.

PART ONE *Tribal Life*

In the tales, presumably man-created and certainly man-related, women are depicted as generally capable and inventive. Of the seven major cultural innovations, a woman is credited with invention or instigation of five: she told a man how to be the first firemaker; told a man "Go get an eel spear," thereby originating the article and the name of the object he forthwith made, thanks to his *keskamzit*; she thought up the first snowshoe and directed its making; a woman named St. Anne taught the first moose-hair weaving; a woman discovered and introduced corn. Man, unaided, invented only bow and arrow, and dyes (see Tales 81–87). As the narrator of the snowshoe tale concluded, "She had more sense than her husband. Providence bestowed more sense on women than on the male."

Stories such as the following are told of women's fortitude and capability (see Tales 88–89).

"A woman had five children. Her husband died. When the people moved away, she was left behind, for no one had room for her in a canoe. She gathered ribs and bark for a canoe and sewed the bark strips together. She could not find cedar, and used bushes for the ribs. When the bark had been sewed, the canoe was well made. Next morning she gathered gum from a spruce tree and put this over the seams, to make the canoe watertight. She placed her children in the canoe, and soon overtook the party. In the old times, anything a man could do a woman could do."

A woman whose children had been spitted and roasted in Mohawk fashion by English soldiers (see Tale 132) became a *buoin* and a *ginap* to "cure her heart," and singlehanded slew the enemy by the score.

Male informants incidentally expressed various opinions about women, particularly when telling stories. Peter Ginnish said: "A man is more manly. Woman's fashion is very soft."

John Newell related the following: "We Catholics do not worship the Virgin Mary. We worship only the Almighty Himself. The Virgin Mary prayed seventy years for water. She went to a large rock and for seventy years prayed on it every day. At the end of this time a big dragon came. When he was close to her, he suddenly thrust his tongue into the rock. It opened a big place and the water gushed out. The women are great people for water. They fill barrels and buckets and rainspouts with it whenever they can get it. If it rained a year and there was water everywhere, I believe the women would be out 'picking' water all the time.

Family, Kin, and Marriage

They are different from us, and they understand their own way. But we men don't understand the women's way."

"Nothing in the world is so good as a good woman, nothing so bad as a bad one," concluded one old man. "When you go into a house in which there is a bad woman, you go to a place where the very devil lives. There is no contentment where such a one lives."

CHAPTER XV

From Birth to Death

DEATH customs of the Micmac are fully described by witnesses from 1606 to the present, but for the opposite end of the life cycle there is no such fund of knowledge. In 1911–12 men had little to say about conception, pregnancy, or childbirth; to fill out the cultural picture, we present here information obtained in 1950 and in 1953 from a dozen women living on reserves in Quebec, New Brunswick, and Nova Scotia, whose present ages range from sixty-five to eighty. These women, who in 1911–12 were aged from twenty-three to thirty-eight, were asked to recall the teachings of their grandmothers as well as their own beliefs and practices; from these interviews the practices and attitudes prevalent when the main part of this study was made are interpolated.

PREGNANCY AND CHILDBIRTH

The importance of children to the success of marriage and great fondness for them is universally expressed. In the old days a medicine was known which would cure sterility, but no one makes it now. Old people say that if a woman has sex relations with too many men, it "spoils" her and she will be unable to conceive, but if she changes her ways, she may thereafter hope to have children.

For abortion there was formerly a native medicine; mechanical means were never used.

During pregnancy a Micmac woman regulates her conduct for her own good and for the well-being of the child. The greatest care must be taken in the first three or four months, while the fetus is susceptible to crippling and blemish. No food is taboo to the expectant mother; on the contrary, it is important that she obtain anything she craves. To touch her face or grip her elbows with the hands during a fit of un-

248

From Birth to Death

satisfied craving is almost certain to mark the unborn child on the corresponding part of the body, perhaps with a spot shaped like the desired food. Fear caused by seeing a clown or a person disfigured by fire may produce a child with a face like a mask or of a fiery, pulpy red.

The pregnant woman must use great care in her relations with persons and animals during the period most dangerous to the child. Discourtesy to a witch may bring a "bad wish" in the form of a patch of fur on the baby. Laughter at cripples, human or animal, will produce a child with the same type of malformation — "mockery will return to you." Hare-lipped, fox-faced, or moose-headed babies have been born to women who teased one of those animals.

Twins are abnormal. The mother is likened to a bitch. Ill luck will fall upon her, and one of the twins is certain to turn out badly. Old men stated this concept in 1911.[1]

Old women tell young expectant mothers, "Don't take something too much into your heart." A child was born with seven fingers and seven toes, twenty-eight in all, and a mouth split like a trout's. During early pregnancy the mother had quarreled with her husband and had called him a lizard. He said, "If you talk that way, you might get a lizard." She cried and brooded over his careless words. She took them to heart.

To ensure an easy delivery, there are several kinds of preventive activity. Universally mentioned was the necessity to go straight through any door approached, and to refrain from looking out a window; hesitating on a threshold or sticking the head out a window will cause the baby to be stuck in the mother's "doorway." It is important to rise immediately on waking. To condition the woman to do so, she is told to follow some simple ritual, for example, to put a glass of water beside the bed, and on rising, walk at once to the door and throw out the water; or to place a piece of soap under the pillow, and the first thing in the morning, get up and turn the pillow over. The soap is probably used as sympathetic magic. Such activities as walking under a clothesline, or knitting, are avoided, for fear the child will be born with the cord wrapped around its neck. Some say these are recent ideas, and that the old-time Indians tabooed the wearing of rings, necklaces, or tying anything around the waist.

Only one informant mentioned the father as a source of prenatal in-

[1] But in June 1950 people of all ages and sexes were proud of a set of twins just born at Burnt Church, N.B., and in 1953 of their sturdy survival.

PART ONE *Tribal Life*

fluence: before the birth of a certain boy, his father teased a seal, and the son was born with a flipper in place of one hand.

Quebec, New Brunswick, and Nova Scotia informants (1911 and 1953) mentioned no restrictions on the father, past or present, during or after a birth. On Lennox Island, P.E.I., it was said (1912) that the father stayed near the wigwam for seven days, and during this time did not enter any other wigwam. Others, it seems, were free to go into the wigwam to see the child. Apparently the father was not avoided and might enter any house or wigwam except his own. No explanation was offered.

Two old women usually assist during parturition. Kneeling is the preferred position. In the old days the woman clung to the center pole of the wigwam. To expel the placenta salt is placed in the woman's hands and she blows hard into them. The placenta is thrown in the stove; the faster it burns, the fewer afterpains will the woman suffer. She is put to bed, given herb drinks, and kept quiet for eight or nine days.

After the stump of the cord falls off, it is buried in a spot favorable to the future career of the child; placed in a tree, it will make a boy a good hunter; buried in the ground, it will lead the owner to gardening; and a cord hidden in a pillow will attract a little girl to bed-making. If the cord is burned, the child will always be poking in the stove.

Many Micmac babies are born with a caul — a most fortunate circumstance. A veiled baby is smart, and has a secret power for good: to foretell the future and to escape perils of fire, drowning, and warfare. He will be a *ginap*, never a *buoin*. The veil can confer protection on others: in both world wars soldiers bought pieces from owners or their parents.

Most women begin to nurse their babies immediately after birth. Colostrum is considered beneficial. The oldest informants had nursed their children for two to three years unless they became pregnant; in that event, they weaned at once. Women of sixty or so consider a year the period they usually nursed. If the mother decides to wean a child, she watches the moon, and when the dark period begins, stops nursing. When the moon reappears, the child will have forgotten the breast.

Two generations ago the first solid food fed to a child was previously chewed by a parent and then put into the child's mouth. Each of two men, aged eighty and seventy years, said that his earliest childhood memory was the taste of bread softened in the parent's mouth; one of them added that his father's chewed bread tasted better than his mother's, because his father smoked. Mothers formerly kept a recently weaned child quiet by giving it a piece of meat fastened on a stick in such a way that the child would not choke.

CHILDBIRTH AND INFANT CARE IN THE SEVENTEENTH AND EIGHTEENTH CENTURIES

A woman without a child was not a woman. To avert the threat of barrenness, women at stated times went to a certain spot in the woods and there, reciting formulas taught them by the oldest and most important women, or by a medicineman, besought the Manitoo to give them a child.[2]

As soon as a woman considered herself pregnant, it was her duty to inform her husband, so that sexual intercourse, considered harmful to the developing child, would cease. "But," said Dièreville, "this rule is not very constantly observed."[3]

Following parturition, women were considered unclean. For thirty to forty days they kept apart from their husbands, and used separate dishes to protect moose and beaver hunters from failure.[4]

Parturition, according to the priests, was a short and easy affair. It never took place within the wigwam: "the men never give it up to them; they remain therein whilst the wife is delivered in the woods at the foot of a tree."[5] A woman accompanied her as midwife and received in payment the knife with which the cord was cut. A normal labor lasted about two hours.

If labor was delayed and the mother was in pain, her hands were tied above her to a pole, her ear, nose, and mouth were stopped up, and the attendant pressed hard on her sides to force out the child. If this failed, a medicineman was called in and was given tobacco to offer to the spirit (literally "worm") which hindered the birth.[6]

Normally the mother rose and at once returned to her work. If birth pains attacked a woman who had gone alone to gather wood, she retired

[2] Maillard, *Customs and Manners*, 51.
[3] P. 145.
[4] LeClercq, *Gaspesia*, 229.
[5] *Ibid.*
[6] Biard, JR, III, 109; Segard, 342; LeClercq, *Gaspesia*, 88–90; Dièreville, 145–146.

PART ONE *Tribal Life*

into the bushes and presently returned home with the wood on her back and the baby in her arms. If she was traveling by canoe, she asked to be put ashore, entered the woods alone, returned shortly with the newborn, and resumed her share of paddling until the end of the journey.

The infant, immediately after its birth, was washed in a stream, no matter how cold the water might be, and made to swallow bear's grease or seal oil. The mother then wrapped it in soft skins and bound it to the cradleboard. That branch of science which has been called "diaperology" is described by Denys:

If it is a boy, they pass his penis through a hole, from which issues the urine: if a girl, they place a little gutter of bark between the legs, which carries the urine outside. Under their backsides they place dry rotten wood reduced to powder, to receive the other excrements, so that they only unswathe them each twenty-four hours. But since they leave in the air during freezing weather the most sensitive part of the body, this part freezes, which causes much mortality among them principally among the boys, who are more exposed to the air in that part than the girls.[7]

The cradleboard, which hung from a broad strap resting over the mother's forehead, had two hooks at the lower end and a narrow strip across the top, two or three fingers wide, to which the carrying strap was attached. Only the head of the child was free. Diapers were sometimes of moss. When not on the mother's back, board and child leaned against or hung from a tree: it was never laid flat. Mothers sang, and jounced restless babies.

The ornamentation of cradleboards and of the soft garments made from fox or beaver fur, swan or goose down, testify to the love which children inspired. Beadwork, wampum, quillwork, and painted figures beautified the cradle, and small colored toys dangled within the baby's reach. The little skin garments were painted, and were adorned with the mother's trinkets.

A stranger visiting a newborn might meet mishap followed by compensation: "If he takes the infant up in his arms and fondles it, the Father and Mother give him a present, in return for such tokens of good will; and if the Child piddles on the person who is holding him, which happens frequently, he is given another present to wipe out the stain."[8]

[7] II, 403. Others described the cradleboard: Lescarbot, *History*, III, 87; JR, III, 101; LeClercq, *Gaspesia*, 88; Dièreville, 146–47.
[8] Dièreville, 147.

From Birth to Death

In primitive hunting days and probably long afterward, children were nursed for two or three years. A woman could not feed two or carry two on a journey and so, "without fear of God or man," if the mother of a nursing child became pregnant, she produced an abortion by means of a secret native drug.

When weaning began, parents chewed meat and put it into the child's mouth.[9]

CHILDHOOD

Old people in 1911 recalled the traditional Micmac attitudes toward the growing child. Soon after birth the infant became a social being. The father entered the wigwam and gave the child a temporary name. When it was two days old, the chief came to the wigwam and, in the presence of the father and the mother, gave a name. In the same *udan*, or settlement, there might be two or more people by the same name. Distinctive names were used for males and for females. Only on a clear day might a name be given.

Boys received little bows and arrows with which to shoot birds, squirrels, rabbits, or other small game, so that they could prepare themselves to kill larger animals. They also improved their abilities by shooting at a target, sometimes in the form of a deer or a partridge carved out of wood by an old man.

"As soon as boys were large enough to run about," said Peter Sock of Burnt Church, "they kept to themselves and did not bother older people. Most boys have a chum. They set snares in the woods for squirrels. They go off early in the morning together. The one who is first up wakes the other. They are like brothers. One tells the other all that he hears. This relationship tends to break up at the marriage of either of them. Until that time they play together, box and wrestle with one another, and are almost constantly together. Girls have comparable chums. They go about together and visit one another daily."

As the age status terms [10] indicate, our culture and that of the Micmac differ in the concept of "child." Youngsters of about ten or twelve years of age were told by the old people how to behave; thereafter they participated in tribal affairs, and heard the old stories. That, according to 1911 informants, was the Micmac way. An etiquette strictly taught pre-

[9] Denys, II, 404; Diéreville, 148; Maillard, *Customs and Manners*, 36; LeClercq, *Gaspesia*, 91.
[10] See above, pp. 233–34.

scribed respect for old people. Boys and girls might not speak to old people unless first addressed by them. When old people came to the house, children had to go outdoors. They might not run in front of old people. They should not step over a person, or over his hands or his feet. This prohibition applied at every age.

An informant (1911) described a stick, with three thongs, used to administer punishment to boys, and a smaller one for girls. In 1850, Silas Rand said: "The rod was used unsparingly to tame rebellion and teach manners. [Children] speak respectfully of parents. They do not pass between their parents and the fire unless there are old people or strangers on the opposite side to be honoured more. Children use of a drunken parent the word *welopskeet*, a gentler word than the usual *katheet*." [11]

The first French writers seem to have been less impressed by the respect of young people toward their elders than amused by its form of expression. In 1612, children and youths sat with knees against chest, and head against knees, in the presence of their father, and of the old, whom they respected. "We laugh at them, and tell them that way of sitting is the fashion with monkeys, but they like it and find it convenient." [12]

All children, it seems, were wanted and cherished, as they are today. This was LeClercq's opinion:

One cannot express the tenderness and affection which the fathers and mothers have for their children. I have seen considerable presents offered to the parents in order that these might give the children to certain Frenchmen who would have taken them to France. But this would have torn their hearts, and millions would not induce them to abandon their children for a moment.

Two hundred years later, Duncan Campbell wrote:

The general treatment of the children by their parents is marked by much affection and gentleness. Observe the untutored denizen of the forest as he returns in the evening of a summer's day to his wigwam. See how his children, who are looking out for him, recognize him while he is yet far off, and run with the utmost glee to meet him, and with what a benignant smile the father's countenance is radiated as he struggles through the older ones to fold in his arms the little "toddling" thing who is crying bitterly on account of her inability to keep up with the rest.

[11] *Legends*, xxxii. In 1950 disciplinary rods — and their effect — were not conspicuous.
[12] JR, II, 133–35.

From Birth to Death

In the aboriginal culture it was around the boy that this affection was institutionalized and celebrated with feasts. The birth of a male child, the appearance of his first tooth, or his first step, brought forth festivities. Some of these seemed to symbolize the particular maturation celebrated: for the first tooth, guests chewed, and rejoiced that the boy would soon be able to do the same; and for his first step, there was much dancing (Lescarbot, Dièreville).

Perhaps most important was the boy's first killing of game.

The family assemble, and all the Indians of the vicinity are invited to this Feast; if they are away on an expedition, it will be deferred until their return, and in the meantime, to preserve the Game better, it will be smoked. At these Feasts, a somewhat special formality is observed; neither the family of the young Hunter nor he himself taste the Game which he has killed, and, no matter how small it may be, it is a point of honor to divide it among all the Guests. Care is also taken to put it into the cauldron last . . . They eat to their heart's content, or rather they devour their food, and only pause from time to time in order to honor the Hunter with cries and joyful songs. All game killed by him in his earliest youth is given to others, to show his skill and courage, but he is not so liberal with his prizes when he has attained the marriageable age.[13]

The humblest of game killed by a small child was important to his father. LeClercq said: "In my presence one time a leading man of the nation threw the foot of an owl into the kettle at a solemn feast, as a sure omen that his son who had killed it at the age of five years, would become some day a great hunter, and the most valiant warrior of the world." In the eyes of the tribe, however, the boy had a long way to go before the day when, having killed his first moose, he no longer ranked with women and girls, but had attained the rights of manhood.

As Denys said, children were the Micmac wealth, future food-gatherers, whose training began early:

The boys aid the father, going on the hunt, and help in the support of the family. The girls work, aiding the mother; they go for wood for the winter and to find the animal in the woods. After the latter is killed they carry it to the wigwam. There is always some old woman with the girls to conduct them and show them the way, for often these animals which it is necessary to go and find are killed at five or six leagues from the wigwam, and there are no beaten roads.[14]

[13] Dièreville, 147–49.
[14] II, 404.

PART ONE *Tribal Life*

ORPHANS AND ADOPTED CHILDREN

The Micmac fondness for children extends beyond ties of kinship and race. In 1911–12 no direct information was obtained about adoption, but the existence of this old and frequent practice was evident in extreme form. At Burnt Church, as on all reserves, white children had been adopted and were, for all social purposes, Micmac. One of these, a baby four months old in 1912, became our informant in 1950 and 1953.

In early accounts of the Micmac, only one type of adoption is described: the substitution, for a relative killed in battle, of a person of like age and sex from the enemy tribe.

When an Indian, old and decrepit, who can no longer hunt, loses an only son in War, overwhelmed by grief and almost in despair, he assembles his friends, entertains them and relates the dismal and disastrous causes of his grief. Moved by compassion they participate in his distress and, at the same time, form a charitable resolve to obtain another Child for this afflicted Father; they give him their promise to do so, and soon after they are working to fulfill it. They go into the Alien Land, where the much lamented Son perished, to seek another Youth for the unhappy Father who had lost his own; they find one, who is brought to him and adopted.

> To this adoption the Young Man agrees,
> And gives assurance by his promises,
> Which in this Race may be depended on;
> And the pretended Father thus consoles
> Himself for the demise of his true Son.[15]

LeClercq noted a group responsibility for orphans and for the children of a broken home. It was the chief's duty to place orphans in the wigwams of the best hunters, where they were to be brought up as if they were children born in the household.

If, following the death of the father of a family, his widow married, the oldest son took care of his brothers and sisters and built for them a separate wigwam. "This is for the purpose of avoiding bad treatment by the stepfather, and in order not to cause trouble in the housekeeping."[16] Today this is generally the grandparents' task.

THE AGED

The aged were treated and addressed with respect. Their opinions had the greatest weight in council and they were the wise instructors of the

[15] Dièreville, 163–64.   [16] LeClercq, *Gaspesia*, 238.

From Birth to Death

young. (See illustration 45 for a typical old woman of 1912.) An informant at Pictou stated that the old-time Indians cared well for their helpless aged; when people moved camp, they were taken in canoes; and on the march, the young and strong carried them on their backs. Lescarbot observed that aged parents were not despised and were supplied with venison.[17]

However, the implications of the *Jesuit Relations* and the statements of Father LeClercq make evident that the aged who were too helpless to care for themselves were either killed or were abandoned at the annual autumnal migration into the woods for hunting.[18]

45. An old woman of 1912.

The end of an aged or seriously ill person and the reasons given for this treatment are described in the following passages.

When our Savages see a person gradually failing from old age or sickness, through a certain compassion they hasten his death; showing him that he must die to procure rest, that it is a wretched thing to languish from day to day, that he is only a burden to them, and offer other similar arguments, by means of which they make the sick man resolve to die. And then they take away from him all goods, give him his beautiful robe of Beaver or other fur, and place him in a half reclining posture upon his bed, singing to him praises of his past life, and of his fortitude in death; to this he agrees, and replies with his last chant, like the Swan; when it is finished all leave him, and he considers himself happy to die rather than to linger on. For these people, being Nomadic, and not being able to continue living in one place, cannot drag after them their fathers or friends, the aged, or the sick. That is why they treat them in this manner. If they are sick, they first make incisions into their stomachs, from which Pilotois, or sorcerers, suck the blood. And, whatever the cause, if they see a man can no longer drag himself along, they put him in the condition above described, and throw upon his navel so much cold water, that, Nature weakens little by little, and thus he dies with great steadfastness and fortitude.[19]

[17] *History*, III, 214.
[18] For example, *Gaspesia*, 92.
[19] JR, II, 151. Port Royal, 1613.

PART ONE *Tribal Life*

In 1646, the priests at St. Charles, Miscou, reported to Paris that the salvaging of a mistreated Eskimo slave had led the Savages

to set down, within a stone's throw of our house two very old and helpless women. We were not willing to let them die of misery before our eyes, or urge that they be embarked again, lest the refusal to assist them, that we might have made, should give occasion to those barbarians rather to deal them a blow of the hatchet on the head, than to take the trouble of dragging them over the snow throughout the winter.[20]

Thus the missionaries found themselves the operators of "a sort of Cabin of Charity" until the Eskimo was cured and the old women died.

DEATH AND BURIAL RITES

Long ago, it was said in 1912, the body was brought home for the funeral rites, no matter how far away a man died. The face of the deceased was covered with red pigment. After a death, all the people in the *udan* (settlement) moved away, perhaps to a distance of five or six miles, even though the deceased was a small child.

At Burnt Church, N.B., the following account of death customs was given: When a person died, a crowd assembled, and the body, clothed as in life, was cremated. They could not dig a grave. Later, when they could dig a grave with an adze and a shovel, they interred the body, after wrapping it in a sheet of white birch bark, a covering that would preserve it for many years. The body was buried full length, face up, arms along the sides. A large stone was placed at the grave, on the right-hand side of the deceased.

As soon as death came, two men took the news to nearby settlements. Those who had assembled around the dying man remained silent. There were no words or songs of mourning until the burial. Sometimes they wrapped a stone with the body, to cause it to sink, and placed the corpse in deep water.

This account does not agree with the testimony of excavated grave sites in the vicinity. In 1911 Patrick Murphy, of Red Bank, N.B., gave me the following description of a burial at that place: The grave was found, about 1850, in clay and sand, near the bank of the South Miramichi River, approximately two miles and a half above Red Bank, and near the end of the bridge that now spans the river. The head was toward the east and toward the river. The body, in sitting posture, was about

[20] JR, XXX, 135.

From Birth to Death

four feet below the surface. The skeleton was intact, and said by the discoverer to have been very large. The head was inserted in a large copper kettle bound with two iron hoops, and was accompanied by steel swords, but by no stone implements. About a mile above Red Bank, on a rise on the east side of Southwest River, James McKinley, later a resident of North Sydney, C.B., while digging the foundation of a house, uncovered a grave which contained two skeletons in sitting posture (supposed, by him, to be man and wife). The skulls were not more than two and a half feet below the surface, in light, sandy soil. They were encased in a wrapping of birch bark which fell to pieces when touched. In the grave were two stone axes, two stone knives, and six arrowheads. No pigment was found in either of these graves. In other burials described to me pieces of red pigment were present. While digging for implements at Musquodoboit Harbour, N.S., I found a small piece of pigment in a deposit which contained two arrowheads.

From Pictou, N.S., there is the following account: The Micmac buried their dead along the shore of a river or of the ocean, but without orientation. A *huwenuetc kwedelaan*, a birch-bark covering, was sewed together with spruce root, placed around the body as bark encircles a tree, and was strengthened with ribs of ash. Bands of twisted yellow-birch twigs were placed around each leg, and around waist and chest. Under and over the body in the grave were placed leaves from any kind of tree. When the grave had been filled in, the ground over it was leveled.

Later, after coffins (*leskwigan*) were introduced, the coffin was made by three or four men, who worked together. While they were making it, none of them spoke or ate. The body was sewed in a cloth sack that fitted very closely and extended from below the feet to immediately above the root of the nose. The arms protruded from sleeves provided for the purpose. The corpse was then put into a coffin made of barrel staves or of rough fir boards. The upper portion of the head of a woman was left exposed. The upper part of the head of a man was covered with a hood. On the day of interment the hood was tied close around the neck.

In some settlements the body was not wrapped or clothed beyond covering the waist with a rag: the remainder of the body was naked, and heads of males were not covered. Black, red, and white, the colors invariably used, were obtained from the *wasaguinu*, that is, the people from heaven (angels?), who dressed in these colors. Sometimes, instead of sewing the body in a sack, a long sash was placed over the left

PART ONE *Tribal Life*

shoulder, passed under the right arm, and wrapped around that arm at or above the elbow, so that it would not slip down. Thanks to this provision, the deceased will be ready to walk right in when he gets to heaven; for there the old clothes will be removed, and this will serve as a substitute. A sash is put around the waist to cover the loins, and another around the chest.

I was told at Pictou that it was formerly the custom to leave the body on an elevated platform until the bones were exposed. They were then buried. The platform was made of small horizontal sticks supported by four upright poles. The camp was then moved. Gluskap told the people this was not the proper way — they should bury in the ground; and so they have done ever since. Sometimes, when not in a hurry, they made a fire under the body and dried it by smoking, as they cured meat. This was employed if the removal of the camp was delayed for two or three days. Social status, it seems, made no difference in manner of burial.[21]

Age and sex of the deceased determined who should place the corpse in the coffin; for example, the body of a little girl was laid within it by two or three little girls in the presence of other girls. Micmac believe this was the ancient custom.

Roth, writing in 1890, said that no Micmac was allowed to die "on any other than a bed of spruce boughs." If he did not take his last breath on the natural Indian bed, he would not go to the happy hunting ground beyond the stars.[22]

It is believed (1911) that an hour or two before death a man whose life has been evil will swear, curse, and rave, not knowing that he is about to die. Or he will take a pack of cards, shuffle them, and swear. The man is then out of his senses. A man who is good and has respected God during his life will, when about to die, not behave in this manner. People do, immediately before death, whatever they enjoyed doing while alive — dancing, drinking, dressing in fine clothes, or whatever. Girls will dress up well and look in the glass to see that their toilet is well made — not knowing that they will die in an hour or two.

[21] I failed to obtain corroboration of Stansbury Hagar's statement that "a form of water-burial, analogous to the Norse, was once practised by the Micmac at the funeral of chiefs"; and found no evidence that it had been their custom, "like the Natchez, Peruvians, and other tribes," to keep "the bodies of their dead in their homes or temples, believing that this would enable the spirits to warn them of the approach of enemies, and to advise with their priests about the affairs of the tribe." HERE, I, 433, 435.
[22] P. 46.

From Birth to Death

All come in to see a man who is believed to be dying. When they think he is in the last throes, they sing the death song, until the end comes. If the dying person is over thirty to thirty-five years of age, or is married, men and women gather and sing. If the dying one is a boy, boys sing during the first night, and girls and boys sing during the second night.

At death the *klidaswaanum* (soul) leaves and becomes a *skadegamutc*. "I stayed with a dying man one night," said John Newell. "His head was covered; but when I awoke, he was dead, and the cover was off his face. This was done by the *skadegamutc* while going away from his face. It is no fun to stay in the night near a *skadegamutc*."

I could obtain no information about the old rules governing the disposition of the property of the deceased, beyond the vague information that it went to someone in the family. All property of a deceased man is sold a very short time after his death. The proceeds of the sale the widow gives to the priest; "then there will be no *skadegamutc* hovering about it." The widow keeps anything which she might be able to use, for example, knives, but all the man's wearing apparel, shaving outfit, and other personal belongings are sold. Many a purchaser buys in order to bestow the money on the widow rather than to acquire the article. "This is really charity on the part of the purchasers," an informant explained. "They pay this to the priest that Mass may be said and the man's *skadegamutc* be helped. It is as though you gave tobacco or matches to someone going along the road, in order to help him."

DEATH AND BURIAL IN THE SEVENTEENTH CENTURY

The quartet of seventeenth-century writers often quoted in this study (Lescarbot, Biard, LeClercq, Denys) covered pages with descriptions of funerals, burials, and mourning. The first two men, it will be remembered, were at Port Royal and on the St. John River early in the century; LeClercq was at the Gaspé Peninsula, at the Baie des Chaleurs, and later on the Miramichi River; and Denys ranged from Cape Breton to Gaspé during the fifty years between 1622 and 1672. Dièreville, who visited Nova Scotia in 1708, contributes only one item.[23]

[23] The following synthesis of the observations of the five men has been made from material to be found in JR, I, 167–69, 215, 261–65; II, 21, 95, 133–35, 229; III, 127–31; Lescarbot, *History*, II, 352; LeClercq, *Gaspesia*, 185–87, 219–20, 228–29, 265–66, 269–71, 300–3; Denys, II, 437–40; and Dièreville, 161.

PART ONE *Tribal Life*

The Dying

The French at Port Royal between 1610 and 1616 were impressed by the ceremonies begun as soon as a medicineman had pronounced his patient's illness impossible to cure. Family and friends gathered around the wigwam of the dying man, who would now take part in his own funeral. Donning his finest robe of otter or of beaver skins, he delivered an oration in which he recited his heroic deeds, gave directions to his family, and said farewell to his friends. Then he chanted his death song. If the sick man had supplies on hand, he held the funeral feast for the assembled friends and relatives. Immense kettles of meat were put over the fire, and dogs were tied together, ready to be slaughtered to precede the soul on its journey, the flesh to be eaten by the waiting guests. The feast was served and eaten, and was followed by song and dance. The dying donor was not fed or nursed; he was already a citizen of the other world. If he lingered too long, great pails of water were thrown over him, or he might be buried half-alive. As soon as he had drawn what was considered his last breath, mourning wails broke forth and continued day and night for perhaps a week.

The chief Membertou, a medicineman and the first baptized Micmac, sang his death song. His children had taken away his otter robe and had ceased to feed him, when he decided to send for the commandant at Port Royal to ask him how a Christian ought to die. Monsieur de Potrincourt arrived and persuaded him to forget the medicineman, to eat and live. "The good man believed and was saved. Today he points out how God has thereby mercifully exposed the malice and deceit of their *Aoutmoins*." Nevertheless, Father Biard also arrived like the cavalry, once or twice again before one (or two) of Membertou's sons in like manner bit the dust.

The Soul

After death in a wigwam, the chief or leading man directed that the bark sides be struck to cries of *Oue Oue*, in order to call forth the soul. If it lingered longingly in its old home, and breathed upon a child, that child would be doomed to die. The soul leaves by the smoke hole. The soul of an infant does not go far from its body, and a deceased infant is buried beside a path, that the soul may slip into the bosom of a woman passing by and animate an undeveloped fetus.

From Birth to Death

Messengers

Only LeClercq mentioned messengers who carried the news of death:

Certain young Indians are appointed to go and announce to all the people, and even to the French settlements, the death of their relatives and friends. These deputies approach the wigwams to which they are sent, climb into a tree, and cry out three times with all their strength that a certain person is dead. After this they approach, and give to those whom they find an account of the circumstances of the illness and of the death of their friend, inviting them to assist in his funeral.

Preparation of the Body

The corpse was carried out, not by the regular exit from the wigwam, but through the portion toward which the sick person turned at the moment of death.

At least two methods of burial were practiced. At Port Royal and in what is now northern New Brunswick, the body wrapped in elk or beaver skins was tied tightly with limbs bent and head on knees, a position the Micmac recognized as that of the embryo; a man should be committed to earth in the same manner in which he once lay in his mother's womb. On a bier of bark, rushes, or planks, the corpse was carried on the shoulders of relatives to a deep grave and there was placed sitting, a position which signified respect.

A form of primitive mortuary science was described to LeClercq:

The chiefs of their nation formerly entrusted the bodies of the dead to certain old men, who carried them sacredly to a wigwam built on purpose in the midst of the woods, where they remained for a month or six weeks. They opened the head and the belly of the dead person, and removed therefrom the brain and the entrails; they removed the skin from the body, cut the flesh into pieces, and, having dried it in the smoke or in the sun, they placed it at the foot of the dead man, to whom they gave back his skin, which they fitted on very much as if the flesh had not been removed.

Lescarbot said the savages embalmed, but "of what kind of balm I could not know."

If a man died during the winter remote from the common burial place of his ancestors, his family wrapped him in bark painted red and black, placed him in the branches of a tree beside a river, and build around him with logs a kind of little fort, to protect him from beasts or birds. In the spring the chief sent the young men of his settlement to fetch the body for the customary funeral rites.

PART ONE *Tribal Life*

Exposure on a scaffold followed by secondary burial was the only type described or mentioned by Denys. No other seventeenth-century writer referred to this practice. A Micmac at Pictou, N.S., who in 1911 described the custom, was born in Cape Breton, and Denys alone of the five early French writers had been in that region; he had lived there for several years. As soon as death occurred, Denys said:

The women went to fetch pieces of bark from which they made a kind of bier on which they placed him well enwrapped. Then he was carried to a place where they had a staging built on purpose, and elevated eight or ten feet. On this they placed the bier, and there they left it about a year, until the time when the sun had entirely dried the body.

The end of the year having passed, and the body [being] dry, it was taken thence and carried to a new place, which is their cemetery. There it was placed in a new coffin or bier, also of Birch bark, and immediately after in a deep grave which they had made in the ground.

Because of the position in which the body was tied and placed, graves had to be deep — four to five feet — and "round like a well." The top was arched over with sticks to keep the earth from falling back into the hole. Over the graves of chiefs or other prominent persons interlacing poles were built up in a pyramid; on that of a man hung bow, arrow, and shield; a woman's bore spoons, packstrap, and strings of beads.

Funeral Rites

Wailing mourners with blackened faces gathered at the wigwam of the deceased. An oration was delivered over the body, "if the condition permit," in which were rehearsed praise of the dead and reminders that all who were born must die and that patience lightens the burden of grief. Mourning continued for three days without food, or until the chief commanded that it cease and invited all to a feast, accompanied by dancing. For holding such feasts, the Micmac gave three main reasons: "first, that they may assuage the general grief; secondly, that those friends who come from a distance to the funeral may be more fittingly entertained; thirdly, that they may please the spirit of the dead, which, they believe, is delighted by this exhibition of liberality, and also partakes of the repast."

Burial was delayed until the end of the feast, and the funeral director, a permanent and honored family officer, proclaimed the moment to go to the grave. Lamentations resumed. Boys engaged in mock wrestling. The

From Birth to Death

actual burial took place in silence. Gifts were then put in the grave or were tied to the poles, each donor being named. Skins, kettles, hatchets, knives, arrows, wampum, beads, and any dogs yet uneaten were bestowed in the early Port Royal days. Denys wrote of competitive display and slow and partial disillusionment:

All the friends of the deceased made him each his present, of the finest and best that they had. They competed as to who would make the most beautiful gift. At a time when they were not yet disabused of their errors, I have seen them give to the dead man, guns, axes, iron arrowheads, and kettles, for they held all these to be much more convenient for their use than would have been their kettles of wood, their axes of stone, and their knives of bone, for their use in the other world.

There have been dead men in my time who have taken away more than two thousand pounds of peltries. This aroused pity in the French, and perhaps envy with it; but nevertheless one did not dare to go take the things, for this would have caused hatred and everlasting war, which it was not prudent to risk since it would have ruined entirely the trade we had with them. All the burials of the women, boys, girls, did not last so long. They never omitted to place with each one that which was fitting for his use, nor to bury it with him.

It has been troublesome to disabuse them of that practice, although they have been told that all these things perished in the earth, and that if they would look there they would see that nothing had gone with the dead man. That was emphasised so much that finally they consented to open a grave, in which they were made to see all was decayed. There was there among other things a kettle, all perforated with verdigris. An Indian having struck against it and found that it no longer sounded, began to make a great cry, and said that some one wished to deceive them. "We see indeed," said he, "the robes and all the rest, and if they are still there it is a sign that the dead man has not had need of them in the other world, where they have enough of them because of the length of time that they have been furnished them."

"But with respect to the kettle," said he, "they have need of it, since it is among us a utensil of new introduction, and with which the other world cannot [yet] be furnished. Do you not indeed see," said he, rapping again upon the kettle, "that it has no longer any sound, and that it no longer says a word, because its spirit has abandoned it to go to be of use in the other world to the dead man to whom we have given it?"

The latest description of grave gifts (Dièreville's) listed a live dog, hatchet, corn, blanket, pipe, clothing, and a musket.

Writing in 1755 of "old days," Maillard alone mentioned human sacrifice: a child and the woman he had loved best threw themselves into a

PART ONE *Tribal Life*

warrior's grave and were buried with him. "Of late," added the Abbé, "the interment of live persons has been almost disused." [24]

Extraordinary circumstances required unusual rites. At Port Royal, those who had drowned were buried with greater ceremony and lamentation. Their bodies were cut open and a portion of the flesh, together with the viscera, was thrown into the fire. This was an offering or appeasement, for the spirits are angry whenever any one loses his life by drowning. The funeral of a man killed in combat was the occasion for assembling to avenge his death. In addition to the customary feasts, dances, and mourning, the chief would rise and speak of the deeds of all who had distinguished themselves or who had died in warfare. A silence followed, broken by the relatives of the dead man, crying for an end to useless mourning and a beginning of vengeance on the enemy. This was customary from Nova Scotia to the Gaspé, and led to almost continuous warfare with Eskimo and Penobscot, for it was almost impossible to engage in a battle that left no dead to be avenged.

Ceremonial cannibalism sometimes occurred at a funeral. LeClercq heard of such a case not far from him, reported to him directly by participants. The deceased had been a prominent man whose serious illness the medicineman could not cure. In the course of an effective oration, the speaker appealed for vengeance against the evil spirit which had caused the death and which still remained in the heart of the man it had slain. All present rushed to the bier on which the body lay, and opened up the belly. The medicineman tore out the heart, cut it into pieces, and distributed these. Each ate his portion, and thus killed the devil.

Cemeteries

The preferred graveyard was an uninhabited island not too near the shore. No one visited the graves except for an additional burial. "The obsequies finished, they flee from the place, and from that time on, they hate all memory of the dead." That was Father Biard's interpretation. Fear of the ghosts would be a more apt explanation of this behavior. Membertou and his people had a graveyard on a desolate island near Cape Sable, thirty leagues from Port Royal. Heron Island, in the southwestern part of the Baie des Chaleurs, was in the seventeenth century an ancient cemetery for Micmac at Restigouche. These graveyards were

[24] *Customs and Manners*, 46.

From Birth to Death

supposed to be secret. A man who pointed out to some Frenchmen a burial ground near Canso was killed by fellow tribesmen.

Everything belonging to the dead was burned, buried, or given to strangers. The name was never again spoken.

Mourning

Relatives mourned for an entire year. In addition to smearing the face with black as did all mourners, they cut their hair, and might not braid it or adorn it with beads or wampum during the year. Neither widow nor widower remarried until the mourning period was over. Denys said that if the widow had children to support her, she did not remarry. During the year in which the body lay on the scaffold, the wives of the dead man, whenever they met, wept together, but not so long as at the first time.

Meat killed by young men was taboo to widows. In accord with the belief that a custom broken brought disaster to the group, a woman might starve to death unless a man who was married, old, or a leader of the tribe would hunt game for her. Father LeClercq thus solved the problem for a hungry woman:

In the winterings I have made with the Indians in the woods, I have seen one of these widows who remained three days without eating, with as much cheerfulness as if she had the best fare in the world. I said everything I could to her to make her break her Lent, for it is thus that they name this abstinence, but it was in vain; and I could never persuade her to eat, although there was meat in abundance in her wigwam. Even her children murmured against me because I solicited their mother to abandon the customs of their ancestors, saying to me that the Indians had their manner of living, as well as the French, and that we should follow our maxims without wishing to oblige them to abandon theirs. This woman begged me to accompany the Indians in a hunt for beaver, to which they had invited me in order to give me the entertainment of it; and she assured me that she would willingly eat that which I might kill, if I had enough cleverness to capture any, because she considered me as their father and as one of their elders. I was fortunate enough to take two of them, of which I broke the heads. I carried them to her wigwam, and made her a present thereof. She ate them both all alone by herself, for she was not permitted to eat with the others, nor the others to eat with her.

Mourning protracted beyond the customary period was not admired and, contrary to Denys' statement, many urged widows to remarry. An admonitory tale (Tale 95) recorded in 1911 tells why widows are for-

PART ONE *Tribal Life*

bidden to cherish the bones of a dead husband. "If your husband is dead, go find another!"

This quality of moderation, combined with evidence of deep personal grief, is reflected in LeClercq's account of a man whose wife and child, during a visit to the Miramichi, had been burned to death at night by a fire in the wigwam.

He often visited their tomb, and there one day, when on his knees, with hands and eyes raised towards heaven, and his heart all rent with grief, he was heard to pronounce these words in the form of a prayer: "O great God, who governs the sun and the moon, who has created the moose, the otters, and the beavers, be appeased: be no more angry against me: and be satisfied with the misfortunes which overwhelm me. I had a wife; Thou has taken her from me. I had a child that I loved even as myself; but I have none any more, because Thou has willed it. Is that not enough? Grant me then for the future as much of good as now I endure of ill. Or, if Thou are not yet satisfied with that which I suffer in my heart, make me die as soon as possible, for it is impossible for me to live thus any longer."

But, at length, as time is a wise physician who administers effective remedies to the keenest griefs, and as, besides, these people do not hold in high regard a man who grieves and is not consolable in even the most grievous accidents of human life, our Indian wished to give unmistakable evidence of the control which he had over his feelings. Hence he assembled [the settlement] to the feast of the dead, which he gave them in accordance with the usual custom of the country. He commenced it by a speech which explained succinctly the reason for which he had assembled them. Then he added a kind of funeral oration, in which he described the fine qualities of his wife and everything that her ancestors had done of most importance for the interests of the nation. At length he finished his discourse by pronouncing a eulogy on his son, claiming that he would have become some day a good hunter, a great warrior, and the worthy heir of the valour and the bravery of his father.

A profound silence followed at once on this speech, and he stopped abruptly with his eyes fixed upon the earth as if he were plunged in the lowest of all the melancholies. This he did in order better to express the bitterness which he had in his heart because of the death of his wife and child. Then suddenly carrying his hand to his eyes, in order to wipe away some tears which he had shed before this assembly, he gave a cry of joy, and said, at the same time, that if he had shed tears which he was unable to refuse to the dead persons whom he had loved so tenderly, he wished, nevertheless, to stop their flow in accord with the esteem which all the Indians had conceived for the greatness of his courage. He added that we were all mortal; that too much sadness and grief made Indians lose their spirit; and that, in fact, it was needful to console

From Birth to Death

ourselves for all the grievous accidents which come to us in life, because He who has made all and who governs all things, has permitted this.

All those assembled answered this speech by three or four whoops which they forced from the depths of their stomachs, saying, as usual he', he', he'. It is thus that they express approval, as a rule, of the reasoning of one who makes the speech. Our Koucdedaoui had no sooner received these public approvals, than he set himself to dancing his very best and to chanting some songs of war and the chase, in order to testify to the assembly that he had banished from his heart all the regret, grief, and sadness he had previously felt. After this he drank a good dram of brandy and gave the rest of the bottle to the oldest men, to be distributed to the assembly with the sagamite of the feast.

CHAPTER XVI

The Modern Micmac

On a summer day in 1912 the little steamer that hauled freight and passengers up and down the Miramichi put out from Burnt Church. On board a young anthropologist called to a Micmac lounging on the pier, "You'll see me back someday — me or my *skadegamutc*."

"Hey!" the old Indian responded, "How you catch 'em that word *skadegamutc*?"

Thirty-eight years later, when we arrived at Burnt Church, the little steamer functioned only in the tales that grandfathers told to children about "old Micmac times," but *skadegamutc* was still a good and surprising word for white people to know. We came — two elderly anthropologists — by automobile, a vehicle not encountered near Micmac reserves in 1912.[1] Now even a few Micmac were car owners. At Burnt Church the finest car — and also cows, a store, and a house with a sun porch — belonged to an old man who had earned them all by hard, steady labor on that small river freighter now rotting on the shore of the Miramichi.

In 1953 there were more Micmac cars and also several trucks; for the three intervening years had been prosperous in the Maritime Provinces, and the Micmac reserves are no longer culture islands inhabited only by isolationists. The great changes that have come to Canada since 1912 — the two world wars, economic prosperity alternating with depression, the old age pension, the Family Allowance, the spread of compulsory education, of newspapers, comic books, and Eaton's mail-order catalog — these have made the Micmac story in the main a Canadian story. Yet Micmac are Canadians with a difference: they pay no taxes; they do not,

[1] For the report of this 1950 trip to New Brunswick and Nova Scotia, see Wallis and Wallis, 1953.

The Modern Micmac

unless they are veterans, vote; and the culture they have taken over combines traits from the two dominant groups of Canada. The language of their schools and churches, even in Quebec, is English; their uniformly Catholic religion brings many of their customs closer to the Canadian French. The attitudes which they express toward their white neighbors, over and above personal reactions, often reflect a strange mixture of times and places. "We don't like French people" may mean no more than the frustration of running up against a second non-Micmac language, a suspicion of people whose speech they cannot understand; while "French people treated the Indians better than the English did" may refer to a traditional attachment to the pre-British regime, much as the French Canadians, ignoring the revolution, flaunt banners with the royal lilies.

Definitely, Micmac still remain a separate people: in the native language spoken in the majority of their homes, in conscious pride, and in the eyes of the Indian Affairs Branch of the Canadian government. To what extent this last factor with its attendant services to those who remain on the reserves is dominant in the preservation of Micmac group identity could not be assessed in two field seasons by two anthropologists whose purpose was to observe life on those reserves and see which traits of Micmac daily life and belief current in 1911–12 had been tough enough to survive over forty years of active contact with white culture.

In Quebec and New Brunswick we found the Micmac living in the same regions where they had been settled a hundred years ago, and in most cases, not far from the spot along rivers and coasts where, as the folktales say, the old people came out of the woods to camp in the spring. The largest of the reserves, Restigouche, is a flat triangle, thrust out into the like-named river, across from the city of Campbellton, N.B. (See illustration 46.) Behind the long straight rows of houses — of weathered shingle, painted clapboards, brick asbestos siding — with their many-colored roofs rise the mountains of the Gaspé which, the Micmac say, are the dried and hardened waves of the primeval sea. Midway in the settlement is the strip of land belonging to the Capuchin Monastery and Church of Ste Anne de Restigouche (see illustration 38), scene of the Micmac tercentenary celebration of 1910; opposite the mission grounds are a Royal Canadian Mounted Police station, a general store, a day school for the children of eight French families resident on the monastery land, the convent, and the much larger English-language school for

PART ONE *Tribal Life*

46. Ste Anne de Restigouche, Que. Old Micmac reserve houses are in the foreground. Across the Restigouche River is the city of Campbellton, N.B., backed by Sugar Loaf Mountain, home of the baleful Pugulatamutc. Micmac legends attribute the great Campbellton fire of 1910 to the supernatural power of mistreated Indians.

the Micmac children. Social rivalry within the Micmac village is expressed by the terms *Wonegg* and *Godunk* (Up Mission and Down Mission) and currently dramatized by a rivalry between baseball teams said to be so fierce that most of their games are held with outsiders. As for hockey the two teams don't even attempt to play together.

Sixty miles farther up the Gaspé Peninsula, on a hilltop between the mountains and the Baie des Chaleurs, live the two hundred Micmac of Maria: convent, store, houses, and roadside stands for selling pop and baskets stretch along a mile of tourist highway. (See illustration 47.) This is the only northern Micmac group which still makes fancy baskets and sweet-grass whisks; finest and best made are the melon-shaped baskets characteristic of Maria. When tourist buses stop at the church the children are sent running, some toting babies to attract lady photographers, tagged by the village idiot, and all with hands extended. When the bus has gone, the wisest of the little girls will pop into the priest's

The Modern Micmac

house to leave her pennies with Father for transportation to the next ballgame.

Eel River, across the Baie des Chaleurs, is a shabby group of houses near the river's mouth, about four miles east of the city of Dalhousie, N.B., and easily identified by the numerous signs reading "Clams for Sale." For the hundred Micmac enrolled here there is a one-room school, a jail, and a canteen, Indian-operated. Here we were told that people spoke only English, and we heard children as young as three so addressed by parents and grandparents.

The four reserves of the Miramichi Agency with their big white churches and St. Anne's Day crosses are along quiet rivers and bays. Big Cove, the largest, on the Richibucto where Micmac met Maliseet and Jesuit in the seventeenth century, with a fine school and new trim

47. Maria, Que. A church shrine and the new type of government-built house are shown. The mountains of the Gaspé are in the distance. The wigwam, built by Micmac men as a basket-selling attraction for sightseers and operated by the priest, is made of small patches of bark, because of the birch blight.

273

PART ONE *Tribal Life*

nursing station, we found almost deserted in early August when all except the aged, infirm, and the young mothers of stepladder families were away for weeks of blueberry picking. The other three reserves are on various branches of the Miramichi where Richard Denys had his trading post and where Father LeClercq observed the customs of the "Gaspesians": Burnt Church, along the bay, continuous with the whites' fishing village of the same name, site of the first Catholic church and cemetery in the region, once a famous tribal gathering place, and the home of Peter Ginnish, now long dead; hilly little Red Bank; and Eel Ground, probably most progressive of the New Brunswick settlements.

MATERIAL CULTURE

To one returning after forty years, the most striking change is in housing. In 1911 ill-made log houses, and tar-paper shacks were the rule; outhouses were the exception; wigwams or tents were common additions, at least in the summer. No tents were seen in 1953, and the only wigwam anywhere was the souvenir booth at Maria (see illustration 47) built at the instigation of the priest. The small neat house seen between it and the church is typical of the hundreds erected at the rate of four or five a year on each reserve since 1946. The better constructed older houses remain in use. An old woman in Quebec, speaking of her hundred-year-old house inherited from her father, complained of the winter cold which killed her flowering plants and said, "We scrub and scrub the house all the time. An ugly old man has to wash his face just the same as a handsome young one." On all reserves, among the bright new cottages stand the old gray shells of aged and empty houses. (See illustration 46.)

The building of new houses and the repair of older units are also going on at the Lennox Island Reserve, P.E.I. The ownership of houses here, as everywhere in the Maritimes, is held in one of three ways. A house built by an Indian or bought with his money from another Indian is his personal property to dispose of by sale, gift, or will, but the recipient must be a member of the band entitled to reside on the reserve: a person adopted from another band in the informal Micmac fashion cannot inherit a house. New houses, built in great quantities by the Welfare Division of the Indian Affairs Branch and assigned primarily to the aged or to very large families may be lived in for a lifetime but may not be rented or sold; they remain government property. It is around the

The Modern Micmac

pleasant little veterans' houses that flocks of small children cluster. By the Veterans Land Act of 1945, a maximum outright grant of $2320 was made available to any Indian veteran of World War II who settles on a reserve, which may be used to buy equipment for farming, fishing, forestry, or trapping, for clearing land, or for the cost of building material and construction. The majority of veterans in the Maritimes have chosen houses; during the first ten years the owner must keep his house in good condition and live in it without an absence exceeding two years, and during this period he may not rent or sell. After ten years it is his house and he may do with it as he likes. That is, like the man who formerly built his own house, he may sell it only to a Micmac of his own band.

One can easily see how the housing program tends to further Micmac group identity and to hold the individual continuously or recurrently in reservation life. The comfort of the houses, the desire to get everything that is coming to one, and the impossibility of turning the house into cash keep many a young man within the tribe and the band. Moreover, anyone can hope to get a government house or at least government repairs some day and in the meantime one does nothing to improve one's property. ("We're going to put on a nice porch as soon as the government puts in a new foundation for us.") But from no point of view — health, morale, or simple humanity — would one wish to see the Micmac living in the fashion of forty years ago. A woman married in 1914 at the age of fourteen to a man of forty-five described their first house. The outside was tar paper with no shingles. There was no foundation and the bare board floor rested on supports. They had a bed of boards and a bedtick stuffed with straw, two small benches, a table, an old stove, and two or three dishes. Her husband made her a rocking chair from an old broken one and there she sat and rocked her babies in the cold moonlight.

At the upper limit of achievement today is the house of a veteran of both world wars who by industry has been able to add considerably to the sum granted by the Veterans Act. Landscaped without and papered and painted within by the family, it is furnished with an electric washing machine and iron, a chrome dinette set, a new upholstered day bed, and a cabinet full of new dishes.

It is in Nova Scotia and Cape Breton Island that the building program has had its greatest social effect. At Eskasoni and at Shubenacadie Wel-

PART ONE *Tribal Life*

fare and Veteran construction together with a centralization policy of administration and resettlement have created what one Micmac called "a real little Indian city." Each reserve contains in addition to several hundred new houses, a church, large school, Band meeting house, hospital or nursing station, Agency offices, and government-operated store staffed in part with Indians, all built from lumber cut in the neighborhood and shaped at a sawmill on the reserve.

At Shubenacadie in June 1950 there was an air of bustle and movement. The sawmill was booming in the middle of the long road lined with new frame houses and in the yards were cars, bicycles, children's wagons, and store-bought swings. Up and down the street passed the cars of Mounted Police and other Agency visitors, of Indians and of tourists, and at noon the big Agency trucks, bringing the sawmill workers home for dinner. Young mothers in bright shortie coats, pushing baby buggies, an Indian constable in blue uniform, swinging his nightstick, old men and crowds of children around the store made lively movement on a reserve that actually was dying before its full-term birth. For in the region there were almost no jobs available. In 1950, with population at the peak of 620, the Indian Affairs Branch reported: "Welfare projects and land clearance continue to be the chief source of work." In 1953, when the population had dropped to 500, welfare assistance in housing, although it had been greatly reduced, "was, nevertheless, through the year the greatest source of employment on the larger reserves of Shubenacadie and Eskasoni." Many of the old people at Shubenacadie, moved willingly or not, remembered the old days and didn't much like "that bunch" from Truro or Pictou, while the minority of old Shubenacadie residents sat apart and also remembered the past. By 1953 enough families had drifted back to their original homes to require the building of new houses and the reopening of schools at more than one reserve.

At Eskasoni in the Bras d'Or region of Cape Breton Sheila Steen in 1950 noted a similar situation. There 692 Micmac were living where in 1941 there had been a group of 257, more than half of them in two groups of related families. The Indian agent lived ten miles away; there was no church and a priest rarely visited the reserve; school was seldom open and attendance was not enforced. Into this closed, inbred community first were moved Micmac from Whycocomagh, and fights were waged day and night. In 1946 Agency officials moved in, and this place

The Modern Micmac

once free of all white interference now had strict supervision in most phases of life. However, as at Shubenacadie, the main jobs were those created by the government program. By 1953 the old reserves at Whycocomagh and Nyanza were having a rebirth; and on the site of a razed schoolhouse a new one had arisen.

Whatever the Micmac do for a living, that living is small. The situation of their reserves, general conditions in the Maritime Provinces, their lack of education and skills, and their attitude toward sustained work, particularly away from their homes, all contribute to this condition.

The old ways of hunting and fishing have gone with the bulk of the game animals. Few individuals trap, and families no longer go into the woods to camp for the winter. Old people at Restigouche spoke of the moose and bear taken fifty years ago; smoked moose soaked for two or three days and then cooked with potatoes or other vegetables "made a good mess during the haying season." Bear which looked and tasted like a big pork-roast also gave a clear, tasteless grease that would stop diarrhea. A Big Cove woman of sixty-five remembered the only moose killed on the reserve in her childhood, of which each household received a share. Porcupine is still generally considered good food if it is properly prepared. The animal should be skinned to avoid the smoky taste resulting from burning off the quills; only the back and hindquarters should be used in the stew. Very few people would touch muskrat; and an insult to Maliseet who think otherwise is to call them "Muskrat People." However, it is now eaten at Burnt Church, where we were told the following method of preparation: "In spring select only a male. A female that has just borne young will be too lean. Put the cleaned meat in brine overnight; boil it in fresh water; throw out the water and add fresh water and boil again; then fry the meat in salt pork with pepper and onions." The same cook saw beaver for the first time in 1953. Knowing that the old-time Indians said the tail was fine, she asked the trapper for a hind quarter. No one would eat the meat. First she soaked and boiled it as she had muskrat, then baked it in a pan with salt pork. The meat tasted just like venison. Rabbits should be snared, never shot, and the blood used in cooking.

Some middle-aged men earn a short-seasonal living as hunting and fishing guides for the "Sports." Recently, one old guide when dying asked his wife to cook frog legs for him, a tabooed food he had eaten with the "Sports." His wife refused to do so. She was, said our informant, a devoted

PART ONE *Tribal Life*

wife, but this was too much. At Shubenacadie in 1950 we encountered a man whom WDW on a camping trip in 1912 had — on a promise of secrecy — induced to eat frog legs. With him we met his ninety-year-old father who immediately remembered what his son had confessed long after the event: "So you're the fellow who — "

Fishing in certain areas for gaspereau in winter and lobsters in early summer is carried on commercially, but it is a small and uncertain business. In 1950 Micmac in the Miramichi were rowing heavy dories to their lobster pots; in 1953 quite a few men had purchased two-hundred-dollar outboard motors on a five-year government loan. We heard frequent complaints about the law prohibiting salmon fishing in the Restigouche River; a man fishing on his own reserve is put in jail!

The occupations of the "old-time" Indians (grandparents and parents of the present-day old people) which still are carried on are lumbering and the making of so-called "Indian wares." As the forests retreated in the Maritimes, Micmac, like their white neighbors, have migrated for seasons or years to the north and west, particularly across the border; as early as 1883 Restigouche men, Indian and white, were in demand in the Minnesota and Wisconsin woods. Of the whites an old newspaper account says: "More of them are there now than remain in their country." At Restigouche, at Burnt Church, and at other reserves old men frequently greeted us with accounts of their experiences in Minnesota; others had spent two years in Labrador. At present men cut pulp on and near their reserve, work on log booms and in the pulp mills of the Maritimes.

Wooden objects known as "Indian wares," often mentioned by aged informants as the chief occupation of their parents, were butter tubs and churns, sap buckets, axe, pick, and peavey handles, snowshoe frames, and hockey sticks. By 1916 government reports indicated that the supply of ash and other suitable wood near the reserves had been exhausted. The work continued, however, though in smaller quantity. In the war years with steady employment open in the steel mills, in lumbering, and on farms, handicraft was carried on mainly by the aged and the physically handicapped; but with the slack years of 1947 and 1948 the government bought handicraft materials and shipped them to the reserves.

The home manufacture of splint potato baskets is the chief occupation carried on by reserve Indians in the 1950s — except for construction of their own new houses. Blueberry picking, the canning of lobster and

278

The Modern Micmac

herring, gathering and selling May flowers, and cutting Christmas trees are various short-term occupations of men, women, and children. The old crafts are carried on by very few. One or two women in Nova Scotia make fancy moccasins, particularly miniatures for the tourist trade. The application of porcupine quill embroidery to birch bark, once general from Restigouche to Nova Scotia, is now nearly extinct; old women know the shapes of boxes their mothers made for the tourist trade and their uses — round ones for jewelry, square for ladies' handkerchiefs, long for neckties. In only two homes were we shown treasured bark-boxes made by forebears. At Shubenacadie, where two women can still do fine quill mosaic, in 1950 several others had developed the making of flowers from basket splints which their husbands sell in Halifax and St. John, and in 1953 we received such flowers as Christmas gifts from a Miramichi reserve. Near each reserve domestic work is available to a few women; for many years it has been most plentiful at Restigouche where fifteen women cross daily to Campbellton.

But in 1953 the principal source of employment for Micmac Indians was in the United States. Young people spent the winter in the factories of Hoboken and Connecticut. From Prince Edward Island at least 35 per cent of the able-bodied men and boys had gone to New England; the same was true for an appreciable number of Nova Scotia Micmac; while New Brunswick reports Indians working on construction in Connecticut and in potato warehouses and fertilizer plants in Maine "in an increased movement to the United States in search of employment."

This is in addition to the annual family trek to the potato fields of Aroostook County. First mentioned in the Indian Affairs reports of 1941, Micmac for at least thirteen years have been leaving en masse each fall to work for individual growers, many of whom send trucks for transport to Maine; back in these trucks, some weeks later, come American electrical appliances, bicycles, expensive toys. In a good year a family can earn enough money to carry them through the winter. Warm clothing is bought and with the recent coming of electricity, lights are installed in the homes.[2] From remote Eskasoni only men migrate for the potato season, but in Quebec and New Brunswick only the old, the ill, and the mothers of numerous very small children, the "potato widows," remain

[2] The prestige of the Micmac home wired for electricity is demonstrated with clarity and charm by the drawings made by children attending the Indian Day School at Burnt Church, in April 1952, eight months after the "hydro" was installed at the reserve. (See illustrations 48 and 49.)

279

48. Man dragging a wood-sled at Burnt Church Reserve, drawn by Ronald Bartibogue, age thirteen.

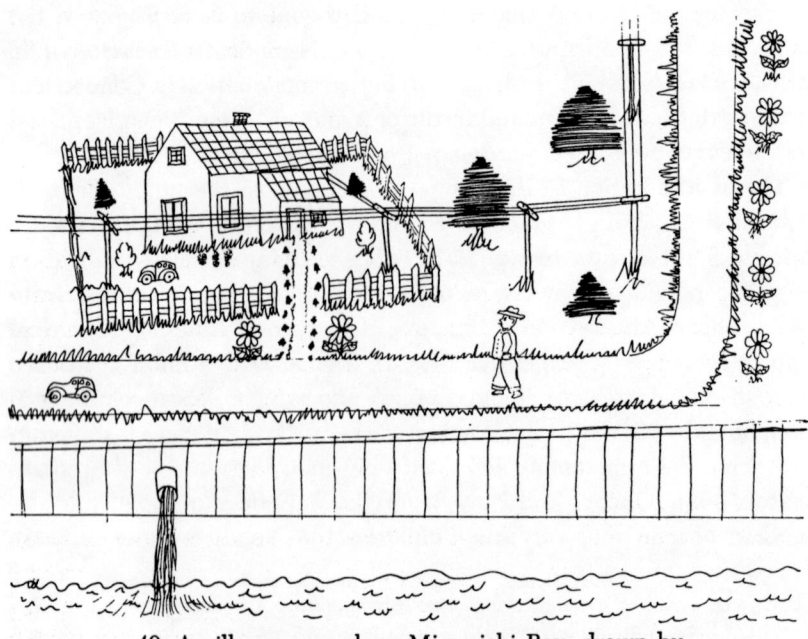

49. A village scene along Miramichi Bay, drawn by Emily Francis, age thirteen.

The Modern Micmac

on the reserves. The scale of this enterprise and its inclusion of both sexes and nearly all ages interlock with many phases of Micmac life. The important contribution to basic income is increased by the manufacture and sale of potato baskets on each reserve which is known to the Maine growers as a source of both labor and materials, and therefore considerable winter employment is also created. The social world is enlarged by the travel across the border and the demand for the white's material culture is greatly stimulated and partially satisfied. Arrangements for employment develop skills in certain men who, while their family pick, work mainly as labor recruiters and contractors. Some Micmac feel that they make easier contacts with white people in the States than with those at home; several mentioned friends they later visited.

The social consequences of the annual potato picking are clearly indicated but not proved. Daily life in the potato fields is hard work, but is also fun. Old friends from all sections of the Micmac and Maliseet territories meet; new acquaintances are made. A group of kin and neighbors live in a shack on the farmer's land; a woman who receives a daily payment from each member, including children, does the food buying and cooking, and may clear a hundred dollars. At the age of eight, children pick steadily;[3] a boy of this age filled thirteen barrels each day; a girl of eleven or twelve will have at least sixty dollars for winter clothes, and the money will be so designated by the parents ("Molly earned all her winter clothes; also Tommie"). The total per child considerably exceeds their share of the Family Allowance which is in abeyance during the working period.[4]

The child as a wage earner has an enhanced status in the family with possibly less show of respect for his elders who henceforth impose less restraint. Certainly the annual period of school attendance is greatly shortened; and this contributes to the picture of the Indian child as backward for his age. More serious and more difficult to assess is the part the weeks of autumn relaxation of social standards may play in

[3] "An Indian child is not required to attend school if the child . . . is, with the permission in writing of the superintendent, absent for a period not exceeding six weeks in each term for purposes of assisting in husbandry or urgent and necessary household duties." The Indian Act, Statutes of Canada, 1951, Section 116.

[4] The Canadian Family Allowance, established in 1945, is a fixed sum per month paid to all mothers for each child from birth to the age of sixteen. Children between the ages of six and sixteen must attend school or forfeit the allowance. The maximum monthly payment at the upper ages is eight dollars. No deduction for dependent children is allowed on the personal income tax; hence Indians, who do not pay this tax, are the greatest gainers from the Family Allowance.

PART ONE *Tribal Life*

the rising birth rate among very young unmarried mothers. This topic, introduced and deplored by at least one woman on each reserve in the summer of 1953, was also mentioned by an understanding Agency superintendent. Not all women attributed increased illegitimacy to group life in Maine (one said, "Too much cars; it's sad for God"); but several mothers and teaching nuns did so. One of the latter said that following the season when members of a working group, not all of whom are related, sleep and eat on the floor of a shack, young girls return to school with a greatly altered manner; two whom she questioned, each under sixteen, admitted to sex relations in Maine. Pregnancies result from contact with boys and single men and with the husbands of the "potato widows." A mother described her daughter as obedient and in the house at nine or ten every night until, when she was past fourteen, she went to Maine without her mother, who was ill. The girl came back independent, "wild," and now at seventeen she is "on the road" late every night. But only the puritanical priest at one reserve has stated that no families ought to go to Maine, an unreal solution to the present economic problems of the Micmac and of the Indian Affairs Branch of Canada.

With all other aspects of Micmac material culture, the traditional dress of ceremony had disappeared. The chief's coats common in 1911–12 have vanished (see illustrations 21, 22, and 33) and, even at St. Anne's Day in conservative Cape Breton, appeared only on the visiting chief from Prince Edward Island.[5] (See illustration 23.) Two old women at Shubenacadie still owned parts of their costumes in 1950, which they sometimes loaned to touring white women who wanted to be photographed so adorned. One of the owners refused to don the squaw cap for us because "I feel all shut in," and preferred a Plains type headband and feather. Old men who showed photographs of themselves attending the dedication of the Canadian destroyer *Micmac* were wearing the feathered warbonnets of the Plains. All said that when in recent years they had worn their costumes on St. Anne's Day they had been greeted with amusement by the younger people; and a New Brunswick Micmac woman who had recently spent a holiday at Shubenacadie described the costumes as "not real Indian, more like a show." They were not worn in 1950.[6] However, one instance — survival, revival, or travesty — existed in 1953 at Eel Ground, N.B. There the chief, perhaps

[5] Parsons, JAFL, 39:460–85 (1926).
[6] Martin and Sayres, unpublished notes.

under the influence of a previous radio appearance, had acquired a "chief's coat," made in Cape Breton, of cheap blue cotton cloth, decorated with a little coarse beading. Donning this for our benefit, he added a red sash, a headband, and a feather to which were sewn two long braids of black yarn.

RECREATION AND HOLIDAYS

St. Anne's Day at Burnt Church in 1953 brought everyone out in best clothes, new and fashionable, if possible, and in any case clean and well pressed. Most of the younger women and girls were dressed in quiet good taste; a few showed the careful grooming which Indian women throughout Canada learn in the tragic setting of the tuberculosis sanitarium.

As for the Micmac "national holiday," which was the union of the aboriginal summer council meeting with the feast of St. Anne, the last of the tribal features described in 1911-12 by Peter Ginnish and John Newell are gone forever. Because of its past importance to the Micmac it seems worth while to present what we know of transitional stages later than the memories of the two old informants of forty years ago.

Among Micmac settlements the most conservative are probably those situated in the Bras d'Or region of Cape Breton. There on Chapel Island, said to be the spot where Father Maillard preached his first sermon, Indians gather each year on July 26. In recent times the occasion was still a combined religious rite, tribal council in charge of the Grand Chief (a figurehead left over from the Wabanaki Confederacy), an attraction for tourists, and a good time for the Micmac. The earliest dated account we have (1903) unfortunately stresses mainly non-Micmac religious elements:

> During the week the large wigwam opposite the church is used as a court house, where the chief, assisted by the captains, and guided by the advice of the priest who has charge of the mission, disposes of any disputes that may have arisen amongst different members of the tribe.
>
> The chapel itself, which is of course dedicated to St. Anne, differs little from the ordinary Roman Catholic church in the poorer districts, except that it possesses a shrine of the patroness, brought out from France by the good Father Maillard himself, which is regarded by the Indians with the deepest veneration. . . .
>
> The most interesting day during the mission is the Sunday nearest St. Anne's Day. Mass is said at ten by the priest, who occupies the only

PART ONE *Tribal Life*

house on the island. One of the Indians acts as server. After the sermon, which is in English, the chief addresses the congregation, partly translating the words of the priest and partly, as the present chief told the the writer, speaking to them in his own words. The musical part of the services is supplied by the Indians themselves and is in Micmac. Their chanting, which is mainly in the minor tones, is weirdly sweet and haunting. After mass the shrine of St. Anne is placed upon a litter, and the Indian women proceed to drape the canopy with lace curtains and bright colored cloths. At the same time the figures of St. Anne and of Our Lady are crowned with flowers, as well as draped with bright colored vestments. Meanwhile, the men are employed in marking out, with poles surmounted by white flags bearing red crosses, the course for the procession, which goes from the church to the spot where Father Maillard preached the first sermon, returning thence to the church.

Early in the afternoon all the preparations are completed. A small cannon, brought from Louisburg, fires a salute and the procession starts from the church in the following order: —

> An aged Indian bearing the processional crucifix.
> The priest and the chief walking together.
> The sacred shrine, borne by four Indians, wearing blue sashes
> and supported by four maidens, walking two on each
> side, dressed in all the colors of the rainbow, and
> each bearing a vase of flowers.
> An Indian bearing a blue banner with three crosses.
> The choir, the leader of which sings from a huge manuscript
> book made from a leather-bound ledger, which is carried
> before him by two younger Indians, wearing green
> sashes, who walk backwards during the whole
> procession.
> The whole body of the faithful men, women and children,
> many of them carrying flags and banners.

During the progress of the procession the choir chant the Magnificat and other hymns and the cannon is discharged at frequent intervals. All the men walk with bared heads and the greatest reverence and decorum are observed. When the sacred spot itself is reached, the procession halts, whilst some prayers in Micmac are recited. All the Indians then approach the shrine of St. Anne one by one, make the sign of the cross, kneel a few seconds in silent prayer, deposit their lowly offerings of a few cents, kiss the feet of the saint and reverently withdraw. The procession then returns to the church. When it has gone about half way from the sacred rock a halt is made and the whole multitude kneel in prayer for a few minutes, presenting a striking picture as the bright rays of the afternoon sun illume their awed and devout faces. The procession then proceeds round the church, which is then entered, the shrine being deposited in the centre of the aisle, whilst a brief Micmac service is held. Later in the afternoon vespers are said.[7]

In 1923 the observer at Chapel Island was an anthropologist, the late Elsie Clews Parsons, who lived in a Micmac wigwam throughout the celebration, which lasted from July 26 to August 8. The total present in that year was 150. Twenty years earlier (the date of the preceding account) there had been 117 tar-paper wigwams around the permanent chapel and glebe house for the priest; in 1923 there were 75 set up by Micmac from Whycocomagh on St. Patrick's Channel, Bras d'Or, who came by boat, and others from Sydney, Eskasoni, Middle River (all Cape Breton); from Pomquet near Antigonish and Truro, N.S.; and the chief and his wife from Rocky Point, P.E.I.

In the temporary wigwams old-time etiquette in seating was rather well observed. The "kitchen" was to the right of the door; and the water bucket to the left. The wife's place was next to the "kitchen," the husband sat above her, a blanket or box was put opposite the entrance for any distinguished guest. Less important but welcome guests were invited to come up higher. Children never passed between adults and the fire.

The old ceremonial on arrival of the visiting party survived only as a joke made at the expense of a very shy chief from Prince Edward Island, who, a jester said, had come in slyly when no one was looking, in order to avoid having to stand up to his knees in water for the old-time greeting.

The Indians described the island as "holy land" where the first French priest had lived. A rise of land at one end, called Sarusalem, was crowned by a large cross; the ten stations on the way to it were marked by smaller crosses.

There was a remnant of the old courting customs. *Elmedek*, the "road up," leading to the cross, was a cleared way suitable for boys and girls, sometimes sex by sex, sometimes together, to go on walking parties. Parsons saw only one couple walking there, arm in arm, a betrothed couple soon to be married by the priest. After dark was the usual Indian time. At the close of the church service on Sunday, the Grand Chief exhorted parents not to oppose marriages of their daughters; here was a good chance with the priest at hand; it was "safest to let them marry, not to have them around at nights."

[7] Vernon, 1903, 112–14.

PART ONE *Tribal Life*

Prominent in this Cape Breton celebration was an element completely lost in other parts of the Micmac world, although introduced in recent times. The office of Grand Chief, instituted with the Wabanaki Confederacy (c. 1750–1850) and elsewhere forgotten or ignored, continues here, and with it certain other Iroquois traits which functioned during the period of defensive union, such as wampum and the wampum record-keeper. Parsons' account, abridged and rearranged, follows:

Sunday, Procession Day. Between the church and the store, flags were standing, four on one side, five opposite. All standards were removed at the end of the day except that of the Grand Chief. The flag consisted of a red cross on a white ground, in the upper corners in red a crescent and a five-pointed star. Micmac explained that the cross was for the church, and that the moon and the star were "Indian flag."

Following Mass, the visiting chief from Prince Edward Island, the most distinguished guest, gave a long talk, with many gestures. He alone wore the old time chief's coat, and his wife was the sole wearer of the former style dress and pointed cap. Then came a midday meal, and later the procession.

A small red cross was carried at the head of it. Two men followed, a chief of one of the bands and the wampum record-keeper; the priest then walked between the Prince Edward Island chief and the Grand Chief; four men carried the heavy image of St. Anne and the Virgin, and on either side walked two little girls in white dresses. Next a choir of six or seven men, and then the crowd of worshippers. From the church door the procession passed through the little avenue of flags and poplar branches . . . and on to the boulder-set iron cross, which they encircled anti-sunwise, and set the images down. After the choir sang a hymn in Micmac, the priest announced in English that he had a reliquary to be kissed. He offered the enshrined relique to the mouth of each worshipper, wiping it between kisses with the sleeves of his vestment. Others pushed up to the images of Mother and Daughter to kiss their feet and *throw* charity.

About a hundred white visitors had arrived on an excursion boat from Sydney — welcome as a source of prestige and of revenue. These paid to be rowed from the steamer to the island, for their seats at Mass, and now collection boxes were circulated among them with the priest's suggestion, "The Indians are poor, the Mission is expensive, give all you can." Returning to the church the procession made an anti-sunwise circuit around it before entering.

Monday, Crawling to St. Anne. The procession to the church and up to the image began some distance from the building. First a prayer was made by the Grand Chief, and then all on their knees, the procession started, headed by the men, who moved forward three or four knee-lengths, movement and prayers alternating. As persons passed over the church threshold they kissed it, moved on up the center aisle, and then turned to the left to kiss the images' feet, and to *throw* small coins. For those sick who have a strong pure heart, it is a sure cure "to go to see St. Anne on your knees."

Wednesday Assembly, mawagenu'temamik; War medicine dance, nes'-kawet. Dinner, which took place at 4:30 p.m., was purely a ceremonial affair. Bread and tea or a money equivalent were contributed by each wigwam and carried to the grand wigwam, *kichi wigwom,* the poles of which were covered with canvas and the entrance closed with a frame door. Within, the chiefs, the wampum record-keeper (*pudus*) and the captains were to eat; other men and boys of all ages were outside facing the door. All inside and out sang a grace, and the meeting concluded with "Thanks to God." The eating inside was over in ten minutes. The men then took seats in a circle around the wigwam entrance, and from within an address was made, lasting about five minutes. Then there was a shout and a song, acclaiming a captain. Out stepped the captain, wearing the insignia, a moon-crescent medal hanging on his chest. Beginning with the man sitting on the right of the wigwam entrance the captain shook hands around the circle (*pusoliwit, bonjours*) in anti-sunwise circuit. In conclusion he stood at the entrance, and with sweeping gesture, waved his hat, wishing good luck, while the circle of men shouted "*eh!*" Another captain followed. After a considerable interval the chief from P.E.I. appeared, sang for a moment, with body inclined slightly forward, took dance steps, a stamp with the right foot, then left. He went anti-sunwise around the circle, shaking hands, and at each quarter circle broke off to sing, dance, receive shouts from the group, and shake hands again. Two men of no particular consequence followed with similar behavior.

From within the tent the wampum record-keeper made an address, following which all men crowded into the wigwam for the final ceremony which the observer, a woman, was not permitted to see. At the close the church bell tolled for evening service, the angelus.

After service people gathered around the dance ring in front of the Grand Chief's wigwam, a rutted ring with a diameter of about 18 feet. A man stood in the center, beating a doubled piece of brown paper in lieu of birchbark. He sang two or three words or syllables, in repetition, for one-minute periods. When he stopped singing, the circle stopped dancing, and shouted. After six or eight such songs and breaks, another man took his place. The dancers progressed in anti-sunwise circuit, one behind the other, their step a rapid clog, their arms loose. Most of them were young men, but a man of 72 and a boy of 3 years joined, as did one middle-aged woman and, when pushed into the circle, one young girl.

PART ONE *Tribal Life*

Our final account of St. Anne's Day on Chapel Island is based on the observations of another anthropologist, Sheila Steen, made in 1950. For the occasion a French priest came from Quebec. The Indians, all from Cape Breton settlements, set up tents, tar-paper wigwams, and even a few of birch bark around the church and the priest's house. Some of the Micmac expected relief from illness through the blessing of St. Anne. Games of chance were operated by Micmac who also ran ice-cream stands. There were no Indian dances; they were last held in 1943, ended, some said, by the priest's orders. Others said they did not know why dancing stopped. Except for the very young at Eskasoni, according to Steen, most of the Micmac still know how to perform the old-time dances.

From Shubenacadie, N.S., we have for the same year (1950) the fuller account of the holiday as seen by Martin and Sayres, then graduate students of anthropology at Harvard. This was a two-day celebration, July 26–27.

On July 26th, mass was said at 8 a.m. At 2 p.m. the procession formed to carry the statue of St. Anne from the church to the cross in the cemetery. It was headed by four girls who held the ends of two poles beneath an open-sided, roofed superstructure containing the statue. They were followed by: small girls in white dresses from the reserve; older girls in clean dresses and uniform white berets from the Residential School; boys from the Residential School in uniform khaki shorts and horizontally striped T-shirts; a small group of Indians of all ages from the reserve, talking and looking around; the priest saying Hail Marys; nuns from the reserve and the Residential School; the rest of the parish. The priest led the procession up to the cross where the statue was placed, with a collection dish on the floor of its enclosure.

During the procession and the following ceremony, old men sang in Micmac. Parishioners in a line now slowly approached the statue. Each in turn knelt, crossed himself, threw a contribution into the dish, and kissed the feet of the statue. The atmosphere was reverent and quiet. Those who had passed through the ceremony relaxed and talked with one another.

On the return of the procession to the church, at a given point all knelt for a minute. The statue was returned to the church, a short prayer was said by the priest, and the religious part of the festival was over.

The recreational features, called "The Picnic," centered around the Band hall. Suppers were served inside; in booths built outside hot dogs, pop and ice cream, candy, cigarettes, and cigars were sold. A dance platform, fenced in on three sides, was erected in the open, with a small shelter on the fourth side for the musicians, guitarist and fiddler,

The Modern Micmac

both local Micmac. Games of chance were: bingo; darts; "crown and anchor," and "seven and under," two dice games; ball-throw.

Bingo was the big money-maker. The priest ran it, assisted by two Micmac. Numbers were announced over a loud-speaker. Players were mainly elderly and predominantly women; several of these stayed at the bingo table most of the time. Whites came later each day than did Indians; after evening dancing began at nine o'clock or so, most Indians drifted away to watch it and players were mainly white. Dice games were patronized principally by young men and small boys.

Chances were sold on a $50 prize, a baby sweater, a cowboy suit, a tablecloth; punchboards were circulated for a doll prize, and paper roses were sold, some of which had small attached prizes. Salesmanship and showmanship were amateur and often inefficient. Food-handling was unsanitary and nobody cared.

Soft-ball games were a prominent part of the picnic; informal games were played each afternoon by Indians from 10 to 29 years of age. Each evening there was a game against a white team from Shubenacadie.

The dance stand was in a sense the focus of activity and interest on both evenings. A small microphone was attached to the violin and the guitarist played into a standing mike: both were attached to an amplifier. Square-dances were hop-polkas set to breakdowns, with about every fourth set to a waltz. Each evening there was one "lantz" [Lancers?] . . . with eight couples and three figures to the set. There were also waltzes for couples. Each evening, the dancers through two-thirds of the time were all whites. Indians began to dance late in the evening; men were "shy," girls, eager to dance.

Comments of Indians on the picnic were that it was not altogether satisfactory because: it lasted only two days; there were fewer kinds of recreation than in former years; the crowd was smaller; prices were too high and all entertainment was staged to make money rather than to provide fun.

No features of this St. Anne's Day could be considered Indian or Micmac. For a short time each night, before other activities began, a couple of old men would get up and step-dance; they would take a few steps, laugh, and quit. No visitors from other reserves are mentioned.

Our own experience with a modern St. Anne's Day in 1953 included attendance at the Burnt Church celebration and a view of preparations at Restigouche and Maria. Under the guidance of the Capuchins of the monastery and parish church of Ste Anne de Restigouche a festival attractive to the religious French and profitable to the church was in the process of organization. Brown-robed, bare-legged monks bent their backs and their tonsured heads to the nailing of booths for

PART ONE *Tribal Life*

the sale of refreshments and articles which would include the handiwork of the white French women's guild and the Micmac Homemakers Club, instituted by the Indian Affairs Branch and administered by the Sisters of the Holy Rosary who had just celebrated their fiftieth year of residence at Restigouche. The Micmac women were to sell their quilts, cradles, dolls, and nicknacks at a separate booth. A midnight mass was to be held on July 25–26, and during the following week, there was to be an evening pilgrimage from a different French parish, with a procession of cars carrying lights.

Some Micmac at the reserve looked on all this with a definitely cool eye. There were murmurs (not checked) that on St. Anne's Day they had to give up the church pews for which they paid to the strange French visitors. And there were reminiscences of earlier days when the only outsiders were Indians who came in canoes. "We went to church and had a big Indian dance. People came from Maria, Burnt Church, Eel Ground. When Father Pacifique was alive, they even came from Prince Edward Island and Nova Scotia. The families here had to take them in and feed them all."

At the small Gaspé reserve of Maria a few children were gathering flowers for the church but there was no great anticipation of the holiday. Those who could afford it planned to go to Restigouche, and here too we heard of the days of Father Pacifique who always came to Maria on the Sunday following St. Anne's Day. There is no "picnic" and ice cream and soft drinks are no longer sold. A procession carrying tapers goes from the convent down to the beach and up again to the church for benediction.

At our earlier visit to Burnt Church in 1950, two old men, co-informants, gave their version of current festivities: "People now come to Burnt Church from every other settlement — from Nova Scotia, Prince Edward Island, and Restigouche. When this visiting began, the hosts made only soup for the visitors. They killed small fat dogs for this purpose. The celebration then lasted for two weeks, and there were dances and festivities. Now the visitors remain usually only two or three days, and there is not so much dancing. Visitors pay for their meals, and this money goes to our church; for this settlement is the Micmac capital. Men, women, children, and whole families, come from other settlements; also many French-speaking persons, especially from nearby rural districts. Sometimes a Mountie or two are present [to preserve order]."

The Modern Micmac

Our return to Burnt Church in 1953 was after the death of our two old friends. To us St. Anne's Day seemed a typical annual celebration of a French Canadian parish. On the preceding Friday and Saturday evenings, an "evangelistic" priest from New Castle preached at benediction. On Sunday morning the 26th there was an 8 o'clock mass. Booths roofed with green boughs had been set up outside the Band hall for bingo and other games of chance, all operated by Indians, with the priest on hand to help. Chances were sold on a box of candy and a doll. In the early afternoon whites began to arrive in cars and standing in heavily loaded trucks. At once they began to play bingo. Indians and whites mingled in the crowd, talked to each other but mainly on the basis of previous acquaintance. All Micmac children were well supplied with money for pop and ice cream cones.

The service in the church began in the late afternoon, as the usual prelude to the procession carrying the statue of St. Anne to the shrine. (See illustration 39.) Then rain came, as it had on the two preceeding years and ended the religious part of the festival. That night there was a dance in the old Band house, and about 200 attended, a smaller crowd than expected had there been no rain. The second night (Monday) there was also a dance, bingo, and other games. Church women sold sandwiches, and men sold pop and ice cream cones. Dancing went on until two in the morning. Not a trace of the old Micmac tribal gathering is left. In 1953 priests at all Miramichi reserves held St. Anne's Day "picnics" to raise money for their churches by attracting whites. And so the old custom of gathering at Burnt Church is dead.

At Big Cove, largest of Miramichi reserves, St. Anne's Day, because it fell on a Sunday, was purely a religious day. The picnic which was advertised in the Moncton newspaper as well as in nearer and smaller towns ran for five nights following, with baseball and dancing each night. Crowds came which proved, according to a white informant, how much the people like the Indians. It could also prove how little there is to do in that part of New Brunswick. However, the attendance indicates that the affairs are well run and the Micmac of today do not withdraw suspiciously from their neighbors.

The universally celebrated Christian holidays with religious and recreational aspects came late into Micmac culture. About 1935 the first Christmas trees were set up at Burnt Church; now every home has one decorated with tinsel and artificial snow and every child believes in

PART ONE *Tribal Life*

Santa Claus. In 1912 old women would say, "Don't let the children know about Christmas." Now, all agree, you couldn't keep it from them, with the newspaper, radio, and the Newcastle store windows available to all. At Eel Ground women of sixty said that as children they received presents only if their parents were working in the States. Santa Claus was introduced about 1940 and now after the coming of electricity, every house along the highway has a lighted Christmas tree. Midnight mass is also a recent introduction.

Twenty years ago, everyone at Eel Ground and Burnt Church made pies in preparation for Easter Eve, when groups of young people went from house to house singing hymns. They would collect the pies and take them to one of their homes for a feast. The custom is not kept up by the present young generation. At remote Eskasoni, where a priest seldom came, the Micmac organized their own observances. Old and respected men led prayers and chants, and Micmac song and dance accompanied Christian ritual. This ended in 1947 when a resident priest came to the greatly expanded reserve. Micmac now, concludes Sheila Steen, are spectator-participants in the government and church-managed ceremonies.

The Canadian national holiday, Dominion Day, was not celebrated in 1950 at reserves in Nova Scotia or in 1953 in New Brunswick. This is, of course, a British not a French Canadian day and Micmac festivals are patterned closely on those of their church group, though every Micmac home, however poor, showed allegiance to "our Queen" by one or more pictures of her and often of the Duke and the royal children.

Personal holidays have recently put in an appearance. A Micmac of any age may receive a birthday cake; children blow out candles according to white custom. And the long commercial arm of Mother's Day and Father's Day has gripped the more acculturated families.

On holidays — and any other days — baseball is the favorite recreation of most men and boys. Mention has already been made of the sport as played at Restigouche and Shubenacadie. At Burnt Church, where old men claimed it was originally learned from sailors off a Yankee boat, the whites considered the team excellent and the players fine sportsmen. Movies shown by the priest in the town hall of white Burnt Church help to raise the money to transport the team to games off the reserve, a sort of circular recreation which pleases a good many. The new settlements at Shubenacadie and Eskasoni play baseball and hockey in government-

The Modern Micmac

inspired intergroup competition, and also attend movies and engage in square dancing organized for them.

Gambling, the oldest Micmac sport, needs no nudge. The game is no longer *waltes*. In two summers we met only two women who could still play the game and we did not see one bowl. One of the women gave us three dice made from moose shoulder-bone and engraved with the characteristic designs, each worn to a slight hollow from scraping it to remove particles which are excellent as a painkiller for toothache and mumps. Five or six *waltes* sets existed in 1950 among Eskasoni Micmac, where Steen saw the game played, though infrequently; once a china plate was used. Many teen-agers did not know the game, and others had to consult old people about the scoring.

The modern gambling games are poker, primarily for men, and bingo and rummy, favored by women. However, at Burnt Church men and women of all ages play bingo on Sunday afternoons in the Band hall.

WEDDINGS AND FUNERALS

The celebration of weddings and funerals follows in the main the European Catholic pattern. The marriage and nuptial mass are held in the reserve church; fashionable young ladies at one reserve prefer the whites' church in the nearest good-sized town. Following this there is a big party with tables set all day. At some reserves everyone is invited; at Shubenacadie one woman said that since expansion and resettlement only friends are invited. A recent bride at Restigouche told us that she wrote notes inviting her friends but she would see other people pass the house where they were feasting and she would run out and ask them to come in. All weddings described to us and by Martin and Sayres ended with all-night dancing in the hall, but at Eskasoni in 1950 Sheila Steen attended two which consisted of the mass and little else. "Formerly, a wedding used to involve much celebration. The families of the engaged couple planned for months in advance. Food was stored up, liquor was made and bought from bootleggers, and many people were invited. There was great feasting, merrymaking, and fun. Now the authorities live on the reserve and 'Good Times are no more'."

Death customs include the Catholic practices of covering the walls with white sheets, holy pictures pinned to them ("like the statues in the church are covered every year at Our Lord's death"), and a wake held for the two nights before burial. Some people are unkindly said to

PART ONE *Tribal Life*

attend merely to see what the grieving relatives will serve. ("If one has a roast and another offers only sandwiches, he is no good.")

When a Micmac at Maria is dying, people gather and sing hymns, believing that salvation is assured if death takes place while they are singing.

The corpse of an adult Micmac is always placed in the coffin by an adult of like sex. Children place infants and children in coffins; informants differed about the sex, some saying that little boys did the service for all babies. Either an old woman or a very young one might wash an infant's corpse. Pallbearers are men except that little girls may carry a baby girl's body to the grave.

There is one death custom which with different application has a long Micmac history. In describing a St. Anne's Day of long ago, old John Newell, of Pictou, told of secret auctions of the belongings of a poverty-stricken person to hunters who then went forth to get the food they had pledged to the starving family.[8] Following a funeral, many Micmac now hold auctions of the deceased's personal property to contribute money for masses. The custom is no longer observed at Restigouche but it still functions in the Miramichi and in Nova Scotia. While informants said that clothing and such small belongings as scissors and pocketknives are the only things sold unless the deceased is the last of his family, the superintendent of a large reserve who had bought a good bed for an old woman shortly before her death was immediately thereafter petitioned for another by her husband because his wife's bed had, of course, been put up for "The Sale."

MEDICINE AND DISEASE

In their treatment of illness, the stubborn retention of folk medicine exists along with an abrupt termination of traditional practices in childbirth and infant feeding. The list of nostrums described by New Brunswick women today is as long as that obtained in 1911. Only a few of the items are identical in content and application; one's own medicine has always been a little better than the other fellow's. One prescription recommended in both periods is "black roots" as an aid in childbirth and dismenorrhea; this refers to viburnum, black haws, which had not entirely disappeared from the recognized pharmacopoeia of American

[8] See above, p. 187.

The Modern Micmac

gynecologists forty years ago. The Indian women take great pride in this remedy but the greatest confidence is expressed in their secret heart-disease medicine which, they claim is so efficacious that the Canadian government has tried to buy it from them. They, of course, refused and will not tell the name of the plant to the visiting nurses. Two elderly women who said they had gathered the roots last spring readily gave us the Micmac name, which turned out to be "heart-disease medicine." The plant is washed, and threaded like beads, to dry. Two of the dried roots are grated and steeped in a quart of lukewarm water for two or three hours, and administered to adults in four daily glassfuls. A teaspoonful in warm water is given to a baby in convulsions. Elsewhere, we were told that the plant is called "little turnips"; actually the bulb on the root is not turnip-shaped but is small and round. The plant, which grows eight to ten inches or higher, has white flowers shaped like a morning-glory and with red veins on the inner side of the petals. The medicine brewed from the roots is not as effective as another which the old people get from Nova Scotia. They are most secretive about the plant; however, the informant knew that it was digitalis.

Leaf poultices still appear on the arms of patients who bring their wounds and sores to the nursing stations. A New Brunswick woman told of her precocious performance in treating wounds by this method: When she was ten and alone in the house, an old man came to the door with a terrible axe-cut which he had filled with chewed leaves. The little girl took the family salve box containing tallow and calamus root and picked some big plantain leaves. She laid the leaves flat on the stove until they softened on the ribbed side, smeared the wound with the salve, laid the leaf on top, rib side next to the cut, and bound it in place. The next day all infection had been drawn out and another leaf was laid on the wound, this time with the smooth side against it to ensure healing.

The medicines now include more elements of European folk-doses than was true in 1911, such as a liniment made by shaking seven razor blades for seven days in a quart of vinegar, a potion brewed from wheat, white cotton, and red ribbon to arrest miscarriage, and generous applications of animal dung, without or within. Epilepsy is now treated by signing the victim with the cross; formerly blood was taken from the tip of the nose with a penknife and, we learned, old Peter Ginnish, the 1911 informant, had been a skilled practitioner. Some people are said to have one specific power to cure by touch an ill such as toothache.

PART ONE *Tribal Life*

Wood from a tree struck by lightning will also alleviate toothache, and several old men always carry a splinter in their pockets. The same persons recommended the application of hailstones to sore eyes.

It is probably safe to say that what the Micmac consider Indian medicines, although still in fair to high repute and in use by individuals who also demand the latest antibiotics by name, are gathered by only a few, almost entirely women, and that no one is much interested in perpetuating the practice. One possible exception should be made: the gathering of mountain ash for use in the disease no doctor can cure, sent by a witch's bad wish.

In contrast to this lingering life-or-death state of Micmac medicine, obstetrics has become suddenly and completely modern. Ancient midwives and breast feeding have been abruptly replaced by hospitalization and the universal nectar called "C'nation."[9] Hospitalization obviously is free. The beliefs and practices concerned with pregnancy and the prenatal period described in Chapter XV are known to all young women and followed by most of them, but two of the old childbirth superstitions cannot flourish under modern conditions of parturition. The cord will drop off in the hospital, and the doctor pierces the amnion without noting the rare and power-invested caul.

BELIEFS ABOUT THE SUPERNATURAL

The persistence of belief in the power of the caul and in all manifestations of supernatural power in 1953 and the modification of certain aspects since 1911–12 excite speculation and raise problems not easily answered. (For tales of the supernatural told in 1953, see pages 338–47.)

In the first place, has belief really changed, or are we dealing with individual differences of memory or of acceptance among informants? And in the two periods of study was the material gathered from comparable persons? In 1911–12 all informants about the supernatural were men, including old and young, whose backgrounds embraced all the Micmac areas; the region least represented was Quebec. Basic concepts agreed from man to man and from place to place. In 1950 and 1953 informants were men and women living at Quebec or New Brunswick reserves who referred occasionally to Nova Scotia and Prince Edward Island as the source of their statements. The ages of each sex ranged from fifteen

[9] Wallis and Wallis, 122.

The Modern Micmac

to over eighty. Much less talk about the miraculous was initiated by men, who, perhaps because of greater contacts with whites, appeared to be somewhat self-conscious and slower to speak of things that might arouse ridicule; or who actually had less interest in their culture and therefore less memory of things heard in their youth. There were, however, notable exceptions among the more talkative and relaxed; and several men in response to direct questions contributed information comparable to that given by their fellows.

Women frequently introduced such topics as ghosts, "bad wishes," and babies born with a veil; and mere mention of the word *buoin* usually brought forth vivid accounts of personal encounters. About the cause of this freer expression in the women, one can make some obvious guesses: that because approach to the subject followed talk about pregnancy and childbirth — subjects which in all cultures, one might say, attract superstitions — Micmac women found the transition to *ginap* and ghost gradual and easy; that they were more naive than the men in accepting the anthropologist's use of Micmac terms as evidence of greater knowledge than she possessed (at one reserve feminine rumor said we were Indians); or that they may have known a great deal more than did the men.

Pooled information given by men agreed with and covered nearly all topics discussed by the women; fundamentally it was the same as that obtained forty years earlier, and it therefore seems probable that the most marked and repeated differences between the two periods are real. Item for item they will be compared below.

Second, who holds these beliefs today? Does the degree of acceptance vary obviously with age, sex, amount of education or of white blood, and is it conspicuously present or absent on certain reserves? So far as we could judge on the basis of our sample, interest and adherence is much the same throughout Quebec and New Brunswick; however, on one large reserve there was avoidance and denial of anything touching on the supernatural. The evidence of emotional disturbance that the suggestions aroused was reinforced by eager and circumstantial talk from Micmac residing elsewhere about the current activity of witches in that particular settlement.

The majority of our informants were people from sixty to eighty years of age who had had very little schooling; the two old women who had attended a convent for a number of years were almost at the two ex-

PART ONE *Tribal Life*

tremes of belief. A man aged thirty-two, a partially disabled veteran, who lived by preference in a very small and isolated settlement and had never been to school, but had an easy social manner, spoke at enthusiastic length about dreams, ghosts, and other manifestations. The best educated of the young women with whom we talked, a white girl adopted as an infant by a very conservative old Micmac woman, entered eagerly into the conversation of her "grandmother," telling of her intense emotional reactions to various supernatural experiences they had shared. Three old women, indicated to us by Indians on their respective reserves as knowing a lot about old Micmac times, turned out to be French Canadians who had married into the tribe when young. In each instance they contributed numerous items, mainly about witchcraft and the caul, which they felt were Indian in origin — "those old squaws knew everything." Finally, on a reserve where we had heard that no knowledge of ghosts and dwarfs was given to children, child informants told a different story.

The supernatural power inherent in Micmac was named and defined by one old man as *gi'na ta bu' e*, "manitou"; the power passes from one person to another, and one who has it can give away half of it. The word suggests the *ginap*, one who possesses strength and mystic power. The power resides in the group and in the individual. Repeatedly informants in 1953 stated the old concept: "On every reserve there is at least one person, and on some reserves two, who have the power. A man who had such power when these persons were born knows that they possess the power; no ordinary people know who these elect are and the elect may not themselves know that they possess it. However, in a time of great need for help they will manifest their power and save their people." The designation *ginap* is applied to these hidden saviors. *Ginap* attributes given in anecdote or tale are the same as in 1911–12: great physical strength (usually); appearance at any age and in both sexes; ability to drink boiling oil; to make themselves invisible; to travel under water; to get great quantities of game or modern goods; to predict the future.

More clearly than in 1911–12 is the distinction between the quality of the two often associated powers: *ginap* is good; *buoin* is bad. To punish enemies of the Micmac the *ginap* may perform deeds which, from the point of view of the target, would not seem beneficent: such as the slaughter of Mohawk (still told in 1953) and the destruction of whites in the Miramichi and Campbellton fires (see Tales 136–37). In 1911–12

The Modern Micmac

tales the Miramichi disaster is kindled by an avenging flame issuing from the ground or from a cloud; in one present-day story the flame appears; in a second, a priest who receives a warning that whites are going to kill Indians burns the letter outdoors, and the sparks from the flaming paper start the conflagration; in a third version the fire is minimized and the hero is a Micmac with "the power" who protects his people.[10] Campbellton fire stories continue to describe the vengeance of a *buoin* or the just punishment by a *ginap* sent upon whites who refused a Micmac a drink of water. One of these tales illustrates the point at which *ginap-buoin* traits may fuse: At the tercentenary celebration in 1910 when a white man in Campbellton refused to give water to Joe Knockwood, the latter said, "You'll be needing some!" Another Micmac said to Joe, "Don't do it!" That is, do not be so angry that your wrath will produce calamity. A *ginap*, like a *buoin*, can injure a person by thinking about it; in fact any good person may bring about evil in a moment of extreme anger because all Micmac are potential possessers of this peculiar power.

However, *ginap* power is usually bestowed in one of various widely recognized ways. A person may hear someone say in a dream: "I'll give you a good power. You can go for two or three hundred miles and no one will see you." Thereafter, even if the dreamer nowadays decides never to use the power, it will show itself in an emergency; for example, a woman, who had had a *ginap* dream, when thrown from a boat into deep water could not sink lower than her knees.

By far the most frequent mention of "the good power" is in connection with the caul; so frequent, in fact, that one suspects genetic drift has produced an abnormally high rate of little veiled Micmac.[11] Added to the typical *ginap* powers of strength and second sight, the child, if even a tiny piece of the veil is kept for him, will be safe from fire, drowning, or any other accident. Moreover the powers extend to a purchaser, particularly as protection against drowning and as fire insurance. Micmac

[10] In another tale there is a curious medley of the so-called Council Fire (headquarters) of the Micmac section of the Wabanaki Confederacy, formerly in Cape Breton; and the beliefs concerning the Miramichi and Campbellton fires: "A long time ago the Micmac had a big meeting. They had to have a fire. If anything serious should happen, that fire must work. They made a law that they would have a fire to protect us. A man from Cape Breton said: 'I shall take the fire to Cape Breton.' They have a fire there now, and can use it for protection, as was done in the Campbellton and the Miramichi fires."

[11] This suspicion first occured to that fine geneticist Dr. Sheldon Reed.

PART ONE *Tribal Life*

mothers sold many pieces to soldiers during the two world wars, and, of course, to sailors. One claimed she got ten dollars a snippet during World War II. The most satisfied possessor we met was an old woman who paid seventy-five cents, thirty years ago, and thus, in spite of a hard and sad life, she now is fine and has no worries. ("It all comes now," meaning, the old age pension.) Between the veil and the veiled there may exist a sympathetic connection: a young man had always stressed his ownership of his caul, saying, "That's mine for war and for sailing." He kept it wrapped in tissue paper and in a little box locked in a trunk. After his death, his parents unlocked the trunk and found an empty box.

No mention of the caul or of its powers was made in 1911–12, probably because there were no women informants; although the chief purchasers seem to have been men. These beliefs about the veil, common in western European folklore, have all been recorded in French- and in English-speaking Canadian groups.[12]

The concept of the *ginap* as a whole seems to be definitely aboriginal and to have remained unchanged in the past forty years. The *buoin*, however, although most of the features dear to Peter Ginnish and John Newell are still present, has taken on a more decidedly European folk air. Elements of old Micmac origin, such as smoking a pipe as a preliminary to a "bad wish" and playing *waltes* to help vanquish an enemy, have dropped out. The curing factor remains very slight (the sale of medicine to end sterility and of love charms). All *ginap* qualities are retained, such as prediction of the future, fast travel, and walking under water. Contests of strength between *buoin*; a "good" *buoin* protecting a bad one; the animal appearing in a dream which must be killed by the dreamer; the endless stories of the request denied; the witch who must return to remove her curse — these have long been and still are beliefs shared by Canadian British, French, and Micmac. The 1911 statement that a witch draws a picture of a victim and then shoots it is now expressed as advice to the victim to practice against the witch. European

[12] For this and other beliefs, see John G. Campbell, *Witchcraft and Second Sight in the Scottish Highlands* (Glasgow, 1902); Paul Sébilot, *Légendes, Croyances et Superstitions de la Mer* (Paris, 1886); and the following articles, all from JAFL: William W. Newell, "The Ignus Fatuus," 17:39–60 (1904); W. J. Wintemberg, "French-Canadian Folk-Tales," 17:265–67 (1904); F. W. Waugh, "Canadian Folklore from Ontario," 31:4–82 (1918); W. J. Wintemberg and Katherine H. Wintemberg, "Folklore from Grey County, Ontario," 31:83–124 (1918); E. Z. Massicotte, "Croyances et Dictons Populaires des Environs de Trois-Rivières (Canada)," 32:168–75 (1920); and C. Marius Barbeau, "Anecdotes Populaires du Canada," 33:173–272 (1920).

The Modern Micmac

traits prominent now but not mentioned in our earlier period of study are these: sharpened mountain-ash as protection against witches; needles to draw the witch to one; injuries done to infants in utero and to living children; a plague of insects sent by the witch; and the direct statement that the animal seen in one's dream is not the witch but his "familiar."[13]

Contradictory ideas about the origin and prevalence of witches are expressed today. It is wise when inquiring about *buoin* to suggest that they have disappeared, and most listeners agree, even though they immediately describe an accident to their car, last week, after they had refused a ride to that old woman at such-and-such a reserve. Reactions are "There are a few still performing but not many." "They have no great strength now." At Eskasoni, it is said that the witches have all left for the remote reserve of Nyanza and at Restigouche that there are none here but a lot live in New Brunswick. Weakening power may be explained as absence of pure Micmac blood; or as in a tale of extraordinarily smart operators of long ago that "they got their witchcraft in France." The devil, who is often named as the source of evil power — perhaps under priestly guidance — is said to run a circus; that is, high-wire performers are regarded as *buoin*.

The avid way in which personal and pseudo-personal encounters with witches dead or now living are narrated gives the impression that the enmities of small-community life frequently find outlet in these patterned accusations. With a flare for psychology, an old man said: "People can make a witch. People said that an aunt of mine was a witch. They said so at this house, that house, and another house. Someone told the priest she was a *buoin*. He said, 'I will find out whether it is true.' People took her to church. She went up to the priest. He said, 'The people say you are a witch.' She said, 'I'll show you whether I am a witch.' She sank through the floor to her knees and then rose up to the floor again. She said, 'All the power I have comes from above.' [What did the priest say?] 'He couldn't say anything.'"

Contrary to hopes expressed by old men in 1911, the power of witches is not on the wane, but *keskamzit*, the sudden magic good luck, has not much life left in it. The word is generally familiar to old people and all of them know it must be kept secret. Skill in woodcraft, hunting, berry picking, and foreign languages were mentioned without elaboration as

[13] *Ibid.*

PART ONE *Tribal Life*

gifts bestowed. It was attributed half-heartedly to a Pugulatamutc, a Migamawesu, and to God, none of whom were so accredited in 1911–12. However, one man mentioned the ethical aspect characteristic of the earlier beliefs: *keskamzit*, he said, could be lost through excessive pride in its possession. Most commonly now the luck comes for finding small coins and is quickly lost because the finder cannot refrain from telling about it, as in the case of an old woman who said she had to explain to her husband that she was not getting money from other men. No one in Quebec and New Brunswick now brings home bizarre objects pregnant with personal *keskamzit* (see illustrations 36 and 37), and it is very doubtful that they do so in Nova Scotia where in 1950 we had an experience that shouldn't have happened to seasoned anthropologists. From Shubenacadie we brought home a stone roughly resembling a partridge and described in our notes as a gift from a man who offered it "somewhat sheepishly," without a word and agreed that "it might be *keskamzit*." The same man, a similar object, a similar manner reappeared in the notes of Martin and Sayres, which were also made at Shubenacadie in 1950.

The fear of *skadegamutc* is probably as widely spread as it was forty years ago, and as it well may be among the Micmac's French and British neighbors, but the guise in which he appears is slightly altered. The thoughts of the dying no longer seem to escape the body to rattle the dishes on the shelf; the cry of the whooper owl is not commonly heard as the voice of *skadegamutc*; and chases through the dark woods were not mentioned to us. The night-long fights with the man who at dawn is an old stump are now seldom recalled and not as personal experiences; but many people have met the ghost of a person about to die. *Skadegamutc* is the ghost of the dead, also, sometimes called back by his bones; and one woman said that her son had recently left home because she and other people had seen his *skadegamutc* and he felt this was a warning.

Again and again we heard about the *skadegamutc* who is a "fire ghost" seen in the sky or over the river; sometimes a human form is visible, covered with fire, and although all appearances of this kind warn of death by accident or drowning, the human apparition seen in the jack o'lantern's light is the most direful. Other concepts stressing European elements and not recorded in 1911 include ghosts who at midnight sit up in their graves or knock on the door asking for prayers, and a chilling

The Modern Micmac

visitation described by a woman who in her childhood had the misfortune to say she would like to see a dying cousin.

Children are early taught to fear *skadegamutc* who will come out of the grave and catch them if they stay out at night, and a boy and girl, each fifteen, told us that following fright-producing tales related by a grandparent, ghosts caught them in dreams. Priests sometimes say sternly that there is no such thing as a ghost, but others equate *skadegamutc* with the devil as a means of instilling the fear of evil, and others, one suspects, having been raised as rural French Canadian boys, quite understand the Micmac apparitions.

However, in 1953 *skadegamutc* is sometimes a figure of fun. Charley Mitchell, of Burnt Church, told humorous stories about a ghost who had been so bad that he was afraid to be buried and go to hell, and about two ghosts who were afraid of each other. One hears reminiscences of playing ghost — pranks that often boomerang on the prankster — and accounts of the investigation and rational explanation of haunted houses.

Of those races and peoples who in 1911 seemed almost a part of the reserves only the Pugulatamutc are universally known, and the acquaintance is no longer intimate. Even the oldest men have had no personal encounters with the Halfway People, who are said in New Brunswick to have left for Nova Scotia. Migamawesu are vaguely described as woods-dwellers who give supernatural skill to lumberjacks, and perform tricks usually associated with Pugulatamutc. One man said that his father's stepfather once lived in the woods with a Migamawesu woman and emerged later covered with hair like a beast. The following story, told at Eel Ground, N.B., embodies the old concept of the Migamawesu:

"Migamawesu appear in the woods; a man sees a female, a woman sees a male. Fourteen years ago here, at Eel Ground, a young woman whose husband was away from the reserve went to a spring, each night, in the woods. One night while she dipped water she saw a man. He was handsome and wore fine clothes. He spoke to her in Indian. She said to him, 'I'm in a hurry.' She wasn't frightened. He replied, 'I'll see you again.'

"The next morning when she went for water he was at the spring, and he carried her pail home. He asked, 'When shall I see you again?' She didn't answer.

"The following day she did not go to the spring. At night, while she

PART ONE *Tribal Life*

was milking the cow, he appeared. At his fourth appearance, the next morning, he said, 'I know you are married.' The girl had not told him this. 'Kill your husband and come away with me. You'll be rich.' 'Where do you come from?' she asked. 'Not far,' he answered. The young woman went home and told the whole story to her mother. 'That,' said her mother, 'is a Migamawesu. Don't go into the woods.'

"The young wife, now thoroughly frightened, never went into the woods again."

The Pugulatamutc, some Micmac say, are the only small race now living near the reserves, but others insist they also have gone and name the destination as New Glasgow, N.S., or as Cape Breton. But at Restigouche and Maria everyone knows they are on the top of Tracadegash Mountain in back of Carleton on the Gaspé where Gluskap told them to stay and let the Indians alone. No longer are their tiny footprints seen on the beach at Restigouche, and they have not recently engaged in such tricks, typical of the French *lutins*, as tying horses' manes in knots and stealing babies out of cradles at Maria. But if one climbs the mountain, one finds that Pugulatamutc are not good. There is a yearly pilgrimage to the mountain top, and twice the Pugulatamutc threw down the wooden cross erected on the summit. Now a priest from France has built a stone church and a cement cross there and the Pugulatamutc are licked. Even so, informants have seen them there in recent years. They are still described as "tiny but just like us," "Tom T'umbs," who sometimes kindly warn people of an approaching epidemic or pick over nuts for them.

A woman of seventy told of three childhood meetings between her son and daughter and a Pugulatamutc:

The first time they were at Red Bank with a small cousin, picking potatoes and carrots. Her daughter, the oldest of the children, then aged ten, described what they saw. On the shore was a tiny man with whiskers and a peaked hat. He was dressed in red clothes. He "walked important," like a big man. He looked at the three children; all of them saw him. Then he knelt down and drank river water and wiped his mouth. The little girl was not frightened: "He was smaller than I am." She turned away and when she looked back, he had vanished.

Another time in full moonlight the same children were outside playing near a big cellar on the river bank. They saw a man of the same size as the first one but couldn't see his face.

The Modern Micmac

Two years later—the daughter was then twelve—at the same place the children were playing with an old chain. One child hid it. Next morning the child was sent out for potatoes. She ran home and said, "Mama, the chain is fastened between two stakes. There are tiny bare-foot prints around it." The mother went out and saw footprints the size you would expect of a year-old baby. That was the third and last time she heard about Pugulatamutc from these children.

The status of Pugulatamutc concepts in the 1950s is perhaps adequately summed up by the comfortable fusion of the seemingly unfusable in the mind of Leo, aged twelve:

Leo: "Pugulatamutc? You mean the little fellers?"

"Yes. The dwarfs."

Leo: "There was this queen and then there came Snow White . . ."

"Did you ever see a dwarf?"

Leo: "My grandfather did. He used to see a little man in the daytime, singing and dancing around the house. And I've seen a dwarf too. I saw him in front of the hardware store in Newcastle. He was only that high. He was twelve years old and he'd never grown."

According to the Grand Chief of Cape Breton, if Gluskap ever returns to protect the Indians against white attack, he will bring the Pugulatamutc with him, so the whites will hesitate. "Probably that won't happen," added a man at Burnt Church, "because the English people have done all right in their rule in India and Africa and Canada. They have grubbed the people well in all those countries."

In 1953 our first inquiries about Gluskap at Restigouche, Maria, and Burnt Church brought an unexpected response: a *gluskap* is a habitual liar, someone who tells such big stories that no one would believe him. Once that was out of the way, the figure of the rather remote and lonely culture hero of the Wabanaki was presented much as he was in 1911–12. His position among Penobscot and Maliseet, if known at all, is no unifying symbol. A Maliseet who was aware of the existence of Gluskap legends in other tribes said to us, "We don't have any superstitions any more. But Gluskap is ours!" Micmac simply accepted him as theirs, a great personage, maybe a god, something big, the inventor of material culture, transformer of the landscape, and reducer of animals to comfortable size. In 1911–12 all informants agreed that his home is beyond the clouds; in 1953 that he lives in a mountain cave in Cape Breton where there is always a roaring sound and an entrance that closes

PART ONE *Tribal Life*

down smaller and smaller as one approaches until it is only a tiny hole.

On the Last Day Gluskap will return. "That," said Charley Mitchell, "is when we'll all come together, body and soul. If you can believe that, Gluskap, too, can come again."

MICMAC ATTITUDES

The Micmac are not thinking much about that Second Coming. Gluskap legends may be unchanged but few know them and we heard them only from people over sixty who no longer dominate the social scene. The two great changes that forty years have brought are the replacement of the apathetic looking backward to an idealized tribal past by a vigorous desire to be like the whites in all phases of material life; and the emergence of leadership among the younger men. The shift in the prestige of age status is obvious in the selection of chief and councilors. This body, set up under the Indian Affairs Branch, gives power of veto but not of choice of office holders to the Agency superintendent. The council has little authority, but it can have influence, and recent elections on several reserves suggest that it is a school for developing political skills. In 1950 at the three reserves we visited, each chief was under the age of fifty and one of them was thirty; in 1953 two of them had been replaced by former chiefs who were elderly men, one of whom, over seventy, was an outstandingly prosperous man and a leader in the North American Indian Brotherhood. At the largest reserves, the chiefs were young, aggressive men, and in a coming election one of these was opposed by a candidate still younger. All reserves had men of thirty or younger on the council.

Under this regime, the once all-powerful old men are respectfully treated but not deferred to; when they speak, the young men listen, but may disregard the opinions expressed. The old men in their turn do not habitually make derogatory remarks about "the young fellers." They have taken the change as part of the world. This philosophical acceptance is probably assumed the more easily because the newly established old age pension relieves the old from worry about their future at the hands of a less respectful younger generation. Realizing now that they must adapt themselves to the white world, they feel that the younger men, with more education than they, are better fitted to deal with the problems.

The Modern Micmac

This admission of the need for some education does not, unfortunately, mean that it is as yet highly valued, nor is the necessary amount and kind understood. As evidence of its poor effects, older people say that too much thought turns hair gray. The ideal Micmac character is described as *ge'o lik 'wa ni skik*, one who likes everybody and everything. Undesirable qualities are the opposite of this, as manifested by one who is cross to his family, a severe, "hard" person, lazy. On the reserve where these evaluations were made, two old men, one now over seventy, the other dead in 1952 at eighty, had by the non-Indian way of hard work and saving become the successful owners of property. The younger of the two is the present chief; the older man, suspicious of banks and probably sharing the general wish to conceal property from the government who might otherwise restrict benefits, lost all his savings when his house burned to the ground. None of our informants mentioned the career of these two men as achievements of which the Micmac should be proud, but prominent white men in the neighborhood did so. Micmac greatness is still too often expressed as small ingenuities beyond the native possibilities of the whites and of reiterations of the possession of supernatural power.

In such intellectual climate it is not strange that few boys and girls have gone beyond the eight-grade day schools. However, in spite of the general fear that education takes the young farther away from the group, a slow beginning has been made. Each year a few young people enter nursing, commercial courses, and trade schools; and whether or not they use the educational facilities, the Micmac want opportunities equal to those of the whites.

At the present time two inducements tend to keep even the best educated close to the reserves: one of these, house ownership, has been discussed; the other is a claim against the government for benefits which all might hope to share. On practically every reserve there is such a claim and an endeavor to implement this claim to an extension of boundaries, fostered by a prevalent belief, usually without foundation in fact, that previously the reserve was much larger and that whites have "stolen" large portions of it. The so-called treaties on which these claims are based and the legends recited regarding them are pathetic illustrations of the need of educating at least a few Micmac to the point of realizing what is evidence in the outside world. For example, at one reserve the chief said: "The treaty of 1774 about the land for our Eel

PART ONE *Tribal Life*

Ground Reserve was made between King John Julian and King George III who came over in a ship which anchored at the mouth of the Miramichi River. King John Julian went out to the ship in a canoe. King George III gave the Eel Ground people six miles on both sides of the Southwest Miramichi and Little Southwest Miramichi." In proof he displayed an old, vaguely worded agreement, recently copied from government archives, signed "Milan, Governor of New Brunswick."

It is difficult to assess the extent to which present problems and organized inducement have aroused an Indian nationalism in the Micmac. On each reserve there are some men, of ages from thirty to seventy or more, who think their salvation lies in joining with other Indians of Canada, and perhaps of the States also, in bringing pressure upon the government to grant their "rights." From some reserves representatives go to meetings of the North American Indian Brotherhood, held in Ottawa; some men are Brotherhood Councilors, and a representative of that federation has visited Micmac reserves. When such pressure has been brought and the results achieved, the federation gets the credit, even though these are measures which are already on the books and would be granted in due course.

But whatever the Micmac desires — clothes, cars, automatic washers; the right to vote; and particularly the right to buy alcoholic beverages with the freedom that whites have — he wants to realize them without the breakup of the reserves, with no diminution of government support, and, above all, without loss of ethnic identity.

General Bibliography

Anderson, William P. *Micmac Place-Names*. Ottawa: Geographic Board of Canada, 1919.
Bailey, Alfred. *The Conflict of European and Eastern Algonkian Cultures, 1504–1700*. PNBM, MS, No. 2, 1937.
Barbeau, Marius. *Québec où survit l'Ancienne France*. Quebec: Garneau, 1937.
———. *Saintes Artisanes*. Cahiers d'Art Arca, Vols. II and III. Montreal: Editions Fides, 1945.
Barrat, Joseph. *The Indian of New England and the North-Eastern Provinces*. Middletown, Conn.: Pelton, 1851.
Bellenger, Joseph M. "Le Veni Mecum d'un Missionaire Mikmakiques." 1817. Manuscript in the library of the Archbishop of Quebec.
Biggar, H. P. *Voyages of Jacques Cartier*. Ottawa: Acland, 1924. Publications of the Public Archives of Canada, No. 11.
Bird, Will R. *A Century at Chignecto: The Key to Old Acadia*. Chaps. I, VIII, XIV. Toronto: Ryerson Press, 1928.
Birket-Smith, Kaj. "Folk Wanderings and Culture Drifts in Northern North America," JSAP, n.s., 22:1–32 (1930).
Bourinot, J. G. "Cape Breton and Its Memorials of the French Regime," TRSC, 9:172–343 (1891).
Byers, Douglas B. "The Environment of the Northeast," in Frederick Johnson (ed.), *Man in Northeastern North America*. PPFA, 3:3–32 (1946).
Campbell, Duncan. *Nova Scotia, in Its Historical Mercantile and Industrial Relations*. Montreal: John Lovell, 1873.
Campbell, John. *The Affiliation of the Algonquin Languages*. Toronto, 1879.
Canada. Annual Reports on Indian Affairs. Issued by the following:
    1868–1873, Secretary of State
    1874–1879, Department of the Interior
    1880–1933, Department of Indian Affairs
    1934–1949, Department of Mines and Resources, Indian Affairs Branch
    1950–   Department of Citizenship and Immigration, Indian Affairs Branch
Chamberlain, Alexander F. "Indians of the Eastern Provinces of Canada," *Annual Archaeological Report 1905*. Pp. 122–36. Toronto: Minister of Education, 1906.
Chamberlain, Montague. "Indians of New Brunswick in Champlain's Time," *Acadiensis*, 4:280–95 (1904).
Champlain, Samuel de. *The Works of Samuel de Champlain*. 6 vols. Edited by H. P. Biggar. Toronto: The Champlain Society, 1922–36.
Charlevoix, P. de. *Histoire et description générale de la Nouvelle France, avec le Journal historique d'un voyage fait par ordre du Roi dans l'Amérique septentrionale*. 3 vols. Paris, 1744.

PART ONE *Tribal Life*

Clark, Jeremiah S. "Micmac Place-Names in the Maritime Provinces of Canada," in Silas Rand, *Micmac Dictionary*. Pp. 179–92. Charlottetown, P.E.I.: Patriot Publishing Company, 1902.
Clarke, John M. "The Micmac Tercentenary," in *8th Report of Director of Science Division*. Albany, N.Y.: New York State Education Department, 1912.
Cooney, Robert. *A Compendious History of the Northern Part of the Province of New Brunswick and of the District of Gaspé, in Lower Canada*. Halifax, 1832.
Cuoq, J. A. "Auotc Kekou," in TRSC, 11:137–79 (1893).
Dawson, Principal. "The Name 'Acadia'," CANJ, 5:84–88 (1876–77).
Dennis, Clara, *Down in Nova Scotia*. Toronto: Ryerson Press, 1934, 1940.
———. *Cape Breton All Over*. Toronto: Ryerson Press, 1937.
———. *More about Nova Scotia*. Toronto: Ryerson Press, 1937.
Denys, Nicolas. *Natural History of the People, of the Animals, of the Trees and Plants of North America, and of Its Diverse Climates* . . . Translated by William F. Ganong. Toronto: The Champlain Society, 1908. 1st ed.; Paris, 1672.
Dièreville, le Sieur de. *Relation of the Voyage to Port Royal in Acadia or New France*. English translation by Mrs. Clarence Webster, edited by John Clarence Webster. Toronto: The Champlain Society, 1933. 1st ed., 1708.
Dixon, Roland B. "The Mythology of the Central and Eastern Algonkins," JAFL, 22:1–9 (1909).
———. "The Early Migrations of the Indians of New England and the Maritime Provinces," PAAS, n.s., 24:65–76 (1914).
Drake, Samuel G. *Biography and History of the Indians of North America*. 5th ed.; Boston, 1837.
Elder, William. "The Aborigines of Nova Scotia," NAR, 112:1–30 (1871).
Fauset, Arthur Huff. "Folklore from the Half-Breeds in Nova Scotia," JAFL, 38:300–15 (1925).
Ferland, Abbé. *Cours d'histoire du Canada*. 2 vols. Quebec, 1861.
Flannery, Regina. *An Analysis of Coastal Algonquian Culture*, CUA, AS, No. 7, 1939.
Gallenz, Mathias C. "A Survey of Micmac Culture Traits." Unpublished thesis, Catholic University of America, 1928.
Ganong, William F. "A Monograph of the Place-Nomenclature of the Province of New Brunswick," TRSC, 2 (Sect. II): 175–289 (1896).
———. "The Cartography of the Gulf of St. Lawrence, from Cartier to Champlain," PTRSC, 7:54–55 (1889).
———. "Indian Nomenclature." 1917. Manuscript in New Brunswick Museum, St. John, N.B.
———. "Indian Place Names of New Brunswick." 1922. Manuscript in New Brunswick Museum, St. John, N.B.
Garneau, François Xavier. *History of Canada, from the Time of Its Discovery till the Union Year*. Translation by Andrew Bell. Montreal: L. Lovell, 1860.
Gates, R. Ruggles. "Blood Groups and Other Features of the Micmac Indians," JAI, 68:283–98 (1938).
Gatschet, Albert S. "Micmac Fans and Games," BFMUP, 2:190–94 (1900).
Gaulin, Antoine. "Rélation de la mission . . ." ANCP, Série K, Vol. 1232, No. 4, pp. 109–25.
Gesner, Abraham. *The Industrial Resources of Nova Scotia*. Halifax, 1849.
Giles, John. "Memoirs of Odd Adventures, Strange Deliverances, etc., in the Captivity of John Giles, Esq., Written by Himself," in Samuel G. Drake, *Indian Captives*. New York, 1856. Pp. 73–109. Originally published at Boston, 1736.
Gilpin, John B. "Indians of Nova Scotia," PTNSIS, 6:260–81.
———. "Micmacs of Nova Scotia," in *Canada: An Encyclopaedia of the Country*. Edited by J. C. Hopkins. Vol. I, pp. 241–45. Toronto, 1898.

General Bibliography

Gordon, Arthur H. (Lord Stanmore). *Wilderness Journeys in New Brunswick in 1862–1863*. St. John, N.B., 1864.
Hagar, Stansbury. "Micmac Magic and Medicine," JAFL, 9:170–77 (1896).
———. "Melange of Micmac Notes," PAAAS, 44:257–58 (1895).
———. "Micmac Customs and Traditions," AA, 8:31–42 (1895).
———. "Weather and Seasons in Micmac Mythology," JAFL, 10:101–6 (1897).
Haliburton, Thomas C. *An Historical and Statistical Account of Nova Scotia*. 2 vols. Halifax: Howe, 1829.
Hallowell, A. I. "Some Psychological Characteristics of the Northeastern Indians," in *Man in Northeastern North America*. PPFA, 3:195–225 (1946).
Handbook of American Indians, "Micmac." Vol. I, pp. 858–59. Washington, D.C.: Government Printing Office, 1907.
Harvey, D. C. *The French Régime in Prince Edward Island*. Chap. XV. New Haven, Conn.: Yale University Press, 1926.
Hatton, Joseph, and M. Harvey. *Newfoundland*. Boston: Doyle and Whittle, 1883.
Hewitt, Harry W. "Customs of the Micmac Indians." Manuscript of 33 pages, read before the Nova Scotia Historical Society, April 21, 1908, and preserved in the files of that society.
Jack, I. Allen. "Acadienses: The Indians of Acadia," in *The Canadian Indian*. Vol. I, pp. 331–37. Owen Sound, Ont.: John Rutherford, 1891.
Jenness, Diamond. *The Indians of Canada*. National Museum of Canada, Bulletin 65. Ottawa, 1932.
Jesuit Relations and Allied Documents, The. 72 vols. Edited by Rueben Gold Thwaites. Cleveland, Ohio, 1896.
Johnson, Frederick. "Notes on Micmac Shamanism," PM, 16:53–80 (1943).
——— (ed.). *Man in Northeastern North America*. PPFA, Vol. 3 (1946).
Jukes, J. B. *Excursions in Newfoundland*. 2 vols. London, 1842.
Kain, Samuel W. "Indian Names in New Brunswick," SJDS, January 14, 1886.
———. "Trade Pipes," *Acadiensis*, 3:255–58 (1903).
Kauder, Charles. *Manual of Prayers, Instructions, Psalms and Hymns in Micmac Ideograms*. New ed.; Restigouche, P.Q., 1866.
Langelier, Jean C. *A Sketch on Gaspesia*. Quebec: J. Dussault, 1884.
Lauvrière, Emile. *Pages glorieuses de l'epopée canadienne*. Chap. II. Paris, 1927.
LeClercq, Chrétien. "A Syllabary of Micmac Language." Manuscript in the library of the Archbishop of Quebec.
———. *New Relation of Gaspesia*. Paris, 1691. English translation by W. F. Ganong. Toronto: The Champlain Society, 1910.
———. *First Establishment of the Faith in New France*. 2 vols. Notes and translation by John Gilmary Shea. New York: Published by the translator, 1881. 1st ed.; Paris, 1691.
Leighton, Alexander. "The Twilight of the Indian Porpoise Hunters," NH, 40:410-16, 458 (1937).
Leland, Charles G. *The Algonquin Legends of New England, or Myths and Folk Lore of the Micmac, Passamaquoddy, and Penobscot Tribes*. Boston and New York, 1884.
——— and John D. Prince. *Kuloskap the Master*. New York, 1902.
Le Loutre, Abbé Jean-Louis. "Autobiographie." Edited by A. David. In *Nova Francia, organe de la Société d'Histoire du Canada*, 6(No. 1):1–34 (1931).
Lescarbot, Marc. *The History of New France*. 3 vols. English translation by W. L. Grant. Toronto: The Champlain Society, 1914.
Levinge, R. G. A. *Echoes from the Backwoods: Or, Scenes of Transatlantic Life*. London: Darling, 1849.
MacLean, John. *Canadian Savage Folk*. Toronto, 1896.
———. *The Indians, Their Manners and Customs*. 4th ed.; Toronto, 1907.

PART ONE *Tribal Life*

Maillard, l'Abbé (Antoine Simon). "Déclaration faite par les Sauvages Micmacks au Sr. Gooront (Gorham) Officier anglais et a luy donnée par ecrit pour être portée a M. Cornwallis Gouv. a Chibouctou. Ecrit au Port Toulouze cinq jours avant la St. Michel, Sept. 24, 1749," ANCP, 6:88. (Earliest known document in Maillard's Micmac ideographs.)

———. *An Account of Customs and Manners of the Mickmakis and Maricheets, Savage Nations, Now Dependent on the Government of Cape Breton*. London, 1755.

———. *A Micmac Grammar*. New York, 1864.

———. "Grammaire de la Langue Micmaque, Redigée et mise en ordre par Joseph M. Bellenger, Ptre.," in *Shea's Library of American Linguistics*, No. 13, 1864.

Mallery, Garrick. "Picture-Writing of the American Indians," ARBAE, 10:424–29, 501–11 (1888–89).

Martin, William C., and William C. Sayres. Field Notes Made at Micmac Reserve, Shubenacadie, N.S., 1950. Unpublished.

Maxwell, Louise M. Beckwith. *An Outline of the History of Central New Brunswick to the Time of Confederation*. Sackville, N.B.: The Tribune Press, 1937.

Mechling, William H. "Micmac Texts." Manuscript in the Division of Anthropology, Canadian National Museum, Ottawa. Collected 1911–13.

———. "The Malecite Indians, with Notes on the Micmacs." Manuscript, deposited with above, 1914.

Michelson, Truman. "Micmac Tales," JAFL, 38:33–54 (1925).

———. "Preliminary Report on the Linguistic Classification of Algonquian Tribes," ARBAE, 28:225–90 (1912).

Micmac Messenger. Restigouche, P.Q., 1903–21.

Murdoch, Beamish. *A History of Nova Scotia or Acadia*. 3 vols. Halifax, 1867.

Nicolar, Joseph. *The Life and Traditions of the Red Man*. Bangor, Me.: C. H. Glass and Co., 1893.

Pacifique, Père. *Leçon grammaticales et théoriques pratiques de la Langue Micmac*. Restigouche, P.Q., Bureau du Messager Micmaque, 1939. Reprinted from AACFAS, Vols. 4–5, 1938–39.

———. *Etudes Historiques et Géographiques*. Restigouche, P.Q., 1935.

Parkman, Francis. *The Jesuits of North America in the Seventeenth Century*. Boston: Little, Brown, and Co., 1867.

Parsons, Elsie C. "Half-Breed," *Scientific Monthly*, 18:145–48 (1924).

———. "Micmac Folklore," JAFL, 38:55–148 (1925).

———. "Micmac Notes," JAFL, 39:460–85 (1926).

Partridge, Emelyn N. *Glooscap the Great Chief and Other Stories and Legends of the Micmacs*. New York: Macmillan, 1919.

Perley, Charles. *History of Newfoundland*. London, 1863.

Piers, Harvey. "Brief Account of the Micmac Indians of Nova Scotia and Their Remains," PTNSIS, 13:99–125 (1912).

Pilling, James C. *Bibliography of Algonquin Languages*. Washington, D.C.: Government Printing Office, 1891.

Prest, Walter H. "A Suggestion for Anthropological Work in Nova Scotia," PTNSIS, 13:35–39 (1911).

Prince, John Dynley. "Algonquins," in HERE. Vol. 1, pp. 319–21.

———. "A Micmac Manuscript – Nine Tales and a Song with English Version," ICA, 15(Pt. I):87–124 (1906).

Rand, Silas. *Dictionary of the Language of the Micmac Indians*. Halifax, 1888.

———. *Micmac Dictionary*. Edited by J. S. Clark. Charlottetown, P.E.I.: Patriot Publishing Co., 1902.

———. *Micmac Reader*. Halifax, 1875.

———. "The Legends of the Micmacs," AAOJ, 12:3–14 (1890).

———. "Glooscap, Cuhkw, and Coolpurot," AAOJ, 12:283–86 (1890).
———. "The Coming of the White Man Revealed," AAOJ, 12:155–59 (1890).
———. *Lectures.* Halifax, 1850.
———. *A Short Statement of Facts Relating to the History, Manners, Customs, Language, & Literature of the Micmac Tribe of Indians, in Nova Scotia and Prince Edward Island.* 1850.
———. Manuscript volume of stories. In the library of the Museum of the University of Pennsylvania, Philadelphia.
———. "The Micmac Indians," OFC, 2(No. 4):10–12 (1888).
———. *Micmac Place Names: Collected 1852–1890.* Ottawa, 1919.
———. *Legends of the Micmacs.* New York, 1894.
———. "Dreams, Visions and Religion in Common Life." 241 pages. Manuscript at Wellesley College. Unbound.
———. "Legends of the Micmac Indians and Extracts from the Micmac Prayer Book with Interlinear Translations into English . . ." Manuscript at Wellesley College.
———. "Legends in English and Micmac." 96 lines. Manuscript at Wellesley College.
Raymond, W. O. *Glimpses of the Past, History of the River St. John, AD 1604–1784.* SJDT, 1905.
Roth, Luther. *Acadieland, the Acadians.* Chaps. II–IV. Utica, N.Y.: L. C. Childs, 1891.
Sagard-Théodat, Gabriel. *Histoire du Canada et voyages que les Frères Mineurs Recollet y ont faictes.* 4 vols. New ed.; Paris, 1866.
Schmitt, Joseph. "Chasses des Sauvages a l'Ile d'Anticosti," ICA, 15(Pt. I):213–14 (1906).
Shea, J. G. "Micmac or Recollect Hieroglyphics," HM, 5:289–92 (1861).
Siebert, Frank T. Review of Père Pacifique's *Leçon grammaticales et théoriques pratiques de la Langue Micmaque*, AA, n.s., 42:331–33 (1940).
Smethurst, Gamaliel. "A Narrative of an Extraordinary Escape out of the Hands of the Indians of the People of St. Lawrence. London, 1764." Edited by W. F. Ganong. CNBHS, Vol. 2, 1905.
Souvenir of the Micmac Tercentenary Celebration. Rimouski, Que., 1910.
Spaulding, Albert C. "Northeastern Archaeology and General Trends in the Northern Forest Zone," in *Man in Northeastern North America.* PPFA, 3, 143–67, 1946.
Speck, Frank G. *Penobscot Man.* Philadelphia: University of Pennsylvania Press, 1940.
———. *The Double-Curve Motive in Northeastern Algonkian Art*, CDM, GS, AS, No. 1, 1914.
———. "The Family Hunting Band as the Basis of Algonkian Social Organization," AA, n.s., 17:289–305 (1915).
———. "The Eastern Algonkian Wabanaki Confederacy," AA, n.s., 17:492–508 (1915).
———. "Bird-Lore of the Northern Indians," *Public Lectures*, University of Pennsylvania Faculty, 7:349–80 (1921).
———. *Beothuck and Micmac*, INM, No. 22, 1922.
———. "Montagnais and Naskapi Tales from the Labrador Peninsula," JAFL, 38:1–32 (1925).
———. "Culture Problems in Northeastern North America," PAPS, 45:272–311 (1926).
———. "Penobscot Tales and Religious Beliefs," JAFL, 48:1–107 (1936).
Steen, Sheila B. "The Psychological Consequences of Acculturation among the Cape Breton Micmac." Unpublished M.A. thesis, University of Pennsylvania, 1951.

PART ONE *Tribal Life*

Tache, J. C. *Soirées canadiennes.* Vol. 1, pp. 27–96. Quebec, 1861.
Vernon, C. W. "Indians of St. John Island," *Acadiensis*, 3:110–15 (1903).
———. *Cape Breton, Canada, at the Beginning of the Twentieth Century.* Chap. XIV. Toronto: Nation Publishing Co., 1903.
Vetromile, Eugene. "Aborigines of Acadia. An Address before the Maine Historical Society in 1861." Manuscript in the library of the University of Pennsylvania.
———. *The Abnakis and Their History, or Historical Notices on the Aborigines of Canada.* New York: James B. Kirker, 1866. Sold for the benefit of the Indians.
Wallis, Wilson D. "Medicines Used by the Micmac Indians," AA, 24:24–30 (1922).
———. and Ruth Sawtell Wallis. "Culture Loss and Culture Change among the Micmac of the Canadian Maritime Provinces, 1912–1950," in memorial volume to Walter B. Cline, *Kroeber Anthropological Society Papers*, Nos. 8–9, pp. 100–29, Berkeley, Calif.: University of California, 1953.

PART TWO *Folktales and Traditions*

Introduction

BY WILSON D. WALLIS

THE tales and traditions of the Micmac here presented were recorded in the summers of 1911 and 1912 at reserves or settlements in New Brunswick, Nova Scotia, and Prince Edward Island. Most of them I gathered at Burnt Church, N.B., and Pictou Landing, N.S.

No published folklore covers the entire Micmac area. The fundamental work of Silas Rand, between 1848 and 1869, was done with informants in Nova Scotia and Prince Edward Island; Speck (1915) and Parsons (1925) collected stories from Cape Breton. I have not studied the distribution of motives through the various Maritime reserves, or followed out the wider affiliations of the tales to the traditional literature of Algonkin tribes to the north and west, which can be seen in Margaret Fisher's recent study.[1]

Primarily my interest in the tales, as explained in Part One, Chapter I, was ethnographic, as an approach to informants and a means, direct or indirect, of getting information about the old tribal culture. All stories were recorded in English, without the aid of an interpreter. One of the more unusual items secured was a story about the origin of stories:

"Among the first generation of old-time Micmac there were no stories. The second generation told a true story about the first generation; the third generation made a story about the second, and added it to the other. The process continued and today a great many stories are known to us all."

There is a certain appealing philosophy in this concept of the myth-

[1] "The Mythology of the Northern and Northeastern Algonkians in Reference to Algonkian Mythology as a Whole," in Frederick Johnson, ed., *Man in Northeastern North America*.

PART TWO *Folktales and Traditions*

making process, a process obviously active in historic times, as the tales of encounters with Mohawk, French, and English attest. Nor has it ceased to function in recent years. In the summer of 1953, at the Eel River Reserve, N.B., I was told the following tale of a historic happening across the narrow Baie des Chaleurs:

"Two dogs arrived at Ste Anne de Restigouche to warn the Indians that a French warship was coming to attack them. They had never seen a Frenchman or a ship.[2] When the vessel appeared and pointed its guns at the shore, a Micmac with the 'power' rendered them useless. Not one cannon could be fired. The Indians killed all of the French aboard and then sunk the ship. It has now been raised, and you can see it over there next to the church."

The final statement is true. In 1936 Father Pacifique received permission and funds to realize a long-held plan to raise the *Marquis de Malauze*, an unarmed French supply ship sunk by the British off Restigouche in 1760 during a small naval engagement. The raising of the vessel and its place in local history received publicity in the English-language press and was the feature story in the final number of Father Pacifique's Micmac-language paper, the *Messager Micmac*. Eel River Micmac, who read English and live only a few miles from the city of Dalhousie, could hardly have escaped knowing what actually happened two hundred years ago. But with total disregard of available facts, the defenseless *Marquis de Malauze* was given a second two hundred years of age, grafted to a typical hero story, and made legend. I might add that at Restigouche, where sightseeing taxis stop each summer day before the remains of the old ship, no Indian mentioned it or its origin as either myth or reality.

The manner of telling the tales in 1911 was much the same as that described by Rand. A story was usually prefaced with *mado wiga djik ki ci gu*, "there, at the home place, among the old people."[3] Auditors responded with *geskwa*, "go on." The introductory word, or phrase, was used only in this context. In relating the tales there was no apparent effort at rhetorical effect. The narrator proceeded as one giving information on some point in which all were interested. During the telling of a story, auditors did not interrupt with question or remark, except to grunt,

---

[2] The first Frenchman was actually Jacques Cartier, who entered the Baie des Chaleurs in 1534.
[3] See Rand, *Legends*, 82–83.

Introduction

now and then, as an expression of assent, or to interpose a note of surprise or of derision, or otherwise indicate interest or emotion.

There was not in 1911–12, is not now, and has not been, as far as I could learn, any occasion or time of the year especially appropriate to the telling of stories; and there were no taboos or restrictions with regard to the telling of any particular stories.

Certain persons were recognized as good storytellers; in no reserve, however, did one or more persons have a monopoly on storytelling. In general, men appear to be superior to women as storytellers. This impression may be due in part to my limited acquaintance with Micmac women. But the impression is substantiated by the lack of reference on the part of the Micmac to any woman as a gifted performer. However, a woman who told me stories about Mohawk and about Beothuck said she had heard them and many others from an aunt of hers, then deceased, who appears to have had an unusually ample repertoire of war tales. Among Rand's informants were five women, three of whom told several tales each; one woman told many. In 1953 two old men who were raised in the same household told me that a grandmother of one of them had related many tales to them when they were children.

With few exceptions, only the older men, and indeed only a few of them, knew many tales. For stories as for other information my best sources were two old men: Peter Ginnish, at Burnt Church, and John Newell, at Pictou Landing. They were equaled, however, by a young man, Thomas Meuse, then probably not more than thirty years of age, who knew a large number of stories of the old days and frequently entertained the old men with them. He was a rover, who traveled throughout the Maritime Provinces, had no steady occupation, and seemed to spend a considerable part of his time in telling and in listening to stories.

In addition to telling all types of stories recorded in this book he related, as did others, what, with a few Micmac embellishments, were standard European fairy tales. Since even the most generous of publishers imposes limitations of space, stories most obviously European in origin are not included here. One of Tom Meuse's most elaborate productions in the genre, about a personage called Epitoplapesi, is a 3500-word amalgam of the King of the Fishes, the Extraordinary Companions, and the Marooned Rescuer — told without pause. On a later occasion he began what seemed to be the Enchanted Horse with *ginap* accouter-

PART TWO *Folktales and Traditions*

ments, and proceeded for seven hundred words. At this point in the narration, seeing the Chatham boat approaching, he suddenly decided he must go up the river on it. He accordingly asked for his pay, borrowed a dollar, and I did not see Thomas again. Forty years later, when I returned to the Miramichi, I heard with great regret that he was dead. To the end of his life he was a wanderer and a great teller of tales.

CHAPTER I

Tales about Gluskap

GLUSKAP, the culture hero of the Wabanaki tribes, appears in the following tales, as in previous collections of Micmac folklore, as teacher of all arts, transformer of the landscape, protector, and prophet. He has said his farewell and departed; but men have visited him in his retreat, and in an hour of dire need he will return to save the Micmac.

The stories are arranged as follows: adventures and activities predominantly aboriginal in content; animal and vegetable transformations; transformations of landscape; adventures centered on European or Christian plots and elements.

The first tale illustrates Margaret Fisher's statement concerning "the unsatisfactory state of the Gluskabe material," which reflects "even in the earliest collections . . . unmistakable indications of the dwindling vitality of native traditions." Here we have Gluskap dwelling with father and stepmother, or (Tale 4) with grandmother, accompanied by a shadowy brother of animal form, and engaged in adventures such as duping the awl-elbow witch and substituting cranberries for poisonous lice, which are common exploits of ordinary heroes throughout the Algonkin area.[1] In "Gluskap and the Two Kings" (Tale 13), while he is introduced in the most exalted terms, much of his activity in international diplomacy is similar to that of the Micmac hero-*buoin* Julian or Duneil. This story with its rich borrowing, including the island episode from the European Marooned Rescuer, is a perfect justification for Stith Thompson's conclusion after his analysis of many Micmac versions of European fairy tales: "Three centuries of contact with the French have resulted in such amalgamation . . . as to make them hopelessly confused."[2]

[1] Fisher, 228, 250.
[2] Thompson, 385, 404–5.

321

PART TWO *Folktales and Traditions*

1. GLUSKAP'S EARLY ADVENTURES

Gluskap had left his stepfather. He made for himself a bow and arrow. He lived by the seashore, but had gone into the woods. When he returned to his wigwam on the shore, his mother and stepfather had left him. He called that he would not go with them; he would leave them.

He called to his mother, who was then in a canoe: "Put my puppy in the *waltes* [wooden game bowl] and send it ashore to me." It came ashore, and he picked it up. He decided to go around the island, and he and the dog started. The first thing he saw was a man, whom he found sitting. "Where are you going?" the man asked. "I am going around this bay." "Well, my good friend, I'm afraid you'll not get around. There are many enemies, and you will be killed by them. Go on. You will see a man sitting by the shore. He will be rubbing his elbow on a rock to sharpen it. He will want you to stop with him that night. He will kill you with his elbow. If you escape him, you will come to the wigwam of a woman. She will try to kill you. She will coax you to stay overnight. She will coax you to look at her head and pick lice off it. She will say to you, 'Take those lice and bite them!' They will poison you. When you have passed there, other women will run after you."

Gluskap came to a place where a man was rubbing his elbow. He stayed all night. His dog growled all night and kept this man away when he tried to jab Gluskap with his elbow. "Chase your dog out of doors! I believe he will bite," said the man. "Oh! no; he is the only company I have." So Gluskap escaped.

He came to the woman who was lousy. Before he arrived there, he found cranberries. He picked them, and put them in his bosom. "If she wants me to eat lice, I will crack cranberries." She said, "Get these lice and eat them." He would get them, and crack cranberries. She thought it was lice he was cracking. So he escaped from her. Next he met the women, and they pursued him. He could not get away. He climbed a pine tree. When they were close to him, at the top, he bent it down, swung himself down, and when on the ground, said, "Turn into cones!" These women are now pine cones.

He escaped from them, and came to a place which he did not know how to cross. He sat down. He had a bow and arrows. He sang a tune. By and by a whale came. It was deep water. "Now, I want you to take me across!" said Gluskap. "Get on my back!" He got on the whale's back, and started.

Tales about Gluskap

He could see land. The whale asked Gluskap, "Can you see land?" — he knew it was not far away. Gluskap said, "Yes; I can just get a glimpse of it." He knew it was a sandbank, and that if he ran the whale ashore, he could step off without getting wet. The whale cried, "Now you have killed me! I can't get off!" Gluskap said, "Oh! I'll get you off!" He took his bow and arrows, put them underneath the whale, moved him out, then shoved him off into deep water. "Now you are all right!"

Gluskap came to the place where his mother and stepfather had gone ashore. He had a little brother. Gluskap found their wigwam. He asked it, "How many days since they left?" The wigwam replied, "Two or three days ago." He traveled on, and found another wigwam. He asked, "How many days since they left?" It replied, "One day." At last he overtook them. His mother was carrying his brother on her back. "Mother," said the little boy (who was facing the opposite direction from that in which she traveled), "my brother is coming!" "Oh, you'll never see your brother again. We left him at Adjadjidjanetc." They made a camp. Gluskap joined them. His stepfather said, "Go get me some water." He gave him a birch-bark vessel. Gluskap went to the brook and got water. His father looked at it and threw it out. "This is no good! Go get me another." Gluskap thought, "Now, what shall I do?" He filled the vessel with black mud and took it to him. His father looked into it. "Oh, take that away!" He grabbed it and dashed it on Gluskap's face. Then a row commenced. Gluskap killed his stepfather. He said to his brother, "Brother, turn into a marten." The marten is Gluskap's brother. I don't know what he did with his mother. JOHN HAMMOND [3]

2. GLUSKAP AND THE ANIMALS

Two caribou were traveling. It was a hard winter; the snow was deep. They thought they would go somewhere, notwithstanding, though they could not travel well in the woods. In a deep ravine between two high mountains there was a settlement of porcupine. When they arrived there, they called at the first wigwam and saw an old woman Porcupine.

Wolverine and Otter had arrived ahead of the caribou. Old woman Porcupine had gathered a lot of hemlock bark to dry. Wolverine was making fun of the old woman, who had kindled a fire. She resented his

---

[3] The first tale by each of the three most prominent storytellers, Peter Ginnish, Thomas Meuse, and John Newell, carries the name in full; subsequently only initials are used for these three. When given, the names of other informants are in full.

PART TWO *Folktales and Traditions*

ridicule. She went out, brought in more bark, and was constantly making the fire hotter. Wolverine was very warm. Otter was never warm. He said to the old woman, "Gracious, Grandmother, you have not made any fire at all. Make a warm fire."

Long ere this, Wolverine had been roasted to death. It was so hot that no human being could endure it. The old woman was making too much fire. She herself could not endure it. Her belly was burning. You can see the burned mark around the porcupine today. She was so warm that her teeth began to fall out.

Wolverine revived. He and Otter left, and traveled on. They went to a large, tall pine at Medabogiak, the Point where all animals assembled.

The two caribou came to the grandmother's wigwam. They walked in. Grandmother Porcupine started to make the fire hot again, as she had done before. She failed to roast these two out, though she tried to do so. They asked for lodging. She replied, "You two boys go into the woods, bring me some hemlock bark, and I will make you some snowshoes, a pair for each of you." The caribou were anxious to have the snowshoes. The following day they put them on. The caribou were much pleased. "We will repay you, old woman, by making you a pair of moccasins that will last you until the end of the world."

They made moccasins, and the porcupine wears them, and will wear them until the end of the world.

They said to Porcupine, "I think we, also, will go to the Point." They went to the Point. Gluskap was there. All kinds of fish were in the water around the Point, also snakes, and, in fact, everything that lives in the water. Gluskap was a kind of judge [chief?] over them. They behaved as tame animals, though all were wild, and all talked to Gluskap, asking for this or that. All wanted to go into the woods; none were willing to live in the water — it was too cold and contained too much ice. Gluskap, however, would not allow all of them to go into the woods, but sent most of them there. He told each animal how it might get its living. He sent a great many into the lakes, a great many onto the high mountains, a great many into the water — ocean and salt water — and the cow, cat, dog, and all the others into the woods close to the water. He did not wish all of them to be wild — he wished some of them to be tame.

After this he went out in his canoe, and took Wolverine with him. He left his dog on the land. The dog is still somewhere on the shore — I

Tales about Gluskap

do not know where. This happened somewhere between Cape Breton and Pictou. The dog turned into a rock, and can be seen today. He is called Elmutc Ulugwetc ["Dog Howling"] because he is mourning the loss of Gluskap. The dog came out and sat down on the Point, for he had smelled his master. Gluskap was then in his canoe, fifty miles away, and said he could not come back, because Wolverine was with him. Until the end of the world, people will not know what Gluskap has done; they may know part of it, but not the whole of it.

This is a true story. Gluskap came to land somewhere north of Baie des Chaleurs. I do not know where — no one knows the exact place.

He went to the Pugulatamutc.[4] He told the Pugulatamutc to be civilized. If they wish to do something, they must first ask Gluskap's permission. He is chief over all of them. The Pugulatamutc live in double wigwams, far in under the mountains. The wigwams are covered with boughs. The place is very cold.

Gluskap stands in the entrance to their country. When he turns, the wind blows, always in the direction in which he faces; when he turns, the wind takes another direction. Sometimes he is lying down, quiet, and is sleeping, or smoking; at these times there is no wind; it is calm everywhere. He turns or rests at his own sweet will, and there is no means of influencing him even the very least. He keeps a big fire. When he removes the ashes, he throws them over the entire earth. When they fall in water, or on bogs, a vapor rises. That is what causes a fog. Sometimes it is so thick you cannot see through it. THOMAS MEUSE

3. GLUSKAP TURNS PEOPLE INTO FROGS

A *buoin* [medicineman] by the name of Welamadox ["Honorable"] went into the woods. He heard an owl. Welamadox was by the fire. The owl sat on a bush near him — for an owl is very fond of a fire. Welamadox took his bow and arrow and shot the owl. With his knife he carved a piece of wood into a likeness of the owl as it was sitting on the bush when he shot it. Next day, he left the owl and traveled on. He saw a spruce partridge flying about. He saw something in the nest where the spruce partridge had been sitting. (They were eggs, but he did not know what they were.) He broke one. "They are not hard," he said. He went to the river. "I will make an egg of stone," he said.

[4] For further accounts of Pugulatamutc, see Tales 41–45.

PART TWO *Folktales and Traditions*

He traveled a long way, then came out of the woods. He did not know where he was. He was lost. On the third night that he was in the woods his wife sent his dog to find him. She tied a small piece of bark around his neck and said, "Now, go get your master!" The dog found the place where his master had spent the first night, and after that he found the place where the man had spent the second night. He knew, then, that his master was not far away. The master heard his dog barking and recognized his bark. The dog was glad to see his master, and his master was glad to see the dog. The man had had nothing to eat. He and the dog went to the lake, and the man caught a trout. He carved a likeness of it in wood, to take home to show his people.

He was starving. He tied up these things he had carved: an owl, a snake, an egg, a trout, and went into the woods. Toward evening he met a man from his settlement.

This man had a moose which he had killed. That night they made good cheer. Welamadox told him what he had made, and what he had seen. "I haven't anything to take home to my children." "I will give you half of my moose." "All right." They wrapped up the moose and started. While they were walking through the woods, they saw a light moving along. It was Ladybird.

In the morning they arrived at a lake. They did not know much about how to cross water. They made a hoop out of a long stick, cut holes around the edges of the moose hide, fastened it to the circular stick, and put the load in this coracle [bull-boat]. "Get in the canoe!" said Welamadox. They got in, and paddled across the lake. (It would have taken them a week to go around it.)

When they reached home, their families were nearly starved. Each took home with him one half of the moose. The people wondered at the figure of the owl which he had made like the bird as he had seen it. They looked at the egg and at the fish, and wondered at these, too. He had stopped in the woods to make them. He had caught a trout, and had carved one out of wood. The trout itself he threw away—he did not want it.

There was dancing for a week. Whenever they saw any wonder, they would dance. They would examine it thoroughly, and then have a dance. Sometimes this lasted all night, and every night, for a week. They danced for a long, long time. Finally, Gluskap told them not to dance all the time.

They did not obey him. They danced steadily for about three months.

Tales about Gluskap

Gluskap then went to see whether they were still alive. He found that all of them were frogs. When they stopped dancing in the morning, they were frogs, though at night they looked like men and women.

I have the egg that was made by Welamadox. I dug it up at Merigomish, when I found some other stone things.[5]   JOHN NEWELL

4. GLUSKAP WINS A CONTEST WITH PESADASIXUNJI [SCALPED]

Some men found a little boy in a well, scalped. The lad was nearly three years old. They took him to their wigwam and kept him nearly a year.

Everything he said would be true — it would have to come true. One day he said, "I shall go to Gluskap's house." "Perhaps he will not see you." "Yes, I must go." Gluskap was glad to see him. He stayed there all day, until evening. "We shall have a heavy frost tonight," he said. "Yes, maybe," said Gluskap. That night, there was a terrible frost.

Gluskap's grandmother and Marten were frozen. Gluskap goes to their house and only with difficulty can keep the fire going. Next evening, he goes to see this boy, who says, "I think there will be a heavy frost tonight." That night, the frost is so heavy that Gluskap can not even leave. They try to outdo each other. Next day, they go hunting. They see no game, and neither of them knows where he is going. They arrive at a small lake. Gluskap puts his bow and arrow into the lake, and vaults over on the end of the bow. The boy tries to do the same, but his bow sinks into the mud, and he cannot jump over. Accordingly, he goes around it. It was a small lake, but that fellow is going yet.

5. ANIMALS AND PEOPLE GET MUSCLES

At Broad Cove, Inverness County, Cape Breton, a big whale went ashore. Outside the cove there is now an island which has the shape of a whale. All the people and animals in the vicinity gathered to see it.

Each species took muscles from the whale and put them on itself. Moose put them on his back. People put them along their legs. They took nearly all the muscles from the whale. Gluskap took up his bow and arrow, pushed them against the whale's head, and shoved the whale off.

---

[5] As he made this statement, the informant produced the "egg," an oval stone having a close resemblance to a partridge egg, but much larger. He had kept it carefully stowed away in a chest for several years, but was eventually prevailed upon to surrender it. (See illustration 36k.)

PART TWO *Folktales and Traditions*

It became an island, and is still an island. Later, Partridge arrived. He was sorry to have missed a share of the muscles. Gluskap said, "Put yellow birch around your legs here (below the knees)." If you notice this bird, you will find a clearly marked ring there. Now everyone [every species of animal] has muscles.

Gluskap took the whale from a lake, where it endangered people, and put it into the ocean where it could injure no one.

6. GLUSKAP HAS POWER TO GRANT WISHES

A woman took a piece of bark and mashed the head of her child to pieces. The child was found, and was brought home in the bark. Its forehead was mashed down so that they could not see its eyes. Gluskap looked at him; "That's my nephew." "All right."

Gluskap built a big wigwam near the sea. He is there yet. If you want to get anything from him, go to the wigwam. There you will find a peavey, such as is used for rolling logs. Raise his forehead, so that he can see you. He is a big man, but he cannot move. Tell him you came to see him, so that you will have plenty of money. He will say, "Take that peavey, raise me up a little, and take some of that rotten wood out from under me. You will then get what you want."

A long time ago two men went there. One wished for an endless supply of moose, clothes, and good luck. He did have good luck all the time. The other wished, "I want to live a long time." "All right; go to the entrance; stand up straight there." He wanted to live two hundred to three hundred years. Next morning there was a big tree standing there. It is still there.

Gluskap is on the other side of the clouds. If you go to see him, he will know you before he sees you. There is an island on his place, and he will take you there. If you can stand the noise of the thunder, you will obtain what you wish: If long life, you will get that; if money, you will be rich; if good luck in hunting, you will get many moose and other game.   J. N.

7. GLUSKAP LEAVES INSTRUCTIONS WITH THE DOGS

Gluskap took the lead in everything. He brought two dogs and a wolf with him. He gathered all the people together and told them to inform all the other Indians that he had come. He gave his two dogs the ability to talk. He said to the people, "I shall now leave you. I will show you how to behave all your lifetime. This is the way to make your living: catch beaver, moose, deer, wild cat, bear." To the dogs he said, "Who will take care of these people?" Wolf: "I shall do so." Dog: "No; I'm going to take care of these people. If you find a moose or other animal, your master will not hear you. You will kill it. But we will call our master." "All right," said Gluskap, "always call your master." "Yes." Now, when the dogs find anything in the woods, they call their master.

8. HOW THE BEAVER GOT HIS TAIL

When Gluskap was in Cape Breton, he obtained a canoe. He had such power that he took for this purpose a big stone which is now at St. Peters, Cape Breton, and resembles a canoe with a person in the middle and a paddle alongside him. He went to the Bras d'Or lakes. He saw a beaver and a muskrat. The muskrat had a tail like a paddle, the beaver had a poor round tail. Gluskap said to him, "That tail does not suit you — it is too small." He asked Muskrat, "Will you exchange?" "Yes." Gluskap took the tail off Muskrat and gave it to Beaver. "This will make you strong." He gave the other tail to Muskrat: "This will suit you. It is just your size." Beaver had a wigwam in the water, and a little poplar tree about twenty yards from the water. Beaver started out with the tail he had gotten from Muskrat, went to the poplar, stood on two legs to bite it, and cut it down. He gnawed first high, then lower. The big tail he had procured held him up like a third leg. But Muskrat merely watches and dives quickly. Gluskap had so much power that he could do anything he wanted to do.   JOHN PAUL

9. GLUSKAP GIVES THE FROGS THEIR VOICES

The frogs became jealous of the noise which the Micmac make in producing thunder. Gluskap said, "You may make noise just as well as the Micmac." "All right." "Whatever noise you make, you will have that noise every day." The frogs are trying to beat the Micmac thunderers, but the frogs' noise is always the same noise; whereas the thunderers vary their tones: they are short, sharp, and loud, when the young people speak, and low, rolling, long drawn out, when the older people speak.

10. THE ORIGIN OF THE CEDAR'S TWIST

Two men were traveling through a swamp and were having great difficulty in wading through the mire. They struggled and agonized to

PART TWO *Folktales and Traditions*

get free of it, but in vain. Gluskap took hold of the head of one of them and twisted it round and round and round, and pulled it up into the air. That is the cedar. There it stands today, still twisted; and it is not rotted by mud or water.

11. THE ORIGIN OF THE CANOE

Gluskap made the first canoe. He took as his model the breastbone of a bird. He procured a bird by killing it with a stone. From its flesh he had a good dinner. While he was picking the meat off the bird's breast, he thought, "If something of this shape were made, it would float on the water." He went into the woods to procure some bark. "If I should kill anything out on the water, I could go out for it in this, and would not have to swim."

Gluskap was a Micmac. At Middle River, Cape Breton, he procured a beaver. About a hundred and fifty years ago the Indians found there the bone of a year-old beaver, one end of which bone fitted the hat of the finder. One end of the bone of the beaver's leg was a large as the man's head.

12. GLUSKAP AS TRANSFORMER

Stories of Gluskap's success in changing the terrain from Gaspé to Cape Breton, often incidental to his operations against the giant beavers, have been printed and reprinted in folklore collections, school histories, and tourist guides to the St. John River and the Minas Basin. The two tales selected for inclusion here, one by each of the principal 1911 storytellers, describe fairly orderly journeys around the New Brunswick coast of the Baie des Chaleurs and the Gaspé Peninsula. The Malbaie named in the second version is about ten miles north of Percé; from Gaspé to Matane is some two hundred miles farther than Peter Ginnish placed it.

AT BAIE DES CHALEURS

At Caraquet, you can see in the rock the bones and head of a fish that Gluskap ate. After eating it, he went to Bathurst, far up to the Falls, and there cooked salmon. He roasted them over a fire. He put up a split stick to hold each of them in turn. He left the stick there, and it can be seen today. No one can move it. The bones of the fish, also, are there. Along the whole length of the backbone you can see where the knife went. He left a piece of the tail of one there. After this he went to Restigouche

Tales about Gluskap

and on to Matapedia. At Matapedia he left one of his fish. It is now rock, but remains as it was when he killed it. It is in the water on the side of the river bank where he brought it and left it. The bones of fish that he cooked are there too.

When he came to Tracadegash Mountain [behind the present town of Carleton] he called to the Pugulatamutc and told them to come out. They came out on top of the rocks. He asked them whether they had a good place. "Yes." "Stay there. Do not leave. Stay there until I come back. Do not tire of waiting. I shall surely return. You have plenty to eat, plenty of clothes, and plenty of room there. Do not meddle with the people down here on the river or with those on the other side of it." He left there and went to Percé. Here he stopped to fish and trap. He soon decided to leave there. He said to his grandmother, "I am going away. I shall return; do not grow weary of waiting for me." (He has not come back yet.)

Gluskap was along the bay, near Dalhousie, and wanted to drive his beavers over to the other side of that body of water. He pulled up a handful of turf, and then another, and threw these at them, to frighten them over to the other side. The pieces of turf that fell into the bay are now the two islands off Dalhousie.

Gluskap was a great man, and he must have been a good man. Probably he is still living. Whether he is a Frenchman, Englishman, or Indian, it would be difficult to say; but inasmuch as he was here before the white man came, he must be an Indian.

J. N.

AT GASPE

Gluskap had an island about a mile off Percé [Gaspé Peninsula], which served as his boat. It was about half a mile long. It sloped on one side. While he was towing it, one side of it went aground, which accounts for the slope that is in the island today. At Malbaie he wintered. There is now, at that place, a very large spring, from which a large brook flows. He thrust a stick out into the river. It is there now in the form of a large, pointed, solid rock. About a hundred miles from it is another one, placed there by Gluskap. Near Malbaie he put up stakes on which to dry his meat. They turned to stone. From Gaspé he traveled along the shore, about twenty miles, to Mete [Matane?] [6] whence he crossed [the St.

[6] A tradition reported, in 1787, about Nantucket suggests some analogies with the Micmac Gluskap legend: "On the west end of Martha's Vineyard, are high cliffs,

PART TWO *Folktales and Traditions*

Lawrence] to the northern shore. From here he went to the Saguenay, and on as far as the country of the Eskimo. He told the Eskimo, "You have a good country here, but you cannot farm. You live on salt-water meat. Do not leave this place." He returned, for there were no Indians beyond there.

He next went to Newfoundland. He told the people there, "Do not leave your country. You cannot farm well here, but you can get plenty of meat." (The people in Newfoundland were Eskimo.)

He left there and traveled to another place on the shore, where he met a man. With him he stayed two nights. The man told Gluskap, "It will be useless to go on. You cannot go farther. There are only rocks and high mountains which extend abruptly into the water." Gluskap decided to go back. "But I shall return some time. Do not tire of waiting for me." Gluskap shook hands with him. The man whom Gluskap met is there yet — he has not died.

When Gluskap comes back, he will get his grandmother. All Gluskap's work can be seen today as in his own day. Nothing has been lost, except his grandmother and the dogs; these rocks have crumbled and fallen into the sea at Ship Head. I think Gluskap will soon come. He is now on the other side of the sun. He is not dead — he will not die. When the last day comes he will fight with the devil. If Gluskap wins, very good; if he loses, very hard will be our luck. If he wins, he will then go to hell, five times, to rescue people. If he loses, it will be bad for us. (The Bishop told me this latter part, and said it was in Scripture.) PETER GINNISH

13. GLUSKAP AND THE TWO KINGS

Gluskap is the same as Jesus Christ, or the Thunder Christ. The Day Christ is the Devil. To the point on the north shore of Baie des Chaleurs

of variegated coloured earths, known by the name of Gayhead. On the top of the hill is a large cavity, which has the appearance of the crater of an extinguished volcano, and there are evident marks of former subterraneous fires. The Indians who live about this spot have a tradition that a certain deity resided there before the Europeans came into America, that his name was Manshop; that he used to step out on a ledge of rocks which ran out into the sea, and take up a whale, which he broiled for his own eating on the coals of the aforesaid volcano, and often invited the Indians to dine with him, or gave them the relicks of his meal. That once to shew their gratitude to Manshop for his very great kindness to them, they made an offering to him of all the tobacco which grew upon the island in one season. This was scarcely sufficient to fill his great pipe, but he received the present very graciously, smoked his pipe, and turned out the ashes of it into the sea, which formed the island of Nantucket. Upon the coming of the Europeans into America, Manshop retired in disgust, and has never since been seen." *Columbian Magazine*, 1:525 (1787).

Tales about Gluskap

[Ship Head Gaspé] where Gluskap left his grandmother, a big whale came. His grandmother was in Percé, and he left his trap there. It is there today, in the form of a rock about two hundred feet high, just as he left it, its shape exactly that of a steel trap with a spring on one side, and a hole through which the spring could work. In that hole the gulls lay their eggs. A man once climbed up there, and never returned. He must have died, and rotted there. Gluskap went from there to Gaspé Bay. At that place where he cooked his dinner you can see, even to this day, the bones of fish, now turned to stone. He sank in the ground up to his ankles, and every step can be seen there, in the rocks, today.

He told his grandmother that he would go away, and added, "I shall return and take you away from here. These two dogs will take care of you." One dog, now a rock, looks in the direction in which Gluskap left.

A whale came. Gluskap had his bow and two arrows. The whale went aground, and could not get off. Gluskap, with his bow, shoved him out into the water, until it was deep enough for him to float. The whale then opened his mouth. Gluskap walked in, and the whale closed its mouth.

When Gluskap arrived in England, he had left the whale, and was on a small island. The island was about a fourth of a mile in circumference. It was the first island the English people had ever seen, and they thought it very pretty. It contained woods with trees so high that only with difficulty could they see to the top of them. The King ordered a man to try to find the man who was in charge there. A ship was sent out, and a boat from it went to the shore of the island. They found a man there and asked him, "Where are you from?" "I am from out there," said Gluskap, pointing westward. "Do you intend to remain here?" "To be sure, I shall stay here."

The English began cutting wood, to put in their ship. He told them not to do so — "All the wood on the island belongs to me." The King sent the ship back to get the man. The Captain went ashore and said to him, "Come aboard; the King wishes to see you. We will put you ashore." "No; go back; tomorrow morning I shall be there." They reported his words to the King. On the following morning it was found that the island was close to the shore. The King told Gluskap to come ashore. "I am not ready to go yet," said Gluskap; "I shall go when I am ready." The King threatened to kill him when he did come ashore.

Accordingly, the King built a big pile of wood and had ready for use a large flask of oil. Gluskap went ashore, and all the while kept very quiet. Two officers took him, handcuffed him, and put him on the pile of wood. Fire was placed to it. It blazed high, and finally the pile was burned to the bottom. When it had burned out, Gluskap was found sitting in the midst of it, just as they had placed him, smoking his pipe. The King saw him, and was frightened. Those who were standing by said, "We must kill that man now." They rammed powder into a cannon, and put him in as a wad. The cannon was fired off; Gluskap walked out and asked, "Where is the King?" The King was called. He went to Gluskap and wished to shake hands with him. Gluskap said, "I cannot touch your hand, for it is of no account — it is like yourself. You, too, are no good; you are a very hardhearted man. When you called me from out there, I thought you would accord me better treatment than I have received. You have treated me very badly: you have put me in the fire, you have put me in the cannon."

The King then knelt before him. "Get up," said Gluskap; "I don't want that. But do not treat people in such manner as you have treated me, for you do not know whom you may encounter. You may be the Master of this World, but there is another who is Master over you. I shall leave you now. If I had not shown myself more powerful than you, you would have killed me. But even I, as well as yourself, have a Master." The King told his sailors to take the man to his palace. "No; I do not want any of you or any of your people near me. Your people are of no account — they are not trustworthy. If I were not able to withstand you, I should now be a dead man. However, you have had your last opportunity to injure me."

When he left them, he got into no boat, but walked on the water, as though it were a floor, went over it to his island, and remained there during the rest of the day. Next morning, he went to France on his island. France had heard of this island — Silver Island. The French then had a King. The King dressed, and went on a boat to the island. There he saw Gluskap's wigwam and smoke coming from it. Gluskap knew the King was coming. He lay down on one side of the wigwam, in his habitual pose when reclining — on his back, the sole of his right foot flat on the ground, his right knee raised, his left foot over the right knee, and moving them to and fro. When the King came to the entrance, Gluskap rose and went to the door. The King offered his hand.

Gluskap took it, and said, "Come in. Take a seat." The King did not

Tales about Gluskap

understand, for this was spoken in Micmac. Gluskap, however, understood all languages.

The King of France invited Gluskap to his palace. "Oh no; I can't go there. I can't go to visit you in your house. I cannot go with you. I have already called on one King, who treated me very badly, and I think you, too, would treat me that way. I came here merely to see your country. I shall not return until the time comes." He did not explain what time he meant. The King said, "I should be very much pleased if you would come and see my country." Gluskap said to him, "I do see your country. It is very nice. But within your palace all is not well. If you are not careful, you will not retain your power; I can see as much from here." The King, when he heard this, almost fell down, and could not reply.

There is now no king in France. P. G.

14. GLUSKAP VISITS THE KING

This is a story hard to believe, and yet it is what I have been told. The King sent for Gluskap to come see him, but Gluskap would not go. Three times the King sent for him, and then Gluskap went. He got on his island, made two paddles, and off he started, to see the King. When he arrived at his destination, some sailors of the King came from their boat to the island and cut down a great many of the trees. That night, Gluskap went to their ship, pulled up the anchor, and drew the boat to the shore and high up on the beach. Next morning the sailors found themselves stranded on the high land. They besought Gluskap to put their ship into the water. He said, "Then you must not come back here and cut down any more trees." They said, "We may never come back, or we may come back; but this is sure: We shall never cut down any more trees, whether we come back or not." Gluskap then put their ship into the water, and let them go. When the King heard about it, he told his men to bring Gluskap there. Three times, he asked Gluskap who he was. They took Gluskap, put him into a big gun, and shot it off. When they looked into it, they saw Gluskap sitting there, smoking his pipe.[7]

NEWELL GINNISH

15. GLUSKAP SUPPLIES A FRENCH WARSHIP

There was a French man-of-war and an English man-of-war. They

[7] A similar story was heard from the Maliseet on the St. John River, N.B., and other variants among the Micmac.

PART TWO *Folktales and Traditions*

had no provisions, wood, or coal. There was a thick fog, and the wind was blowing hard. They were anchored in a fine harbor.

They saw two wigwams. One was Gluskap's, the other was his grandmother's.

The French went ashore and asked the old woman and the little boy, Marten, what place that was. "I don't know — ask my grandson, Gluskap; he will tell you." "May we get some water?" "Yes." "May we get some wood?" "Yes." "May we get some food?" "Yes," the old woman said. She gathered an armful of wood, which she gave to the sailor, also a bark vessel of water, some flour, and some meat. She said to the Captain, "Put the wood on board where the wood is kept, the water in the tank where the water is kept, the flour where the flour is kept. Follow exactly the instructions I give you."

The Frenchman did as directed. Next day they looked and found that the place where the wood had been put was full. The tank in which the water was put was full, and the bin in which the flour was put was full. Gluskap was that strong. They went away.

The English would not do this — they would not go to the old woman. The French had to give them supplies in order to keep them alive.

16. GLUSKAP ASSISTS THE INDIANS IN A FIGHT

A few years ago the English were fighting the Indians out west, in Alberta. The English would not allow them to kill buffaloes. The government sent a consignment of meat to them, in care of the agent. The agent kept it until it was rotten, and then distributed it among the Indians. The Indians went to the agent and told him they would not eat that rotten meat. After a while, they began fighting.

The Indians took the guns from those of the English whom they killed. After a while, a strange Indian said, "Come on, boys, we will kill all of them." Under his leadership and guidance, all the English were killed. That man was Gluskap. He is around somewhere, and if the Micmac were to have war with the English, he would come and assist us.

Gluskap was present at a big fight which the Indians in northwest Canada had with the English a few years ago. He went about among the Indians and said to them, "Do not give up; keep on; I will help you." The Indians won. I do not know where he went after that. He has not been seen since then. He is something like a king for the Micmac. I do not know where he is, but if the Micmac need help, he will come and help them.[8]

JOHN PAUL

17. GLUSKAP'S PROPHECY FULFILLED

Gluskap taught our people to make bows, arrows, fishhooks, and stone pipes, and showed the Micmac how to fish, hunt, and make a living, and also what to procure as medicines. He was born in the same way as any of us. He must have been a leader among his people, the old Indians said, because he knew everything so well. Gluskap said, "You are now free to get your living where you like. But there will come a day when you will be prevented" (referring to the game laws and property of the English settlers and present inhabitants). He was correct. Now we may not go out and kill moose and partridges.

[8] Not all Micmac believed that Gluskap came off first in encounters with Europeans. In 1890 they told Roth: "The mighty Glooscap was not able to cope with the white invaders who came into his domain. He was vexed with the English beyond all endurance. And the end of the matter was that once, in a mighty storm, he broke down his beaver dam, kicked over his camp-kettle, which is now known as Spencer's Island, turned his two huge dogs into stone, left them standing on the mountains, and took an unceremonious departure. But tradition asserts that he will one day return, his inverted kettle will be righted, his petrified dogs spring into life, his royal wigwam will be again set up, and his unbounded hospitality dispensed more freely than before." Roth, 42.

CHAPTER II

Supernatural Beings

Kitpusiagana

KITPUSIAGANA ("Born-by-Caesarian-Operation" or "Taken-from-Guts" according to taste) is a supernatural hero most fully known to the eastern Micmac. This account was given in Nova Scotia; two others published thirty years ago are from Cape Breton.[1] Another hero born in similar fashion is Tcikapis, the Montagnais-Naskapi dwarf.

18. KITPUSIAGANA'S BEGINNINGS

Kitpusiagana's power was second only to that of Gluskap. Before his birth his mother was captured by enemy Indians. They had killed all the Micmac at the settlement except this one woman. They said, "We will take this woman to our chief." They captured her and took her with them. The chief accepted her as his wife. The chief's father lived in another place.

The chief accepted her and her little boy. Every day he hunted, and every night returned home. One day he became surly, tired of the woman, went to his father, and said, "Go, now, to my place, and get that woman."

The old fellow started, and took his toboggan. When he arrived at his son's wigwam, the woman treated him as well as she could. She entertained him until about the middle of the afternoon. He lay down on one side of the wigwam, and stuck his iron cane into the fire. When it was red hot, he struck the woman with it four times, and killed her.

This man was Djenu [a cannibal]. He took Kitpusiagana, the woman's baby boy, and said to his own little boy grandson, "Take this little

[1] Speck, JAFL, 28:61–64; Parsons, JAFL, 38:56–57.

Supernatural Beings

brother of yours to the brook and put him in it." The boy did as he was told.

He took the little young one and put him into the brook. Miktcitck [Turtle] was there. Miktcitck took the little boy, who was floating.

The old man went home and hauled the body of the woman on a toboggan. The little boy was left alone in the wigwam. When the chief returned, his wife was gone, and he saw only the little boy, who said to him, "A man came, stayed until the middle of the afternoon, killed my mother, and took her away."

The chief went away again each day, and the boy stayed alone in the wigwam. Later he went to the brook, and found the little boy, playing. He stayed with him for a long time — until he heard the chief calling him. He did not tell what he had seen. At last the chief asked, "Why do you stay so long at the brook?" He tried to find out. The boy told him, "This made me stay so long — I played with my brother every time I went to the brook."

The chief asked him to bring his brother to the wigwam. They could not induce the child to come. At last, the chief decided to go in the morning to a certain place near the brook and try to see that boy. He did so. He saw the little boy in the wigwam. All day they played there. When they heard the chief coming, they ran to the brook. Three times Kitpusiagana went to the wigwam before he was captured there. The chief pretended that he would be away during the entire day. When, however, he saw the boy in the wigwam, he went to the middle of the entrance, and sat there. It was not possible for the boy to get out. He cried and cried. They did everything to please him, but nothing comforted him. To please him they showed him all sorts of feathers, little birds' tail feathers, and the prettiest feathers of birds. The very last feather he took. This was Crane's tail feather. He took it, and laughed. He asked for more feathers; and promised to stay there.

Kitpusiagana stayed contentedly with them. He grew so fast that soon he was as large as any man, and nothing was too difficult for him to do. No matter how strong the bows and arrows which the chief made, the boy broke them. He himself made a bow. He said to them, "You fellows do not know how to make a bow." The bow was ten times stronger than any man there could bend.

He and his brother hunted. Every day they brought home moose, caribou, and bear. The chief was a bit excited at seeing the boy carrying

PART TWO *Folktales and Traditions*

them. The boy was very strong. He said to his brother, "Now we will build us a wigwam — a larger wigwam than this, so that we will have room to play inside." They commenced to plan what they would do.

The older boy used to tell Kitpusiagana about their mother. He said to his brother, "I shall kill all the Djenu in the world." They made a strong wigwam of dry hemlock and pine. They made the wigwam of three-ply hemlock and pine logs. They made a door of six heavy logs. When they had finished it, they went out and gathered many strips of birch bark. They tore the bark into fine shreds and hung it all about the wigwam in little bunches, until they had covered the inside with fine bark, and until only fine bark could be seen. When the chief came, he saw what they had done: they had made a big wigwam. They said to him, "We now have a good wigwam. We have plenty of room for fun and play." The chief was a bit surprised and frightened; when he saw how much work they had done, he did not know what to think of them. They said to him, "When we go in, put the entrance flap up for us." The old man could not do it. The younger one did it.

They commenced to pack. They gathered up the best arrows and arrowpoints, and packed these away.

At midnight, the boy induced his older brother to go out. The chief was sleeping. Kitpusiagana took fire, went three times around the interior of the wigwam, and set the birch bark on fire. He ran out, and shut the heavy entrance flap upon the old man. When the chief awoke, the inside of the wigwam was in a raging blaze. He cried, "*Ak tciga na miwotualuk*" ("Save the younger one"). (He wanted the older one to take the younger one out.) They sat outside the wigwam, watching, and heard him crying this, to the very last. The entire wigwam went up in flames. They found his bones. Kitpusiagana piled these bones in one place, with two stones mashed the bones into a fine powder, and, when he had beaten them to powder, made a wish. The bones came out in three sizes: big, medium, and very small. He threw the big ones into the air, and made a wish. They became the houseflies.

He made a wish and pitched up the medium-sized bones. They became mosquitoes. He made a wish and tossed up the smallest. They became sandflies.

He said, "Now we shall go to see our grandfather." The older brother did not know, of himself, what they would do, but always asked. They went to see the old man. When they arrived at his wigwam, the old man

Supernatural Beings

would give them no satisfaction. Kitpusiagana told his brother, "You must not be discouraged. I will shoot that old man with my bow and arrows. When I shoot him, hit him with a club." The older boy did this. They killed him. They cut out his liver, and said, "We will take this to grandmother." Each went in a different direction, to search for the old woman.

Before they reached her, they met a bear, which was very ugly. Nevertheless, they killed it. A little way farther on, they met a moose. They killed it. They took from the moose only its heart. They found the place where their grandmother was. When they walked into the wigwam, the old woman was lying down. She would pay no attention to these boys. The younger one said, "We will cook this for grandmother, so that her dinner will be ready when she gets up." They placed the liver and the heart on spits, before the fire. When it was cooked, they woke her. Her first words were, "Kitpusiagana has done these things." Kitpusiagana said not a word, but pulled out his tomahawk, and cut off her head. Thus they got rid of those three: the chief, and the entire family.[2]

LOUIS GLODE

19. KITPUSIAGANA GETS SUMMER

Kitpusiagana wanted Summer. It was guarded by an old man and an old woman who sat in a wigwam near it, constantly shaking their arms and elbows, to keep it from escaping. An old woman went out of her wigwam, and looked around. She knew Summer was in the wigwam on the other side of the lake. She cut off a piece of fat meat, and put it into her pocket. She went along the river until she was opposite the place

---

[2] This Kitpusiagana tale in a hundred years of telling shows strikingly the changes in Micmac interest and narrative ability. Rand, who collected stories between 1848 and 1869, published a version which follows the same episodes as this 1911 tale but in so much greater detail that it fills seven pages of fine print. The story begins at the village from which the woman is captured, and all relationships are more clearly defined. In 1953, the question Do you know any stories about Kitpusiagana? brought the following reply from a man at Burnt Church, N.B., a ready talker with an interest in old times:

"A woman died. She was going to have a baby. Her husband or her father operated and cut the baby out. This boy when he grew up traveled a lot by canoe and by walking. In those days the Micmac used to kill each other. They lived in small groups who were jealous over hunting and fishing rights; several families living in a small settlement might be killed. This woman was killed in that way. She was thrown in the water and was drifting. A man found her before the baby within her had died. He cut out the child and buried the mother. The child at birth knew his name was Kitpusiagana."

where Summer was kept. There she saw Muskrat swimming along the shore. From time to time he stopped, as if listening for something. She took the fat from her pocket, and threw it on the water, near Muskrat; then she threw a piece toward him, but nearer the shore; and so on, until she had coaxed Muskrat to the shore. She asked Muskrat what he was doing.

"I am going to get Summer." "Do you know where it is?" "Yes, in that big wigwam." She said to Muskrat, "If you do not tell that I told you, I'll give you plenty to eat. I will give you this tallow. It will keep you as long as you live." "All right. In the morning I will cut a hole in their canoe, and I will chew the paddles. I will go to the other side and get a root. They will think it is a moose in the water, and will put out in their canoe to kill it." That night the old woman crossed the lake at that place. She caught Blue Jay, and said to it, "Now, fly!" It flew up above her head, but made a noise with its wings. "No; you won't do."

She got Gugwetc [Owl], and told him to fly. He made no noise at all. "Now, go get Summer!" she said to the latter.

Woodchuck was with Gugwetc. Now, Woodchuck is a great fellow to laugh (meaning his bark). She said to Woodchuck, "Now, do not laugh!"

"I cannot help it," pleaded Woodchuck. "Well, laugh now, and get laughed out!" He laughed a long, long time. Gugwetc pushed his nose against the wigwam, to see Summer, and awaited a chance to take it away.

"What's that?" asked an occupant of the wigwam. "I don't know," replied the questioner's companion. "Take a firebrand. If it is somebody, or a living creature, it will move." Gugwetc was burned on the nose, and shows signs of this today. He now has a small nose, whereas previously it was long and large. Then some one cried out, "A moose!" All went after it; and the visitor took Summer. When the occupants of the wigwam returned, Summer had gone. They cried, "Summer has gone! Summer has gone!" They launched the canoe and paddled as fast as they could in pursuit of the thieves. Soon, however, the paddle broke, for Muskrat had gnawed it. Moreover, they were nearly drowned, as a result of the hole he had put in their canoe. Then Woodchuck laughed long and loud. So they brought Summer back with them. Kitpusiagana was pleased, and stopped crying.

Supernatural Beings

20. DJENU AND KITPUSIAGANA

Djenu was the strongest man in the world. When he became angry, he grew. He is under the ground, alive, to this day. Djenu lies as he was buried. Kitpusiagana was another strong man, not dead, who is buried in the ground. One who goes where he is buried obtains medicine. Twelve men go every three months and turn him from one side to the other, from his face onto his back, and then onto his face again. Everything grows above him. When you pull something that is growing above him, you obtain good medicine. A limb of a tree or a bush which grows there will cure anything. He is buried to the east, Djenu still further to the east. They fought, and many people died because of the noise they made. I do not know on what month or day he is turned.[3]   P. G.

Djenu

Djenu, cannibal giants, eat the flesh of their own bodies. John Hammond, narrator of the following brief tale, said that these beings could kill by their voice alone, so loud was it, worse than thunder, and audible for thirty or forty miles.

21. A DJENU TAMED BY KINDNESS [4]

A family lived in the woods. They heard Djenu crying out. He came to their wigwam, and stopped at the door. The woman spoke to him, and called him "Grandfather." He did not hurt anyone. He stayed there a while. The husband came home, and spoke in friendly fashion to the Djenu. They heard another Djenu. "Now we shall be killed!" said the first Djenu, "but I will help you." It was a female, and among the Djenu this sex is the stronger of the two. "I shall fix a club. If she and I take hold of each other, pound her with the club. That will weaken her." The two Djenu fought and the man pounded the female Djenu with the club. He killed her. The victorious Djenu commenced to eat her, but her flesh was too cold. He told the Indian to make a fire and burn her up.

---

[3] The locating of these mythic personages to the eastward is possibly of some significance, inasmuch as the full-fledged stories about the Djenu and Kitpusiagana flourish in Nova Scotia, whereas they seem to be little known, and only partially known in New Brunswick. The turning of Kitpusiagana every three months by twelve men suggests the change of seasons, but I could not learn whether this is really its significance. This is the only recorded version of the story that contains the last-mentioned motive.

[4] This motive is typical of Wabanaki tales. Fisher, 248.

PART TWO *Folktales and Traditions*

22. THE DJENU ARE CANNIBALS

Three boys went to hunt moose. Only one of them had any success. A woman made the unfortunate two boys victims of a bad wish, and turned them into moose. The first brother killed and ate them. Because he ate his own kind, he became a Djenu. In the summer the Djenu goes north and remains there until the approach of winter, then goes south. Wherever he goes, he will sweep [i.e., destroy] everything. Such is the temper of his wildness.[5]

23. A NEWFOUNDLAND DJENU [6]

Djenu lives on ice. He can grow suddenly into a big man whenever he wishes to do so. There is a large lake in Newfoundland across which he went at its narrowest point. A Micmac on the other side of the lake saw him crossing it. He was a big man and carried nothing with him. The Micmac who had seen him walked all night toward the south, for he knew the Djenu would not go in that direction. His liking for the cold would take him north. He is a Micmac.

24. A MAN AND A WOMAN BECOME DJENU

A Micmac and his wife were camping in the woods, hunting. The man, when alone in the woods, saw a Djenu coming toward him. Djenu eats people — he eats everything. The man went to the wigwam and said to his wife, "When that man comes, we will do the best we can. Call him 'Father.' We will surely be eaten."

The woman went to him, shook hands with him, and called him "Father." She went out to tell her husband about it. "What did you call him?" "I called him 'Father'." The man went in and also called him "Father." "I have just arrived," the Micmac said. The Djenu sat there all day, crouching. The man said to his wife, "The day after tomorrow a big woman is coming. Cut down as many big maple trees as you can fell in two days." "All right."

The man dug a big hole. Two days later a big woman came, pulled

---

[5] The Cree are acquainted with Weettako, "a kind of vampire or devil, into which those who have fed on human flesh are transformed." John Franklin, *Narrative of a Journey to the Polar Sea* (Everyman's Library), 72. Compare the Ojibwa (Chippewa) Windigo, a cannibal giant.

[6] The designation is said to be Atceu in Montagnais. A similar creature, Djecactodjnehwan, appears in a tale from the Lake Waswanipi Cree just east of the Montagnais. Speck, JAFL, 28:77.

Supernatural Beings

these trees out by the roots, and with them they hit the Djenu over the back. Wherever they struck off some flesh, it grew on again. The man said to the woman, "When the flesh comes off, put it on the fire and burn it." They did so, and finally killed him. It took the fire two days to consume his heart, which was solid ice. They boiled water in two pots. The man drank all of it — he was thawing out his insides. "We can do that. We must lie down during the winter, put ice on our neck, leave it there until it melts, then put another piece on, and another, until the heart gets cold. Then we can grow up quickly to a very large size, start for the far north, and live on ice."

He tells the woman, "Take a stick and hit me on the back with it as hard as you can." She does so. He vomits. "Strike again." She strikes again. He vomits more ice. Djenu had the power to make others like himself and send them to the far north.[7]   J. N.

Tcipitckaam

Tcipitckaam, a serpentlike being, lives in lakes and woods. Its head is as big as that of a horse and its eyes are two great crystals.[8]

The water in a certain spring in the woods rises in big ripples and is very muddy, as though a big snake or other beast were in it. A boy had first seen it. Later I saw the spring with its water thus troubled and muddied. I would not want to go near that place.   J. N.

25. A MAN BECAME A TCIPITCKAAM

Two brothers were hunting. They saw a trench. "What is that?" one of them asked. It had been made by a Tcipitckaam. One of the men lay down in it. He became larger and larger and stronger. The other could not get him out of the cavity. He followed it down into the water. He came back and narrated a big story: Tcipitckaam is a female. The man went to the bottom of the lake, and there found a wigwam. He went in. There he saw an old man, a woman, and a girl. A boy came in. "This is my son," said the woman. "Your brother-in-law came in only a few minutes ago," the woman said to her son. "All right."

[7] In two tales of human beings transformed into *chenoo*, the setting is on the Saguenay in the Tadoussac region. Rand, 246 and 250.
[8] A popular European import, this dragonlike creature appears most frequently in tales containing many French motives. See Rand, Tales 2, 4, and 13, all of which have been analyzed by Thompson.

PART TWO *Folktales and Traditions*

The people from whom these two brothers came were Micmac. Among them was a medicineman.

The medicineman said, "If he sleeps with her under the same blanket, we cannot bring him back. If he does not do so, we can." The medicineman went out, dug a trench, put water in it, and placed medicine upon this water. He climbed a tree and trimmed off the branches. Soon he saw two big dragons approaching. The dragons made a big noise. One came to the tree where the medicineman was, curled around and around it, and thrust up his head in the middle of the coil. The medicineman said to the returned brother. "All right. That is your brother." He was now a big Tcipitckaam, and the brother could not go near him. With a wooden knife the medicineman cut off the creature's head, and removed the entire body of the man. His wife was beside herself with joy. She jumped, danced, and shouted. The medicineman gave the man medicine which caused him to vomit. The brother said: "When I tried to converse with him, he made a noise like a Tcipitckaam — he could not speak properly." If he had stayed there another day, it would not have been possible for him to come back. This is true. We know it because the old Indians have handed it on to us.[9]

J. N.

26. A MAN IS CHASED BY A TCIPITCKAAM

A man who was drinking from a large spring in the woods noticed that the water was rising and falling in a peculiar manner. The oscillation increased. He left off drinking and backed away. He saw a big black object coming from the earth and knew that it was a Tcipitckaam.

He ran, and every now and then dodged by turning at right angles. The Tcipitckaam could not turn as rapidly as could the man, and the man outdistanced it. The man came to a cleared path.

While he was running along this, at top speed, he came to some men who were sitting alongside it. "What are you running from?" they asked. "A Tcipitckaam is after me," he said. "Run into the house over there and keep still," they told him. He went into the house, and the men hid themselves near the road. After a while they saw the Tcipitckaam coming, its head raised high in the air. It went past them, then got mixed up on the tracks, turned around, and started back. They had a rifle and a gun

---

[9] Franklin (*Journey to the Polar Sea*, 69–72) speaks of a being "whom they term *Kepoocikawu*," to whom the Cree "make offerings," and to whom they pay considerable respect. The description of this being, however, differs considerably from the Micmac portrayal of Tcipitckaam.

Supernatural Beings

with buckshot, and they shot the monster again and again, until it was dead. It was so big that a five-year-old horse could not move it. It required two horses to drag it off the road.

27. AN ENCOUNTER WITH A TCIPITCKAAM

While I was hunting in the woods with another man, we saw, on the other side of the brook, a big snake. Its body, at the neck, was about the size of a stovepipe, and its head was about the size of that of a small dog. Its head was raised high in the air. I said, "I shall shoot it."

"No," said the other man, "perhaps we will not be able to kill it." "Yes, we can kill it. Not kill it!" I said, "I have a rifle with a magazine full of cartridges, and you have a gun with buckshot. Of course we can kill it. I shall shoot it." "No, do not do so," he said; "we might not kill it, and you do not know what it might do to us." We did not disturb it.

I do not like to be in a canoe on a lake back in the woods. One of those large snakes might pull you under, and you could not help yourself.

CHAPTER III

Mythic Peoples

THE mythic races whose activities the Micmac so circumstantially describe are to them real peoples. Though in a narrative the informant may sometimes employ the English words "fairy," "dwarf," or even "Liliputian," the terms are used as approximations which Europeans can understand. These are old races with old powers, not supernaturals.

The two groups most commonly mentioned in 1911–12 and best remembered in 1953, the Migamawesu and the Pugulatamutc, are sometimes confused by the Micmac; or the name of one people is used to describe feats usually characteristic of the other. This is an old Micmac custom; the same confusion or transfer of traits from one set of supernatural beings to another is found in Rand's tales, where the cannibal giant is known as Chenoo (Djenu) or as Kookwes (Gugwes).[1]

28. THE VERY LARGE AND VERY STRONG PEOPLE

An Indian lived on the seashore. He went to shoot some birds.

He fell asleep in his canoe. It went adrift. When he awoke, no land was visible, and he did not know where he was. He arrived at some islands. He decided to go ashore. There was no one to give him information. He saw a canoe coming around a point. It was a large one.

"They saw me. They talked Micmac. A girl in the party said, 'I shall take that for a doll.' She put her paddle under my canoe. She took it home. She said to her father. 'I found a doll.' 'No, that is a Micmac.'"

[1] See Tales 100 and 102. In a tale told at Lequille near Annapolis, N.S. (1923), Genub, Megumooweso, and Chenoo (Djenu) are three individuals who visit Gluskap. Most of the exploits are Genub's, whose strength and cleverness pass all of Gluskap's tests. Chenoo is taken home to his own country in the cold regions of the north. The others fill their ears with fat and escape the cannibal. Megumoowesoo stays in the mountain country. Genub goes on with Gluskap to create the lakes of Nova Scotia. Fauset, Tale 13, 309–14.

348

Mythic Peoples

These people were so strong that any one of them could pick up a moose and carry it on his back.

"Have you any children?" they asked the Micmac. "Yes; a wife and four children." "I shall keep your canoe and make another one for you." They made another canoe for him and went on. There was a very small dog. The strong man said to the dog, "Take this man to the place from which he has drifted." To the Micmac he said, "Go in whatever direction this dog points his nose." The dog looked in a certain direction, the man headed his canoe that way, and the dog went back, and lay down. Finally, they reached the shore, and the dog jumped out. "I fed him and he played about. I wished to keep him. I called to him, but he jumped up and ran away, over the water."

That happened before this country was discovered. P. G.

29. THE HALFWAY PEOPLE

There are many Indians everywhere, all over the world, even in the bottom of the bay. In the halfway place the lower part of the body is like a fish, whereas the upper part is human. Sabawaelnu, "water-dwelling people," is the name of these people. Sometimes they come up to the surface and ask for tobacco or a knife. If they are treated well, they do no harm; but if they are treated badly, they will raise a big storm, and do great injury. Before a storm, you can hear them singing; when they cease, the storm breaks. The child which I found [2] was one of these people. [In proof of their existence the informant mentioned other corroborating accounts, and the fact that when he dropped the child, it went at once down into the deep water.] When the storm is over, they resume their singing. Not everyone hears them singing, and not everyone has seen them. A great many old people, but not many of the younger generation, have seen them. Some of these people are male, and some are female. P. G.

30. THE APPEARANCE OF THE HALFWAY PEOPLE IS OMINOUS

About the seventh of August, some thirty-five years ago [about 1875], when I was out fishing and was lying in the bottom of the canoe, I felt

[2] See Tale 31.

PART TWO *Folktales and Traditions*

something queer come very fast all through my body. I rose, and pushed a pole down into the water. Something black and indistinct came up toward the surface of the water. When he was about two feet from the surface, he stopped, looked up at me, and laughed.

I felt something go through my face, as when I am ashamed. He stayed there, perhaps three minutes, and then went down. About five minutes later, between my canoe and another, I saw a frog going around and around, and growing gradually larger, until it was about the size of the base of a stack of hay. I said to the boy who was with me, "We will go ashore; we'll get no fish today, but we'll get plenty of them tomorrow."

When I was ashore, I got some shad and herring, and pounded two bucketfuls for bait.

Next morning all went to fish. We threw out three hundred pounds of ballast, and piled in mackerel until the water came to the edge of the canoe. Every canoe was full.

"Boys," I said, "I told you we would get plenty of mackerel today. Tomorrow we shall have a big storm. If anyone wants to go home with me, let him come along." Next day I hauled my canoe up on the shore. That night a storm came, and raged for three days. When it was over, and the men came back, they said, "Peter, maybe you are the master of that storm. You told us it would come, but we did not go home. If we had listened to you and had gone home, we would not have been out in it." P. G.

31. THE HALFWAY PEOPLE MUST BE RESPECTED

I was buying salmon around the bay, from Portage Island, Fox Island, and other places, for Mr. Sewall, about forty years ago [1870], and was carrying the purchase money with me. A fisherman on Portage Island promised me some salmon if I would call for them the next day. Next morning, at six o'clock I started for Portage Island. "I have five salmon for you outside there," he said, when I arrived. "We'll go after them." The tide had been very high. When I walked ashore, I found the ground was very soft, except for the firm strip where the tide had been. I looked ahead of me, and soon I saw something on the sand. The fisherman, too, saw it and said, "What is that?" It was a little child, his face about three inches wide, and his head about as big as my fist. He had little hands and tiny fingernails. Where he lay, milk had run out of his mouth and

Mythic Peoples

stained the ground. The fisherman wanted to bury him there in the ground. I lifted him up and told the fisherman to come with me, and we would put him into deep water. When we got him out to deep water and dropped him, he sank right down. (There must be people underneath.) When I came home I told my mother about it. She said, "You did well when you put him into the water. If you had treated him badly, you might suffer bad luck; but because you have treated him well, you will have good luck."

P. G.

32. THE GIRL WHO VISITED AADAIIK [HALFWAY]

An old man and his wife and daughter were traveling by canoe, near Green Point. When they came to the cove, his wife said, "You should kill one or two ducks for dinner." The woman paddled, the man sat in the front of the canoe, and soon was close enough to the ducks to shoot and kill two of them. They went farther, and he killed two more ducks. He reloaded his gun and went toward the shore. When he commenced to paddle, a very nice person, whose head only was visible, came up out of the water. He looked at the old man in the canoe, and then at the old woman. The old man in the canoe laughed at him. After a while he came up alongside the canoe, and shook hands with the daughter. He took her out of the canoe and down into the water. The old man cried [grieved at the loss], and the woman cried and nearly fainted.

The wife said to her husband, "If we had gone ashore after the first shot, we would have our girl now." She continued to cry, and talked a great deal. "We can't help it now," replied the father; "she was a very nice girl — she worked hard, and made us no trouble. But we can't help it now."

After this the old man and his wife would not go out to sea, but went along the shore to Shippigan. (At that time there was no settlement at Shippigan — only two or three white people lived there.) The old woman was almost crazed with grief. At Shippigan they saw two lone [abandoned?] wigwams, and the old woman said, "We will go there." They stayed at that place until autumn.

They went to Burnt Church for St. Anne's Day, then returned to Shippigan. Three or four canoes came there at that time. During September the old woman cried, and ate hardly anything. But the old man was more manly — woman's fashion is very soft. The old woman was crying; the old man lay stretched out behind her, smoking his pipe. They heard someone coming. The visitor raised the flap of the wigwam. "Mother, are you asleep?" The mother raised her head. "My girl has come back! The girl who went away with the man whose face we saw in the sea!"

The father asked, "Where did you come from?" "I came from home." "Where is your home?" "I do not know, father. I have been in the water. Since I left you suddenly, I have been in the water. I do not know how fast I went with my man. I went with him until I arrived at his abode. His father and mother were very glad to see me, and they treated me nicely. The people were very nice and good. I had to shake hands so much that my hand was worn out. One day my husband's father said to my husband, 'Take your wife back to her father and mother.' I was pleased when I heard those words. I started, and I do not know how fast I went. When we arrived at the gully, my husband looked around, pointed to a wigwam, and said, 'You see that smoke? That is your father's [wigwam].' I asked my husband, 'What time will you come back?' 'I shall be back, and I shall see you here at the gully,' he said."

Soon after the daughter's return she gave birth to a male. Her father and mother were very much pleased. "He will cut our wood and do our work for us when he grows up," they said. A week or two later the daughter was able to go about again. Her husband came to the shore, though he consisted of only a head, so far as people could see. He told his wife's mother to bring the boy to the shore, for he wished to see his son. The boy's grandfather was in great fear that the father would take the boy away. The father was very glad to see his boy. He told his wife that she must return with him in October and stay until spring; in the spring, he would take her to her father's.

The daughter told her mother that in the place where she had stayed, "the people are very good, very quiet, and very clean. The grass is always green. At each crossroads a band lives. Mother, you can't see a spider or a worm or anything on the ground — it is so clean that you can lie where you wish; and there is no noise."

Autumn came, the boy was two or three months old, and the daughter knew that soon she must return to her husband; but she did not like to speak of it to her mother. She told her mother that they should go into the woods. Her mother repeated this to the father. He said, "No; later we will build in the woods." It was now autumn; the daughter knew that her husband would soon come for her, but said nothing about it, lest she worry her father and mother. If she should go away suddenly,

Mythic Peoples

this would not be so hard on them. The old people wished to keep the girl with them.

When she had come back to them, some months previously, it was in the morning; now, in the evening, she went away. The old people, when they returned home in the evening, were always glad to see the child, and they fondled it. Now, the daughter and the child were gone. The husband said, "They will return in the spring." So the old people did not take it very hard, knowing that the daughter and her child would come back. One morning, when the old man went outside, he saw on the shore a large dead horse-mackerel. He walked farther, and found two dead seals. These had been taken to him by his son-in-law. He went home and said to his wife, "I found a dead horse-mackerel and two seals. Bring them home, split them, clean them, and store them for the winter." In this manner the son-in-law brought supplies from time to time, and supported the old people throughout the winter. Time after time, when the man went out, he found fish. He did not wish to track moose or caribou, for it was easy to pick up fish. The people nearby found out how the man got his living.

In June, the daughter again came to her mother and father, and spent the summer with them. "Father," she said, "the entire time I have been away seems like only two or three days. It is a very nice place there. The people eat no flesh, fish, or fowl." "What do they eat there?" "For breakfast, dinner, and supper, they bring only berries. When you have eaten one of them, you have enough, and do not eat anything more until the next meal." "Do they have wigwams?" "Yes; everybody has a wigwam. They are all over the place. No one does any work — they merely walk about."

This happened in my father's time. Just a year before the girl disappeared, a boy from Burnt Church visited Aadiik [Halfway] and returned to tell his tale. The stories must be true, because they are the very same in all essential details. The boy called the name of the place "Halfway" and the girl gave it the same name. There must be people living below us.

I believe it because the stories come together and are right [i.e., correspond and therefore corroborate each other] and what he says is what she says. Djoseph was the name of the girl's father; Kago, the name of his wife. The daughter's name is not known.

[Subsequently, the narrator of these stories about the halfway place

PART TWO *Folktales and Traditions*

wished to make the following addition, which he said he had forgotten when he told the stories.] There are people who live in the ground below us, just as there are people who live in the sea, and they are all the same people. We call them Sabawauegaumg.

This is not my story. It came from the girl and the boy who had visited the halfway place. No other person has been there. The girl said, "One time, when my man came home, he laughed. When he had laughed a while, he said, 'There is a big storm, and there are many boats across the way, on the water.' That is all he said. His mother said, 'That is not good; a bad storm is not good; too many people die.'" The boy said about the same, except that he made no mention of storms. He said, "There is no cold, no ice, no fire. At night they lie on the grass — it is so soft and warm." The boy told his father and mother that if they would go back with him, he would take them. But he could not persuade them to go. Both the boy and the girl had to go back — they could not stay [with their Micmac relatives] whether they wished to do so or not.[3]

P. G.

33. THE SALSTOG

There is a tribe of Indians called Salstog, who are smaller than the Micmac. They are about the size of a fourteen- or fifteen-year-old boy.

They do not put up wigwams, as do animals. I have not seen them, but the old people told me about them. The oldest people I knew talked about them. They live on nuts, berries, and the flesh of wild animals. They live more like animals than like people — like the muskrat or the ground hog. They are very wild. When they see people coming, they suddenly disappear into the ground and stay there. The old people knew how these people live. They have never been civilized. They believe nothing that is told them, but continue their own way of life.

In the winter they collect beechnuts off the ground and store them. Everyone has a great pile of them. There are three kinds of these nuts which they gather and live on. They grow very fat on the nuts, which are sweet, fatty, and of good flavor. They eat all kinds of small animals, the squirrel, muskrat, ground hog, fisher, and others. They shoot these with their bows and arrows. They do not kill any of the big animals, for

[3] On another occasion, when giving place names, Peter Ginnish mentioned two sites close to Pokemouche, one as the spot where the girl fell out of the canoe ("Fast Gulley") and the other as the home of her father ("Red Ground").

354

example deer or moose; it is only the smaller animals that they can carry home; the larger ones they cannot carry. They put these animals on the coals and roast them.

Both men and women are well built and good-looking. Both sexes wear only a breechclout, merely sufficient to cover the private parts. They have canoes, torches, and a little spear for taking fish. They wear the skins of smaller animals, especially those of the fox, squirrel, fisher, mink, and sable. In every respect they live as formerly did the Micmac, except that they roast their meat over the fire, instead of boiling it.

If two or three men hunt together and kill, for example, two or three muskrats, they apportion the game equally, and each man carries his own share.

After they kill an animal, they leave nothing; even the blood they keep, and use as a gravy. When they eat nuts, they take two or three mouthfuls of these, then a mouthful of meat. When they cut off a piece of meat, they dip it in the blood, which is on a plate nearby. They are very good singers. Some nights you can hear them singing in the ponds and lakes in the woods. They travel mostly at night. Only when they are hunting do they travel during the day. They must come home before sunrise. There is something very queer about them.

The [narrator's] informant had seen only two or three of these people. "I talked with them," he said, "and they understood every word I said. They talked Micmac. They live at Hutcheson Bay [Hudson Bay?], in the woods. I don't know where that is, but it is a very cold place. It is only one day's travel from the coast. They are so wild that they are afraid of everything, and do not like to come out." He did not know how many there were. "Maybe too many," he said. "They do not mind the cold in the winter, for they live in the ground. They have no houses or buildings of any kind. They can hide very easily, for they merely have to go into the ground." The informant would not go into the hole where they stayed — he thought it was not safe to do so. "They had no guns, only axes, knives, bows and arrows; but they were very good marksmen, even when shooting the smaller animals. They are so wild that it is not possible to coax them out of their houses. When I met them, the men inquired where I was from, how I got my living, and so on. When I asked one of them the same questions, he could not tell me — he merely said that they lived in the woods. They had no town, no houses or wigwams, but all lived in the ground."

P. G.

PART TWO *Folktales and Traditions*

34. THE PUKTESADULKWULTIDJIK [THE PEOPLE WHO SMOKE]

These people were Indians, and a shade of red in complexion. They lived in the ground, like animals, and dug holes in the earth below the frost line, as a pismire does. No one knows how numerous they were. They lived in the woods, in places where you now see little hillocks. They would not live on level ground. They occupied only mounds and hillocks, never big mountains such as the Stone People used. They were very queer. In some respects they were very strong. They lived on the best of animals: moose, caribou, deer, beaver, the very best. They had a splendid opportunity to kill these animals, because they themselves were so very small. The animals would think, They are so small — they will do us no harm. They hunted with bow and arrow, and with a small stick a foot or a foot and a half in length. This was bent through a crotched stick [the shape of the letter Y], and the ends were tied fast with thongs. A small stone was laid on this stick and shot from it [as a sling]. They could kill gulls with it, and it would kill a man if the stone struck him in the head. By this means they killed their game. A chief or headman was master of all of them. They are sometimes heard singing; and they are very good singers. At the least sound or movement, they suddenly disappear; for they are very wild. If you are lost in the woods and need help, they will tell you the various directions and, sometimes, will show you the way home. They will not injure an Indian; in fact, they like to learn our customs and habits.[4]

P. G.

35. THE MIGAMAWESU

Night and day the Migamawesu keep watchful eyes over the Indians. The old-time Indians called upon them only in the woods, and only if an Indian was alone. If you tell anyone that you are going to see them, or that you intend to ask their help, you will not see them or obtain their assistance. They are so strong that they could stop a train on the tracks; but they do not do such tricks. If I should go into the woods and sing, keeping time with a stick, they would soon come, for they would know immediately that something was wrong.

[4] The slinglike weapon of these people was said to have been used by the Micmac before they obtained snowshoes; after that they could drive animals to the encampment. It was alleged that this weapon was too dangerous, hence was abandoned. The name given was *likpe maa nukt*. Further inquiry convinced me it was the white man's sling and not a native device.

Mythic Peoples

36. MIGAMAWESU CURE DISEASE

A man met a Migamawesu in the woods. The following conversation took place: "What do you wish?" "I want medicine for sickness." "What sickness would you cure?" "Spitting of blood, blindness, deafness, rheumatism, sore head, sore tooth — everything." "It is well; I shall help you now. Come with me." The Migamawesu takes three or four steps, finds green leaves growing, and pulls them up by the roots. He takes them in his hand and counts them. "I give you these. Whenever you go into the woods, you will find them. The first branch of the root will cure spitting of blood and tuberculosis." From this one branching root the man obtained seven medicines.

A man with the secret power to cure any ailment met a man who was stone-blind. "How did you become blind?" "This morning when I arose, I saw that it was light. But at sunrise I could see nothing." "I will try to help you." The man who had said this went into the woods, obtained a root, and said, "I want you to cure that blind man." He obtained four such roots, carried them home, and washed them. He broke and crushed them. He told the afflicted man to lie down, and put these on his eyes. "If they itch, do not rub them much." Before sundown, his eyes began to itch. That night, while he was rubbing them, he felt something on his finger, and pulled off a thin film; he did the same with the other eye. Next morning his vision was normal; and during the remainder of his life he did not suffer from blindness. The man who obtained the medicine had *keskamzit*. Probably he got his *keskamzit* from a Migamawesu.[5]

P. G.

37. THE MIGAMAWESU FACILITATE TRAVEL

In the winter, while there was a great deal of snow on the ground, I was driving a horse. I felt something strange, the lines got a little tighter, and I could see the entire road ahead of me, even where it went in and around the woods and trees. [The narrator had been raised into the air by the Migamawesu.]

My father was in the woods, about seventy-five miles from Campbellton. After he had walked about twenty-five miles, on his way home,

[5] For *keskamzit*, see Tales 74–78.

PART TWO *Folktales and Traditions*

he felt himself rising into the air, and then sailed along like a bird, all the way home. He made the remainder of the trip in five hours. When he arrived at his destination, he went to his employer. "I didn't expect to see you before tomorrow," he said to my father. "When did you leave?" "At such and such a time," said my father. "And how did you come?" "I walked." "You don't mean to tell me that any man can walk seventy-five miles in that time?" he said. But my father made no reply. The Migamawesu had transported him.

38. AN ENCOUNTER WITH A MIGAMAWESU

If a Migamawesu yells, you will never see him — not if there are a thousand of them. They can do anything. My grandfather saw one. He said: "We were putting up deadfalls in the woods. When I was about to go to sleep, I heard something singing. I, too, was singing, but I did not know when I had begun to sing. No one was with me. Next evening, the same thing happened. Next day, I went into the woods, into a region of big trees, with large open spaces about them. I thought I saw someone, behind the trees, coming toward me. It was a nice woman about twenty-five to thirty years old, dressed like the old-time Indians, in skin — for it was only lately that they obtained blue cloth, beads, and ribbons. She wore a peaked woman's hat covered with beads, her hair was plaited, and hung down in front of each shoulder. Her first words were, 'You are a poor man.' 'Yes.' 'If you believe what I tell you, no one can hurt you. I will help you, at any time, so that no one can kill you. Even if you kill one of your relatives, a brother, sister, or other near relation, I will help you.'"

My grandfather said: "I didn't know what to do. I walked straight ahead and did not want to look around. When I had taken ten or twelve steps, I looked behind me. No one was visible." JOHN PAUL

39. TWO MIGAMAWESU AT BURNT CHURCH

A man came here [Burnt Church] on St. Anne's Day, and stayed among the Indians. No one noticed him. They did not know who he was, but knew he did not live here. A man went to another and said, "He is a stranger. He does not live here." They asked him, "Where are you from?" He became angry, and would not answer. A second and a third time he was asked; but he would not state whether he belonged to Richibucto or some other place. After a while, in a flash, he disappeared. He had given no answer, and he was not seen to disappear — he simply passed out of sight, like the wind. The young man who had first given information about him said, "We must find that Indian tonight. He will be here and perhaps will do some considerable damage. It is not easy to trust that man." The people listened to him, because he had been the first to find out that the man was a stranger. The stranger had disappeared, just like the wind, and no one knew where he had gone.

Two men hid back of the reserve, where the post road to Neguac now runs. One of them hid on the ground, and the other nearby. At about eleven o'clock, the stranger was seen coming back. At almost every other step he stopped and looked around, and constantly turned his head this way and that. He walked between these two men. They jumped up, caught him, and brought him before the chief and the people.

When he was taken before them, he said nothing. Chief: "Where are you from?" Stranger: "From the woods." Chief: "Where did you belong before you came from the woods?" Stranger: "I belong everywhere. Wherever I go, there I belong." Chief: "Very well. It is this way: No one wishes to hurt you or do you harm. But you must come out [disclose who you are] like any other man." "I am not afraid. You cannot hurt me. You cannot kill me."

The men who had caught him said, "You have heard the chief. When you have finished talking with him, go away from here and never come back. If you return, we shall surely kill you. We can injure you, but we do not wish to do so." Chief: "How long were you here before you appeared publicly?" "Three days." "How long did you intend to stay?" "I should like to stay another three days — a week in all." "If, at the end of three days, you go away, all right; but if, at the end of three days, you do not go away, there will be trouble." The young man who had discovered the stranger was the only one who could master him.

When the chief had finished, he offered his hand. "Good-by." "Good-by." They shook hands. Chief: "Your business is finished here now. Start off." He started off straight into the woods, singing. He sang steadily for three days and two nights; everyone heard him. He never came back. We did not know what he might do. He might poison a person or kill someone, and no one else would ever know who had done it. The young man kept on the lookout for him. At the end of the three days, he

PART TWO *Folktales and Traditions*

had left the place where he had been singing, and was never seen since. His name was Migamawesuke. He never died. He is an Indian. At various times, though not very often, we hear him singing. I have heard him, but I never heard anyone now alive say that he had heard him.

There is a very pretty, good-sized, fat, and healthy woman in the woods, just like him. One minute, you see her, then, in a flash, she is gone. You hear no noise, but open your eyes, and there she is. Then, suddenly, she is gone. Once, in April, I saw her in the woods. I was making peavey shafts out of maple wood. She came within eight feet of me, and began to talk. I was chopping a stick with my axe.

When she had finished speaking, I said, "No." She repeated her words. Again I said, "No." She said it again; and again I replied, "No." She then said, "You had better take care after this, for something will happen to you." Then she was gone.

While I was chopping wood again, suddenly I heard ice crack. My foot went down, the blow of my axe was deflected, and the axe cut into my wrist [the big scar was shown] and, as a result, for seventeen months I was unable to work. That woman brought this misfortune upon me. She told me she would do me harm; but I did not believe her. That is what she did to me, because of my skepticism. Since that time I have had no desire to see that man or that woman. They stay in the woods. But only those who like them can see them — no one else can.[6]   P. G.

[6] Penobscot describe twin beings, called Mikamwesu, as Micmac creatures, little fellows, "waist high who entice maidens into the depths of the woods. Women who consort with them never wish to marry . . . They come when wished for. If sought for and found . . . they may become spiritual helpers. When hunters slept without shelter in the woods in winter, they put their snowshoes over their heads, the ends thrust into the snow, to avoid the maliciousness of a *mikamwe'su* who might pass by and push their brains out. Such a fate was said to have overtaken any hunters found dead in the bush." Speck, JAFL, 48:16–17.

Timagami Ojibwa describe Memegwesi as "a species of creature which lives in the high remote ledges. They are small and have hair growing all over their bodies. The Indians think they are like monkeys, judging from specimens of the latter they have seen in the picture-books." Frank G. Speck, *Myths and Folk-lore of the Timiskaming Algonquin and Timagami Ojibwa*, Anthropological Series, Canada Department of Mines, Geological Survey, No. 9 (1915), p. 82.

Sister Bernard Coleman, writing of Ojibwa in northern Minnesota, describes "the Memegwicio or men of the wilderness. Some called them a 'kind of monkey.' They were somewhat like our fairies, and were described as being about the size of children of ten or eleven years of age. Since their faces were covered with hair, the Memegwicio covered them with their hands whenever they noticed anyone approaching. They lived in the rocks on the shores of great bodies of water and were frequently seen paddling their stone boats across the water. The Indians left tobacco, food, or clothes on the rocks for them to keep these beings propitious." Sister Bernard

Mythic Peoples

40. MIGAMAWESU AT A LUMBER CAMP

Two Indians were employed by lumbermen. About twenty [white] people were at the place. It was almost Christmas, and the people were talking of going to the shore to spend Christmas. They asked the Indians whether they intended to go to the shore. "Yes." "You shall not go; you shall stay here in the camp." On the following night they talked about this plan again. All of these twenty men were opposed to the Indians. One of the Indians said, "What can we do? We cannot fight a bunch of that size. We should go tonight." "No fear; I will put a stop to their plans now." To the white men: "You men make an end of this! We wish to have no trouble." "Shut up, you Indian devil!" The Indian looked at the speaker, then at the ground, picked up a little stick, sat on a wooden bench, and sang. While he sang, he tapped on the bench with the stick.

When the Indian started to sing, the white men looked at him, and one of them said, "Look at that damned fool! Shut up, you Indian!" The Indian continued to sing. Soon he heard people coming. The white men who were watching him rushed into their camp, shouting, "Great God! A host of Indians are coming — we do not know how many!" The new arrivals went to the Indian, and he talked with them. He said, "If they carry this any further, I shall let you know about it." The Indian went into the hut. No one said a word.

Next morning, four Englishmen [English-speaking whites] went home for Christmas, leaving sixteen men in the woods. A Frenchman [French Canadian] said to the Indian, "Sing again! I want to see your men come again tonight." An Englishman slapped the Frenchman in the mouth and said, "Shut up, you damned Frenchman!" After this the Indians went to the shore, and were home in half a day. After they had gone, the overseer said to the other men, "Leave them alone, for God's sake! You do not know what an Indian can do. If he had gotten cross last night, he might have killed all of us."

This is a true story — every word of it.   P. G.

Coleman, "The Religion of the Ojibwa of Northern Minnesota," *Primitive Man*, 10:9–10 (1937).
    James Bay Cree left offerings for the Memegwecio, "the diminutive being who looks like a human except that he is covered with hair and has a very flat nose." Regina Flannery, "The Culture of the Northeastern Indians," in Johnson (ed.), *Man in Northeastern North America*, 269.

PART TWO *Folktales and Traditions*

41. THE PUGULATAMUTC [STONE INDIANS]

Only in the afternoon do the Pugulatamutc come out for a good time, they begin their sport about five or six o'clock. They then come out of the mountain, and both men and women sing. They have very good voices. Some have very strong voices; some of the singers are men, and some are women. After singing, they dance. I never saw them, but one can hear them, and if one listens, find out what they are doing. They begin about dusk. They have a little horn in which there are pebbles, and this they shake, as a rattle. The dancer holds the horn in his right hand and strikes it sharply on the open palm of his left hand. Thus they sing and dance, on and on. By and by, about the middle of the night, you can hear them shake the horn vigorously. The leader holds it out in a vertical position in front of him, gives it a sudden shake, and shouts, "Kiluwalo! Kiluwalo!" which means "dinner time." Later you can smell smoke and can see the glow of the pipes which they are smoking. After they have smoked, the leader holds the horn in vertical position, as before, shakes it sharply, and cries, "Hau! Hau! Hau!" and the dance begins again. The leader stands in the middle of the dancers and beats the horn on his open palm [to keep time].

The old man who told me [the informant] about them said: "One night I listened for about an hour. Next morning I went to the place where they had held the celebration, and I could see absolutely no signs of their having been there. (They come out in this fashion only during the night.) I saw a great many of them — men, women, and children — but I could not go near them. Once, when I was in the woods, a man, a woman, and a child walked past me. In the path of the child was a log which he could not step over, and I wished to lift him over it. As soon as I moved, he and his mother were off in a flash, like lightning. Ever after that I have been afraid of them. I have wanted to steer clear of them, for one does not know what they will do. If they poison a person, that person will die at once.

"When a big meeting is to be held, a man comes out and cries, 'Hau! Hau! Hau!' long drawn out and in a strong voice. Then another, and another, and another cries out 'Hau! Hau! Hau!' All assemble, and there will be a meeting. When they talk among themselves, it is like birds talking together, and no one can understand them. But when they talk to me, I can understand them. [That is, they speak Micmac.]

"The big mountain on Baie des Chaleurs, opposite Dalhousie, is full

Mythic Peoples

of them, as also all the mountains along the bay east of that place. One can see the small tracks of their bare feet. They wear no hats.

"One time I saw two or three going through the woods. I never found out where they went, but in the evening they returned with loads on their backs. 'Where are you from?' I asked. 'From away over the mountain,' was the reply, 'I wanted to go through to the St. Lawrence, but that is not possible.' If they had wanted to go there, they could have done it easily — they are no human folk.

"I am told that you cannot tire of looking at them, no matter how long you watch them. Among themselves they talk in quiet little tones, like birds; but when they talk to other people, they speak out, just as we do.

"All go barefoot. Both men and women wear only a strip of cloth, to hide the private parts. You can scarcely tell the men from the women, except by their hair. The men put their hair up in braids, and coil them around the top of the head, or tie them up at the back of the head; whereas the women let theirs hang at full length, and do not dress it at all. Some of the women have long hair that reaches below their buttocks. They fashion very neat stones, about four feet long, which they put on their head and carry away to a place where they store them. They can work stone as though it were wood, though no one knows what they do with the worked stones. It is not surprising that they are called Pugulatamutc, for they act like Stone Indians. They are very small, but they do a big work."

These are not my [the informant's] words, but the words of the old Indian who told me. P. G.

42. APPEARANCE AND HABITS OF THE PUGULATAMUTC

The Stone Indians travel like lightning. They are so called because they used to write on stone. They are about three feet high, and live in the mountains. In the evening you can hear them; they come out, dance, smoke, and play. When they smoke, you can see the smoke. Sometimes one sees a few in the daytime. They have little canoes, about a fathom in length. They catch salmon and trout.

When they go home, one of them puts the canoe on the back of his neck and carries it up the mountain; the other carries the fish and the baggage. They go, always, two together. They are very strong, and carry on their heads stones which contain fancywork that they have executed. Sometimes, at twilight, one can hear them singing; but at dark, the sing-

PART TWO *Folktales and Traditions*

ing ceases. If you should get hold of one, you would not be able to lift him. He could take you in his hand and lift you up over his head, no matter how big you are. They are very dangerous to tamper with, for in no respect are they civilized. They act, in every respect, like old-time Indians and are, in fact, Micmac. They cannot be seen in the daytime. They live in the rocks. When they wish to come out, the rock opens, like a door.

They live on fish and berries. They come to Indians, but to no one else. They are shy, but at times, if not well treated, are very dangerous. They are very quick and strong, and are exceedingly powerful. They are naked, except for a little belt and a covering for the loins. Men and women dress alike. They live in the same manner during winter and summer. They have an abundance, always, and are never in want. They have a chief; whatever he says must be done. He is their mainstay.

Fish they spear, and large animals they shoot with bow and arrow. Large animals are not afraid of them, for these people are very small. To them, all animals are tame; the animals have no fear of these people, and sometimes walk up to them and smell of them, to find out what they are.

They sport in canoes on the rivers, and in the ponds and lakes in the woods. They paddle and sail in a canoe of birch bark modeled like our canoes. They put up a pole for a mast, and with this they pierce a piece of cedar bark at its two ends to serve as a sail. When the wind shifts, they turn the sail to catch the breeze. To keep it toward the wind, a man holds thongs attached to either side of this bark sail. On the mast they sometimes have two or three of these bark sheets. If the wind blows very hard, they remove one of the top pieces of bark. P. G.

An Indian about fifty to sixty years of age met one of these people, and said, "I do not wish to do you an injury. I merely wish to find out about your customs. Do you go hunting in your canoes?" "Oh, yes." "What kind of place is it at which you live?" "It is very warm and nice; it is never cold; and it is light, never dark." "Do you have guns with which to shoot?" "No, we use the bow and arrow." "I should like to see you shoot." "All right." He thrust one end of a little stick into the ground, put a little stone, about the size of a pea, on top of the stick, stepped back about fifteen feet, and shot off the stone without touching the stick. He did this a second time.

Mythic Peoples

"Are there many people where you live?" the Indian asked. "A hundred thousand. On the other mountain, yonder, are two hundred thousand — that mountain is full. They, however, do not come out. Only when there is need of us do we come out." "To what need do you refer?" "If there should be war, we would come at once. I would not try to kill you. We are brothers, of one blood. I would not try to kill you." They shook hands and said "Adieu." After the man had walked about eleven yards, the little fellow suddenly disappeared from sight.

Some are male, some female. They live on a high mountain opposite Dalhousie and on other mountains in Gaspé, along Baie des Chaleurs. No one can discover where the entrances are, though we know they are immense rocks. One time many Micmac who were on top of one of these mountains lost their senses, and never got down. That was about sixty to seventy years ago. A priest has placed a cross there, and now people do not become crazed when they climb this mountain.   P. G.[7]

A man told me [the informant] this story: "I was going down the river and saw two Stone Indians. They go ashore. One of them carries the canoe on his neck. I grasp the other. He throws me into the air with both his arms, and after he puts me down, I am done for. He picks up the canoe and the baggage and goes up the mountain. Soon, both disappear into the mountain."

Sometimes they come down to the shore, and can be heard singing. In the morning, however, they will be gone, and leave no sign of having been there, except small footprints in the sand. There are a great many Stone Indians under the ground, everywhere, but they seldom come out.

43. AT CAPE BRETON

At Cape North, Cape Breton, you can sometimes see fire going back and forth on the mountain, as though someone was pitching stones to and fro.

My grandmother and I went up there, and fell asleep. When we had gone down a certain distance, we were not so sleepy. My grandmother told me the Pugulatamutc had made us sleepy. We found twenty beads of stone, about the size of robin eggs, which belonged to the Pugulatamutc.

---

[7] A chapel now stands on the mountaintop back of Carleton, Quebec. Each summer there is a pilgrimage and a mass.

PART TWO *Folktales and Traditions*

I was going up a mountain in Cape Breton with my wife when I saw a ball of fire move on a mountain, far away from us. Then it went back. We watched it for some time. It was the Pugulatamutc playing ball.

At the mouth of a cave near Eskasoni have been seen the footprints of little folk. These were made by the Pugulatamutc. A dog went into the cave. When he came out, all the hair was off him, except a little bit at the end of his tail, above his eyes, and around his neck. The dog wished to go in again, but his owner, who was there, would not permit it. The Pugulatamutc had caught him and had done this.

In a rock about a mile high is a large cave which is said to be Gluskap's house. Some men went into it. They could see only gravel. They put a big stick up at the entrance. (If you go into a cave, you should put up a stick to keep it open; the stick, no matter how small, will prevent the cave from closing.) The party had forty torches of bark, twenty to use when going in, and twenty to use when returning to the entrance. The cave was of the same appearance everywhere, and there was no sign of anything unusual.

Once people went through there into another world. Gluskap made his power so strong that he drew a man and his daughter into this cavern. They had shot two birds which, at high water, floated into the cave. They unsuspectingly paddled into the cave. It was as if they had gone into another world. They saw an island on which were wigwams. These were the property of Indians. They thought that perhaps the Pugulatamutc had brought them in. They spent two weeks there. A man asked, "Perhaps you want to go home?" "Yes." He said to a boy, "Take them back." The boy took them in a canoe. As quick as a flash of lightning they were out in their own world. The Pugulatamutc had taken them into the cave.   J. N.

44. AT MOUNT KATAHDIN

An old man shot at a bird over the lake on Mount Katahdin. He was sure he had struck it, but the shot did not injure the bird in the least. Soon it seemed as though the whole mountain were thundering. This [the echo] was caused by the Pugulatamutc. Moreover, along the shore were tracks of small human feet. These tracks he pointed out to his companion, a white man. The latter was then convinced of the presence of the Pugulatamutc.

Mythic Peoples

45. THE PUGULATAMUTC HELP THE INDIANS

An Indian went to hunt. He was alone. He wished to get fur. He traveled and traveled, and at last, did not know where to go. Nearby was a mountain. He met two little fellows and knew they were Pugulatamutc. They asked him, "Where are you going?" "I don't know. I am going for fur." "Stop overnight with us, and we will show you where to get fur." They went to a cliff. There was a door in it. They opened the door and told him to walk in. He walked in. There was a room. They were playing all kinds of games. He stayed with them [as their guest]. When his visit was over, they tied up fur for him, as much as he could carry. They tied up two bundles more, and said, "We will help you to carry this almost to your place." All the most valuable furs that could be got, they carried to his house, for him. When he reached home, his people asked, "Where were you? We thought you had been killed, and had died in the woods. We inquired, and could not find you." He had been away two years, and thought that it was only two days. The Pugulatamutc told him, "If you want fur, come to us, and we will help you."   JOHN HAMMOND

CHAPTER IV

Ghost, Will-o'-the-Wisp

Skadegamutc

SKADEGAMUTC is a dread being of various facets which to the Micmac eye appear more clearly unified than to the anthropologist's listening ear. It is the ghost of the dead, and as such can be seen by night and more rarely by day. It is the thought of the dying expressed in action, and the mind of man when "outside the head," the separate soul. The will-o'-the-wisp is *skadegamutc* and can chase one; and it is the phosphorescence of tree stumps which will fight a man throughout the night.

46. PERSONAL ADVENTURES WITH *SKADEGAMUTC*

One night a woman at Pictou chased a *skadegamutc*. She was standing with others by the Point and told them she would chase the *skadegamutc*. They advised her not to do so. However, she went. The woman became smaller and smaller, and the *skadegamutc* grew larger and larger. She caught it under her arm and brought it back. While she was returning, it became smaller and smaller, and when she was nearly back, it became merely a piece of birch stump. All the other women ran away in fright. She took it into the house, put it on the fire, and burned it. For a week afterward that house stank so foully that no one could go into it.

Two men were hunting through the entire woods. The night was dark, and it was wet. On their backs they had a big supply of provisions, and they decided to travel by the old roads. They hit the trail and went to an old camping place. Said one, "Let us stay here tonight."

They camped. The other wished to go further, but the first one had started a fire. It was comfortable, and they were sleepy.

Ghost, Will-o'-the-Wisp

The other, meanwhile, was busily thinking. A headless man came into the camp and lay down by the side of the sleepy fellow. The other man, in a corner, was watching the visitor to see what he would do. (This is a true story.)

He could hear the intruder gnawing at the throat of the other man. He knew he was powerless to help his comrade, so he jumped up and ran with all his might. He ran about thirty miles before he was out of the woods and in a clearing. He heard some one whooping. It was the *skadegamutc*, which was now pursuing him. He did not answer, and continued to run with all his might.

He arrived at a lake. It was autumn, and some men were skating there. He ran onto the ice, and the *skadegamutc* was pursuing him. *Skadegamutc* said, "It is well your friends are here on the ice; otherwise there would be no man here tomorrow."

Skadegamutc had been trying to take this man's life. It was three or four hours before the man could speak or recover his breath. He then told the people of the death of his comrade in the camp. They found the corpse, but it was only bones.

Near where the men had stayed in a shedlike structure were the bones of a person who had starved there; the *skadegamutc* had come from these bones.

In the camp they found the body of the man's comrade. All the blood had been sucked out of it. They took his body away and buried it, and also the bones which they had found there; and burned the shelter.   T. M.

A man fought a *skadegamutc*. He was going through the woods by a fifteen-mile short cut. All evening he had been thinking about *skadegamutc*, and he was afraid to go outside. He was what we call at Burnt Church *nesit*, and in Pictou, *giwakit*, that is, frightened and nervous. Sometimes a person is frightened and afraid to go out.

About ten o'clock, when he was only halfway through the woods, he met *skadegamutc*. Immediately they fought. They fought along the road until they arrived at the reserve, for *skadegamutc* continued to pursue the man.

They fought hard all night. The man then stepped back and said, "Now I shall show you what kind of man I am." They fought until daylight. The man then saw that the thing which he was twisting and striking was only a stump.

PART TWO *Folktales and Traditions*

He had been chased by a stump, and had thought it was a man. During the night it had been a man, and at daylight had changed into a stump.

47. ONE WHO WAS NOT AFRAID OF *SKADEGAMUTC*

Some people are afraid of *skadegamutc*. I am not afraid of them, though I was once chased five miles by one.

I was walking along the railroad track, looked behind me, and saw a man wearing a dark gown with ribbon hanging from the right side of his waist. When he came within about fifty feet of me, I ran. At the crossing, I yelled. Some people were living in a house close by. I dropped, and was unconscious until morning. They had carried me into the house. But I am not afraid of *skadegamutc*, although this one did chase me five miles. *Skadegamutc* are good runners; and the more you run, the better they like it.

T. M.

48. AN ENCOUNTER WITH *SKADEGAMUTC*

One night I was out after midnight. On the way home I saw someone standing in the road. When I was near him, I dropped my head to look. He wore a black dress, fastened to the top of his head. I go on. When I am close to him, I put out my hand and take hold of him. It is a dry spruce, in the middle of the road. I bring it to my gate and put it inside the fence. Next morning when I get up, it is not there.

Another time a big person was standing, dressed entirely in white. It had two eyes, a nose, mouth, and so on, just like a human being. I took hold of it. It was a piece of lumber. I threw it on the fire and burned it.

P. G.

49. THE BEHAVIOR OF *SKADEGAMUTC*

Three of us, all men, were standing by a bridge with guns in our hands, watching for ducks. We saw a light up the road. One man was near the end of the bridge. I cocked my gun and was about to shoot. But the light went in front of a house, then over to that man, who fell down instantly. The creature had nose, eyes, mouth, and was completely covered with flames. When he came to the bridge, we fired at it. He dropped on the other side of the bridge. Soon we heard a noise there like the rolling of thunder thrice intensified. A *skadegamutc* will not pass a pin or a needle. I always carried a pin with me at night. A sharp stick or a splinter is useless. Sixty years ago an old cousin told me that. Many people say that. [This is a well-known European way of stopping ghosts.] No one can hold a ghost; when you try to grasp it, it evades you like wind.

50. SKADEGAMUTC IS A FEARLESS FIGHTER

A man went from Burnt Church to Tabusintac to get eels. He had taken more fish than he could carry. So he borrows a hand sled on which to haul his bags of fish. He arrives at a dark portage in the woods. Here something comes toward him. It takes hold of his shoulder. The Indian says, "Hell, what are you doing?" There is no answer. He then says, "Hold on!" [That is, Be careful!] He takes the sled rope from his shoulders and says, "Now fight!" They fight from early in the night until morning. When daylight comes, he is fighting a rotten stump of hard wood. The Indian says, "I'll go home now, but I shall come back and fight you to the finish." But he never fought with it again.   P. G.

51. FEAR OF SKADEGAMUTC

Skadegamutc is the only dangerous creature in the woods. If you hear a *skadegamutc* cry out, make no reply. He may cry again. Do not answer. He yells when he travels. If you answer, he will find you, and you will surely die. He comes with a noise like the onrush of a train, and goes past. English people here call him "whooper." He is very often heard about twelve o'clock noon, or in the afternoon.

I have heard him twice. I was back in the woods all alone. I heard a noise toward the west. I remained quiet. Soon it whooped again. The third time I heard it, it was close to me, but went by. It gave another whoop, went past, and gave another whoop, far off toward the east. Whenever he whooped, I felt it all over my body. It does not affect me like the whoop of a person or the cry of an animal.[1]

I started late one afternoon for Neguac to get a tin ink-pot soldered for the priest at Burnt Church. When I started home, I was frightened, for it was very dark, and the road was narrow. I almost fainted. I ran until I reached the priest's house. He came out, looked at me, and said, "What is the matter?" "Nothing." "Anything frighten you?" "No." But I was so frightened that I had almost fainted on the road. He told me to come in, and pray. I did so. He read from a little book, then blew on my head. He read again, and again blew on my head; read again, then

---

[1] The "whooper" thus referred to seems to be the large owl.

PART TWO *Folktales and Traditions*

again blew on my head; and repeated this a long time. He then said, "Get up, and do not become frightened again." After that, I was never frightened in the dark.
P. G.

[While WDW was walking with an old Indian along the lonely wooded road from the bridge at Boat Harbour to the reserve at Pictou Landing, this Micmac stopped almost within sight of the nearest house and related the following.]

Do you see that telephone pole up there? I was coming along here one clear night, with my gun in my hands. There was no moon, but the stars were shining. I did not see anything, and I heard nothing. But when I arrived here [indicating the exact spot] I felt that I could not go a step farther. It was as if there were a hundred guns in front aimed at me. I did not see a thing, I did not hear a thing. I retreated about ten feet. I forgot I had a gun. I started again. But when I arrived here, it was the same thing — I could not go a step farther. I went back. I said, "My God, I'll go past you," and started again, determined to go on. This time I went a little bit farther than before. If I had taken one more step, I think I would have fainted. I felt weak, and I was as wet with sweat as if I had been out in the rain all day. I came back, went up that road to the right, through that field, and in to Jim MacKenzie's, then back into the road up there [a considerable detour]. After I reached home I told the people about it, and two men told me the very same thing had happened to them along here. [He would give no explanation.]

52. *SKADEGAMUTC* CLOTHED AS A WOMAN

[John Newell and WDW were walking single file through the woods. At a narrow place, well enclosed by a forest's dense second growth, John stopped and related the following.]

Some people say there are no ghosts. I saw one here one night. I was coming home from near Glasgow where I had been hewing all day. I carried my broadaxe with me. It stood right there, a woman, dressed entirely in white, as in a shroud, and about five and a half feet tall. She did not move. I thought I would have to turn back to the road and go around that way. I started back, then remembered that I had my broadaxe with me. A *skadegamutc* will not go close to steel. I took the paper off the edge and held the edge toward her.

Then I walked on. Almost immediately in front of her I stumbled

Ghost, Will-o'-the-Wisp

over a log and was stamping in the mud and water on the other side, trying to regain my balance. I was pretty close to her, and she leaned over to one side, but did not say a word. "You had better look out for your skirt," I called out to her. "You had better look out for your skirt or you may get it spoiled."

Then it seemed as if a thousand hands caught hold of me and lifted me up so that I hardly knew whether I was walking or not. But I walked away all right.

53. SKADEGAMUTC

One night Francis Marble was coming up the road to Pictou Landing and had just crossed the bridge at Boat Harbour [a lonely, forsaken road bordered here by a dense foliage of trees and bushes]. He felt strange — a bit frightened at something. A little farther on he saw an old woman sitting on the side of the road. She wore an old-time Indian hat, and her bowed head rested on one hand. He looked at her hard, kept to the other side of the road, and went past. She did not move, but remained in the posture in which he had first seen her. As soon as he was past, he walked along pretty lively until he arrived home, but he did not run.

J. N.

54. SKADEGAMUTC CAUSES THE ECHO

["I guess there aren't any ghosts?" said an old man one day, by way of testing the anthropologist's faith. "I don't know," WDW replied; "some people say there are, and several have told me they have seen them." "Well, I know there are, for I have seen them. One night I saw an old woman — she was wrapped up in white. What I tell you now has happened to me several times."]

Yesterday, when I was in the woods cutting wood, I heard someone chopping whenever I cut. When I used the wedge, I heard someone hammering a wedge. That has happened to me several times. But it does not happen only to me — many Indians here have had the same thing happen to them. I do not know what does it. Some people say it is a *skadegamutc*. There are a great many dead people around here who [when alive] used to cut trees in the woods, and we think it is their spirits.

If you hear a *skadegamutc* coming behind you, you must not run. If you do, it will catch you. Walk along as if nothing had happened. When it is at your heels, jump to one side quickly, and if you can speak, say, "Go ahead!" It will then go on and not bother you.

PART TWO *Folktales and Traditions*

Another way to be rid of a pursuing *skadegamutc* is to stick a needle into the ground at the back of your heel track, with the needle's eye open in the directions you have come and are going. Then move on. When *skadegamutc* comes to this, it will have to go through it. It will probably be there, in this attempt, the entire night.

Sometimes, when you are walking alone at night, you hear someone walking behind you. You stop and look back, but see no one. You go on, hear the footsteps following you again, and again you look back — but always with the same result. [On one reserve several men confessed to having had this experience at night, especially when running.] *Skadegamutc* will not cross a bridge unless you are on the other side and say, "Come over." It will not cross a bridge unbidden.

55. A GHOST STORY

My uncle, his son, and I were along the Ottawa River. I camped alone near a place at which a man had been killed by a falling limb. At night I heard a sound like someone driving oxen. I looked out, but there was not a mark on the snow, and no one was near. The wind blew the door open and nearly put out the fire. I set an empty barrel against the door. A sudden gust blew the barrel to the other side of the hut. I heard a sound like the whinnying of a horse, and then something walking over the top of the flat cedar roof. The second time this happened, I fired a gun. The visitor went away. There was not a sound during the remainder of the night, but I could not sleep — sleep was miles away. JOHN PAUL

56. *SKADEGAMUTC* CAN BRING HELP

In a wigwam at Black Brook, below Chatham, N.B., two women were fighting. They pulled one another's hair as is their wont, as well as that of the men, when fighting. When *skadegamutc* is asked to come and help, it is there at once. And this is what happened. That night a woman who had been sick and had died a short time previously was found to have one hand full of hair. Her *skadegamutc* had been appealed to, had promptly responded, and these were the proofs positive of the success of its mission.

57. *SKADEGAMUTC* OF A DROWNED MAN

I was coming home one night, just after dark, and saw a man in the yard, lying at full length on his back. He wore high leather boots, a dark

Ghost, Will-o'-the-Wisp

coat, a collar, and a necktie. There was a mark on the left cheek. I supposed he had drunk too much whiskey and had lain down there, unable to get home. I walked over to him, knelt on one knee, and put out my hand, to feel his face. My hand went to the ground without touching anything, and the man was gone — not a thing was there. When my hand went through his face like that, without touching anything, my backbone felt cold, and my hair stood straight up. When I went into the house, I learned that a man had been drowned the day before, and the people had not been able to find his body.

Next day, I joined in the search for it, and found it. When I drew the dead man into the boat, I saw that he was just like the *skadegamutc* that I had seen the night before; he wore high leather boots, a collar, and a tie, and there was a mark on his left cheek, just as on the "man" I had seen.

58. SKADEGAMUTC IN THE HOUSE

When I was a young boy I saw [the ghost of] a man in an empty house near ours. He stood and smiled at me. It was dusk. I ran to my father, who was cutting wood close to our house, and told him I had seen a man in that house. He took the axe and went over and looked. But when he arrived, the man was not in the house. I had seen a ghost.

About three years ago I was in the woods with a Yankee, fishing. In the house, that night, we heard footsteps come up the landing, like someone walking. I said it was a ghost. "No," the gentleman said, "it is a rabbit or something like that." "No rabbit ever made noise like that — it was [the ghost of] a man walking," I told him. But he would not have it so.

Three days later he read in the paper of the murder of Mr. White in New York. Mr. White had been with us on previous trips and his ghost had returned to us.

CHAPTER V

Supernatural Powers

Ginap[1]

59. A YOUNG *GINAP* AT RICHIBUCTO

A LITTLE five-year-old *ginap* at Richibucto said he could carry a barrel of pork. He picked it up and carried it from the wharf to the place where he wanted it. A man could do it, but it is a wonder that so young a boy could do it. He is dead now, for he showed too much [strength]. There is a *ginap* in each reserve. He may be very pleasant and kind, and no one knows that he is a *ginap*. A boy who shows too soon that he is a *ginap* will die. This is usually the fate of young *ginap*, they show their power too much.[2]

When this little boy at Richibucto was in the woods setting snares, a rabbit came to him and said, "Do not kill us too rapidly. You kill nearly twenty a day. We wish to breed in the springtime, as the other animals do." The boy repeated to his mother what the rabbit and various birds had told him. He always had plenty of game, and people wondered how he could get so much. Soon after this he died. Before dying, he said, "I want a crane to eat today." It was winter. No one knew how to get a crane in the winter, yet the boy wanted it. If he could get a crane, his life would continue. They could not get a crane, but got a lake hawk-fisher, *kwus meneedj nutkwidamet*, which has long legs and a bill much like that of the crane. So that he should not see it the old woman cooked it while the boy was in bed asleep. She removed the broth, put the flesh in his bowl, tasted it, and gave it to him. He said, "That tastes like

---

[1] These powers and their possessors are described and discussed in Part One, Chapters IX and XVI.
[2] A *ginap* does not necessarily possess other than great physical power, although he is sometimes also a *buoin*.

kwus meneedj nutkwidamet." That he was able to distinguish this food is astonishing. After that he died. T. M.

60. A *GINAP* IN CAPE BRETON

A man in Cape Breton, who is now living, can unassisted haul a schooner up on shore. He can turn it over and tar it, then drag it back into the water. No one except himself knows how he does it. People see merely that it has been done. This must be true, else the story would not have come so far — if it was false someone would have corrected it. P. G.

61. A *GINAP* AT CAMPBELLTON

A *ginap* who was seen by an Indian who visited Campbellton some forty-five years ago had shoulders three and half feet broad. He overexerted himself, lost his health, and died. On one occasion, by using only his hands and his knee, he bent the barrel of a flint-lock musket until the end of the barrel touched the stock. He intended to use it as a club rather than as a gun. He said that with one shot he could wound only one man of an attacking party, whereas with a club he could kill several men. This musket can now be seen, and the load is still in it.[3]

62. A *GINAP* IN DISGUISE [4]

I heard this story from my old grandfather. It was in the time of the oldest Indians of all, when there were no French, English, or anyone

[3] An account by Cooney (1832) seems to give some basis for the Micmac stories about their *ginap*:
"The following incident exhibits the ferocity, as well as natural bravery of the men, with whom the early settlers had to deal. Pierre Martin, an Indian of remarkably large stature, and athletic make, made, when two English marines attempted to put him in irons, a most desperate resistance. In the course of the contest he particularly distinguished himself; but on this occasion all the haughtiness of his soul came to nerve the energy of his arm. It is said that he absolutely strangled the two men in the scuffle, and that after he had received two or three severe wounds from some others who attacked him, that he wrenched a bayonet from one of the sailors, and by the force of a blow which he aimed at the disarmed man, drove the weapon through one of the stanchions of the vessel. Being at length overpowered by numbers he fell apparently dead, and literally riddled with wounds. But the Micmac spirit was not yet extinguished; lingering existence still fluttered in his bosom; for when the almost inanimate corpse lay bathed in blood, gashed with wounds, and quivering with agony, Martin rallying the dying energies of his soul, sprang to his feet, and fastening upon the throat of one of his companions, whom he upbraided with cowardice, had nearly succeeded in strangling the poor wretch, when he received his death blow from one Robert Beck, an Irishman." Cooney, 45–46.

[4] For a similar story, see "The Little Boy Who Had Fits," Tale 125.

PART TWO *Folktales and Traditions*

else here, except Indians. In the autumn, the people went into the woods. At each settlement there were many wigwams. It was about a day's journey from our settlement to the nearest one. The settlements, on account of the game, were separated by considerable distances. If they were too close to one another, the people would frighten the game away.[5]

In a certain band lived Llui, the king of them all. He lived on the outskirts of the winter settlement, not in the midst of it. He had only one grandchild, Ginap by name; and Ginap left his home settlement to go elsewhere. He had no father or mother, and had been raised by his aunt, or by someone else. He was poor, not rich, but had a great deal of power. He did nothing to get a living, and minded [was afraid of] nothing. When he was leaving home, he said to his [foster] mother, "I am going away. If I have good luck, I shall return and get you. In the meantime, do not leave, but wait here until I return. If I should have an opportunity to get a wife while I am away, I shall marry. But I have nothing to carry with me." His mother gave him a little skin pouch, and said, "When you want clothes, or a wife, or anything else, look in this pouch, and you will find what you want."[6]

The young Ginap went away. He wore no clothes except a piece of deerhide which covered his back and part of his chest. He arrived at the dwellings of a band in which the events of this story took place. At the first wigwam he removed his snowshoes and buried them in the snow.[7] In the wigwam sat an old woman and a boy, who lived by begging, because the boy killed nothing and the woman could not kill anything. She was very glad to have the stranger live with them because of the help he could give in cutting wood.

The news spread through the settlement that a young man had come to the house of this old woman; he was good-looking, but did not wash himself, or comb his hair.

The chief of this band had a daughter. A curtain was across the wigwam, and most of the time she was kept behind the curtain. A great many young men had sought to obtain her as wife. But the old woman, her mother, who was more the master in the wigwam than was her

---

[5] Informant: "In the spring of the year the people came down to the shore."

[6] In another version of this story, the same informant, Peter Ginnish, listed the mother's gifts: "In a little packing-box she put two women's dresses, two suits for her son, a comb, and four or five yards of ribbon with which plaited hair is tied."

[7] So that no one would observe their great size and recognize his supernatural power? See Tale 125.

husband, would not consent that she marry any of the suitors. The stranger boy, whose name was Ginap, wished to have the girl as his wife. He said to the son of the old lady with whom he was staying, "Say to your mother that she should tell the parents of the girl that they ought to have another man in the wigwam to help, for they are getting old."

Accordingly, the son went to her and said, "Tell these people, 'My companion here wants to help you — you need help.'" The old woman took a cane and went to the chief's wigwam. When the chief saw the old woman coming, he thought there was something strange about it. The old woman went to him and said, "I am not coming to this wigwam for nothing; I am coming for something. A young man came to my wigwam and, because you are getting old and need help to do the cooking, he wants to help you and your old woman." The chief bowed his head and thought a long time about it. "Yes, I have a girl here, and I will give her to him." The old woman was satisfied. After she had gone, however, the chief's wife raised a disturbance. He said, "Shut up! Not one word more."

The old woman returned home and said to Ginap, "I have had good luck. The old chief favors you."

The young man went to the chief's wigwam. When he arrived there, the old chief said, "Come in." The boy entered, and the girl came out from behind the curtain and sat beside him. The chief said to her, "That is your husband. You must work for him. From now on, I have no claim on you."

Thus they were married. Her hair was plaited in two braids and hung down over her temples, a strand over each temple. The mother took hold of one braid, cut it off, and threw it on the fire; then grasped the other, and treated it the same way — so angry was she. When the old man came in and saw what the woman had done, he was very angry and wanted to slap her. The daughter said, "Do not do it. She is my mother." The girl was a very obedient child, and was not angry with her mother. The mother, however, did not like the young man, and the chief, in his anger at his wife, rushed out of his wigwam and shouted, "We will move away." (If a chief says that, they will move; move they must.) All were surprised to hear this, but all moved away and took their provisions with them.

The chief's daughter, left without clothes or provisions, and with her hair cut off short, went to the wigwam of her husband, the home of the old woman and the boy. The old woman said, "Sit over there, on that side.

PART TWO *Folktales and Traditions*

That will be your place." Ginap said to the old woman, "Don't move away. The others will return."

There was no meat for supper. Before sundown the young man went away. He walked only a short distance, found two deer, drove them close to the wigwam, and killed them. He struck one on the head with a small tomahawk, and left it embedded in the deer's head. He came in. "Oh! I forgot my tomahawk!" He asked the boy to get it. The boy went out and found it sticking in the head of the deer.

Next morning, while his wife was eating breakfast, he said, "Come here." She went and sat by him. He placed his hand on her head, and asked, "You are sorry that you lost your hair?" "Yes; everybody laughs at me, and I cannot go out. I am ashamed." He puts his hand inside his coat, brought out a pouch, laid his finger on it, and wished a comb. He found it there, and put it on her head. He wished hair, took it from the pouch, put it on her head, and pulled it down into a braid, like the one she had lost. "How long was your hair?" he asked. She showed him its length. He made the braid as long as one's arm, and as soft and silky as downy feathers. He looked at her, brought clothes, and said, "Take off your clothes and put on these." They were very fine ones. He did not put on any fine clothes.

The boy was cutting wood for him. Ginap went out and said, "Do not do that. I shall cut my own wood. Take all the meat you want." Next day, he put on his snowshoes, and got meat — deer, caribou, bear, the bear a very fat one — and brought them home. A man returned to the settlement, to see Ginap. He and the others had had very hard times. He saw four or five animals — moose, caribou, bear — lying there, and not skinned. Ginap gave some of the meat to the man. "Here, take a load and go home. Tell my father-in-law to come and get his share." Ginap had driven all the animals to his place.

Because the other people could not get any, all of them returned. His father-in-law came to his wigwam. The young man said, "You had no right to leave that way. Wherever you put up your winter wigwam, there you should stay." The people thought a great deal about this young man, because he always had plenty of provisions. The next time he went to hunt he killed a moose and two caribou. When the people went out and saw the animals lying there, not skinned, they wondered at it. Ginap did not say much. In his pouch he had a suit of clothes, made in the old-time way. One day, while he was having a gay time, he put these on. He looked fine. All were surprised to see him so well dressed. The men said, "Chief, you should not have treated the man that way. He is very nice — and we do not know who he may be. He may be like a king." The chief thought this man must be something more than an ordinary man.

Ginap went away to get his mother. He traveled a long distance, and at last arrived at the place where his mother was. She was very glad to see him. "My son, what luck have you had while you were away?" "Very good luck," he answered. "Yes, I hear you have a good wife." "I have come for you; I want you to live just as I live." He took his mother home with him.

The old chief was very glad to see them. Ginap said to him, "This is my mother. I have no father; and I could not do without her any longer. I had to go and bring her home. You must treat that old lady just as you would treat your mother." The chief went outside and said to Ginap, "I shall treat her better than my mother treated me, for my mother treated me very badly."

He continued, "I don't want you to go away again. You can accomplish a great deal. You can drive the animals to the camp any day." The chief told Ginap's mother not to be bashful [i.e., to feel at home]. Ginap said, "I can drive to this place any kind of animal I want; I always have plenty of meat. When poor people come, I give them skins for clothing, and meat to eat." His wife said to her father, "Do not go away again; stay close home. Do not go to hunt. There is plenty of meat, and plenty of skins, here. This man has great power — he can do anything."

His father-in-law, mother-in-law, mother, brother, himself, and wife — six in all — left the camp. Ginap said to his wife, "Tell your father to make me a pair of snowshoes; mine are broken and worn out." She told her father. He said, "Yes." He asked his son-in-law, "What size snowshoes do you want?" Ginap said he wanted them nine feet long [that is to say, of more than eighteen feet of wood], and "plenty wide in the middle." The old man got the wood, prepared it, and made the snowshoes. The old woman prepared the thongs for them. Ginap struck three blows on them, then said to his father-in-law, "They are good; but if they were stronger, they would be better." "If I had asked you before I commenced, I could have made them the way you wanted them," the old man said. A great many people came to see the snowshoes. They were surprised at their size.

Ginap said to his wife, "I must get some meat — I must kill some

PART TWO *Folktales and Traditions*

animals." He put on his snowshoes and departed. Almost immediately he fell into the snow (not by accident, but on purpose, for fun). When he got up, he saw his wife watching him.

At the next step he took, he again fell. She went in and said to her father, "He cannot use those snowshoes." "Why not?" "Because, at the first three steps, he fell down into the snow." "Go and look again."

She went out to look, came back, and said, "He is all right now."

Her father went out to see what progress the man was making. He found only five full depressions on the snow; from that place on there were only little round impressions in the snow. He went into the wigwam.

After about two hours, the youth returned. He was driving three moose and a big bear — a very fat **one** — and killed them near the dwelling. He went in, took off his snowshoes, set them up, and said, "That was great traveling!" The wife said to her father, "Come outside. There are three moose and a fat bear near here. He killed them with his tomahawk." There was plenty of meat for everyone. The people said, "We should make that man chief; he does a great deal for us. He is very quick and fast, and he is never hungry." Another said, "No; we can't do that; no; we can't do that — not until our chief dies, can we do anything." (And he was very right; they cannot make another man chief until the incumbent dies.)

Soon after this they heard a man emerging from the woods and calling to them, "The Mohawk are coming!" They knew then that there would be fighting immediately. Ginap said, "Don't be afraid; I'm going to meet them." He went to the place where they were, and walked into their camp to see what they were doing. "Tomorrow," they said, "we shall give the Micmac some hot water." When he walked away from them, he was wearing his snowshoes. He commenced to sing. The Mohawk were surprised to hear the man sing, and stood and looked at him. He walked in a circle around them, put on his hat, and yelled, "Kwe! ya!" (at the same time making a sweeping horizontal movement with the hand, elbow at the side, right forearm and extended hand pointed toward them). Next morning everyone of them was dead. Next day, he walked around them and shouted, as he had done on the previous day. Whoever heard him shout those words died.

Ginap returned to the camp, on the day after he had left it, and said to the people there, "Have no fear; they'll not come. All of them are asleep. I have been there the entire morning, until dinner time, and I cannot wake them." The old chief said, "I know what that means; he has killed all of them. He walked around them, singing, 'Kwe! ya! Kwe! ya!' and in that way he has killed all of them."

No beast in the woods could escape from that man. He could drive the animals wherever he wished. Sometimes you could not see his tracks, although you could see the tracks of the animals that he had been chasing. You could see only plenty of meat and skins. That man did not die. When he was a hundred years old, he was just the same as when he was a boy. I do not know whether he is alive now. That is exactly the story given me by my old grandfather about those old times. The people had only fire, stone, and wood; they had none of the tools and metals that they now have.

His father-in-law, wife, mother, and brother remained in the winter camp. The man said to his father-in-law, "I shall go away for a while, into the woods, and I shall take my wife with me." He said to his wife, "Come into the woods with me for a two days' journey." He stopped at a brook, put up a little wigwam, for the meat, and made a fire. In the morning, he went to this brook and proceeded upstream, along its bank, to see how much water was in it. He thought he might find beaver dams. He saw the tracks of someone. He did not know who had made them. He broke off branches, and with them covered the tracks where they crossed the brook. Before he had gone into the woods he had said to his wife, "Do not go along this brook; do not go there." Two or three times he said this. She laughed and said, "All right."

After he had gone, she thought, "What does this mean? There must be something in that place!" She went and saw the brush in the brook and the water running over it. While she stood there, she saw three men approaching.

She felt that she must stand there until they arrived. They asked, "How many people here?" "Only one." "Is he a big man and able to withstand a big fight?" "No." "Tonight, when he comes, cut the strings of his snow-shoes, so that he cannot use the shoes. If you promise to do this, we will spare you; if you do not promise, we will kill you now." She was frightened, and promised to obey. "When we arrive at the wigwam, at midnight, make no noise."

When the husband came home, he said to his wife, "Did you go up that brook?" "Yes." "Why did you do it, after I had told you not to go? What business had you to do that? Now you will be the cause of my

PART TWO *Folktales and Traditions*

death. If you had not gone, I would not lose my life. I knew they were coming. If you had not gone, they would not know where I am." After supper, he asked her what they said. "They asked me, 'Is he a strong man?' 'No,' I said. 'When he comes home, cut the strings of his snowshoes; and when we come at midnight, do not tell him.'" He said, "I knew what they told you." She cut new strings for his snowshoes.

At midnight, they came with torches, gave a war whoop, and surrounded the wigwam. He sprang up, jumped out of the wigwam, and went around them. After he had completed the circuit, he cried, "Kwe! ya!" and waved his hand [as described above]. All dropped dead — the women, children, and men. When morning came, the woman said, "We must go away from here; I cannot stay among so many dead people." After they arrived at their former home, she told her father about the adventure and mentioned how many people her husband had killed. Her father said, "I do not know about this man; but all those people have been killed, and they will never trouble us again."

This was the story told me by my grandfather. Ginap was the man who did all these things. He was the grandson of Llui. P. G.

People Who Live under Water

63. THE MAN WHO LIVED UNDER WATER

This is a story of events after the white people came. I think it is not much more than a hundred years old. I do not know whether it is true. I am not certain about its correctness. The story says:

Off the south coast of Nova Scotia, two white men were tending the lobster traps. One of them fell overboard. After he had gone down into the water a certain depth, he was in a second water, below the first layer of water. This second water did not seem like water. All about him were fish and lobsters. He went to a big rock. A large lobster went toward him, but did not hurt him. Later it brought him things to eat. He was there about a week. At the end of this time the man who had been there with him at the traps saw human excrement rising to the surface of the water. He knew his former companion was there. He secured a schooner and a diver — the two of them cost him five hundred dollars. The diver went down. At first the lobster attacked him, but he drove it away. He called to the man, put a rope around him, and signaled to the people above to be drawn up. They drew him up. The rescued man would not

Supernatural Powers

tell very much about what he saw while he was down there under the water, although he had been there eight days.   J. N.

64. ATWEUMISEL, THE MAN WHO SAID HE HAD LIVED UNDER WATER

In the autumn, a man went about seventeen miles from his home. He was moving to another place. He took all his possessions on a toboggan. The ice broke under him. Only himself and his wife were there.

The old man grasped his wife, and they sank to the bottom. (This is a story that only the man himself could tell.) The people tracked him, found the hole through which he fell, and said, "They are dead."

When the man reached the bottom, he walked toward the shore and built a wigwam. His wife assisted him. They remained there a long while. In April (he must have known something about the time of the year), people came there. A canoe passed over the place at which he had gone down during the previous autumn. He came to the surface, and lay there, as a seed floats. He looked about, saw a canoe not far away, and called to the occupants, "Come back!"

The canoe returned. He and the man in it shook hands. "Where are you from?" "I'm from here — I want some fresh herring." "I should like to go home if you will take me; if not, I shall return to my home."

"Agreed." The man went down and said to his wife, "Get the toboggan and our possessions; we shall go home." When they arrived at their old home, on the land, a great many came to see him. They asked him where he had been. He replied, "When we fell in, it was so cold that we went down, built a wigwam, and remained there all winter. [In the spring] smelts came and said, 'Old man, winter is gone; it is spring now.' I came up and saw a canoe." He said to the people, "I can live as well under water [as on land], because there is no wind there, only the tide; and it is not cold." "How did you cook?" "I did not cook. I ate as Eskimo eat their meat. I ate nothing cooked — only raw food." The Indians talked about this all the time and remarked, "Atweumisel" [i.e., a man who tells long stories, and too many stories]. This name was given that man. They did not believe his story, and gave him that name.   P. G.

Buoin

65. ATUEN

A hunter was sitting in the woods. He decided on a plan of action. He shot at and killed five ducks and two geese. The other ducks and

PART TWO *Folktales and Traditions*

geese went to deeper water. On the following day the hunter watched for them.

At flood tide, the geese returned. He watched them. One side of the place was bounded by a curving cove. He made a plan which would enable him to kill a great many. When he pointed a straight-barreled gun at the flock, he killed only two or three birds. He bent his gun, and then killed fifteen; whereas on the previous day he had killed only five. He straightened his gun, so that no one noticed that it had been bent.

He told his friends, "I bend my gun, so that I kill a great many, for the shot goes all around." The people said it was not true.

However, he could do anything he wished to do. He was altogether queer. Always, whatever he said came true. The oldest man [in the settlement] said, "Let him do what he likes. Keep away from him and follow your own plan. His plan may not be good. Leave him alone."

In the autumn the people were catching fish and curing them for the winter. A man said to this man, "Have you any fire with you? I want to make a fire." He replied, "No; where is your pipe? Put it in your mouth. Now, puff." Smoke came. He could cause smoke to come whenever he wished to do so. No one else can do that.

When he approached a place, all the beasts, birds, and other creatures immmediately loft.

I saw him. He was not a big man. He was a very fine-looking man. But he died when his time came. Atuen was his name. P. G.

66. A *BUOIN* SAVES HER SON

Two men who are walking along the shore of a lake see two girls combing their hair. One of the men starts to drink the lake dry. The water goes down about six inches. One of the girls says to one of the men, "You cannot drink this lake dry, for your name is not there."

"Who are you?" he asks. "I am a Micmac." "Who are you?" she asks the man. "I am a Micmac." The other girl drinks all of the water, except a very little. The man's mother is a very strong witch. He wishes to summon her. Finally he sends his spirit to her. The old woman is in the wigwam. The flap is pushed aside. "You had better hurry or your son will be killed." "All right." She sends a loon. Soon the loon is above him, circles round and round above the water, then dives down, and saves this man, whom, by this time, the girl's strong witchcraft had drawn into the lake.

Supernatural Powers

67. TCEDJAGINWIT

Tcedjaginwit ["Clean Life"] was the name of an old Indian medicineman. He had seven wives. He saw the French when they first came here. The priest asked him, "What name would you like to have?" "Mary." "That is a woman's name, not a man's name." "I would like to be called God." "Only one person has that name. He is in Heaven, whence he sees the whole world. Try again; MacDonald, Peter, John, Noel — all of these are English names." "Devil," said he. The priest could do nothing with him — he was such a strong medicineman. He had a son. Someone asked him how strong he was. (Whatever the man said would come true.) A man hurt his foot with a hard stone. Tcedjaginwit said, "He has one foot of stone and one of flesh." "How did you effect that?" he was asked. "I caused it to be so," was the only reply he would make. He broke the stone foot at the ankle, and soon the boy had a good foot in its place.[8]

When Clean Life was dying, he told the people to come to his grave at the end of seven years. "On that day it will be as clear as glass, and you will not see a cloud. At twelve o'clock you will see a little cloud near the sun, and will hear thunder." On the day appointed, at the end of the seven years, the priest did not want them to go. Tcedjaginwit had said, "I will come out as a young man twenty-five years of age." On the day after the appointed one the people went to the grave and saw that the ground above it was cracked — the man had almost gotten out. He was buried, about a hundred years ago, on an island about four miles from Pictou. My wife was sixty-five years old when she died, and at the time mentioned she was not born. My father shot a seal near this island and could not get it, for it had sunk. I told him, "You should get that seal — my children are starving." My father and I arose early and went to the place where he had shot it. The seal was high and dry on the shore, ten feet from the water. If, when you pass the island, you make a request of this man, you will have the luck for which you ask.

68. A *BUOIN* IN RED BANK KILLS A WOMAN IN CAPE BRETON

A man at Red Bank and a woman in Cape Breton have a dispute. No one else can hear it. Their messages are like present-day telephone mes-

[8] At this point the narrator produced a stone, having a rather remarkable resemblance to a foot, which he had found while digging out earth in the process of making a camping place, and which he believed was the stone foot in question. Some, however, did not agree with him. The hero of the story had made a stone foot like

PART TWO *Folktales and Traditions*

sages. Finally the man says, "You have too much to say; go easier, or you will go over my head." "I can go over your head and jump back over you again." She is dead immediately. Next morning the man says, "A woman in Cape Breton is dead." No one believes him, for Cape Breton is a great distance away. A few days later, a letter from there states that the woman is dead. While she was dying she told her parents, "I have been quarreling with a man, and he has taken my life. He got the better of me. If I had overcome him, I would have killed him. But it is my fault, and now I am about to die." A letter comes to Red Bank with this news. The man says, "It is true. If she had not been fighting so much, she might still be cooking lobsters in Cape Breton." I do not know what these buoin have or where they obtained it; but they have something, howsoever they obtained it. The woman knows she cannot step over [conquer?] the man — the man is sure to prove himself her master. What the woman says must come true, yet the man is mightier than she.   P. G.

69. A *BUOIN* CAUGHT AT HER OWN GAME

When I was nine or ten years of age, two men from Red Bank went into the woods to hunt. When they came out, they had a good catch of beaver and otter. Upon their return, an old woman — a very large one — thought she would receive some of the meat which the men had brought with them. However, she received none, and in consequence, was very angry. When they again went into the woods, she determined to do them injury. She caught a [small bird?], put it into a trap, and walked on ahead of them. They were surprised when they arrived and saw [this small bird] in a trap, for they had never seen that. One of the men could not forget this thing. That night he dreamed about that old woman in Red Bank.

In the dream, she said, "You would not give me any meat; now you shall suffer."

The man put the old woman in the trap; it caught her over the shoulder, and held her nose tightly in it. Next morning, when she got up, the people said, "What is the matter?" "Oh, I have a sore neck."

The man came back, saw the woman, and said, "You will die here." This happened after New Year's. On the fifteenth of May that old woman

the wooden one which the French used when making shoes. This stone foot is now in the George G. Heye Collection, Museum of the American Indian, New York City. (See illustration 36g.)

Supernatural Powers

died. She was compelled to stay doubled up, as in a trap, with her nose between her knees.

She was an old *buoin*. I saw her, and heard the story of the fight and the cause of her death. The man was stronger than she.   P. G.

70. OLD SALLIE AND THE CONDUCTOR

Old woman Sallie, who now [1912] lives at Pictou, and is said to be one hundred years old — she is the head of four generations — went on the train to New Glasgow. The conductor, a stickler for fares, would not permit her to stay on the train, for she did not have enough money. She got off. A little farther on, the train ran off the track. Later, it again went off the track. While they were putting the engine on the track, after this second mishap, the conductor lost a finger. He felt that something was wrong, and said to old Sallie, "Mother, get on and go inside." After this the superintendent at Moncton told the conductor, "Whenever an Indian wants to go, take him whether he has the fare or not."

71. THE RESULT OF A WISH

I was walking along the road, carrying a heavy load. A man in a wagon passed me, and I asked him to take me in. "I have load enough," he said, and drove on. About three miles from that place, a wheel came off his wagon. That was his luck.

One winter I was carrying two dozen axe handles. The crust on the snow was heavy, it broke under me, and I was very tired, because of my load. A man passed me in a sleigh, driving two horses. "You wouldn't take a tramp in?" I called to him. "I'm in too much of a hurry," he said.

A little farther on there was a bridge. The ice had frozen hard and high in the middle of this, leaving a slope to either side of the road. I don't know whether a horse had a ball of snow in the frog of its foot, or what the trouble was, but one of the horses fell on the bridge and dragged the other down with it. When I arrived there, the man was trying to get them to their feet. "My dear man," he said, "for God's sake help me." "I'm in too much of a hurry," said I, and walked on. You should have seen the look he gave me! But I was that mad I could have seen him and his horses in the hottest part of hell and not felt the least bit sorry for him.

After a while another man drove up to me. "That is a heavy load you have," he said. "Not very heavy," I replied. "Get in and ride," he said. "My bundle is too big," said I. But I put it in, and I got in. I told him about

PART TWO *Folktales and Traditions*

that man and our adventure. I don't know whether he was a cousin or some relation, but he didn't say a thing — he merely laughed.⁹   J. N.

72. WALKING UNDER WATER

A man shot, from the bushes, near the reserve at Pictou Landing, at a seal. He struck it. It went down. He was sorry to lose it.

His children were crying, because they were hungry. He stripped off his clothes and walked along the bottom for about two miles, from a place near the piles of the present lighthouse. He obtained the seal, and brought it back. That was his power. He could do that, or walk on the water, any time.

73. A *BUOIN* TRAVELS FAST

My grandfather lived near the point at Burnt Church, where he had a small house with two doors. A great many people used to meet there. One evening he told this story:

A strange man arrived and said that he came from Cape Breton. It was difficult traveling, for there was no railroad, the highways were poor, and there was no travel by water. A canoe brought the man, his wife, and two children. People spoke of him as a stranger, though he was welcomed, for he was a Micmac.

After supper he went to the house of my grandfather. He sat down, folded his hands, bowed his head, and smoked his pipe. My grandfather asked him, "What is the news from your settlement?" "War." (Whether it was war with the English, the French, or the Yankees, I do not know.) "Are you sure of that?" "Yes, I saw it. I ran off, for I did not want to be killed. I saved the lives of myself, my wife, and my children."

The news spread here. The Indians at Burnt Church said, "This is harsh. We do not know what we should do. The war may be so bad that we cannot help our people." (My grandfather spoke of them as "our people.")

A man who had heard the news spoke, "I am going to Cape Breton. Yes, I shall go by water." He walked onto a rock (which is pointed out

⁹ This tale was told by way of illustrating how people come by their "luck." I suspect that John Newell thinks his own personal powers had something to do with these misfortunes, though he did not explicitly say so. I remember his once saying to me, in a moment of gratitude for some small favor, "My power isn't very strong, but I wish you good luck wherever you go!" I dare say he attributed some efficacy to his wishes for misfortune as well as to those for good fortune.

390

Supernatural Powers

to this day), jumped into the water, disappeared, and the following day was in Cape Breton. He walked under the water to Cape Breton.

To the people there he said, "Not all of you have been killed." "No." "I wanted to come. A man brought the news to Burnt Church that there was war here; that the Yankees, English, and French have made war, and intend to wipe out the Indians. Is that true?"

When the chief heard about the man from Burnt Church he got up. It was night. He went to see the man and asked, "What man told you such news?" "He is from Buctouche. Is he sane?" "No; he is crazy; do not listen to him. If any trouble comes such as he spoke of, you will know it soon enough." The messenger jumped into the water and emerged at the place where he had entered it. He asked the visiting bearer of news, "Whence have you come?" "From Cape Breton." "When did you leave?" "Two weeks ago. There was war there and I ran away." To this the man said, "Go away from here. I was in Cape Breton last night and left there today. We do not wish to have a fool like you with us." They did not kill the bearer of false tidings. "If trouble comes, we shall get news of it. If we do not," this man says, "I shall go there and find out. I can walk in the water."

That is all true. Some Indians [Micmac] can do almost anything. Some Indians you see playing, and the next minute they have disappeared.

P. G.

Keskamzit [*Magical Good Luck*]

74. FOR FINDING MONEY

MY WIFE was very lucky at finding money. One morning, about six o'clock, in full daylight, while she was walking alone, she saw a big pile of silver dollars in the place on which she was about to step. She raised her foot over it and then it came down with a jolt. She looked behind her at the place where she had seen this pile of money, and not a thing was there. After that, she always had good luck at finding money. Not every time, but nearly every time, she went to town, to Pictou or to New Glasgow, she found money — sometimes a dollar bill, sometimes a five-dollar bill, sometimes a coin. She found a big package of bank notes, but did not know what they were, and threw them away. When she described the package and the paper to me, after she came home, I knew they were bank notes. If she had told this [her propensity] to anyone, however, she would have lost her *keskamzit*.

To find anything queer or odd in the woods, if you do not tell anyone, is *keskamzit*. If you are hunting for a certain kind of tree that is hard to find, and find it straightway, that is *keskamzit*.

75. FOR VIOLIN PLAYING

Keskamzit for violin playing was acquired in the following way:

The favored man was in an empty house near Bathurst, and had his violin. While he was playing a tune, a man knocked at the door. The musician said not a word. The door opened, and the stranger entered. He walked to the player, and asked leave to play a certain tune. The player made no answer. The stranger whistled the tune, the Micmac played it after him, and soon had it in good form. Soon he was in a

Keskamzit

ballroom, where finely dressed men and women were dancing, and he was playing many different tunes. This continued until morning. When daylight came, he saw the old house, as he had seen it before dark on the previous evening, the floor covered with dirt. In this dirt there now appeared nothing except the tracks of rabbits' feet. Ever since that time this man has had a big genius for the violin. [His experience was said not to have been a dream but a real wide-awake one. The story was no doubt implicitly believed by the man who narrated it and who descanted on the musical abilities of this gifted individual.]

76. FOR MAKING TUBS

A boy was badly treated by his stepmother, as is usually the fate of stepsons. To escape her nagging, he went into the woods with the men who were making staves for coopering. He found a small stave. Next day he made five tubs — a big number. In about two weeks he was making a dozen tubs a day! He did not have to take a measure, but merely looked at things, measured them with his eye, without the slightest error, and put them together as easily. That was *keskamzit*.

77. FOR CUTTING WOOD

[*Keskamzit* improves the individual in only one respect. He can do a thing so well and in such a short time, and make so much money by these brief efforts, that he becomes lazy and indolent the rest of the time. The following story about Martin Francis, of Frederickton, whose extraordinary *keskamzit* is talked of from the Miramichi to the straits of Canso, illustrates the point. The narrator of his prowess was, in this instance, an old man by the name of John Paul.]

I cut wood with a man, one winter. We sharpened the axes. I turned the grindstone. He gave each axe two or three vigorous rubs on each side and said, "That is enough." It was almost as if a child had done it, but I noticed something strange about those axes while he was sharpening them. We separated and started to cut. At the end of the day we met; we had then cut the trees that stood between us when we started. I looked back over what I had done. I am only an ordinary woodcutter, but, upon my life! I never saw anything like that before! I never had cut nearly as many trees as I cut that day. "Throw this axe you have been using over into the bushes there, as far as you can fling it, and put the other

PART TWO *Folktales and Traditions*

axe on a shelf at home and tell people that they are not to touch it," he said.

Later I saw him in a saloon, drunk, with bottles all around him — he was the biggest drunkard that ever walked on shoe leather. Next morning I returned and asked him whether we would cut trees that day. To my surprise, he was sober. "Yes," he said. He had two bottles. He took a swallow from one of these, then said, pointing to the untouched one, "I shall put that on a shelf where no one will touch it." He told the saloon-keeper where he had put it, and said, "Do not allow anyone to disturb it." We went out. When we came to the railroad track, the bottle from which he had taken a drink he threw against a rail, with all his might, and broke the bottle to pieces. We took our axes and began to cut wood. He marked a place on the handle for [the grasp of] my upper hand, toward the blade, and said, "Don't let your hand come down over this mark!" I cut an awful amount of wood that day. But it wasn't my *keskamzit*, it was his that did it.

[Thus, it seems, *keskamzit* is an influence or power that can be transferred, or is acquired for the time being by one who comes within the circumference of its powers. Usually, a man who sees another's *keskamzit* in action thereby destroys it.]

78. *KESKAMZIT* INDICATED BY HEARING A BELL

Four of us were in the woods, picking gum. When we came around a hill, we heard a cowbell, about a hundred yards away, but did not see the cow. There was a house nearby. I heard the bell. The sound ceased.

My son came up, and heard the bell. "There is a house here." "Yes, there is a house here." The sound ceased. A third member of the party came up, and the bell sounded again. We went around the hill, but no house was there. One of the party climbed a tree and hallooed, for we were lost. "Did you hear that bell?" "Yes." Three times we heard it. If we had then gone in search of it, we might have found gold or silver. It was our *keskamzit*. Later I went there three times and hunted for the bell, but could not find it.

CHAPTER VII

Supernatural Places

79. HALFWAY RIVER

"Near Pictou there is a place where no one can stay overnight, neither a small nor a big crowd. 'Better stop here for the night,' we said once, a small party of us. We had plenty of wood and a good fire was burning. About nine or ten o'clock we heard whistling. Again and again we heard it. By and by, there came a heavy shower of rain. We couldn't keep the fire going. We could hear crying and bawling which was worse than that of a bull, and whistling, and something like the snorting of a horse. Then snow fell." [The informant was quoting what someone else had told him.]

The people had to leave. They went about a mile from there, and everything was then all right. This was told me [the informant] by three different Indians. It happened at Puktaaktaegan. Near this place is a lake on which, in the evening, you can see stones floating about like fish.

80. THE LAKE WITH THE WATER LILY

In a lake or big pond, near Antigonish, is a water lily which has a root as big as a man's neck. On a certain day, every year, it comes to the surface and floats, then goes below the surface, and is never seen again until the following year on that day. I have seen the pond. I did not see the lily, but a man who did see it told me about it.

This was told by the old Indians, and told again by the younger ones, for a great many years after all the old ones who had seen it were dead. One time, they decided to go look for it. They knew, from hearing this story, where it was; and they found it to be just as the old Indians had said.

J. N.

CHAPTER VIII

Origins of Material Culture

81. FIRE-MAKER

A WOMAN says to her husband, "If you get dry wood, make hard sticks, put one of these in a piece of wood, and turn it, fire will soon come." The old man decides to try. He takes a dry, hard limb from a tree, and twirls and twirls it. After a while, he feels it. He twirls it very rapidly, faster and faster, until smoke comes. He twirls it some more, and fire comes. The twirled stick was beech; the trough, birch; punk was placed in the hole; and the twirling was done by the unaided hands. [The informant could not remember the names of the man and woman mentioned above, but said they were "very queer names."]   P. G.

82. BOW AND ARROW

The first bow was made by an old Indian who lived here at Burnt Church. He went to the shore, saw some birds feeding there, but could not kill them. He went into the woods, gathered cedar wood for the purpose of making a canoe, and went to the shore to split the wood. He took a splint about five feet in length, bent it over his knee, and shaved it a little at each end, where it was too thick and heavy. When it was thinner, its action was quicker. He made two arrows, fastened a thong to each end of the cedar stick, and returned to the shore. The birds were less than twenty feet away. They were not wild, for there were no people about to bother them. He stood, shot an arrow, and struck a bird in the head. With another arrow he struck a second bird in the head. He went out into the water and procured these two ducks.

When he arrived home with them and the cedar stick, a man asked him, "How did you get them?" "I shot them." "With what did you shoot them?" He showed the man the strong cedar bow. "How did you get

Origins of Material Culture

that?" the man asked. "When I went there, I wanted something with which to kill those two ducks, but I did not know how to do it. I went back, took a stick about two inches wide, and whittled it at the ends." "Why did you whittle it at the ends?" "That makes it quicker; if it is too thick, it is not so quick." And he was right, that old Indian. If it is thin at the ends, it goes more freely. He told the man how he had killed the ducks. Other people came by and asked how he thought of that. "I hardly know. I found a round stick out there, and after I bent it and tied it, I did not want it. I split a cedar, whittled it at the ends, made a groove at each end, and bent it over my knee. I then made an arrow of light cedar wood, and shot it."

Those old people were surprised. The first bow was made of cedar. Some bows were six to seven feet long, and some were very strong.

My grandfather told me this story. Matio was the man who made the first bow. After this the people made even better bows and of different kinds. With them it was possible to shoot a hundred yards. P. G.

83. ORIGIN OF THE EEL SPEAR

A man saw eels. He obtained a long stick and told his wife to get long roots. He made a pole and two spear points. He used a dry spruce limb and scraped it with flint until the end of the limb was very sharp.

He held a piece of cedar bark in one hand, to serve for a light, the spear in the other hand, and his wife paddled the canoe. She said, "You can do nothing; go ashore and get the *pasigawadi* [eel spear]." He got the *pasigawadi*, and removed the bark from it. This invention was *keskamzit* — no one had told him how to make a spear. His wife gave the spear its name. He had a big catch and shared it with all the people. This man, Matio, had *keskamzit* for spears as well as for canoes. When the woman was asked how she could give the eel spear its name, she said, "Oh! it came right out of my mind."

84. ORIGIN OF THE SNOWSHOE

In the olden times, at the very first, the Indians could not travel through the woods in deep snow. An old man who one night came home covered with snow up to his head, and carrying game on his back, said to his wife, "It is very difficult to continue in this way; it is difficult traveling." The wife said, "If you do not do better than that, we shall starve. Make for yourself snowshoes for traveling over the snow." "How can I

PART TWO *Folktales and Traditions*

do that?" "If you have no plan, I shall get one and make them." The old man went out and cut a small yellow birch of considerable length. The woman told him to bend it, place a stick across the middle, and fasten the toe. "Yes, that is very good."

He then put a small stick across the toe, and one at the heel. He made them exactly the width of his foot. His wife said, "It will be well to put them out a little farther, so that they will not hurt your foot when you walk." To hold the sides together, he used a little stick which had notches on each end, for he had no way to bore a hole. The old woman cut thongs with a knife, and with them tied these sticks in position; for she did not know how to bore a hole.

The old woman split a piece of rawhide into strips, for thongs. When she had a piece three or four fathoms long, she began to knit the [mesh of the] snowshoes. She said to the old man, "Now see if you can fill in the frame of this snowshoe." He thought it would be very difficult to do. First he looped the strap about the frame, to hold the frame in position, filled in the toe, then the heel, and left the middle part open. The woman, meanwhile, was busily cutting skins into thongs. He commenced with the middle. He started on the left side of the toe stick, crossed to the middle of the frame opposite, then to the left side of the heel stick, and back to the left side where the toe stick joins the frame, going here and there until it was filled in. He then crossed the frame from left to right, and made the middle net solid. After the snowshoes had been filled in from side to side, he crossed them lengthwise, so as to pull the net away from the frame and the crosspieces, and leave these adjacent spaces open. At first the thread at both heel and toe went from side to side; but the second time, while finishing it, they ran lengthwise. He then put a strap on, to hold the shoe to the foot, and to keep the foot from slipping off it. The woman assisted the man a great deal in filling in the frame of the snowshoes. He said, "How shall I wear them? There is no place for my foot." "Come here."

She held a strap, told him to put his feet on the shoes, and arranged the strings under his feet. She tied this string to the top of the toe of the snowshoe, then to the heel of it, wrapped it tightly about his foot, and said, "Now move your feet." The snowshoes held fast. When people heard about it, they came from all about, to see the shoes. The man was the chief of that settlement. I have never heard his name, or the name of his wife. She was a smart woman.

She had more sense than had her husband. Providence bestowed more sense on her sex than on the male. P. G.

85. ORIGIN OF WEAVING

Moose-hair weaving was taught by an old Indian woman, St. Anne. At that time there was no iron in use here, only wood. Her husband's name was Swasan. St. Anne was not born here, but somewhere else. This was three or four hundred years ago, when the French first came. They gave the Indians implements, tools, clothes of modern style, also blankets [*elabicit*], worn by both men and women, which were doubled, thrown over the shoulders, covering the right arm, and pinned under the left arm and in front. P. G.

86. ORIGIN OF DYES

A man was building a canoe, and chewed some of the chips. He spat, and saw that the saliva was black. In this way the people obtained that color. Later they boiled everything to find out what colors various things would produce; and so obtained all their dyes.

87. ORIGIN OF CORN

A woman and a little girl were lost in the woods. When they arrived home, it was dusk. On their way home they found in the clearing [plants with] many long narrow leaves. There was a big patch of them. The little girl asked, "What is that?" "I do not know." She picked one. "Take that home," said her mother. She took the corn home and pulled the husks off.

"What is this?" she asked her mother. "Perhaps it is good to eat," was the reply. The girl was hungry and ate a mouthful of it. The substance was soft and mushy. Her mother tasted it. "Maybe it is poison," she said; "it would be wise to leave it alone." There was a big patch of it. They put it on the fire to roast. She left it there a long time, roasted it, and ate it. Finally her mother said, "Give me a taste of it." Her mother liked it. Next morning she visited the wigwams and showed this to the people. It was the first grain they had to eat with meat. When, four or five days later, her husband returned from fighting, all the people went to obtain some of it. They found a big patch of it and gathered it.

I cannot tell you how they knew it was corn. I once asked an old man, "Did anyone bring that word to you so that you would know how to call it 'corn'?" "No," he said, "they knew its name just as they knew the name of all the animals in the woods." At last, the people said, "We should save this for winter, roast it, boil it, and make soup of it by cooking it with moose meat." They put the corn around the fire, roasted it, and had a dance around it. Now the song it called the "Green-Corn Dance" [1] [*piek-amiamalkewaan,* said to be a native Micmac word]. It is a kind of thanksgiving dance. We know what to call it, but we do not know where it came from.

J. N.

[1] The Green-Corn Dance is a northern Iroquois ceremony.

CHAPTER IX

Human Adventures

Deserted Women [1]

88. ORPHAN GIRL

An orphan girl was left alone in a wigwam. The little girl went from one wigwam to another. Finally she found a fire. She was hungry and cold, and for two days she cried. It was cold. One morning she went out and saw at the door a large beaver which had been killed. She did not know who had killed it. With difficulty she took it into the wigwam. With a stick she broke the skin, inserted her fingers, and removed the skin. After two months the people returned, thinking "that little girl died long ago." In a few months the people of the wigwam, who had deserted the girl, began to shake with the palsy: first the man, then the woman, and finally all of them. This is the explanation given for the palsy, now that the people know more. It was sent by the Almighty. "Who brought the beaver? It was her luck."

89. A WIFE ESCAPES MURDER

A woman and her children lived on Pictou Island. Her husband struck her, thought he had killed her, and killed all her children. He went, in his canoe, to what is now Pictou Harbor. It was autumn. She found a seal on the shore. She had nothing with which to cut it up; with a stone, she broke a piece of flint, and thus procured a knife. She took slabs from rotten logs (these sluff off easily), and made a wigwam with them. These she covered with spruce boughs. She gathered the driftwood on the beach and used it as fuel. With yellow birch she made a snare for rabbits.

[1] These two are selected from a larger group of similar tales.

PART TWO *Folktales and Traditions*

Their skins she sewed into a dress for the winter, using a sharp wooden stick for a needle, and rabbit muscle for thread.

During the following spring her brother and another man came to the island to hunt seals. She thought it was her husband coming to kill her. When she discovered that the man was her brother, she went to him. "You did not come out of the grave?" he asked. "No," she said. (Her husband, upon his return, had said his wife was dead, and thus explained his failure to bring her back with him.) Her brother did not look for seals. He told his sister to get into the canoe. They started toward home. When he was near the camp, he saw his brother-in-law approaching. He told his sister to lie down in the canoe. When the husband saw his wife, he ran away. He never returned. If the husband had remained at the settlement, his brother-in-law would have killed him. There was then no value on a man's life. If you did me wrong, I might kill you. I would know that if I did not do so, perhaps you would kill me.   J. N.

Marriages

90. A MARRIAGE THAT RECONCILED TWO COMMUNITIES

The Burnt Church Indians said to some others, "If you wish to come here, you must adopt our customs." The visitors were too much civilized.

When St. Anne's Day arrived, they wanted to come here. Six or seven of them met and had a conference. They talked it over, pro and con, and finally decided that they must conform to Burnt Church custom. They went slowly, in their canoes, to the bridge [over Church River]. A Burnt Church man called out to them, "If you do not do as we do in Burnt Church, beware! If you do not adopt our ways, you may not stay with us. But if you do as we do here, all will be well." A Burnt Church man had his daughter with him. The group of visitors was from Pokemouche. The Burnt Church people saw dried eels, gave some money to the girl, and said to her, "Go to the Pokemouche Indians, buy three or four eels, and cook them." The eel-man and his wife had a young man with him. He was one of those who had been warned to do as the people do here, at Burnt Church.

The girl goes up to the Pokemouche people and asks, "Have you any dried eels here?" "Yes; do you see that woman there? She has them." To her, "Have you some eels?" "Yes; how many do you wish?" "I should like to have six."

The girl pays her a dollar. The woman says, "That is too much." "No, take it all. Are you satisfied with what you have?" "Yes, *lusuwesk* [daughter-in-law]." All hear the old woman, and all laugh. Her son is standing nearby, listening.

Upon the girl's return, her father asks, "Did you obtain them?" "Yes." "Where?" [Here the whole proceedings, as given above, are narrated by the girl; the storyteller omitted nothing.] Her mother says, "That is your husband. After supper you must go to him."

After that, and until this day, the people at Burnt Church and those at Pokemouche have been friends; for a girl and a boy from these two places were married. P. G.

91. TRANSACTION IN EELS THAT RESULTED IN MARRIAGE

An old Indian from Pokemouche, and another from Red Bank, came to Burnt Church. The one from Pokemouche had a fine girl with him.

On the way there he caught some eels, a dozen or more, and cut them up and dried them. The other Indian wished to buy them from him. Some Indians had already obtained some of his eels. A certain young man who saw them asked, "Where did you get those eels?" They replied, "From that man over there."

The boy goes to get some for his father's supper. When he approaches, he sees the girl. He asks her mother, "Have you still some dried eels?" "Yes." She looks at him, and answers very slowly. The girl is standing there, and remarks to her mother, "Answer this man, if you please." The girl's father turns around and sees the boy. He says to his wife, "Have you still some of those eels?" "Yes." "Give this man what he asks for." She asks, "How many do you wish?" "Three." The daughter says, "You may as well take four." "Yes, I may as well take four; and if I see more, I will take more." Her father replies, "All right, *entlusuk* [son-in-law]. Have you the eels?" "Yes." "Come back tonight."

The boy takes the eels to his mother and says, "Mother, I have bought four eels from that man down there. I know they are very nice. When I went there and asked for eels, the old woman was very slow to reply. Her daughter said, 'Answer this man, if you please.' The old man turned his head around and saw me." [The above conversation is repeated.] The old woman listens to the words of her son. When his father comes home, she tells him. "Oh!" he says to the son, "that is all right; go where your wife is." P. G.

PART TWO *Folktales and Traditions*

92. MARRIED AT A CRANE-PICKING

An old man killed a crane down-country, and brought it up here [to Burnt Church]. He said to his wife, "Cook that crane — roast it." (Roasting was better than boiling; the old-time people always roasted their meat.) Two young men came to his wigwam, for the man had a very attractive and lively daughter. They saw her mother picking the crane. While they watched, one of them said to the bird, "You will not fish any more on the flats; now your career is at an end." No one made a response. The daughter said, "[It will be] the same with you. When you die, you will not be able to do much." The old man laughed, the old woman laughed, then all laughed. "Well done," the young man said, and started to leave. After he had taken two or three steps, the father of the girl called out, "*Entlusuk* [son-in-law], come back after this has been cooked." The boy said to his mother, "I have been over there where the old woman was picking a crane. The girl's father said to me, '*Entlusuk*, come back after this crane has been cooked.'" His mother responded, "Yes, you have been caught. She is your wife. You must go back." P. G.

93. A GIRL WHO WAS MARRIED WHILE CATCHING TROUT

At Tabusintac a young girl was fishing for trout. Her father had cut two holes in the ice through which she might fish for trout the following morning. Nearby there were many wigwams, and many Indians were fishing for eels, trout, and other fish. She was a very fine-looking girl, fit to be married any day. They looked at her, but she made no response to any of them. A certain young man came up and saw her catch six or seven trout. The trout flopped around a great deal on the ice.

The young man had come, not to see the girl, but merely to look at her catch. He said, "How is the fishing?" "Oh, the fish are very scarce — they have not come yet. They are very small fish — *aptcadjidjidjit*." To which he replied, "*Aptcadjidjidjit apdjedjutc* [small fish are like a small girl] *alimtunui djidjit* [jumping around]." She said, "*Alimtu nui djidjit istigealim* [they flop around, and are still flopping]."

He left the girl and went up the river to fish. The girl caught more fish and carried them home. At dinner, she said to her father, "This morning that young man came up from Burnt Church and passed by me. I said to him, 'I have very small fish'" [and so on, repeating their conversation]. To this the father said, "He is your husband."

The young man came to the settlement, but did not go to her wigwam.

Human Adventures

He stayed in another wigwam. Her father sent for the boy. He went. When the boy opened the door and entered, her father said, "Come in, son-in-law." He used this greeting because the marriage had already taken place.
P. G.[2]

94. HOW A CERTAIN SNOWSHOE TRAVELER WAS MARRIED

This happened after we had been given the name "Micmac" and began to observe Sunday; after we were civilized and Catholicized.

It was Easter Sunday. The Indians did not know it was Easter Sunday, for they had not obtained the Catholic religion. Two men here [Burnt Church] and two at Richibucto were very fast travelers on snowshoes. They knew the next day was Sunday and that they must observe the Sabbath [by not traveling]. One said, "I shall go home now." The other replied, "No; we will go tomorrow morning." "No, that will be Sunday. We shall not go then." (I do not know what they called Sunday in the old days.)

From here to Richibucto in a straight line is forty-five miles. They went on snowshoes, to spend Easter Sunday at Burnt Church, rather than at Richibucto. "I do not want to spend it here," said one, "I should rather be at home." "Well, we shall start in the morning." A Richibucto man said, "I shall go with you tomorrow." A young woman who was present said, "I shall go with you tomorrow." To this one of the men objected, "You cannot go to Burnt Church; you cannot keep up with those men." They started at daylight, while the sun was coming up. The woman obtained snowshoes, and went with them. While the first church bell was ringing, the people saw a man approaching, then another, and another, and finally a fourth.

The sun was at about eight or nine o'clock. The young woman was back of the best traveler, and ahead of the other two men. (Some women can travel faster than men.) The people here asked when they had left. "At sunrise." They arrived here in time for Mass. That was very fast traveling. The Indians here talked a great deal about that woman, who was not married. She went to the chief's house, and stayed there.

A young man went to his father and said, "Father, that woman is a

---

[2] Peter Ginnish told three other marriage tales, two circumstantially set in the Miramichi area and a third which, after his customary beginning, developed as the European fairy tale of the Magic Pebble.

A story identical with Tale 93 was told at Lequille near Annapolis Royal, N.S., in 1923; see Parsons, JAFL, 38:100.

PART TWO *Folktales and Traditions*

fast traveler on snowshoes. She is better than the men here." The father replied, "Well, you now have a good opportunity — you have a good opportunity to get that woman, if you want her." "I want her, if it is possible for me to get her." His father responded, "Take your axe, go to the wigwam of the chief, cut some wood, split a handful, carry it into the wigwam, and say to the chief, 'I brought you *noksemaan* [fuel].' Do not say one word more. Walk out immediately."

He did as directed. He said to the chief, "I have brought you *noksemaan*." The chief replied, "*Ken welalin, entlusuk* [Thank you, son-in-law]."

The chief, however, had no daughter. The chief's wife said to her husband, "You terrible old man! You have no daughter to give that man as wife; and yet you thank him as [though you were] a father-in-law."

The chief: "You know very well I have a daughter. If she were not my daughter, she would not come here. The man brought *noksemaan*, and she is his wife."

The girl laughed. The boy returned home. His father asked him what he had done. He related all that had happened. "Oh!" the father exclaimed; "She is your wife! Go to her wigwam tonight." He went. "*Mik tcik ubugik iktebidem*," said the chief to the young man ["Go over there and sit by your wife"]. He sat by her. Thus the chief had the man marry the woman, for the lad had brought him firewood.

Next morning the news went abroad that such and such a boy had obtained "the snowshoe traveler," as she was called. The father and mother of the young man said, "*Pusul, lusuwesk* [Greeting, daughter-in-law]. Go to your place." After this she had a right to one half of the wigwam, and all was well. When the Richibucto man returned, he carried news of this to that place. He told the father and mother of the girl, "Your daughter was married on Easter Monday." "Who had her married?" "The chief." They bowed their heads and thought it over. "How did that happen?" [He narrated all of the happenings: how she outdistanced all except one of the men on snowshoes, the favorable impression which she made at Burnt Church, the actions of the young man, and so on, in full detail, the informant repeating, as the newsbearer to Richibucto, all that preceded.] The old woman remarked, "I did not think my daughter would be married when she went to Burnt Church. I thought she went merely for Sunday."

The father said, "That was her time. It was right for her to obtain a husband then. The time had come to go help her husband. Now she has gone."

In this way "the snowshoe traveler" was married. P. G.

95. A WIDOW MUST NOT CHERISH THE DEAD HUSBAND

Three men are preparing to go to hunt. One of them says to his wife, "Three weeks from now I shall return, and whatever I have procured I shall bring with me." The second man says to his wife, "Do not expect me before the end of three weeks." The third man says, "I am going away. You have provisions enough to last until I come back. If your provisions fail, go to my father." He goes to his wife and lays his pipe close to her. "If this pipe becomes bloody," he says, "you will know that I have been killed, and that I shall not return."

The three men go to hunt, a long way off. A week after he had left the pipe, the third man was sick. The first man returned unharmed. The second man returned unharmed. The third had not returned. At the end of a week they say, "Something must be wrong, we shall hunt for him." They find him lying on the snow, dead. Before dying, he had folded his upper garment, put his right hand on one side, and his left hand on the other.

One of the party said, "We must take the body back." Another said, "We have too many things to haul; we cannot take him." The first replied, "We must haul him back to his father and his wife." They put the body on a toboggan.

When the party was nearing home, the wife said to her husband's father: "My husband left me this pipe and said, 'I shall return in three weeks. If the pipe is filled with blood, I shall not return.' It is filled with blood." The old man takes it to his wife, tells her what the daughter-in-law has said, and adds, "Our son is dead." The old man said, "I do not want to cremate the body until all come." The others said, "No, you cannot keep it that long — it will smell badly and make the others sick."

When the body was nearly consumed, it was noticed that some flesh remained at the root of a toe of one foot, and was scarcely burned. The father said, "I shall keep that flesh." The others said, "Why should you want it? Eat it! Eat!" The father put it in his mouth and ate all of it. The wife of the deceased was surprised to see her father-in-law eating this flesh. One night, in a dream, she talked with her deceased husband. She said, "I saw your father eat your toe — the portion which was not

PART TWO *Folktales and Traditions*

consumed in the fire. A man had said, 'Eat it! You can keep it in no other way.' Your toe is in your father's intestines."

"Tell my father I will take that bone out of his intestines. I do not want him to eat a bone of mine. My father and my mother procreated me, but my body is my own."

Next day the widow says to her father-in-law: "Last night my husband talked to me. He said, 'Although my parents gave me existence, they have no right to eat me.'" (His big toe had been eaten.) The old man vomited, in an attempt to get the bone out, and continued to vomit, until he died. (It was very seldom a man died in the old days unless killed in battle; some lived to be a hundred or a hundred and fifty years old.) The old man who thought that the only way he could keep the flesh was by eating it was cremated. After all the flesh and bones were burned white, so that, when touched, they would fall apart, the deceased's wife came and uncovered the end of his toe, which was very hot. Two men who were standing there, watching, stirred up the flames, and remained by the body until it was merely ashes. The old man's wife held a piece of his bone on her knee. The men who were watching asked what she intended to do with it. "I want to keep it. I shall wrap it in a rag, put it in a box, and think of him when I see it." "I suppose you will eat it." "No, I shall not eat it. He treated me well; I liked him; he will never come back, and I want to have this much of him." "No, you may not keep it. All must be burned."

When she saw the man stirring the ashes, she cried. He said, "Do not cry any more. He cannot come back. Go find another husband."

After this, every woman wants to do as this one had tried to do. The man said, "Hereafter, if a woman wishes to keep her husband's bones, I will not allow her to do so. When your husband is dead, go find another." (In the old days a woman could not get along without a husband.) The man said, "I shall take charge of this, and will not allow women to do this any more. When a man is dead, he will never come back."

Lari was the name of the third hunter, the one who was brought home dead.

Hunting Stories

96. A MAN WHO KILLED MANY BEARS

A long while ago, when people went to hunt, always two men went together. They would be gone for a long time, sometimes for several months, and would not return until June. Sometimes a man took his family with him.

A man and his wife who were hunting were chased by a bear. The bear caught the woman and tore her to pieces. The man ran until he came to a lake. He swam out into it. The bear pursued him, and only the lake saved him from being torn to pieces. (The bear will not put his feet into water.) When the man returned to camp, he told the people about the bear, and described how it had killed his wife. The wife's brother said he would kill the bear. He and the husband went to the place where the bear had killed the woman. They saw only pieces of her clothes. The bear attacked them. The woman's brother said to the husband, "Climb this tree; and I will kill the bear." The husband climbed the tree. Many bears pursued the man. He had only a tomahawk; with this he killed all the bears except one. There were fifty bears. One escaped. The man who had killed them put them into one big pile, brought a great deal of brush, and burned them until there was nothing left except ashes. He killed, all told, almost sixty bears.[3]

JOHN TENASS

97. DJAKO: A STORY OF ACCULTURATION

My grandfather often told this story about Djako. Every year in the late autumn Djako moves into the woods, where there are enough wild animals to keep him alive. Only his wife knows where he has gone. He does not return until spring. The day after they went into the woods, they built their wigwam. They had no children, and were alone. He said to his wife, "Tomorrow I shall go away and kill an animal for our provisions." The snow was only about six inches deep; so he could not wear snowshoes. That day his wife was left alone. She went out to bring in some dry wood for the fire. She looked about and saw an animal coming straight toward the wigwam. She did not know what it was, and was frightened. She brought a knife to the door, took her bow and arrow, and prepared to shoot. She watched the approaching animal. Soon it halted near the wigwam. The woman, holding up the flap of the wigwam, about twenty feet from the beast, took aim and shot. The arrow penetrated the animal's throat. The beast jumped, then started to walk around the wigwam. When it was nearly back to the place at which it had been

---

[3] Tales like this must have been widely told sixty years ago. Old women of eighty now (1954) recall their childish horror of "sad stories, with people torn to pieces by bears."

PART TWO *Folktales and Traditions*

shot, it fell. The woman went to it, removed the arrow, and cut the beast's throat.

That evening, Djako brought home only a partridge. He saw blood and thought that perhaps someone had killed his wife. She had cut off some of the meat and cooked it. He brought home only a partridge. "Has someone been here today?" "No, only an animal. It came here. I was getting some fuel. It came straight toward me; I thought it would run against the wigwam. About twenty feet from the wigwam it stopped and looked about. I shot it in the throat. The entire arrow shaft was bloody, except a little bit at the end of the shaft." "Did you kill that moose without any assistance?" "Yes." "I saw blood." "It was from the moose." "You did very well." She had also removed the skin and the intestines of the beast.

Next morning, while Djako was at home, two men arrived. They were friends, and were very glad to see Djako and his wife. They said, "We traveled all day, but tracked no beast like that." "Return now, take meat with you, and say, 'Djako's wife killed a moose yesterday; here is some of the meat.'" The following morning, Djako again went into the woods. He said to his wife, "I am glad you watch so much. I shall now fix a bow and arrow." He tightened the bowstring and straightened the arrow shaft. "Do not make the string any tighter. Be ready, and keep watch all the time. You may have another opportunity like that one."

About noon, she heard something coming. There was a little opening in the wigwam; through this she looked, and saw a big bear approaching. It came straight toward the wigwam; it had smelled the meat. She was surprised to see such a big bear approaching. She took the bow and arrow. The bear stopped at the place where the blood of the moose had fallen. He smelt of it, stood up, and looked around. She raised her bow and arrow, shot, and struck the bear on the side of its head. She went to it. The bear wobbled from side to side, then dropped, and soon was dead. She was frightened. She punched him with a stick. He moved not a leg, head, or any part of the body, and she knew he was dead. She pulled the arrow out of his head.

Djako saw the track of a big bear and found that it led straight to his wigwam. After a while the wigwam was in sight, and he saw the slain bear.

He went in. "What luck?" "None," said his wife. "Who killed that bear?" "I killed it. It came straight to the wigwam. I shot it with the bow and arrow. See the hole in its head where the arrow went!" "If you do that all winter, I shall not have to hunt much. You are a lucky woman!" The bear was very fat all over.

Next day, two other men came. They said a man had told them to follow his track and they would find the house of Djako, whose wife had plenty of meat. Djako said to them, "I have been away twice, and have killed nothing. The first time, I secured only a partridge. When I came home, I found a moose had been killed. Next day, when I came home, I found a bear had been killed. The old woman had shot it in the head — see!"

They said to the woman, "You are a lucky woman." "Yes, I cannot go anywhere; I must stay here and watch." She gave them fat and meat to take back with them, and said, "If you want to come here, come." To this they replied, "There is not enough snow yet to haul [a sled over]." Later, the first of these pairs of men came and built wigwams; then the second pair of men came and built wigwams. After Djako had prepared the bear, he again went away. His wife stayed home and kept constant watch. She saw an animal approaching. She thought, 'That is the queerest animal I ever saw. It has roots all over its head.'

It was a male deer with large antlers. When he stopped and looked around, the woman shot him in the head. He moved only once, then fell, dead. That night her husband brought a very large porcupine. He said to his wife, "I have brought a porcupine. Did you get anything today?" "Yes, look over there."

He looked, and saw the deer. The first day, Djako brought a partridge, the next day, nothing; the third, a porcupine. His wife had killed a moose, a bear, and a deer.

The father of Djako's wife, an old man, heard that she was killing plenty of animals. Thereupon he and his wife started for Djako's wigwam. They were very glad to see their child. He asked his daughter, "How did you kill that moose?" "I will tell you. It came straight to our wigwam and stood there. I was afraid it would break into the wigwam. I took my bow and arrow, tightened the string, and shot the moose in the head. The entire arrow penetrated, except a little bit at the end of the shaft. The moose dropped there. I knew it was dead, and immediately cut its throat. I was so much pleased that I forthwith removed the skin from its neck, took off the meat, boiled it for Djako, and, when he came, it had been cooked. Next day a bear came." "You are very lucky," said her

PART TWO *Folktales and Traditions*

father. "I killed a deer, too." Djako killed only a partridge and a porcupine. Wherever he went, he found no animal.

In March, Djako and his wife moved away. He said to his father-in-law, "You should move from here. Soon the snow and the ground will be soft." "Yes." All five families moved away. Djako left, and on the following day the others left. He went to the shore to look about. He walked about three miles farther, and when he was leaving that place saw something on the shore: a man lying there, dead. A vessel laden with flour and other provisions had been wrecked, and all of the crew were dead. When Djako saw the dead man and the vessel, he was frightened. He scarcely knew what the vessel was. He started back. Djako acted like a crow. (When a crow finds something, it tells all its friends.) "I found something on the shore and I saw some wood with a hole in it, and food there." (He could not say "barrel.") They went to the place. There was a great quantity of provisions on board the ship — food, guns, powder, and bullets. The Indians obtained a great quantity of clothes. No one else came, for there was no one except Indians near there. Djako had plenty of blankets, clothes, and other things. The Indians salvaged all they could.

The next autumn, Djako again went into the woods. He built a big wigwam, and stored it with flour and other things. He did not know how to use flour — he had never seen it before. Finally, he had an idea. He put water into it, mixed it, and cooked it in cakes, on the coals. Others split wood, put cakes between the pieces of wood, fastened each piece tightly with spruce root, put the end of the stick into the ground, and thus cooked the cakes. From time to time they turned the stick around, so that the cakes would cook evenly on all sides. With the cloth they made shirts and other clothes. The Micmac then began to discard their old skin clothes. I often heard my grandfather tell about this. Djako's wife did a big work. Djako made the first bootjack.[4]   P. G.

[4] This last assertion is obviously a later addition, inspired by the resemblance between *Djako* and *jack,* "bootjack." The name itself may be a modification of English *Jack,* or French *Jacques.*

CHAPTER X

Animal Stories

RABBIT and Gigwadju, the Wolverine, each by turn trickster and dupe, appear again and again in stories so similar that Tales 99 through 101 cover all the main patterns. In four additional pursuit tales collected in 1911–12, Rabbit is chased three times by Wolverine, once by Otter. In all of these, the transformation flight motive takes a European, not native, form. All four end with the ship; preceding incidents include a sleigh ride and a city hotel; Rabbit as old woman and priest; the Crane's-neck bridge. Wolverine's adventures with the Star Wives and Crane, which bring him to a maggotty though temporary death, are duplicated in a tale about Jay Bird.

To Micmac narrators these two tricky animals bear different characters. Rabbit is sometimes smart, sometimes stupid, and a thief. Gigwadju is downright destructive, as described in Tale 101 and also in an omitted story in which he baby-sits for Rabbit and through misunderstood instructions kills the children. In 1911 he was likened to a monkey, always up to tricks. The name is said to be cognate with *gwadaeck*, "frightened." He is sometimes called Indian Devil. Rabbit, as more than one informant described him, is a gentleman.

98. RABBIT THE GENTLEMAN

Rabbit[1] is a great gentleman. He wears snowshoes all the time — he can walk on top of the snow. "Why have you no tail?" "I sat in an armchair so much that I broke my tail. I spent too much of my time writing." "Why do you have that groove across your nose?" "I always carry my pencil there." "Why do your ears stand up in that fashion?" "When I am

[1] *Ablegamutc* (rabbit) at Pictou, N.S.; *webus* (hare) at Burnt Church, N.B.

PART TWO *Folktales and Traditions*

hunting, I must listen for game." "What makes your dung so round?" "Oh, I am always eating crackers with the gentlemen." "Why is your urine so red?" "Oh, I take so much brandy with the gentlemen in the woods. That is why my urine is so red." "Why is your foot like that?" "Oh, I always wear my snowshoes."

Rabbit is a great gentleman. He always answers you no matter what you ask him.

P. G.

99. RABBIT AND HIS GRANDMOTHER

Rabbit and his grandmother [*Ablegamutc ak Ogamidjal*] had a wigwam. Rabbit hunted, but seldom brought anything home. One day, while he was hunting, he came to a big wigwam. He went there again. Here lived Bear and his grandmother. Bear said, "Come in, my nephew." Rabbit went in and sat in the place of honor, in the front part of the wigwam [actually at the back, opposite the entrance]. Bear said to his grandmother, "Grandmother, put on the pot. My nephew has come. Let us give him a dinner." His grandmother said, "Child, we have nothing to cook for him!" Bear said, "Well, put it on anyway!" When the water was near the boiling point, Bear took a knife, turned toward the corner, cut pieces from his paw, and put them in the pot. When he had cut off two or three pieces, the pot was filled with fine fat bear meat. Meanwhile, Rabbit was observing, and thought it very easily done; he thought that he, too, could do it. They had a good dinner. Rabbit stayed there until nearly evening.

When he was about to go home, he said to Bear, "Now, uncle, be sure to come see us tomorrow." Next day, Bear strolled out to see Rabbit and Rabbit's grandmother. When Bear arrived, Rabbit said, "Come in, uncle." Bear came in, and sat up front in the wigwam.

Rabbit said to his grandmother, "Put on the pot. Let us have a feast for my uncle."

She replied, "We have nothing." "Put it on anyway."

When the water was at the boiling point, Rabbit took a knife, sat down in a corner, and began to carve his foot. As soon as he cut into it he drew his foot back, for he felt a sharp pain. Nevertheless, he cut off a small piece of flesh, and put it into the pot. He cut two or three hairs out of his foot [put them into the pot?], and looked in the pot. There was nothing in it. He tried again. By and by, Bear asked the old woman, "What has my nephew been doing? His foot is bleeding." Rabbit's foot was bleeding. "Well!" says the old woman. "Oh! that foolish nephew of yours! Perhaps he saw someone do that." Bear had pity on him, took the knife, turned toward the corner, cut a few pieces from his paw, filled the pot, and they had a fine feast.

Bear went home. Next morning Rabbit again went out. In the course of the day he arrived at a wigwam. It was the wigwam of Otter — of Otter and his grandmother. Otter said, "Come in, my younger brother." Otter said to his grandmother, "Put on the pot and make a feast for my younger brother." His grandmother answered, "We have nothing." "Put on the pot, anyway." When the water was beginning to boil, Otter went out, and Rabbit peeped through a hole to see where he was going. He saw him jump into the river, dive into the water, and in a short time come in with a big string of eels.

They put the eels into the pot, and had a big feast. Rabbit thought he surely could do that, easily. When taking leave, he said to Otter, "Brother, be sure to come see us tomorrow." When, next day, Otter came, Rabbit said, "Come in, my older brother." He said to his grandmother, "Put on the pot."

When the water was boiling, Rabbit went out and dived into the well. He didn't stay long, for he was out of breath and was glad to come back [to the surface]. He got nothing, and tried a second time. He got nothing that time, and began to feel cold.

After a little while, Otter looked out to see where Rabbit had gone, and saw him sitting by the well, shivering. He asked the old woman, "What is wrong with my little brother? He is out there, sitting by the well, wet and cold." "Oh! that foolish brother of yours! Perhaps he has seen someone doing that sometime." Otter took pity on him. He jumped out, dived into the brook, and in a short time had a string of eels.

Next day, Rabbit again went strolling, and arrived at another wigwam. "Oh!" Woodpecker said, "Come in, my friend. Come forward." Woodpecker said to his grandmother, "Put on the pot. I shall give my friend a fine feast." When the water was boiling, Woodpecker went out and jumped into an old tree, near the entrance, pecked it, and drew eels out of it. Rabbit thought that was easily done, and that he could certainly do it. (Actually it was worms the woodpecker was getting out of the tree.) They made a feast. He said to Woodpecker, "My friend, be sure to come see us tomorrow."

When Woodpecker went there, next day, Rabbit was in great glee. He

PART TWO *Folktales and Traditions*

thought he surely would have a fine meal for his friend that day. Rabbit told his grandmother to put on the pot; he said he would give his friend a fine feast. When the water boiled, Rabbit went out and pecked at an old tree. At the first blow, he smashed his nose. Rabbit now has a very blunt nose. He bled at the nose freely.

After a while, Woodpecker looked out and saw that Rabbit was full of blood. He asked the old woman, "What is wrong with my friend? He is covered with blood." "That foolish friend of yours! I'm sure he has seen someone do that." Woodpecker had pity, and went out and got some eels (worms).

Later, Rabbit went to Otter's wigwam and stole eels. Otter was angry, and tracked him. He swore vengeance on him, and declared that if he caught Rabbit, he would kill him. Rabbit took the eels home to his grandmother. He was chased by Otter, and ran as fast as he could. He knew Otter was close to him. He entered a swampy place, and there made tracks in every direction. He went to a little spruce tree, and sat by it.

When Otter arrived, Otter thought he was in a town. The streets ran every direction, and he lost Rabbit's tracks. He arrived at a big house. A man was walking back and forth on a piazza, wearing a long white coat. (Rabbit had made himself look like this.) Otter asked him, "Didn't you see a rabbit going by this way?" "No" (very slowly and deliberately), and the man shook his head; "I don't know what rabbit it was." "His tracks came into this town." "No," the gentleman said, "I didn't see him. But you must be tired. Better come in." Otter was hungry, and more than glad to come in. The gentleman left him in the kitchen, and went into the living room. He brought him a glass of wine and a few round biscuits. Otter ate them greedily, and drank his wine. The gentleman came in again, brought him a bottle of wine, and a few more round biscuits, and told him he might need them on his travels. Otter ate the bread and drank the wine, became drunk, and slept. He slept there and did not awake until after nightfall.

When he awoke, he was lying alongside a little bush. Where the house had been there was only a little bush, and Rabbit's tracks were alongside him. He felt in his pocket for the bottle of wine. It was only *mkwoawetck* [a little plant said to hold water like a pitcher; probably the pitcher-plant]. It was filled with Rabbit's wine [urine]. What had been biscuits were only Rabbit's dung, and Rabbit had gone. Otter was very angry, and said he would this time kill Rabbit, surely. But this time Rabbit ran very fast. He knew that Otter was close behind him.

He came to a little pond. In the pond there was a small island, and on it were two or three dead trees. Rabbit changed these into a big ship, and the pond into a big bay. When Otter arrived at the pond, he thought it was a bay and a big ship was anchored on it. A gentleman, wearing a little white coat, was walking to and fro on the deck. Otter said, "You are Rabbit! You can't trick me again!" and swam directly to him. When Rabbit saw him coming, he shouted to his men, "Look at that Otter coming! Shoot him. His fur is of great value in our country." Otter saw them, was sure they were men, and turned back. While he was returning to shore, he was nearly drowned. SIMON BASQUE

100. RABBIT AND WOLVERINE VISIT KITPUSIAGANA

Rabbit remains at home all week. On Sunday he says, "I am going to see my friends." Rabbit goes to see Kitpusiagana. (Kitpusiagana is an animal that is difficult to see. I have never seen one, and I have never heard anyone say that he has seen one.[2]) Kitpusiagana is at home, entertaining guests from everywhere.

Rabbit passes many of the animals — moose, caribou, and others — and says with a flourish of his paw, "Oh, I know what you fellows are eating." Kitpusiagana gives this company a good dinner, which includes all kinds of foods. He lives on everything and consequently is very tough and strong.

Kitpusiagana: "Did you stop at the chief's wigwam?" Rabbit: "No, I did not stop there." "Did you call at the wigwam of the second chief?" "No."

Kitpusiagana: "Did you call at the wigwam of the third chief?" Rabbit: "No." (The first chief was Moose, the second chief Caribou, the third chief Deer.)

Kitpusiagana: "Well, we must have a good time today."

To everything Rabbit replies, "Yes." To Kitpusiagana's wigwam come Mouse, then Skunk, and a great many other animals. They had escaped from Gugwes,[3] all in one canoe. Kitpusiagana asks them how they have gotten along.

[2] See Tales 18–20.
[3] Gugwes is a grotesque creature; in 1911–12 he was commonly compared to a baboon; in 1950 he was described as a giant and was used as a bugaboo for the

PART TWO *Folktales and Traditions*

They told him the following story of their escape from Gugwes: Skunk: "I have power to make him go to sleep, and in this way I escaped." Down the river is a log over the water. On this sits Gugwes, intent on catching someone. Gugwes says, "Whoever is in the first canoe that comes down the river I shall get for my dinner." Skunk, however, thinks matters may turn out otherwise. Gugwes: "I shall have a good dinner — no matter who, even if it is my grandmother in the canoe." Mouse and Skunk are in the canoe, and get past Gugwes; the log is high enough to allow the canoe to go under it. After Mouse and Skunk have gone past him, Gugwes awakes, and says, "Hee! if I get you two fellows, I shall have a good dinner today." Skunk replies: "We shall meet again." Gugwes: "When we meet, what will happen?" Skunk: "I shall show you that you cannot stand a shot." Gugwes: "I shall not say anything. I am not afraid of you, but I dislike touching you. I thoroughly hate you."

Mouse says, "That fellow would eat me quickly." Gugwes: "Yes, I guess I should eat you quickly enough. When you talk, you seem to be a big man; but when you walk about the place, you are worthless — a body can scarcely see you. It is difficult to find you, and even so you are not worth eating. There is no taste to you, because you are too small."

Kitpusiagana has finished asking questions, and has heard the entire story. "Don't be afraid to go home, boys," he says, "I myself will take you home." Rabbit again feels lonesome. He says good-by to Kitpusiagana — "I am going home." Kitpusiagana's canoe is anchored along the shore. He pulls in the anchor, pushes the canoe out, and says to Mouse: "Get aboard, and we will find out what kind of storm we shall have." It be-

children on at least one reserve. In 1603 Gugwes was a well-known horror to Micmac and to Frenchmen, including Samuel de Champlain:

"Many savages have assured me . . . that near the Bay of Heat [Baie des Chaleurs] toward the south, there is an island where a frightful monster makes his home, which the savages call Gougou, and which they told me had the form of a woman, but very terrible, and of such a size that they told me the tops of the masts of our vessel would not reach to her waist, so great do they represent her and they say that she has often eaten up and still continues to eat up many savages; these she puts, when she can catch them, into a great pocket, and afterward she eats them; and those who had escaped the danger of this awful beast said that its pocket was so great that it could have put our vessel into it. This monster makes horrible noises in this island, which the savages call the Gougou; and when they speak of it, it is with unutterable fear, and several have assured me that they have seen him. What makes me believe what they say is the fact that all the savages in general fear her, and tell such strange things of her that, if I were to record all they say of her, it would be considered as idle tales, but I hold that this is the dwelling-place of some devil that torments them in the manner described. This is what I have learned about this Gougou." Champlain, *Works*, I, 186–88.

Animal Stories

comes very rough, the boat is half-filled with water; Mouse thinks he will drown and will never reach shore. The others are on the shore. Mouse says, "It is rough. I hope I shall never have fishing as my occupation." To this Kitpusiagana says, "Then you would do well not to become a fisherman. You should come to the shore and stay around the wigwam. That is all you are good for, anyway."

Kitpusiagana says to Skunk, "Now, you should get into the canoe." He takes Skunk into the canoe and goes out with him, as he had done with Mouse. Skunk has a hard time of it but, nevertheless, fishes. He cannot fish successfully, for the waves are too high, and there is much thunder and lightning. He comes to land close to Gigwadju. Skunk thinks Gigwadju is a fish.

Kitpusiagana says to Rabbit, "What do you think of that?" Rabbit: "A bad storm. Skunk smells bad." (Rabbit does not know that Gigwadju is on board.) "Do not keep him on board. I will not fish with him."

Kitpusiagana: "If you think you can fish alone, go ahead." Rabbit: "Goodness, who could stand the odor of the canoe? If I wish to fish here with you, I shall bring my own canoe." (Rabbit has no canoe, but is always bragging.) Thus Rabbit excuses himself from going out to fish. "Well," Rabbit says, "I shall go home."

On his way home Rabbit arrives at Otter's wigwam. He looks into the wigwam. Otter is not at home. "Where is Otter?" he asks. "He went out long ago. Please, would you mind chopping a few sticks of wood and chucking them in here for me?" the old woman asks. "Yes, ma'am," he says. He turns around and chucks in old dirt and a few chips, very carelessly, turns his head up and sees a *wabogan* [fish spear] on top of the wigwam. "Ha! Ha!" he says, "that is mine." He takes it, runs off to his own wigwam, sees his grandmother, says, "I am going out to get a few sticks of wood." He runs away with the *wabogan* which he has stolen, and thinks that with its help he can make a living. He runs all night.

Otter comes home and says, "Who was in here while I was out?" The old woman replies, "Rabbit was here and chopped me a few sticks, then left. I do not know where he went — he went home, I think." Otter does not miss the *wabogan* until next morning. When he looks for it and fails to find it, he says, "Rabbit has taken it." He dives into the water, and swims to Rabbit's wigwam. When he reaches there, he asks the old woman where Rabbit is. She replies, "He went out last night, saying he was going to get a few sticks of wood; and has not come back." She asks

PART TWO *Folktales and Traditions*

him why he wishes to see Rabbit. "Well," he says, "I wish to see him," and refuses to tell her why. He merely says, "I must see Rabbit," and follows Rabbit's tracks. Otter runs with all his might.

Rabbit thinks he will soon be caught, and makes cross tracks everywhere, as you see them on the snow, and so confused that he himself could not tell by them what way he has gone. Otter arrives at these cross tracks and cannot discover what direction Rabbit has gone in. Rabbit, however, has taken a straight course. Otter says, "Aha! I guess I know where you are going, chummy — I guess I can follow you farther." He runs and runs, but he cannot catch Rabbit.

Rabbit thinks that he will soon be caught, and wishes he is a bartender in a hotel. Rabbit arrives at the hotel. He is the bartender there. Otter comes to the hotel and walks in. Rabbit wears a white waistcoat, white hat, has a long mustache, and his entire nose is split. He is behind the bar. "I am glad to see another customer coming in," says Rabbit to Otter. Otter, who does not recognize Rabbit, asks, "Did you see Rabbit go by here on this road?" "No," replies Rabbit; "I am so deaf that from here I could not hear a thing out-of-doors. You must have a drink." Otter takes a drink, a second one, and wants a third. After a fourth drink, he is so drunk that anyone could deceive him. Rabbit says, "I have made him like a bum — fussy talk, and dancing around the bar; that is the way I wish him to be." Rabbit: "Are you hungry?" Otter: "Yes."

Rabbit tells the servant girl to give him crackers and a bottle to put into his pocket. They put Otter in one corner of the barroom, drunk, with a bottle and crackers in his pocket. After Rabbit knows that Otter is drunk, he leaves, and takes the *wabogan* with him. He stands by Otter and says to him, "You think you are a sensible man, but you are not. People who think they are sensible get fooled sometimes. The light stuff I am making will cause you to sleep." Rabbit goes away. When Otter gets up in the morning, he finds himself in the water, among stumps of blown-over trees, and amid ice, snow, and slush.

Rabbit travels on, taking the fish spear. After Otter gets up, he says, "I shall catch you sometime." While he runs, he feels sick — he has a headache, and wishes for good water, a good breakfast, and a drink of whiskey (the things which he had had on the previous night). Otter turns around. "He gave me a bottle last night. I shall have a good square drink." He puts his hand into his hip pocket and pulls out a piece of rotten pine, the size of a bottle. He becomes angry again, and says, "You will not deceive me next time." He sits down and cries, sorry that he drank the liquor the previous night. He turns around again, and says, "Oh, yes, he gave me crackers last night, to carry away to eat." He feels in his pocket, finds his handkerchief and the crackers, which latter prove to be a piece of mud tied up in his handkerchief.

"Well," he says, "I think I shall pursue you; you have done too much to me" — and follows Rabbit's tracks. "I know you," he says, "that is you, Rabbit." Rabbit thinks he will soon be caught. He wishes himself in a church, for Otter has now traveled a long way in pursuit of him. Rabbit hears a very strange sound. (Rabbit had never before heard a church bell.)

Otter remarks, "Goodness, I shall go over there to see what kind of place that is." He arrives at the church, and sees a great many people enter. Many people are going in. "I, too, may as well go in." He sees people kneeling (it was a Roman Catholic church), and he kneels.

Rabbit is dressed in white, and is saying Mass, apart to himself. Otter sees the lighted candles, and hears the priest and the people singing in the church. He had never seen things done that way. He falls soundly asleep. Rabbit notices that Otter is asleep, and goes away. He carries the *wabogan* with him, and once more fools Otter. He takes a straight course to the shore.

When Otter rises in the morning, he finds himself on top of a large pine tree. (He had climbed up on top of the church.) He says, "It will be very difficult for me to get down." Nevertheless, he does get down.

After he has gotten down, he says, "I shall test you once more. If you fool me again, I will give up. But if I catch you, I shall kill you." He starts off again, in pursuit of Rabbit. Again Rabbit thinks he will soon be caught. He wishes he may have an establishment with all kinds of geese, ducks, and waterfowl that make a big noise — all females. Otter comes up and is surprised. He is somewhat bashful when he sees that all the people are ladies, and wear white dresses. "Goodness; I guess there is no Rabbit around here, in this part of the country." When they see Otter coming, all begin to tease and torment him. Otter says, "I have not much to say, girls. Did you at any time see Rabbit go past here?" "Oh, that is what you are looking for! He might go by in the night, or in the daytime, and we would not see him." He tells them why he wishes to find Rabbit. The girls invite Otter to remain overnight. Rabbit has been in the house, and jumps out when Otter comes in. They go in and give

PART TWO *Folktales and Traditions*

Otter his supper. Otter gets up; "I shall surely catch you this time, for you are certainly along the beach."

Otter again travels all day, a great part of the time in the water, where he travels best, though sometimes he travels by land. Rabbit again thinks he will be caught. He wishes he were a captain on a war vessel. He is on such a boat, and is the captain. He wears a white waistcoat and white trousers. It is summer and he is beginning to turn black in a circle around the middle of his body. He uses this ring as a watch chain. Otter arrives and sees the boat that Rabbit is on. "Ah," he says; "here he is again!" Otter says to Rabbit, "There you are, standing in white waistcoat, white collar, white jacket, white shoes, and white everything. You begin to turn black in the spring; that is why you are wearing your watch chain. I know you!" and into the water he dives. When Rabbit sees Otter dive into the water, he says, "Shoot him, boys." They shoot: bang! bang! but do not kill him. Rabbit: "If these shots do not kill you, there will be others later that will."

Otter goes on board and meets Rabbit. He says to Rabbit, "Now, you had better be careful what you do after this! I have been pursuing you ever since you left home. You have been talking about how I shall die. I think you may as well talk about how I shall live. We are friends again — shake hands." He takes pity on Rabbit, because he has seen things which Rabbit has never seen. "We are friends again, though you told me that other shots would be fired and would kill me. Not every man will shoot me — the shots of some will miss me." Rabbit could not say much. Otter continued, "I wish now to say a few words more. There is nothing that can kill you except Fox. You will have no wigwam, and you will be compelled to keep moving continually, for fear something will kill you. I, however, shall have my wigwam. There is only one young fellow who will go in pursuit of you — that is Fox." "Good-by, Otter." "Same to you, Rabbit — *adiu ginnik* [Good-by, Otter]."

Meanwhile, Kitpusiagana has Skunk, Gigwadju [Wolverine], and Mouse together. Skunk says, "Let us walk up the river to our place." They start.

Gugwes is still on the log. When they are close to him, Gugwes sees Kitpusiagana coming, and remarks, "We cannot do much, boys." He has seen Kitpusiagana approaching, and cannot say much. Mouse remarks, "I do not amount to much — I have not much body. I have been working for this man. He has not paid me, for he intends to defend me."

They are not yet close to Gugwes, and Gugwes can move if he wishes to. He is large and strong and thinks himself a bully, though he isn't.

Skunk: "It is not only you whose part Kitpusiagana will take. He will defend me, too, because I have been working for him." [To Gugwes]: "You see we have been fishing. Do you see this fish that we have here?" (referring to Wolverine). Gugwes says to Skunk, "You are trying to make a friend of me again!" Wolverine: "No, he does not wish to make friends with you again. In fact, you never had a friend."

Said Gugwes to Wolverine, "Who may you be?[4] I passed by you a hundred times along the shore. You were dead — no good — rotten."

Gugwes contradicts every statement Wolverine makes, and says he does not wish to be his friend. Wolverine: "This is the boy who will never die" (referring to himself). Gugwes cannot answer this. Kitpusiagana: "He has met his match in the three of us." Gugwes: "What will the fourth one do?"

Kitpusiagana: "The fourth one will soon show you — if you will get off that log."

Gugwes understands this as a challenge to move, and is checked again, for he does not wish to risk his life. Kitpusiagana: "You had better get off that log. You do not know how many people may come and wish to cross on it. Clear off!"

Gugwes clears off, and is glad to get away. Skunk and Mouse then continue in the canoe, up the river, to their home.

Kitpusiagana returns to his home. He leaves Wolverine, who then walks down to the shore. He meets three boys. They have little bows and arrows, and are shooting birds along the shore. Wolverine: "What kind of bows and arrows have you there?" The boys show them to him. Wolverine takes one of them, pulls back the string, and breaks the bow. When the boy sees his broken bow, he sits down and cries. Wolverine: "Never mind, do not cry. Do you see that point away off there? That is my home. I have a bow and arrows at my home." Wolverine has broken all their bows, and all the boys are crying. "Never mind," he says, "I have good bows and arrows at my home; they are made of bone and stone. I shall give you some of them. Let us start and go to that point." They start. Wolverine, like the others, throws stones. (Wolverine is like a boy; he plays around, but has no home.)

[4] The intent of the question is almost equivalent to our "Who the hell are you?" Or, "Who do you think *you* are?"

PART TWO *Folktales and Traditions*

They arrive at the point, and walk up the bank to the top of it. No home is there. The boys ask, "Is this the point you meant? Is your home here?" Wolverine: "No, I did not mean this point, I mean that one up there."

They start again. They arrive at the next point, but it is the same thing — there is neither home nor arrows. Wolverine says, "Excuse me, boys. I thought this was the point. It is that one up there." They arrive at the third point.

Again, they find nothing. The oldest boy says, "We had best kill that rascal."

"Let us make a big box, like a canoe," they say to Wolverine, "and we shall have some fun with it." Wolverine replies, "Yes, let us all turn to and make that box — we shall have great fun." Accordingly, they make the box, procure a cover, and say to Wolverine, "That box has just about the same length as yourself."

"Yes, there is not much difference." The smallest boy goes into the box, lies on his stomach, and says, "The box is too long for me." "I think it is the right length for me," says Wolverine, who goes in and lies down on his stomach. The little boy jumps out, and they cover up Wolverine, for they are trying to kill him. They shove Wolverine out into the river, to drown. The box drifts around, here, there, and everywhere, but none of this suffices to kill Wolverine. The boys go home. Wolverine lands somewhere.

Down the river two daughters of the old Indians are lying in their wigwam at night, looking up through the smokehole. The older one says to her sister, "What kind of husband would you like to have — one with big eyes or one with small eyes?" The younger one replies, "It makes no difference to me provided it is a man — big eyes or little eyes, it is all the same." "Well, I will take the big eyes." "Well, if you take the big eyes, I will take the small eyes." The older says, "Turn your head and look at those stars. Which would you like to have [pointing], those two there, or those two over there?"

The younger and the older each choose two stars in the east. They fall asleep. When next morning they awake, they are in the other world, one in one wigwam, the other in another, each with a husband. One husband has big eyes, the other has little eyes. The girls look about, but do not recognize the place. The men say, "We must go to work. We have been

Animal Stories

working this morning, and we must put in another half-day." The girls are now in the place where the stars have been. The men, before they leave, say to the girls, "Do not raise a stone or a piece of wood or dirt. Do not disturb any thing. Remain where you are." The younger girl says, "We must get a mess of *sageban* [wild potatoes] and prepare them for dinner." They dig a hole in the ground, to search for these. They move a stone. One says to the other, "Oh, look down! I see another country." The older one looks into the hole; "I know that country. There is our wigwam way down there by that pine."

One of their husbands, who are working a long way from home, says to the other, "We should go home and find out what is wrong. Something is wrong. They must have moved a rock, or a stone, or something else." The husbands run with all speed to their wigwams. When they reach home, they ask, "Did you raise a stone, or something else? Answer at once." They tell him about moving the stone. The men ask them whether they wish to return. They say "Yes," they are lonesome, and not willing to remain in that place. The men tell the girls they will cover their [the girls'] faces, and that they must not remove the cover until they hear the crow and, later, the robin. "People will tell you to open it, and you will hear various birds singing; but do not open it until you hear, first, the crow and, then, the robin." Later the younger one says, "Those fellows told us to uncover our faces when we hear the crow." "No," replies the older, "he said we should uncover our faces when we hear the robin." "No, he said, 'crow'." "All right, as soon as we hear the crow, we will uncover our faces and find out where we are." While they are coming from the sky they hear geese, ducks, and almost everything, some of them telling the girls to uncover their faces. When they hear the crow, they uncover their faces. They are then in the top of a big pine tree — for the crow was on top of it — and there they are stuck. There are no limbs on this pine tree, except at the very top, and they cannot get down.

Gigwadju had gotten out of the box. Someone had opened it and had found him rotting. He came to life again, for he had not [actually] died. The wigwam of the girls was on the ground.

Bear passes by the tree while the girls are up in it. They call to Bear, "Say, Uncle, take us down — even if you are only a sort of man." "Oh, I have not time to go up there and take you down. How did you get up there? You must have gotten up some way." Moose walks past the tree,

PART TWO *Folktales and Traditions*

traveling the very path which the girls took when they went to the spring to get water. They call to him, "Take us down, Uncle." "Oh, no; I do not have time to go up there. Why did you climb up there, anyway?" The other animals which walk past the tree likewise refuse to take the girls down. Gigwadju comes. He is traveling along the path, whistling vigorously. The girls say, "Here is Gigwadju. He will take us down, surely."

Gigwadju comes in a straight line, not looking up at all, and whistling gayly. "Take us down, Uncle." Gigwadju: "Whom are you addressing as Uncle?" "You. We wish you to take us down." "Oh, I haven't time."

The girls: "Do you know what we will do if you will take us down? We will stay with you forever. You may marry my sister or you may marry me."

Gigwadju: "If you have a wigwam, I will marry you, and I will take you down." "Yes, we have a wigwam; now take us down." Gigwadju takes them down.

The girls plan what they will do with Gigwadju. The second girl to be taken down ties her garter to a limb. Gigwadju takes both of them down. When they are starting toward their wigwam, the younger one says, "Oh, my! I have forgotten my garter and left it up there on a limb. You will have to climb up again and get the garter." Gigwadju goes back, climbs the tree again, and gets the garter.

The girls go straight home and kindle a little fire. There is so much smoke in the wigwam that it is impossible to see anyone. One girl says, "In this corner let us put the porcupine quills and the porcupine, and over all that part of the wigwam there, the bees." Gigwadju climbs down from the tree, and while he walks toward the wigwam, thinks, "Lunch will be ready for me when I arrive." He walks in.

When he is inside, the wigwam is so full of smoke that he cannot see anything. He hears the porcupine say, "Tetlia! Tetlia!" that is, "Come to this side." He thinks it is one of the girls speaking to him, and carelessly jumps in that direction. He is stung, wriggles off, and says, "Oh, I am going to hug this one." He has heard a noise on the other side, the dull buzz of the bees, and thinks it is the laughter of the other girl. Accordingly, he springs to the other side, and jumps into a swarm of bees.

Gigwadju complains, "Your sister has too many pins all over her back and everywhere else; I shall not marry her." While he is feeling around, trying to find the other sister, he breaks the hive, and the bees escape. When they sting him, he says, "Who would marry you? You are too

Animal Stories

busy. No matter what kind of husband you might get, you would never get a husband who could stand the smoke." [Meanwhile] the girls run away as fast as they can. Crane is fishing nearby. When the girls arrive at the brook, they say, "He, Uncle! Will you take us across? Gigwadju is pursuing us." He has a sore neck, is very reluctant to comply, but finally says, "I suppose I shall put you across." He places his neck across the river, thereby making a bridge, and tells the girls not to walk too rapidly or be too rough, but to step lightly; otherwise they will hurt his neck. So they are able to cross.

Gigwadju runs, follows their tracks, and says, "Oh, I shall get you!" When he comes to Crane, who is again fishing there, he says, "Will you put me across, old man?" "Yes, I will put you across. But I want you to walk slowly, and do not jump or dance on my neck." "Oh, no fear, old man, no fear." Crane stretches his neck across the river. Gigwadju starts over on Crane's neck, and when halfway across, begins to dance, jump, and yell. Crane is hurt, and pulls his neck back with a jerk. Crane does not care whether Gigwadju should drown, for he told Gigwadju not to jump. Gigwadju goes down the river, here and there. I guess he is going yet, and Crane is there yet, as far as I know. Gigwadju finally comes to the shore at a cave which has a peculiar name; but I have forgotten what the place is called. T. M.

When Gigwadju realizes that he is in the water, he makes a wish that he shall float to his native country. Accordingly, he floats downstream until he comes to Esaqwesagwadikc Nematkikc [the name of the place where he wishes to land].

Two boys who are going out to shoot sea birds see something lying on the sand. They have bows and arrows. The youngest one says, "I shall shoot that thing." He shoots at it, and his arrow strikes it. "Koktca," says the object which he has hit. "What made you hit that old man?" the other boy asks. "It is a man." They go to him. It is an old man. "His eyes are full of maggots." The old fellow says, "Oh, that's only a little dirt in my eyes." The younger boy says, "Look at his mouth and nose — [they are] full of maggots." Gigwadju says, "That's nothing — *misida nadimcal* [a running from the nose]." The boy continues, "Look at his ears — full of maggots." Gigwadju says, "That's nothing — *nokikamtcik* [ear wax]." He jumps up, shakes himself, and shakes all the dirt off. He is as whole as ever. He says to the boys, "Let me see your bow and arrows." The older boy gives him

PART TWO *Folktales and Traditions*

the bow to try. The old fellow breaks the bow. He asks for the younger boy's bow. The little boy gives it to him, and he breaks it also.

He asks the boys, "Where do you live?" They point a finger toward the wigwam. The boys cry; they have no bow. He says to them, "Don't cry. I have a wigwam here. I'll show you where it is. I will give you bows and arrows made of gold and silver, or of steel, or of anything else you like." The two boys go to the place indicated, but find no wigwam. There is no wigwam at that place.

During the night the two boys return home. They are tired. They say not a word, but lay down and sleep. In the morning, they discover that their grandmother has been killed; Gigwadju did that. They do not know what to do.

They wish that all the big animals should come and follow Gigwadju. The big animals come and follow him, but can do nothing. They wish for all the small animals. They too can do nothing with Gigwadju. They wish for the small birds. The small birds can do nothing with him. They wish for Crane. Crane comes. He says, "I shall kill that thing." He takes off his hat — they get that much [reaction] from him — and returns home. Hawk comes. His coat is off — he has stripped. Then comes Loon. His trousers are off — he has stripped for diving. Another bird comes — *tcigagago* [black crane]. He removes his moccasins. Eagle comes home and goes after Gigwadju, saying, "I shall kill him."

Eagle gets him. He takes hold of Gigwadju while the latter is running. He carries Gigwadju up into the air. While Eagle was flying up with him, Gigwadju said he wished to go still higher. He sang:

Ne'msiala'li	*te'leptaniane'ck*	*ke'mitkinu*	*esta'ietc*
Still higher	covered with boughs (said when he looked down upon the earth)	the world	like

ki'sinaga'sigel.	*"Ta'liwe'dji*	*nudji'tc kc?"*
covered with foliage.	"What are they saying,	grandson?"

te'luwe'djikc:	*"Kasunowe'osul*	*e'dunabes*
They said:	"High up where you are going	?

ela'ledja."
with that one."

(Free translation: Still higher, where we now are, the world seems to be covered with boughs; it appears to be covered with foliage. "What are they saying, grandson?" They said, "High up where you are going [?] with that one.")

Animal Stories

Eagle then drops him. When Gigwadju realizes that he will be dropped, he wishes that his backbone should come to the earth safely. He falls on hard rocks and is thoroughly smashed, except his backbone, and that comes apart easily. His limbs are apart. He wishes that his head should come out from his backbone. Immediately, it comes. He wishes that his arms and all the parts of his body should come, and immediately they come; all except his testicles. He cannot get them, but he hears them talking. They are in between two rocks, and cannot go to him. He leaves them there, and takes little stones in place of them. He jumps up, as happy as a king. He dresses himself as a woman, and goes to a place where there are many wigwams. The people say, "A strange girl has come to this place." Every boy is eager to see that girl. The chief's son thinks he will marry her at once — for she is a stranger. He is the only boy in the family, but he has three sisters.

He marries this stranger. They have a splendid time, for he is a rich boy. The first night they have separate beds — that is to say, they lie together, but have separate blankets. Gigwadju says to him, "In my country it is the custom for young people not to have intercourse for several months after they have married." He believes everything Gigwadju says; and Gigwadju has a glorious time with the three girls.

Gigwadju's husband and the latter's father go away to hunt, and leave him with the girls. He has them make two *atkiwaan* [cradle boards] in the finest style possible; then bids all go outside.

The old man kills a bear which has two young cubs in her. The old lady then makes two little suits of the very best fur that she could obtain. Gigwadju puts the two little cubs on the cradle boards, and asks the people not to look at the children or lift the cover for three months, lest they [the children] become cross-eyed. Young people come in to see the babies, but are not allowed to see their faces. Before the end of the three months, he runs away. He abandons the two young ones and his husband. The young girls discover what is in the cradles. When they look, there is a little cub in each of them. They do not know what to think, or say. They say they will kill Gigwadju. They pursue him a long way, but cannot catch him. They determine to kill all the [Gigwadju] females, but they find only males. They do not dare to touch these.

Again Gigwadju travels, and visits the animals. He comes to a den in which there are seven [raccoons]. They will not have him there. He travels on and comes to a place where there are four Indians — boys and

PART TWO *Folktales and Traditions*

girls. They will have nothing to do with him. He comes to another place where there are four [foxes]. They know him and try to make way with him. He goes on until he arrives at a river. There he sees three girls on the bank of the stream. They have no canoe, cannot cross, and are very anxious to go to the other side. He cannot cross. He likes the appearance of the girls. He cuts a long rod and thinks it will reach across the river. He urinates on it and puts it across the river for them to catch hold of. No one can walk on it or do anything with it except take hold of it. Then he cuts his penis off, puts it on the end of the stick and hands it to the girls. When he puts it back, he gets it on wrong; and you can see that to this day it is on wrong.

[The story is said to resume with the episode of the girls who crossed on Crane's neck, but the informant was not familiar with that portion of it.]

LOUIS GLODE

101. WOLVERINE'S BEHAVIOR

Wolverine will go up a tree and watch you. As soon as you leave, he will go into your wigwam and destroy things and often, in tearing about, set fire to it. He will carry out of the wigwam all that is edible. What he can't eat he will take up into a tree.

There was very little in a certain wigwam way off in the woods. The occupants had merely some powder. They put it by the fire to dry and left it there. Wolverine put it on the fire. It exploded and he was blinded in both eyes. He couldn't get out. They heard a noise, and when they returned, there was Wolverine inside — he couldn't find his way out.

102. GUGWES AND THE ORIGIN OF MOSQUITOES

Gugwes cannot go into a Christian country, for if he sees a church, he will die.

A long, long time ago, Gugwes used to go about and eat people. He killed a pregnant woman. He ate her, and put the child from her womb into a well. The husband came home, and learned that his wife had been eaten.

Gugwes was there. The husband went to the well to get water. He saw the child in the well, and took it out. It was alive, and spoke to its father: "Gugwes ate my mother. Gugwes put me into the well." An old woman said, "Neither axe nor bow and arrow will kill him. Put the child's clothes into a stove, close the door of the house, and keep Gugwes

Animal Stories

in the house until the clothes have been consumed." The husband put the clothes of all his children into the stove. Gugwes wished to go outside. He bellowed and made a big rumpus, but the husband would not allow him to go out. The woman said, "Take an axe, crush his bones fine, pitch them into the air, and say, while you do so, 'You are all mosquitoes!' "

["This seems to be so," said the narrator, "because you can drive flies away, but you can never drive mosquitoes away. They like to eat people. We have talked about that [story] several times, and think it is very nearly true." See Table 18.]

103. A BOY WHO LIVED WITH THE BEARS

The bear is a very queer animal. He eats nothing during the winter, but merely lies sleeping. When bears pick blueberries, they eat all they can, and the remainder they pack in a *putckadju* [birch-bark box], and keep throughout the winter. One fall all the Indians were picking blueberries. A boy was lost. A bear caught him, intending to eat him, and gave him a hug. The boy screamed, and happened to squeal like a young bear. The bear released the boy, and the latter followed it. The bear put him in the midst of his winter den, with the cubs, and kept him warm throughout the winter. During this season they ate only the berries in the *putckadju*. In the spring, all went out, and allowed the boy to stand on the ground. Every spring, about May, smelts come up the streams. When the smelts had started to run, the big bear sat down by the brook, and the cubs stood on either bank. The boy drove the smelts to the bear, and she threw them out with her paws.

People heard the boy. "We must get that boy!" they said, "the one we lost last summer." They did get him. He had hairs on his back like those of a bear, but he cried like a person. His relatives would not hurt that bear, because she had spared the boy. They would kill other bears, but not that one; though I do not know how they could distinguish it from the others.[5] The descendants of this boy are now represented by the Thomas families at Pictou Landing, whose Indian name is Bear [Muin].

104. THE MAN WHO WAS TRANSFORMED INTO A SNAKE

A man's brother goes into a big hole, and when he comes out, is a snake. Medicine is put on his head. His head splits, and the man comes

[5] Another informant said the smoke of the fire rose straight up when the friendly bear appeared.

PART TWO *Folktales and Traditions*

out of the snake skin. He looks around, but cannot speak. His brother puts more medicine on his head. In a little while, he arises, but his feet and arms are straightened out stiff, and he can move only his head. More medicine is put on him, and his limbs loosen up. Other medicine is put into his mouth; this he swallows. He vomits until his insides are completely cleansed. Matio's son gave him this medicine, and said, "One who sees a hole in the rock must not go into it. It belongs to the occupant." He had warned his brother not to go near it. His brother had put his head in, and had been drawn into it. When he was in it, two or three hundred yards from the entrance, he was told to hurry. He could not speak. His legs and arms became stiff. He was wearing, as clothing, the skin of a snake. Two or three snakes came out before the man was able to identify one of them as his brother. In deep holes, there are strong poisons. The man who cured him obtained his medicine from the ground.

P. G.

105. THE CROW WHICH FOUND A WHALE

About the last of March or the first of April, the Indians had very few provisions — there was no game or fish. A big storm came. [Peter Ginnish's] grandfather heard a crow flying toward him. It came close to him, then cawed and cawed. He noticed it appeared to be greasy, and was wiping and cleaning its bill on its feathers. It cawed and cawed, then flew off to one end of Portage Island. He told his father about the crow. They went out with another man, put on their snowshoes, and crossed on the ice to the island.

Something had come ashore. When they arrived at the place, they found it to be something large, like a ship, and black. It was a big whale. They found a big whale! There was seven inches of fat in addition to the meaty part. The men returned, each with a big load. Next morning a man went on snowshoes to Richibucto, one to Red Bank, one to Shippigan, and even to Bathurst and Restigouche, to take the news. From all these settlements the Indians came and hauled away pieces of the whale — every piece of it. They left only the bones.

The Indians are never stingy. They are like a crow. It is never stingy. When a crow finds provisions, it brings the news to the Indians. It came to tell the people at Burnt Church about the whale which it had found at Portage Island.

P. G.

Animal Stories

106. THE SERVICE RENDERED BY PIGEON AND BY CROW

We talked a great deal about how the Indians acquired their language, but could not solve the problem. We think it was changed at the tower of Babylon. We talked a great deal about the ark. Only two of each kind went in; then where did the Indians come from? What kind of crow was in it? I explain the matter in this way:

When the world was under water, and the ship had started, they were out twelve days, then sent a crow to find dry land. (In those days crows were white.) It did not return. They sent a pigeon. At last the pigeon found the crow. It was eating [the bodies of] the people who had been drowned and had been washed ashore. It became greasy and black all over, and has been so ever since. The pigeon, however, went to the shore and ate blueberries. Look at his mouth and his feet — they are blue! Where did the Micmac come from? The boss on board that barque hadn't the power. God had the power. He took the two who went onto the island. No one now knows where that island is. God's power took us out and put us on dry land. Even if we put all our power together, we cannot excel God; for he has more power than that of all things on earth put together.

P. G.

107. THE DOG AND THE OTTER

A dog used to come through the channel into Pictou Harbor, bark, swim far up the river, return to the Straits, then return, dive, and not be seen or heard of again for perhaps a month. The Indians said it was the devil, trying to frighten them. The priest erected a cross by the shore. A sea otter went up the river and fought with the dog. They raised foam like that caused by a ship at full speed. Later they were seen out in the Straits, and finally far out beyond Merigomish, though nothing was then visible except the splashing water. The dog was never seen again.

J. N.

108. EAGLE AND FISHHAWK

In the old days the birds and the beasts had the same language as people.

An eagle is sitting on a tree. He sees a fish on top of the water. He makes a swoop, thrusts his foot into the water, and takes the fish. A fishhawk is looking at him. Eagle asks, "If there is a storm, and the water becomes very muddy, how will you get your living?" Fishhawk: "You see how I make my living?" Fishhawk goes out, flops his wings,

PART TWO *Folktales and Traditions*

and soars above the water. Suddenly he dives, and secures a fat fish. He takes it ashore. "That is the way for you to do." "No, I get my living in my own way." Eagle flies down and secures a fish with his claws, as before. "I can have my breakfast, dinner, and supper." Fishhawk: "What will you do in the winter?" "I stay here in the winter, but you go south. I wear a big warm coat. I'll stay here until the ice comes, and, perhaps, all winter." Kingfisher says to Fishhawk, "Don't you believe that fellow. Get your food as I do." Kingfisher dives into the water and gets some food. Eagle: "Because of the way in which I get my food, I live longer than you. You live only a few years; I live one hundred years."

This is the story an old man told me. Formerly birds and people must have had the same language.

109. WHALE [*PUDAP*]

Four canoes went up a river. All the people in them, except two, were killed. A monster about a fathom long came out of the lake and killed them. The surviving man and woman returned to their settlement down the river.

All the people in the settlement then went to that place. They found the bodies of the dead, and buried them. About twenty men went, chopped wood, and set fire to this pile. They cut a pine stick and stripped off the bark.

They went along the shore. They raised two big logs and watched [behind these?]. Soon these beasts came along. When the monsters put their heads on the log, the Indians cut them off and threw them on the fire. They continued this until midday of the following day, one man relieving another. Then they stopped. A man went away, made a larger circuit around the lake, and more of the beasts came. They killed all these, then made a still larger circuit. This time, none came; all had been killed. The men stayed here.

There were many beavers and all kinds of game. One foggy morning they went off in canoes to the other side of the lake. The lake was covered with foam. When they returned home, the foam had settled, and they saw a big beast coming toward them. It was so long that they called this snake a whale. They were paddling away from it as fast as possible, but the canoe was not moving, for the monster was drawing it to him. Finally, a man, John Tait, stood up and shot at it with bow and arrow. He shot again. The beast died, and made a wave which nearly upset them. They went home and prepared to leave at once, because another monster was coming. They paddled as rapidly as possible. They heard a big noise.

They went from the big water into a smaller stream, and looked back. The monster was raising water a hundred feet high. It could not go up the river, so turned and went back. Another time they went to that lake. The monster is called *pudap* [whale].

110. WHY THE WHALE CHEWS HIS FOOD

Three moose-hide canoes were crossing a bay and were upset by a whale which repaid himself for his trouble by devouring the crew. Gluskap said that was not right. He put his hand on the whale's head and told him not to do that again. Since that time, the whale has not been able to eat even a mackerel without chewing it.

111. HOW THE BEAVER OBTAINED HIS BROAD TAIL

Muskrat and Mole had a contest as to who could stay under water the longer. Mole won. Muskrat then went into the mud and burrowed into the ground.

Mole and Beaver had a dispute about their tails. Mole had a long flat tail, and Muskrat also had one. Beaver had a tail like that which Muskrat now has. Mole said to Beaver, "I know a man who can trade with you." "Who is that?" "Do you know a cousin of mine — his name is Kalus? He has a tail that will suit you." "Where is he?" "Go down that river. Some flax grows along it. He is there." The reference was to Muskrat — Kalus [Rand: Keooasoo]. When Muskrat heard this, he said, "Who sent you?" "Mole told me you had a tail which you would trade."

Muskrat went up the river to scold Mole. "I didn't tell him," said Mole; "I have no eyes. Look and see whether you can find any eyes." Muskrat looked, but saw no eyes. Beaver said, "You should trade. Your tail suits me." "What will you do [with it]?" "I am building a dam. I could use your tail as a trowel." "All right!" They exchanged. Beaver now has a broad tail, and can make a big dam.[6] J. N.

112. ADVENTURES WITH GEESE AND SPIDER

There was a man who always denied everything he saw or knew. One day he went into the woods and saw Crane sitting on the other side of

[6] This is a widely spread motive. I have recorded it, in a slightly different version, among Canadian Dakota.

the river. "What are you doing there?" "I'm getting fish." "You can't get fish—your neck is too slim, and it is too short." He broke off a stick the shape of Crane's neck and showed it to him. "See that! That is like your neck. Don't try to catch fish." The man went away.

That night many geese and ducks came. He invited them into the wigwam. They came in. "When I give you a signal," he said, "shut your eyes." All closed their eyes. "I shall dance around the fire. Don't open your eyes until I have finished. If you open your eyes while I'm dancing, you will lose your sight."

He danced one round. During the second round, he caught them by the neck. He had told them he would touch them on the second round, but that they should not open their eyes. He crushed their heads with his teeth. He killed all on one side. A black duck on one side then opened one eye, just a little, saw what was going on, and said, "Quack! Quack! Quack!" All opened their eyes and flew away, but he had gotten many of them.

Next day the man walked about in the woods, wondering what he could get to live on. He saw a woman in a wigwam, went in, but did not like the people there, and did not stay. He walked, walked, walked, and at last arrived at a river. He did not know what kind of river it was. He tasted the water, but did not know what river it was. He was frightened; he feared the river would hurt him. At night, he went far from the river and camped under a bush, afraid that the river would pounce upon him. At last he saw coming toward him what he thought was a bear with a big lump on its back.

"Where is your wigwam?" he asked. "I have none." "Where are you going, Grandmother?" "I am going to set my net." "Where is your net?" "Here on my back—with it I catch beasts, birds, and anything in the water." "Let me see, Grandmother, how you set your net." She goes up and spins a web around and around. "But how can you catch birds and things?" "Come here." The man discovered that he was caught, and could not escape. Spider laughed and laughed, until he stretched his arms. Up to that time they were short; but ever since then they have been long. The man begged her to take him out [of the net] and save his life. She did so. He said he would go away. She told him how to reach home. She had set many nets on the path. She directed him to go along the path in which these nets were set.

Spider followed him. He did not see the net, and walked into it. She

Animal Stories

arrived. "Why do you spoil my net?" "I didn't see your net, Grandmother. I can't get out."

She took him out, and he went on. He walked into another net. She took him out, and told him not to go into any more nets, lest he spoil them. He was going to the shore. He told Spider to go out on a long point (showing her where this was), called *Kukinaidjinanenik* [Grandmother's Point]. She went there, and couldn't get back. (This point resembles an old woman, sitting, and smoking a pipe. There is one such, known as Bell's Point, at Baddeck, and one between Cheticamp and Margaree.)

113. MOOSE AND CARIBOU

A moose and a caribou were with their mothers. They were ready to go away, by themselves. They traveled together. They were together from spring until fall. In the fall they decided to part company. One went south (this was Moose) and the other went north (this was Caribou).

Moose visited two porcupines [Matawes]. They were old people, lived alone, and had no children. He was given beans to eat. He spent the night with them, and kept the old man talking all evening, directing him [Moose] where to go to find more people.

In the morning he left, and found another little camp. In this wigwam he found only four people: two old ones, a young girl, and a young boy. They were Muspitc [Minks], which are always four in number. He was given, to eat, something that grows in trees. They pulled down a great many seeds and made a fine dinner for Moose. He stayed there all night, getting the old man to talk and direct him where to go.

Next morning, he left. He found a little wigwam with six in it — Aliistaneot [Martens]. He spent the night there. He had a gay time with the young fellows. He had the old fellow talking all evening, telling him where to find more people.

He traveled on and came to a little wigwam in which there were two old people. That was in a den. They were Muin [Bears]. They induced him to stay all night. He persuaded the old man to talk and tell him where to find more people. The old man took his knife, cut something from the soles of his feet, and put this in the pot. Moose had a first-rate dinner from it. Moose thought he had never eaten anything as good as that. The old man asked him where he was going. He did not know

PART TWO *Folktales and Traditions*

precisely, and wanted the old man to direct him to a place where he would find more people.

He traveled on. At the next place there was no wigwam. They seemed to be very poor people. Anyway, they lived happily. They were only two. Their name was Abaligamutc [Rabbits]. He ate dinner there. The meal was very nice.

Next morning he traveled on. He went a little way and found a wigwam with six in it. In the evening he had a very fine time with the young fellows. They bade him spend the night with them. He did so. They were Pulawetc [Partridges]. He had a nice dinner with them. He induced the old man to talk and direct him where to find others.

He traveled on and found a wigwam with four in it. The first words from the old man were "There is my son-in-law coming in!" (There were two girls in the wigwam.) They invited him to spend the night. He persuaded the old man to talk and direct him where to find more people. He did not promise to stay.

He left, and traveled until he came to a lake. At the lake, he met two young fellows. They asked him where he was going. He said he did not know. He visited with these people. A young fellow said, "It is not very safe for you to cross the lake; the ice is not strong enough to hold you. It will be best for you to go around the lake; if you do so, you will find some people."

He did so. He found a place with four in it. He went in. They invited him to enter, and asked him where he came from. He said he had come a long way, and had seen all those people [mentioned above]. The young fellow bade his mother put the pot on the fire, and prepare dinner. She did so. The young fellow went out, twisted a little branch of yellow birch, and tied it around himself. He went to the lake, where there was a hole in the ice, and dived into the water. Soon he returned, and brought a string of eels. That was Otter [Giwanik]. The old lady cooked the eels, and they had a fine dinner.

Next morning, he left. He went around the lake until he came to another wigwam. There were only two occupants. They seemed very saucy, but he paid no attention to them. He stayed there a long time. Before any of them would speak, they merely laughed a little while at each other. After a while the old man spoke. He said, "Which way are you going?" He did not know. This was Woodchuck [Munamkwetc]. They are saucy. The first thing they do is laugh.

Animal Stories

He traveled on and came to another little place where were four: two old ones and two young fellows. When he stepped in, they jumped out of their wigwam — every one. They were Skus [Weasels]. They came back and looked in. Whenever he moved, they jumped away from him. It was a very, very, cold night, and they had to come in. So they did. Every one of them came in while Moose was sleeping.

In the morning he traveled on. He could get no information out of the old man or any of them. He came to Amaltcigwetc [Raccoon]. There were seven, all females. They stayed with their mother. When he looked into the wigwam, the old woman said, "Aha! there's my son-in-law coming in! Now, my boy, get ready and take your choice of these girls. Whichever you like, you may have as your wife." He went in, and promised to stay.

The old lady said, "Now, boy, you must do this: you must sleep with me the first night." Thus he was told what to do. She made a bed of moose and bear skins and took nine skins with which to cover him. He had a little knife, and cut every skin that she lay over him, so that there was an opening through which he could breathe. Every now and then the old lady would feel him over the heart, to see whether it was still beating. At last he said, "What is the matter, old woman? I want to sleep. Lie still! I want to sleep. I'm tired." It was then nearly daylight. The old woman was angry, because she could not smother him. She took all her skins, crossed to the opposite side of the wigwam, and lay down there and slept. He had a gay time with the girls all day, and took the best one — the youngest.

Toward night the old woman said, "Now, son-in-law, we must get some wood." He agreed. They started. They came to Aksuskeget [Hemlock]. The young fellow grasped a long pole, bent the tree [with it], then jumped to one side. Every piece of bark on the tree came to the ground, like a shower of pins. He made a bundle of this hemlock bark and carried it home to be used for firewood. The old woman returned home angry, because she could not kill Moose. He said nothing, but had a gay time with the girls.

Next morning the old woman said, "Now, boy, we shall go fishing [*weskikwa*]." She said to him, "There is your harpoon — *njlebietc muktabama.*" In the canoe she kept one hand on her bosom, and paddled with one arm. When he saw her coming toward him, he raised his spear and struck her. He held her on his spear until the shaft broke. Down she went.

PART TWO *Folktales and Traditions*

He saw salmon, caught them, and took them home. The girls asked about their mother, but learned nothing. They did not know she had returned. She did not come in until after they had gone to sleep. In the morning the old woman felt so sick that she could not eat breakfast. They asked, "What is wrong with you, old woman?" She pretended that nothing was wrong — until they saw the spearhead that had penetrated her arm. He said, "Hello! old woman! How did you get this spearhead into you?" He put his foot on her, grasped the spearhead by the butt, and drew it out.

A few days later she had recovered, and was as well as ever. "*Nahea tahisak menawek* [We shall go to the island to gather the eggs of wild fowl]." They did so. They started toward the island in a canoe. She planned to leave him on the island. They went to the island and gathered eggs until they had a good load. He did not know where she was. After a while she came out. They were almost ready to go.

Then she came. She said, "*Nahe entalusak maniskeau amalaadjkal waal kesonoweskewidjit wilul* [You go, son-in-law, and get the spotted eggs of all colors that I left at the place where my jacket is hanging]." She had picked the best looking eggs to take to her youngest child, who was her favorite, and also was his wife. He ran. He hunted for her jacket, but could not find it. He ran a long way. While he was searching for the jacket, the old woman took the canoe, and left him on the island. When he returned, the old woman had gone. He did not know what to think, and did not know how to plan to get across. There were many young birds nearly ready to fly. He picked up a large number of them and strung them together. When they raised themselves to fly, he took hold of them, and, thus transported, came ashore ahead of the others. The birds landed him there.

The girls asked about their mother. He told them, "She is coming in the canoe." They asked, "How did you get home before she did?" He had brought home several dead, and several live, birds. "This is how I did it: the birds brought me across, because she had left me on the island." She came home. All ran down to help her out of the canoe and onto the shore. The old woman said not a word. But she was furious, because she had not been able to detain him on the island. The girls prepared dinner.

When they had eaten dinner, the old woman said, "Now, *entalusak* [son-in-law] this will be the last thing for us to do." So she said. The

Animal Stories

young man asked what they would do. She asked him, "Can you wrestle well?" He said he did not know how, but would try. They went to a wrestling place, where she was accustomed to wrestle. There, where she had wrestled, he saw many bones. When they stood up and took "backholds," she made a wish:*"Makam saksegie kiskodanak ulun* [May the flint come out sharp and he be thrown upon it]!" Thus had she always done. They wrestled. The young fellow threw her and smashed her up.[7]

LOUIS GLODE

114. PARTRIDGE AND HIS FAMILY

Every day Partridge hunted, to get food for his family. When he obtained no game, he took little strips off his back, and soon had a load to take home. Because of this, he became weak and was fagged. Every night, upon his return home, he went to bed early. He lay down by the fire, opposite his wife, and warmed his back. In due time, old wife Partridge noticed that her husband was becoming slow and sluggish. She decided to investigate, and found out what was the matter with the old man. They had only two children. One night, when the old man was asleep, she went to him and lifted his shirt. Behold! His entire back was stripped, and every particle [of flesh which had been there] had been eaten.

She pitied him, and decided to leave him. She waited, next day, until he had gone to hunt. She removed the wigwam pole which was next to the entrance, sat down by the hole, and cried. She cried until she had cried herself down into the hole from which she had removed the pole. She left the surface [of this world] and entered another world, a very pretty country. She traveled over this country until she came to a brook. There she sat down and washed. She washed herself, and combed her hair. She put red ocher on her cheeks, and made herself very beautiful.

Thus painted, she traveled on until she came to a very large encampment. She went into a little wigwam. Here lived Marten and his grandmother. They were poor. Marten ran from wigwam to wigwam, trying to get enough for the woman's supper. The rumor spread that a pretty woman had come to the settlement. Every man wanted her as his wife.

[7] The story now resumes with Caribou, who makes a similar round of visits to various animals and has similar experiences. He visits otter, beaver, mink, raccoon, fox, wolf, deer, and stag. Unfortunately, I did not hear the remainder of the story. See Tale 2.

PART TWO *Folktales and Traditions*

She told the people, "The one who first gathers food enough to make a big feast I'll marry." Next day all the young fellows went to hunt.

There lived in that place an old crow, a widower, who had several children. He got busy and tried to make a feast, in order to obtain the pretty woman. He told his children to go in every direction and gather up all the dog manure, "the whiter it is, the better — it's the fattest." He filled his cooking pots with this. In a short time, all were ready for the feast, and he told one of the little crows to bring his [the latter's] stepmother. She said to him, "I don't want your dog manure feast." The little boy ran home. "Well, what did your stepmother say?" "She said she did not want your dog manure feast." "Well, how kind she is! Now, children, make a feast for yourselves." The chief's son was the first man to bring in a moose, and he made a feast. A wedding celebration was held, and for several days there was dancing and feasting.

Old Partridge and his children were living where they were when the wife and mother left. He became lonely, and asked his children, "What was your mother doing when she went away?" They answered, "She took up the entrance pole and cried until she went down into the ground." The old man did the same. He, too, passed from the surface [of this world] into the other world. There he saw the tracks of his old wife. He followed her tracks to the brook. There he washed, applied red ocher, and made himself into a very beautiful man. He followed the tracks of his wife to the encampment. He stayed a little while at the first wigwam, where Marten and his grandmother lived. The old woman told him his wife had come to the settlement and had married. He remained there. When wife Partridge heard that such a man had come, she knew he was her husband. She told her present husband to kill the stranger and make of his skin a flap for the entrance to their wigwam. That was done. They killed poor old Partridge, skinned him, and with the skin made an entrance flap for her.

The little partridge boy and the little partridge girl became lonely. They took out the entrance pole and sat down and cried, as their father had done. They, likewise, went below the surface, and came to the other world. They found the tracks of their father and those of their mother, followed them to a brook, washed themselves, put red ocher on their faces, and made themselves into very pretty children.

They arrived at the wigwam of Marten and his grandmother. They stayed there. The old woman knew at once who they were. She told them

Animal Stories

their mother had come to the settlement and had married, their father had come, and had been killed. They stayed there two days. One morning, the woman made them wash, fix themselves up, and go to the chief's wigwam, to see their mother.

She told them, "Don't run to her or act as though she is your mother. Merely see what she will do." They went to their mother. The little boy was the younger. When they went in, he was about to make a leap toward his mother, but the little girl held him by the sleeve and stopped him. The mother pretended that she did not see them. After a little while she rose and threw down two pieces of meat from the pole on which they hung, and said to the children, "Go back to the old woman. Something might hurt you." People thought that the little boy looked much like the man who had been killed there, and that the little girl looked much like the woman, the chief's son's wife, and they suspected something [foul play]. The children's mother thought about this, and was afraid people would discover the truth. She therefore made a plan. She said to the people, "It is always bad luck if two children, by themselves, come to a place. Something serious will happen. It would be well if all should leave and go somewhere else."

They moved. She said, "Let us tie those children up in a tree." They did not kill the children, but tied them high up in a tall tree. She then went about and put water on every fire in the camp, to douse them. Marten and his grandmother were the last to leave. The grandmother said to Marten, "Can you gnaw the straps with which the children are tied?" She threw to him an old moccasin, and he bit through it. "Yes, I can do it," he said.

His grandmother held a piece of *elgadu* [a punk-like growth on the outside bark of trees] near the fire and, when it became red hot, hid it. She gathered all the hair and put this around the tree at the top of which the children were tied. This would prevent their being hurt when they fell down. The chief's wife said to the old woman, "Hurry!" "Well, I'll have to fix Marten's moccasins — they are very poor." So she continued to mend them. When the others had started, he jumped up and gnawed the straps. The children fell on the hair and were not hurt.

The old woman made a little fire for them, and told them not to allow it to go out. Marten and his grandmother then left. The people were waiting for the old woman. The chief's wife told someone to go and see what was delaying her. She did not like the way the old woman was

PART TWO *Folktales and Traditions*

acting. They found her, and asked what was the trouble. "Well, Marten had such bad moccasins that I had to stop now and then and mend them." They traveled on, and camped in another place.

Meanwhile, the children were alive. They went about, gathered what scraps of food they could find, and at last made a wish for a plan. They wished for mice. Mice came in hundreds. They killed the mice for food, and lived on them. They wished for squirrels. When they were tired of these, they wished for rabbits. Another time the boy cut two sticks out of *habok* [said to be a small bush of white wood which does not grow to considerable size]. He wished that the size of themselves the next morning be the size [i.e., the length] of the sticks. These lay by them while they slept. When they arose, his stature was the length of his stick, and her height was the length of her stick.

It was winter. The boy, however, had grown, and could not go out, for the snow was deep. The girl made small snowshoes, and at night put them outside. Next morning, outside, there was a pair of big strong snowshoes.

The boy hunted, went around in a big circle, and drove all the moose into one place. The girl had long hair, which she used to comb. Every evening the boy came home. Every day a bear came and licked the girl's hair. The boy asked his sister what was the matter with her hair — every evening it was ruffled. She told him a bear came every day, when he was away, and licked her hair. He became angry. He said he would kill the bear. Next day, he followed the bear and overtook it. Before he shot it, the bear told him not to shoot his body, but, when he moved his paw, to shoot the undersurface of his foot. "And don't eat my flesh — give it to your enemies."

Meanwhile, the others had no provisions. They hunted, but got nothing, and at last became very hungry. They had eaten all the food in the settlement. The little boy had told the old woman she would know by this sign that they were safe: Marten would run around the wigwam and would find an arrow with fat about it. After every snowstorm Martin ran around the wigwam, and found an arrow covered with fat. He then knew that the children were still alive.

Every time a man went to hunt he found the tracks of snowshoes ahead of him, and he obtained no game. Finally the people were very hungry. Crow remembered that the children were tied up in the tree, and thought that if he went there he would get something. He went to that

444

Animal Stories

place. When he went inside, there were racks filled with meat. He was somewhat ashamed, did not like to go in, and flew around above the place, calling, "Caw! Caw! Caw!" Finally the boy said to his sister, "Call Uncle in." She called him in, and fed him. When he was ready to go home, she asked him whether he could take something home to his children. He said he could not take a very heavy load, but could take the intestines, wrapped around his neck. That night, when he arrived home, he threw the intestines in a circle around the fire. The little Crows made so much noise that the chief's wife heard them, and said, "Run over to Crow's, and see what they have gotten." When he heard them coming, Crow gathered *elagadutc* [punk from an old stump] and threw it over the intestines. They learned that he had intestines there, and took them away. Old Crow was angry, and flew high up into the air. "Caw! Caw!" he said, "those children who were tied up together were saved."

They then knew where he had procured the moose intestines. She [i.e., the chief's son's wife; she was sometimes referred to as the chief's wife] told them to go there again. They returned. Yes, there was plenty of meat. She said to them: "You are my own children." She showed them her breasts and said, "That is where you were nourished." They gave the people meat to eat. Next day they gave the bear meat to all of them except Marten, his grandmother, and the Crows. Next morning all the people who had eaten bear meat died. Grandmother, Crow, and the children lived happily ever afterward.[8]　　　　　SIMON BASQUE

115. THE KALU

Some children were playing in a valley. They saw a little deer. Kalu came with a sweep, like that of an eagle after salmon, and took the deer up to its young. The children ran away, but Kalu captured a boy and took him up to his nest. He intended to feed the boy to the little birds. They always kill their prey before they devour it. The boy held out his bow and arrow and kept the Kalu off. The Kalu took him into the nest. He lay down there. (At that time people could live on raw meat.) He ate raw deer meat, which the Kalu brought him on the top of this high mountain. Later it brought him down. He came home. All were surprised to see him alive. He described his adventures. There were four of these birds. Every day two of the Kalu brought the flesh of animals; but they never brought fish.　　　　　JOHN PAUL

[8] The concluding sentence suggests a recent addition.

PART TWO *Folktales and Traditions*

Two birds had a nest on the tower of Babylon. They were strong enough to kill a moose and carry it up there. A Micmac was taken there by these birds. Kalu is the name of this bird. There were two little ones. They carried up a moose, a caribou, and a bear.

[The informant quotes the Micmac who was carried to the nest] "I used to cut them up and feed the flesh to the little birds. There were holes there and plenty of water, and we all drank from them. One day the bird brought up under one leg a big bundle of wood. He told me to make a fire. While it was raining, the little one went under the wing of the large bird, and I did likewise. One day, I killed one of them, took its skin, wrapped myself up tightly in it, and went down. When I was about a fourth of a mile away, I heard them coming. I cut the skin away, and ran toward the woods. I heard them overhead in the trees, breaking limbs more easily than a man can break them. I ran all day."

That is how we know about those birds. There is now a big lake around the tower of Babylon. The tower settled into the ground, and water gathered around it.

CHAPTER XI

History and Tradition

THROUGH most of these stories of relations with Maliseet and Mohawk, with English and French, and with present-day Canadians, there runs one simple theme: everyone fears the supernatural power of the Micmac. In legends a single Micmac *buoin* conquers an entire raiding party of the Mohawk who, in actual life, were feared at least as late as 1911. The same type of victory characterizes the conflicts with European soldiers; and Mohawk crimes, such as roasting children on spits, are attributed to French or English. Many highly similar variants of Mohawk and English-French fight tales have been removed from this 1911–12 collection.

In the accounts of devastating fires at Miramichi in 1825 and at Campbellton in 1910, retribution visits whites who abuse Indians; this concept is also present in Tale 70 of "Old Sallie and the Conductor." In 1953 it was still expressed, sometimes with the explanation that the evil falls without any "bad wish" consciously made by Indian against white. Micmac just have the power.

Other Tribes

116. MALISEET

On two occasions, all the Maliseet were nearly killed. When the whites first settled near them, they gave these Indians five pounds of flour. The flour had been poisoned. A Maliseet woman said, "Do not eat that! First give some of it to the dogs." Accordingly, they gave cakes made from it to two dogs; and soon both dogs were dead.

When a Maliseet meets a Micmac, the former appears to be unaware of the presence of the latter and walks past him without, apparently, knowing of his existence; then, after he has walked past, he turns and

PART TWO *Folktales and Traditions*

comes back. The Maliseet, the Micmac say, like to be close to the Micmac, because the former are so small [they are, as a matter of fact, not smaller than the Micmac]; and have never fought the Micmac [some deny this], because they were never sufficiently numerous. On the other hand, they aided the Micmac. Some Micmac, likewise, say that they have never fought the Penobscot.

117. MONTAGNAIS

The Mountaineers are as afraid of us as are the Maliseet. I was in Labrador. I went ashore. There were several in a bunch. After a while, I went toward them. Soon every one of them went away and left me alone.   J. N.

118. WESTERN INDIANS

A Micmac was out west, in an Indian tribe. The men were sitting close to a spring, waiting for moose to come. That is the way they hunt moose. He rolled a piece of bark into a horn, and called the moose. Soon a moose came, and he shot it. Next morning he did the same. They talked among themselves, and one of them then asked him who he was. "I am a Micmac," he said. After they heard that he was a Micmac, they went away and left him, and he never saw them again.   JOHN PAUL

All the other Indians were afraid of the Micmac. This was because the Micmac had very powerful medicinemen. A man from here [Pictou Landing] was in the far west, in the harvest fields. Two Indians came toward him. They were on horseback and looked big and fierce. When he saw them, he was a bit frightened. They looked very wild. They asked him who he was. He said he was an Indian. "We thought you were an Indian," they said. "What tribe are you?" "I'm a Micmac." When they heard the word "Micmac," they seemed to dodge on their saddles, and they looked uneasy. He asked them to visit him, and they said they would. They went away and never came near that Micmac again. He told his employer about this encounter. The employer said, "They are afraid of the Micmac; you will never see those Indians again."   J. N.

119. MOHAWK

The Mohawk have great fear of the Micmac. Two or three of them come here every year, selling beads, but they do not stay with us. I saw one at Pictou. I asked him to stay at my house for two or three days — "It won't cost you anything," I said. "We are busy on this side, all day selling beads," he said, "and the ferry doesn't run after six o'clock." "Come Saturday night," said I; "it runs until nine o'clock Saturday night." "I'll try," he said. When he said "I'll try," I knew he meant that he would not come. They never stay with us — they are that much afraid of us.

The enmity between the Micmac and the Mohawk came about in this way: A Micmac and a Mohawk boy killed a white squirrel, and each wanted to take it home. The boys fought, and the Mohawk boy killed the Micmac boy. That is how the fighting started. J. N.

120. GAINSKUGWAK

Gainskugwak are Mohawk who come from Quebec. In the daytime they are in the form of squirrels or of birds, and at night throw stones at the wigwams. They never do any other injury. Some of them go around selling beadwork. [The word means "those who go sneaking around."]

Fifteen or twenty years ago the Gainskugwak were in every reserve, and about half a dozen were captured. They were in the shape of men. A Micmac met them in a path. They asked him, in English, about good places to hunt, and so on, and were dressed in English style. The Micmac replied, "I do not know of any game in this little strip of woods. It's a peculiar question that you fellows ask me. Why don't you go way up country [i.e., up north] where there is plenty of woods?" They were then in Cape Breton, in a small cluster of trees surrounded by an open space. The Micmac, after encountering these strangers, ran rapidly around the clump. He saw them hiding their coats and other clothes, getting ready to turn themselves into birds, or into some kind of animal. He thought, "I shall get you fellows this time." He went to his wigwam and procured a knife, bow, and arrows. He killed five of them. The sixth was wrapping up his clothes into a bundle and had not noticed that the others had been shot. The Micmac jumped toward them, took one of them by the throat, and said, "I know you fellows are not out to hunt or to look for game. I think you have found all of the game you want today."

With this he took out his knife, cut off the man's ears, a piece of skin from each cheek and from nose, mouth, and chin, and told him to go home and say to his people, "This is what the Micmac did to me." The man is alive today in Caughnawaga. Since that time no one has come here to throw stones at our houses. When the Mohawk arrived home, he said to the people, "This is what the Micmac did to me. I could not defend myself. They were in the bushes, watching, when it happened."

T. M.

121. MOHAWK MAGIC AND MICMAC MAGIC

Two Micmac left Merigomish, to go to the northwest. They saw two big salmon, on the ground, shaking their tails, as a bird does. They killed them with sticks, cooked them, and ate a portion. Two Mohawk were with them.

The Mohawk would not eat of these fish, for they knew the flesh was poison. (Mohawk are poison; and these salmon were transformed Mohawk.) The Micmac ate a great deal. The Mohawk expected them to die. "Why don't you eat? There is plenty of them in our country," said the Micmac. "What is your country?" "We are Micmac." The Mohawk were frightened. The Micmac did not die. Next morning they ate some of the fish.

They went farther, and saw in the woods a "lobster" with small legs, not big legs like those of our sea lobster. They ate it and did not die. They came to a big lake, and crossed it on a raft. They camped about half a mile from the river. At night they heard a noise as loud as thunder.

The Mohawk started to run away and leave the Micmac to the mercy of these beasts. It was a tremendously loud noise. The Micmac got up and looked about them. The beasts were as big as hogsheads, and had large claws. They sank into the ground, when they trod, to a depth of about six inches. A Micmac grabbed a firebrand and gave the monster a blow on the head. The beasts retreated. The Micmac shouted, and finally the four Mohawk returned.

In the morning, one of the Micmac said, "Why did those beasts come here?" "I do not know," replied the Mohawk. "Yes, you know. If you do not know, I'll tell you, so that you will know: You wished to torture us before you killed us. If I had wanted to kill you, I would do it myself. I would not enlist the services of a monster." The Micmac rose. His brother-in-law said, "Don't hurt them," and restrained the man. Next morning, the Mohawk were so weak from fear that they could not get up. The Micmac gave them some medicine which enabled them to recover their strength. The Mohawk then went away.

History and Tradition

The Micmac crossed the lake, on a raft. That night, the beasts did not come. One of the Micmac wanted the other one to go away with him from the water because the beasts might come if they remained there. The other said, "No, I do not want to go far away from the water." Next morning, one of them said, "Now we will go straight over there." They asked the Mohawk, "Will you go with us?" "I do not know. We cannot walk on the water." The Micmac took off their moccasins and gave them to the Mohawk to see whether they would fit. The moccasins went around in a circle and came back to the Micmac. The Micmac said to his brother-in-law, "Watch where I put my foot on the water, and put yours exactly in the same spot." He did so, and thus they crossed the lake. He said to the Mohawk, "If I had wanted to kill you, I would have done so." In those days, the Micmac were so full of magic, that they could do anything. J. N.

122. MOHAWK FIGHTS AT BARNEY RIVER

This happened at Barney River, near Merigomish. The Mohawk killed all the Micmac who were there, except one woman. They roasted two children on spits. She hid in eel grass, and counted the Mohawk when each jumped over a stick. Next morning, canoes started out from a nearby camp, and their occupants saw the children who had been roasted. One child, who was not killed, had lost the entire scalp. The child told a man from the canoes, "I was here alone, father." The man placed his head on the child's head, and its head was healed. They went to Little Harbor. There the man, a *buoin*, went ashore. It was a calm day, but the water was as rough as on a windy day.

The *buoin* said to the Mohawk, "Why didn't you go to a settlement [instead of killing children]?" He cut off the nose and the lips of the Mohawk. The Micmac chief had said to his "captain," "Tell the Mohawk chief there are about one hundred of us here — don't tell him there are four hundred." The Mohawk chief asked, "How many are you?" "Not many — only about a hundred. We haven't good fields, and cannot grow good crops." "One hundred of you will be a good crop — you will make good manure." Next morning, four hundred Micmac came out. The Mohawk did not kill one Micmac. The boys went to the opposite shore and played as if nothing were happening. The Micmac chief said to the Mohawk chief, "Do not go to the Micmac again! If you go, you will get

PART TWO *Folktales and Traditions*

what you deserve. Yes, if you try to do that, we will serve you the same way, and there will not be one Mohawk in the world."

The Micmac went out and stayed close to the road which the Mohawk took when leaving. They heard someone yelling, and this continued throughout the night. The Mohawk were passing by there until break of day. Perhaps they were ghosts, or something strange.

The Mohawk then went home. It was the last time they fought with the Micmac. J. N.

123. A MICMAC *BUOIN* AND HIS WIFE FIGHT MOHAWK

A Micmac man and woman married and went away to live in the woods. The woman became lonesome. The husband, too, felt lonesome and thought of going home.

He was not well pleased. The wife was cooking a kind of moss, called *agasan,* gathered from the stones along streams. She intended to make soup of it. The husband came home and commenced to eat supper. He said to her, "What would you say if the Mohawk yelled at us?" "I would not say anything — merely spill this soup on you." (The dish was slippery.)

The Mohawk yelled, and she spilled the soup on her husband. He jumped out of the hole in the wigwam and walked over the heads of the Mohawk. With an axe, she killed them, one by one, as they came in the entrance, until the entrance was filled. She heard her husband giving the war whoop.

He fought them all night. He shouted to her to run away if she could. While her husband was fighting the Mohawk, she ran out between their legs. Next day, he ran away. She went in a canoe. He killed a dozen or more of those who tried to stay him; then another bunch of about a dozen who tried to intercept him; the fourth time this happened, he had reached the canoe. When the man and his wife arrived at the settlement, they said to the people there, "Get us clothes." Both were naked.

Four canoes went up the river. They found hundreds and hundreds of unburied bodies. The Mohawk had lighted fires, and were cooking breakfast. A Micmac went alone to the Mohawk, and said, "Why did you not go farther down the river? There is a settlement farther down. Why did you fight with my children? Go home and tell your people that you saw a man and a woman in a wigwam, and next day you saw two other Micmac. I will give you a mark so that we will know you when you come

History and Tradition

back." He then cut off the nose, ears, and lips of the Mohawk, who died, and did not get back, ever.

This was before the whites came.

124. FIGHTS WITH MOHAWK AND ENGLISH

Nine men left Merigomish. The Mohawk chief was at Pugwash, with warriors. The second in command went to the Micmac camp, and announced, "Tomorrow we will have a meeting." "All right." The Micmac went to the place of meeting. The chief was there, with his hatchet and some punk. The Mohawk chief made a gesture toward the Micmac chief, signifying that the latter should sit by him. The Mohawk trimmed off some of the punk, as tobacco for his pipe, then stabbed the Micmac in the leg with the knife which he had used. If the Micmac had shown signs of fear, the Mohawk would have stabbed him through the heart. Even so, two Micmac were killed that day. Three Maliseet were with them. These Maliseet said, "In a few days all of us will be killed."

A Micmac, who was a Migamawesu, said, "We will kill them." A Maliseet who was likewise a Migamawesu, said, "Brother, I will help you." The Migamawesu sat by the Mohawk. The Mohawk drew his knife. The Micmac suddenly stabbed him, and killed him. Another Mohawk came in and sat down in the place where his comrade had been killed. The Micmac killed him, in the same way, and took the body out. Then a Mohawk objected, "That is no way to play. Soon, all of us shall be killed." The Migamawesu said, "I took pity on you, else two of my men would not have been killed. Do you not know me?" "Is that you?" They shook hands. The Micmac said, "If I had not taken pity on you, all of you would have been killed." "Tomorrow our young men will play." They indicate the time of day [by holding out a fist with the thumb pointing upward].[1]

They met. The Migamawesu had taken his life [his soul] out and hidden it in a bush.[2] The Mohawk had an old musket — no one knows where he got it. The Mohawk perceived that the Micmac did not have his life, and he [the Mohawk] did not know where to shoot in order to kill him. The Mohawk had put his own life on the middle of the barrel of the musket. The Micmac stabbed it, and killed the Mohawk. The Mohawk fell, his body in one place, and his head in another, with the

---
[1] This indicates the position of the sun above the horizon.
[2] This is a European concept.

PART TWO *Folktales and Traditions*

scalp off. Then the fighting stopped. Two Maliseet had participated in the fighting.

After supper, a big eagle sat on top of the wigwam. A Micmac picked up a bow and arrow, and killed it. He thus killed the best man the Mohawk had.

Later, a fish hawk perched in the same place. He shot at it three times, but could not hit it. The fish hawk flew away, and later returned. Again he shot at it, and again failed to kill it. That settled the matter.

Some time after this, two Micmac who were in the woods felt that something was wrong. They returned to camp. The wife of one of them was gone. The Mohawk had come from the Mississippi [!] and taken her away. When the Mohawk arrived home with her, his people asked who she was. "I think she is a Micmac." "Was she married?" "Yes, for we saw something which belongs to men." They said, "In the spring you must take her back, because, otherwise, they will come for her." She learned to talk Mohawk.

The Micmac men went to Quebec, and stayed there until spring. In the spring, the young Micmac said, "Father, I shall go to see my wife. She will be lonely." The wife went to the river to get water, and heard her husband singing. When she returned, the Mohawk asked, "Did you hear anything?" "No." Next day it was the same.

The Mohawk took the woman to her [Micmac] home. After she arrived in the settlement, there was good cheer. They asked her where she had been, and how she had been treated. She said she had been treated well, in regard to both food and clothing. "Did you come alone?" "No, a man brought me. He went home a few minutes ago." Her Mohawk escort was a powerful medicineman. Next morning, one of her brothers was dead. The fourth night, another one died. The medicineman had killed them. The woman who had reached home told her story, then died. Witchcraft had caused her death.

The Micmac men left Quebec, and went to Red Bank. They traveled up the river and met two Mohawk, who were lost. They made good cheer. The Mohawk said nothing. They stayed there a week, and hunted. Then a Mohawk asked, "What direction do we take for Quebec?" The Micmac made a map on birch bark, with charcoal, showing the rivers and the route. The Micmac stayed there through the winter and the following spring.

One of these Micmac went to the river, where he saw salmon. He

History and Tradition

sharpened a stick and speared a salmon. He was far from his home — he did not know where he was. While he was roasting the salmon on two sticks, before a fire, he saw a canoe approaching. He went away and hid.

The people in the canoe were talking. He learned they were Micmac. They saw the fire and smoke and began talking about who had made it. Meanwhile, they made preparations to kill him. He called to them, "I am a Micmac." They gave him something to eat. He asked the name of the river. "The Mississippi." "How far away am I?" "Three or four months." He told them he had been looking for a good place to settle, and when he found one, would go home and bring his wife. "You should go home with us." They paddled on.

Finally, they saw a camp. "Are these Micmac?" "Yes." All the people came out to see him. The men said, "This is our brother. We found him by the river." He stayed there three or four days, then started toward home. They made a map, and showed him the nearest way home.

He went up as far as Red River. A [English] war vessel was anchored there. Some officers came ashore and asked for the Micmac chief. The chief asked them how far up the river they intended to go. "As far as a war vessel can go." "You cannot go farther than here." "Oh, yes." "No; I shall not allow you to go up." "If you prevent me from going up, you will not have many camps left here." (I suppose the ship had gotten lost.)

Next morning a man came, on horseback, with all kinds of animals. Soldiers went ashore. Soon all were killed, except one man. This Englishman returned to Halifax. He was a slave in the chief's house, where he worked all the time. When they found that he worked very well, and very steadily, the chief said, "We should keep this man." Some [young?] men went to hunt. They said to their fathers, "We shall go to hunt. We will return in a week." Later they said, "Father, we will stay two or three weeks." After the young men started, they said to the Englishman, "We will try to save you; we heard the old people say they would kill you." Three weeks later they arrived at another shore. They gave the Englishman provisions, and left him there. Finally, the Englishman sighted a war vessel. His name was "Micmac." He stole a flag, put a pole on it, and raised it on a point of land. The crew saw the flag, and sent a boat. He replied to their signals, and they took him on board.

This was about four hundred years ago, before North America was discovered. An English war vessel was here before the French discovered America and claimed it. The man who had this experience was

PART TWO *Folktales and Traditions*

the ancestor, by four generations, of the grandfather of the white man who narrated this adventure to the Indians.   J. N.

125. WEDJIBOKWEDJIK [THE LITTLE BOY WHO HAS FITS]: A MICMAC *GINAP* WHO SLEW MOHAWK[3]

Before Wedjibokwedjik was born, his father and mother went on a long trip into the woods. After one day's long hunt, they had nothing to bring home. They saw the Mohawk [tracks] coming [toward them]. The husband went into the woods, broke off branches, and put three or four of them in the brook. In the morning he said to his wife, "Do not go there. Promise me you will not go." "Yes, I promise you I will not go."

When, on the following day, he returned from the hunt, he had killed nothing. The reason was that there was plenty of food at home. Next day, he repeated his injunction to his wife, and added, "Have you been there?" "No." He felt something different — a depressed feeling. He knew she had been there. He asked her again. She answered, "Yes." He said, "I told you not to go." Next day, five Mohawk came and asked the woman, "What kind of man is your husband? Can he withstand a big fight?" "No, he is scarcely able to kill an animal," she replied. "Tonight," they said, "when your husband comes home, partly sever the strings on his snowshoes, so that, when he goes out, they will break and cause him trouble."

The woman, however, did not cut them, but told her husband what had happened. He made for himself new snowshoe strings, and put them in. About ten o'clock the Mohawk came. The man jumped out of the wigwam and fought them until nearly daylight, when he was killed. The Mohawk numbered about two hundred and he had killed all except twenty of them. Those who remained came into the wigwam, took off their left moccasins, and threw them over the wife of the man who had

[3] This story appears in four highly similar versions, three from the Miramichi region of New Brunswick (Red Bank, 1; Burnt Church, 2) and one from Pictou Landing, Nova Scotia. The following account is a synthesis of the four. Likeness to the Ginap tale (Tale 78) is evident. The difference is in emphasis; here Micmac-Mohawk relations are more important than supernatural prowess in hunting.

Remarks by informants, injected during the narration were these: Wedjibokwedjik ("Little Fits") was the strongest man who ever lived. He could make fire by rubbing his thumb and first finger together. When he fought Mohawk, their arms were lifted to thrust spears at him but they were stayed in midair. They never did him harm.

For a version of this tale told at Restigouche (1910) see Michelson, "The Wejiboquet," JAFL, 38:41–51.

been killed, until she was covered with their moccasins. They then picked up the moccasins and put them on, until only one moccasin was left on the woman. The man to whom this moccasin belonged obtained the woman as his wife. He took her with him. She was with child, and soon gave birth to a boy.

The mother did not tell the boy that her Mohawk husband was not his father. When he was about five years old, playing with the other boys, and sometimes, when he was fighting them, they said, "You are a Micmac." Later he asked his mother, "Why do these boys call me Micmac? Every time I play with them, they call me a Micmac," he repeated. One day, however, when her husband was away, she said to the boy, "Yes, that is correct. Your father was a Micmac." He bade her, "Make me a suit of Micmac clothes and a pair of snowshoes." Reluctantly, she made them. He said to her, "Good-by; tonight I shall go away." The mother told him the name of his Micmac uncle. "If you find people using square-toed snowshoes, they are Micmac." (Only Micmac have square-toed snowshoes.)

That night, the boy takes his tomahawk, kills a man, goes to another wigwam, and kills another, six of the ablest and largest. The boy wishes a snowstorm to come behind him and cover his tracks. It snows, snows, snows.

In the morning the Mohawk found the six dead men and learned that the boy had gone. Twelve to fifteen men went after him. Wedjibokwedjik hid under the snow. The pursuers came up and stuck their spears into the snow, all about him, between his arms and his sides, and between his legs, but not once did they touch him. The disappointed Mohawk said, "Wait until the tenth of May — then we will get you." After the Mohawk had returned home, Wedjibokwedjik traveled a few days, and then crossed a track made by square snowshoes. The same happened on the following day. That night he buried himself in the snow. Next day, he found that he was close to a camp of these people.

He removed his snowshoes, lest these should give a false impression. [That is, indicate that he was a Mohawk.] He took out the small snowshoes which his mother had made for him and found that the tracks corresponded exactly with the shape of his model.

He came to a spring. He took balsam [gum], and coals from a fire, rubbed these over his face, and sat down in the snow, near the spring. A daughter of the chief came to get water. She saw this man, with ugly

PART TWO *Folktales and Traditions*

face, sitting there, up to his waist in the snow, went to her father, and said, "A man is sitting by the spring; I do not know whether he is a man or some kind of devil." Her father, the chief, went out, and saw him. "Who are you?" "I am a Micmac," the man answered. The chief was a *buoin*, and he knew at once that this man had some [magical] power. (The man, however, was not showing what he could do.) "Come to my wigwam," said the chief.

The oldest daughter of the chief would not marry the man — she said he was too ugly. She thought he was like a snake — all balsam gum and black. She was a very pretty girl. The younger daughter of the chief married him. He was lazy, and did nothing except stay near the fire in the morning, and sleep. One day he told his wife to bend him a pair of snowshoes. She bent him a pair of snowshoes; he put them on, and went out. After a while, the girl's father said to her, "You should go out and see whether he needs help with those snowshoes."

She went out, and found the man [fallen] in the snow. She helped him to his feet, and he went into the wigwam. "Bend me a pair of larger snowshoes," he said. She bent a pair of very large snowshoes. He went out. People watched him. He was taking steps about ten feet apart.

Later he returned with a moose, which he left at the spring. The father said to his daughter, "Get some water." When she arrived at the spring, she saw a moose. It was not quite dead. She told her father: "At the spring I saw a moose." The following day he [Wedjibokwedjik] went out, and presented his wife with blue Micmac clothes covered with beads. He put on the clothes which his mother had made for him. His mother-in-law did not know him. His wife ran to him, jumped up, sat on his knee, and kissed him — she liked him so much. Her three uncles came in and joined them in a festive celebration.

One day, in the spring, they saw a canoe coming, and soon the entire island was covered with the canoes of Mohawk. Throughout the night these Mohawk held a scalping dance. Wedjibokwedjik then told the people that the Mohawk had killed his father and had carried off his mother. The brother of his own father went out to fight the Mohawk, but was killed. Wedjibokwedjik then killed all of the four hundred to five hundred Mohawk, excepting two. He cut off the noses and ears of these two people and sent them to their homes to tell the people there how their warriors had been treated.

The Mohawk said, "Sometime they will come after his mother. You should return her to the place whence she came, and she will then go home of her own accord." They did this. Wedjibokwedjik saw his mother across the river. He caused a fog to form, walked over on the water, and brought his mother back. That was the last appearance of the Mohawk in the territory of the Micmac.

126. DUNEIL'S ADVENTURES WITH THE MOHAWK

One day a man was going far away in a canoe. He left his wife and family here [Burnt Church]. He went to Restigouche. The people at Restigouche went up the river with him. There were two canoes, carrying four men. They encountered a party of Mohawk. In the Micmac canoes there were only four men. When the Mohawk saw that there were only four men in the Micmac party, they attacked them, and killed three Micmac. He [the hero of the story] was not killed. In the morning he jumped into the water where it was very deep. When he reached Campbellton, there were cuts over his entire chest, and blood was running constantly from his wounds. When he reached the spring at Campbellton, he allowed the water from it to run over his chest. He had lost his man, and two other men had been killed.

When he was near Newcastle he began to sing, while he paddled his canoe. The other Indians listened. It was Duneil. They said, "Something has gone wrong with Duneil." That night, at Treasure Island, he told them, "I have been up the Restigouche River, and have lost three men. I intend to go back in the autumn — not now, but later, when the leaves begin to fall." (While the leaves were on, it was too light [meaning, the days were too long?].) He then removed his shirt and showed them the wounds on his chest, inflicted by the arrows of the Mohawk. He said, "I have a cure. If anyone wishes to follow me, it is well. I wish to fight the Mohawk. They seem hungry for a fight." Accordingly, he took seven men from here. When they arrived at Restigouche, they found a big crowd assembled there, for one of the two men from that settlement who were killed was the son of the chief. They left. In December, about a week before Christmas, they found the Mohawk. Duneil and the seven men from here [Burnt Church], together with the forty or more from Restigouche, began to fight. After a while, Duneil was beside himself with anger, and commenced to fight in real earnest. Not one of his men was killed. He did not allow one of his men to die. He had neither bow nor arrow, and the Mohawk had no weapon that could kill him. Duneil

PART TWO *Folktales and Traditions*

could withstand all of them. When he began in earnest, he killed all of them with one swoop, as one would slay flies with the hand. [The informant illustrated with appropriate gesture.] Duneil: "If you people had not tried to kill me the first time I met you, I would not now be doing this." He opened his shirt and showed the men his wounds.

The entire party returned to Restigouche. He told the people at Restigouche, "Mohawk will never again come here. If they move one step in this direction, I shall know it, and will go to meet them. But they will never again come to this place." Four men, in two canoes, started from Restigouche, with Duneil. Duneil had no canoe, so they brought him here to Burnt Church. He sent word ahead to the Indians here: "I am coming; tomorrow night I shall be home." The Indians came from southwest Miramichi, from Red Bank, and from Eel Ground, to see Duneil. When the canoes arrived, Duneil with his little tomahawk hanging from the belt at his right side, and a little bow and two arrows, got out of the canoe and sang. While he sang, the people answered each refrain, in concert, with, "A he! A he!" Duneil said, "I came home safe. The Mohawk got it all [that is, all the misfortune]. They lost their lives, but I came back alive. After this they will not kill any Micmac." From that day until the present, the Mohawk have not troubled the Micmac.

Duneil, like his parents, was born in the woods. His father died before the child was born. He was born a short while after the death of his father. His mother was very poor. One or two other wigwams were near his father's wigwam. When his mother was in childbirth, in the springtime, Duneil's father's mother said, "We cannot keep that sick woman and her child. They will be too much trouble and bother. It will be best to kill the child — drown it in the river." Her husband pretended to agree to this. He went to the woods, peeled birch bark, made a little canoe, and fastened the bark tightly together at both ends. He then took deer and muskrat skins and put them into the canoe as a lining. He put the child in, rolled it in these skins, and set the canoe adrift in the river. Duneil was only three days old. The canoe was put on the river. (I do not know what river this was.)

Near the river lived some Indians; perhaps there were about twelve wigwams. That afternoon, when one of the Indians came out of the woods, he saw something floating down the river, and a little arm moving out of it. After a while, the canoe drifted ashore. A man went to it, and said, "A child is in here!" He took the child, unwrapped the deer

History and Tradition

and muskrat skins, and looked at him. The man was puzzled. He did not know from what place the child had come. He took it home to his wife, and told her to feed it. All the people nearby heard that he had found the child. It was only three days old. They knew it was very young.

Duneil's mother, when she learned of the loss of the child, cried, and asked her father-in-law and her mother-in-law where it was. Finally they said, "Your child has been taken away — it is dead." She was sick, and not able to walk about.

Duneil grew. When he was six months old, he could sit up. He could then almost walk. The man who had found him liked him very much, even as his own child. When, later, his mother went there, Duneil walked up to her, embraced her, and said, "Mother, I am not dead!" She: "Why do you call me mother?" "I know my mother. My grandfather made me a little canoe, put me in it, and I was one night on the river. In the afternoon of the next day an Indian found the canoe along the river; that is how I came here." The woman then knew it was her child. He grew, and lived with his mother. When he was a year and a half old, he went to live with his mother. She was pleased to have him.

Her father-in-law had told her the boy was dead. He thought the child had been drowned in the rapids. On the contrary, in a year and six months he had found his mother. Duneil asked his mother, "Where is my father?" "Your father is dead. When you were born, your father was dead. When you were three days old, I lost you. My father-in-law's wife said to me, 'We must kill that child; if we don't, it will trouble us all the time.'" "My grandfather did not want to kill me outright, he wanted me to die in the river. But I did not die in the river; and I shall not die until the time comes for me to die. Nothing will kill me." His mother said, "I must now name the boy." She asked the man who found him what to call him. "I do not know." "Give him whatever name you like." "So be it; I shall call him Duneil."

That boy was never killed. If God does not kill him, he will never die. He fought a big battle and was not killed. He is living yet. He can go any place he wishes to go. He can stay in the water for twenty-four hours, like a fish, and he can fly through the air like a bird.[4]　　　　P. G.

127. DUNEIL'S ENCOUNTER WITH THE FRENCH AND ENGLISH

This man, though shot in the face or body with a bullet, was not penetrated by it. No steel could go through him. When he was angry, he

---

[4] Part of the story suggests a version of Moses and the bulrushes.

PART TWO *Folktales and Traditions*

sang; he sang only when something had gone wrong. When misfortune was at hand, he sang. At such times you could scarcely look upon his face, it had such an unusual color. He would not injure Indians. When a white man came within his grasp, he took the white man's head in one hand, grasped his shoulder with the other, twisted off his head, and threw both away. Before the treaty was made with the English, he had done nothing wrong. He was at Shediac Island. When, one evening, a war vessel arrived there, all were frightened. It sent a shell, which burst and scattered fire over the entire island. The Indians went to Duneil and asked him what they should do. He said, "They will do no harm. Go home and sleep." That night, he cut a stick two or three fathoms long, stuck it into the war vessel, and carried the vessel onto a hill in the woods.

Next morning, the crew found that they were in the woods. They thought that all of them would be killed, for only a strong man could do that. Duneil came, looked at them, asked the captain who they were, and what they intended to do. (Perhaps he spoke his own language, perhaps he used English or French — we do not know.)

The captain came, shook Duneil's hand, and said, "My friend, I did not come here to injure anyone. I came merely to cruise about and see the place. Now we are done for. I suppose we shall lose our lives." "No, you will not lose your lives. If you are not trying to injure us, we shall not hurt you. I will put your vessel back into the water."

They offered the Indians money, but the latter would accept none. Duneil told the captain to get on board; then, with his stick, lifted the ship, and put it in the water. The crew were so glad to have the vessel in the water that they left at once. The man would accept nothing — neither money nor tobacco. My grandfather [the informant, Peter Ginnish, was an old man] was then nineteen years old. Soon after this, the treaty was made.

Later a ship came, and the King was on board. Two Indians asked who it was. The King came ashore. Julian, one of these two Indians, would not shake hands with him, but Ginnish, the other Indian, did so. Julian said, "I must kill that King and all the men on this war vessel." But Julian could not carry out this threat while Ginnish was there. If he had been alone, he would have done as he said he would do. The terms suggested by Ginnish did not suit. Julian said, "Go back, and come again tomorrow." The King went back, and next day came again. Ginnish asked, "Is your mind right?" The treaty was not yet made. He sent the King away again, and told him to come the following day; also, that if he was not then in the proper mind, he might not be permitted to go away again.

There was a King on each vessel, that is to say, a French King on one, and an English King on the other. Next day, when these two came ashore, they said, "This is our final proposal. We will not come again." The King said to Ginnish, "This is the last time I shall come ashore with my proposal. As long as the sun shines, the tide rises and falls, and the grass grows, I will support you. I shall give you your living: food and clothes. If you die, it will not be because of any fault of mine; if I die, it will not be because of any fault of yours." The Indians said, "All right." They dug a grave four feet deep. The Indians said, "Put your bayonet in first, the French bayonet on it, and the Indian will put his battle-axe on them. You see me put them in. I shall never take one out. If I do take mine out, I promise you that I will finish you. But I will never take it out, unless it is through your fault." The grave is there to this day. Since that time we have been friends — there has not been much trouble. Some have been killed. We cannot allow them to kill our Indians. If they do so again, we may have to kill them.

Duneil did not have to light his pipe. He merely held out his pipe, and it was ready to smoke. When he smoked, the fumes covered the entire locality, like fog in the morning. He could walk on the water, like a butterfly, without breaking the surface. He traveled very rapidly. It took him no time to go to his destination, and none to return.   P. G.

128. SABIESAGAMAC AND HIS SONS

Three men were traveling along the river, hunting. They had been walking all day. They were a father and his two sons. The old man belched a great deal. After each belch, he said, "Thank you, God [Neskamgean]." The sons said, "We will have good luck, surely." They had been walking steadily for three days, without provisions, and all this time the old man had been belching. The younger one said to his brother, "That is something I do not believe. The old man has had that *welat* [belching] ever since we started, and we have not seen a thing yet. Next time father is taken with one, tell him we are sure he has been telling lies ever since we started."

The old man said, "I wish to sleep a while." He lay down on his face. They allowed him to sleep about an hour. He dreamed of a place where

PART TWO *Folktales and Traditions*

they would catch herring. When he got up, they went on to a place called Pusewitcik [Foam]. Two stayed there, and one son went to Lipkedamuwegadik [the name given indented decoration on birch bark]. The old man and his son found a brook, Pedaweetcik [tea-drinking]. It was night. While the old man was building the fire, he saw bear, deer, and all kinds of game — because he had dreamed of them during the day.

The son who was lost went to a settlement, but could not find Lipkedamuwegadik. He went to a wigwam where he might stay. He looked up at the flagpole. His bow and arrow he had with him. After breakfast, he looked up through the smokehole and saw a very large clam on the flagpole. "I suppose," he said to the family there, "you know that I am lost."

He lay down and asked the girl there whether she would marry his brother. He said that by a three days' walk through the woods they could reach his home. He took up his bow and arrow and was aiming at the clam overhead. The girl: "You should shoot it down — that clam is not fooling." "All right." He shot the clam down.

After breakfast they were lying in the wigwam, looking up through the smokehole, telling stories, and talking. After a while, a big pigeon flew up and alighted on top of the flagpole. The girl said, "This time I shall try a shot." Before she could shoot, the pigeon came down into the wigwam. It flew into the wigwam, and the girl laid down her bow and arrow. The bird said the other people [the clam's people] were not coming, for their headman had been killed; also that he was not of their party, but had come down from a certain part of heaven. She did not shoot this bird, because it said that the Bilwedj [enemy] would not come again, for their chief had been killed. Bilwedj was the clam that had been killed.[5]

"I guess the Bilwedj will not stop here — they will pass by." All the people went to the river to see the Bilwedj going by. There were only small chips floating by on the river.

The bird began to tell how the old man [father of the visiting boy] knew that his son had got lost, and what luck he had had: "When the fire was started, they saw game all about them. The old man went to sleep, dreamed, and next morning knew all that had happened to you." (No one knew where Lipkedamuwegadik was, but the boy had to obey.)

[5] The clam was a Mohawk spy.

History and Tradition

[Meanwhile] the old man said to his second son, "Do not worry about your brother. I know where he is. I suppose you, too, may as well go there. If anything [untoward] should happen, I can let you know. I think I can take care of the game that is here." To this the son replied, "I wish to do whatever you say, but I do not wish to go alone." "Why do you dislike going alone?" "Because I dream of chips that are floating down the river, and I do not know where they will go. If they pursue me, I do not know what I shall do." (The chips were Mohawk.) "Well, hustle and take this meat home. If you are afraid to go alone, we will go together. But you will have hard work to do." "I can work hard, father." They prepared to take the meat to their wigwams in their home settlement. When the old man was ready, he asked his son whether he, too, was ready to go to the place where his brother was. (This son did not know that there was another settlement.) "Oh," he said, "I shall be ready to go at any time, after the meat has been packed away." They departed for the place where his brother was.

When the old man, who lived in the wigwam where the absent son was, got up, he felt a twitching in his right thigh, and said, "I think that a friend whom I have never seen before will come today."

When the old man arrived at the wigwam in which his son was staying, everyone was pleased to see him. All bowed their heads, because he was a stranger and a Micmac. They knelt on the left knee, bowed the head, then rose, shook hands, and said, "*Pusul, widjigadik* – greeting, brother."

There was no water in the wigwam. The birch-bark bucket was empty. The older son had arranged it so.

On his way to the wigwam his younger brother, who had been with his father, had seen a big moose, taken it by the neck, thrown it into a big muddy spring, and said to his father, "See what I do!" Only the head of the moose remained visible.

The young son, who had come with his father, now said, "Father that [?] you gave me made me thirsty. I should like a drink of water." The host told his daughter to get water. She said, "There is none here – the birch-bark bucket is empty."

"Well, go to the spring and dip up some water – there is plenty at the spring." She went to the spring, looked at it, and said, "Goodness, I cannot get water there. There is a moose in it." She threw stones at the moose, but it did not move. She returned to the wigwam, and said to her father, "Father, I could not get water, because a moose is drinking

465

PART TWO *Folktales and Traditions*

in our spring." "What?" She repeated her statement. The old man began to sharpen his knife, and said, "That is what I have been feeling all day; I knew that something would happen." Although he had been sitting in the wigwam, he knew, by the various "feelings" he had had, all that had happened within ten or twenty miles of the place. The old man continued sharpening his knife, and said, "I guess I shall get the moose and have it for lunch." He took the moose out, they got water, and ate lunch.

When all was ready, the old men began to talk. The girl remained quiet, said nothing, and listened, to find out what would happen. After they had talked, they said, "We will have a little wedding party." The old man and his son said they would not carry any of the meat home with them, for they had enough for themselves.

The wedding began. The father of the boys said, "If we are going to do this, we must have two weddings. Your chief will perform the marriage ceremony here, and my chief will perform one after we return to my settlement."

After the marriage, they left, in the middle of an inky dark night. One of the young men acted as guide, "because," said he, "I know the road well, well, well." They arrived at their settlement. The old man said, "I think we have enough meat to start a *malies diabu* [wedding feast]."

The boy who had married is now dead; it is two or three years after his death.

A fight began. (They had a peculiar way of whooping. Such a whoop gives you a creepy feeling, and kills some people. It could be heard a hundred miles. No one now knows just how that whooping was done. It was low and long drawn out, rising and falling, and had an uncanny effect.[6]) Sabiesagamac, the chief over all (he died about eighty-five years ago), whooped. The young men heard the whooping, and said, "I suppose he is chasing the Bilwedj away." They knew that the Bilwedj were not very numerous, and could not overcome the Micmac. The Mohawk broke Sabiesagamac's canoe, chased him down to the water, and wounded him on the right side, under his upper arm. He ran to the cliffs and lay down near a spring, so that the water from it dropped on the long gash in his side.

During the night, the Mohawk came to the shore. They thought he had hidden in the water, and they prodded about with their fishing spears

[6] See tales of Djenu, Tale 20.

and their fighting arrows, trying to find him, and using torches to assist them. Sabiesagamac was in the water, and before morning the spring water had healed his wound. When he came out of the spring, he said, "I am now all right." He gave a whoop directed toward the Mohawk, jumped in the canoe, and paddled across the bay. The Bilwedj [Mohawk] heard him whooping. They knew that Sabiesagamac could not use his canoe, for it was broken through the middle. They said, "There he is; we shall get him, surely." While they were hunting for him, they saw him leaving. He was in the fore part of the broken canoe and was going so fast that the water could not get into the stern end of it, which was broken off completely.

He paddled across to the other side, about five miles, all their canoes after him, but none able to overtake him. When he reached the shore, he gave another whoop, so loud that all the Micmac on that side heard him. Again he whooped for help.

The young fellow who had shot down the clam [seeing the Mohawk] said, "It is the man whom I know. I knocked the clam down, and there it is again. I must see that man. I went to see him in another settlement, but that settlement stopped me. Now I shall surely get him. He has no business turning himself into a clam and coming around in that form. I am going to see him this time. He knows well that I shall go." The young man was very angry. He was only fifteen years old. He was a *ginap*. Sabiesagamac said, "A man like you should not become angry." When they crossed the river, the enemy were waiting there, thinking they had killed all the Micmac. They were roasting children on spits over the fire, had massacred all the women, and had burned everything in the settlement.

When the young *ginap* arrived, he saw a man who looked just like the clam that he had killed. He said to this Mohawk, "I am the man who killed your brother two years ago when, in the form of a clam, he was fooling around that flagpole." He looked about, then continued, "Well, this is an awful mess here — this work of the Mohawk."

Up to this time the old man Sabiesagamac had not spoken. The Mohawk were ready to fight, and the two Micmac, who had just arrived, were equally ready. Not all the Micmac were dead. Only a few had been present at the fight. If they had been more numerous, they could easily have killed the Mohawk. There were only forty or fifty Micmac, pitted against three hundred to five hundred Mohawk. Even so, they had killed

PART TWO *Folktales and Traditions*

about one half of the Mohawk before the latter captured the settlement. The young man said, "I shall find out what treatment has been accorded my relatives. You should have remained in your own country." (This last to the Mohawk.) He was very angry, but did not swear. He said, "I am sorry, because of the fate of my relatives, and I have pity on you who have killed some two hundred to three hundred of my people. We shall now rid ourselves of you, and you will not return to trouble us again. You should go away from here."

To this the Mohawk responded, "Are you sad because of the fate of your relatives? What will you do if we do not leave here?" "Yes, I am sad because of the fate of my relatives, and I shall show you what I will do if you do not leave here." He gave a small whoop, but one of such volume that the Mohawk had never before heard the like, although they had heard a great many Micmac whoops.

At this, all of them fell in a heap: some on their knees, some on one side. He grasped his tomahawk and knife, walked among the two hundred Mohawk, and said, "Now, I shall show you what I will do. Show me now what you will do. Why did you come to fight us in this manner? — five hundred men against five families? You had best go to Bido [said to be Caughnawaga], and stay there. If there are any more of your men here, call them, and we shall send all of them home."

All about were canoes filled with Micmac, who were determined to kill the Mohawk. The young man, however, took pity on the enemy, and did not wish to kill them. "All right," they said, "we will trust in the wisdom of your advice." The old man, Sabiesagamac, gave a small whoop to the four hundred canoes of Micmac that had assembled at this place. The canoes then started to cross, in procession, the bow of one touching the stern of another. The Micmac had their bows and arrows ready for action, and were watching the gulls and all the other birds, for they did not know into what birds the Mohawk might transform themselves. The women and children were in camp, and it was probable that the Mohawk would try to capture them and take them away. After a while, two large hawks came from the woods and looked about, as if in search of something to eat. The young man gave a small whoop: "*Gumemit.*" The canoes stopped and their occupants observed these two birds. The birds, however, wheeled and flew back. If they had not done so, they would have been killed. They could not deceive the Micmac, for at least one Micmac was certain to recognize them as enemies. The birds

History and Tradition

returned to the place where Sabiesagamac and the *ginap* were. To them the other Micmac said, "You did not keep watch over them; those two fellows intended to steal our women."

The Micmac chief had been blinded by the Mohawk, and the *ginap* now acted as their leader. The *ginap* said to the two birds, "It is well you came back. If you had not done so, you would have lost your lives. You shall go up the river today." They rounded up the Mohawk and chased them north. They pointed their bows and arrows toward the Mohawk and said, "Get into that canoe there." If a man hesitated, he was killed at once. They chased them to Caughnawaga, two days' journey from here; and I suppose they are there yet. The Micmac canoes came back from Caughnawaga to the settlement. A few had remained at the settlement to protect the women. Five or six Micmac withstood fifteen to twenty Mohawk. The Micmac were the most powerful of all peoples. There was nothing they could not do. T. M.

Micmac and Europeans

129. COLUMBUS' VISIT

When Columbus came over, he met the Micmac chief. They were sociable. The Micmac smoked, and handed his pipe to Columbus, who smoked. Columbus pulled out a flask — it was either glass or silver — drank from it, handed it to the Micmac chief, and said, "Drink from my pipe." The Indian drank. Soon he felt queer in his head. He was happy, stood up, and danced. He and Columbus shook hands. The Micmac made signs to indicate to Columbus that he was welcome, and the Indians cordially invited him to return.

130. THE FIRST FRENCH VISITORS

When the French [first] came it was raining. The Indians saw the warship. The children thought the thunder had torn a big tree up. They went home, and said to those there, "See what the storm did last night!" "No!" "The thunder has pitched a big tree up, roots and all."

Two years later, another vessel came. The French went ashore. The Indians found their tracks. They did not know what kind of beast this was. Everybody was asking, "Do you know what kind of beast made these tracks?" "No." They asked everyone.

A Frenchman had defecated. They came to the excrement. They did

PART TWO *Folktales and Traditions*

not know what it was. An Indian put his finger in it, placed the finger to his nose, and smelled it. He did not know what it was. Next day, they saw the French. The Frenchmen signaled the Indians to them, and gave them some biscuits. The Indians did not know what use they could be put to, and played with them as quoits. Next day, the Frenchmen gave them a loaf of bread. The Indians tried to strike fire with it [that is, use it as punk]. It would not make fire, so they threw it away.

The French could not civilize them, for the Indians threw away everything that the French gave them. Five years later, a French priest came. Among the Indians was a powerful medicineman. The priest asked him, "What name would you like to have?" "Mary." "No; that is a woman's name. Try again." "God." "No; God has charge of us all." "Devil." "No; he takes care of Hell." Finally the priest left him, for he could not get any satisfaction out of the medicineman. J. N.

Why Micmac Have a Treaty with the King
131. FATHER MAILLARD

After the English came here and dispossessed the French, they used to shoot into the churches when the people were in them, and kill the priest and all who were inside. Finally, a priest and his congregation, thus attacked, ran to the woods. The priest was Father Maillard. The thorns and bushes tore his clothes to ribbons. The Indians made him clothes of skin.

A long time after this attack the English again found them. The Indians were not frightened for themselves, but merely on account of the priest. They ran away. They came to a lake, and started to cross it on the ice and snow. When they were about halfway over, they saw the army of the English behind them. The priest then began to pray for them.

When he had finished praying, he rose, took his bow, and drew a long scratch on the ice, separating the Indians from the English. They then traveled on, over the snow and ice. When the English arrived at this long scratch on the ice, the ice, with a report like a cannon, suddenly broke, and left a stretch of open water in front of the foe, who had to turn back.

After the Micmac had crossed the lake, they met the English. The Micmac fought them for two days and two nights, and killed all of them.

History and Tradition

132. A WOMAN *BUOIN*

A woman dreamed that another army was coming. Before the English knew where they were, all of them were killed. The Indians returned to the priest. Two years later, the husband of the woman who had had the dream was killed by the English. She had three children. She went out to get boughs for her wigwam. She was carrying the old boughs out [that is, replacing the old floor by a new one]. While she was out, some English officers went into the wigwam and saw the children. Two girls ran away, but the smallest one could not run. They thrust a stick through her body, up to her throat, and roasted her on this spit before the fire. The woman returned and found her older two children crying, and the smallest one roasted. She took the dead child away and buried it.

She went to the King and told him she felt badly about the murder of her child. The King said to her, "If you are able to cure your heart, you will do it." She returned to her home, hid her children in a bank, put on her husband's clothes, and went to the King. She said to him, "Here I am. I want some medicine to cure me." "All right!" said the King. She went out. They put fifty soldiers on the battlefield. She had a bow and arrow and a tomahawk. In the field there was a small rock. They called to her, "Are you ready?" "Yes, I am ready." Fifteen or twenty shots were fired at her. She fell down flat, behind the stone, then suddenly jumped up, gave a whoop, and killed all of the fifty. They ordered out another hundred soldiers, and after she had whooped, she killed all of them. They put out a hundred and fifty soldiers. As fast as they came out, she killed them. The King said, "You had best stop! That will do!" The woman said, "No! I will not leave one louse alive in your town." They coaxed her and coaxed her, and gave her things, and finally, she consented to desist. This was at Cape North, in Cape Breton.

133. BILL DUMFY'S STORY

There were few English people in Cape Breton, or in Newfoundland. They stayed there through the winter, getting fur. An Englishman and a little boy came, and the man said, "We will stay here with them, through the winter." The Indians were getting many furs, all the time. The Englishmen did not get nearly as many, and were about to go away. One of them said, "How would it do to kill the Indians and take their furs?" "All right."

Bill Dumfy, a boy who was with them, later told these things to my

PART TWO *Folktales and Traditions*

grandfather. They made that boy, Bill Dumfy, swear that he would not inform on them. He went, on his knees, a distance of about four feet, kissed his master's foot, made the sign of the cross over the Bible, and swore secrecy. That night they went out and ground their axes. They went about midnight, and Bill Dumfy went with them. They saw the two [Micmac] men and a woman lying asleep. They cut off their heads, and also the head of a little girl. One man rose and walked out of the wigwam, but his head had been cut off, and he fell outside. They went home and procured a pick, shovel, and two lanterns. Bill Dumfy went with them. They took two handspikes, rolled a moss-covered log away, dug a trench at the place where it had been, buried the bodies in this trench, and rolled the log back, to cover all signs of the grave. They smashed the wigwam into pieces and set fire to it. Everything was entirely consumed by the fire. They also burned their own log house, and then the murderers left for Newfoundland.

They reached St. Johns, and went ashore with their big supply of furs. While they were ashore, Bill Dumfy took the water barrel and let all the water out. When they came home, they asked for water. "There is no water," they were told. They gave Bill Dumfy a shilling and told him to go ashore and get water. He went. While he was ashore, he went to the [police] office, told them all about the affair, and explained how he had managed to get ashore. "Go upstairs," the officers said to him. They took these two men to jail. Next day, they hailed them into court. One of them said to Bill Dumfy, "If I had known you would tell this story, I would have taken your life long ago." For three weeks they had been planning how to kill these Indians. The men were hanged. For a long, long time the English did not let the Indians know about this, lest the latter should "walk over and sweep the town clean." From time to time they gave them money for seed and necessities, and they gave money to the old and needy. This is their way of paying back for the furs which the English took from those Indians. That is why King George made the treaty with them. J. N.

Miramichi Traditions

134. THE HISTORY OF BURNT CHURCH AND ITS CHURCH

The first ship which came to Canada found the Indians here, on the Miramichi River. The Indians, after seeing the ship, thought it queer, and did not like it. They said, "Go away from here!" Off the English went.[7] The French went ashore in Nova Scotia. The Indians fought them and defeated them. The English came, and the Indians fought and defeated them. The Indians were here, working. A priest came. He had walked a long way, along the shore. He saw the Indians, and stopped. He had them make a large bark wigwam, to serve as a church. He passed the winter here [at Burnt Church]. As soon as he and the Indians could understand each other, he said, "We must collect money and build a church." From June until September he collected money; throughout the winter he collected money, and so until spring and summer again, and all summer and winter again, he collected money. When spring came, and the month of June, the priest said, "I shall go to Quebec, to procure a carpenter who will build the church." He left a box, about two feet long, filled with silver dollars. He went away on board a steamer. Before leaving, he took the box to the chief, and said, "Keep this. Do not open it until I come back." The key he took with him. He was away during the entire month of June.

When St. Anne's Day [July 26] came, the Indians said, "We must find out how much money we have for the church." "There is no key." "No matter; break it [the chest] open." This they did. It contained not a cent — only rocks and sand.

The Indians said, "We must build a church." They put up a log building, in which the priest might say Mass. It contained a very expensive altar of solid gold, a present from the King of France. Later the English drove the French away, and another priest came. He treated the Indians very well. An Indian is like a fox: if you beat a fox, it will play with you at once, and then, in a twinkling, it will run off. This priest said, "We must build a church — that is not a church, it is a log building." The Indians said, "All right." When June came, the priest said, "I must go to Quebec to get pictures. I shall take the altar along to have it fixed." One day, when all the men were away, the priest took it. The women cried, and tried to prevent his taking it, but could not do so. Both priests were French Canadian. The following year, a war vessel arrived. A boat came to shore, took brush to the church, piled it about the building, set fire to it, and burned it to the ground.[8]

[7] Miramichi Bay was first visited, by Cartier, in 1534, and was named by him the Bay of Boats. His vessel was surrounded by so many canoes that the French had to keep them off.

[8] According to tradition, the church at Burnt Church was burned by a party of English from a vessel that was carrying the remains of Wolfe to England. They had

PART TWO *Folktales and Traditions*

The Indians built another church — a stone one. The frost cracked the stones, and the elements blew through them. The Indians filled the cracks with mud. In the spring, they assembled, and tore it down. The stones used in it had come from salt water and, because of the salt which they contained, were of little use. [Apparently, they were soft sandstone gathered along the beach, where the water had exposed the stone.]

Eighty-one years ago [i.e., in 1830], another church was commenced. Two churches were burned [one of them the church built in 1830], and one was torn down.

A French priest came. At first, he was very good; a little later, not so good. Then came another one, also a [French] Canadian, and he proposed to burn this church also. French people will do anything against us. We now allow no French priest to come here.[9] I said to the Bishop,

gone ashore at Neguac, about five miles northeast of Burnt Church, to get water. Here they were attacked by the French, whom, however, they mistook for Indians. To punish this attack, they proceeded to the settlement at the present site of Burnt Church. At the approach of the British vessel, "the few inhabitants fled; and then executing his reprisal upon the church, he set it in flames, from whence the settlement has ever since been distinguished by the name of Burnt Church." Robert Cooney, *A Compendious History of the Northern Part of the Province of New Brunswick, and of the District of Gaspé, in Lower Canada,* Halifax, 1832.

Actually, in September 1758, after the capture of Louisburg in July, Colonel James Murray was sent to destroy the French settlements on the Gulf of St. Lawrence. Murray reported to General Wolfe that he reached Miramichi Bay on the 15th of September; the fleet anchored "in an open road, seven leagues from the Settlement and Three from the Barr, exposed 16 points of the Compass." The men embarked in boats with an artillery sloop for protection and succeeded in getting over the bar at the entrance of the inner bay at high tide and "got safe within Musket Shott of the Settlement about 12 at Night, Joseph the Indian being our Pilot." The Acadians, about 40 in number, had taken to the woods with their priest, Père Bonavanture. Indians, very numerous at that point on the bay, had also disappeared. Because the ship captains were concerned about the hazardous position of the fleet, Murray did not proceed to the French settlements farther up the river. On the evening of the 17th, he reported to Wolfe, "in Obedience to your Instructions [I] embarked the Troops, having two Days hunted all around Us for the Indians and Acadians to no purpose, we however destroyed their Provisions, Wigwams, and Houses, the Church was a very handsome one built with stone, did not escape. We took Numbers of Cattle, Hogs and Sheep, and Three Hogsheads of Beaver Skins, and I am persuaded there is not now a French Man in the River Miramichi."

The burning of the stone church gave to the Indian village of Eskinwobudich the name Burnt Church, which it and the adjoining white village still bear. Adapted from Esther Clark Wright, *The Miramichi,* 1945.

Levinge, writing in 1835, repeats the story that the vessel which carried Wolfe's remains to England put in to shore for water, and later, after suffering an attack from the French soldiers stationed nearby, "was 'brought up' at Burnt Church Point, all the buildings on which were battered down. A chapel, which had cost the French a sum equal to 5,000 pounds sterling, was set on fire and wholly destroyed, whence the point has since borne the name of 'Burnt Church'." Pp. 38–39.

[9] In 1953 the French priest was well liked by his congregation.

History and Tradition

"That is enough. Do not send, surely, any more French priests here. We do not want them. We will not have them." We had $4400 insurance on the church which burned last spring. The priest went to the bishop for the money. He did not get it. He told the chief to raise it. I told the chief not to give them one cent of it. The chief gave $1700 to the priest.

Whatever money was left the bishop got; and now they are building another church. The old Indians were not well pleased, but they made no complaint. When bad weather came, their sentiments came out; in the summer all is quiet. We live with the white people like two brothers. The Frenchman abuses the Indians all the time, but sometimes he makes a mistake. About fifteen years ago, the priest who built the last church died. He was Father Agen [?], a very large Irishman. When Father Agen was our priest, the Indians from all the nearby reserves came here for St. Anne's Day. We had a frolic and dances and games that lasted one or two weeks.

About fifty years ago, when the governor came here from Fredericton, for St. Anne's Day, the Indians made a big tent, also a big wooden cannon. It made a big noise, but burst, though it did not hurt anyone. When the governor had had his dinner, the Indian commissioner said, "The governor wants to see the people do the old-fashioned Indian dance."

P. G.

In the second church built at Burnt Church there was an altar of solid gold. The church was burned by Yankee sailors (some say English) from war vessels anchored off the point. They were trying to get possession of this altar. They took it up the river, and left it in the stream, near the site of the present bridge. It was there for about six months, and was then taken to Montreal, where it still rests in one of the churches. It weighed about a ton, it is said, and was worth, perhaps, a million dollars.

A priest promised to return it, and brought back an altar that looked like the old one. But it was found to be made of pine, and was only covered with gold — it was not of solid gold, like the old one.[10]

JOHN TENASS AND NEWELL GINNISH

[10] "For years the church [St. Anne's, Chapel Island, Cape Breton] possessed a curiously carved French altar, which bore upon the tabernacle the date 1717, and regarding which an interesting story is told. It is said to have been first used in the French chapel at Port Toulouse. When that place was taken by the English, the French carried off the altar and hid it in the neighboring woods. They themselves never returned to seek it, but it was found by the Indians who kept it religiously for years as one of their greatest treasures. Unfortunately, some years back a priest

PART TWO *Folktales and Traditions*

135. SCOTS CIVILIZE THE MICMAC

One winter, the people were fishing for smelts and tomcods. They caught a great many cod and put them in a big pile on the ice. It contained perhaps forty-five or fifty pounds. They caught no smelts. There were hard times that winter. People came and hauled the tomcods away. In the spring a vessel arrived to get lumber. Two men on board were passengers from Scotland. They went ashore at a place about fourteen miles from Burnt Church, and saw Peter Ginnish's grandfather. These men were Gilamore and Rankin.[11] During the second week in July, the ship was loaded, and left. They had procured provisions from the Indians.

Late in October, the ship returned, laden with flour, sugar (no tea), tobacco, blankets, and many other things. All this went to the Indians. Again the ship was loaded. The following year the vessel came again, and traded as before. Rankin told one of the men to plant potatoes. The women prepared the ground and tended them. The Indians thought it strange that these men should give them so much; and the Micmac would not allow anyone else to go near them.

That is how the Micmac became civilized. They then built churches and put up other buildings.   P. G.

136. THE MIRAMICHI FIRE

The Miramichi fire [which swept along the northern shore of the Miramichi river in 1825] burned seven inches into the ground — the ground itself was burned into ashes to a depth of seven inches. That shows for certain that the fire must have come from below. Not one Indian was burned; but nearly all the English people and their property

who at the time had charge of the mission, persuaded them to give it to him for his own church and to replace it with a modern altar decked out with the customary white enamel and gold paint." Vernon, 1903, 112.

[11] Gilmour, Rankin, and Company, shipbuilders, an offshoot of the Glasgow firm of Pollok, Gilmour and Company, was established on the Miramichi in 1812 and there prospered for many years. Alexander Rankin, who remained in charge of the firm's regional affairs, arrived with James Gilmour in the autumn of 1812 to find the bay and river already full of ice. They landed, therefore, at the mouth of the river and walked to Chatham, a settlement then a few years old. Faced with the difficulty of feeding employees during long New Brunswick winters, Rankin encouraged the development of agriculture in the Miramichi country. His reputation for integrity and kindness, as we see above, remained long among the Micmac. According to an old squaw, "there was once a white man who was kind to the Indians, and because of that, when the fire was sent to destroy the white men who were bad to the Indians, his house was spared. His name was Rankin." Wright, 41–42.

were burned and destroyed. When the fire came to the wigwams of the Indians, it went around them, and did not burn them. That was queer — very, very strange. It must have been a punishment on the whites for their treatment of the Indians. There is no other explanation.[12]

The Miramichi fire was caused in this way:

The white people were planning to murder, one night, all the Indians along the Miramichi River. They had guns and powder and were ready to make the attack. Only one man refused to join them in the plot. He owned a mill at Newcastle, and told his employees not to help to kill the Indians, but to come and stay at his house that night. They did so, for they had to do as he commanded. There were many ships nearby. The captain of one of them had said that he would not help to kill the Indians, although the captains and crews of all the other ships were planning to do so. He went ashore to spend the night, took his men with him, and told them they were not to kill any Indians. The people were ready with their guns to go out and kill the Indians. But a dark red cloud came [of the kind which, today, is said to contain fire] and started the fire. Every house of the English except the house of the man in Newcastle who said that he would not kill any Indians — neither he nor his men — was burned to the ground, and a great many people were burned to death. The fire came within a foot or two of the wigwams of the Indians and then went around them, without burning one wigwam, in all that conflagration. All the ships, too, were burned, except the ship of the captain who had said that neither he nor his men would kill any Indians. His ship was not burned at all, although all the others near it were consumed. The ground was burned to a depth of about seven inches. There was something peculiar about that fire — very strange. It must have been a punishment to the white people for having planned to kill the Indians. That must have been it.   T. M.

[12] This was told at Burnt Church. The stories of the Miramichi fire have a close analogue in the following reported by Farrer with regard to the fire in the river parishes near Quebec while that city was being besieged by Wolfe: "At the siege of Quebec Wolfe dispatched an expedition to harry the river parishes. 'Wherever resistance was offered,' says Parkman, 'farmhouses and villages were laid in ashes, though churches were generally spared.' The Church at Beaupré was not spared by the troops; it was set on fire three times, but each time Saint Anne extinguished the flames, and some of the Highlanders confessed the miracle. When the north shore down to Cape Tourmente was blazing, nearly all the farmhouses in which she was specially venerated escaped." *Popular Science Monthly*, 34.

PART TWO *Folktales and Traditions*

At the time of the Miramichi fire there were two camps, six miles apart. Indians were in one, and whites in the other.

The Indians had three sons; there were six persons, all told, in the wigwam. Some of the boys went to the other camp to visit, and intended to return at night. The boss of the camp went out and said there was something bright, like a fire. The boys went out, and at once saw a big fire. They told their father. A big lump was going up here and there, bursting out into a blaze, like someone throwing firebrands. They returned home and went into the water, under some logs at the mill. It was so hot that only with difficulty could they breathe, or endure the water, which was so hot that it almost scalded them to death. They remained awake all night, and throughout the next day. Not one Indian wigwam was burned. All the churches, with one exception, were destroyed. That church was in the midst of the blaze and was filled with people, who were Catholics. All the Protestant churches were burned. The fire swept over the water, as though the water were kerosene. The ground burned to the depth of six or seven feet.

It was their luck for not listening to the Almighty. All the bad people were consumed. That was their luck — what they were given. If you do not believe God, some [bad] luck will come to you. There was so much noise that one could scarcely hear anything. It was in the fall, and people were leaving for the lumber camps. The fire began about two miles from those camps, and traveled like lumps, constantly kindled new fires, and made a noise like thunder, although there was no thunder. J. N.

The English had mills on the Miramichi. The Indians work well, because they are smart [i.e., agile]. The whites said, "We will sweep [destroy] the Indians!" They plotted, and planned to sweep the Indians on the Miramichi River.

The Indians knew nothing about this plot. One man, Ginnish, in Burnt Church, knew about it. When he learned about it, the plans had been made. Two Indian boys and this old man were making traps for beaver, otter, and mink. They went into the woods and spent the night there. The flies were so troublesome that the people could not stay outside, and they slept in a hut. Next morning the old man did not feel right. (This was on account of the fire.) He woke the boys. "Get up! Let's go — something will happen today." They went down the river. When they had gone about ten miles, they saw smoke, in the forest, rising like a

History and Tradition

funnel, and twisting around. The fire started, and swept the whole place. In the woods nearby there was an old dam. There were piles at this place, and water under them. The boys went into the water, under these, and the fire passed over them. They lay there all day and all night, until the fire had left. About a foot and a half of the soil was burned. They left, and arrived home, barefoot. In some places they could find the road, and in some places they could not find it. When they arrived home, they learned that not one Indian had been burned — not one.

One Englishman, a Baptist, and a rich man, was good to the Indians. He had a shop and a store. When the fire came, the Indians went into his barn and his house until these were full, and said, "Now we will die!" That man had not a scratch on his shop, barn, or store, although vessels a quarter of a mile from the shore were burned. Since that day the British have had some sense. Next day, he took out the flour and provisions and distributed them among the Indians.

Such was the Miramichi fire.

The Miramichi fire burned seven inches into the ground. It must have come from below. Not one Indian was burned. Nearly all the English people, together with their possessions, were burned. The fire went around the wigwams of the Indians. It was a punishment visited upon the whites.   JOHN TENASS

137. THE CAMPBELLTON FIRE

[There are several versions of the cause of the Campbellton [13] fire, which, in the spring of 1910, destroyed the town, except for two houses. Most attribute it to the wickedness of the place or, more commonly, to mistreatment of the Indians by the whites. An Indian at Burnt Church, who at the time of the fire was living on the Restigouche reservation, opposite Campbellton, gave the first explanation below. The second and third versions were also told at Burnt Church.]

An Indian was waiting for a train in Campbellton but the train was delayed and would not get in that night. He asked an Englishman to take him into his house for the night. The Englishman was proud, and would not take him. The Indian who had been refused shelter said, "I wish that after a few days he may have to stay out in the open as I do

[13] On Baie des Chaleurs, northwest of Burnt Church on Miramichi Bay and near the Micmac Reserve at Ste Anne de Restigouche, Quebec.

PART TWO *Folktales and Traditions*

now." Three days after this the fire came, and none of the people had shelter.

A white man in Campbellton had refused to sell some things from his store to one of the Indians and had told him to get out. The Indian had wished misfortune on him, and in a day or two, the fire came.

The fire was a visitation upon the place for its wickedness in selling liquor to the Indians at Restigouche, who could purchase it by merely crossing the bay.

I don't know what started the Campbellton fire. Some say one thing, some say another. Some say that it was this way:

The white people went over to Restigouche and put poison in the wells, to kill all the Indians. When the fire started, the people [in Campbellton] could get no water for the fire. They thought there was plenty of water. The firemen, before they left to put out the fire, went into a saloon, to get a drink. They said, "There's plenty of water to put out the fire; we may as well take a drink first." They had always had lots of water; but now, when they went to get it, the reservoirs were dry, and they could not get a drop. So the entire town burned down. Next day, the chief at Restigouche said, "Well, they tried to poison our water and kill the Indians here; now they themselves do not get any water." Everyone said the fire was to punish the whites for what they had done.

At the time of the Campbellton fire, I was in Spring Hill. Mateo Francis [in 1912, chief at Pictou] traveled on the midnight express, and arrived in Campbellton early in the morning. He and an Indian by the name of Gluskap, from Halifax, were there. Mateo was spitting on the floor of the station. The stationmaster told him he should go out and spit. They had some words. At last Mateo said, "You like this floor better than dirt! See how long it will be with you!" They went away. Two or three days later the whole place was swept by fire. Even the iron rails were burned. And all the water tanks were dry!

Tales Told in 1950 and 1953

AFTER the comparative riches of 1912, the almost complete disappearance of folktales in forty years was a disappointing feature of our later visits to the Micmac country. To many elderly people, the names of Gluskap and Gigwadju, Duneil and Kitpusiagana brought up memories of the nights, when, as boys, they went from house to house, begging old men to tell them tales; or when a grandmother lay beside a little girl at bedtime to relate stories about Otter and Rabbit. A few old people in Quebec, New Brunswick, and Nova Scotia could tell one or two good stories, but most tales were at best synoptic variants of long accounts recorded in 1912. Even in more conservative Cape Breton there seems to have been a similar loss of folk literature. In 1950, at Eskasoni, where old people from the whole region had been resettled, Sheila Steen learned that although old and middle-aged people knew stories about Gluskap and "a host of other folktales," there were no longer recognized storytellers, or, one infers, a waiting audience.

Gluskap stories heard in 1950 and 1953 included short accounts of the destruction of the giant beaver dam and the consequent change of landscape, related at Eel River, Burnt Church, and Eel Ground. This tale, now included in Maritime school texts and tourist literature, needs no further preservation. Mrs. Charles Wilmot at Shubenacadie contributed a well-told version of the suppliant for eternal life whom Gluskap turned into a hemlock tree — "good for nothing." The two fragments given here we had not previously recorded.

138. GLUSKAP'S UNCLE

Tugoluptcotc, Gluskap's uncle, has no bones. He was once a very wicked man and strong. Now his forehead has grown and dropped down to his knees, for he has no bones.

PART TWO *Folktales and Traditions*

Formerly he would kill whatever he saw. If a warship came, he could look at it and kill everyone on board; he had so much power. Gluskap said to him, "Lend me your bones; I am going hunting." He did not return the bones, but he will do so at the end of the world. From time to time Gluskap turns his uncle over, and from the side where he has been lying, medicines grow. Tugoluptcotc cannot move himself.¹

139. GLUSKAP AND TURTLE

When Gluskap was here, every beast and bird could talk with one another. Turtle was the smartest man alive, but he made a mistake. Gluskap was lying in his wigwam, having a rest. To tease him Turtle jumped over the wigwam several times. Finally Gluskap said, "Now young fellow, some day you will not be so smart [agile]!"

Now Turtle can scarcely move. Gluskap changed him quite a bit.

[Gluskap is conceived as transformer, never as creator of the earth and of mankind. In telling the following story, Joseph LaRocque of Restigouche used the titles "God" and "Our Lord" but stated, "We do not know the Creator's name." In LeClercq's day, Micmac told a similar tale and designated the Sun as creator.²]

140. THE CREATION OF MANKIND

In old times, after he had made the whites across the sea, God landed in Gaspé and walked along the shore up to the mouth of the Restigouche River where there is a nice sandy beach. God molded a man in the sand and looked twice at what he had made. He gave him the breath of life and stood up. He did not say a word. He bent down again and made a squaw. He got up and said nothing. They were the first Indians.

He made a little dog. He said nothing. The dog got its breath and wiggled around the trees. God said, "Get up. Tell the man something." The dog got up. The man looked at the dog, and language came to him. "Look," he said, meaning look at the dog. The dog said, "See that white bush." He named it and everything around them. "It's all your property, all the Gaspé and farther still."

¹ Micmac in 1954 claimed that all attempts to photograph at this spot a stone which resembles a human image result in blank film. (We wish to thank Nicholas N. Smith of Danforth, Maine, for this information.)
² See Part One, Chapter IX.

Tales Told in 1950 and 1953

God gave the man and the woman each a little square of bread. They were never hungry the whole blessed day. In the afternoon God taught the man to make a wigwam. He gave him the gift to make it. God made a little model for the man to copy. The man cut down bark to cover the wigwam; it was like a little side-tent. Then God told the man how to make traps. God made models of every kind you can mention: for bear, otter and fisher, traps of all sizes. He told where to look for moose and caribou, and how to hang up meat to smoke.

God walked along the river shore. He picked up a stone and shaped it for an axe, round, with depressions along which to fasten thongs. Then God showed the people how to cook: to make birch-bark vessels and fill them with water so that the bottom wouldn't burn. He showed them how to cut up fish right down to the bone with a sharpened stone and to split sticks for roasting fish over the fire.

God stayed three days and three nights with the man and the woman. Then he and the man and the dog set out for a lake. They left the old woman at home. God told the man how to catch fish. God made spears. He broke a limb as dry as whale bone. He used black spruce-root for strings. He made a little model canoe.

After lunch God said to the man, "Go back to your wife. I'm going ahead." The man said, "I don't know the way." The man was scared of the long walk through the woods. "Watch the sun and woods where you started and where you ended. The dog will take you home. Dog, go home!"

The man started off. The little dog ran ahead and smelled their tracks. The man watched the trees which the Creator had said would lean south. Halfway home he recognized a tree. Then he saw smoke from the old lady's wigwam. "I'm all right. I can get back any time."

The man trapped fish as he had been taught. His wife stood on a rock and as fish passed by, she speared a big trout. They cooked the fish, turned it and roasted it nice. They got all their food that way for three years, four years, five years, I don't know how long. (That's the way the old men used to tell the story.)

The Lord went on to the next lake and there made another man and woman. He went all over Canada and at each lake he made a new tribe with a different language. When the people from these lakes met in the woods, they couldn't understand each other.

PART TWO *Folktales and Traditions*

141. THE END OF THE WORLD

Gluskap will arise at the end of the world. Seventy-five or a hundred years from now, Sugar Loaf Mountain, back of Campbellton, will explode. Other mountains will do likewise.

Fish will come out of the water and beasts will emerge to torture mankind. They will bite people and will carry them into the sky. They will kill no one, merely cause them to suffer. The world will end in fire. Only dust will remain. [Told at Eel River, N.B.]

There is an old-time belief about the end of the world: things will gradually deteriorate until nothing will grow. It will be impossible to raise anything. The end of the world will then be near.

In winter at Grand Falls near Bathurst people used to see two white otters which they could never kill. A turtle made tracks from the water to the edge of the cliff. When the turtle gets to the top of the cliff, it will be the end of the world. The turtle is now a big stone shaped exactly like a turtle. [Told at Eel Ground, N.B.]

[Accounts of supernaturals other than Gluskap were mainly limited to personal encounters with Pugulatamutc and Migamawesu. Inquiries about Kitpusiagana brought, in addition to the fragment appended to Tale 18, the information that telling tales about him would cause rain; this is the single instance of a seasonal taboo or restriction on storytelling which we encountered at any time among the Micmac.

[The spirit of Katahdin, the highest mountain in Maine, whose supernatural properties, regarded with awe by Penobscot and Passamaquoddy, have been recorded by such diverse authors as John Giles, Henry D. Thoreau, and the Federal Writers of the WPA, is the hero of a tale told at Shubenacadie, N.S., by Mrs. Henry Sack. Mrs. Sack said she had learned the story from Newell Lulen, a Passamaquoddy, who narrated it at the age of eighty-four, but the reflections of social attitudes and the lively style are certainly her own.]

142. MOUNT KATAHDIN

At Mount Katahdin an old, old kind of people were living.

On an Indian reserve about ten miles from the mountain lived an old couple who had one daughter. They were very, very proud of the daughter. She was handsome. Every fellow wanted to marry her. She wouldn't have any of them. (A boy's parents asked a girl's parents if they would let the daughter marry the boy. Most times, her parents said, "We will if she will.")

The girl said at last, "I'll marry if a fellow comes here and promises to dress me like that mountain. It's green in spring. At the end of summer it's turned all pretty colors. In winter, it's pure white."

Indian men wouldn't want their wives dressed like that.

One day a man came from Mount Katahdin. He looked very young but he was really old. He left his parents at Mount Katahdin, and came to the girl's old parents. (This man's own mother was 200 to 300 years old; she will never die.)

As soon as the girl saw this man, she kind of liked him. He asked her parents if he might marry her. The girl told him what she had told the other men.

He said, "I believe I can dress you like that — in green in the spring, at the end of summer in all different kinds of colors, in winter in white."

The girl said, "I'll marry you."

The old people were glad that at last their daughter was getting married. The man went to his home and brought back things for the party.

For a while the young couple stayed with the old people. They were married in the spring. In the fall the man, Katahdin, said to the family, "Now I'll go hunting."

He went away and stayed quite a while. When he came back, a young son had been born. The child grew fast and was very sensible. The man was proud of him and stayed another year. In the fall he went hunting again, went to his own parents. Next time he came back, there was a young daughter and he was proud again. The two-year-old boy was very wild for so little a child. The other children in the settlement slapped and shook him and the young mother took the child's part, and at last she had few friends.

When Katahdin came home, the child told him all about it. The mother said, "I won't put up with their beating my boy. I'll fight any woman whose child fights my boy."

Her husband said, "That's not the way to do. We'll have to leave this place. People mustn't make bad friends because of children. My parents never allowed that."

She said, "I'd rather go than see my child abused. I think the world of that boy."

He told her parents, "We must leave."

The old people said, "All right. That's a good reason for going."

They hitchhiked to Mount Katahdin. The girl didn't mind walking. The man carried the children and all their belongings. So they came to his old people at Mount Katahdin.

There the girl saw two big snakes lying on each side of the door of a cave in the cliff. She was deadly scared.

Her husband said, "Don't be scared. Those are our dogs. They protect us from danger." He told the snakes, "Keep your heads down. You're scaring the lady and the children."

They went into the cave and it was as nice inside as in a log cabin. By the fireside was an old woman and an old man. The husband's sister was there, too. The old people (they were 200 to 300 years old) were happy to see their grandchildren. They thought the world of them.

The old man said to the young wife, "I've changed my wife into a young woman twice: each time she gets to be fifty years old. I'm going to do it once more. But she can't make me young."

The man was so old that moss grew on his face, arms, and hands. The young wife had to laugh, but she had to believe him, for her husband had told her the old people would never tell her lies.

Katahdin used to go hunting (it was the only way of making their living). One day when he came home, he brought a stranger. This young fellow came from the same settlement that the young wife came from. He had gone out to hunt for her. (She hadn't been his girl; she was his cousin or some other relative. Little boys, you know, get fond of older girls.) While he was out setting traps, he thought he'd like to find the girl, and happened to meet her husband. Katahdin invited him to come to his home. "You might get finer fur around there. My wife said you were a nice kid." (The boy is now a grown-up.)

That same afternoon they came to the cave, and the young fellow was scared by the snakes. "Those are our dogs," said Katahdin. "Keep your heads down and don't scare the visitor." But the stranger nevertheless was still scared.

The wife was very glad to see a man from her settlement. Her young sister-in-law was proud, thinking, "Maybe he will be my boy friend."

All of them played a game. The stranger stayed three or four nights. He thought nothing would change. He said, "I must go now. My parents will be worried."

The young girl gave him a button to remember her by, and said, "Return some day."

Katahdin said, "Can you find your way home?" The stranger said, "Yes, I can." Katahdin said, "I'd better take you as far as the river."

The river was way down below the cave. When they got there, everything looked so changed for an absence of only two or three days! Trees grew where the stranger had left his traps. "This is something wonderful," he thought.

The young man kept on going. Everything had changed. There wasn't even a camp in the settlement. A little farther on he met some Indians and asked them, "Where are my parents?" He described them.

"It's hard to tell you," the Indians said. "Their youngest son is living down there a piece." (This brother was two years old when the young man left home.)

He went to his brother's house. There he found just an old, old man and an old, old woman. The man's name was the same as his brother's.

The old man said, "My brother left the settlement when I was two years old. Everyone then at the settlement has moved away or died. We'll stay here till we die."

My, he was surprised. He still had the girl's button. He couldn't believe all this change had happened in four days. He thought it must have something to do with the Indians in the mountain cave. He thought about the button. He said, "Now I'll go back where my girl friend is."

So he did, and soon he arrived there. They were all glad to see him, and they asked him how he had found everything.

He said, "I'll stay with you. I might marry your sister."

The old man agreed, but the old lady didn't. She said to her husband, "You ought not to let her marry a stranger."

He said, "Our daughter-in-law did that. Why can't our daughter?"

The old lady said, "All right." So they were married.

One time when Katahdin's little boy was getting bigger, he went out of the cave and teased the snakes. The old man came out and yelled at them when they were about to kill the boy: "You can't do that to this child. You're trying to hurt my first grandchild. I order you to get down, both of you."

Both of the snakes were angry. They were big, as big around as a barrel. While they were going down hill, they were tearing up everything, making deep depressions whenever they turned. Next morning

PART TWO *Folktales and Traditions*

water started from the cave and it increased in volume. It flowed down the depressions. It was pretty rough.

That was the Penobscot River. That's how it began.

[Among the many "true stories" told of *buoin*, Old Margaret's exploits cover perhaps the greatest range. The episodes are standard among French, British, and Micmac Canadians, but there is a special interest attached to the woman who gave birth to a shawl. The narrator, a woman of seventy-eight years, living at the Maria Reserve, Que., is the aunt of another informant, ten years her junior, at Ste Anne de Restigouche. According to this younger woman, one of her sisters gave birth to a normal infant with a band of pink flesh from shoulder to waist across its back, long and wide, like a shawl (the chorion or bloody caul). This incident, which was not attributed to witchcraft when related to us, may have been the source of Old Margaret's most spectacularly bad wish.]

143. OLD MARGARET, THE *BUOIN*

Old Maggie, a terrible *buoin*, lived at the Micmac settlement seven miles from Bathurst. No one wanted her mad at them. Once three Indian women set out to walk the seven miles to town. Maggie, the witch, said, "We'll ask some one with a horse to take us." A white man came driving along. She asked for a ride. He said, "I haven't room to take you all. I'll take the one I know." Maggie demanded, "Take me instead." He refused. "I'll be in Bathurst before you are," she told him.

The three women walked on and came to a big hill. At the bottom they saw the man stuck, pulling and pushing in the middle of the road, trying to get his wagon off the road. The three squaws drew near. They saw the horse lying in the road. Maggie, the witch, did not speak. The man said to one of the women, my sister, "My horse fell down dead."

Later he met the witch in town. She said to him, "I got here before you."

The same witch, Margaret, did an evil deed at Restigouche. A young woman, married five years, was childless. The witch had a medicine to cure sterility. She went to the young wife, who had asked to see her. She promised to cure her if she would pay $1.50 for a gallon of ground medicine. The young woman agreed.

Within a year she was pregnant and the husband paid, but the witch again and again begged for more until he, tired of giving meat and money, refused her. The baby was born. At the age of three months it became incurably sick.

An old man at Restigouche, a *buoin*, said Old Margaret was after the baby. He would fight with her. She must come to cure the baby. "When you see her come in, she won't speak. She'll be chewing something. Don't let her give it to the baby. Speak to her and send her away. But what she takes from her pocket and steeps will be good."

That night there was rain, thunder, lightning, and white water in the bay. No boat could cross. But Old Margaret came.

The mother was rocking her baby. The witch came over to them, took the cud out of her mouth, popped it into the baby's mouth, and then the Devil took her away.

The next morning the baby was dead. The old man, the *buoin* came. "You didn't do what I said."

My sister had a fight with that squaw. Old Margaret was staying with her. My sister said, "Go away or I'll take the knife to you." My sister was pregnant. When her baby was born, it wasn't a baby: it was a shawl, rolled up, with the fringe hanging down. The mother nearly died. "You got a bad wish," the doctor told her. He sent for the husband, who took one look, and knew. He took his gun and went to Margaret, saying, "I'll shoot you, or you'll come now and cure my wife." The witch said she couldn't walk. He loaded her on a hand sled and pulled her.

The witch put some medicine on the stove and said, "I'll go upstairs." There were just beams across the ceiling. She was right over the stove. The boards began to creak. She lay flat on her back, asleep, snoring, shivering, her hands moving.

All the time my sister was getting a little better. It was hard to waken Old Margaret. She kept on steeping medicine for a week. When my sister had taken all of it, she was well.

When that old devil was dying, she called her grandson to her and said, "Hold my little finger until I die, and you'll be as strong as I am." But he was afraid to do it.

Margaret's terrible power was shared by her whole family. It was inherited. They foretold only bad things.

Margaret and other members of the family sold love charms. Once when I was having trouble with a fellow, the old witch said, "Give me three dollars. Me fix him." I refused.

PART TWO *Folktales and Traditions*

A girl and her fellow had parted. Another girl had stolen him. Margaret said, "Me fix her. She won't have him long." Within a week the love thief went crazy and acted like a beast. Even the priest said he knew it was the work of the witch.

[One or two tales at most, and, at least, some shadowy remembrance of each group of stories known in 1911–12, remained in 1953. In the category of human adventures, the Deserted Wife was retold, and an old motive new to Micmac collections was added: the girl who married a dog. Animal tales included the adventures of rabbit with bear and with Gigwadju, the wolverine. In a tale of the star husbands, the girls in the pine tree, and the crane-neck bridge, the wolverine's part is played by a jay bird. Kalu, the mythic bird, who carries off children to feed its young, was still remembered. Traditions of early encounters with Europeans are described in the old terms, including Sebastian Cabot's transporting of two Micmac to Europe, and the ubiquitous explanation of the term "squaw" as a white man's misunderstanding of an Indian woman's greeting, *Pis'kwa*, "come in." More than a half-dozen informants mentioned and slightly amplified statements that the Campbellton and Miramichi fires were judgments for mistreatment of the Micmac, and each reserve had its story of buried treasure and attempts to find it; the many incidents of this genre recorded in 1911–12 are omitted from this book.

[Finally, Mohawk stories had dwindled in number and length. Two variants of the Duneil or Dunar story (see Tale 126) told at Restigouche and at Eel Ground have added a Birnam-Wood-to-Dunsinane element to Micmac warfare. At Shubenacadie Mrs. Wilmot and Mrs. Sack each told about the *ginap* Newel Sapir who wrestled successfully with a Mohawk. Mrs. Sack's fuller account, which includes our single collected reference to the Wabanaki-Iroquois Confederacy, follows.]

144. MICMAC AND CAUGHNAWAGS

The Caughnawags used to come and bother the Micmac women while the men were out hunting. The Caughnawags were cruel to the women and they cut off the children's feet and hands, put them on sticks and roasted them. They tied the women's hands and feet.

The Micmac men were mad. One man stayed home from hunting. He hung around until he saw the Caughnawags coming. The Caughnawags saw the Micmac. They already had one Micmac woman and they started off with her. The Micmac man followed them.

The Caughnawags were witches. They would turn into squirrels when the Micmac man came near. He followed the squirrels till he saw light, a camp. The Micmac woman was there. (She wasn't this man's wife or his girl friend.) All fell asleep.

The Micmac man whispered to the woman, "Tie your garters across the wigwam door to trip up the Caughnawags." She did. There was a big fire in the center of the camp [wigwam]. She poured water on the fire and all the ashes came up and burned and blinded them and she escaped.

The Micmac people watched and watched for the Mohawks. About seventy-five years later, three Mohawk men came to Pictou. Old Man Sapir (aged thirty-five) was there. He and his wife were getting eels. He was a tough man. A Mohawk waded out (he was strong) and carried Sapir's canoe to shore.

Sapir got out and the biggest Mohawk said to a young Mohawk, "Hit him!"

"Go away," said Sapir, "you're too young."

Sapir's wife said, "Three to one. They'll kill us. If they get after you, I'll use stones."

Sapir said, "All right. You help me."

The big Mohawk said to Sapir, "Let's wrestle." He grabbed hold. He wasn't fooling.

Sapir got his strength. He grabbed the Mohawk's bare belly and took a handful of skin off. The other two Mohawks tried to help, but Mrs. Sapir threw stones and they ran away. The big Mohawk stopped wrestling with Sapir and ran for his life. Old Sapir found he had a handful of skin from the Mohawk's belly.

Sapir was surprised. He washed the skin the way he would leather and spread it on a stone to dry. The Sapirs got in their canoe and went home. They hung the skin up high.

Thirty-five or forty years later, it was decided to have peace. The Mohawks invited the Micmac to come to their country. The Micmac men had big square pockets [pouches]. Sapir put the skin in his pocket and went with twenty men to Caughnawaga. They walked — from Cape Breton, Pictou, Annapolis, and Halifax, two from every place. They walked to Caughnawaga, and used canoes, too.

PART TWO *Folktales and Traditions*

One Micmac from Annapolis was a witch. The Mohawks had a big old-fashioned pot full of boiling seal oil to treat the Micmac. A Mohawk said, "The first one who drinks that down will be a big man." The one who sat next to Sapir said, "I will." This Micmac took a pint measure of birch bark, filled it with boiling oil, drank it like cold water. The Mohawks pretty near fainted.

The Micmac said, "Let's dance a Mohawk dance. We're on their land. We won't dance an Indian pow-wow dance. That belongs to Micmac. We'll dance Mohawk here."

They started to dance on hard-packed ground, and the Micmac made mud of it. The Mohawks were surprised and got cold-like.

The Mohawk chief said, "We needn't be against each other. Let's be brothers."

The Micmac said, "No. You have been using us very dirty."

Old Sapir said, "If I had been there at the time, I would have helped those babies, because," he said, "I have a piece of leather here in my pocket which belongs to some of you boys here."

An old man stood up, pulled up his coat, and said, "Yes, it belongs here."

The other two got up and said, "Yes, it's the God's truth, because he was so sick after that was taken off we thought he was going to die, but we chewed some herbs and roots and rubbed them on his bare body."

Sapir said, "He may have this back. He might be able to sew it on."

When the Micmac were ready to return home, they made a promise that a Mohawk man won't marry a Micmac woman and a Mohawk woman won't marry a Micmac man. That's a strong promise. They must keep that yet.

Ka'iya. The end.

Bibliography of Micmac Folklore

Fisher, Margaret W. "The Mythology of the Northern and Northeastern Algonkians in Reference to Algonkian Mythology as a Whole," in Frederick Johnson (ed.), *Man in Northeastern North America*, PPFA, 3:226–62. (1946).
Mechling, W. H. *Malecite Tales*. CDM, GS, AS, No. 4, 1914. Memoir 49.
Michelson, Truman. "Micmac Tales," JAFL, 38:33–54 (1925).
Parsons, Elsie Clews. "Micmac Folklore," JAFL, 38:55–133 (1925).
Prince, J. Dyneley (ed.). "A Micmac Manuscript," ICA, 15:87–124 (1907).
Rand, Silas T. *Legends of the Micmac*. New York, 1894.
Speck, Frank G. "Some Naskapi Myths from Little Whale River," JAFL, 28:70–77 (1915).
———. "Some Micmac Tales from Cape Breton Island," JAFL, 28:59–69 (1915).
———. "Penobscot Tales and Religious Beliefs," JAFL, 48:1–107 (1936).
Thompson, Stith. *European Tales among the North American Indians*. Colorado Springs, Colo.: Colorado College Publication, 1919. Gen. Ser. 100 and 101, Lang. Ser. II, No. 34, pp. 319–471.

APPENDIXES, KEY TO ABBREVIATIONS AND INDEX

Appendix A. Zoological Terms

Land Animals

epko'mpk, fisher.
ama'ltcigwes, lynx.
tiageotc', mink.
ki'wesu, muskrat.
a'bukcigan, otter.
abis'tanea'tc, sable.
a'dudu'etc, gray squirrel.
ababa'ametc, ground squirrel (chipmunk).
sa'skcadu, flying squirrel (flying fox).
u'ato'ltc, toad.
ba'ktisam, wolf.
wo'kwis, fox (*me'gweg*, red, *ma'lsteweg*, black, *su'liawe'*, gray, are prefixed to indicate these respective varieties).
pulkut wa'ktaibit, silver gray fox.

EUROPEAN DOMESTIC ANIMALS

kwe'tabet, ox.
leto'alan, bull.
e'lwaduktcitc, heifer.
wendju'diamutck (diminutive of cow), calf, up to about a year and a half old.
te'cibu, horse (Rand: *tasebow*, horse, is derived from French *des chevaux*).
e'lgwaduk te'cibu, mare.
leto'alan te'cibu, stallion.
te'cibuktcitc, colt.
aptci'tc bultigik, pony.
tci'te kilowe'otck, sheep.
tci'te kilowetc'tcitc, lamb.
te'baltc, goat.
ku'lkwis, pig.

EXOTIC ANIMALS

a'udak ki'ni we'djit, monkey.
e'laban, elephant.
mes'tigesbigad'jit, buffalo.

Water Animals and Fish

mu'tcpedji, porpoise.
ko'ukadamp, sturgeon.

wibi'damok, dogfish.
punama'tc, tomcod.
a'mlama, mackerel.
a'dumedj, sardine.
a'nagwedj, flounder or sardine.
glo'etc peda, sculpin.
kamu'ksis, said to be "shoemaker" (has small horns on top of its head, is long, like an eel, has a very large head, and bites fiercely).
e'psamo, shad.
nme'djitc, herring.
ku'spalak, gaspero.
e'tawasu, trout.
ka'tpesa, smelt.
kadjiglagwetc mani, clam (*esk* is also given).
pitowumpk, sand eel.
kat, eel.
ta'awump tcitc, gilt(?).
ko'mp kwetc, suckerfish.
sabadimok, shark.
wabinmek 'wa, white shark (*wa'bin*, white).
n'plamu, salmon.
si'go, bass.
pe'dju, cod.
ca'dkc, lobster.
mtainigetc, crab.
mu'ndama, oyster.
a'ngada'alag, mussel.
kegi na'lawetc, the large "water lizard."
pitalawetc, the small "water lizard" (*ta'ktalok*, lizard).
sa'sap, jellyfish (its tentacles are called *u'kwadal*).
glo'aweddjitc, starfish, "little star."

Birds

LIST OF PETER GINNISH, BURNT CHURCH, MIRAMICHI BAY, N.B.*

tei'mumkwak, wild goose. They hatch up north in a cold place in summer. Heat kills the young ones.
moalewid'tck, brant. It has black legs and a bill like those of a goose, but is smaller. It is sweet meat.
a'ptcitekamutc, wild duck (black). The domesticated duck is called the same.
tama'aniuk, sheldrake. It nests on the shore where grass and bushes grow. It has 20 or 30 young in one hatching. When the young leave the nest, the mother immediately takes them swimming. When frightened, they return to shore. The black duck similarly hatches on a marsh in a wet boggy place.
mo'alewetc, a duck which goes north, as does the goose, to hatch its eggs in a bog. They are the only birds that do so. It nests on soft ground and people must have large snowshoes in order to walk there. "That is what I have heard about them and I know it's all true."
clu'munkwesk is the designation of small (young) wild geese.
moalewi'djis, young brant; *aptcitckamu'djtic*, young ducks (black); *tama'anieshisk*, young sheldrakes.

---

* Peter Ginnish was at the time blind. Many of these birds I was unable to identify. The list and order are his own.

iktc'ikamu'wetcx, sea ducks, hatch on rocks and cliffs.
iktcigwe'tcx, wood duck, hatches in trees, and like a woodpecker digs a hole in the tree.
pu'gweshishx, pond ducks, have, like the black duck, little wings. They make their nests in a pond, at the edge of the water. [All these birds of sea or pond have more than a dozen eggs in their nest, but the informant did not know the exact number.]
tci'ktcanwigane'cic, dipper, or water witch, is a flat-billed duck; small, fat, and has very sweet meat. It builds its nest on the edge of a pond.
pugwe'cic, dipper, a pond duck, nests on the edge of a pond.
mu'iax, canvass-back duck. "When one is killed, it looks like a bag. That is why the English call them canvass-bag. They hatch far away, I do not know where."
nalispam, loon, hatches on a pond.
ni'deyete, salt-water loon, hatches on the shore.
a'duwobu, shag, hatches, as does the gull, on a rock.
be'lagwet, a sea bird.
han'tawesk, the large woodcock, black with red tuft.
a'bo'adetc, woodpecker.
ti'tiesk, blue jay.
miktago'awetc, always in the woods, winter and summer.
kitput, eagle.
eskwaanik, fishhawk.
koarotc, crow.
wa'biguguwe's, winter white owl, never goes to the woods. At haying time he is around. Always hunting.
ti'digalie, cat-owl, is a very queer bird. "If he tries to scare you, you must leave at once, or he will frighten you to death. He sings out at night, talking, talking, and if you do not know him, he will scare you badly. Sometimes he talks Maliseet; I don't know what he talks at other times."
pla'wetc, birch partridge, eats the buds of birch trees. It has a white upper eyelid fold.
widjek, spruce partridge, eats the buds of spruce trees. It has red eyelids.
wasteweye'dtex, one species is the white, and one is the blue, snowbird. When they come, it is a sure sign of snow.
ko'ptcawetcx, robin.
pugudali'skietc, black like a crow, but the size of a robin. It can kill an eagle. It soars down from above onto the neck of the eagle, sticks there, and pecks and pecks until it breaks something on the back of the eagle and causes the bird to fall to the ground. It is the only bird that the eagle cannot kill.
pi'eltcitc, mockingbird.
ki'koli, an old-time bird that knows a great deal. It comes to the Micmac in the night. Whatever it says is certain to be true. It brings news. It repeats "ki' ko li."
unatcputdie'tlu, a very fast bird that flies around about sunset and after dark. It flies in a circle, and comes down with swift swoops. "Ki ka ki aka git! ka ka ki ka git!" it says. This is the whippoorwill (*antrostomus vociferus*).
pugwalecic, chimney swallow.
milida, hummingbird, lays eggs in some place like a garden. It lays four eggs, each about the size of a pea.
o'noiet, dab-chick, or hell-diver, literally, "covered." So called because of the double fold of skin above the eyes, which drops like a curtain.
glo'edjidjit, puffin, cries only after dark. It lays its eggs alongside a river or other stream.
abudawi'sdagedxji'djit, murrelet, marshbird. From *abudawi'sda*, "head first," *gedji'djit*, "doing little tricks," so called because the bird is very quick and it is never

The Micmac Indians of Eastern Canada

possible to tell what way it will go or what it will do. It gets its living on the dikes and ditches. It is a smart bird, and eludes one's surest anticipations.

glo'endietc, smaller gray gull, fishes on salt water, and never goes into fresh water. It gets its living along the beach at low tide, and is so called because it is always hunting. It never lays eggs in a cove, but always on an island or a point of land. If this bird is on the bank nearby, the fishing there is good for all kinds of fish. If you hear them screaming near a sandy point, this is a herald of a coming storm, and you should go ashore. Its flesh is very good.

nikdun'ietc, a larger gull and darker, lays its eggs close to the other gulls, but always a half-mile or so from them. It digs a hole in the sand, covers the bottom of it with grass, and lays its eggs on the grass. The grass is flat and is not arranged in the form of a nest, as is done by other birds.

LIST OF JOHN NEWELL, PICTOU LANDING, N.S.*

magwis', grebe, lives in salt water (*Aechmophorus occidentalis*). Has a flat neck. [1]
kwispumixwadj kwi'nux, lake loon. [2]
kwimu, fresh-water loon (*Gavia imber*). Builds nest on shore, lays three eggs. [7]
kwi'mu, salt-water loon (*Gavia lumme*). Sometimes lays two eggs. Big birds never have many eggs. [11]
wa'bilksuni, white-winged loon. The black guillemot (*Cepphus grylle*). [27]
mactawegal glo'endictc, black gull (*Larus argentatus*). [51; 109, the stormy petrel (*Oceanites oceanicus*), was given the same name.]
wa'betc glo'endietc, white gull (*Pagophila alba*). [39]
ni'xtulanetc, "forked," referring to the tail feathers. The tern (*Sterna hirundo*). [70]
aptcitckamutc, pintail (*Dafila acuta*). Lays many eggs. [A species of loon, in native classification, as signified by the suffix *kamutc kwimu*, loon.] [143]
wa'bietcitckamutc, white duck. Eider (*Somateria dresseri*). [160]
mo'i, surf scoter (*Oidemia perspicillata*). [166]
wa'bisitc, "winter duck." Comes in winter when the gulf is frozen over.
ta'golitc, ta'golidjitcx, goslings, "whistling swan" (*Olor columbianus*). [Probably a wrong identification.] [180]
simamx, Canada goose (*Branta canadensis*). [172]
wi'adjametcx, bittern (*Botaurus lentiginosus*). [190]
sakwatchkamwa'liganetcx, "crest," or "long hair." Heron (*Ardea herodias*). [194]
wabi'tawaliganetcx, white crane (*Grus americana*). [204]
aci'djawigodetcx, sandpiper (*Bartramia longicauda*). [261]
an'xuminxox, plover. [Not identified.]
tci'djawigode'djitc, "sand birds" on shores. Gray and small. [Not identified.]
tci'gadji'djitc, white "sand birds" on shores. Very small. [Not identified.]
wid'jex, grouse (*Canachites franklinii*). [299]
pu'lawetc, Canadian ruffed grouse (*Bonasa umbellus togata*). [300a]
abide'bigi'djatc, "puffing," "expanding," wild turkey (*Meleagris gallopavo silvestris*). [310]
wabol'tidjix pules', "white pigeon." Wild pigeon (*ectopistes migratorius*). [315]
kit'pu (*Aquila chrysaetos*), Golden Eagle [349]
kup'ketc, saw-whet. Small owl. "First heard in March, cries "kup! kup! kup!" at night. If you go out and repeat this after it at night, your house, wigwam, or

---

* The information was obtained by reference to Frank K. Chapman and Chester A. Reed, *Color Key to North American Birds* (New York: Doubleday, Page, 1903). In some cases the informant could not distinguish the variety, and sometimes confused two varieties. (The numbers in brackets refer to the numbering in Chapman and Reed.)

Zoological Terms

clothes will be burned. You will not know where the fire comes from. I do not know the reason for this. It is a very tame bird. In the daytime its eyes are shut all the time. It perches on a bush." [372]

ti'digali, screech owl (*Megascops asio*). [373]

gu'gugwes, owl (*Asio accipitrinus*). [367]

wa'bigu'gugwes, stays on the ice all the time, "white owl" (*Nyctea nyctea*). [376]

a'tawes, woodpecker (*Campephilus principalis*). When warm weather comes, makes a noise with his picking; also in the winter, before a storm. Has *buoin*. [400; 392, ivory-billed woodpecker (*Picoides arcticus*) was supposed identical with 400.]

pe'logwet, parrot. [Evidently derived from the English word.]

tji'gadalig'atc, kingfisher (*Ceryle alcyon*). It makes a hole in a bank and cleans it out. [390]

abo'adjetcxc (*abo'adade'gat*), woodpecker (*Dryobates pubescens medianus*). "He strikes [or drums]." [349c]

widjex, locally, spruce partridge. "All alike." [417]

minido, hummingbird (*Iache latirostris*). [441]

pu'xales, the barn swallow (*Hirundo erythrogastra*). [613]

namat'kalme'sis, wilnilnimta adeg'al, "tail-sticking-up," catbird (*Galeoscoptes carolinensis*). [704]

ma'xtawegsi'sip, blackbird (literally, "black bird").

ti'ti'es, blue jay.

puxto'kdjidji'djit, ivory bell. "Little fire" (bird), so called because of the color of its feathers.

tci'djitwitk'atadjidjit, small ground sparrow (*acidjawit*, the sound of falling water when it runs through a sieve or basket and falls in streamlets, perhaps "trickling" is the nearest English equivalent.)

LIST OF TOM MEUSE

nu'djago'gidj, the moosebird, lays its eggs in March, and is the only bird that lays eggs in winter. It stays in the woods, and never comes out into the open. Four of them work in company, helping each other. Thus the eggs are always covered. No one ever found a nest, but from having watched the birds, we know their home life.

wado'psidjidjit (Burnt Church, N.B.), *geg'watponide'a* (Nova Scotia), from *gegwatpo'nit*, comb (of a fowl). A marshbird. Yellow neck, black on top of its head, and black stripes on its wings.

go'kwetc, a small bird with a large head that sings "go'go!" at night, making a sound like that produced by rubbing one plank on another.

Appendix B. Botanical Terms

ni'punano'ksi, hazel; *epskana'amusi*, black hazel.
so'an, cranberry bush; *sun'aksis*, cranberry; *ni'banmanaksi*, high-bush cranberries.
niske'djaman, moss cranberry.
ka'lidak, or *klidomusi*, raspberry.
winoman, blackberry.
babakte'djkal, gooseberry.
adwom'komin, strawberry.
wis'kiman, a berry, resembling the cranberry, though smaller, which grows on the rocks (*eskwina'am*, "not completely covering").
e'pkuman, blueberry.
maskwes'inaan, wild cherry; *lu'imana'ksi*, black-cherry tree.
e'psemusi, round tree (mountain ash).
ko'gauma'naksi, thorn-bush berries.
abadombiadjik, juniper.
iksusk, hemlock.
kawak, spruce, whether black, red, or white variety. The name is said to be indicative of the noise made by spruce trees when they sway in the wind.
sua'wi, rock maple.
masua'wi, white maple.
kul'djimanaksil, wax root. Said to be from *kete'ls*, cold, and *mana'ksil*, root or stem.
kwa'sanima, waxberry.
wisk'wok, swamp ash.
wisk'wokwabeg', white ash.
maskwe'simana'ksi, cherry tree (*maskwi*, birch, *mana'ksi*, berry).
klum'udjimansksi, white cherry tree.
mkwad'awog, black moosewood.
wa'bog, white moosewood.
tu'psi, elder.
megwegkas'kusi, red cedar (*megweg'*, red).
suo'mo'si, beech.
meskada'djit, princess pine.
mid'i, poplar (*mabeg* and *megweg'*, suffixed for white and red varieties, respectively). "During the time Our Lord spoke with Moses, the people might not speak lest they die. When Moses returned, everything on earth bowed down. The poplar refused to do so. Hence its leaves tremble. For that reason people will not cut it."

NOTE: For the botanical identification of these specimens which I gathered, I am indebted to the late Professor John Muirhead MacFarlane, of the University of Pennsylvania.

Botanical Terms

wik'pi, elm.
ul'migpi, dogwood. (Believed to be cognate with *el'mutc*, dog.)
num'no'an, yellow birch.
mas'kwi, white birch. Rand (*Dictionary*) gives four designations of white birch bark connoting, respectively, when peeled in the proper season, when peeled out of season, when peeled in the winter, when stripped from an old dead log. There are also designations for the bark of a young birch tree, bark for covering a wigwam, bark for building a canoe, the inner bark.
es'toan, fir.
kas'tak, ground hemlock.
aldai'a'awal, vine.
nibu'ktc, a woods or grove.
wig'wan, white bean.
amalabakta'sigal, butter bean, or lima bean ("twines and twines around").
aske'damukgewi, cucumber. ("Eaten raw"; cognate with *e'skimo*, "eaters of raw.")
wen'djusun, apple (literally, "French cranberry").
magoltidek, tomato, i.e., "red all over."
mastaba'anadjitck, pear. (*mastaba'an*, a bowstring, a shoelace, or any tense strand). The same word means jews'-harp; the resemblance in shape is said to be close. (For pear Rand gives the word for "arrowhead.")
bip'toagawe, banana (*bip'toag*, the shape of anything circular or oval and oblong, or flat and oblong, for example, a banana, knife, etc.).
meskigikun, orange, i.e., "big cranberry."
tcu'ktawiganetc, orange. In New Brunswick the same word means raisin; in Nova Scotia, *skadomink* means raisin. From *so'kte min*, "to chew up," or "beat up," fine. The seed of a fruit is *skin'amin*; the core, *lampk*; the skin (also the skin of an animal), *bi'oksig'an*.
bibigwana'tckal, dandelion. (*bibigwa'an*, music, *natckal*, stalk). So called from its use by children, who blow on the stem as a whistle, as they use a blade of grass.
tesipka'ksit, clover (*ni'bi*, leaf, *kamutc*, stem, i.e., "leafed stem").
kulu'mpkcul, wheat.
te'siboiman, oats (*te'sibo*, horse; *i'man*, berry).
bakwi'dawel, buckwheat.
tabadatck, potato.
bie'skaman, corn.
utuua'nabaktcid'jit, a yellow flower (*utuua'ni*, a muscle or tendon, a cord; *tci'dji't*, small).
i'kton, "sea leaf," literally, "out at sea" (*Louchus olenaccus* (?), Hare's lettuce).
eduiwu'lnu'ksit, labrador bush (*edu'i*, "both sides"; *wulnuk*, "smooth," "soft," that is, both sides smooth and soft). *Ledum latefolium* (*Groenlandicum*).
mo'ino'nan, literally, "bear berry" (*Myrica cerifera*, wax myrtle). Ripe in August, eaten by bears, and believed to be stored away by them for winter use.
sasagomana'ksi, a short bush eaten by moose, for the sake of the berries, known as mooseberries (*Corvus canadensis*, bunch berry).
tcigawa'bi, bass root.
labileskbemampkiagaweg (*labilesk*, "black seed," *bemampkiogaweg*, "sand beach"). So called because it grows on the beach (*Polygala, Glaux maritima*, sea milkwort).
mi'tcimsigo, literally, "single leaf" (*Polygonum convolvulus*, Black bindweed). An ivy said to be poisonous. It has only one leaf on each branch.
a'la'weaksil, "pea plant." In the old days this was boiled with fat and eaten. The same name is given the cultivated pea (*Lathyrus*).
ka'adjumanakti, "crow's nest."
sage'ban, "wild potato." A species of wild carrot, grows mainly in low sandy soil.
mtcusabeg'an, a large wild carrot (*Ligusticum scoticum*, Lovage).

mkwot'ck, the large swellings or burls on trees, said to be caused by the collection of a superabundance of sap. If the sap finds egress, the swelling will not form.
ma'susid'jal, sweet-john. A low-growing bush.
wababa'ktcigal, the wild sarsaparilla bush (literally, "white strings," *Aralia nudicaulis*).
a'ldaia'al, "land," bogberry.
pisa'anak, "French soldiers." A very short plant which grows in closely packed single stems. Its tops are said to resemble the hats of French soldiers. Hence the later name, *swa'ganisk* ("soldiers").
sos'kasitc, a forest plant which resembles crowfoot.
wa'bwesawek, literally, "white flower" (*Anophales* (*Antennanea*) *margaritacea*, Woolly cudweed, or large-flowered everlasting).
ka'adjuma, winter berries. Boiled for tea in the winter.
abu'duwe'djiwa'lu, literally, "squirrel's tail," or *madaweswa'lu*, wild carrot (*Achillea millefolium*, yarrow).
inpowabiadjidjkal, a short gray plant.
a uudjidjimanaksi, a swamp willow.
wabu'ukwuo'k, white moss.
ke'cikabi'tckawe'l, a plant that grows in salt-water marshes.
kun'dawey'el (literally, "clinging to rock"), a moss found on rocks.
gig'wesuskwul, "muskrat root." So called because the muskrat eats it. Flagroot.
rusig'iwima'su'si, fine leaf fern (*rusig'iwuk*, sticky, clinging).
rusi'giwi, hay.
kuwas'aumana'ksil, literally, "old moss log stem." Usually grows on an old mossy log.
bis'aganu'kul, bog moss (*bi'soganuk*, "filling" a crack or opening). So called from its employment in filling up the cracks in the wigwam or in canoes; also, the bear is believed to rub this into its wounds. (*Sphagum acutifolium and cymbifolium*, the narrow and broad-leafed bog moss.)
li'pkoda'men, broad-blade swamp grass (*eli'pkadem*, "to indent with the teeth," as when one makes designs on thin birch bark with the teeth). Said to be poisonous. Iris (*prismatica*?).
sada'newim'pkewe (*sedan'ewimpk*, "St. Anne's Day"), the daisy; also the wild pink rose; the "black-eyed Susan."
impkuaksedanewim'pkewe, a flower that blossoms in the bogs. This and the last mentioned are gathered on St. Anne's day.
ga'gipkul, a bush (*gag'ipc*, "rough and irritating"). When boiled, it has a rough and irritating taste. It is believed to be poisonous. (*Kalina augustifolia*, the narrow-leaved sheep's laurel.)
ki'silaba'kodewim'pkge'we, buttercup (*laba'dkod*, a holiday or fast day, said to be June 18); *impipk*, holiday, *wadaptekwas'owek*, "buttercup," is, presumably, an older name.
aldai'alawel, a trailing vine (*Lycopodium clavatum*, Club moss, running pine).
kida'anamusi, staghorn sumach (*Rhus typhira*, or *hinta*).
ma'susi, coarse-leaf fern (*Pteris aquilina* (*Pteridium aquilinum*), brake, or bracken fern).
wis'kimamaksi, "snake-berry bush" (*Oxycoccus Vaccinium macrocarpori*, large American cranberry).
sko'tpigus'uwiwas'awe'ktcitc, May flower, or arbutus (*Epigaea reperis*). *skoto'tpasi*, coming up (*sko'tpigus*, May; *wa'sawek*, flower; *tcitc*, diminutive). Used on the Virgin Mary's birthday.
wade'psidek, literally, "yellow bush" (*Sporoea salicifolia*, American meadow sweet).
msi'tkodjowegan, hairy mullein (*Verbascum Thapsus*).
psina'an, Appalachian tea (*Viburnum cassinoides*).

Appendix C. Anatomical Terms

wagi or *ukti'nin*, body. No word for corpse is in use.
up'sagupk, raw flesh.
wa'anda, skeleton.
un'djiel, skull.
geg'wutpun, scalp.
uktug'wedjan, forehead.
[*che'dakun*, occiput (Rand).]
ehnida'anut, the lower portion of the back of the head around the nape of the neck, extending from the occipital projection to the lower margin of the hair.
ukto'lowagan, (either) side of the neck.
uktco'alkaweg'am, front of the neck from chin to top of sternum.
wibida'tck, the gum on (either side) of lower jaw.
widjimi'au, cheek.
us'il, lip (upper or lower).
usis'kwan, nose.
uk'tun, mouth.
jugigul, eye.
lm'alkagal, nasal aperture (seldom used).
sis'kwumit'ck, depression between the eyes at root of the nose.
wit'kul, eyelid.
umsig'wan, eyebrow.
lamipck, eyeball; also, core of a fruit, for example, of the apple.
[*mpukika ulnoojech*, "little man of the eye" (pupil?) (Rand).]
wa'beg, white of the eye (literally, "white").
wa'sawolbi'gikwat, iris (*wa'sawol*, "shiny," *bi'gikwat*, "place," or "location").
la'muksidiwag'an, interior of the ear; *sidiwa'an*, external ear.
u'sabun, hair of the head.
pru'ksiganagawel, hair of the body.
pri'wedama, hair on symphysis pubis and in armpits.
wi'dul, hair of the face.
utilma'an, shoulder, from the base of the neck to acromion.
upi'dinomun, arm, from acromion to wrist.
upi'tan, hand, from wrist to end of fingers. (There is no name for wrist.)
un'kwiskotc, joint.
u'klui'gan, finger.
uktidjan, thumb.
msku'saweklui'gan, first finger.

NOTE: The terms and equivalents in this list were given by one informant, Thomas Meuse.

da'boiklui'gan, second finger, and so on, the numeral adverb being prefixed to finger for third and fourth fingers. Also, *wi'tckwobugawitck* indicates little finger.
ina'an, right hand.
pa'dadutc, left hand. His "left" or his "right" means left hand or right hand.
lanul'tau, the palm of the hand, including the palm or surface of the fingers. There is no name for knuckles, or for the palm of the hand not including the palm or surface of the fingers.
ko'si, nail of finger or of toe.
ina'anainkatc, right foot.
pa'dadutce i'nkutc, left foot.
to'djumal, toes.
pi'skiskunam, or *utodjimin*, big toe.
aptcedjidjit, little toe.
upus'kun, chest, including sternal length.
epune'bigatc, side, from armpits to lower margin of ribs.
n'tala, surface area around pelvic region.
o'igan, depression along spinal column.
uksug'an, spinous prominence at parting of the buttocks.
ukpiga'gan, ribs. (Bony portion.)
u'musti, abdomen.
wi'li, navel.
kwad'kogan, groin.
ulukwa'kog, depression on inner side of the leg between thigh and symphysis pubis.
mi'stunk, urethra.
duwa'andjitc, testicles (*duwa'an*, "ball," *djitc*, diminutive).
kwe'djikat, upper leg.
uktakalam, posterior surface of upper leg, or of lower leg.
utcig'wan, circumferential surface about the knee. There is no name for kneecap.
wi'tckwo'gwat, anterior surface of lower leg from knee to foot.
u'kwat, surface around ankle.
u'kun, heel.
e'kida'sitc, sole of foot, including solar surface of the toes.
pa'amikut, upper surface of foot from ankle to tip of toes.
a'nakwedj, vulva. "Jellyfish," *mas*, is a vulgar name for the same. The female organ of an animal is *um'usal*. Another vulgar term for vulva is *elma'kasit* (*elma'kit*, "hole"). (Similarly, penis has other appelations: *upu'guma'an*, "club," not a vulgar appelation; *utu'lum* and *mip* are vulgar designations.)
ma'tola, the penis of an animal.
tci'ptci'dja, a "funny word" for penis. The scrotum, including the testicles, is known as *dabadatck*, or *mul'sug*. The sex organs of fowls or birds are designated for males as *skwe'o*, and for females as *na'beo*.
mi'djimic, anus.
mano'i, buttocks.
kwanhuman, heart. It hangs on *uku'mlamuna'bi*, a muscular fiber of semicircular shape attached to the lower part of the neck near the seventh cervical vertebra. (The last mentioned has no name.)
wa'ktias, intestines.
mu'tcian, large intestine.
wis'kan, gall bladder.
ma'ldu, blood.
t'akalan, muscle.
utnuanabi, any large muscle, for example, the biceps muscle.

Key to Abbreviations

AA, American Anthropologist
AACFAS, Annales de l'association canadienne-franc pour l'avancement des sciences, Montreal
AAOJ, American Antiquarian and Oriental Journal
ANCP, Archives Nationales, Colonies, Paris
ARBAE, Annual Reports, Bureau of American Ethnology
BFMUP, Bulletin, Free Museum of Science and Art, University of Pennsylvania
BSGQ, Bulletin de la Société de Géographie de Québec
CANJ, Canadian Antiquarian and Numismatic Journal
CDM, GS, AS, Canada Department of Mines, Geological Survey, Anthropological Series
CNBHS, Collections of the New Brunswick Historical Society
CUAAS, Catholic University of America, Anthropological Series
HERE, Hastings Encyclopaedia of Religion and Ethics
HM, Historical Magazine
ICA, Proceedings of the International Congress of Americanists
INM, Indian Notes and Monographs (Museum of the American Indian, Heye Foundation)
JAFL, Journal of American Folklore
JAI, Journal of the (Royal) Anthropological Institute of Great Britain and Ireland
JR, The Jesuit Relations and Allied Documents
JSAP, Journal de la Société des Americanistes de Paris
MHSC, Massachusetts Historical Society Collections
NAR, North American Review
NH, Natural History
OFC, Our Forest Children (Owen Sound, Ontario)
PAAAS, Proceedings of the American Association for the Advancement of Science
PAAS, Proceedings of the American Antiquarian Society
PAPS, Proceedings of the American Philosophical Society
PM, Primitive Man
PNBM, MS, Publications of the New Brunswick Museum, Monographic Series
PPFA, Papers, Robert S. Peabody Foundation for Archaeology (Andover, Mass.)
PTNSIS, Proceedings and Transactions of the Nova Scotia Institute of Science
PTRSC, Proceedings and Transactions of the Royal Society of Canada
SJDS, St. John [N.B.] Daily Sun; SJDT, St. John Daily Telegraph
SR, Scottish Review
TCI, Transactions of the Canadian Institute
TCSME, Transactions of the Canadian Society of Mines and Engineering
YAS, Yale Anthropological Studies

Index

Abnaki, 14
Abortion, 248, 253
Acculturation, 9, 10–11, 67, 81, 168–69, 170, 183–84, 188, 237, 270–308: Christian elements, 87, 98, 99, 100, 133, 138–39, 144–45, 152, 184, 214, 246, 306, 332, 387, 446, 502; tale, 412
Adoption, 256: of whites, 21, 256
Adornment, 85–87, 89: face paint, 86–87; scarification, 86; tattooing, 86, 242
Adze, 76
Afterlife, 19–20, 149–50
Aged, 109, 256–58, 306
Agriculture, 19–20
Algonkin, language and people, 3, 14, 21, 86, 90, 204–5, 210, 220, 221, 223, 317, 321
Anatomy and physiology, native, 121–23, 505–6
Anderson, William P., 102
Animals: insult to (Maliseet), 40; as weather signs, 101; months based on habits of, 103–4; beliefs about, 106–7; respect for, 107–9, 118; flesh tabooed, 109, 249–50, 251, 267, 277; domestic, 114–16; undersea, 116
Annapolis Royal, *see* Port Royal
Anticosti Island, 16, 53, 207
Armochiquois, *see* Penobscot
Arrow, 32–33, 216
Awl, 76

Baie des Chaleurs, 11, 12, 13, 15, 16, 19, 53, 102, 176, 190, 261, 266, 272, 273, 318, 330, 332, 362, 365, 418
Barbeau, Marius, 41, 89, 90
Baseball, 292
Baskets, 73–75, 76: origin of, 73–74

Bathurst, N.B. (Nipisiguit), 12, 140, 176, 218, 330, 392, 432, 484, 488
Beads, 84, 85–86
Bear, 35–36, 106, 108–10, 277, 408–9, 414–15, 425, 431, 437, 444
Beaver, 34–35, 107, 108–9, 110–11, 267, 277, 329, 330, 435
Beer, native, 66–67
Beothuck, 125, 205–6, 319
Berries, drying of, 66, 431
Biard, Father Pierre, 10, 13, 17, 25, 49, 60, 79, 85, 103, 114, 120, 126, 134, 135, 142, 171, 173, 177, 183, 211, 212, 222, 229, 261, 262, 266
Big Cove Reserve, N.B., 3, 4, 16, 28, 188, 209, 273, 277, 291, 376, 405–6, 432. *See also* Richibucto
Birch-bark containers, 62, 70–73, 90, 93
Birds, 38–40, 117–18, 498–501: songs learned from, 118–19
Blood, 122
Blood-brotherhood, 184, 187
Blood-letting, 122, 295
Blue Jay, 342
Botany, native, 119, 502–4
Bow, 31–32: for war, 216; origin of, 396–97
Bread, 67
British, attitude toward, 11, 203, 210, 220, 333–34, 336, 337, 361, 447, 455, 461–63, 470–73
Brooms, 76
Brother-sister etiquette, 228–29
Buoin (witch), 22, 118, 123, 134, 138, 156–62, 200, 246, 250, 297, 298, 299, 300–1, 325, 376, 385–91, 451–54, 488–90: mountain ash as protection against, 296

508

Index

Burnt Church Reserve, N.B., 3, 4, 7, 14, 16, 42, 47, 48, 49, 57, 61, 77, 78, 84, 87, 88, 102, 103, 129, 151, 154, 157, 159, 162, 163, 168, 169, 174, 176, 184, 188, 189, 208, 233, 245, 249, 253, 256, 258, 270, 274, 277, 278, 279, 280, 283, 289, 290, 291, 292, 293, 317, 319, 341, 351, 353, 358, 369, 371, 390–91, 396, 402–6, 413, 456, 459, 472–79, 481, 498

Cabot, Sebastian, 490
Cadillac, Antoine de la Mothe, sieur de, 15, 16
Campbell, Duncan, 61, 228, 245, 254
Campbellton, N.B., 170, 271, 272, 279, 298–99, 357, 447, 459, 479–80, 484
Canada, Department of Citizenship and Immigration, Indian Affairs Branch, 271, 274, 276, 279, 282, 290, 306
Cannibalism: in war, 217; ceremonial at funerals, 266, 407–8; Djenu, 338–41, 343–45, 348
Canoes
    Birch bark, 18, 30, 42, 330: construction, 42–46; anchor, 46; paddles, 46; sails, 46–47, 49, 364; size, 47, 49; navigability, 47–48; disappearance of, 50; adornment, 89, 175; mythic origin, 330
    Dugout, 51
    Hide, 50–51, 326
    Spruce bark, 50
Cape Breton, 3, 4, 7, 11, 12, 13, 16, 21, 22, 34, 95, 106, 107, 114, 144, 152, 153, 155, 156, 157, 161, 163, 174, 183, 190, 194, 201, 203, 205, 206, 207, 209, 220, 224–25, 231, 238, 243, 259, 261, 264, 275, 282, 283, 285, 286, 299, 304, 305, 317, 327, 329, 330, 338, 365–66, 377, 387–88, 390–91, 449, 471, 481, 491
Caribou, 106, 111, 323–24, 417, 437, 441
Cartier, Jacques, 10, 318
Carving, stone and wood, 92
Cats, 116, 324
Caughnawaga, *see* Iroquois
Caul, 250, 296, 299–300, 488
Cemeteries, 266–67
Champlain, Samuel de, 11, 418
Chapel Island, C.B., 283, 285–88, 475–76
Charlevois, P. de, 15, 150
Chesnaye, Aubert de la, 15

Chief, 171–75, 176, 184, 185, 188, 379: insignia, 85, 172, 287; succession, 171; duties, 172, 173–74; assistant to the chief (Watchers), 174–75, 184, 238; grand chief, 176, 209, 225, 285, 287, 305.
Chief and Council (*1953*), 306
Chignecto, N.B., 12, 17, 102, 203
Childbirth, 108, 250, 296
Children: care and training, 227–28, 253–55, 303; as wage earners, 281–82
Chippewa, *see* Ojibwa
Clothing, aboriginal, 78–81: raincoat, 81; cleaning, 81; traditional, 82–83, 282
Cold, 100
Coleman, Sister Bernard, 360–61
Columbus, Christopher, 469
Cooney, Robert, 21, 78, 377
Corn: cultivation of by Maliseet and Iroquois, 19–20; mythic origin, 399–400
Cow, 116, 324
Cradleboard, use and ornamentation, 92, 252
Crane, 428, 435–36: crane-neck bridge, 413, 427, 430, 490
Cree, 344, 361
Crime and punishment, 172–73
Crow, 432–33, 442, 444–45

Dalhousie, N.B., 273, 362, 365
Dancing: at feasts, 180–81, 182, 186, 187, 191–92, 287, 289; war dance, 218
Day, divisions of, 104–5
Death, 108, 258–69: cremation, 258; interment, 258–60, 263; messengers, 258, 263; secondary burial, 260, 264; the dying, 260–61, 262, 294; disposal of property, 261; death customs (*1953*), 293–94
Deer, 36, 111, 417
Degeneration, physical, 120, 408
Denys, Nicolas, 13, 15, 34, 35, 37, 39–40, 41–42, 49, 68, 78–79, 80, 178, 179, 241, 252, 255, 261, 264, 265, 267
Denys, Richard, 274
Design, 89, 92, 93–96: double curve, 96
Dew, 100
Dièreville, le Sieur de, 13, 15, 17, 60, 86, 111, 125, 126–27, 142, 146, 148, 171, 221, 222, 229, 251, 255, 261, 265
Diet, effects of, 122–23
Directions, finding of, 54
Disease: and its treatment, 123–35, 294–96, 357; causes of, 123, 266, 296

509

Distances, reckoning of, 54
Divorce, 243
Djenu, see Cannibalism
Dodge, E. S., 91, 92
Dogs, 33, 63, 114–16, 122, 166–67, 212, 324–25, 326, 328–29, 433, 482–83, 490
Dragon, see Serpent
Dreams, 138–41, 159–60, 211, 299
Drowned persons: resuscitation of, 126–27; offerings to spirits, 266; ghost of, 374–75
Drum, 180, 191, 287
Ducks, 107, 436
Dyes, 87–89, 399

Eagle, 118, 428–29, 433–34
Economic occupations (1953), 278–81
Education: Canadian, 23, 307; by Ursuline nuns, 89–90
Eel Ground Reserve, N.B., 3, 4, 16, 28, 49, 157, 175, 176, 274, 282–83, 290, 292, 303, 308, 460, 481, 484
Eel River Reserve, N.B., 3, 4, 16, 273, 318, 481, 484
Eels, drying and smoking of, 62–63
Eggs, 65
English language, use of, 22, 23, 24, 271
Eskasoni Reserve, C.B., 16, 225, 275, 276, 279, 285, 288, 292, 293, 301, 366, 481
Eskimo, 11, 66, 80, 90, 100, 206–8, 219, 220–21, 229, 245, 258, 266, 332, 385
Etchemin, see Maliseet

Fairy tales, European, 319, 405
Family, 171, 226–33: recital of genealogies, 179; allowance, Canadian, 270, 281
Feasts, 178–83, 185–86, 189: "eat-all," 178; marriage, 178, 242–43; war, 203, 212
Fire-making, 396
Fires: Miramichi, 101, 169, 298, 447, 476–79, 490; Campbellton, 170, 298, 299, 377, 447, 479–80, 490; Rimouski, 170
Fish: method of smoking and cooking, 62–63; beliefs about, 113; trout, 326
Fisher, Margaret, 317, 321
Fishing, 27, 277, 278: hooks, 27; spears, 27, 397; nets, 28; weirs, 28–29; through the ice, 29
Flannery, Regina, 361
Fleché, Jessé, 10
Flute, 191

Fog, 100, 325
Folktales, as reflecting culture, 6, 25, 234, 246, 317
Food: preferences, 5; supply in aboriginal times, 18, 25–26
Fox, 112, 114–15, 430
French, relations with, 10, 11, 203, 209, 210, 217, 334–36, 361, 399, 447, 461–63, 469–70, 473
Frog, 277–78, 327, 329
Funeral rites, 264–66, 407–8. See also Death

Gambling, 20, 195, 244, 293
Games, 195–201: songs at, 193. See also Waltes
Ganong, William F., 68, 69, 102
Gaspé, 3, 4, 12, 16, 21, 22, 53, 60, 80, 91, 102, 103, 149, 173, 174, 207, 210, 212, 213, 214, 218, 220, 243, 261, 266, 271, 272, 273, 304, 330, 331–33, 365, 482
Gaspesians (designation of Micmac), 14, 16, 69, 125, 150, 240
Geese, 435–36
Geography, native, 102–3
Germain, Father Charles, 203
Gesner, Abraham, 223
Ghost, see Skadegamutc
Giants, 154, 343, 348–49
Gigwadju, see Wolverine
Gilmour, Rankin and Company, 476
Ginap, 156, 157, 174, 184, 185, 187, 246, 250, 298, 299, 300, 376–84, 456–59, 467–69, 490–92
Ginnish, Mrs. Peter, 8, 42, 84
Ginnish, Peter (informant at Burnt Church, N.B.), 7, 8, 14, 42, 47, 73, 77, 99, 102–3, 117, 161, 188, 235, 245, 246, 283, 295, 300, 319, 323, 354, 378, 405, 432, 476, 498
Gluskap, culture hero and transformer, 13, 42, 51, 112, 153, 155, 166, 209, 304, 305–6, 321–37, 348, 366, 435, 480, 481–82
Gugwes, 348, 417–18, 422–23, 430–31
Gulls, 118–19

Hagar, Stansbury, 56, 155, 260
Hairdo, 83–85, 379: hairstring, women's, 85
Harpoons, 30
Hawk, 118, 428, 433–34
Heye Museum (Museum of the American Indian), 89, 93, 387
Hoe, 76

Index

Holidays, 291–92: Christmas, 291–92; Easter, 292; Dominion Day, 292; personal days, 292
Hospitality, 177–78
Housing, 274–75
Hunting and trapping, 29, 30–40, 172–73, 277: calendar, 25–26; localities, 53; allotment of territory, 172; stories about, 408–12
Huron Indians, 90, 92
Husband and wife, duties, 229–30

Ideal character, 307
Ideographs, 12, 23–24
Incest, 229
Indian Island Reserve, N.B., 16
Infant feeding: nursing and weaning, 250, 296; first solid food, 250–51, 253
Iroquois (Caughnawaga, Mohawk), 18, 90, 96, 118, 156, 175, 194–95, 202, 206, 208–11, 219, 223–25, 246, 298, 318, 319, 447, 448–61, 463–69, 490–92

Jesuit Relations, 9, 13, 14, 15, 205, 220, 257
Jesuits, *see* Missions and missionaries
Johnson, Frederick, 144, 156
Joking relationship, 233

Kalu, 445–46, 490
Katahdin, Mount, 366, 484–88
Kauder, Father Charles, 23
Keskamzit, 42, 146, 153, 162–66, 301–2, 357, 392–94, 397
Kettles, 68–69
Kingfisher, 434
Kinship, 230–33
Kitpusiagana, 338–43, 417–18, 422–23, 481, 484
Knives, stone, 75

Ladybird, 326
Landmarks, 54
Language, 21–24, 143, 483: Maliseet, 202–3
LeClercq, Father Chrétien, 12–13, 14, 19–20, 23, 35, 37, 38–39, 54, 60, 64–65, 69, 85, 86, 91–92, 103, 111, 122, 123, 126, 127, 134–36, 142–45, 146–47, 149–50, 156, 158, 172, 173, 208, 211, 212, 218, 222, 228, 229, 230, 236, 241, 243, 254–57, 261, 263, 266–69, 274, 482
Leighton, Alexander, 30
Le Jeune, Father Paul, 21

Leland, Charles Godfrey, 207
Le Loutre, Abbé Jean-Louis, 203
Lennox Island Reserve, P.E.I., 3, 4, 16, 158, 165, 208, 239, 250, 274
Lescarbot, Marc, 9, 10, 13, 19, 20, 28, 32, 33, 35, 49, 67–69, 75, 79, 84, 109, 126, 134, 135, 171, 205, 211, 212, 213, 218, 219, 220, 241, 244, 255, 257, 261, 263
Lice, 65, 322
Lightning, 99, 296
Lizards, 109, 113
Loon, 386
Lorette (Huron Mission), 90, 92

Magic, 166–67, 199–200, 212–14, 450–51: sympathetic, 249. *See also Buoin*
Maillard, Abbé Antoine Simon, 9, 12, 13, 23, 68, 86, 143–44, 149, 179, 202, 214–17, 237, 242, 245, 265, 283, 470
Maliseet, 11, 14, 16, 18, 19, 40, 50, 52, 53, 69, 90, 95, 202–5, 208, 210, 214, 217, 223, 237, 273, 277, 305, 335, 447–48, 499
Manitoo, 143, 146, 149, 243, 251, 298
Mankind, origin, 144
Manslaughter, 37, 172–73
Maple sap and sugar, 67
Maps, 54–55, 454
Maria Reserve, Que., 3, 4, 16, 272, 273, 274, 289, 290, 304–5, 488
Marquis de Malauze (French ship), 182, 318
Marriage, 184, 188, 234: tales, 234, 379, 402–7, 465–66; true stories, 235–36; choice and consent, 236, 240; age, 237; missionary influence, 237; tribal arrangements, 237–39, 285; polygyny, 239–40; probationary year, 240–42; ceremonial feast, 242–43; weddings, 293
Marten, 323, 327, 437, 441–44
Martin, William C., 282, 288–89, 293, 302
Massé, Father Enemond, 16
Meat, smoking and cooking, 63–65
Mechling, William H., 22
Medicineman, 134–36, 156, 251, 266: as diviner, 146–49, 174–75, 242
Medicines, 127–34, 294–96, 343, 357, 432
Membertou, 10, 16, 17, 20, 120, 146, 175, 178, 182, 209, 240, 262, 266
Memory, 137
Menstruation, 108, 244–45

511

Mermen (Halfway People), 303, 349–54
Messages, 55–56, 175
Meuse, Thomas (informant), 7, 110, 117–18, 121–22, 151, 193, 319, 323, 501, 505
Michelson, Truman, 22, 456
Micmac Messenger, 24, 318
Migamawesu, 155, 302–4, 348, 356–61, 453, 484
Migration, seasonal, 25
Mind, 137
Mink, 437
Miramichi Bay and River, 10, 12, 16, 19, 60, 62, 102, 103, 124, 157, 169, 173, 175, 201, 202, 203, 224, 258, 261, 268, 270, 273–74, 278, 280, 291, 294, 298–99, 308, 320, 447, 456, 472–79
Miscou (St. Charles Mission), 12, 13, 15, 115, 207, 214, 219, 221, 258
Miscouien (designation of, Micmac), 15
Missions and missionaries, 10–12, 14–15, 237; Jesuits, 10, 11, 12, 115, 120, 207, 220, 240, 272
Modeling, clay, 92
Mohawk, *see* Iroquois
Mole, 112, 435
Montagnais, 11, 15, 18, 52, 53, 205, 206, 210, 218–21, 338, 344
Months, 103–4
Moon: eclipse, 98; calendrical, 103–4; phases, 104, 250; worship, 143–44; helper in childbirth, 144; oath, 214
Moose, 36–38, 63, 101, 106–7, 108, 111, 127, 277, 417, 425, 437–41
Moose-hair embroidery, 92
Morgan, Lewis H., 232–33
Mosquitoes, origin, 340, 430–31
Mourning, 258, 267–69
Mouse, 417–18, 422–23
Murder, 172–73, 401
Muskrat, 277, 329, 342, 435

Name of Micmac tribe, 14–16
Names, 253: nicknames, 121
Navel cord, 249, 250, 296
Newell, John (informant at Pictou Landing, N.S.), 7, 8, 100, 102, 106, 114, 117, 118, 120, 138–41, 153, 159–61, 166, 175, 184–88, 194, 195, 205, 235, 238, 246, 261, 283, 294, 300, 319, 323, 372, 390, 500
Nighthawk, 118
Nipisiguit, *see* Bathurst
North American Indian Brotherhood, 306, 308

Numerals, 105
Nyanza Reserve, C.B., 277, 301

Ointment, animal fat, 21, 87
Ojibwa, 205, 229, 344, 360–61
Old-time Micmac, concepts of, 25, 38, 101, 120, 122–23, 408
Omens and signs, 167–70, 214, 500
Oratory, 179–80, 181, 182
Origins, 73, 144, 330, 337, 396–400, 482–83, 488
Orphans, 256
Ottawa (tribe), 50, 205, 218, 223, 224
Otter, 323, 415–17, 419–22, 433, 438, 484
Owl, 117–18, 119, 151–52, 325, 326, 342, 371, 499, 500–1

Pacifique, Father, 22–24, 102–3, 145, 290, 318
Parkman, Francis, 204–5, 477
Parsons, Elsie Clews, 225, 231, 285–87, 317, 405
Partridge, 101, 325, 328, 438, 441–45
Passamaquoddy, 3, 14, 55, 202, 223, 484
Peabody Museum, Salem, Mass., 91–92
Penobscot, 3, 14, 16, 40, 90, 202–6, 210, 219, 223–24, 266, 305, 360, 448, 484
Percé, Gaspé, Que., 11, 12, 16, 207, 221, 330, 331, 333
Physical traits, native designations, 120–21
Physical type, in the seventeenth century, 20–21
Physiology and anatomy, native, 121–23, 505–6
Pictou Landing Reserve, N.S., 3, 4, 7, 16, 47, 51, 76, 88, 94, 113, 116, 128, 130, 140, 151, 160, 166, 184, 200, 201, 204, 206, 208, 235, 257, 259, 260, 264, 276, 294, 317, 319, 368, 372, 387, 389, 390, 392, 395, 401, 413, 433, 448, 449, 456, 480, 491, 500
Pigeons, 118, 433
Pins, 81
Pipes, 68
Place names, 102–3
Poor, assistance to, 176–77, 186–87
Population, 17
Porcupine, 63, 101, 112, 277, 323–24, 437
Porcupine quillwork, 86, 89, 175: boxes, 89–92, 279
Porpoise, 29, 30–31
Port Royal (Annapolis Royal), 10–13, 18,

Index

62, 79, 103, 114, 120, 126, 146, 147, 171, 178, 203, 210, 212–13, 241, 261–63, 265, 266
Power, supernatural, 156–66, 202, 298, 447
Precocity, 138
Pregnancy: prenatal influence, marking, 248–49; easy delivery, 249; sexual intercourse, 251
Promiscuity, sexual, 237
Prophecy, 157, 174
Psychology, native, 137–41
Puffin, 117
Pugulatamutc, 47, 155–56, 302–5, 325, 331, 348, 362–67, 484

Quiver, 33

Rabbit, 277, 413–22, 438, 481
Raccoon, 112, 429, 439–41
Race mixture, 21
Rainbow, 98–99
Rand, Silas, 22, 47, 48, 51–52, 53, 66, 103, 104, 134, 146, 177, 190, 202, 207, 227, 232, 233, 254, 317, 318, 319, 341, 345, 348, 435, 503, 505
Rats, 116–17
Rattle, 186, 191
Recollect (Franciscan) Fathers, 11, 12
Red Bank Reserve, N.B., 3, 4, 16, 50, 102, 120, 157, 175, 176, 217, 258, 259, 274, 304, 387–88, 403, 432, 454, 456, 460
Reed, Sheldon C., 299
Religion, 142–50
Reserves, Micmac, in 1954, 16, 271–77
Restigouche Reserve, Que., 3, 4, 12, 16, 23, 24, 50, 51, 65, 102, 103, 116, 145, 160, 169, 175, 176, 209, 266, 271, 272, 277–79, 289–90, 292–94, 301, 304–5, 318, 331, 432, 456, 459, 479–80, 482, 488
Retribution, supernatural, 169–70, 447
Richard, Father André, 210–12
Richibucto, river and region, 16, 19, 102, 176, 202, 221, 273. *See also* Big Cove Reserve
Rivière-du-Loup, Que., 12, 16, 53, 92
Roth, Luther, 104, 144, 260, 337

St. Anne, 87, 170, 184, 399, 477
St. Anne's Day, 83, 104, 134, 175, 183–90, 194, 225, 237–38, 239, 282, 283–91, 294, 351, 358, 402, 473, 475, 504

St. John River, 3, 11, 16, 17–19, 153, 176, 202–3, 208, 219, 261, 330
St. Lawrence, Gulf, 15, 207, 214
St. Lawrence River, 12, 15, 16, 18, 53, 92, 102, 170, 205, 331–32
Ste-Anne au Cap-Breton, 12, 183
Ste Anne de Beaupré, 170, 183, 477
Ste Anne de Restigouche, 10, 12, 23, 182, 271–72, 289–90, 318, 479
Salstog, 155, 354–55
Salt, 65–66
Sapir, Jacob D., 192
Sark, John (informant at Lennox Island, P.E.I.), 95, 158–59
Sayres, William C., 282, 288–89, 293, 302
Schappelle, Benjamin F., 41
Sea cow, 242
Seal, 29–30, 113, 242
Seasons, 103, 343: summer, 341–42
Serpent: sea serpents, 113–14; Tciptcka-am, 114, 345–47
Settlements, Micmac, 175–76: insignia, 175
Shellfish, 27
Shield, 33, 217
Shubenacadie Reserve, N.S., 3, 4, 16, 92, 275–79, 282, 288–89, 292–93, 302, 481, 484, 490
Signalling, 56
Signs and omens, 167–70, 214, 500
Skadegamutc (will-o'-the-wisp, jack-o'-lantern, ghost), 6, 137, 151–53, 157, 261, 270, 302–3, 368–75
Skinning animals, 40–41
Skunk, 109, 111–12, 417–19, 422–23
Sky, 97
Sleds, 51–52, 115
Smethurst, Gabriel, 65, 224
Smith, Nicholas N., 482
Smokehouse, 61–62
Smoking, 68, 178, 242
Snakes, 107, 109, 113, 114, 326, 431–32, 486–87
Snowshoes, 32, 52–53, 397–99, 405–6
Songs, 118–19, 184, 192–95, 201, 287: magic power, 214
Soul, 137, 261, 262
Souriquois (designation of Micmac), 11, 14, 15, 19, 205, 223
Speck, Frank G., 3, 16, 41, 224–25, 317, 360
Spies, 190, 208–9, 210, 464
Spoon, 76

513

Spider, 436–37
Springs, 100
Squirrels, 107
Star Husbands, 413, 424–25, 490
Stars, 98
Status: age, 233–34, 253, 306; women, 243–47
Steen, Sheila C., 276, 288, 292–93, 481
Sterility, cause and cure, 248, 251
Stones, moving, 128
Storehouse, 62
Stories, origin, 317
Storytelling, 5–7, 317–18, 481, 484, 490
Streams, 100–1
Summer, theft of, 341–42
Sun, 97–98, 101: eclipse, 98; worship, 142–46; oath, 214; invocation and sacrifice, 215–16
Supernatural, the, 151–67: beings, 153–54, 338–91; races, 154–56; belief in (*1954*), 296–306; places, 395. *See also* Migamawesu, Pugulatamutc
Sweat lodge, 123–25
Sweet grass, 129

Taboos following childbirth: father, 250; mother, 251
Tadoussac, Que., 12, 15, 16, 53, 210, 221, 345
Tanning hide, 41–42
Tcedjaginwit (Clean Life), 165, 387
Tcipitckaam, 114, 345–47
Teas, native, 66, 129
Tercentenary (*1910*), Micmac, 10, 182–83, 209, 271
Thompson, Stith, 321, 345
Thongs, 77–78
Thunder and lightning, 99, 332
Time: divisions, 103–5; magic passage of, 353, 367, 487
Tobacco, cultivation, 68
Toboggan, 51
Tracadegash Mountain, Carleton, Que., 304, 331, 362, 365
Tracking the enemy, 217
Trade: with French, 15, 26, 69, 86, 179, 183, 202; with Algonkin tribes, 86; with Maliseet, 202; with Penobscot, 205
Travel, 18–19, 53–54, 202
Treasure, buried, 490
Treaties, 204, 221–22: treaty song, 194–95
Tribal gatherings, 183–190: ceremonial arrival, 184–85, 188, 285

Trumpet, 191
Truro, N.S., 3, 4, 7, 16, 209, 276, 285
Turkey, 118
Turtle, 156, 484
Twins, 249

Underwater life, 384–85
Unmarried mothers, 282
Ursuline nuns, 89–91

Vegetable foods, 66
Veterans Land Act, 275
Vetromile, Father Eugene, 217
Vieuxpoint, Father Alexandre de, 183
Vimont, Father Barthelemy, 183
Virginity, 234, 237
Voegelin, C. F. and E. W., 22

Wabanaki: tribes, 14, 67, 75, 153, 305, 321, 343; Confederacy, 56, 176, 223–25, 283, 286, 299, 490, 491–92
Walrus, 30, 205
Waltes, 94, 95, 157, 184, 186, 195–200, 213, 244, 293, 322
Wampum, 56, 222–25, 286, 287
Warfare, 55, 203, 205, 207–8, 209–19: role of women, 194, 213–14, 216, 218, 219–20; torture, 194, 216, 217, 219; captives, 194, 219–21, 455; war alliances, 210, 222–25; causes, 211, 216; war paint, 212, 215; declaration, 216–17; trenches, 217; honor to heroes, 219
Warriors, return: song, 195, 218; head trophies, 218; war dance, 218
Weasel, 112, 439
Weather and weather signs, 101
Weaving: moose-hair socks, 87; sashes, 96; mythic origin, 399
Webster, J. Clarence, 17
Whale, 106, 113, 154, 323, 332, 432, 434–35
Whites, attitudes toward, 5, 8, 22–23, 67, 120–21, 169–70, 289, 291, 307, 336–37. *See also* British, French
Whycocomagh Reserve, C.B., 225, 276, 277, 285
Widowhood, taboos, 108, 267
Wigwam: construction, 57–61, 288; decoration, 95; Beothuck, 206; social life, 226–28; etiquette, 226–28, 285
Witch, witchcraft, *see Buoin*
Wolfe, General James, 473–74, 477

Index

Wolverine, 112, 323–25, 413, 417–19, 422–30, 481, 490
Women: duties and skills, 243–44; occupations shared with men, 245; originators of culture, 246; men's opinions of, 246–47, 399
Wood, Wilson, 130–34

Woodchuck, 342, 438
Woodpecker, 415–16, 501
World, end of, 484
Wowenock, 14
Wright, Esther Clark, 474, 476

Zoology, native, 106–19

Made in the USA